HELLENICA

HELLENICA

A Collection of Essays

ON GREEK POETRY PHILOSOPHY

HISTORY AND RELIGION

EDITED BY

EVELYN ABBOTT, M.A. LL.D.

KENNIKAT PRESS
Port Washington, N. Y./London

74-9223

HELLENICA

First published in 1880
Reissued in 1971 by Kennikat Press
Library of Congress Catalog Card No: 76-86577
ISBN 0-8046-1196-3

Manufactured by Taylor Publishing Company   Dallas, Texas

KENNIKAT CLASSICS SERIES

PREFACE.

THOUGH each of the Essays in this volume has been written independently of the rest, they are all in a certain sense connected with each other, and I have endeavoured to indicate the link of connection by the common title " Hellenica."

We have not done with the Hellenes yet. In spite of all the labour spent, and all the books written on them and their literature, we have not yet entered into full possession of the inheritance bequeathed to us. It has, indeed, been said that we know nearly as much about the Greeks and Romans as we shall ever know; but this can only be true of the mass of facts, to which, without some new discoveries, we are not likely to add greatly. It is not in the least true in regard to the significance of Hellenic history and literature. Beyond and above the various interpretations placed by different ages upon the great writers of Greece, lies the meaning which longer experience and more improved methods of criticism and the test of time declare to be the true one. From this point of view much remains and will long remain to be done, whether we look to the work

of the scholar or to the influence of Hellenic thought
on civilisation. We have not yet found all the
scattered limbs of Truth; it may be that we are only
commencing the search.

It is not likely that the great authors of Greece
will ever become, like the Hebrew Scriptures, a text-
book of daily life. The rapt utterance of the prophet
is far mightier " to sway the soul of man " than the
calmer reasoning of the philosopher, who often loses in
intensity what he gains in breadth. But they may
do a great deal more for us than they have hitherto
done, if we will allow them. The *Gorgias* of Plato
and the *Ethics* of Aristotle are more valuable than
modern books on the same subjects, for the simple
reason that they are nearer the beginning. They
have a greater freshness, and appeal more directly to
the growing mind. No age can neglect them without
suffering a definite and appreciable loss, least of all
the present age, for the study of the writings and the
contemplation of the lives of men who sought after
knowledge as after hidden treasure, who found, or
seemed to find, the one great Good, which all men,
consciously or unconsciously, were everywhere seeking,
who observed the facts of the world around them with
calm judgment, and built thereon their own lofty
theories of what human life might and ought to be—

> " Serene creators of immortal things,"

—become more and more valuable as the course of

history tends to put things material and practical in the place of things intellectual.

In many respects modern civilisation contrasts favourably with ancient; it is, for instance, a trite thing to point out the care taken in modern times of the criminal and the idiot. On the other hand, it is possible that this gain has not been without some accompanying loss. While we are anxious to hide or relieve the degradation to which human nature can sink, we tend to become less careful of the elevation to which it can rise; we put feeling in the place of thought, and throw away half our birthright. But if a single generation were able to keep before it an ideal of culture which should blend all the elements of human knowledge "into an immortal feature of perfection," if a whole country could unite in one effort to appropriate in any real manner the best that has been thought and written on the great interests of life, we should indeed make a great stride forward, but we should also find that the brightest hope of the future is not far removed from the truest interpretation of the past.

At present such an effort is impossible, partly because much of the best literature of the world is in the exclusive possession of the few. The most direct method of breaking down this exclusiveness, and bringing the great writers of Greece within the immediate reach of English readers, is no doubt to translate them; but it is hoped that a volume like the present, while it helps to increase the interest taken in Greek literature, will also show how that literature may be of service in the present day.

E. ABBOTT.

BALLIOL COLLEGE, OXFORD,
December 1879.

CONTENTS

PAGE

AESCHYLUS

ERNEST MYERS, M.A., Fellow of Wadham College, Oxford   1

THE THEOLOGY AND ETHICS OF SOPHOCLES

EVELYN ABBOTT, M.A., LL.D., Fellow of Balliol College,
Oxford 33

THE THEORY OF EDUCATION IN PLATO'S *REPUBLIC*

RICHARD LEWIS NETTLESHIP, M.A., Fellow of Balliol
College, Oxford 67

ARISTOTLE'S CONCEPTION OF THE STATE

ANDREW CECIL BRADLEY, M.A., Fellow of Balliol College,
Oxford 181

EPICURUS

WILLIAM LEONARD COURTNEY, M.A., Fellow of New
College, Oxford 244

THE SPEECHES OF THUCYDIDES

RICHARD CLAVERHOUSE JEBB, M.A., LL.D., Professor of
Greek in the University of Glasgow 266

XENOPHON

HENRY GRAHAM DAKYNS, M.A., Trinity College, Cambridge 324

POLYBIUS

JAMES LEIGH STRACHAN-DAVIDSON, M.A., Fellow of Balliol
College, Oxford 387

GREEK ORACLES

FREDERIC WILLIAM HENRY MYERS, M.A., late Fellow of
Trinity College, Cambridge 425

AESCHYLUS.

THE three sons of Euphorion the Athenian, Kynegeirus, Aeschylus, and Ameinias, all earned the gratitude of their country and of the world, for all fought in the great battles of the Persian war, and helped to save the brightest hopes of the human race, which then stood in jeopardy of death. But to Aeschylus belongs another and a still more conspicuous fame, for he is the Father of Tragedy; nor have any of his spiritual sons, save perhaps one, been able to claim a right to the boast of Sthenelus.[1] And since all European drama derives from the Athenian, it is more than mere idle speculation to say that without Aeschylus there might possibly have been no Shakespeare.

Aeschylus was born in the year 525 B.C., and died in 456, twenty-five years before the Peloponnesian war began, so that of him, more truly than of Sophocles, it might be said that he departed οὐδὲν ὑπομείνας κακόν,—taken away from the evil that was to come. When the Persian war was over, during the latter part of his life, he seems, like other poets and artists of the time, to have visited Sicily and Syracuse, once at least, more probably twice, or even thrice. We need not regard the gossip of later times, which attributed his absence from Athens to jealousy of the rising fame of Sophocles, who had become more popular than himself in the Athenian theatre. We may feel sure that the personal relations of Aeschylus and Sophocles find far truer expression in that passage in the *Frogs* of Aristophanes, where Aeacus tells how, when the younger poet came

---

[1] *Iliad*, iv. 405.

down among the dead, he clasped the hand of the elder and
embraced him, and would not suffer that he should yield his
throne. Syracuse was at that time a common resort of men of
art and letters ; and the sympathy of Aeschylus may well have
been aroused, as Pindar's was, for the Hellenic people and
prince who had fought so well against the Carthaginian and
Etruscan in the West, while the Hellenes of the mother country
were beating back the Persian in the East. Whatever were
the cause, there is no doubt that Aeschylus did at least once
exchange the fair curve of hills that stand about the Athenian
plain for Etna's solitary cone, and the rock-fretted ripple of
Ilissus for smooth-sliding Anapus and his reedy banks. In
honour of a new-founded Sicilian city, he wrote a play called *The
Women of Aitna,* but of this unhappily only four lines remain,
so that we cannot know " how fair a fountain of immortal verse
he made to flow "[1] for his hosts, among whom he came like
Alpheus rising blended in the Arethusan spring,

> " bearing bridal gifts,
> Fair leaves and flowers and sacred soil of Hellas."[2]

In Sicily death overtook him, and his ashes were buried at
Gela with the honours of a public funeral. On his tomb was
engraved a brief epitaph, attributed to himself; and we may
well believe that he wrote it, for it makes no mention of the
triumphs of his art, only of his share in the common duties of
a citizen when he fought in the ranks at Marathon.

His choice of the new and native field of tragic poetry was
symbolised in the legend which told how, when as a boy he
had fallen asleep in his father's vineyard, Dionysus appeared
to him in a vision, and gave command that he should serve
him after this sort at his festival when the vines grew green.
So amply had he fulfilled before his death the charge enjoined
on him by the God, that no less than seventy dramas, of which
only seven have descended to us, were even at the lowest
reckoning ascribed to his hand.

Such external evidence touching the bent and genius of
Aeschylus as has been left to us in the shape of contemporary

---

[1] καί κε μυθήσαιθ' ὁποίαν Ἀρκεσίλᾳ
εὗρε παγὰν ἀμβροσίων ἐπέων.—PINDAR, *Pyth.* iv. 298.

[2] ἔδνα φέρων καλὰ φύλλα καὶ ἄνθεα καὶ κόνιν ἱράν.—MOSCHUS, vi. 3.

or nearly contemporary criticism and comment, is naturally meagre. The most striking and copious is that found in the *Frogs* of Aristophanes. In the *Frogs*, Aeschylus is introduced to be contrasted with, and to triumph over, Euripides. The glorious and endearing associations of the elder time find vindication in the victory of the elder poet. The contest is not unlike that waged between Honest and Dishonest Pleading in the *Clouds.* Simplicity, directness, dignity, heroic magnanimity, and contempt of the frivolous, the egoistic, the morbidly ingenious, are arrayed, to the eyes of Aristophanes, against affectation, meaningless subtlety, inartistic carelessness and triviality, voluptuousness, shallow and violent passion. It would be difficult to find a modern parallel to Euripides, but if, to illustrate the situation, we imagine some modern English critic, whose indignation had determined him to see nothing but prosaic coldness in Wordsworth, nothing but bad workmanship and theatrical declamation in Byron, nothing but voluptuousness in Keats or Mr. Morris, nothing but pretentious oddity and "a well of English defiled" in Mr. Browning ; a critic who further saw all these qualities, not dispersed among several poets, but concentrated in the writings of one, and that one far more popular than any of these, and with a popularity which the critic believed to be one of many signs of a fatal degeneracy of the age ; and then if we imagine this critic matching such a poet against such another poet of old time as the "God-gifted organ-voice of England," employing a wit as unscrupulous as brilliant to expose the degeneracy of the later-born, we may thus form some idea of the purpose accomplished by Aristophanes in the *Frogs.* One-sided as that play is, it is still a most valuable relic of nearly contemporary criticism. But the exigencies of comedy, and possibly even an imperfect appreciation on the part of Aristophanes himself, leave the *Frogs* very far from satisfactory as a criticism not only of Euripides, but also of Aeschylus. And probably the manner in which Aeschylus is there introduced has done something to incline modern estimates of his genius toward judgments which a careful study of his works must pronounce superficial.

Without doubt, of all the tokens whereby we may estimate a poet, his style is the chief ; but if we go no deeper we shall be apt to err even in our estimate of his style. And the style of

Aeschylus, characteristic as it is, has misled some critics by not being viewed in the light of less obvious elements in his work, as well as by having undue emphasis laid on its most salient points ; and the same has been the case in inferences from the structure, the stories, and the *dramatis personae* of his extant plays. Because his diction is always lofty, and sometimes grandiose and excessive in its wealth of ῥήμαθ᾽ ἱπποβάμονα, words on horseback,[1] because among his characters are Titans and Furies, he has been accounted one whose delight was pre-eminently in the colossal and the terrible for their own sake, and whose prevailing passion was for stupendous effects produced by a recklessly gigantesque imagination. In the *Frogs*, this is made a chief point of Euripides' attack, and the one defect which Aristophanes seems to allow to exist in his hero. And since then the difference in modern taste has been equally ready to recognise, though less ready to blame, those picturesque extravagances. It is not merely that criticism is always willing to lighten its task by making the most of the salient features in its object, but also the standard of comparison between different kinds of literary and artistic merit is very commonly other than it was in the time of Aeschylus and Pheidias, and will sometimes be found wanting in its application to that time. The value of vigour and passion, of vividness of all kinds, was at least as amply recognised in theory and exemplified in practice by the artistic genius of that age as by that of any other ; but its larger view never lost sight of the supremacy of measure and harmony, the powers whose gracious influence was present in every great effort of the Hellenic mind. And thus in the drama of Aeschylus, behind all the lurid clouds of a mysterious destiny, above the mountainous waves of conflicting passions, the star of his Athenian soul is never quenched, nor refuses to eyes that wait for it the pure and grave serenity of its light.

And probably it is the critics' fancy for striking contrasts, above referred to, with the effect produced by the *Frogs*, which has led also to a somewhat false estimate of the attitude of Aeschylus toward the political and speculative movements of his age. In the *Frogs* he is made generally a *laudator temporis*

---

[1] *Frogs*, 821.

acti, though without commitment to any especial political opinions. Later authors speak of his having been a conservative of the school of Aristeides and Kimon, and opposed to certain innovations made by Pericles and Ephialtes ; it has been also asserted that the honours paid to the Court of the Areopagus in the *Eumenides* were intended as a protest against the encroachments on its power which the last-named statesmen made. On this point, however—the question of the significance of the *Eumenides* as regards the Areopagus,—it will generally be agreed now that the views of K. O. Müller, expressed in his valuable dissertations on the play, must be accepted with considerable modifications. As Grote has pointed out, the privilege of the Areopagus on which Aeschylus is dwelling in the *Eumenides,* namely the judicial power in cases of homicide, is the very privilege which Pericles and Ephialtes left untouched; it was the senatorial power of the Areopagus which they took from it, and on this point Aeschylus does not reveal either satisfaction or dissatisfaction. To some at least of its readers the play would lose much of its perfection and impressiveness if it seemed no longer to breathe that spirit of peace and concord before which party conflicts are forgotten, and to speak throughout allusively, as well as directly, of those agencies of renouncement and reconcilement to which Aeschylus looked for a solution of the perplexities of gods and men.

The supposed anti-democratic tendencies of the poet have been by some critics exaggerated even to absurdity. We find a widely-read English commentator saying, " His feelings evidently incline to an excessive reverence for kings, . . . and a degree of grandeur is thrown over their state such as is wholly incompatible with real dislike or contempt for it." This is indeed to pervert evidence of dramatic instinct which Aeschylus certainly had into evidence of political leanings which he certainly had not. It would be easy enough to show, from the *Persians* especially, but also from other passages where he is concerned with a comparison of Oriental with Hellenic manners and customs,[1] that Aeschylus was to the full possessed of the Hellenic contempt for that barbarian surrender of the rights and

---

[1] Such are *Agam.* 918-22 ; *Eum.* 185-90 ; *Suppl.* 368-80, 398-401.

duties of citizens into the hands of a single person chosen by accident, which brought freemen to the level of slaves.

" Among the Easterns all save one are slaves."[1]

Indeed, neither the oligarchic nor the democratic party in Hellas, though we find both, and especially the former, afterwards tampering with the Persian king, had at that time any of that natural affinity to despotism which in modern times both the courtier-noble and the ochlocratic leveller not unfrequently display. Nor is there any reason to suppose that Aeschylus attached himself to any extreme party or ideas. Both his own genius and character, and also his chronological position, furnish reasons against assigning to him a share in the party spirit which raged so fiercely in Athens and the other Hellenic States in the middle and end of the fifth century B.C. In his time the strife between oligarchy and democracy, while it had somewhat subsided since the days when it had been embittered by the greater pressure of poverty on an increasing population, the fear of demagogic city despots, and other causes, was not yet exasperated by the alternating revenges for which the Peloponnesian war gave opportunity. Aeschylus was intensely Athenian and intensely Hellenic. He could not be the first without being democratic; he could not be the second and adhere to any principles which would divide the Hellenes in the face of the barbarian.[2] The battles of Marathon and Salamis and Plataea formed the central point to which his political ideas referred themselves. We can readily believe, as tradition tells, that Aristeides, a hero of the Persian war, the man pre-eminent for his reverence of that altar of Justice as whose priest Aeschylus so often appears, would attract the poet's political as well as personal confidence. But it must be remembered that it was Aristeides, conservative as he was, who proposed the law by which the civil offices were thrown open to election from the

---

[1] τὰ βαρβάρων γὰρ δοῦλα πάντα πλὴν ἑνός.—EURIPIDES, *Helen.* 276.

[2] Among many instances of the Pan-Hellenic feeling of Aeschylus, one less obvious than others may be referred to. We learn from Plutarch that in the drama of *the Eleusinians*, (*Fragments*, 48,) Theseus obtained from Adrastus the burial of those who had fallen before Thebes by friendly treaty, not by force of arms, as Euripides afterwards represented in the *Suppliants*. Nor is there any passage in all that remains to us of Aeschylus containing words of hostility or disparagement toward a Hellenic State.

whole people. Very far removed were such men from the oligarchs who, in the year 411, traded on the agony of their country. And indeed the later oligarchical movements were connected with a sophistic and cynically individualistic spirit, which Aeschylus, and most conservatives of his time, would have disliked far more than the spirit of innovation encouraged and directed by Pericles. Even later, it was rather a change of persons, and sometimes of policy, than a change of constitution, that the Athenian conservative opposition of the older school desired: we may see this in the *Knights* of Aristophanes, where there is no desire to dethrone Demos, but only to bring him to his right mind, and to inspire him with distrust and contempt of the demagogic schemers who enthral him and lead him into trouble. In Aeschylus, the passage most directly bearing on Athenian politics is the speech of Pallas in the *Eumenides* (681-710), and the central warning of that,

> " Bright watersprings with mixture of foul mire
> Stain not, or never hope for wholesome draught," [1]

is one which no democrat, who is not a mere ochlocrat, need repudiate.

Passing onward, then, and upward from the misconceptions of *littérateurs* and commentators, and the travesty of playful burlesque, let us proceed to the only valid material for a just estimate of Aeschylus—his seven remaining plays,—first very briefly viewing them in relation to their antecedents and surroundings in action, thought, and art. He appeared at a time when Athens was just entering on her prime, on the years when she was to justify the oft-cited eulogy of Pericles, when he called her "the school of Hellas;" when to her sons "the love of beauty brought no extravagance, the love of knowledge no lack of manly vigour;" when no element seemed wanting to train both heart and head into admirable and harmonious life. The progress of thought, rapid as it was, had not yet the destructive aspect which it afterwards assumed. Already the public law-courts, the increased acquaintance with foreign modes of thought, the joyful exercise of intellectual powers, were shaping a taste for dialectical inquiry; but the multiform spirit, which

---

[1] κακαῖς ἐπιρροαῖσι βορβόρῳ θ' ὕδωρ
λαμπρὸν μιαίνων οὔποθ' εὑρήσεις ποτόν.—*Eum.* 694-95.

may roughly be called sophistic, was yet undeveloped. The old religion, thanks to the elasticity of Hellenic theology, and its identification with the national cause in the Persian war, still kept a strong hold on the minds even of the most thoughtful. Pallas had fought for Athens, and the Parthenon was her thank-offering. Tradition seemed to be reconciled for the time with reason, as aristocracy with democracy, and artistic with political energy. Thus from the union of a sense of self-reliance and completeness with an eager interest in the spectacle and the action of life, there arose that state of calm without languor, vivid feeling without distracting passion, which provides the best atmosphere for artistic development. Thus of all the great literary and artistic epochs of Europe this was the most propitious to literature and art. In the Hellenic prime there was more of life and freshness than in the age of Virgil, not to mention that of Corneille and Molière, more sanity and serenity than in medieval Italy in Dante's time, or than in either England or Italy at the Renaissance, or during the religious wars of the Reformation; more also, it need hardly be said, than in any of the European countries which felt the stimulating shock of the French Revolution. Of this age in Hellas the chief artistic interpreters to us are Pindar, Aeschylus, Pheidias, and Sophocles. Three of these are Athenians. But it must be remembered that, splendid as the achievements of Athens were in poetry, she only appeared late upon that field. The genius to which we owe the poems of Homer, though Ionian, was assuredly not Attic; and in all the famous roll of lyric and gnomic poets who filled the sixth and the beginning of the fifth century, the only Athenians are the ancient Tyrtaeus, who dwelt among Dorians and made his war-songs for the Spartan host, and the lawgiver Solon. Solon, indeed, was both an Athenian patriot and a true, though not a great, poet, so far as we can judge from a few fragments. In the twenty or thirty iambics of Solon's still extant, we can already detect some prefiguring semblance of the mighty march of the Aeschylean line. But Solon was primarily a statesman and lawgiver, engrossed in training the first shoots of that law-abiding freedom which was in the appointed time to bear such rich fruits of art. That time was come when Aeschylus received his first mission from Dionysus. Homer had sung for the warrior-prince, and Hesiod for the toiling husbandman, Sappho for the

lover, and Pindar for the glory of youth; but the word of
Aeschylus was for the citizens of an august commonwealth,
whose acts and thoughts were destined

> " To cast the kingdoms old
> Into another mould."

A new form in poetry was demanded, a form which should be
congenial to those stirring times of action, and this demand
Aeschylus supplied by an unsurpassed effort of original genius.
Thespis, Choerilus, Pratinas, and even Phrynichus, are to us
mere names, but all testimony agrees in regarding Aeschylus
as the virtual creator of the drama.[1] For more than a century
before his birth, Hellas had been alive with lyric song, and the
fragments of that poetry of the sixth century B.C., the loss of
which is one of the heaviest in all literature, show us with
what wide range all the chords of personal feeling were swept
by it in turn. Moving in a parallel stream with these utterances of personal feeling was another kind of lyric poetry of
graver ends and more chastened treatment—the Dorian odes
and hymns, the " solemn music " which accompanied triumphal
and religious joy. When toward the beginning of the fifth century the common Games and the common worship of the greater
Gods were at the height of their dignity, when the forces of
Hellas were becoming concentrated, and the national life intensified, Pindar appeared, and gave the final lyric expression to
this side of Hellenic life. Aeschylus also was one of the
greatest of lyric poets, but as he grew up he found in the beginnings of the Athenian drama a new kind of art arising, which
was to draw aid from all existing kinds, and combine them into
a thing of new beauty and power. When a generation of men
is filled with high emotion and interest, as were those who saw
Salamis or the wreck of the Spanish Armada, it craves some
poetic expression, and has found none happier than the drama,
which shares with music the power of uniting an audience by
sympathy in a common interest and delight. And in the
Hellenic drama music itself was retained in the choric song
alternating with iambic dialogue, the form in which it seems to

---

[1] It is truly astonishing to think that a second actor was only first introduced by Aeschylus. Phrynichus, his most eminent predecessor, seems till
then to have employed in his dramas (if they might so be called) only choric
songs and dialogues of one actor with the chorus.

have been combined with acting with less incompatibility than in any other that has been tried. In such expression the vague body of emotion which might have wasted itself in idle or pernicious channels finds relief in the work of a great artist who interprets souls to themselves, and lifts them into a larger air. Different kinds of poetry shade into each other ; one of the greatest of all poems, Dante's *Commedia*, cannot be classified—it is not a drama, for there is no action, yet there is a unity which makes it more than a romance. The lyric is the essence of poetry, its simplest form, and can flourish under much more precarious conditions of mental soil and climate than either the epic or the drama. The epic is between the drama and the romance, and probably the so-called epics of the Cyclic poets might more properly be classed as romances.[1] Hellenic drama sprang from the lyric and the epic both, though primarily from the lyric; while the elegy and the weighty gnomic line lend their forces blended and transformed. The flexible iambics which had expressed the satire of Archilochus or the wisdom of Solon are developed into the poetic rhetoric of the dialogue, and the lyric odes still appear in the Doric songs of the chorus, the original nucleus from which the drama was expanded. Aeschylus, as has been said, is one of the greatest of lyric poets, but he calls his dramas " morsels left from the great banquets of Homer." In the erection of the Athenian theatre there is the same blending of the new and old, of the venerableness of tradition with the vigour of revolution, which is the especial glory of the Athenian people, who, whether as grasshopper-wearing αὐτόχθονες or Eupatrid descendants of gods and heroes, were yet ever the first to spread sail in quest of new adventure, whether in the physical or in the intellectual world. The legends of Thebes and Troy, of the acts and passions of Gods and sons of Gods, were an ancient treasure of the race ; but in the hands of the dramatist they yielded new meaning and delight. There is no stiff and formal allegory ; the figures are scarcely less life-like and real than they are in Homer, but a deep and serious meaning breathes through all : they are individuals still, but they are also more than ever types, and through their separate action is

---

[1] See Aristotle's *Poetics*, c. 23.

revealed the action of universal laws. The plot is so implicit in the situation that we are irresistibly led to compare the Aeschylean drama to groups of sculpture of the same age, such as those which filled the pediments of the Parthenon. Not that poetry has here foregone its privileges among the arts ; action there assuredly is, and such as potently effects that "purgation of the terrors and pities of the mind" which Aristotle conceived to be the drama's aim. Yet through the whole the sense of some harmonising unity is never absent ; we never feel that we may be hurried to some inconsequent disappointment by the mere caprice, as it were, of the writer or of his characters ; all is under the guardianship of those powers of measure and harmony already spoken of, in the general conception as in the details and the feeling. Intensity without extravagance, dignity without coldness, grace without enervation—these qualities are found in Aeschylus, as they are found everywhere in the best Hellenic art, though in degrees and proportions varying with the various artists. In the portrayal of human passion, the tragedians, like Homer, are strong and terrible, yet human. Their tragic agonies have neither the wild and portentous violence which sometimes in the Elizabethan drama kindles the ebullient blood to almost preternatural outbursts, such as seem to remove the stage from the dominion of reason altogether, nor yet have they the languor and the self-consciousness which mix so often with the melancholy of poets of the present age,

> "ove i lamenti
> Non suonan come guai, ma son sospiri."

The heroes and heroines of Hellenic story cry aloud in their pain ; the torrent of their anguish is full and strong, yet we feel in it an expression of natures not self-conscious, though sensitive and highly and harmoniously organised, and thus it has something of health in its very disorder, which seems a latent antidote to its bitterness. It is what we feel in Achilles' cry to the vision of his dead friend :—

> "But ah ! come near, let each with each embracing,
> For one short moment feed our fill of woe."[1]

---

[1] ἀλλά μοι ἆσσον στῆθι· μίνυνθά περ ἀμφιβαλόντε
ἀλλήλους, ὀλοοῖο τεταρπώμεσθα γόοιο.—*Iliad,* xxiii. 97-8.

The dramatic achievements of Aeschylus, and the poetic
qualities of imagination, diction, and versification which give
him his high place among poets, have often been dwelt upon;
and if it might avail to describe what can only be felt, it would
be hard to say enough of the terrible and beautiful things which
he has revealed to us, of the imploring agony of the Danaid or of
the Theban suppliants; the chivalrous and benignant constancy
of the king Pelasgus; the war frenzy of the sons of Oedipus and
the seven chieftains in arms before the seven gates; the baleful
splendours of Clytemnestra; the piteous soul-solitude of Cassandra; the indignant woe and solemn vengeance of Agamemnon's children; the confusion of the Persian invader; the pæan
of the Hellenic patriot; the great heart and high bearing of Prometheus on his bed of pain. Although the simple structure and
few persons of the drama in the time of Aeschylus precluded
him, even had he been capable of it, from the " myriad-minded "
craftsmanship in human types which Shakespeare showed, yet in
Aeschylus also we feel that each character, simple as it is, is an
organic whole, a true creation, but the offspring of a brooding
imagination rather than of conscious analysis. This is the
secret of the great effects which he produces with his severely
limited means. Each of his persons, notwithstanding their
similarity of diction, seems almost always to bear about him an
atmosphere which makes his presence unmistakable. We can
readily believe the tradition that on the stage their silence as
well as their speech had its meaning and its eloquence: the
long silences of the Niobe and the Achilles, whom we know not,
sitting beside their dead; of the Atossa, the Cassandra, the Electra, the Prometheus, whom we know. Let any one imagine to
himself what the effect must have been when, " at the limit of
the world," the Titan had been thrown upon the rock by the
huge hands of Power and Force, and nailed there by unwilling
Hephaestus, and after listening to their dialogue above his
helpless body in scornful silence, in silence also let them
depart, and so remaining till the place should be, as it were,
purified of the presence of the ministers of injustice, at last broke
the stillness with his despairing yet august appeal:—

> " O holy Heaven, and ye swift-wingèd winds,
> And river-fountains, and the ocean-waves'
> Innumerable laughter; Mother Earth,

And thou all-seeing Sun, I summon you,
Behold me, how these Gods entreat a God.
   See in what stress of torment
   Ten thousand years of pain
   Here must I agonise."[1]

If poetry is akin on one side to sculpture and painting, on another side it is akin to rhetoric; and when Aeschylus wrote his plays, that great school of eloquence had been founded in free-speaking Athens which afterwards produced the oratory which has served as a model to the world. Homer had found a place for oratory in his epic, much more might Aeschylus do so in his dramas. The suppliant Danaüs and Orestes would hardly have pleaded so persuasively, the dialogue of Prometheus with Hermes, or of Apollo with the Furies, would hardly have been so apt and telling, had not Aeschylus been at least a listener to those pleadings of Athenian law-courts which obtained so wide a fame for evil and for good, to the eye of Aristophanes a mere solvent of morality, to the eye of the modern historian an origin of moral philosophy. But in Aeschylus the poet was always foremost, the logic-chopping to which the genius of Euripides descends is alien and remote from him. Even looking to expression alone, to him belongs a witchery of words far beyond that of the orator or the rhetorician; metrical and verbal harmonies born only in a poet's mind. His imagination is of that most genuinely poetic kind which is concerned primarily with the truthful transfiguration of the real and abiding elements of human life; but he knows well how to use as accessories the images on which genius of an inferior order might be principally and ultimately employed. Although a child of daylight and the dawn, he has learnt secrets of the encompassing night. No poet has surpassed him in his power of thrilling the mind with a sense of mystery and presentient awe. None has presented more impressively the dim border-land which lies, as men fancy, between the material and the

---

[1] ὦ δῖος αἰθήρ καὶ ταχύπτεροι πνοαί,
ποταμῶν τε πηγαὶ ποντίων τε κυμάτων
ἀνήριθμον γέλασμα, παμμῆτόρ τε γῆ,
καὶ τὸν πανόπτην κύκλον ἡλίου καλῶ·
ἴδεσθέ μ' οἷα πρὸς θεῶν πάσχω θεός.
δέρχθηθ' οἵαις αἰκίαισιν
διακναιόμενος τὸν μυριετῆ
χρόνον ἀθλεύσω.—*Prometheus Bound*, 88-96.

spiritual. With dreams and visions he deals habitually. In the
seven extant plays we find five places where he bodies forth
apparitions of the night. There is the dream of Atossa, in
which she saw her son Xerxes mount his chariot behind the
unequally-yoked pair of woman-steeds, to be hurled to earth by
the fierce and fair sister who cast away his yoke from her neck,
and turned and rent the harness of his car. There is the dream
of Clytemnestra on the eve of her death-day, when she seemed
to herself to have brought forth a serpent that sucked from her
milk and blood, and a great cry rang at midnight through the
palace, where on the morrow her son's sword was to be at her
breast. There is the vision of the Furies, when Clytemnestra's
phantom rises to upbraid them for their slackness in avenging
her blood. There is the vision of Menelaus, born of his yearning desire, the vision that seemed Helen, but when he stretched
his arms to it was gone, " with wings that follow down the
ways of sleep." Lastly there are the dreams which Io tells,
the very reading of which seems to make a midnight awe and
ghostly stillness in the air :—

> " For ever to my virgin chambers came
> Strange visions and soft voices of the night,
> Importunately pleading : Happy maid,
> Why tarriest thou so long in maidenhood,
> Seeing how high espousals are awaiting
> Thy choice ? for lo, the love of highest Zeus
> Yearns for thy love, to enfold thee as his own." [1]

Aeschylus would seem to have inclined to some such transformed survival of a primitive belief as we find referred to in a
fragment of Pindar,[2] that in sleep the mind is open to influences

---

[1] ἀεὶ γὰρ ὄψεις ἔννυχοι πωλεύμεναι
ἐς παρθενῶνας τοὺς ἐμοὺς παρηγόρουν
λείοισι μύθοις· ὦ μέγ' εὔδαιμον κόρη,
τί παρθενεύει δαρὸν, ἐξόν σοι γάμου
τυχεῖν μεγίστου ; Ζεὺς γὰρ ἱμέρου βέλει
πρὸς σοῦ τέθαλπται καὶ ξυναίρεσθαι Κύπριν
θέλει.   —*Prometheus*, 645-51.

[2] καὶ σῶμα μὲν πάντων ἕπεται θανάτῳ περισθενεῖ,
ζωὸν δ' ἔτι λείπεται αἰῶνος εἴδωλον· τὸ γάρ ἐστι μόνον
ἐκ θεῶν· εὕδει δὲ πρασσόντων μελέων, ἀτὰρ εὑδόντεσσιν
ἐν πολλοῖς ὀνείροις
δείκνυσι τερπνῶν ἐφέρποισαν χαλεπῶν τε κρίσιν.—(*Frag.* 96.)
(And the body indeed is subject to the great power of death, but there
remaineth yet alive a shadow of life ; for this only is from the Gods ; and while

and capable of intuitions which in waking moments are denied. In one place he says :—

> " For oft in sleep comes light upon the soul,
> But in the day their fate is hid from men ; "[1]

and in a different but still more memorable passage :—

> " In sleep there doth before man's heart distil
> A grievous memory of ill,
> And makes the unwise wise against his will."[2]

These last words may not unnaturally lead us to another part of the subject, when, descending below the poetic qualities of the plays, we seek to discover the religious and the moral ideas which underlie them. These are by no means identical, or even closely connected ; among the Hellenes morality grew up separate from religion, and then as it were turned round to it to demand its aid. Gods had always been stronger and more beautiful than men ; men now demanded that they should be also better and greater. In the form Xenophanes had given to this demand it shook rudely the whole fabric of theological belief. Now, whatever opinion may be held as to the existence of the supernatural, it can hardly be denied that when a belief in it becomes forbidden to art, art loses one of its most precious means to attaining elevation and impressiveness. To sculpture and painting—especially to sculpture—the possibility of dealing with supernatural beings is of immense importance. No other adequate symbolism has yet been found for expressing visibly that idealisation of itself which must always be the object of humanity's highest and deepest reverence. From the Hellenic Olympus and the Christian Paradise has come all that is noblest in glyptic and pictorial art. Poetry too, though its resources are less exhaustible, must feel it a chilling hour when the ancient shrines have shuddered at the murmured words, *Let us depart hence.* No theology, indeed, in its popular shape,

---

the limbs stir it sleepeth, but unto sleepers in dreams discovereth oftentimes the judgment that draweth near for sorrow or for joy.)

[1] εὕδουσα γὰρ φρὴν ὄμμασιν λαμπρύνεται,
ἐν ἡμέρᾳ δὲ μοῖρ' ἀπρόσκοπος βροτῶν.—*Eum.* 104-5.

[2] στάζει δ' ἔν θ' ὕπνῳ πρὸ καρδίας
μνησιπήμων πόνος· καὶ παρ' ἄ-
κοντας ἦλθε σωφρονεῖν.—*Agam.* 179-81.

has been pure enough to express unmodified the highest moods of the highest minds, and it was so especially in that time of quickened intellectual activity and of increased acquaintance with new modes of thought. Yet the old religion still kept, as has been said, a real hold on the minds even of the most thoughtful. But if Pindar and Aeschylus treated the primitive theogonies with reverence, it was not the reverence of a primitive theogonist; although the happy blending of tradition with advance enabled them, as it were, to build a New Testament on the foundations of the Old. Pindar's attitude toward Hellenic mythology is comparatively easy to decide; he flatly refuses to believe or report evil of the Gods, and when tradition conflicts with morality he will not scruple to alter tradition before he admits it to a place in his pure and stately song. At the same time, it is obvious that no complicated or reflective scheme of theology is to be gathered from his poems, and therefore no attempt to gather such has been made. It is otherwise with Aeschylus. Right and wrong, sin committed and curse inherited, the intervention of protecting and punishing supernatural powers, form so large a part of the matter with which Aeschylus deals, that he has left materials which have employed the most earnest and ingenious analytic endeavour to discern among them the outlines of a system of moral theology of which the poet was the prophet and evangelist. In such analysis the most prominent subject for inquiry must be found in the nature of his conception of the moral government of the world, and the hands in which it is placed. The old belief in the infatuation by a supernatural power as the cause of guilt, which is the primitive expression of the bewilderment with which the remorseful soul looks back upon its sin, and the belief in inherited curses and evil destinies which cling to devoted races—these beliefs are treated by Aeschylus in a way which makes them at once more moral and more scientific. According to him, man is only blinded and hastened to destruction when he has voluntarily made an evil choice.

"When the fool to folly hasteth God shall speed him to his fall"[1]

---

[1] ἀλλ' ὅταν σπεύδῃ τὶς αὐτὸς, χὦ θεὸς συνάπτεται.—*Persians*, 742.

are the words which the phantom of the dead Darius pronounces on the câlamities of his son. Thus, while it is only
consistent with the nature of things that wrongs done among
kindred beget wrong, and that tendencies to wild deeds are
inherited, yet each deed stands on its merits for judgment, and
fairly so, because each has its cause in the passions and will of
the doer. The family curse is only one form, though a very
impressive one, of the means which it is the especial office of
tragedy to employ to express the terrific significance and far-
working effect of the human actions and passions with which
it deals. When the developed human spirit begins to reflect
on the terrors and perplexities of its destiny, the "blind
hopes"[1] which Prometheus gave them as his first boon grope
for some solution or consolation, and the prophet or the poet is
moved to reveal it to them in the shape of a moral government
of the world, discerned in the history of the generations of
mankind and in the conscience of the individual man.

In whose hands Aeschylus supposes this government to lie
is harder to decide. We have but a tithe of his works left in
evidence, and even these are not all agreed. If from the seven
plays were excluded the *Prometheus*, we might perhaps find it
easier to construct from them by conjecture a systematic theology. In all the other six Zeus occupies a position which is
almost monotheistic, so unlimited are the might, majesty,
wisdom, and goodness assigned to him. He is the All-causing,
All-sufficing, Almighty, All-seeing, All-accomplishing ($\pi\alpha\nu\alpha\iota$-
$\tau\iota\sigma\varsigma$, $\pi\alpha\nu\tau\alpha\rho\kappa\eta\varsigma$, $\pi\alpha\gamma\kappa\rho\alpha\tau\eta\varsigma$, $\pi\alpha\nu\delta\pi\tau\eta\varsigma$, $\pi\alpha\nu\tau\epsilon\lambda\eta\varsigma$) Lord of Lords,
Most Holy of Holies.[2] "In thy hands is the balance; what
can mortals accomplish without thee?" asks one Chorus;
another, "What without Zeus can befall any man?" To Zeus
Apollo refers every oracle that issues from his shrine;[3] even
Justice is called by Eteokles the child of Zeus. It is Zeus

---

[1] $\tau\upsilon\phi\lambda\grave{\alpha}\varsigma$ $\dot{\epsilon}\nu$ $\alpha\dot{\upsilon}\tau o\hat{\iota}\varsigma$ $\dot{\epsilon}\lambda\pi\acute{\iota}\delta\alpha\varsigma$ $\kappa\alpha\tau\acute{\phi}\kappa\iota\sigma\alpha.$
(Blind hopes I brought to dwell among mankind.)—*Prom.* 250.

[2] $\ddot{\alpha}\nu\alpha\xi$ $\dot{\alpha}\nu\acute{\alpha}\kappa\tau\omega\nu,$ $\mu\alpha\kappa\acute{\alpha}\rho\omega\nu$
$\mu\alpha\kappa\acute{\alpha}\rho\tau\alpha\tau\epsilon.$—*Suppliants*, 524-25.

[3] $o\dot{\upsilon}\pi\acute{\omega}\pi o\tau$' $\epsilon\dot{\iota}\pi o\nu$ $\mu\alpha\nu\tau\iota\kappa o\hat{\iota}\sigma\iota\nu$ $\dot{\epsilon}\nu$ $\theta\rho\acute{o}\nu o\iota\varsigma,$
$o\dot{\upsilon}\kappa$ $\dot{\alpha}\nu\delta\rho\grave{o}\varsigma,$ $o\dot{\upsilon}$ $\gamma\upsilon\nu\alpha\iota\kappa\grave{o}\varsigma,$ $o\dot{\upsilon}$ $\pi\delta\lambda\epsilon\omega\varsigma$ $\pi\acute{\epsilon}\rho\iota,$
$\ddot{o}$ $\mu\grave{\eta}$ $\kappa\epsilon\lambda\epsilon\acute{\upsilon}\sigma\alpha\iota$ $Z\epsilon\grave{\upsilon}\varsigma$ $'O\lambda\upsilon\mu\pi\acute{\iota}\omega\nu$ $\pi\alpha\tau\acute{\eta}\rho.$
(Ne'er spake I yet from my oracular throne,

who "leads mortals to wisdom, in that he ordained that to suffer is to learn."[1]

To the acceptance of this lofty conception of Zeus as the final and consistently held theological theory of Aeschylus, there is one obstacle, but that is one of great importance,—the *Prometheus Bound.* The loss of the *Prometheus Fire-bearing,* and still more of the *Prometheus Unbound,* is a loss of which we cannot more accurately calculate the magnitude than to be certain that it is immense. In all literature there is no blank so cruel to our highest desires. But whatever reconciliation may have completed the story, nothing could altogether efface the impression which the poet unmistakably means to convey, that the Power which stretched on his painful rock and hurled to Tartarus the giver of good things to men, was in that act overstepping the limits of wisdom and righteousness, was guilty, in some measure, of the reckless violence which in other plays he judges and abhors. Zeus does not indeed appear himself in the play, but his messenger and representative Hermes cannot but be taken as expressing the spirit of his rule, against which the "anima altera e disdegnosa" of Prometheus is exasperated by his own wrongs and the wrongs of men. This Hermes is not the righteous protector of Agamemnon's children and of the suppliant Danaids, not the embodiment of calm and friendly skill and grace, such as Praxiteles wrought him at Olympia, but the harsh official taunter of a fallen adversary, alert with a boyish insolence of new intoxicating success. And his very errand, his threaten-

---

Of man, of woman, or of commonwealth,
Answer unbidden of the Olympians' sire.)—*Eum.* 616-18.
And compare *Fragment* 79 :—
στέλλειν ὅπως τάχιστα, ταῦτα γὰρ πατὴρ
Ζεὺς ἐγκαθίει Λοξίᾳ θεσπίσματα.
(Send with all speed, for thus the Father Zeus
Gave Loxias charge to speak his oracle.)

[1] τὸν φρονεῖν βροτοὺς ὁδώ-
σαντα, τὸν πάθη μάθος
θέντα κυρίως ἔχειν.—*Agamemnon,* 175-77.

Accumulation of instances in this sense may be found in Dronke's *Religiöse und sittliche Vorstellungen des Aeschylos und Sophokles.* The author does not seem to feel so strongly as I do the force of the arguments in a different sense which the *Prometheus* affords.

ing inquiry of the secret which would save his master from
ruin, confesses the limits of the wisdom and power, no less than
of the goodness, of Zeus.

To bring this drama into consistency with the rest, there
would seem to be two considerations especially to be taken
into account. The first is, that the utterances on the powers
and attributes of Gods are, after all, dramatic, even when
proceeding from the Chorus. For the Chorus is always in
Aeschylus a personage concerned in the drama; it has ceased
to absorb the whole, as in the dithyrambic songs from which
the drama arose; but it never stands quite outside the whole
action, as in Euripides, and to some extent in Sophocles.
Thus we must remember that when the Danaid or Theban
suppliants, or even the chorus of Argive elders in the *Agamemnon,* deeply moved as they are for the fate of their king
and city, invoke an all-just and all-ruling Power, this is
primarily and essentially the expression of that longing for a
saviour in the day of trouble which can intensify belief held
lightlier in lighter hours, and can even develop what seem
intuitions of powers and influences unthought of, because
unneeded, before.

The second consideration is, that there are indications, though
grievously scanty, of the reconciliation which was effected in
the *Prometheus Unbound.* This much we know, that Prometheus was delivered by Herakles, son of Zeus and of the mortal
Alcmene, the seed of the woman Io, who had received recompense for her maddened wanderings when she rested by the
banks of Nile. On his release Prometheus tells the fateful
secret, and the danger is turned away for ever from the Olympian throne. In Pindar the revelation is made, not by Prometheus, but by his mother Themis, in that majestic passage of
the seventh Isthmian ode, which may here be cited to fill the
gap in the Aeschylean story, and tell the end of the tale of
divine renunciations in obedience to that $Mo\hat{\imath}\rho\alpha$, or Allotment,
which seems a mysterious universal behind the individualities
even of Gods, a personification of the law which constrains all
forces, personal and impersonal, in nature to fulfil the law of
their being by which the cosmic order is sustained :—

"Thereof was the Gods' council mindful, what time for the
hand of Thetis there was strife between Zeus and glorious

Poseidon, each having desire that she should be his fair bride, for love had obtained dominion over them.

"Yet did not the wisdom of the immortal Gods fulfil for them such marriage when they had heard a certain oracle. For Themis of wise counsels spake in the midst of them how it was predestined that the sea-Goddess should bear a royal offspring mightier than his father, whose hand should wield a bolt more terrible than the lightning or the dread trident, if she came ever into the bed of Zeus, or of brethren of Zeus.

" 'Cease ye herefrom : let her enter a mortal's couch, and see her son fall in war, who shall be as Ares in the might of his hands, and as the lightning in the swiftness of his feet. My counsel is that ye give her to be the heaven-sent prize of Peleus, son of Aiakos, whom the speech of men showeth to be their most righteous, an offspring of Iolkos' plain. Thus straightway let the message go forth to Cheiron's cave divine, neither let the daughter of Nereus put a second time into your hands the ballot-leaves of strife. So on the evening of the mid-month moon shall she unbind for the hero the fair girdle of her virginity.'

" Thus spake the Goddess her word to the sons of Kronos, and they bowed their everlasting brows. Nor failed her words of fruit, for they say that to Thetis' bridals came those two kings even with the rest."[1]

Renouncement and reconcilement—these are the inseparable healing agencies to which the mind of Aeschylus turned, when he contemplated the tumult of passions and ambitions, whether found in the Assembly of Athens, or in the palace of Mykenae, or in the Olympian council-hall of Gods. The conception which would seem most nearly to solve the difficulties of the subject seems to be one which would certainly also be congenial to the genius of Aeschylus ; it is that he recognised a certain progress and education even among Gods, that in the interval between the binding of Prometheus and his release, Zeus and the new Gods, while retaining supremacy, had not been without their share of care and fear, though not of actual misfortune, and had learnt and unlearnt much of the great teacher, Time.[2]

---

[1] Pindar, *Isthm.* vii. 26-47.

[2] ἀλλ' ἐκδιδάσκει πάνθ' ὁ γηράσκων χρόνος.

(All things are taught by the great teacher, Time.)—*Prom.* 981.

Thus, while he dramatised the deliverance of Prometheus, he seems to have adopted also the tradition which spoke of how the dethroned Kronos had been released from his bonds,[1] and had been given, as Pindar tells, an abode in the Islands of the Blest, not unvisited by his son, and ruling among the spirits of the good and great.[2]

Both the considerations which have been urged on this subject are expressed by that most striking passage in the *Agamemnon,* where the Chorus most emphasise their appeal to Zeus :—

> " Zeus, whosoe'er he be, if this name please his ear,
> 　　By this name I bid him hear ;
> 　　Nought but Zeus my soul may guess,
> 　　Seeking far and seeking near,
> 　　Seeking who shall stay the stress
> 　　Of its fond and formless fear.
> 　　For he who long ago was great,
> 　　Filled with daring and with might,
> 　　Now is silent, lost in night :
> 　　And the next who took his state
> Met his supplanter too, and fell, and sank from sight."[3]

Here, while Zeus is made the object of glorification and earnest appeal, the mythic account of the divine dynasties is yet accepted, and the strange vagueness of the opening address symbolises the poet's half-unconscious sense of the insufficiency of the mythology to satisfy his aspiration toward an embodiment of the highest good. It is difficult for a modern European, accustomed to a religion with a body of doctrine formulated by Greek metaphysic and Roman law, to realise the fluctuating, though always individual, character of the Hellenic Gods, or how

---

[1] *Eumen.* 645.　　　　　　　　[2] Pindar, *Ol.* ii. 70.

[3] Ζεὺς, ὅστις ποτ' ἐστὶν, εἰ τόδ' αὐ-
　　τῷ φίλον κεκλημένῳ,
　　τοῦτό νιν προσεννέπω.
　　οὐκ ἔχω προσεικάσαι
　　πάντ' ἐπισταθμώμενος
　　πλὴν Διὸς, εἰ τὸ μάταν ἀπὸ φροντίδος ἄχθος
　　χρὴ βαλεῖν ἐτητύμως.
　　οὐδ' ὅστις πάροιθεν ἦν μέγας,
　　παμμάχῳ θράσει βρύων,
　　οὐδὲν ἂν λέξαι πρὶν ὤν.
　　ὃς δ' ἔπειτ' ἔφυ, τριακ-
　　τῆρος οἴχεται τυχών.—*Agam.* 160-72.

a belief in them which cannot be called unreal was yet consistent with acquiescence in the saying of Herodotus that Homer and Hesiod first settled their genealogies and attributes. A similar but still greater fluctuation seems to have prevailed, and to prevail still, in India; and even in Catholic Europe something like it appeared, in spite of the lateness of the time, when the central controlling force of the Papacy was shaken and maimed; while another unsettlement of the attitude of worshippers towards objects of their worship seems to have occurred among Mahometans when they separated into Sunnis and Shiahs. The Hellenic Gods, while always regarded as stronger and more beautiful than men, only acquired that special claim to allegiance which a moral interference can support, when specialised, so to speak, in relation to some human duties placed under their guarding care. The instinctive idea that God will protect the right finds indeed such utterance as the exclamation of the old Laërtes in the *Odyssey*, when he hears of the slaying of the wooers:—

> " Still then ye live, Zeus and Olympian Gods,
>   If verily vengeance hath the wooers found." [1]

But it was only Ζεὺς Ξένιος, Ἑρκεῖος, Ἱκέσιος, the Guardian of Host and Guest, of the Landmark, of the Suppliant, who, to the ordinary believer, was reckoned a present God who would avenge or aid. It was thus that the forces outside humanity, which the Hellenic imagination conceived as Gods, took shape and definite relation to human conduct; a relation in which both sides had, at least for Aeschylus, their several obligations; for Apollo himself shrinks from the thought of having the blood of Orestes on his head:—

> "For dreadful among Gods and men alike,
>   The suppliant's curse, if uncompelled I yield him." [2]

One very striking proof, among others, of what has been said, occurs also in the *Oresteia*.[3] It is by the Erinyes, the avengers

---

[1] Ζεῦ πάτερ, ἦ ῥα ἔτ' ἔστε θεοὶ κατὰ μακρὸν Ὄλυμπον,
   εἰ ἐτεὸν μνηστῆρες ἀτάσθαλον ὕβριν ἔτισαν.—*Odyssey*, xxiv. 351.

[2] δεινὴ γὰρ ἐν βροτοῖσι κἂν θεοῖς πέλει
   ἡ προστροπαίου μῆνις, εἰ προδῶ σφ' ἑκών.—*Eumen.* 233-34.

[3] Under this name is generally known the trilogy composed of the *Aga-*

of blood, that Orestes is pursued for slaying his mother, and yet it was also by foretelling the wrath of these very Erinyes that Apollo urged him to the deed.[1] So fluctuating is the personification, though the idea is clear beneath each shape it takes.[2] And we feel that the real worship of Aeschylus, though it may attach itself to this God or to that, to Zeus, Apollo, or Pan,[3] when he comes to avenge the orphan nestling or the orphan child, is really independent of the persons, and belongs to the moral law which they execute and represent.

It is not however for the poet, especially the dramatic poet, directly to inculcate moral or religious doctrine; the essentially important question under this head is, In what region of ethical feeling does he chiefly move, what ethical qualities and laws does he present most impressively, and what ethical ideal do they indicate and indirectly communicate to the spectator or reader of his work? Here Aeschylus ranks with Dante and Milton, and in some ways above both. We may distinguish two ethical qualities especially which he has glorified, and with which he is above all to be identified. One is the self-control, the sound-mindedness ($\sigma\omega\phi\rho\sigma\sigma\acute{u}\nu\eta$), and respect for the rights and feelings of others which the artistic

---

memnon, the *Choephoroe*, and the *Eumenides*. But when in the *Frogs* of Aristophanes Euripides requires Aeschylus to recite the prologue of the *Oresteia*, he answers by the first lines of the *Choephoroe*. The evidence against the statement (commonly accepted since Welcker wrote) that dramas were habitually exhibited in trilogies or tetralogies, is succinctly stated in a paper by Mr. H. Richards in the *Journal of Philology*, 1878.

[1] ἄλλας δ' ἐφώνει προσβολὰς 'Ερινύων.—*Choephoroe*, 283.

[2] It must of course be understood too, that even after Homer and Hesiod an immense body of infinitely various local traditions as to supernatural persons remained, which the most curious theologian could not expect to master entirely. Thus for instance we read in Pausanias that the legend of Glaucus was told (plainly for the first time) to both Pindar and Aeschylus when they were at Anthedon, the legend's home, that Pindar made some slight mention of it in his poetry, while Aeschylus took it for the subject of a play.

[3]   ὕπατος δ' ἀΐων ἤ τις 'Απόλλων,
       ἢ Πὰν, ἢ Ζεὺς, οἰωνόθροον
       γόον ὀξυβόαν τῶνδε μετοίκων
       ὑστερόποινον
       πέμπει παραβᾶσιν 'Ερινύν.—*Agam.* 55-59.

The use of the indefinite τις is of still further significance.

instinct of the Hellene helped to make a capital and constant virtue in his ethical ideal. With this virtue the Pythagoreanism of Aeschylus,[1] like the Catholicism of Dante and the Puritanism of Milton, may have mingled something of asceticism, but with him, as with those other two, it was very far from the morbid asceticism of the fanatic, who thinks that by maiming his own humanity he shall gratify a fiend disguised as God ; it was an asceticism based on a recognition of a supreme and harmonious order, by conforming whereto, and so only, human nature entered through discipline into the possession of its full privileges and capacities. The other quality is more peculiarly emphasised in Aeschylus than in other Hellenic poets, partly owing to his individual character, partly to the time when he lived, and the mighty acts in which he had borne a part : this was the virtue of indomitable resistance to unjust oppression, and of valour in a righteous cause. The issue of the Persian war seemed to the Hellenes the most signal judgment—more signal even than any overthrow of their own city-despots and oligarchies—which had ever descended on that sin which was the opposite of the virtue of measured self-control, the sin of $\H{\upsilon}\beta\rho\iota\varsigma$, of insolence, ready to trample in violence over law and liberty to gratify selfish lust and pride. The feelings of the religious Hellene who had fought at Salamis and Plataea were in this like those of the English Puritan who had fought at Marston Moor and Naseby ; so clearly did a righteous God seem to have triumphed through their arms. Nowhere could this feeling be so strong as in Athens, where the ruins of her temples in the Acropolis, profaned and burnt by the invader, had looked down a few months after on the Persian wrecks round Psyttaleia. And when Aeschylus wrote the *Persians*, Athens as yet bore her exceeding weight of glory with majesty and self-control. Perhaps even a more peculiar triumph for her than

---

[1] It is impossible that anything definite should be known of the relation of Aeschylus either to the Pythagoreanism or to the religious mysticisms of his day. As to the latter, the results of such interesting and valuable researches and speculations as those of Kreuzer and Guigniaut, and the like, seem to point to the conclusion that this period of Hellenic civilisation was less inclined to mysticism than either the earlier time in which the worship of "pre-Dorian" divinities was more prominent, or a later time which inclined to ascetic or sensual rites and mysteries of the East.

Salamis itself was when the allied fleet turned away from the corrupted Pausanias, affecting with his Persian dress, with his Egyptian and Median bodyguards, the bearing and habits of a despot, to Aristeides, simple and open, strong and self-controlled, the perfection of an Athenian gentleman, a trusted leader among soldiers, an equal citizen among citizens, dwelling ever with high thoughts and working for great and patriotic ends, and chose him with one accord to be their chief. And Aristeides was the object of Aeschylus' warmest devotion, the man to whom he did felicitous and noble homage in the lines in which the Theban messenger describes Amphiaraüs,

> " Who bare no blazon on his shield,
> Who only cares to be, not seem, the best,
> Gathering the harvest of a soul profound,
> Wherefrom grow forth his counsels pure and high."[1]

But it was the companionship of that other virtue of indomitable valour in a good cause which made so bright the gentle moderation of Aristeides and of Athens, the spirit in which the city of Pallas had arisen to face the invader alone, when in the other states of Hellas " there were great searchings of heart," when some of the mightiest quailed, and shrank more from danger than from the coward's curse—the curse pronounced by the Hebrew Deborah against the men of Meroz, " because they came not to the help of the Lord, to the help of the Lord against the mighty." No Athenian could ever forget the day when a second storm of invasion threatened his devastated land, and there came into his Agora the Peloponnesian envoy, who prayed Athens to forget the desertion of her allies and stand forward once more as the bulwark of Hellas; and over against him the Macedonian prince, who in the name of the Persian king offered her safety for herself and dominion over her fellow-Hellenic states, on that one easy-seeming condition, " if thou wilt fall down and worship me ;" nor how each had his answer from the Athenian people : how they told the Spartans that they thanked them for their offer of shelter and supplies, but that

---

[1]   σῆμα δ' οὐκ ἐπῆν κύκλῳ·
οὐ γὰρ δοκεῖν ἄριστος, ἀλλ' εἶναι θέλει,
βαθεῖαν ἄλοκα διὰ φρενὸς καρπούμενος,
ἀφ' ἧς τὰ κεδνὰ βλαστάνει βουλεύματα.
                    The Seven against Thebes, 591-94.

was not what they desired; let Sparta send men to fight beside them against the barbarian : how they bade the Macedonian go back to those who sent him, and say that so long as the sun should hold his course in heaven they would be the irreconcilable enemies of the invaders who had desolated their homes and burnt with fire the temples of their Gods.

One worthy poetic monument of the great war has been left to us by Aeschylus in unmistakable form in the drama of the *Persians.* It is the counterpart of that colossal statue of Nemesis which stood eloquent upon the plain of Marathon. But the spirit of the struggle can be discerned also in the *Seven against Thebes;* that drama, as Aristophanes called it, " full of the War-God,"[1] and more profoundly still, even if less obviously, in the *Prometheus Bound.* It may be permitted to dwell briefly on the consummate art with which, under the simplest and severest forms, Aeschylus has made the mighty central figure stand out, how admirably its qualities are relieved and accentuated by the successive surrounding personages, even in the one play which is left to us. It would indeed have been of the deepest interest to have known from his treatment of the story how the Deliverer's Deliverer, Herakles, was in turn portrayed in the *Prometheus Unbound;* how these great souls greeted one another in the wilderness, when in the year of redemption the process of the ages had brought them face to face. In the Prometheus who remains to us, the time-serving good-nature of his would-be counsellor Oceanus, the sight and foresight of the sufferings of his fellow-victim Io, the remorse of Hephaestus under constraint of his hateful office, the taunts and threats of Hermes, or of the giant Power, all call forth the bitterness of just resentment, and intensify the grim and scornful endurance which he has summoned to meet his torment. One softer element there is to relieve the sombre sternness of the whole,—the bright and tender personality of the daughters of Ocean, who come to visit Prometheus in his woe, and form the chorus of the play. Aeschylus was reproached by the partisans of Euripides for making small account of female character in his works, but whether this was due to real indifference or to a reserve which will bear another interpreta-

---

[1] Ἀρέως μεστόν.

tion, may at least be questioned. A Beatrice was impossible
to Hellenic art; this was the one thing lacking to it; but
within Hellenic limits, and they were not narrow, Aeschylus
was less deficient on this point than has been supposed. He
is more careful to preserve the feminine attributes of Electra
under her dire mission of vengeance than is either of the other
great tragedians. His judgment of Helen is sterner than
Homer's, but the vision he evokes of her is not less magi-
cally fair. For pity and beauty nothing in poetry can surpass
his contrast of the hour when Iphigeneia's pleading eyes " as in
a picture " struck her sacrificers to the heart, with the happy
times when her pure voice sang free and joyously in her home,
to gladden the same father whom fate now made her murderer.
But no character is more truly womanly, more winning in its
weakness and in its strength, the weakness of inexperienced
timidity, the strength of self-forgetful devotion, than is the fair
collective personality of these sisters of the sea. Their first
approach is perceived before they are arrived; Prometheus
breaks off the " large utterance " of the iambics of his first
soliloquy, he feels another presence than he had known of late:

> " Ah, ah, but what fragrance
> Is wafted anear ?
> What murmur comes stealing
> Untraced to my ear,
> Of God, or man, or blended of the twain ? " [1]

Tears are in their eyes, and words of compassion on their lips,
while yet at first a half-timid glee at their own daring in
visiting the victim of the wrath of the new king of heaven, an
eager curiosity as to his eventful story, give a touch of childlike nature to their speech. Their traditional sympathies are
with the old order of things which Zeus has supplanted, but
they cannot see how it can be of profit to resist the supreme
power once established as supreme; they are little conversant
with ideas, and when Prometheus unfolds the history of his
championship of the human race, and enumerates the benefits
he gave it, they are but slightly moved to sympathy with the

---

[1] ἆ, ἆ, εἅ, εἅ
τίς ἀχὼ, τίς ὀδμὰ προσέπτα μ' ἀφεγγὴς,
θεόσυτος, ἢ βρότειος, ἢ κεκραμένη ;—*Prom.* 114-16.

" creatures of a day," whom they have never known; they are still absorbed by the sight and prospect of the Titan's pain, and press him to end it, even if it must be by submission. But when Hermes, baffled and scorned by Prometheus, bids them flee from the wrath to come, which is to hurl the rock they stand on into hell, then at last their reply makes it plain that it was from no selfish indifference to the hero's honour, but only from an over-anxious care for his wellbeing, that they counselled him before:—

> " Other bidding bear if thou wouldst bend us ;
> Tak'st thou us for traitors to our friend ?
> Nay, with him, with him, unbowed to baseness,
> Be it ours to suffer to the end." [1]

On their heads then be the consequences of their folly—such are Hermes' last words : and he is scarcely gone when the wrath of Zeus descends upon the rock, and Prometheus' last cry of indignant defiance is heard amid the tempest and the fire :—

> " Lo in deed, no more in word, the earthquake !
> Hark, the thunder ! lo, the lightnings leap !
> Dark with dust and torn with warring whirlwinds
> Crash the skies, confounded with the deep.
>
> Zeus himself amid the awful onset
> Hurls me hellward to Tartarean gloom :
> Earth, my mother ! Heaven, thou light of all things !
> Hear ye, see ye, my unrighteous doom ? " [2]

---

[1] ἄλλο τι φώνει καὶ παραμυθοῦ μ'
ὅ τι καὶ πείσεις· οὐ γὰρ δή που
τοῦτό γε τλητὸν παρέσυρας ἔπος.
πῶς με κελεύεις κακότητ' ἀσκεῖν
μετὰ τοῦδ' ὅ τι χρὴ πάσχειν ἐθέλω,
τοὺς προδότας γὰρ μισεῖν ἔμαθον,
κοὐκ ἔστι νόσος
τῆσδ' ἥντιν' ἀπέπτυσα μᾶλλον.—*Prom.* 1063-70.

[2] καὶ μὴν ἔργῳ κοὐκέτι μύθῳ
χθὼν σεσάλευται·
βρυχία δ' ἠχὼ παραμυκᾶται
βροντῆς, ἕλικες δ' ἐκλάμπουσι
στεροπῆς ζάπυροι,
στρόμβοι δὲ κόνιν εἱλίσσουσι,
σκιρτᾷ δ' ἀνέμων πνεύματα πάντων
εἰς ἄλληλα

The *Prometheus Bound*, as is the case with a few of the highest works of genius, is laden with mighty meanings which wait on Time to be unrolled. Prometheus himself may be called a type at once of the Past and of the Future; he belongs to the primeval race of deities, but he suffers for having anticipated the process of the ages, for having helped the new-born race of man, for having acted on his own vision of things to come which others could not see. Zeus represents the Present, with its exigencies, its imperiousness, and its force; for the time he forgets the traditions and benefits of the Past, and ignores and would stifle the Future; his only concern is to keep in being the order and administration with which he is identified, and to which it is not unnatural, it is almost necessary, though it is still unjust, that he should be resolved to make all claims bow. There have been situations in modern revolutions which might well remind us of this contrast.

It could hardly be that the august and beautiful conception of a champion and saviour of men, enduring for their sake the extremity of agony, yet not suffered to remain in Hell, should fail to strike the Greek-speaking Christian Fathers as a prefigure-ment of the great tide of human yearning which found its most impressive manifestation when the western world swore alle-giance to the Son of Man crucified on Calvary, foreshadowed by the Son of Earth crucified on Caucasus, and claiming the supremacy of Godhead by virtue of his oppressors' taunt, *He saved others, himself he cannot save.*

The only work of Aeschylus later than the *Prometheus* which we possess is the trilogy in which he tells the fortunes of the house of Agamemnon. If it is the passion for freedom which finds pre-eminent expression in such Aeschylean treatment of the story of Prometheus as remains to us, it is the equally vital desire for Order and Harmony which is satisfied in the last play which came from the poet's hand, the *Eumenides.* From this

---

στάσιν ἀντίπνουν ἀποδεικνύμενα·
ξυντετάρακται δ' αἰθὴρ πόντῳ.
τοιάδ' ἐπ' ἐμοὶ ῥιπὴ Διόθεν
τεύχουσα φόβον στείχει φανερῶς.
ὦ μητρὸς ἐμῆς σέβας, ὦ πάντων
αἰθὴρ κοινὸν φάος εἱλίσσων,
ἐσορᾷς μ' ὡς ἔκδικα πάσχω ;—*Prom.* 1080-93.

we may indeed divine somewhat of how the *Prometheus Unbound* must have ended. Here the half-blind worship of half-blind forces, though arrayed in its full pomp of terror, yields to a more excellent revelation. In so doing it yields in fact to what is best in itself. *Blood for blood*, the old law had said: this was enough for it. The new law is awful as the old, but juster, and will distinguish between degrees of homicide. Vengeance for Iphigeneia may be the plea of Clytemnestra, as vengeance for Agamemnon is the plea of Orestes. But the new tribunal shall discover beneath the plea of Clytemnestra the selfish motives of lust and guilty fear. The plea of Orestes shall be allowed to save the slayer, though after an agony such as must needs follow a deed of so wild justice. For, as has been said, the old law yields to what was its own best part. The Eumenides are not deprived of their office, but resume it in allegiance to the new dispensation. All through the *Oresteia* the moral judgment is appealed to by revenges and recrimina- tions of varying justice. And thus the stories of Orestes and of Hamlet, while they have much of likeness, have much more of difference. The interest in *Hamlet* is primarily in the persons and in the situation: the interest in the *Oresteia* is primarily in the disentangling of the laws which govern the moral development of the race.

It is significant that the last arbitrament which lays finally the demon of the house of Tantalus rests not with the Zeus of either the upper or the under world,[1] but with a council of just men, as though to show that to the conscience of humanity the ultimate appeal must lie. It is only when the votes of the Areopagites are equally divided that Athene adds hers, and turns the balance for acquittal. Then the whole tumult of conflicting passions, rights, and duties is resolved in an august harmony, and passes upward into a stormless air.

If we are thrilled and awed by merely reading this majestic drama, what must it have been to see and hear as it was pre-

---

[1] See the *Suppliants*, 230-31 :—

    Κἀκεῖ δικάζει τἀμπλακήμαθ', ὡς λόγος,
    Ζεὺς ἄλλος ἐν καμοῦσιν ὑστάτας δίκας.
    (Among the dead, they say, that other Zeus
    Holds a last judgment of the sins of men.)

sented on the Athenian stage ?   And when at evening the play
was played out, and its solemn voices still were in his ears,
the Athenian whose path home lay north-westward passed
thither under the very hill of Ares where the momentous
verdict was pronounced, and beside the cave haunted by the
dread powers so hardly appeased; but his lifted eyes met the
sunlit western front of her shrine who had prevailed for mercy
and right, and could discern the statuary of the pediment, the
monument of the primeval triumph when she won his Athens
to be her own.

This was the last drama written by Aeschylus, and its calm
ending, while it deprives it of none of the solemnity of tragedy,
seems to cast back a mild light over all the terrors which his
spell had called into being before, over the troublous mysteries
of theology and human fate. He leaves us rejoicing in the
triumph of the two brightest and wisest, the "highest and
most human," of all the Hellenic divinities. One is Athene,
queen of light, the most cherished child of Zeus,

> " Who only of gods may know that chamber's keys
> Where sleeps the sealëd thunder of her sire,"[1]

yet for her people's sake is now most patient, and "will not
tire of speaking gentle words"[2] to the resentful brood of Night.
The other is Apollo, "la lieta delfica Deità," the god invoked
as healer and helper in time of pestilence and war, the Apollo
on whom Herakles called to guide his arrow straight against
the eagle which preyed upon Prometheus, when the hour of
his deliverance drew nigh.[3] And those whom such coincidences affect may remember that to these two deities, among
all the Gods of Hellas, belong, as it happens, the only two certainly ascribed temples of which more than the merest ruins
are still standing on Hellenic soil. Athene's is on the Acropolis of Athens, beneath which a new life struggles feebly, yet
not all ignobly, toward some glimmer of the ancient day.
Apollo's is at the lonely verge of the Arcadian mountain-

---

[1] καὶ κλῇδας οἶδα δωμάτων μόνη θεῶν
ἐν οἷς κεραυνός ἐστιν ἐσφραγισμένος.—*Eum.* 827-28.
[2] οὔτοι καμοῦμαί σοι λέγουσα τἀγαθά.—*Eum.* 881.
[3] Ἀγρεὺς δ' Ἀπόλλων ὀρθὸν ἰθύνοι βέλος.
(Hunter Apollo guide my arrow straight.)—*Frag.* 191.

forest, high above forgotten Phigaleia, and looking south beyond Eira and Ithome toward his unredeemed Cretan home.

Until Aeschylus was forty-one years old no play of his was crowned at the Dionysiac competition, and again in his later years the growing fame of Sophocles seems to have somewhat overshadowed his. But he had dedicated his works to Time,[1] and the dedication was approved. To his plays the Athenians assigned the unique privilege that they should be acted after his death at the public cost, and to Hellenic colonies he became, in the phrase of M. Victor Hugo, the guardian of their minority, their preserver from barbaric contamination.[2] In a quaint but touching simile M. Hugo has compared the function of the colossal poet among these children of Hellas to that of the huge and kindly elephants ("ces bontés énormes") who watch over infants at play in the jungle round an Indian homestead. To us at this distance of time and thought his relation must rather be expressed by some figure of less familiar intercourse. There are a few great poets of past ages who seem to us, by a not dishonourable illusion, even greater than themselves, who have become in our eyes as it were invested with the attributes of the wonderful and beautiful things of inanimate nature, of ever-flowing rivers and solemn hills, or of the signs of heaven. And we may liken Aeschylus to some golden-armoured constellation, whose first rising was when the sky was thronged with potent fires, yet found there no radiance of which his own was less than peer. Then the mists and storm-clouds of barbarism hid him a long time, and when he again became visible he seemed to have receded far into the vault; he reveals a mere fragment of his effulgence, and of his seventy stars but seven. These at least remain to us, and shall now be taken away no more. Well is it for the reasoning soul that has received their influence on her birth, and can still feel their presence in the firmament, austere and yet benign.   E. M.

---

[1] Athenaeus, viii. 347.

[2] Le théâtre eschylien était comme chargé de surveiller le bas âge des colonies.—Victor Hugo's "William Shakespeare," p. 216.

THE THEOLOGY AND ETHICS
OF SOPHOCLES.[1]

IN his own generation Sophocles was eminent for his piety. Though he lived at a time when most men were disengaging themselves from their traditional religion, he remained true to the old faith; he believed in the gods of his age and nation. At the same time we find in his writings some of the noblest thoughts on religion and ethics recorded in antiquity. Thus it is that two elements of Greek religion, the mythological and the ethical, are combined in his dramas, and, incongruous as these elements often are, there is no attempt to separate them. Zeus is the upholder of the eternal laws of justice; he dwells beyond the reach of time, in a light "which no man may approach unto." Zeus is also the lover of Semele and Alcmene, the father of children half-human, half-divine. The inconsistency of such a presentation of the divine being would be fatal if the dramas of Sophocles were a treatise on theology; but when we remember that they are pictures of a mind partly influenced by the contemporary age, and partly in advance of it, the contradiction is intelligible and true to nature. It is from this point of view that I have attempted to describe the attitude adopted by Sophocles towards the deities of his national religion, and to indicate some of the ethical and religious thoughts underlying the situations and characters which he has chosen to depict.

I.

The gods of the old Homeric mythology appear in Sophocles, but while some are little more than names, others are represented as having a real influence on human life and action,

---

[1] Dronke, *Die religiösen und sittlichen Vorstellungen des Aeschylos und Sophocles.* Leipzig, 1861.

and take a prominent part in the development of the dramas. For this reason we may conveniently speak of these deities of mythology under three heads. There are, in the first place, the deities mentioned only in connection with certain places or isolated facts, local and tutelary gods, present or absent as the case may be, and having no influence beyond their own sphere; then there are the deities which are mere personifications of human passions, Eros and Cypris—deities which obviously must take a prominent part in any representation of human life; and thirdly, distinct from either of the foregoing, is the great triad of Greek mythology—Zeus, Apollo, and Athena. Without being of any intrinsic value in analysis, this triple division will enable us to bring out the aspects under which the gods of mythology appear in Sophocles.

Under the first head come all the gods of the Homeric Olympus, and even more, with the exception of those set apart in the other divisions. For the most part these deities are mentioned in the choruses only. Sophocles adds little or nothing to their attributes; he speaks of them in reference to certain places or facts, as any other Greek of his time might do. Thus in the final chorus of the *Antigone* Bacchus is the god of Thebes. As in the myth, he is the "joy of the Cadmeian bride," "dwelling beside the seed of the fell serpent," seen by the gleaming fires on Parnassus, sent forth with loud acclamations from the vine-clad shores of Nysa. Bacchus is also the Iacchus of the mysteries, and therefore, as we read, the hymn becomes more mystical in tone : "O leader of the fire-breathing stars, master of the voices of night, O son and seed of Zeus, beam thou upon us with thy Thyiads from Naxus, mystic maidens who in nightlong dance glorify thee, their lord Iacchus." Bacchus loves to wander near Colonus, which is also the haunt of the Muses, of Aphrodite, and Poseidon, and has been made famous by their gifts. In Homer, Ares is, of all the gods who dwell in Olympus, the most hateful to Zeus. He is "the two-faced deity to whom strife, war, and battle are ever dear." [1] In Sophocles, Ares is the personification of all evil powers. He

---

[1] μή τί μοι, ἀλλοπρόσαλλε, παριζόμενος μινύριζε·
ἔχθιστος δέ μοί ἐσσι θεῶν οἳ Ὀλυμπον ἔχουσιν·
αἰεὶ γάρ τοι ἔρις τε φίλη πόλεμοί τε μάχαι τε.—*Il.* v. 890.

is the pestilence which desolates Thebes (*O. T.* 190); he is the god whom the gods put far from honour (*ib.* 215). Ares lifts the cloud of misery from the eyes of the Salaminian mariners (*Aj.* 706), *i.e.* it is Ares who has placed it there. Artemis is implored to come to the aid of plague-stricken Thebes, in which city she has a temple (*O. T.* 160 ff.); she is also the goddess whose torches flash along the Lycian hills, the sister, that is, of the Lycian god of light, whom the Greeks identified with their own Apollo. In the *Electra*, l. 563, Artemis is said to have caused the many winds to blow at Aulis in consequence of an outrage inadvertently committed in her precincts by Agamemnon, and thus she brought about the sacrifice of Iphigeneia. Of Hera, the queen of heaven, there is no mention in the extant plays of Sophocles, except in one passage, *Electra*, l. 8, where she is mentioned incidentally in connection with her temple at Argos. Demeter and Persephone are spoken of in reference to the holy mysteries at Eleusis (*O. C.* 1049 ff.), " the torch-lit shore, where the queenly goddesses cherish their rites for men on whose tongue rests the golden key of the ministrant Eumolpids." Persephone is also the goddess of the dead, the unseen goddess (*O. C.* 1556), to whom Antigone goes down, the last of a sad company. In *Philoctetes*, l. 391, the chorus invoke Cybele, the all-nurturing mountain-goddess, by whose bounty Pactolus flows with gold, whose chariot the lions draw. Aidoneus, " the king of the benighted," is entreated to suffer Oedipus to pass easily into his realm (*O. C.* 1557). Hades, the god of night and death, is of course frequently mentioned; in *Ajax*, l. 1035, he is the cruel workman who wrought the baldrick by which Hector was torn to death. Prometheus, the fire-god, is one of the deities of Colonus (*O. C.* 56). But of none of these can it be said that they are brought before us in an aspect peculiarly Sophoclean, or that they enter in any great degree, if at all, into the action of the drama, and influence the plot. They hold here the place allotted to them in the ordinary Greek mind, which connected certain places with tutelary gods, and looked to particular deities for protection under particular circumstances.

More important than any of the deities hitherto mentioned

are the Eumenides, the deities which occupy so prominent a place
in the theology of Aeschylus. Yet even they, as we find them
in Sophocles, must be brought under this head. They cannot
be said to exercise any influence on the actions of any of the
extant dramas. They are, it is true, the cause of a scene in
the *Oedipus at Colonus*, but only in so far as they are the local
representatives of higher and more universal powers. Local
customs are needed to propitiate them as local goddesses ; as
universal deities Oedipus claims to be reconciled to them by
his long-suffering and humiliation. Nor is it the Eumenides
who have brought him to ruin, but Apollo (*O. T.* 1329), and
from Apollo and Zeus comes his restoration. In many cases
where we might expect to find the operation of these goddesses,
we do not find it in Sophocles. In the case of Oedipus and
Polynices it is Zeus and Apollo who undertake the work of
vengeance, and demand expiation. There is no trace of the
Eumenides in the Sophoclean Orestes ; and though Electra
invokes them to come to her aid in avenging her father, the
deed of vengeance is really accomplished under the guidance
of Apollo and the auspices of Zeus.

In any delineation of human life and action there will
necessarily be a place for those deities which are the personifications of human passions. Such are Eros and Aphrodite,
or Cypris, the deities of passionate love. Tradition tells us
that Sophocles knew their power too well. In his poems Eros
is invincible in strife ; his power none can escape, whether
mortal or immortal ; and he who is wise will not contend with
him. Eros puts madness in the heart, and leads astray the
soul of the righteous ; he stirs up strife between kindred blood,
and desire sways a sceptre no less powerful than justice.
Without the intervention of Eros the *Antigone* would have no
dénouement. The love of Haemon for Antigone leads to the
altercation of father and son, and to the suicide of the latter on
finding his betrothed dead. The death of Haemon is the direct
cause of the death of his mother Eurydice. Thus it is through
the operation of Eros that the vengeance of the gods overtakes
Creon, and a natural passion becomes the instrument of divine
justice.

In another passage the personification is less complete.

The passion is more than the deity.   Love, we are told in *Frag.*
162 (Dindorf), is a pleasant plague, which may be figured thus :
When the air is frosty, and children take the dry ice in their
hands, at first the experience is something strange and sweet;
but soon the ice is frozen to the hand, and the pleasure passes
into a pain, of which the child would fain be rid,—and even
such is the impulse which sways the lover.[1]

Here Eros is spoken of in a figure, but not personified.
Indeed, the Greeks, however acutely sensible of the power of
Eros, had not made up their minds whether he was a god or
not.   He is at once a human passion and a "great spirit."

Equally important is the action of Aphrodite in the
Trachiniae.   Cypris is triumphant ever; she beguiled the son
of Cronos, Hades, and Poseidon; from her came the famous
strife of Achelous and Heracles for the hand of Dejanira; and
now she has ensnared Heracles in a new passion for Iole.   The
fear of a rival in her husband's affections induces Dejanira to
send the fatal robe; and thus Cypris brings about the death of
Heracles, and takes part in the accomplishment of the will of
heaven.   In a beautiful and well-known fragment (678) we
are told that Cypris is not Cypris only, but a goddess named of
many names.   Death and Immortality, Frenzy, Passion, and
Grief,—these are her titles.   Eagerness, gentleness, violence, are
blended and united in her.   She enters into all living things
and consumes them : hers are the fish that swim in the sea,
the four-footed kind that tread the earth; her pinion waves
among the birds, in creatures of the field, in men, and heavenly
gods.   Even in the heart of Zeus—for the truth is blameless,
though we speak it of the gods—Cypris is queen; without sword
or spear she cuts down the counsels of men and gods.

In Aphrodite or Cypris the personification is more complete
than in Eros.   But personifications of this kind are of course no
invention of Sophocles.   What we can perhaps claim for him
is, that he was the first to make them of importance in the
progress of the dramatic action, and to point out the manner in
which they assist in the development of divine purposes.   The
motive of love is well known to Homer: it is present in

---

[1] οὕτω δὲ τοὺς ἐρῶντας αὐτὸς ἵμερος
δρᾶν καὶ τὸ μὴ δρᾶν πολλάκις προσίεται.

both the *Iliad* and *Odyssey*, but it can hardly be said to govern the events and assist in the catastrophe of either poem, though it is true that the love of Helen and Penelope forms the basis on which the poems are built. "None can blame the Trojans and Achaeans that their strife for such a woman is long and sore." "I too know well that Penelope is not beautiful as thou art: she is mortal, and thee nor age nor death can touch: still, even so, I yearn to visit my home and behold the day of return." These passages remind us of touching scenes, in which the charm of beauty is deeply felt, and brought into contrast with the love of home and country. But Sophocles has gone much further than Homer. He has distinctly recognised these passions as elements in a dramatic action, binding individuals together so that wrong cannot be done to one without affecting another, or as forming the weak and assailable point in some otherwise superhuman character.

Zeus, Apollo, and Athena are deities far more exalted and sublime than any hitherto mentioned. Yet even they are not always, or at least the first and greatest of them, Zeus, is not always represented by Sophocles in the same light. Zeus is at times the god of the old Olympus, at others the god of the Athenians of the age of Sophocles, while, in other passages, the poet seems to be speaking his own thoughts, and to elevate Zeus, with Apollo and Athena as his ministers, into a supreme deity of justice and truth. How such various conceptions of one and the same deity—which was also the great national god—became possible, the history of Greek religion will explain. The interval between the earliest conception and the latest was a long one, but the Greeks did not allow the mythology which stood to them in the place of doctrine to restrain them from the endeavour to bring their conception of the Supreme Being into harmony with their conceptions of justice and law. Their religious conceptions became ethical at an early period, and continued to be so to the last, ever growing higher and higher as the conception of life and duty became more elevated. To this development and progress Sophocles contributed his part, without breaking away from what was traditional in religion or imposed upon him by the limits of poetry.

As a god of the old mythology, Zeus is the son of Cronos (*Tr.* 127, etc.); Earth is his mother (*Phil.* 391), Hades his brother (*Tr.* 1041), Apollo his son (*O. C.* 623). By Semele he is the father of Bacchus (*Ant.* 1116); by Alcmene, of Heracles (*Tr.* 1148, etc.). His daughters are Athena (*Aj.* 91) and Artemis (*Aj.* 172). He is the progenitor of Ajax (*Aj.* 389); he slays Capaneus (*Ant.* 134 ff.), descends in a shower of gold upon Danaë (*Ant.* 950), and punishes Ixion (*Phil.* 680).

Here we find Zeus mentioned as the lover of Semele, Alcmene, and Danaë. These connections, so far from being regarded as out of harmony with his nature as a god and the first of gods, are rather brought into prominence as connecting certain cities or families more directly with the deity, and making them, as it were, his elect. The inconsistency of connecting immoral actions with a moral being is hardly felt. In the same way, Aeschylus in his *Supplices* speaks of Zeus as ἔφαπτορ Ἰοῦς—*i.e.* the sensual story is adopted to bring the daughters of Danaus under his immediate protection,—but this does not prevent the same chorus in the same ode from appealing to Zeus as the highest and most perfect of the gods.[1] In the *Prometheus Vinctus*, on the other hand, the conduct of Zeus towards Io is spoken of as tyrannical in the extreme.

In other passages of Sophocles Zeus is addressed by epithets which express the popular contemporary feeling from a moral or religious point of view. Such are ἀγώνιος (*Tr.* 26), ἀλεξῆτορ (*O. C.* 143), ἀραῖος (*Ph.* 1182), ἑρκεῖος (*Ant.* 487), ἐφέστιος (*Aj.* 492), ἱκέσιος (*Ph.* 484), πατρῷος (*Tr.* 753), τροπαῖος (*Ant.* 143). These epithets are interesting as showing how Zeus is brought into relation with various sides of human life and action. A path is thus prepared by which polytheism can pass into monotheism, the special spheres of human life being made special sides, as it were, of the universal providence. Zeus is still Zeus, whether invoked as ἀγώνιος or ἑρκεῖος, but the epithets may not be interchanged, and he who invokes the god by a wrongly chosen epithet will not, such was the Greek conception, obtain a hearing.

---

[1] ἄναξ ἀνάκτων, μακάρων
μακάρτατε καὶ τελέων
τελειότατον κράτος, ὄλβιε Ζεῦ.—AESCH. *Suppl.* 524.

In a similar manner, Zeus was popularly connected with certain localities, as Oeta, Athos, and Lemnos.   Other passages (as
O. C. 1464, 1502, 1650; *Phil.* 1198, etc.) represent him as lord of
the thunder and god of the physical world.   From a more elevated
and ethical point of view, Zeus is almighty and all-wise— Ζεὺς
πάνταρχος θεῶν, παντόπτας (*O. C.* 1086); παγκρατής (*Phil.*
680); πάντ' ἀνάσσων (*O. T.* 904); πάνθ' ὁρῶν (*Ant.* 184).   Zeus
and Apollo know the affairs of mortals (*O. T.* 498).   But in all
these passages, and in many more which might be added to
them, the poet is only reproducing the religion of his day, and
using language which any pious Athenian would naturally
use.   Those who believed in gods at all, believed in the Power
dwelling in heaven, whose eye beheld and hand guided all
things.

There is yet another point of view from which is presented
to us, so far as we can tell, the poet's own conception of the
Supreme Being.   Zeus is the eternal ruler in heaven, the upholder of the highest laws of morality and religion, exalted
beyond the reach of human pride and power.   The poet has
attained to the idea of an order of the world which is just and
good, and this order he identifies with the empire of Zeus.   In
Zeus the highest laws of the family and the state have their
origin and birth, and though these may clash with the appetites
and ambition of men, and bring "not peace, but a sword," Zeus
is nevertheless a just and righteous ruler.   His kingdom is
founded on law, not on caprice.   "It was not Zeus," Antigone
declares, when speaking of the edict of Creon, "who made this
proclamation, nor Justice, who abides with the deities of the
under-world; they have established among men the laws which
I obey" (*Ant.* 450).   That is, Zeus and Justice uphold the laws
of family affection and the burial of the dead.   The power of
Zeus is also eternal and immutable.   "Thy power, O Zeus,
what proud advance of men can repress?—that power which
sleep never overtakes, nor the divine unwearying progress of
the months.   Through undying time thou dwellest in the
brightness of Olympus; thy laws are all-pervading; they have
been and shall be for ever" (*Ant.* 605-614).   Reverence for
Zeus is reverence for the highest law, so that Electra in her
abnegation of self in the cause of her dead father is pious towards

Zeus.[1] Loftier still is the conception of Zeus in the *Oedipus Tyrannus*. Here indeed the name of Zeus seems too narrow for the poet's thought : " O Zeus, if thou art rightly named, let it not be hidden from thee and thy everlasting rule that men are disregarding oracles, and that religion is passing away " (*O. T.* 902). The poet appeals to the highest of divine powers, for which he has no other name than Zeus, whether that be the right name or no.[2] In another passage he substitutes Olympus for Zeus, as though the highest laws were the outcome of the whole host of heaven : " May it be mine in every act and word of life to preserve the piety and purity ordained by those high laws of which Olympus is the only sire, whose birth was in the sky above,[3] and nothing human gave them being. In them is a divine power, which grows not old " (*O. T.* 863).

Of the two deities which remain, Apollo is prominent in the *Oedipus Tyrannus*, the *Oedipus at Colonus*, and the *Electra*. It is however necessary to distinguish between two deities called Apollo. There is Apollo the son of Zeus, who announces and executes his father's will—Apollo Pythius, the Delphian Apollo,—and there is also Apollo Lyceius, the protector of his worshippers and destroyer of their enemies, whose temple is at Argos (*El.* 7), and whose shrines are found beside the palace-doors (*El.* 635). To this latter god oracular functions are not ascribed in Sophocles, nor is he connected with Delphi, or regarded as the prophet of Zeus.[4] But Apollo, the Pythian god, is the son of Zeus, and makes known by oracles his father's will. The oracle of Delphi occupies a very prominent place in the Sophoclean drama. It influences largely the development of the action in the two plays concerned with Oedipus. It was

---

[1] ἃ δὲ μέγιστ᾽ ἔβλαστε νόμιμα, τῶνδε φερομέναν
ἄριστα τᾷ Ζηνὸς εὐσεβείᾳ.—*El.* 1095.

[2] Cf. Aesch. *Ag.* 160 : Ζεύς, ὅστις ποτ᾽ ἐστίν, εἰ τόδ᾽ αὐτῷ φίλον κεκλημένῳ.

[3] Cf. Bergk, *Litteratur-Gesch.* p. 330. The idea that the highest laws have their birth in the " heavenly ether " is perhaps, as Bergk suggests, an intimation that the highest law is realised in the movements of the heavenly bodies. Cf. Heraclitus, *Fr.* 29 : Ἥλιος οὐκ ὑπερβήσεται μέτρα· εἰ δὲ μή, Ἐρινύες μιν δίκης ἐπίκουροι ἐξευρήσουσι, and Wordsworth's *Ode to Duty*,

" Thou dost preserve the stars from wrong,
And the most ancient heavens through thee are fresh and strong."

[4] Aeschylus, *Ag.* 1080, identifies the Apollo "of the street" with the god whom Cassandra rejected,—the Delphian god of prophecy.

the oracle which induced Oedipus to fly from Corinth in the
hope of avoiding the doom foretold to him—that he should slay
his father and marry his mother.   It was the oracle which induced Laius and Jocasta to expose their child to death.   It is
the oracle which gives the true reason for the plague which has
visited Thebes, and requires the expulsion or death of the murderer of Laius.   It is the oracle which announces to Oedipus that
he shall, after many wanderings, find a place of rest and reconciliation.   It is the oracle which induces the Thebans to make the
attempt to recover Oedipus, so that his bones may lie in their land.
In the *Electra* it is the oracle which supports Orestes in his
attempt to avenge the death of his father, and points out the way
in which vengeance is to be taken.   In the *Trachiniae* also it is
the oracle which warns Heracles, before his last venture, that
he will either fail, or, if successful, enjoy rest for ever.   In
nearly all these cases the oracle points out what will certainly
happen.   No place is left, apparently, for the freewill of the
doer.   Oedipus is destined to slay his father ; Laius is destined
to fall by his son's hand.   Both Oedipus and Laius take measures
to avoid the doom foretold, but in vain.   Apollo therefore
would seem, in some cases, to be the prophet of a harsh fatalism which has no regard for guilt or innocence, and which no
one can escape.   But the other side of fatalism is human weakness, and the prophetic announcement of destiny is no more
than the complete foreknowledge of what will happen as the
result of such weakness.   Laius knows that his child is destined
to slay him, but this does not prevent him from becoming the
father of the child.   Oedipus is aware of the doom in store, yet
οὔθ᾽ ὁρῶν, οὔθ᾽ ἱστορῶν he slays a man in his haste, and takes to
wife the queen of Thebes.   From thus announcing the suffering
which will fall upon men, Apollo is sometimes regarded as the
author of that suffering.   Thus Oedipus (*O. T.* 1330) declares
that it was Apollo who brought to pass upon him the miseries
which the chorus behold.[1]

---

[1] In such passages as these something must be allowed for the supposed
etymology (Ἀπόλλων ἀπόλλυμι), a play upon words for which we have distinct
authority in Aesch. *Ag.* 1080 :

  Ἄπολλον, Ἄπολλον,
  ἀγυιᾶτ᾽, ἀπόλλων ἐμός.
  ἀπώλεσας γὰρ οὐ μόλις τὸ δεύτερον.

Rebellion against the authority of Apollo, and disregard of his oracles, are regarded by Sophocles as the height of impiety, inasmuch as Apollo is the servant of Zeus, and directly conveys his will to man. This rebellion is conspicuous in Jocasta, and makes that character the darkest in the Sophoclean drama. In impiety Jocasta far surpasses Clytemnestra; her language not only excites a certain impatience in Oedipus, but is denounced in no measured terms by the chorus, who are at once startled and shocked by her declarations. We may observe that the feeling entertained by Sophocles for the great religious institution of his time, the Delphian oracle, stands in marked contrast to the attitude of Thucydides.

If the conception of Apollo inspires awe, inasmuch as it shows how a man's weakness and want of foresight may act as an inevitable doom, the picture of Athena in the *Ajax* of Sophocles is perhaps more terrible still. When Ajax parted from his father Telamon to join the host for Troy, he received the wise counsels of age,—" My son, strive for victory, but with the help of God ! " Proud and impious was the answer: "With the help of the gods, O my sire, even a mean man may win the victory; I, without them, trust to make this glory mine." And when, at a later time, Athena offered the hero her aid in battle, he replied with scorn, bidding her go elsewhere: " Where I stand the battle shall not break bounds." Such words betrayed a spirit too proud for a human breast, and brought upon Ajax the anger of the goddess. She sends madness upon him, so that he slays the sheep and oxen of the spoil, believing them to be the Atreidae and Odysseus, and on his recovery he is overwhelmed by such sovereign shame that he takes his own life.

At first sight there seems to be something inhuman and cruel in the cold nature of this goddess, who punishes her victim without the least regard to his nobler qualities, and exhibits him in his degradation to the eyes of Odysseus, his greatest enemy. But a goddess is necessarily superhuman ; to speak of a want of humanity or of cruelty in Athena is as though we should complain of the cruelty or inhumanity of the laws of nature. These go on their way without regard to time and circumstance, and often cause great suffering, but this does not in the least affect their excellence and perfection as laws. In a similar way Athena is a controlling intellectual force, offences against which bring their own punishment. Ajax has rejected her, and spoken scornfully of her help; he has presumed "beyond the goal of ordinance," and exalted human power at the expense of the gods. Hence the wrath of Athena visits him. Yet the visitation is but for a day, and could Ajax have been preserved through that day his life was safe (*Aj.* 756).

The scene at the beginning of the *Ajax* exhibits the operation of this law of vengeance. Just as a natural law may paralyse the body, so has this divine power paralysed the mind of Ajax. In this phrenetic state he is exhibited to Odysseus, not to excite exultation—for Odysseus knows the limits of humanity too well to triumph over a slaughtered enemy,—but to awaken his compassion and deepen his sense of the frailty of human nature, and the dependence of all men in all things on the gods. It is thus that Odysseus is brought to insist on the burial of Ajax. He alone, with Calchas, knows the reason of this frenzy, and he shrinks from depriving an enemy when dead of the funeral rites which are fitly his.

Athena then is the spirit of σωφροσύνη—she is the divine power who keeps watch over the impulses of men, and punishes them when they would pass beyond the appointed limit. Those who most acknowledge their dependence on the divine power she is most willing to aid, but she punishes with all the resistless and relentless persistence of a natural law all who rebel against her. In her we see that intellectual conception of life which makes men responsible for their mistakes as well as their crimes, and punishes with equal severity the presumption and the baseness of men.

II.

From this examination of the conception of Athena in her relation to Ajax we may pass on to the wider question: "In what way does Sophocles conceive the relation of man and God?" Often, instead of naming any special deity, the poet speaks vaguely of θεός, ὁ θεός, θεοί, δαίμων—words which seem to be used, without much difference of meaning, for the divine power; but which have the effect of emancipating us entirely from the old mythology, and enabling us to put the question just mentioned in its widest form.

We cannot read much of Sophocles, or of any Greek tragedian, without arriving at the conclusion that the relation of man to his God is conceived under two different and almost contradictory aspects. On the one hand, God is beneficent, the author of good to his creatures; just and holy; the upholder of right, the avenger of wrong. On the other hand, God is the author of evil, and men are even divinely deceived in order to bring them the more certainly to their ruin.

In support of the first or optimist view, we may refer to the passage already quoted from the *Oedipus Tyrannus* (1. 871), in which the high laws are divinely sustained : " There is a mighty divine power in them, which grows not old." In the *Antigone* the gods are the guardians of justice (1. 369); and justice is said to have her home with the deities of the underworld (1. 450). In the *Ajax* (1. 1343) the gods require the burial of the dead. To the gods also Philoctetes looks for vengeance of the wrong that has been committed against him: " Ye will perish for the wrong that ye have done to me, if the gods have regard for justice; and that they have I know : never would ye have made this voyage hitherward for a helpless man had not some heaven-sent yearning for me impelled you." [1] In like manner Electra trusts to the gods for vengeance of her wrongs.[2] The justice of God may however in appearance be at variance with the justice of man : " With God to lead him, a man may wander from the way of justice, for where God is guide reproach follows not."[3] The gods are holy as they are just; Oedipus in his horror of the crime which he fears that he may have committed appeals to the " pure

---

[1] εἰ μή τι κέντρον θεῖον ἦγ᾽ ὑμᾶς ἐμοῦ.—*Phil.* 1039.

[2] οἷς θεὸς ὁ μέγας Ὀλύμπιος
ποίνιμα πάθεα παθεῖν πόροι.—*El.* 209.

[3] ἀλλ᾽ ἐς θεοὺς ὁρῶντα, κἂν ἔξω δίκης
χωρεῖν κελεύῃ, κεῖσ᾽ ὁδοιπορεῖν χρεών·
αἰσχρὸν γὰρ οὐδὲν ὧν ὑφηγοῦνται θεοί.—*Frag.* 234.

holiness" of the gods.[1] They are also beyond the reach of human pollution.[2]

As a natural result of their justice and holiness the gods punish the wicked. In *Electra*, l. 1383, Apollo is entreated by Electra to show to the world what are the wages of impiety. This divine vengeance may linger,[3] or it may come quickly,[4] or the sins of the father may even be visited on the children.[5] But whether the vengeance is swift or slow, that it will come, that all morality and religion depend on its coming, is the faith of Sophocles.[6] As the gods disregard and punish the evil, so they love and honour the good.[7] They are helpful to men, and from them comes the wisdom of the wise. It was by divine aid that Oedipus was enabled to save Thebes from the Sphinx.[8] No one is truly wise whose wisdom is not from above.[9] The utterances of the gods are indeed dark at times, but the wise will understand them, and those who will not will nevertheless find them true.[10] In understanding the mysteries of life a righteous and loving soul sees further than cunning or

---

[1] ὦ θεῶν ἁγνὸν σέβας.—*O. T.* 830.

[2]
εὖ γὰρ οἶδ' ὅτι
θεοὺς μιαίνειν οὔτις ἀνθρώπων σθένει —*Ant.* 1043.

[3] θεοὶ γὰρ εὖ μὲν, ὀψὲ δ' εἰσορῶσ', ὅταν
τὰ θεῖ' ἀφείς τις ἐς τὸ μαίνεσθαι τραπῇ.—*O. C.* 1536.

[4]
συντέμνουσι γὰρ
θεῶν ποδώκεις τοὺς κακόφρονας βλάβαι.—*Ant.* 1103.

[5]
θεοῖς γὰρ ἦν οὕτω φίλον,
τάχ' ἄν τι μηνίουσιν εἰς γένος πάλαι.—*O. C.* 964.

[6] *O. T.* 883 ff.

[7]
τοὺς δὲ σώφρονας
θεοὶ φιλοῦσι καὶ στυγοῦσι τοὺς κακούς.—*Aj.* 132, and *Ant.* 288.

[8]
ἀλλὰ προσθήκη θεοῦ
λέγει νομίζει θ' ἡμὶν ὀρθῶσαι βίον.—*O. T.* 38.
On this point the relations of Athena and Odysseus as described in the opening scene of the *Ajax* are abundant evidence.

[9] σοφὸς γὰρ οὐδεὶς πλὴν ὃν ἂν τιμᾷ θεός.—*Frag.* 234.

[10] καὶ τὸν θεὸν τοιοῦτον ἐξεπίσταμαι,
σοφοῖς μὲν αἰνικτῆρα θεσφάτων ἀεί,
σκαιοῖς δὲ φαῦλον κἂν βραχεῖ διδάσκαλον.—*Ibid.* 707.

cleverness,[1] and even the capacity for sound judgment is derived from the gods.[2] Lastly, the gods have power to remove misery.[3]

Such is what may be called the optimist relation of man to God: we find in it that which is the "central light of all religion," the justice and truth of God; but we miss from it many ideas with which Christianity has made us so familiar that they seem to us a part of the necessary relation of the human and the divine. There is little trace of the paternal relation so prominent in modern conceptions of the same subject. No doubt, in Greek religion Zeus is the father of men and gods, but not much is meant by the title. There is nothing said of the love of God for his creatures, or of their love for him. The picture is severe, even in this the most favourable light.

What then is the darker side of this relation of man and God? The poet does not hesitate to speak of the gods as heartless.[4] They are the fathers of human children, whom they leave to perish miserably, even as Heracles was consumed by fire. They are also jealous of the power of man. In the *Ajax* the divinely-inspired bard Calchas says of Ajax, and those like him—"Men over mighty in stature are plunged by the gods into dire misfortune."[5] They also injure men, so that the evil may outstrip the good,—such at least is the utterance of Ajax in his despair.[6] It is the gods who, for purposes

---

[1] ψυχὴ γὰρ εὔνους καὶ φρονοῦσα τοὔνδικον
κρείσσων σοφιστοῦ παντός ἐστιν εὑρετίς.—*Frag.* 88.

[2] *Ant.* 603.

[3] νῦν γὰρ θεοί σ' ὀρθοῦσι, πρόσθε δ' ὤλλυσαν.—*O. C.* 383; 394.

[4] μεγάλην δὲ θεοῖς ἀγνωμοσύνην
εἰδότες ἔργων τῶν πρασσομένων,
οἳ φύσαντες καὶ κληζόμενοι
πατέρες τοιαῦτ' ἐφορῶσι πάθη.—*Tr.* 1266 ff.

[5] τὰ γὰρ περισσὰ κἀνόνητα σώματα
πίπτειν βαρείαις πρὸς θεῶν δυσπραξίαις
ἔφασχ' ὁ μάντις, ὅστις ἀνθρώπου φύσιν
βλαστὼν ἔπειτα μὴ κατ' ἄνθρωπον φρονῇ.—*Aj.* 758 ff.

[6] εἰ δέ τις θεῶν
βλάπτοι, φύγοι τἂν χὠ κακὸς τὸν κρείσσονα.—*Aj.* 455.

of their own, have sent on Philoctetes his pain and loneliness,[1] while the chorus in their dismay at the frenzy of Ajax can only say, "I fear that some heaven-sent evil may have overtaken him."[2] When God so determines, the change from evil to good is easily brought about, and no one can escape the "stroke of God."[3] Not only are the gods the authors of misery, but they even lead men into calamity, and deceive them to their ruin. "It was wisely uttered of old," so we are told in the *Antigone*, "that evil often seems good to the man whom God is leading to his ruin" (*Ant.* 623). In a fragment, Phaedra excuses her fault by saying that no one can escape the evils sent by Zeus.[4] It is the gods who have placed strife between the two sons of Oedipus—the gods assisted by an evil mind.[5]

Thus the religious feeling which runs through the plays of Sophocles does not scruple to attribute to the gods the evil which falls upon men. And the power of the gods is supreme; man is absolutely helpless before them. The gods are indeed just and holy, and regard the good before the evil : but this justice is consistent with the suffering even of the good. Hence we cannot expect to find in Sophocles a cheerful view of life, or a high value placed upon existence. And in truth, if there is one point on which the poet insists more than another, it is the "Nichtigkeit" of human life. However light-hearted and happy we may picture the inhabitant of Athens to have

---

[1] θεῖα γάρ, εἰ καὶ κἀγώ τι φρονῶ,
καὶ τὰ παθήματα κεῖνα πρὸς αὐτὸν
τῆς ὠμόφρονος Χρύσης ἐπέβη.—*Phil.* 192 ff.

[2] *Aj.* 278.

[3] ἐν γὰρ βραχεῖ καθεῖλε κὠλίγῳ χρόνῳ
πάμπλουτον ὄλβον δαίμονος κακοῦ δόσις,
ὅταν μετάστῃ καὶ θεοῖς δοκῇ τάδε.—*Frag.* 572.

θεοῦ δὲ πληγὴν οὐχ ὑπερπηδᾷ βροτός.—*Frag.* 656.

[4] αἴσχη μὲν, ὦ γυναῖκες, οὐδ' ἂν εἰς φύγοι
βροτῶν ποθ', ᾧ καὶ Ζεὺς ἐφορμήσῃ κακά,
νόσους δ' ἀνάγκη τὰς θεηλάτους φέρειν.—*Frag.* 611.

[5] νῦν δ' ἐκ θεῶν του κἀξ ἀλειτηροῦ φρενὸς
εἰσῆλθε τοῖν τρισαθλίοιν ἔρις κακή.—*O. C.* 371.

been, his reflections on life were melancholy and sombre. Life is an evil: it were better not to be born at all; and next best to die in infancy. Life is only good so long as youth continues, and the joys of youth are idle follies (κοῦφαι ἀφρο- σύναι, *O. C.* 1225 ff.). Mortals in the prime of life are but as nothing. No one gains more than a mere phantom of happi- ness, and even this he loses in the gaining (*O. T.* 1186 ff.). We are as shadows, and wander to and fro, a superfluous burden on the earth (*Fr.* 682). " I know," says Theseus in his glory to the outcast Oedipus, " that I too am a man, and that in the morrow I have no greater share than thou hast" (*O. C.* 567). Odysseus, gazing on the ruin of his enemy, is saddened with the thought that "all of us who live are no more than phantoms, than fleeting shadows" (*Aj.* 125, 6). The misery of age is intolerable; age is the home of every evil; the hand of the aged is feeble, his mind fails, his thoughts are nothing worth.[1] Even when life is most prosperous a change may quickly come, and no man's happiness can be estimated till the day of his death.[2]

Against this melancholy picture we have little to set on the other side. There is a chorus of the *Antigone* in which the inventive genius of man is celebrated. By the help of his art he has made himself master of sea and land, of beast and bird and fish. By this he has found out the secret of language and reason and civic life; the comforts of house and home and remedies from disease. Yet these victories only remain to him so long as he cherishes a righteous and pious mind; they are lost to the daring and the impious. In the *Trachiniae*, the women of Trachis comfort their mistress with the thought that " heaviness endureth for a night, but joy cometh in the morn-

---

[1] *O. C.* 1235 ff.

πάντ᾽ ἐμπέφυκε τῷ μακρῷ γήρᾳ κακά,
νοῦς φροῦδος, ἔργ᾽ ἀχρεῖα, φροντίδες κεναί.—*Frag.* 684.

[2] οὐ χρή ποτ᾽ εὖ πράσσοντος ὀλβίσαι τύχας
ἀνδρός, πρὶν αὐτῷ παντελῶς ἤδη βίος
διεκπεράνθη καὶ τελευτήσῃ βίον. (?).—*Ibid.* 572.

The sentiment is repeated in other words at the end of the *Oedipus Tyrannus* and the *Antigone*.

ing." [1] But even in these words of comfort, joy and sorrow are
closely united, and the issue of the play shows how "ironically"
they are spoken, for in another sense, and with a deeper meaning, there comes on Dejanira χαίρειν τε καὶ στέρεσθαι.

But the sadness of life is a theme as old as the lyric poets,
and equally old are the sorrows of age. Mimnermus has told
us what existence is worth when the joy of youth is gone ; the
sentiment that judgment cannot be passed on life till its close
is attributed to Solon; it is the central thought in his famous
dialogue with Croesus, a dialogue which, if genuine, would have
to be placed about a century before the literary activity of
Sophocles. Moreover, to most of the sentiments about the
sadness of life here illustrated from Sophocles parallels could
be found in the History of Herodotus. They are the strongly
expressed maxims of the moral philosophy of that period. In
truth, the melancholy view here taken of human life is no
fancy of a poet sighing after an impossible happiness, or of a
diseased mind which finds the world out of joint. The Greek
was no doubt free from much that distresses and almost
paralyses the modern world. In him there was not that
struggle of inward and outward, of flesh and spirit, which
plays so large a part in modern ethical reflection. Yet in other
respects life pressed upon him far more heavily. Few were
the years in which the Greek was not at war for interests
more or less vital; few the households in which there was not
one slain in battle. And even in peaceful times the race of
life was severe. The battle went to the strong. Here and
there we find passages which betray a certain tenderness towards suffering and weakness, but these are exceptions to
the general rule. The Greek at his best was a fierce
partisan, who rejoiced in the calamities of his enemies.
At his worst he did not scruple to rob the weak and helpless, the orphan and the widow, while relentless vengeance
on an enemy in an unguarded moment was exalted into a
moral duty. And when a man turned his eyes away from
himself, there was little to comfort him. The gods might

---

[1] μένει γὰρ οὔτ᾽ αἰόλα
νὺξ βροτοῖσιν οὔτε Κῆρες οὔτε πλοῦτος,
ἀλλ᾽ ἄφαρ βέβακε, τῷ δ᾽ ἐπέρχεται χαίρειν τε καὶ στέρεσθαι.—*Tr.* 131 ff.

indeed be good and just; it was dangerous to speak evil of them; but they were certainly jealous and exacting. Their wrath was easily kindled, and no one could tell how their anger would be shown. For there remained the inexplicable mystery that evil overtook the good as well as the wicked, a Nicias as well as an Alcibiades. Poets spoke of a future world beyond the grave; but did it really exist? Or was it more than a place of punishment? Even if all that Pindar said were true, how could a life beyond the grave compensate for misery in this life? Thoughts such as these must have passed through the minds of many Greeks in the time of the Peloponnesian war; so that Sophocles is true to nature in his picture of the evils of human existence, and if we find him attempting to explain them, he is explaining a fact and not a fiction.

The deepest note is touched in the passage already quoted from the *Antigone:* "With wisdom was it declared of old, that good often appears evil to one whose mind God is leading to ruin." The passage occurs in the ode in which the chorus dwell on the woes of the house of the Labdacids; and nothing can represent life under a more hopeless aspect than that picture of a house stricken with a curse which penetrates from generation to generation, till every member of the family is destroyed. This hopeless ruin, though induced immediately by frenzy and infatuation ($\lambda\acute{o}\gamma ου \ \tau'\ \mathring{a}νοια\ καὶ\ φρενῶν\ 'Ερινύς$), is nevertheless part of the ordinance of Zeus—"whom neither age nor sleep can touch, who sits supreme throughout neverending time in the splendour of Olympus." Even the hopes of mankind are but deceptions, leading them unawares to destruction; the heart of the doomed is blinded, so that good is evil, and evil good, and few are the days that are not days of sorrow ($πράσσει\ δ'\ \mathring{o}λίγιστον\ χρόνον\ \mathring{e}κτὸς\ \mathring{a}τας$).

This chorus is, no doubt, in designed contrast to that which immediately precedes it in the play, and which tells us of the power and inventiveness of man (cf. *supra,* p. 49). It raises the question, "Is this unhappy condition of man—whose wisdom is so great—this angry temper of the gods, due to the wickedness of man, or is it mere caprice on the part of potentates desiring to keep within due bounds a rebellious race, or is it a severe inexplicable destiny? The presence of misery in the world is shown by abundant testimony. What explanation can we give of it?"

In part the misery of life is due to the foolishness and pride of men. Pindar had spoken of ἄτη as the child of ὕβρις, and Sophocles is penetrated with this feeling. A rebellious spirit breaking the bounds imposed on humanity (θνητὸς οὐ θνητὰ φρονῶν) will not go without punishment. It is this which brings upon Ajax the punishment of Athena (cf. supra, p. 44), and the goddess herself declares that this is the lesson to be drawn from the picture of Ajax sitting among the dead sheep and oxen.[1] In such a punishment the justice of the gods is apparent. Ajax has sinned, and he suffers. But even here the punishment, in its worst form, is not inevitable. For one day only will the wrath of Athena pursue him. If for this day he can be saved, he will hereafter be free. The frenzy will pass away, and with it the sense of humiliation. Ajax will return to a better mind.

But the instances in which this close connection between the fault and the punishment is apparent are few in Sophocles. We may trace it, of course, in Clytemnestra, and, though the case is widely different, in the Creon of the Antigone. But of Antigone herself what can we say? Is she to be placed beside Ajax, or beside Creon? Is her death the punishment of a rebellious spirit, or is she a martyr in the cause of sisterly affection and the rights of the dead? We must not answer this question according to our own views and feelings; we must ask, What was the view and the meaning of Sophocles? As A. Böckh has seen, a strong case may be made out against Antigone. She defies the civic authority; she goes beyond the limits imposed upon a woman. Her own sister Ismene regards the deed which she contemplates as rash and un-womanly. It is in fact impossible, and the mere attempt is foolishness.[2] The chorus also, aged chiefs of the State, speak with strong reprobation of Antigone's conduct. Her act is the

---

[1] τοιαῦτα τοίνυν εἰσορῶν ὑπέρκοπον
μηδέν ποτ' εἴπῃς αὐτὸς εἰς θεοὺς ἔπος.—Aj. 127.

[2] ἀπόρρητον πόλει, l. 44; νόμου βίᾳ, l. 59; βίᾳ πολιτῶν, l. 79; ἀμηχάνων ἐρᾷς, l. 90; ἄνους, l. 99.

rash deed of youth, prompted by folly and infatuation.[1] It is an offence against justice; the work of defiant passion.[2] Böckh is also of opinion that unless it be assumed that Antigone, no less than Creon, is guilty of rashness and rebellion, the play is deficient in unity. This view has been examined elsewhere. It is enough to say here that the words of Ismene and the chorus cannot be taken to be the judgment of the poet, and that an action which involves a double catastrophe is not necessarily wanting in unity; it may be the manifestation of a single central idea. The leading idea of the *Antigone* is not merely that rebellion is a crime; rebellion against injustice, and such is Antigone's rebellion, can never be placed on the same footing as the outrage of natural rights consecrated by religion, in which lies the guilt of Creon. It is rather that the laws of nature are not to be overridden by the law of the State. That the assertion of this law involves both Antigone and Creon in destruction does not in the least destroy the unity of the drama.

But we may perhaps, from another point of view, ask : If Antigone is in no way guilty, is not her death, in the language of Aristotle, μιαρόν, or shocking? Does not the play decline in this respect from the standard of the *Poetics*,[3] where we learn that a character, to be tragic, must be good, but not perfect?

The explanation is, that men fall by their good qualities as well as by their bad qualities; and it is possible to be daring and incautious in the cause of right no less than in the cause of wrong. The ἁμαρτία τις, which Aristotle regards as a necessary part of the tragic character, is not to be limited to moral imperfection. It implies any flaw, however slight, of temper or prudence. Such a flaw we may allow in Antigone without detracting from her heroic character. She is hasty with her

---

[1] ἐν ἀφροσύνῃ καθελόντες, 1. 383 ; λόγου τ' ἄνοια καὶ φρενῶν Ἐρινύς, 1. 603.

[2] προβᾶσ' ἐπ' ἔσχατον θράσους
ὑψηλὸν ἐς Δίκας βάθρον
προσέπεσες, ὦ τέκνον, πολύ.
. . . .
σὲ δ' αὐτόγνωτος ὤλεσ' ὀργά.--*Ant.* 853 ff. 875.

[3] *Poetics*, c. 13, § 2.

sister, abrupt and resolute in her own determination, and contemptuous towards Creon. Her nature is by no means conciliatory; on the contrary, it is made up of extremes, a passionate tenderness and love alternating with no less passionate resolution. This intensity of nature is not to be put on a level with moral guilt. Antigone is righteous in her transgression (ὅσια πανουργήσασα). Ismene and the chorus may stand apart from her—they have neither her vision for right nor her will to do it,—but the gods justify her actions, as does also the popular voice of Thebes. In defending her conduct she speaks the law of nature and God, though she breaks the ordinance of a man who identifies the law of the State with his own will. Her suicide is her own act; it is a rash deed, and for it we may gently blame her, pleading in her defence that she takes a life already doomed, and hastens from a lingering death to be at rest with those whom she loves.

In Antigone then we must admit that we have a case in which the lower nature (Creon) and the lower law is allowed to triumph over the higher one. The triumph is short-lived, it is true, and the scale is quickly turned. But the victory of her cause cannot restore Antigone to life; she is beyond the reach of earthly comfort; she suffers, so far as we can see, without offence and without compensation. The evil has prevailed against the good, and this, if false to any supposed canons of art, is true to human nature.

Let us turn now to the two dramas which deal with the fate of Oedipus. Here again we ask: Is it not μιαρόν that a character so noble and exalted as Oedipus should be involved in unmerited destruction? For who can say that his sufferings are deserved? Throughout he defends himself as an unconscious actor in the crimes which have brought him into the abyss of ruin. "I was the victim in wickedness, the victim, be God my witness, for nothing in it was my own deliberate act."[1] When in the *Oedipus at Colonus*, the chorus would speak of his deeds, he cries: " Deeds they were not; I did nothing; I accepted a gift, which

---

[1] ἤνεγκον κακότατ', . . .
ἤνεγκον ἑκὼν μὲν, θεὸς ἴστω,
τούτων δ' αὐθαίρετον οὐδέν.—O. C. 521.

I would that I had never taken."[1] And again, in reference to his incestuous connection with Jocasta, he declares, " She was my mother, and we knew it not, and to her shame my mother bore me children."[2] Indeed, the plea that the evil was unconscious cannot be denied. There is nothing in the character of Oedipus that can be brought forward as any sufficient reason for his calamities. Headstrong, rash, and over-confident in some respects he is, but once more we must not confuse weakness of this kind with moral guilt. How different, for instance, is Oedipus from Jocasta!

There still remain the instances of Philoctetes and Dejanira. The question whether the years of agony endured by Philoctetes in Lemnos are brought upon him in retribution of some crime of his own, or whether he is to be regarded as wholly guiltless, has been much discussed. Hasselbach and others contend at great length for the guilt of Philoctetes; Hermann and Schneidewin are in favour of his innocence. There can hardly be any doubt that the latter are right. The passages most to the point are these :—In l. 192 ff., when making reply to the chorus, who express their sympathy with the loneliness and misery of Philoctetes, Neoptolemus says : " By heaven's will, if there be wisdom in me, these sufferings came upon him from the ruthless Chryse."[3] And he adds the reason for the suffering : Troy was not to be destroyed before the appointed time, and the affliction of Philoctetes was the divinely-appointed means for delaying the destruction. Again, in l. 1326 ff., Neoptolemus tells Philoctetes : "This affliction is sent upon thee by a divinely-ordered chance, in that thou didst approach the guardian of Chryse, the hidden serpent, who keeps watch and

---

[1] οὐκ ἔρεξα . . . ἐδεξάμην
δῶρον, ὃ μήποτ' ἐγὼ ταλακάρδιος
ἐπωφέλησα πόλεος ἐξελέσθαι.—O. C. 539.

[2] ἔτικτε γάρ μ' ἔτικτεν, ὤμοι μοι κακῶν,
οὐκ εἰδότ' οὐκ εἰδυῖα, καὶ τεκοῦσά με
αὐτῆς ὄνειδος παῖδας ἐξέφυσέ μοι.—Ibid. 982 ff.

[3] θεῖα γὰρ, εἴπερ κἀγώ τι φρονῶ,
καὶ τὰ παθήματα κεῖνα πρὸς αὐτὸν
τῆς ὠμόφρονος Χρύσης ἐπέβη.—Phil. 192 ff.

ward in the open shrine."[1] These passages are as much
evidence as can be reasonably required to prove that there was
no intentional violation of the sanctuary of Chryse, whoever she
may have been, by Philoctetes. For the righteousness of his
dealings with his fellow-men we have evidence in a passage
where the chorus speak of him as one " who did no wrong to
any, nor defrauded him,—a just man among the just."[2] Other
passages may no doubt be quoted, as, *e.g.* l. 446 ff., in which
Philoctetes displays a certain vehemence against the gods; but
this vehemence is induced by an experience of life in which the
evil has outstripped the good. If Philoctetes wonders that such
things as the triumph of Odysseus and the Atridae can happen
in a world governed by just gods, he is not alone in his wonder.
And with him such impatient thoughts are only on the surface.
He is not at heart sceptical of the justice of the gods; he even
recognises it in his own case.[3]

The misery which descends on Philoctetes is therefore due
to a θεία τύχη. It serves a definite purpose in the economy of
the world, inasmuch as it delays the vengeance of the Greeks
upon Troy till the time appointed.[4] Dramatically, it serves
to bring out the character of Philoctetes in its strongest and
most sublime lines. It is therefore a fit object for a dramatic
poet to delineate, and Sophocles, as a rule, does not inquire into
the motive of a legend which he finds serviceable for dramatic
purposes. It is the more remarkable that in this instance he
has chosen to raise very clearly the further question of the
guilt or innocence of the sufferer.

Lastly, in the case of Dejanira there can be hardly any
question of guilt. Her action, perfectly innocent in itself,
except in so far as it may be called an experiment, is done
without the least suspicion of the results which flow from it,

---

[1] σὺ γὰρ νοσεῖς τόδ' ἄλγος ἐκ θείας τύχης,
Χρύσης πελασθεὶς φύλακος, ὃς τὸν ἀκαλυφῆ
σηκὸν φυλάσσει κρύφιος οἰκουρῶν ὄφις.—*Phil.* 1326 ff.

[2] ὃς οὔτ' ἔρξας τιν' οὔτε νοσφίσας,
ἀλλ' ἴσος ἔν γ' ἴσοις ἀνήρ,
ὤλλυθ' ὧδ' ἀναξίως.—*Ibid.* 684 ff.

[3] *Ibid.* 1306.   [4] Cf. Aesch. *Ag.* 365, 736.

and for a motive which cannot be condemned. She sees the beauty of Iole, she knows the weakness of Heracles, and seeks to keep for herself the first place in the affection of her husband. We may accuse her of ἀβουλία—want of prudence,—but of nothing more. Even Heracles, at first so furious and eager for vengeance upon the wife that has destroyed him, and Hyllus admit, in the end, her complete innocence.[1] The miserable end of Heracles is one divinely appointed for him; and Dejanira was but the agent in carrying out the divine purpose.[2]

In all these cases, from Antigone onwards, the calamity which overtakes the actor in the Sophoclean drama is not to be attributed to moral guilt. Rashness and want of circumspection there may be, but the punishment is out of proportion to such weakness. It is hopeless to attempt to find in Sophocles a poetical justice measuring out sorrow and joy to every one according to his deeds; and such "poetical" justice would be unworthy of so great a poet, because it is out of harmony with the facts of human life.

Yet the gods are just,—of this Sophocles has not a doubt. And so once more the question presents itself, How are we to account for the calamities which overtake the noble and high-hearted among men? What is the meaning of the suffering inflicted upon them?

Can we fall back on the idea of an inherited curse? In Aeschylus this conception runs through a large part of his theology, and is brought forward very strongly in the *Seven against Thebes* and the *Agamemnon*. The Erinyes will not leave the accursed house of the Atreidae, but remain there from generation to generation till the last blow of divine vengeance is struck. But in Sophocles this conception plays a far less important part, though there are clear traces of it. In the chorus already quoted more than once from the *Antigone* we find it stated that when "a house is shaken from heaven,

---

[1] κἂν σοῦ στραφείη θυμὸς, εἰ τὸ πᾶν μάθοις . . .
. . . . . . ἥμαρτε χρηστὰ μωμένη.—*Tr.* 1134 ff.
[2] ἐμοὶ γὰρ ἦν πρόφαντον ἐκ πατρὸς πάλαι,
πρὸς τῶν πνεόντων μηδενὸς θανεῖν ὕπο,
ἀλλ' ὅστις Ἀιδου φθίμενος οἰκήτωρ πέλοι.—*Ibid.* 1159 ff.

calamity never leaves it; it advances upon the whole race; and one generation frees not another : a god dashes them to earth and there is no release." [1] In the *Electra* we find the evils of the house of the Pelopidae traced back to the murder of Myrtilus by Pelops.[2] Oedipus, in looking back on the misery of his life, can only account for it by saying, " Such was the will of the gods ; perhaps they cherished some anger of old against my race." [3]

Of these passages those taken from the *Antigone* and the *Electra* occur in the songs of the chorus, where the poet is perhaps expressing the popular view of such miseries as those of the Labdacids and Pelopids. The language of Oedipus hardly amounts to more than a conjecture : " It may have been some guilt of my father's which caused my woe; it was certainly not any guilt of my own." In the case of Philoctetes and Dejanira there is not the slightest allusion to anything of the kind. They do not suffer for their own sins nor for the sins of their fathers. Nor again is there in the play of *Oedipus Tyrannus* an allusion to anything of the kind. In truth the notion of an inherited curse, if held in its naked strength, is calculated to limit the freedom of the individual so much as to make a drama of character nearly impossible. But the drama of Sophocles is a drama of character.

The mystery of suffering has not been cleared up yet, and Sophocles may well have found it an almost insuperable difficulty. His conception, so far as we can gather it from the fate of Oedipus, Antigone, Philoctetes, and Dejanira, would seem to be that suffering is part of the appointed order of the world, alternating, at the best, with happiness, as night with day. But to him suffering is not altogether an evil. It may further the purposes of divine wisdom, as in Philoctetes ; it may develop,

---

[1] οἷς γὰρ ἂν σεισθῇ θεόθεν δόμος, ἄτης
οὐδὲν ἐλλείπει γενεᾶς ἐπὶ πλῆθος ἕρπον . . .
οὐδ' ἀπαλλάσσει γενεὰν γένος, ἀλλ' ἐρείπει
θεῶν τις, οὐδ' ἔχει λύσιν.—*Ant.* 584 ff.

[2] ὦ Πέλοπος ἀ πρόσθεν
πολύπονος ἱππεία,
ὡς ἔμολες αἰανὴ τᾷδε γᾷ, κ.τ.λ.—*El.* 504 ff.

[3]   θεοῖς γὰρ ἦν οὕτω φίλον,
τάχ' ἄν τι μηνίουσιν ἐς γένος πάλαι.—*O. C.* 964.

deepen, and enlarge a character, as in Philoctetes or Oedipus; it may establish a higher law, as in Antigone. This is the end of suffering in its highest aspect; but Sophocles does not exclude the fact that there are accidents in life such as that which caused the supposed death of Orestes, though even these accidents, as we see from the case of Philoctetes, who suffers ἐκ θείας τύχης, are often divinely sent and of high importance in life. There are, besides, the rash acts of men in moments of excitement, the sins of ὕβρις, and the suffering caused by deliberate wickedness extends to those who are in no way guilty. But the truth which underlies these facts of human nature is that the moral order of the world does not of necessity mean the happiness of all men. From some it may demand endurance and sacrifice, and he that loses his life shall find it.

Yet two questions still remain:—

1. Is there no compensation for the suffering which falls upon the guiltless, as part of the divine government of the world?

2. Do the gods intentionally bring calamity upon men in order to accomplish certain ends? or, to put the question more plainly, Do the gods deceive men to their ruin?

In the *Philoctetes* a definite recompense is made to the wounded hero. Troy cannot be taken without him. Heracles, the type of triumphant endurance, is sent to announce to him the divine will. Heracles has won immortality by labour and endurance, and Philoctetes has a similar lot.[1] Philoctetes will be deemed the foremost warrior at Troy (l. 1425). He will slay Paris, the arch-enemy, sack Troy, and return home to the plain of Oeta with the prize of valour. Aesculapius will be sent to cure his wound. He is not left without his reward; it comes to him in full measure, and it comes to him before his death.

Oedipus again is greater in his death than in his life. His position as king of Thebes is only apparently majestic; the true majesty is seen when the Eumenides permit him to enter their holy place, when Theseus gives him welcome, when Thebes strives in vain to recover possession of his body, when Poly-

---

[1] καὶ σοί, σάφ' ἴσθι, τοῦτ' ὀφείλεται παθεῖν,
ἐκ τῶν κακῶν τῶνδ' εὐκλεᾶ θέσθαι βίον.—*Phil.* 1421.

nices prays for his help in the attempt to regain his throne,
and, above all, when the divine voice summons him to his last
resting-place; and he is allowed to pass away from life in a
mysterious manner, taken, as it were, to his rest without the
trial of death. His tomb becomes a holy place, bringing prosperity to those who possess it. The life of suffering has its
reward in the final triumph of him who endured nobly.

Moreover, as has been pointed out by Dronke, calamity when
undeserved is represented by Sophocles as having no power
against the inward conviction of rectitude. " Thou wilt keep
him in perfect peace whose mind is stayed on thee." These
words of the greatest of Hebrew prophets, uttered at a time
when ruin was impending on his nation, denote the peace
which Israel may yet gain by trusting in Jehovah. No Greek
could have uttered them, for no Greek was ever so deeply
penetrated with the love of the Deity for the nation. But
what Isaiah extends to the nation Sophocles can say of the
individual. The peace of the spirit which rests on the highest
and holiest deities is not easily disturbed. Secure in that
repose, it can rise above the distress of unconscious errors and
involuntary crimes. If Creon accuses Oedipus, the accusations
only serve to reveal his own baseness. He is not worthy to
tread the soil of Attica, but Oedipus may recline in the hallowed
shrine of the Eumenides.

But Antigone: In her case there is no final triumph. The
consolation offered by the chorus, that her death is glorious,
exempt from disease and bloodshed, is rightly rejected by her
as no equivalent for the brightness and hope of life. There is
no compensation for Antigone in this life, and what does
Sophocles tell us of the next?

Even when she is brought face to face with death, and the
"pity of it" becomes more deeply felt, Antigone speaks with
cheerful hope of that other world in which she will join her
friends: "When I come there, such is the hope I cherish, I
shall find love with my father, love with my mother, and love
with thee, my brother." [1]   The life which will be hers then will

---

[1] ἐλθοῦσα μέντοι κάρτ' ἐν ἐλπίσιν τρέφω
φίλη μὲν ἥξειν πατρί, προσφιλὴς δὲ σοί,
μῆτερ, φίλη δὲ σοί, κασίγνητον κάρα.—*Ant.* 897 ff.

be far longer than the life of this world.[1] And in that future
life there will be no misapprehensions and mistakes. " Justice
has her home with the gods below." [2]

Hence for the righteous there is a good hope in death, and
the life to come is a real existence in which the broken ties of
this world will be united, never to be severed again. Heracles
is now an immortal being abiding in heaven.[3] Electra speaks
of her father's spirit as alive (*El.* 459), and Clytemnestra will
live in the under-world (*El.* 437). By thus conveying the
mind to another life, Sophocles in some measure softens the
weight of injustice and misery in this. Antigone, in the consciousness that her act is accepted before the higher powers—
" in those pure eyes and perfect witness of all-judging Jove,"
—is content to undergo the sentence which man pronounces
upon her. And her death achieves the victory which her life
could not have achieved. Not only is her brother buried, but
the ordinance of burial is established by higher and holier laws.
We see then that in a certain sense compensation comes to
those who suffer innocently—such compensation as a noble
spirit would seek to gain. But there are passages which seem
to intimate that God leads a man to ruin. And if this be so,
how can we any longer speak of the justice and truth of God ?
In *Antigone*, l. 623, the passage so often quoted, we are plainly
told " that evil seems good to a man whom God is leading to
ruin " (p. 48). This is the reflection of the chorus on the house
of Labdacus, and it probably reproduces with accuracy the
ordinary Greek conception. Many a man looking back on
actions done in moments of passion or excitement can hardly
give any other account of them than that he was not himself
when he did them. So Helen excuses her weakness—ἄτη με
παρήγαγε, and in a religion where dualism was unknown, this
deception or bewitchment is naturally referred to the gods.
But if the chorus mean this sentiment to apply to Antigone in
the sense that she has confounded good and evil in her act of
self-devotion, neither Sophocles nor we can agree. In the life

---

[1]   ἐπεὶ πλείων χρόνος
     δν δεῖ μ' ἀρέσκειν τοῖς κάτω τῶν ἐνθάδε.—*Ant.* 74.
[2] ἡ σύνοικος τῶν κάτω θεῶν Δίκη.—*Ibid.* 451.
[3] ἀθάνατον ἀρετὴν ἔσχον, ὡς πάρεσθ' ὁρᾶν.—*Phil.* 1420.

of Oedipus we have indeed evil seeming good. His success at Thebes in destroying the Sphinx and gaining the hand of Jocasta is an instance of the way in which evil may seem good; but it is the shortsightedness of man rather than the deception of God which brings him to ruin. Oedipus, who has been forewarned of his destiny, acts οὔθ' ὁρῶν οὔθ' ἱστορῶν in the death of Laius and the marriage of Jocasta. In the case of Dejanira we may also observe a similar want of caution. The suffering in either case is not a thing apart from the ἀβουλία of the sufferer. The deception of God is not to be charged with that which is due to the blindness of man. If man were all-wise, and could in every act proceed with perfect knowledge, he would be saved from much, if not all, the suffering which comes upon him; being imperfect, he must accept the suffering which comes from ignorance as well as that which comes from crime and its punishment.

Still it is possible to ask—Is this divine order of the world, which entails suffering on men, more than mere destiny? Can we deny, in spite of the lofty tone of many passages, that in Sophocles man is the slave of a relentless destiny whose will he is powerless to resist or escape?

It is often assumed that the tragedy of the Greeks, especially in the hands of Aeschylus and Sophocles, is no more than a tragedy of destiny. That is, it exhibits man not as suffering in consequence of his own misdeeds, or as the slave of his own passions, but as the sport of destiny—doomed at birth to a certain pre-ordained fate, which he strives in vain to resist. Every man has his μοῖρα, and the interest of the tragic situation lies in showing how this μοῖρα is fulfilled. Often this μοῖρα is announced in an oracle, often it is not known till the end of life, but, known or unknown, it is inevitable and uncontrollable by the will of man. Even those who do not find this "destiny" in the work of Sophocles regard it as the groundwork of the tragedy of Aeschylus.

If destiny, as something apart from and superior to the will of the gods, plays such an important part in Greek tragedy, it is remarkable that Aristotle should have no allusion to it in his *Poetics*. It is more than remarkable,—it is impossible that if he entertained such a view of destiny he should have written

the description of the "tragic" character in the thirteenth
chapter of that work. For with Aristotle the truly tragic
character is not, as we might expect, a good man struggling
with an evil destiny, but a good man failing δι' ἁμαρτίαν
τινά. The tragic character is not *teres et rotundus*, a perfect
sphere on whose smooth surface no speck can be found,
but a character with faults, and yet suffering beyond the
desert of the faults. Such a character implies freedom of
will, which on the hypothesis of an overruling destiny is
annihilated. And therefore in any severe system of fatalism
tragedy becomes impossible. There must be room for the
individual choice, for the individual development of character,
or the "tragic" element becomes "shocking" (μιαρόν). There
is no relation between a man's moral guilt and his actions,
without which a drama is impossible. Hence Aeschylus, in
whom, if anywhere, we may look for the idea of destiny, is
nevertheless at pains to show that the actions of men are free.
It is open to Eteocles to go forth to meet his brother Polynices,
or to remain. He declares that he *must* go, that it is the
curse of his father which is driving him along a fatal path.
But the chorus plead against his resolution, though they plead
in vain. In the same way it is open to Agamemnon, if he will,
to return home from Aulis, and save his daughter from sacrifice.
But he will not return—πῶς λιπόναυς γένωμαι; and thus both
Eteocles and Agamemnon place themselves within the reach
of the curse of their house. In Sophocles, Antigone urges
Polynices not to pursue his march to Thebes, but to save himself from the curse of Oedipus by returning to Argos. But
Polynices, like Agamemnon in Aeschylus, cannot be false to
his army. He goes on his way, though he is going to certain
destruction. The principle which urges these heroes to their
doom is not unlike that false sense of honour which has prevailed in modern times. It is not destiny.

Again: Such an idea of destiny as that described is impossible
when the gods have been recognised as omnipotent and just.
So long as there is a question about the justice of the reign of
Zeus, the "triple Moerae and mindful Erinyes" may have power
against him, but this power is gone when Zeus is himself the
centre and source of justice. An unjust destiny is at variance

with the will of the Almighty ; a just destiny is merely the expression of his will : in no case is there room for destiny outside and above the deity. There is therefore no destiny apart from the will of God. By obedience to that will man may escape from evil, by opposing it he may bring evil on himself and on his descendants. Labdacus consciously opposed the will of heaven ; Oedipus, when informed of the evil in store, does the very actions which he should most have avoided. In the case of Antigone there is no question of destiny at all. She acts of her own will, in defiance of an authority which has the power to punish by death. Dejanira dies by her own hand, in consequence of her own act. Her conduct may have been a part of an order of things which the gods foreknew, but there was no irresistible destiny compelling her to act as she did. She acts from human motives ; she takes human counsel, and her act is a mistake. Philoctetes suffers ἐκ θείας τύχης, by an accident, as it were, which serves the purposes of heaven. Whether he could have escaped his accident or not it is useless to inquire, for the drama of Sophocles is founded on the fact that he did not escape it. He has his reward, and his suffering is not due to a blind destiny, but to the conscious purpose of the gods.

Aeschylus and Sophocles are not religious teachers as the Hebrew prophets and St. Paul are religious teachers. They are not conscious of a divine mission, or carried out of themselves in an ecstasy of faith and love. They are poets, desiring to give to a nation the pleasure which poetry can give. But the greatness of the themes on which they wrote, and of the times in which they lived, brought them into close contact with the truths and difficulties underlying all faith and morality. These they did not pass over, or treat in any merely formal manner. To them, therefore, and to Plato, we must look for the best that the Western world can tell us on the nature of God, on the relation of the divine and the human. In the popular Hellenic view, all the calamities of men were either the result of crime in the individual, or some ancestor of the individual, or they were the work of a capricious power known as " destiny." This popular conception Aeschylus strove to elevate and refine. He eliminated the caprice of destiny as irreconcilable with the justice of the divine nature, and sought, in every case, to connect the calamity of the sufferer with some deliberate act of wrong-doing :—" Sin and sorrow, the old, old story." [1] In this severe conception the justice of God is, if we may use the expression, saved at the expense of facts. The popular view is right in maintaining that the guiltless do suffer : yet how can destiny be anything but the will of God ? and how can the will of God be anything but just ? Here Sophocles takes up the problem. He accepts the mysterious fact that the guiltless do suffer, but seeks to explain it by taking a higher view of the nature of such suffering. For him the calamities of the guiltless are part of human life as a whole, not punishments dealt out to individuals. They are often necessary to the development of character ; without them we should know nothing of the strength and majesty of Oedipus or Philoctetes. They assist in the general purposes of humanity ; and thus at times, as in the case of Antigone, suffering comes near to the modern conception of self-sacrifice. They help to bring before us the true nature of life, and separate the accidental from the real. It is not prosperity and success, it is often failure and endurance, which become the most effective and truly real factors in the advancement of mankind. Hence it is only a superficial judgment that can ascribe to the injustice of the gods or the caprice of destiny the evil which overtakes the good. In part, no doubt, that evil is the result of some want of foresight, which, though not morally culpable, is yet sufficient to bring calamity upon a man, or even on a race. In part it arises from the imperfection of a world in which justice and power are not always in the same hands. It may also arise from the wise purposes of the gods, " whom no weak pity moves " to regard the happiness of one man more than the elevation of all, more than the illustration of some great moral truth. In any case, it must not be taken alone ; it must always be considered in reference to the whole, just as in human life isolation is impossible. Calamity, again, is a wholesome check on the conceit of knowledge and power. To the Greek prosperity was a snare ; it tended to raise him above the appointed limit, and kindle ambitions which brought about their own overthrow. Even in the ordinary course of life

---

[1] δράσαντι παθεῖν τριγέρων μῦθος τάδε φωνεῖ.

it was difficult to know the bounds of human nature and " think human thoughts." To live entirely free from danger in this respect would require perfect wisdom, the knowledge what to do and what to leave undone in every circumstance, every moment of life. Such knowledge is not attainable by men; it is divine; and only by submission to the divine power may we hope to gain something of it. For the gods are accessible by oracles, and declare their will to men, darkly indeed, but yet in tones which a simple heart may understand. Finally, when calamity has been thus separated from guilt—so Sophocles seems to teach us, and the lesson is the more striking in a nation so excessive in its regard for prosperity and its dread of misfortune as the Greeks—it loses half its terrors. It has still an outward power in so far as it may bring poverty and distress; it may mar the body and make life heavy to be borne, but it has no inward power against the mind. Vain is the remembrance of his past agony, vain the prospect of helpless distress to subdue the mighty heart of Philoctetes in his lonely island; vain are all promises of glory and dominion to move the spirit of the outcast Oedipus. Each is the guiltless victim of a grievous calamity, and the inward consciousness of innocence makes the outward suffering of less moment. In the end the reward of patience, endurance, and submission comes, either in this world or the next. The lowly is exalted, the rejected is victorious. The undertone of divine vengeance running through the dramas of Aeschylus seems in Sophocles to pass away into an echo of divine compassion, and we move from the gloom of " sin and sorrow " towards the dawning of a brighter day in which strength is made perfect in weakness.

E. A.

THE THEORY OF EDUCATION
IN THE *REPUBLIC* OF PLATO.

SOME apology may seem to be due for printing an Essay
upon a subject so well worn as the Platonic conception of
Education, the more so as I have no new discoveries to detail
and no new theories to advance. But it seems true that
Greek thought is in a sense ever young ; that while its lessons
are always being learnt, they are always being forgotten and
misunderstood; and that though much has been done for its
interpretation, and the study of it has established itself in the
curriculum of our schools and Universities, we are still in many
respects only at the threshold, and often see it through a veil of
conventional platitudes, pretentious antiquarianism, or senti-
mental finery. All that I have here attempted is to draw
renewed attention to some of the salient and familiar points in
a subject which concerns us all, and to suggest reflection upon
our own corresponding theory and practice.

The subject of Education is treated by Plato in the
Republic as an integral and vital part of the wider subject
of the wellbeing of human society, and it is scarcely possible
to give an intelligent account of his treatment without first
indicating the scope and plan of the work as a whole. The
Republic opens by asking the question, What is the nature of
justice ? and the first four books of it pursue the answer to this
question without any serious deviation. The real bearing of
the question is but poorly represented to us in its English
dress ; it would be better expressed, if (following the suggestion of Plato himself[1]) we substituted for it the question, How

---

[1] 1. 344 e ; 352 d.

are men to order their lives so as to live best ? which naturally involves the further question, What is to live well ? Various representative answers to these questions are first propounded and examined; the personal experience of the good old man of the good old time, the half-understood maxims of the educated man of the world, the sounding formulas of the unscrupulous and cynical rhetorician,—all these are passed in review, and found to be inadequate, ill-considered, or self-destructive. Then the voice of society or its leaders is listened to; current theories of the origin of law and morality, which resolve the one into arbitrary convention and the other into a calculation of rewards and punishments, or a system of indulgences, are exhibited in their most naked form; until at last we seem to be left with the whole of popular opinion and experience arrayed upon the side of what is called injustice, and upon the other side nothing but a bare conviction, to which the moral sense of man still clings, though unable to justify itself for doing so.

Such a justification Socrates is now called upon to give. We have had enough of verbal discussions [1] in which everything seems to depend upon the sense in which the particular disputant takes the particular word in dispute; nor can we rest satisfied with theories which reduce morality to its material consequences, whether in this world or the next. If justice and injustice, right and wrong, are not merely the same thing viewed from different sides, but express real and radical distinctions, they must admit of being exhibited " as they are in themselves," that is, not in their current equivalents of wealth, success, popularity, and the reverse, but as forces working for good or ill in the very soul of man.[2] With the demand for such an exhibition, the inquiry passes from the domain of verbal definition and popular opinion to that of psychology, and the question, How are we to order our lives for the best ? becomes the question, What is the nature of the living principle[3] within us which Plato calls the soul ? Though, however, this is the real import of the transition now made in the dialogue, it is made in a form which would be little expected

---

[1] 2. 367 b, μὴ οὖν ἡμῖν μόνον ἐνδείξῃ τῷ λόγῳ, κ.τ.λ.

[2] 2. 366 e ; 367 b and d ; 358 b.

[3] Cf. 4. 445 a, αὐτοῦ τούτου ᾧ ζῶμεν.

by a modern student of moral psychology. Instead of meeting the new requirement by analysing the human soul, Plato proceeds to analyse human society. The reason for this is to be found in his conviction that in society (to interpret his own familiar simile[1]) we see man "writ large;" in other words, that in the broad outlines of the state, with its classes, its trade and industry, its military and political institutions, the secret and subtle elements of human nature come to the surface, take visible shape, and are unmistakably legible to the observer. If then we would study human life successfully, we must begin from the outside and work inwards; we must take the obvious facts and principles without which society would not go on, and ask, what they mean, of what inner facts and principles are they the exponents? And in order to do this, we must have a method. It will not do to take society at any chance point on its surface and probe it there; we must begin at the beginning, we must look at it "in its growth."[2] Not, however, in its historical, but in its logical and psychological "growth;" for this seems to be the explanation of the picture which Plato gives of "the genesis of the State." He has begun with what he considered the lowest stratum of life, at the point where it is most nearly the mere keeping life alive, the mere satisfaction of necessary wants; to this rudimentary basis he has gradually added the higher factors of human nature, with their accompanying needs; and throughout the structure, alike in its lower and its higher ranges, he has shown us the same principle of efficiency and well-being, a principle writ large on the face of society,[3] but to be ultimately traced back to its analogue in the constitution of the human soul itself. That principle, to which he gives the name of justice, may be briefly

---

[1] 2. 368 d.   [2] 2. 369 a, γιγνομένην πόλιν.

[3] Cf. 4. 443 b-c, where it is stated that the principle of the division of labour in trade and industry was a sort of "initial outline" (ἀρχήν τε καὶ τύπον τινὰ) of justice, the first suggestion and rudimentary form of it, and further, that this principle was really only "an image" (εἴδωλόν τι) of justice, the truth being that justice is not merely concerned with "the external doing one's own work," but with "the inward doing of what is in very truth one's own;" so the harmonious working of the soul within itself is the really essential condition of which external organisation is merely the "image" or outward expression.

explained as follows :—Every man has wants, of which he cannot get rid, but which he cannot himself satisfy.[1] They are as various as the want of food and clothes, the want of protection from external violence, the want of assistance against his own lower nature ; but whatever their character, they make him individually insufficient for himself. On the other hand, while all men need others, all men are, or may be, needed by others ; the same limitation which forces the individual into society also makes him a useful member of it; for the diversity of individual character is not a mere diversity of atoms, but has in it the capability of organisation, or, in other words, of forming a whole. These primary facts suggest, as the true principle of human life, that each social element should do that which it is most fitted to do, thus contributing to the common stock the best that it has to give, and receiving from each other element that of which it is itself most in need. The more society is so ordered that this twofold principle of division and association of work is carried out, the more nearly will it approach its most natural and most perfect form. The main part of the first section of the *Republic,* from the middle of the second to the end of the fourth book, is occupied with the sketch of a society as it might be conceived to be if this principle of harmonious co-operation were realised, and it is as an element in its realisation that what may be called the first system of education is developed.

Before considering that system in its details, it will be well to see what was Plato's conception of education in general, for by it his whole treatment of the subject is in a great measure determined. We know in our own time what a difference it may make in the spirit and working of an educational method, whether the idea with which it starts is that of culture, or of training, or of useful accomplishment. Plato's idea of the essence of education is most simply and comprehensively

---

[1] The "insufficiency" of the individual is first illustrated from the most obvious sphere, that of the necessary wants (2. 369 c ff.) ; but it holds good in higher spheres too ; cf. 9. 590 d-e (the divine reason which it is good for a man to be governed by, if he has not got it in himself, is supplied to him from outside). Similarly the industrial principle of association is applied to the relation of the philosophers to the society of which they are members (7. 519 e—520 a).

expressed in the word "nurture."[1] To him the human soul
is emphatically and before all else something living, something
which in the strict sense we can neither create nor destroy,
but which we can feed or starve, nourish or poison. As in
the case of other living things, of plants and animals,[2] the
stronger and better the nature of the soul, the more important
is it what nourishment it gets, and a gifted soul in a corrupt
society is like a good seed sown in a strange soil; it grows
crooked and unlike itself, loses its proper virtue, and sinks at
last to the level of its surroundings. And in another famous
passage,[3] to which we shall have to refer more than once, the
young citizen who is being educated is compared to an animal
at pasture ; from the things which he sees and hears about him
he assimilates, little by little, the good or the evil which they
embody, till "many a little makes a mickle," which becomes
part and parcel of himself. It is this feeling of the assimilative
power of the soul which leads Plato to attach such immense
importance to the circumstances and environment of life, and
makes him on the whole more disposed to attribute moral evil
to bad nurture than to inherent vice. Amongst the various
elements which make up the complex creature man, he conceives that there are few which are not open to good influence.
Of what are usually called the lower desires there are indeed
some that are radically "wild,"[4] and with these there is only
one course possible, to stop their growth ; but the others admit
of being "tamed," and made to take service under the higher
self. And thus it is with a sort of compassion that Plato[5]
looks upon some of the great criminals of the world, who in
his eyes had the capability of being its greatest benefactors,
and owe their failure to its corruption or neglect. Against the
all-powerful influence of society,[6] he thinks that no private
teaching can hold its ground. It is not the so-called enlightened leaders of public opinion, the sophists of the day,
who really teach and demoralise the youth ;[7] the real educator

---

[1] Cf., for the use of τροφή or cognate terms, 3. 401 b, e ; 402 a ; 403 c ;
412 b ; 4. 424 a ; 6. 491 d-e ; and *Phaedrus*, 247 e ff., where the metaphor
is enlarged upon.

[2] 6. 497 b ; 491 d—492 a.   [3] 3. 401 c-d.   [4] 9. 589 b ; 591 b.
[5] 6. 491 e.   [6] 6. 492 c-e.   [7] 6. 492 a-b.

and the real sophist is public opinion itself, whose voice, resounding in the assembly and the law-courts, in the theatre and the camp, is practically irresistible by the isolated efforts of individuals. Such a power for evil can only be counteracted by creating a power for good as penetrating, as unconscious, and as universal, and to do this is the true function of a public system of education. On the other hand, while the inherent vitality of the soul makes the question of its nourishment all-important, it also precludes a merely mechanical treatment of it. We can place it in a healthy atmosphere, but we cannot compel it to assimilate only the healthy elements. The "eye of the soul"[1] is not, as some "professors of education" seem to think, a blind eye into which knowledge can be put; its power of vision can neither be originally produced by education, nor entirely destroyed by the want of it; it can only be "turned to the light," for which it has an intrinsic capacity. And the same holds good of the lower extremity of human nature; as in the "wild" and unteachable element there is a power of growth which can only be dealt with by being repressed, so among men there are found moral "incurables," for whom society has no course but to put them out of the way.[2]

The very simplicity of these ideas, as in the case of some others of Plato, is apt to conceal their importance. Everybody admits in theory that the human self is a living being, requiring a certain environment in order to grow properly, and capable of growing improperly in an immense variety of ways. But it is mainly in dealing with the material circumstances of life that the truth of the principle is practically realised, because there the consequences of its neglect are palpable : when we have to do with the mental atmosphere we are liable to forget it. Then again, the greater specialisation of modern life makes it difficult for us to keep our hold on universal elementary truths, which to the Greeks seemed neither old nor simple. Modern education inevitably divides itself under many heads ; it is primary or higher, technical or liberal, scientific or religious ; the distinctions are real and cannot be ignored ; but in

---

[1] 7. 518 b-c.   [2] 3. 410 a ; cf. 10. 615 e.

the controversies to which they sometimes give rise it is well, just because it is hard, to remember, that the ultimate subject of all education is a living organism, whose vital power, though divisible in thought, is really one and undivided ; that its vital wants are equally such, whether they be for fresh air, for useful knowledge, or for religious truth ; and that it will starve or degenerate in mind if its natural mental nourishment be denied it, as surely as it will in body if its bodily wants be neglected.

Such being Plato's general conception of the nature of education, we may expect that any system of education which he propounds will be a system for providing proper nurture to the growing soul, or for adjusting its surroundings to its higher needs. It is also clear that the particular character of the system for attaining these ends must be determined by the conception of the human nature which has to be fed, and the needs to which its circumstances have to be adjusted. And thus, in order to understand Plato's theory of education, we must understand his psychology.

In giving some account of the psychology of the *Republic,* we shall have to notice that, while the ground-plan of the account of the soul remains on the whole the same, the position assigned to its various elements changes considerably in different parts of the work; and these changes are necessarily accompanied by changes in the view taken of education. We will begin with the psychology of the first section of the work, only combining that of later sections where it seems to be in substantial agreement. From this we gather that Plato regarded the human soul as a complex whole, consisting of three "forms," "kinds," or "parts,"[1] as he variously calls them. The first of these, beginning at the lower end in the scale of worth, is ἐπιθυμία or "appetite." Plato[2] was aware that in what he called the "appetitive" form of the soul he was dealing with something too various to be easily described by a single name. He seems to have chosen the name in question because the bodily appetites, to which it was most commonly appropriated, are, from

---

[1] εἶδος, 4. 435 c ; 439 e, etc. ; γένος, 4. 441 c ; 443. d ; μέρος, 4. 442 b.
[2] 9. 580 d-e.

their intensity, the most obvious and conspicuous instances of their class. He has, however, another name, suggested, not by the degree of intensity of the activity, but by what seemed to him its most typical object;[1] "because wealth is the principal instrument by which the bodily appetites are satisfied, we call this element of the soul the wealth-loving or gain-loving element." This close association of things sometimes supposed to be so far apart as sensuality and avarice,[2] is very characteristic of Plato; and we shall see later on by what facts he illustrates it. For the present it is enough to observe that, though Plato by no means confines the word translated "appetite" to the above-mentioned instances,[3] yet when he speaks of the "appetitive" as a specific form or part of the soul, he intends primarily those desires of which bodily satisfaction and wealth are the typical objects. Of such appetites he distinguishes in a later book two kinds, "necessary" and "unnecessary."[4] Necessary appetites are those which we cannot get rid of, or those of which the satisfaction does us good; unnecessary are those which are superfluous or harmful. In these latter,[5] again, there is a subdivision into those which, though in themselves unproductive and wasteful to the organism, are yet capable of regulation, and those which are incurably "wild," "bestial," "lawless," which make themselves felt, even in the best men, when reason is in abeyance, but which, unless repressed or reduced to a minimum, bring ruin into life. These distinctions are graphically reproduced in a somewhat generalised form in one of the allegorical figures under which Plato represents his conception of human nature. He asks us to imagine a being having the outward semblance of a man,[6] but combining within three creatures, a man, a lion, and "a beast with many heads, heads of beasts tame and wild, and able to breed and change them at its will." Of the first two there will be more to say presently; in the third we readily recognise the psychological element of appetite in the sense just described. The hydra-like creature has in it an inherent capacity of growth and reproduction; some of its off-

---

[1] 9. 580 e—581 a.
[2] 3. 390 b—391 c ; 4. 442 a ; 8. 548 a-b.
[3] Cf. *e.g.* 5. 475 b; 9. 580 d.
[4] 8. 558 d ff.
[5] 9. 571 b ff.
[6] 9. 588 b ff.

spring can be "tamed" and "domesticated,"[1] and made serviceable to life; others are radically untameable, the inorganic,
inhuman, "unnecessary," and possibly destructive, appendage
of our nature, which, while it can never entirely divest itself of
its humanity, touches God at one extremity and the beast at
the other.

Though Plato represents appetite as the element which
occupies the largest space in the soul,[2] and though the men who
live for appetite more than for any other part of themselves
are, in his view, the majority of mankind, we shall not expect
it to occupy the chief share of attention in his system of education. The degree of education of which the appetites are
capable is expressed by his own word "taming,"[3] and by this
he seems to mean such a regulation of them as shall prevent
them from interfering with the higher psychical activities, and
train them to contribute to the good of the whole soul that
basis of healthy physical life which is the necessary groundwork of those activities.

The second element in the Platonic analysis of the soul
is not quite so easily described or understood. The Greek
words θυμός, τὸ θυμοειδές, by which it is designated, are commonly translated "spirit," and though this term covers only a
part of their meaning in the *Republic*, it will serve as well as
any other in the absence of a real equivalent. "Spirit" is
first introduced as being the indispensable foundation of courage,[4] that element of hardihood and intrepidity which is common
to men with dogs and horses, and which makes them "never
say die;" at the same time it is represented as the source of
pugnacity and aggressiveness, with their possible developments
into ferocity and cruelty. It is only another form of the same
view, when "spirit" is said to be that part of the soul which
is peculiarly fostered and stimulated by athletic exercises;[5] it is
the "hard" element in human nature, which, if rightly nurtured,
becomes true bravery, but if exclusively encouraged degenerates
into blind brutality, surliness, quarrelsomeness, or self-will. In

---

[1] 9. 589 b, τιθασεύων.
[3] Cf. 4. 442 a ; 8. 559 a-b ; 9. 591 c d.
[2] 3. 410 c-d ; 411 c-e ; 9. 590 a-b.
[2] 4. 442 a ; 9. 588 d ; 4. 431 c.
[4] 2. 375 a-b.

all this we at once recognise the "lion" of the allegorical figure of man mentioned above.

So far the account of the "spirited" element is simple enough. It has two other senses which are not quite so obvious; the one attaching to the sense of anger which θυμός so commonly has, the other to that of pugnacity. From the former point of view "spirit" appears as what we may call righteous indignation. It is that which makes a man's blood boil at the consciousness of suffering unjustly,[1] while it is characteristically absent when the suffering is felt to be deserved. It is that, again,[2] which makes a man angry with himself when he feels that he has let his appetites get the better of his reason, whereas no one ever feels this anger when he has let his better judgment prevail over his appetite. These observations lead Plato to represent "spirit" as the natural ally or servant of the rational or better self;[3] not that it is never irrational, or may not be perverted by bad education,[4] but that it never seems to act with the lower appetites against the reason; or, to use more modern phraseology, if we are once convinced that in refusing to satisfy an appetite we are acting reasonably, we may feel dissatisfaction, but we do not feel indignation. In its third and last distinctive use,[5] "spirit" is the root of ambition or the competitive instinct. In this sense it is, as was said, a modification of the fighting spirit, for the essence both of ambition and of pugnacity is the desire to do better than somebody else. And as in the other two senses, so here "spirit" may have a good or a bad development, into honourable rivalry on the one hand, on the other into mere contentiousness.

It is not difficult to see how these various representations of "spirit" may be connected. In all of them there is an element of what we may call self-assertion and self-consciousness. It is this, in the form of not choosing to be "put upon," which makes us resist what we think injustice; it is this, in the form of honourable pride, which makes us face danger without flinching, and prompts us to measure ourselves against others; it is the consciousness of a self which deserves respect that makes us angry when we have disgraced ourselves; and it is

---

[1] 4. 440 c-d.   [2] 4. 440 a-b.   [3] 4. 140 b.   [4] 4. 441 a.   [5] 9. 581 a-b.

the feeling that there is no such self to fall back upon which weakens us when we know that we are in the wrong; and lastly, it is often an exaggerated sense of our own importance or power which breaks out into aggressiveness, hardens into self-will, or is nursed into bad temper.

It now remains to consider the third, and in Plato's mind the highest, element in the constitution of the human soul, that which he calls "the philosophic." And here much more than in the case of the other two we shall have to notice considerable modifications in his account in different parts of the *Republic*.

Beginning with what we have called the first main section of the work, we find the "philosophic" element at first characterised in a way very far removed from what the English word would lead us to expect. It is introduced[1] as a necessary psychological complement to the element of "spirit." Unmitigated or unbalanced, the latter element would be a source of mere indiscriminate pugnacity, and would result in a destructive war of all against all. Clearly if human nature is to be adapted to the higher functions of civic society, it must contain some counterbalancing factor, some quality of gentleness to soften ferocity, some tendency to union to counteract the feeling of mutual antagonism. The germs of such an element Plato finds in some of the lower animals: the well-bred dog, who had been already chosen to typify the quality of "spirit," is found to exhibit, along with the greatest fierceness towards strangers, the greatest gentleness towards those whom he knows; and this suggests, what is found to be the fact when we come to look at human nature, that this combination of qualities so opposite is not only possible but natural. But the question arises, Why call this softening, unifying element "philosophic"? Here again, half-playfully perhaps, yet not without a deeper meaning, Plato helps himself with the analogy of the dog. The dog judges of friends and enemies by the test of knowledge;

---

[1] 2. 375 b—376 c. In this passage a selection of men is being made who are to be "guardians" of the ideal state which is being constructed. But it is clear (cf. 9. 581 a-c ; 4. 435 e—436 a) that while here appearing to pick out certain qualities for a certain purpose, Plato is really enumerating the qualities which he conceived to be present in different proportions in all human beings.

those whom he knows he treats as friends, those whom he does
not know as enemies; with him, in a word, to know is to be
fond; and as it is the feeling of knowing those whom he knows
which excites his fondness, he may be said in a sense to be
fond of knowing, much as a person who likes the society of his
inferiors might be said to be fond of superiority. In so far
then as the quality of gentleness attaches to the consciousness
of knowledge and the pleasure which that consciousness excites,
it may be said to arise from fondness of knowledge, and this is
almost equivalent to " philosophy " in its literal sense of " love
of knowledge " or " wisdom."

The first and simplest application of this somewhat curious
train of thought is obvious enough. Every one has felt in one
form or another the power of knowledge or familiarity to breed
a sort of liking. It is an instinctive feeling, which often does
not rise to the height of affection, but remains a sense of quiet
pleasure or comfort; it attaches to things, to places, to persons;
much of the love of home and of country, and even of humanity,
is traceable to its presence; much of the antipathy to foreigners
or to novelties, to its absence. In such a rudimentary feeling
of attachment for what belongs to us Plato saw the first germ
of that which seemed to him highest in human nature. We
shall see shortly how the germ developed under his hands.

Our next introduction[1] to the " philosophic " element of the
soul is in a somewhat different context. It is still, indeed, the
" gentle " or " tame " part in contradistinction to the " wildness "
and " hardness " of the " spirited " part, and it is still intimately
associated with knowledge; but the gentleness of which it is
now said to be the source is the result of culture instead of
dog-like attachment, and the knowledge in which it takes
delight is the sense of something understood rather than of
something familiar. It now includes susceptibility to the
influences of language, of music, of painting, of beauty in the
widest sense of the word; it includes also the quickness of
perception which makes learning pleasant and welcomes every
fresh form of truth. It has also a more purely moral aspect;
it is that which produces love of order and quietness, the

---

[1] 3. 410 b—412 a.

impulse to obey rather than to resist, and to use persuasion rather than force. Like "spirit," it is capable of exaggeration and perversion; under the exclusive or excessive influence of culture and refinement it develops softness and effeminacy, or nervous sensibility and unstableness.

When we again[1] meet with the highest form of the soul it is no longer under the name of "philosophic;" the intellectual character in it now predominates over the emotional; it is the calculative, deliberative, reasoning element in the soul, that in virtue of which it guides and rules, that which when fully developed becomes, not love of wisdom, but wisdom. Its relation to the "spirited" element is also changed; from being a merely complementary factor to it, it has come to be its natural master, from whom issue the dogmas and principles which in the well-trained soul "appetite" cheerfully obeys and "spirit" fearlessly carries out.

Such is the account of the "philosophic" part in the first section of the *Republic;* in its most primitive character it is the impulse of attraction to what is familiar because it is familiar; then the substratum of gentleness and of culture; lastly, reason in its regulative and ruling capacity.

To sum up then briefly the results thus far arrived at, the human soul, in Plato's view, is a triple being. It has for its largest constituent appetite, the simple craving for present satisfaction, capable of indefinite expansion, mostly amenable, but also partially unamenable, to reason. Secondly, it implies an element of self-assertiveness and pugnacity, which gives rise to qualities as various as courage and brutality, ambition and contentiousness, just indignation and unreasoning bad temper. Lastly, there is in it a capacity of attraction and receptivity, which if not perverted into weakness of character, develops, on the one side, into gentleness, sociableness, love; on the other, into refinement, culture, and wisdom.

Proceeding now to the later modifications of this psychology, we find, as has been already observed, that they are modifications not so much in the general constitution of the soul as in

---

[1] 4. 439 d ; 441 e ; 442 c. In the fourth book the word φιλόσοφον is dropped, and the highest element in the soul is generally called λογιστικόν or (436 a ; cf. 9. 580 d) ᾧ μανθάνομεν.

the relationship of its constituent elements. They consist mainly in the widening and deepening of the conception of the "philosophic" element, and in the assignment to it of a much more predominant position in the formation of human character and' the regulation of human conduct. It is scarcely possible to make this clear without again referring shortly to the general structure of the *Republic.* The first four books of it, as we saw, contain the discovery and exhibition of a principle of human life, social and individual, such as, if carried out, would realise the greatest wellbeing of which man is capable. That principle is most simply described as the harmonious co-operation of various elements, whether those of the individual soul or those of the state; and the ultimate hypothesis upon which the principle rests is that these various elements have the capacity of forming a whole, and that, therefore, in performing each their separate function in the best way, they are also in the best way working for the good of the whole. According to this view, in a normally constituted society each class would consist of those individuals in whom a certain psychological quality predominated, and who were therefore best fitted for a certain kind of work; and the chief interest and duty of the society would be to secure, firstly, that each of its members should have his proper place in the organisation of work; and, secondly, that having found his proper place, he should be fitted by education or other means to do the particular work of his life as well as possible. Of the work necessary to the wellbeing of a state, Plato thought that there were three principal kinds, the work of producing the material commodities essential to life, the work of protecting the state against external enemies and of preserving order within it, and the work of legislation and government. For the class of citizens engaged in the first kind of work he apparently did not think that any public system of education was necessary, a fact which, however much at variance with modern ideas, will not startle any one who is familiar with the position of the industrial classes in Greek society, and with the opinions entertained of them both by the public and by philosophers. It was then for the classes who are engaged in military and political functions, that is, in what a Greek would consider the functions of a citizen proper, that the education sketched in the earlier part of the *Republic* is exclusively intended. That education is a method for providing the natural and proper nurture for the souls of the persons in question. Its character (to anticipate for a moment what must be said later) is emphatically non-technical; it teaches no knowledge or mental accomplishment having a direct bearing upon the functions eventually to be exercised by those who receive it; it comes to an end at about twenty, when those functions have not yet begun, and its main object is to predispose the soul, intellectually and morally, to the perception and execution of ideas and principles of which it does not as yet understand the full bearing, but upon which it will afterwards find that the welfare of itself and society depends.

We may now return to the point at which it was necessary to make this digression. It seems to have been in Plato's mind,[1] even at the time when he was writing the first part of the *Republic*, that the system of education contained in it was imperfect and inadequate. Whether it was from design that he deferred the expression of this feeling, or whether it was forced from him by subsequent criticism, this is not the place to discuss; it is at any rate certain that in what may be called the second section of the work, comprising the fifth, sixth, and seventh books, the education described in the preceding books is referred to and criticised as insufficient for the purpose of preparing citizens for the exercise of the most important public functions. This attitude of criticism adopted in the later towards the earlier section is however by no means the only symptom of change on the part of the writer. The question under discussion, the tone in which it is discussed, and the answer which is given to it, are very different in the two parts. In the first the question is, What is the true principle which should regulate human life, and what would be the form of a society in which it was carried out? In the second it is, How could such an ideal society, with all the consequences which it seems logically to entail, be actually realised, and what is the root

---

[1] Indications of this feeling are found 3. 414 a and 416 b, compared with 6. 503 a-b, e. The want of "exactness" or completeness in the account of education in the early books is parallel to that in the psychology (cf. 4. 435 d with 6. 504 a-e.

of the existing evils of mankind which hinder its realisation? In the first part, again, the tone is that of a man who certainly sees much to criticise in existing institutions, but who is nevertheless disposed to make the best of them, and does not despair of doing so. In the second it is that of one oppressed by the sense of the evil in the world, hoping for salvation only from remedies which are themselves almost hopeless, diffident and yet defiant, daringly paradoxical and yet terribly in earnest. And lastly, the two answers are different. To the earlier question the answer is: Allow, and if necessary compel, human nature to develop normally, and provide it with the nurture which its development demands; the rest will manage itself. To the later it is: The cause of the ills of mankind is ignorance of their true good and neglect of their noblest natures; train those natures rightly and they will see what is the true good of mankind; give them unlimited power and they will carry out what the good requires. Such is the significance of the startling demand made in the fifth book of the *Republic*, that philosophers should be kings. We are here concerned with it, not in its political, but in its psychological and educational, aspect; in other words, we have to see how Plato's conception of what we have already learnt to know as the "philosophic part" in the soul has expanded to the point at which we now find it, giving its name to the whole man, embodying all gifts and excellencies, and claiming to rule the world.

Between the account of the "philosophic" element which we have gathered from the first four books of the *Republic*, and that of the "philosophic nature" which we are about to gather from the following three, the references made to the same subject in the ninth book seem to occupy an intermediate place,[1] and to form a kind of transition. In the ninth book, taking his departure from the triple division of the soul with which we are now familiar, Plato divides mankind into three "primary kinds,"[2] according as one or other of the three psychical elements predominates in the character. To those in

---

[1] I do not mean to imply that the ninth book was necessarily composed before the sixth, though there is some ground for the supposition.

[2] 9. 580 d ff.

whom "appetite" predominates, the chief object in life is the
wealth by which appetite is satisfied; to the "spirited" class it
is the honour which rewards successful competition; while to
those in whom the "philosophic" side is the strongest, it is
truth. And accordingly they are called respectively lovers of
gain or wealth, lovers of contention or honour, lovers of learning or wisdom, that is, "philosophers," and of these the last are
said to enjoy the fullest experience and to live the highest life.
Here then we find the love of knowing, which has all along
underlain in different senses the "philosophic" form of soul,
interpreted as the love of "knowing the nature of the truth," [1]
or, to use an equivalent Platonic phrase, "the nature of what
is," and further, when present in sufficient force, giving its
name to a definite type of character, and that the highest.
The allegorical figure of man in the same book, to which reference has already been made, supplies some more additions to
the conception. In the triple creature which we are there asked
to imagine, the "man," or, as he is called to distinguish him
from the external human semblance, the "inward man," clearly
represents the "philosophic" element; and from this we see
that in Plato's view it is this element which constitutes the
real humanity, and therefore the real personality, in our complex nature. But this is not all. The "inward man" is distinctly asserted to be that which is "divine" or "the most
divine" in man.[2] To Plato there is a revelation of God in the
human soul, as there is in the physical world; his "celestial
city"[3] is not only a visionary type, it is also, like the "kingdom
of heaven," within us, and he who will may enter in and dwell
there. And once more, as it is this divine humanity which is
in the truest sense the self, the other parts of human nature
are conceived by Plato to find their highest activity and their
most real satisfaction in following and serving it as far as they
are able; to become as human as possible, to live for humanity
in this sense, is the highest end of the half-animal nature which
forms the larger part of man.

Turning now from the ninth to the three central books of

[1] 581 b, e ; 582 b, c.
[2] 9. 589 d, e ; 590 d; cf. too, 6. 497 c, and 10. 611 e.   [3] 9. 592 a-b.

the *Republic*, we find the attributes with which the "philosophic" nature is invested in the former confirmed and developed in the latter. The point of departure is the same: the "philosopher" is described, in accordance with his name,[1] as one who loves knowledge or wisdom, and "philosophy" is the instinctive and indiscriminate craving to learn. The man endowed with this passion is like a man with a great appetite and a strong digestion; everything that will stay the hunger of his soul is welcome food. Or again, he is like a man who is in love, not once or twice, but always and everywhere; as the lover finds nothing that is not beautiful in the face of his beloved, so to the man born to be a "philosopher" there is nothing in the face of truth which is not loveable. This is the germ, the elementary condition, of philosophy; it does not of itself make a full-grown philosopher, any more than the possession of "spirit" necessarily makes a brave man; but no true philosopher can be without it, any more than a spiritless man can have real courage. But (and here Plato takes his next great step)[2] these elementary qualities are not only the germ of the true philosophic character, but of all human excellence as well; or rather, the philosophic spirit cannot exist in its fulness and integrity without involving all that is called good and noble in human character. Plato explains this somewhat startling idea by showing how the whole company of virtues flows naturally and necessarily from the single passion for truth. In one whose desires "set strongly" towards one all-absorbing object, the channels of the bodily appetites must run dry; and the "vision of all time and all existence" which he enjoys will make human life seem but a little thing, and death nothing to be feared. In a mind which "reaches out after all that is human and divine" there is no room for meanness or pettiness, nor can such a mind be harsh or unfair in dealings with other men, for the motives which make others so—avarice, conceit, or fear—do not touch it. Add to these ethical qualities the intellectual gifts without which love of knowledge is impossible, quickness to learn and slowness to forget, with that mental grace or proportion which

---

[1] 5. 474 c—475 c; 6. 485 b.
[2] 6. 485 b—487 a; 489 e—490 c.

predisposes the soul to receive truth, and we have a fully-endowed nature, such as " the god of blame himself could find no fault in."

We have here reached the culminating point in the development of Plato's conception of " philosophy" in the *Republic.* Beginning with the instinctive attraction to what is familiar, passing on into the ready receptivity for all that is admirable in nature and art, with the unconscious grace and refinement which accompanies it, it has now become the consuming passion for what is true and real, at once the most human and the most divine attribute of the soul, the crowning gift and complete embodiment of perfect manhood.

Neither the later uses of the word "philosophy," nor its literal interpretation as "love of wisdom," will much help the modern reader to enter here into the spirit of Plato. Philosophy to most of us is too much wrapt up in the associations of books and systems, of technicalities and jargon, to let us feel the living spirit which it still is when it is anything more than a set of phrases. And the love of truth, in spite of the boasts of modern science, is still but rarely found to dominate the character and mould the life as Plato conceived that it might do. The difficulty of understanding him is further increased by the dispersion and differentiation which his idea has undergone. When he spoke of "the truth," or of "what is," we see that there entered into his feeling not only the enthusiasm of the scientific discoverer, but also the passion of the poet for beauty and the devotion of the saint to the object of his worship. It would be beyond our present scope to dwell at length upon this point; a reference to two passages in the *Republic* will sufficiently illustrate it. One is that in which he describes the philosophic spirit as the desire for union of the mind with reality :[1] "It is in the nature of the real lover of learning to be ever struggling up to being, and not to abide amongst the manifold and limited objects of opinion; he will go on his way, and the edge of his love will not grow dull nor its force abate, until he has got hold of the nature of being with that part of his soul to which it belongs so to do, and that is the part which is akin to being; with this he will draw near, and mingle

---

[1] 6. 490 a-b.

being with being, and beget intelligence and truth, and find knowledge and true life and nourishment, and then, and not till then, he will cease from his travail." The imagery of this passage shows us that to Plato the process of knowledge was very far from being the mechanical and external operation as which we are apt to regard it. To him the world of reality or fact, that which really is in spite of what appears or what we fancy, is something of kindred nature with what is highest in the human mind ; the impulse to know is the impulse to become one with that which is " bone of our bone and flesh of our flesh," and truth is the birth which allays the " travail of the soul."

In another passage [1] the effect of the same spirit upon the formation of character is brought out in a way equally remote from ordinary modes of thought. " The man whose mind is really set upon the things that are, has not leisure to look down at the concerns of men, and to fight with them, and fill himself with envy and bitterness ; that which he sees and gazes upon is set fast and ever the same, it neither does nor suffers wrong, but is all reasonable and in order. This he imitates, and, as far as is possible, becomes like it, for it surely cannot be that a man can live in fellowship with what he admires without imitating it. So then the philosopher, living in fellowship with what is divine and orderly, grows himself orderly and divine as far as man is able." Such is Plato's conception of what in modern phrase we should call the genuine study of the laws of nature and the world. In the unchangeable order and beauty of the universe he sees the image on a vaster scale of the same reason which is imperfectly reflected in human life, and he might have said to Justice what Wordsworth has said to Duty :

"Thou dost preserve the stars from wrong,
　And the most ancient heavens through thee are fresh and strong."

We have now passed in review the main elements of that human nature for which, as Plato conceived, it was the function of education to provide nurture. It may seem, perhaps, that a disproportionate space has been given to what belongs not to education but to psychology. But it is just the inseparableness of the two that is so characteristic of Plato's treatment, and,

---

[1] 6. 500 b-c.

whatever we may think of his analysis of the soul in its details, we shall hardly escape the conclusion that some such analysis is an indispensable condition of a really rational theory of education; in other words, that neither a state nor an individual can undertake to educate in a systematic way unless they start with some idea, not only of what they wish to teach, nor only of the type of character which they wish to produce, but also of the living being to which the matter to be taught is relative, and upon which the given character is to be impressed. The "practical" man, who believes in "results," will be disposed to regard such psychological considerations as fanciful or far-fetched. And yet the most fatally unpractical thing in the world is to go on testing methods by results which take every factor into account except the one upon which the whole result ultimately depends. That factor in man is the human mind, in Englishmen the English mind, in different classes of Englishmen the minds of those classes; and to discuss what kinds of education are in themselves the best, without considering mental organisation, is as idle as to discuss what is the best kind of food in the abstract without regard to the stomach which has to digest it.

Before passing on to our main subject, the methods by which Plato proposed to meet the educational needs of the soul, one preliminary observation must be made. It appears from what has been already said that there is a certain want of continuity in his psychology. Instead of following the soul in an unbroken series from its earliest to its most advanced phase of development, he has first given a picture of its education up to a certain point, which is apparently meant to be final, and has then made a fresh start, and represented the previous course as a merely preliminary stage in a larger and more elaborate system; and this fresh start coincides with a fresh point of departure in the account of the highest or "philosophic" element in the soul. The questions suggested by these facts as to the composition of the *Republic* do not concern us now; whatever they may be, and however they may be answered, it may be assumed here that Plato, at some time in his life, intended the sections of the *Republic*, as we now have it, to form parts of one work. On this assumption, the accounts which it contains both of the soul and of education have been considered in this Essay as forming a logical if not a literary whole, and as supplying a fairly complete and coherent representation of what Plato conceived human nature in its fulness to be and to require. It must, however, be remembered once for all that the *Republic* gives us, not a detailed treatise on education, but certain leading principles which admit of being applied under various circumstances and in various ways. Our present object is not primarily to discover the modifications which these principles admit or require, but to exhibit the principles themselves in their clearest light and fullest bearings.

The education of the average Greek gentleman, like that of the average English gentleman, comprised a certain amount of mental cultivation and a certain amount of athletic exercise. The former, besides reading, writing, and some elementary mathematics, consisted mainly in the reciting and learning by heart of poetry, along with the elements of music, and sometimes of drawing. Perhaps because so much of the poetry was originally sung or accompanied, the word "music" was sometimes applied to the education in literature as well as in music proper, and it is in this wider sense that Plato habitually uses it. Under the term "gymnastic" was understood the whole system of diet and exercise which, varying with the customs of different states, had for its common object the production of bodily health and strength, and the preparation for military service. In this twofold method of education, which the wisdom of the past had handed down, Plato sees an unconscious recognition of the psychological requirements of human nature on its two most important sides.[1] At first sight it would seem that "music" and "gymnastic" were related to one another as mental to bodily training, and this was no doubt the ordinary way of distinguishing them; but Plato, while himself adopting the popular phraseology at first, afterwards corrects it by asserting that the soul, and not the body, is the primary object of "gymnastic" as well as of "music,"[2] and appeals

---

[1] 2. 376 e, ἢ χαλεπὸν εὑρεῖν βελτίω τῆς ὑπὸ τοῦ πολλοῦ χρόνου εὑρημένης; cf. 3. 411 e, θεὸν ἔγωγ᾽ ἄν, κ.τ.λ.   [2] 3. 410 b-c.

to the fact that exclusive devotion to physical exercises affects the character no less markedly than exclusive devotion to literary and æsthetic culture. The truth is, that "music" educates,[1] not the soul merely, but specifically the "philosophic" part of the soul, through the medium of the eye and ear, while "gymnastic," through bodily exercises, not only produces bodily health and strength, but disciplines the psychological element of "spirit." It is through the gentle, responsive, loving element that the soul is open to the influences of literature and art; it is this which makes it quick to assimilate, ready to obey and to imitate, open-eyed and open-eared to catch the sights and sounds of the living world. To satisfy its cravings with the right food, to offer true nobility to its admiration and true beauty to its love, to keep its perceptions wakeful and clear, to refine and balance its emotions, these are, in Plato's opinion, the functions of "musical" education. But it will not be truly "musical," truly "harmonious," unless it be counterbalanced by something different.[2] If the "philosophic" side of the soul be exclusively fostered, its gentleness will turn into effeminacy, its sensitiveness into irritability, its simple love into feverish desire.[3] It is not enough (though this is important) that the material presented in "music" should itself be such as to brace the softer qualities in the soul; it must be supplemented by nurture of an altogether different kind acting upon altogether different qualities. This is the office of "gymnastic," which, by bodily exercises, develops and educates the element of "spirit." For "spirit," though it has an instinctive tendency to ally itself with reason, requires training if the tendency is to become a habit. Proper "gymnastic" will discipline the wild impulses of violence and pugnacity, developing the intelligent courage of the citizen-soldier, instead of the blind ferocity of the barbarian or the wild beast,[4] while it will counteract the yielding, voluptuous, or nervous tendencies by encouraging competition, endurance, and presence of mind. On the other hand, excessive attention to it brings with it evils as great as its undue neglect. The body then

---

[1] 3. 410 c—412 a.

[2] 3. 412 a ; cf. 9. 591 d.

[3] Cf. 3. 403 a ; 404 d-e ; 410 a.

[4] 4. 430 b-c.

gradually swallows up the mind; the whole man swells with
the pride of conscious strength; by degrees his courage sinks
into brutality, and his high spirit into insolence; his senses,
the windows of the mind, are clogged and darkened, and his
intelligence, neglected and starved, grows "weak, deaf, and
blind." The problem then of education is to adjust these two
complementary but conflicting elements in human nature.[1]
The soul is like a stringed instrument, and education has to
tune it, tightening here and slackening there, that it may
become one instead of many, and its life a harmony instead of
a discord. The man who can thus educate himself or others,
who can "combine music and gymnastic, and apply them in due
proportion to the soul," deserves, far more than any musician,
to be called a "musical" man.

Of the two branches of education, "music," in its widest
sense,[2] will clearly begin before "gymnastic," for we tell stories
to children before they can take athletic exercise. The means
employed by "music" in the Platonic system are literature,
music proper, and the other fine arts. Each of these, in its
different way, is capable of expressing certain ethical characteristics, and by each these characteristics are conveyed, through
the eye or ear, to the soul.[3] Of the various means, literature,
in the shape of stories and poetry, naturally comes first,[4] and
the questions which Plato[5] raises regarding the educational
use of literature are two, firstly, what should it express? and
secondly, how should it express it? The first question explains
itself; the second concerns literary form or style, and, as the
ethical influence of form depends mainly, in Plato's view, on
the degree to which it is dramatic, this question to him comes to
be, How far is the dramatic element in literature good or bad for
education? Such a problem would not arise until a comparatively late stage, for in young children the susceptibility to
literary influence is as yet too embryonic to admit such distinctions as dramatic or undramatic, personal or impersonal, and
the like. The first question then is not as to the form but as to
the substance of literature, regarded as an educational agent.

---

[1] 3. 412 a; cf. 4, 443 d-e.   [2] 2. 376 e.   [3] 3. 400 c—401 a.
[4] 2. 376 e; 377 a.   [5] 3. 392 c; 398 b.

"In all work the beginning is of the greatest importance, especially when we have to do with a young and tender creature, for then, more than at any other time, it receives the particular fashion and stamp which we wish to impress upon it,"[1] and so, "what the child hears when it is young generally becomes fixed fast and indelibly in its mind."[2] This is Plato's reason for giving so much consideration to the beginnings of education. The young soul, like the young body, is plastic and malleable, and mothers and nurses, who take such care that their children's limbs shall grow straight, should remember how much more care is needed in the handling and shaping of their minds.[3] What then are the ideas which should be impressed most deeply on the minds of children? Speaking generally, they will be such as we should wish them to retain when they are grown up.[4] The education of childhood should lay a foundation of character which will not have to be cut away as years go on, but will invite and sustain the superstructure of manhood. Such a foundation Plato would see laid in certain religious or semi-religious ideas; he would, in other words, have the fundamental elements of character developed in the first instance by habitually putting before the minds of the young the true nature of God and of what is most godlike in man. In this sense, then, that he would represent the primary moral ideas to children as embodied in divine or superhuman beings, Plato may be truly said to invest those ideas with a religious sanction, and to give his system of education a religious basis. The child is to be bred up in the belief that beings greater and better than himself have behaved in a certain way, and his natural impulse to imitate is thus to be utilised in forming his own character.[5] It would, however, be an inversion of the real order of Plato's thought, to say that he conceives the ideas in question to owe their validity to their superhuman embodiment. On the contrary, it is clear that with him the moral is

---

[1] 2. 377 a-b.   [2] 2. 378 d-e.   [3] 2. 377 c.

[4] 2. 377 b, ἐπειδὰν τελεωθῶσιν ; cf. 383 c, εἰ μέλλουσιν, κ.τ.λ.

[5] This impulse is mostly insisted on by Plato in connection with what is bad (2. 378 b ; 3. 391 e), but it is implied in all that he says of early education. Cf. 6. 500 c, ἦ οἴει τινὰ μηχανὴν εἶναι, ὅτῳ τις ὁμιλεῖ ἀγάμενος, μὴ μιμεῖσθαι ἐκεῖνο ;

the criterion of the supernatural, not the supernatural of the moral; and that if, and so far as, a religious sanction means a sanction derived from a story of miraculous events, he considers that sanction to belong to a rudimentary stage of education and intelligence. This will appear more plainly if we examine the form in which what we may call religious truth is supposed by him to be imparted. Education, Plato says,[1] must begin with literature, and "literature is of two kinds, true and false; it is with the latter kind that education must begin, for the literature which we read to children consists of myths, and myths, speaking generally, are false, though they contain elements of truth as well." The whole circle of Greek religious ideas, so far as they found expression in language at all, did so mainly in the form of myths. Instead of an authorised collection of more or less historical books, with a mass of authorised doctrine more or less directly depending upon it, the Greeks had a number of floating mythical stories, local and national, some of which, receiving glorified shape from the genius of poets or artists, exercised a special ascendency over the popular imagination. The bulk of these stories Plato unhesitatingly pronounces "false," and what he means by "false" appears from a passage[2] where he is enumerating the cases in which "falsehood in speech" may be useful and admissible. One of these cases is "the falsehood of the poet:" for " in mythology, owing to our ignorance of the actual truth of what happened long ago, we make the falsehood as like the truth as we possibly can, and so render it useful." The old myths, then, are untrue, not because they necessarily misrepresent facts, but because the lapse of time prevents us from knowing whether any facts underlie them, and what those facts are. They are like pictures of which we are no longer able to test the accuracy. And yet, in the same sentence which tells us that myths are false because we do not know the truth of what they say, we are told that we can " make them like the truth." The explanation of this apparent contradiction is found in an important distinction in the sense of falsehood. In the sense that they can at best be only an uncertain approximation to the truth, all myths and mythic

---

[1] 2. 376 e—377 a.   [2] 2. 382 d.

poetry are necessarily untrue. They may, however, be untrue
in another, and, to Plato, more serious sense; they may not
only veil our want of historical knowledge, they may also contradict our fundamental ideas about the subjects of which they
treat; they may be not only unhistorical, but morally or meta-
physically inconsistent and illogical.[1] Their subject-matter is
the divine nature, gods and demigods; of this nature we must
have a more or less definite conception, and wherever a myth
contradicts that conception, we must pronounce it false. It is in
this sense that Plato speaks of the poet "telling his falsehood
badly,"[2] "when he makes a bad likeness in language of the
characters of gods and heroes, like a painter who paints a
picture not at all like what he means to copy." And he gives
numerous illustrations of his meaning; the dismal accounts of
Hades are "not true;"[3] the stories of the changes of Proteus
and Thetis, of the robberies of Theseus and Peirithous, are
"calumnies;"[4] and it is a sort of "blasphemy" against Achilles
to say or to believe that he was so avaricious as to accept
Agamemnon's presents, and not to give up the body of Hector
without a price.[5] In one sense, then, (to recapitulate) all myths
must be false, in so far as we cannot know whether they represent what actually happened; in another sense they may be
true or false, according as they do or do not conform to the
logical laws of their subject-matter. And as Plato seems to
consider myths to be the appropriate form for speaking of the
divine nature, when it has to be spoken of as a person or
persons, he would seem to conceive of specifically religious
truth, so far as it implies such a personal representation, as
belonging to a rudimentary stage of mental development. On
the other hand, he clearly sees no objection to employing this
admittedly inadequate form of expression as an agent in education, nor to telling children religious stories which cannot pretend to be historical.

This entire subordination of historical to moral truth in
religious education, strange as it may seem to us, was natural
to Plato. The mythology which occupied the Greek mind

---

[1] 2. 380 c, οὔτε ξύμφωνα αὐτὰ αὑτοῖς.   [2] 2. 377 d-e ; cf. 3. 388 c.
[3] 3. 386 b-c.   [4] 2. 381 d ; 3. 391 c-d.   [5] 3. 391 a ; cf. 2. 381 e.

was its own creation, the offspring of its early contact with nature, developed by subsequent reflection; and the mind from which it sprang felt itself competent to judge it. The element of dogmatic fixity in their religion attached much more to its ritual than to its ideas; these latter were a plastic material, growing in accordance with the secret laws of psychology and language, or the conscious design of poets. In applying to them canons of criticism resting on no authority but that of his own moral consciousness, Plato might expect to offend many popular beliefs and prejudices, but they would not be the beliefs or prejudices of a priesthood or a church. It seems to be incident to religious movements and ideas, that they rapidly gather round them an accretion of mythical events and conceptions, and neither the Jewish nor the Christian religion is an exception to the general rule. But there is this great difference between them and the Greek religion, that the literature to which the former attach themselves, large as is its infusion of poetry and mythology, still purports in its most important parts to be historical, and that with its historical character its religious significance has come to be almost inseparably associated. And thus, in religious education, we are not only met by the question which Plato asked, Whether the whole of this literature is consistent with our ideas of the divine nature? but we have also to settle the question, which did not present itself to Plato, Whether it is consistent with our canons of historical evidence? Had Plato been writing now, he would have found the second a more prominent question than the first, and we cannot say with certainty what his advice would have been to those who find themselves in the dilemma of teaching, or seeing others teach, their children religious stories which they themselves do not believe to be true. We may, however, conjecture that he would have made the moral worth of those stories the final test, and that if they had seemed to him to embody ideas really vital to human life and character, he would have retained them, trusting to the child's mind to assimilate what was valuable, and to later education to preserve or to rectify its sense of historical truth.

The increased appreciation of the distinction between truth of fact and truth of idea, is often and rightly represented as a characteristic acquisition of modern, as compared with ancient, thought. Yet, in its ultimate analysis, the distinction is seen to exist only in abstraction. Neither " mere " facts nor " mere " ideas form any part of our knowledge, but facts which are interpreted into our mental experience, and ideas which are referred to something independent of that experience. The importance of a historical fact must depend, in the last resort, upon its moral or ideal significance, or, in other words, upon what it tells us of our own nature ; and our conception of the use and value of evidence is in advance of that of the Greeks, not because we have discovered a new sort of truth which was unknown to them, but because our whole mental horizon has enormously expanded, and we are far more vividly conscious of the possible bearings of one part of our experience upon another. Our truth of fact is more pregnant with thought than theirs, and our truth of idea goes back into a deeper reality.

We have seen in what sense Plato bases education on religion, and how he conceives that the mythical form in which religious ideas are presented may be, in different ways, both true and untrue. The next question is, What is that religious truth which mythical literature may approximately express, and by its conformity to which its educational value is to be determined ? Clearly it can be no other than the most perfect and consistent conception which can be formed of the divine nature. Plato accordingly begins by laying down certain " outlines of theology, which the makers of stories must not be allowed to transgress," for " God must always be represented as he really is, whether in epic or in tragedy."[1] The doctrines of Plato's state-religion are only two, but they go to the root of the matter; the first is, that God is good and the cause of good only ;[2] the second is, that God is unchangeable and true.[3] Thus simply stated, they are the common property of all higher religious thought, but Plato's application of them is to some extent peculiar. The primitive conception of the deity as the simple embodiment of power, readily leads in one direction to the belief that he sends good and evil upon man

---

[1] 2. 379 a. [2] 2. 379 a—380 c. [3] 2. 380 d—383 b.

according to his caprice, and in another to the idea that he is
jealous of human success.   To these deep-rooted tenets of the
Greek popular religion Plato opposes the simple logical position, that what is in its essence good cannot produce what is
not good.   As to the difficulty of accounting for the undoubted
preponderance of evil in the world,[1] " either we must say that
it is not the work of God; or that, if the work of God, its in-
fliction is just and good, and those who suffer it are the better
for being chastised. . . . To say that bad men are miserable
because they need chastisement is allowable, but not to say
that God is the cause of their misery.";[2]   In the emphasis with
which Plato insists on this truth, we see not only the resolution of the philosopher to uphold his logical conception of the
divine nature, but also the anxiety of the legislator and teacher
to press home human responsibility.   To encourage the natural
tendency to lay to the door of an irresponsible being the evil
which we ourselves have caused or deserved, is what no state
will do " if it is to be well governed."[3]   In the oracular words
of the daughter of Necessity to the souls about to enter on their
earthly life, " Virtue owns no master; as a man honours or
dishonours her he will have more or less of her.   The guilt is
with him who chooses.   God is guiltless."[4]

The application of the other great religious principle is
still more strongly coloured by Greek or Platonic ideas.   The
liability to change by external influences, whether in organic
bodies, or in products of art, or in the human soul itself,
seems to Plato a universal symptom of inferiority or weakness; least of all in the divine being, the absolutely best,
can he admit any variableness.[5]   Nor again in another and
more obvious sense can he conceive of God as liable to
change.[6]   The metamorphoses which play so large a part
in the stories about the Greek divinities are impossible to
a being who is already perfect; for no one, God or man, will
voluntarily change for the worse.   It is not the representation
of the deity as having shape or similitude which offends Plato,

---

[1] πολὺ γὰρ ἐλάττω τἀγαθὰ τῶν κακῶν ἡμῖν, 2. 379 c.   [2] 2. 380 a-b.
[3] 2. 380 b ; and cf. 10. 619 c, οὐ γὰρ ἑαυτὸν αἰτιᾶσθαι τῶν κακῶν, κ.τ.λ.
[4] 10. 617 e.   [5] 2. 380 e—381 b.   [6] 2. 381 b-e.

as it did the great Jewish teachers, but the indignity offered to the divine essence by supposing it capable of wantonly taking lower forms. Lastly, it is inconceivable that God should be otherwise than true,[1] whether in the peculiarly Platonic sense of untruth,[2] in which it means want of conformity in the mind to fact, ignorance of that which it is vital to know, the " delusion " which makes us " believe a lie," or in the ordinary sense of deceiving others by word or deed.[3] In the first sense no man, much less God, could choose to be untrue ; in the latter, there are some circumstances under which men think lying admissible, but none of these circumstances can apply to God.

Such is Plato's conception of the divine nature ; and as such, in its essence and its operation, he would have it presented by poets to the imagination of his future citizens, " if they are to be men who reverence God and are like God as far as it is possible for man to be so."[4] These general religious ideas, however, are not the only ideas which he would see embodied in poetry, and by which he would judge of its right to a place in the education of a people. It should be its function also to exhibit the moral ideal in all its various manifestations ; and we have next to ask how Plato conceived of that ideal, and what are the specific qualities and principles which he considered to be at once the true elements of moral greatness, and the legitimate material of poetical art. Plato's " whole duty of man " is comprised in the following list : honour to parents, love of fellow-citizens, courage, truthfulness, self-control. Each of these deserves a few words of notice. The honour due to father and mother is set by Plato next to the honour due to the gods,[5] and he denounces the stories of the treatment of Cronos by his son Zeus as " the greatest of lies about the greatest of things." The mixed sentiment of awe, admiration, and modesty, which the Greeks associated with the untranslatable word αἰδώς, and which they regarded as the germ of all youthful virtue, has its earliest and simplest expression in the feeling of children for their parents ; and to diffuse this feel-

---

[1] 2. 381 e—383 b. [2] 382 a-b. [3] 382 c-e.
[4] 2. 383 c. [5] 3. 386 a ; 2. 377 e ; 378 b.

ing through society, knitting old and young together by an instinctive bond, and superseding the law of the state by the finer law of family affection, was one of the fairest though most impossible dreams of Plato's life.[1] Equally important in his eyes was the sense of fellowship amongst citizens.[2] The false tales of the battles of the gods with one another are not to be told to children, who should see in the Olympian community the glorified image of their own. Rather they are to be taught that it is "very disgraceful lightly to quarrel amongst themselves," "that citizen never falls out with citizen, and that it is wicked to do it." Thus the earliest lessons of education are to appeal to that element in the soul which, as we have seen, Plato regarded as the highest and most distinctively human in man, the element in virtue of which he is not a mere isolated atom and centre of resistance, but capable of attraction both to what is higher than himself and to what is like himself.[3]

From the common groundwork of citizenlike feeling we pass to the specific virtues of public life, and the first of these is courage,[4] or, as we might more literally and more instructively translate the Greek word ἀνδρεία, "manliness." Plato's treatment of this quality is characteristically Greek. The child who is to be one day a soldier and to fight for his country must learn before all things not to be afraid of death. Death, as the inevitable end of youth and strength and beauty, as the entrance to a joyless and ineffectual phantom world, seemed to the Greek imagination of all terrible things the most terrible, and the man who could face it without flinching the most worthy to be called a man. Plato, as usual, has both a speculative and a practical interest in banishing from poetry the ghastly pictures of Hades; they "are not true,"[5] and they "do no good." "Not true," for to Plato it is clear that a good man can have no reason for being afraid of death;[6] and "they do no good,"[7] for whatever scope they may give to descriptive power, and however pleasant it may be to feel the pulse quicken and the skin creep at reading them, they only unnerve the

---

[1] 5. 463 d ; 465 b.　　　　[2] 3. 386 a ; 2. 378 b-c.
[3] Cf. 2. 375 c-d, and 376 b-c, with 378 c.　　　[4] 3. 386 a—388.
[5] 3. 386 c.　　　　[6] 387 d.　　　　[7] 387 b-c.

character, and are bad for children who are to learn "to be freemen, fearing slavery worse than death."[1] But if a man need not be afraid to die himself, neither need he be afraid for his friend to die,[2] and the expenditure of tears and lamentations over the departed is both uncalled for and unmanly, for a man ought to learn as far as possible to lean upon himself, not upon others. And if it is weak to give way to excess of grief, it is no less so to give way to the opposite emotion ; laughter, like tears, is not to be allowed to get the better of us, for the violent expression of one feeling tends to produce an equally violent reaction.[3]

These precepts, to which Plato is led by his conception of moral truth, remind us of those which Lessing arrived at by thinking out the laws of artistic propriety. Perhaps few Englishmen will feel themselves or their children to be much in need of such precepts. Many of us would be only too glad sometimes if our sense of the pathetic or the ludicrous could find more relief in expression. To the Greek of Plato's time, as to some southern peoples now, the tendency to sudden and violent revulsions of feeling was a real cause and symptom of weakness of character. To us, taught as we are from early years by example and temperament to be neutral and moderate in our language and gesture, an analogous danger may perhaps be found in the tendency to nurse suppressed emotion until it becomes a drain upon the mental forces or breaks out in extravagant action.

In his treatment of truthfulness,[4] the virtue which comes next upon his list, Plato is short and simple. Elsewhere,[5] in passages where truth is identified with "what is," we find him basing the obligation to truthfulness upon the desire to be in harmony with fact ; here, where he is concerned primarily with early education, he connects it naturally with obedience. He would have the young citizens continually conscious that they are living under authority, and that "to say the thing that is not"[6] to their elders is as "deadly and destructive to the community" as it would be for the sailor to lie to his officer or

---

[1] 387 b.　　　　　[2] 387 d-e.　　　　　[3] 388 e.
[4] 3. 389 b-d.　　　[5] *E.g.* 6. 485 c ; 486 d.　　　[6] 3. 389 c.

the patient to his doctor. Obedience too is the basis of the remaining virtue of σωφροσύνη,[1] which in its literal sense describes the man who remains " sound in mind," or, as we might say, " keeps his head," under the stress of appetite and passion. " To obey those who are in authority and to have authority over one's-self "[2] is the fully-developed virtue of which the sentiment of αἰδώς is the instinctive germ. It is this law-loving spirit, whether the law be the external law of the state or the voice of reason within us, which is the enemy alike of forwardness and insolence, of gluttony, drunkenness, and lust, of meanness and avarice. The principle of balance and control, which so pervades the Greek life and philosophy, comes out nowhere so prominently as in the conception of this virtue. It is a principle which no longer appeals strongly to the modern mind, to which it tends to suggest rather the complacencies and prettinesses of morality than its inward victories or struggles. But to a people like the Greeks, combining such an extraordinary sense of proportion with such an extraordinary capacity for excess, a perfect self-mastery might well seem as high an ideal as the humility and purity which take its place in the Christian code.

The elements of moral greatness just enumerated form the second main category in the legitimate material of poetry in a well-ordered state. To trace them out in the lives and actions of national heroes and great men, and to give them fitting expression, is the true function of the masters of language. The divine and the heroic, however, are not the only subjects which Plato would allow to poets. There remains the whole sphere of human life and nature, to discover some principle in which was the original problem of the *Republic*.[3] How then are poets to deal with this vast material? What canons can be laid down to which their imagination should conform in drawing human nature, corresponding to the canons of religious and moral truth which they are not to transgress in drawing the divine? Is the world really what it is popularly represented, a scene of confusion and caprice, in which the

---

[1] 3. 389 d—391 d.   [2] 389 d-e.
[3] 3. 392 a, περὶ ἀνθρώπων τὸ λοιπὸν ἂν εἴη.

unjust are happy and the just miserable ?[1] The answer to these
questions is the *Republic* itself. If, as Plato would have us
believe, justice is the health, and injustice the disease, of human
life, individual and social;[2] if the triumph of what is most
divine in the world is also the triumph of what is most human,[3]
and man can only realise himself by living at his highest;[4] if
the life of the just man is in the hand of God, who orders
all things for good whatever the appearances may be,[5] and if,
when we come to look at the facts, even in the judgment of
the world justice more often prospers than not ;[6] if this is the
truth, then children must be taught it, and poets must sing
it, and the contrary representations of popular literature
are as great calumnies upon man as they are upon gods and
heroes.

Many reflections must be suggested to a modern reader of
the part of the *Republic* to which we have been referring, partly
as regards the nature and method of early education, and partly
also as regards the position and functions of poetry and literature. One of the first points which must strike him, accustomed
as he is to hear the methods of imparting knowledge, and the
kind of knowledge to be imparted, made the main subjects of
discussion, is the almost exclusive attention given by Plato to
the method of developing character, and the kind of character
to be developed. We are not indeed to suppose that Plato
intended children to be brought up in ignorance of reading,
writing, and arithmetic ; besides this elementary knowledge, he
evidently contemplated some teaching of the rudiments of such
science as then existed.[7] But he does not dwell upon this early
scientific education, except to say that it will be comparatively
unsystematic,[8] and that it should be made as little compulsory
as possible, "for the acquisition of knowledge ought not to be
made a slavery to any free man."[9] Thus it remains true on the
whole that Plato regarded the formation of character in childhood and early youth as a much more important part of education than useful instruction or the training of the intellect. It

---

[1] 3. 392 b. [2] 4. 444 d e. [3] 9. 589 c—590 a.
[4] 9. 586 d-e. [5] 10. 612 e—613 b. [6] 10. 613 b-e.
[7] 7. 536 d ; 537 c ; cf. 6. 498 b.
[8] προβάλλειν, 536 d : χύδην, 537 c. [9] 7. 536 e.

would, however, be a mistake to suppose that because this branch of education finds a comparatively small place in modern theoretical discussions, it is therefore neglected in modern practice; on the contrary, it is probably just because it receives so much attention at home and at school, that it is thought capable of taking care of itself. The successes of our public school system have lain, much more than in any particular stimulus that they have given to literary or scientific activity, in the production of certain types of character and the preparation for the art of life, and in these points we naturally feel less need for method or even for consistency. And yet perhaps our very feeling of security should make us diffident. The names of "Christian," "scholar," and "gentleman," are as much in our mouths as those of the cardinal virtues were in the mouths of the Greeks; but the ideas of religion, culture, and manhood, which we attach to them, are not less confused, and often not less untrue, than some of those which Plato found in the current literature and opinion of his day.

Our neglect of the theory of ethical education as compared with Plato has also another explanation. In a small Greek State, with the whole or greater part of its effective citizens taking part in the conduct of affairs, the influence of personal character upon society and politics was more direct and unmistakable than it can be in the vast organisation of a modern nation, where the members at the circumference may be almost unconscious of their connection with the centre. Ultimately, no doubt, it is as true now as it was in the times of Plato and Aristotle that the character of a people is responsible for its social and political life, and that education is mainly important because it produces or modifies that character and thus affects the public interests. But the steps by which ethical and psychological agencies come to the surface in politics are much more numerous now and much more difficult to trace, and it is proportionately more easy to isolate particular aspects of the national life and to treat them as if they had no connection with each other or the whole. And thus, while it has become a commonplace that many of the evils of modern society can only be cured by education, few people probably can see the connection between the evil and the remedy as clearly, and express it as simply, as Plato did when he said that the encouragement of ghostly fears and superstitions tends to make bad soldiers, or that changes of fashion in popular music are symptoms of political revolution.

But the difference between ourselves and Plato in the relative importance attached to the education of character is not greater than the difference in the means employed for that education. In the first place, we have no really national mythology which takes, or could be made to take, such a position in education as did that of the Greek people. The Arthur legend has indeed been recently made to yield the picture of an "ideal knight," and the still more recent treatment of the Scandinavian Sagas has shown that the ideas which stirred our forefathers are still alive in ourselves. But the position of Mr. Tennyson and Mr. Morris in this respect is very different from that of the Greek dramatists. The myths with which the latter worked had been handed down by a continuous tradition, both literary and popular; and however freely a poet might transform or modernise them, he was still sure of appealing to the popular imagination, of which his material had come to form an integral part. The characters of Celtic and Scandinavian mythology are no longer domesticated amongst us; we no longer regard them with either familiarity or reverence; the ties which bound them to us have been shattered beyond repair, and it is only here and there that we dimly catch sight of them behind the crowd of classical and Christian figures which has pressed in between us and them.

The place thus left vacant in education by our want of a national mythology has been partially filled by other forms of literature, of which the books of the Old and New Testaments are the most conspicuous, while alongside of them there has grown up the miscellaneous mass of stories, romances, allegories, and fairy-tales, comprised under the head of "literature for the young." It is from these two sources that our early conceptions of the divine and the heroic are mainly derived. What would Plato have thought of them? He would no doubt have been surprised at the hard and fast line which it is usual to draw between sacred and profane literature, which robs the former of much of its legitimate literary effect, and the latter

of much of its educational power. There may seem to be a
certain incongruity in applying high canons of criticism to
the story-books of children; and indeed their miscellaneous
character and rapid multiplication makes such an application
almost impossible. Yet it would be a fruitful work for a competent person to make such a collection from the religious
books, mythologies, and popular tales of different peoples and
ages, as should appeal to and stimulate the best elements in a
child's imagination, without either spoiling its simplicity, over-
exciting its sensibility, or nursing its conceit. In such a
collection the most appropriate stories from the Bible would
find their natural place. The circumstances which have led to
the Biblical writings being treated as a single book, while
investing them all with the same promiscuous sanctity, have
greatly increased the difficulty of using them as a text-book of
religion and morality. There is much in the Old Testament
which Plato's canons would exclude from the education of the
young, and some of the worst expressions of Jewish fanaticism
have served as the watchwords of modern cruelty or cant. On
the other hand, the direct influence of example is much less in
the case of the Old Testament than it was in that of the Greek
poets. The heroes of Jewish history do not live in the English
mind as types to be imitated in the same way that the Greek
heroes lived in the mind of their own nation. It is to the
words with which their names are associated, rather than to
the deeds, that the influence of the former is due, and this
makes it all the more important that their words should be
purged from the baser matter which adheres to them, and fitted
to be in truth what they are now only in name, a revelation
of the divine nature to the English people. With the New
Testament the case is different. Here it is the story of a life
and a character to which, more than to anything else, the power
of the book has been due; and Plato, if he might have warned
us gently against that literal imitation which is really no imitation, would have found there all and more than all the ideal of
heroic manhood which he sought for in vain in the figures of
his native mythology. And yet we must see that the very
exaltation of that character and life makes it difficult to present it to children without falsifying it, and that we are not

teaching them to be like Jesus, either on the one hand by making him so familiar to them that they can "play at being him," or on the other by introducing him to them in a buckram of ecclesiastical dogma. To us, as to Plato, the problem of early religious education is, How to express the highest truth in the most appropriate and the least inadequate forms. But in the interval of more than two thousand years which separates us from him, the spiritual inheritance of Europe has been both enormously enriched and enormously encumbered; enriched by the advent and expansion of new and potent religious ideas, which have carried the human mind to heights scarcely dreamt of by him, but encumbered also by an undergrowth of theological tangle which makes it harder for us to keep in view the grander outlines of the truth and the light towards which they tend.

The demand of Plato that poets should be teachers, and their subject-matter limited accordingly, will generally be received with disgust or derision in the republic of letters. This is due partly to the extreme simplicity and even crudity of Plato's language, and the difficulty of translating it to suit the complex conditions of our modern civilisation, partly to a narrow conception of the scope of education on the one hand and the responsibilities of literature on the other. Plato in the *Republic*,[1] as he tells us himself, "is not making poetry, but founding a commonwealth, and the founder should know the outlines within which the invention of poets should be exercised; but it is not his business to invent himself." Hence to any one who thinks of the exuberant variety of the poetic activity, these "outlines" are apt to seem a Procrustes-bed, and Plato's poet is pictured as a literary tailor who cuts his wares to order. And this feeling is intensified by the fact that Plato is much more concerned to criticise the current literature of his time than to suggest fresh lines for writers to work on, thus leaving the impression of an entirely hostile attitude to poetry in general. Moreover, in reading proposals like his, we are naturally more apt to seize upon the difficulties or mistakes in them than on the essential truth which they may contain. We

[1] 2. 378 e—379 a.

are all agreed that a public censorship of poetry would be impossible and self-destructive; we also see that as a matter of
fact the greatest poets have not often been educators of their
people. We forget that this idea of a censorship is an accident
of Plato's mind and circumstances, and that the truest ideas are
often those which are most slowly realised in history. For
what is the requirement here made, if we look at it on its positive, not merely its negative, side ? It is that the poet should
take his place in the commonwealth, not as an ornamental
luxury, a caterer for the pleasure of intellectual epicures,[1] but as
an integral part of it, with a work of his own, imprinting[2] the
first indelible ideas upon the souls of the young, revealing[3] the
inscrutable nature of God in forms of imaginative truth, nerving[4]
the heart and chastening the emotions by the power of heroic
examples, interpreting[5] to the fancy the language of facts, and
surrounding[6] the mind with an atmosphere of health and beauty.
This is not a position of which any poet need be ashamed.
Few, if any, have ever risen to it; but not a few, and those not
the least, have claimed it. The abilities of the poet, says
Milton, " wheresoever they be found, are the inspired gift of
God, rarely bestowed, but yet to some—though most abuse—in
every nation : and are of power, besides the office of a pulpit, to
inbreed and cherish in a great people the seeds of virtue and
public civility ; to allay the perturbations of the mind, and set
the affections in right tune ; to celebrate in glorious and lofty
hymns the throne and equipage of God's almightiness, and what
he suffers to be wrought with high providence in his church ;
to sing victorious agonies of martyrs and saints, the deeds and
triumphs of just and pious nations, doing valiantly through
faith against the enemies of Christ ; to deplore the general
relapses of kingdoms and states from justice and God's true
worship. Lastly, whatsoever in religion is holy and sublime, in
virtue amiable or grave, whatsoever hath passion or admira-

---

[1] 2. 373 b, where poets and artists are included in the list of "unnecessary"
luxuries in the τρυφῶσα πόλις.

[2] 2. 377 c.   [3] 2. 382 d.   [4] 3. 387 c ; 389 e.

[5] 3. 401 c, τοὺς εὐφυῶς δυναμένους ἰχνεύειν τὴν τοῦ καλοῦ τε καὶ εὐσχήμονος φύσιν,
and cf. 402 c, where the "images of the letters," which "music" has got to teach
us to read, seem to be works of art.   [6] 3. 401 c.

tion in all the changes of that which is called fortune from
without, or the wily subtleties and refluxes of man's thoughts
from within ; all these things, with a solid and treatable smooth-
ness, to point out and describe."

High words like these will perhaps provoke a smile or a
sigh in those who remember the bathos of unsuccessful attempts
to carry them into effect ; and when to this is added the thought
of the pressure of modern life, so feverish and yet so mechanical,
so interesting and yet so unlovely, the poet himself will sometimes lose heart, and become, instead of "the trumpet which sings
to battle," "the idle singer of an empty day." Yet those who
fancy that the lamp of imagination is waning before the dawn
of industry and science might reflect that our scientific insight
into nature is scarcely more in advance of the crude fancies of
the Greeks than our imaginative interpretation of it is in
advance of their naïve mythology. And if others are inclined
to retire to a " shadowy isle of bliss," and to leave education to
school boards and ministers, they should remember that the
"immortal garland" of poetry must be " run for, not without dust
and heat." They might consider too (to adapt Milton's words
once more), " What nation it is whereof they are, and whereof"
(if they knew it) " they are the governors ; a nation not slow and
dull, but of a quick, ingenious, and piercing spirit ; acute to
invent, subtile and sinewy to discourse, not beneath the reach
of any point that human capacity can soar to." Such a nation
is worthy to be educated by men who have the genius to do it.

We have heard Plato's answer to the first of the two questions which he raised about poets—the question, What ought
they to say? and may now pass on to the second, How ought
they to say it ? What is the manner or form of poetry best
fitted to the functions which have been assigned to it in education ? By the form of poetry Plato understands merely the
mode in which the poet represents the personages in his poem,
that is, whether he speaks in his own person and simply
describes what they say and do, or whether he puts himself in
their place and makes them speak and act for themselves.[1] The
first of these manners he calls " narrative,"[2] the second " imita-

----

[1] 3. 392 c ff.   [2] 3. 394 c.

tive ;" the two may of course be employed separately, or combined in various proportions in the same work. The type of
the " imitative " manner is the drama, that of the " narrative "
certain kinds of choric hymns, while the epic introduces them
both. We shall, however, understand Plato better if we banish
from our minds this triple division of poetry, with its modern
associations, and fix them upon the real question which occupied him. That question is, Whether " imitation," or, as we
might better say, impersonation, should be the ruling principle
in poetry, or whether some other principle should rule ; or, in
other words, Is the poet to put himself into as many and as
various interesting personalities and situations as he possibly
can, and is the greatest poet he who can do this to the greatest
extent, or is he to observe some principle of selection other
than that of the merely interesting, and is there some other
criterion of poetic excellence than the degree of " imitative " power ? That this is the real issue in Plato's mind
appears from the following passage : " The well-regulated man,
when he comes in his narrative to a speech or a deed of a good
man, will, it seems to me, want to give it in the very person of
that man, and of such imitation he will not be ashamed ; he
will imitate the good man most of all, when he acts without
stumbling or folly ; to a less extent and degree when he has
been upset by disease, or love, or drunkenness, or any other
calamity. But when he comes upon a person unworthy of
himself, he will not like seriously to assimilate himself to his
inferior, unless it be on the few occasions when he does something good ; partly he is unpractised in imitating such people,
and partly, too, it goes against the grain to put himself into
the mould of natures worse than his own ; his mind scorns
to do such a thing, unless it be in fun." [1] On the other hand,
" the lower the nature of the poet, the less will he discrimi-
nate in what he says, or think anything unworthy of him,
so that he will try to imitate anything and everything, in
sober earnest and before a large audience, such things even as
thunder and wind and hail, the noises of wheels and pulleys, the
tones of trumpets, flutes, pipes, and all kinds of instruments,

---

[1] 396 c-e.

and the voices of dogs, sheep, and birds."[1] We see that Plato is
here grouping together forms of imitation which would be distinguished by a modern writer. As art and literature advance,
the primitive delight of mere mimicry gives way to that of
subtler kinds of reproduction, and tends to confine itself to the
less educated classes of society. But though the dramatic poet
stands on a different level from the actor, still more from the
pantomimist, they all agree in one point, that they are endowed
with more than ordinary capacity of losing their own personality in that of others. It is in this common capacity that
Plato sees a danger, a danger both to the artist who possesses
it, and, in various degrees, to the audience which is able to follow him in the exercise of it. His whole conception of the true
form of human society is based, as we saw, on the principle that
each member in it should have his work to do, and should do
it.[2] He is convinced of the impossibility of one man's excelling
in many trades or professions; the same natural law which
makes every man the possible helpmate of others imposes on
him the necessity of accepting help from them. And if one
man cannot do many things well, neither can he imitate many
things; and Plato (at least when he wrote the *Republic*) did
not think it possible for the same poet, or even for the same
actor, to excel both in tragedy and comedy. This law of the
limitation of human nature, which he found to hold good in
arts and professions, he would see observed in the greatest of
all arts and professions, the life of the citizen who is engaged in
the public service of the state. To men for whom the good of
the commonwealth is to be the paramount rule of conduct,
whose " craft "[3] is to be to maintain the liberty of their country,
what need is there of doing or being anything except what bears
upon their work ? and if not of doing and being, why of imitating ? For imitation, bodily or mental, cannot remain mere
imitation; if it begin early and continue long, it results in a
second nature.[4] If, then, the young are to put themselves into
other characters at all, let it be such characters as we wish them
ultimately to be, but no others, " lest from the imitation they

---

[1] 397 a. [2] 3. 394 e—395 c ; cf. 2. 370 a-c.
[3] δημιουργοὺς ἐλευθερίας τῆς πόλεως πάνυ ἀκριβεῖς, 3. 395 c. [4] 3. 395 c-d.

catch something of the reality." And thus the only poets who will have work to do in a well-ordered State, will be those who will " imitate what is right, and that only ;"[1] who will express in their works the true type of character, and thereby help to produce it. As for the great pantomimic genius, " the man with the skill to turn himself into all kinds of people, and to imitate everything,"[2] he may be allowed to be " divine and miraculous and delightful ;" but he will find no audience in a society where " twofold and manifold men do not exist, but everybody does one thing."

The mitigated attack made upon the drama in the third book of the *Republic,* is renewed by Plato in the tenth with greater vehemence and a more elaborate array of argument. We need not here enter into the general theory of the nature of artistic production which he there advances in order to refute the extravagant claims of omniscience made for the poets by their admirers ; but his account of the psychological effects of dramatic poetry may be noticed, as it develops and illustrates that given in the earlier book. Plato charges dramatic writers, firstly,[3] with depending mainly upon illusion for their success ; and secondly,[4] with weakening character by over-stimulating the emotions. The meaning of the first charge is best seen from the analogy of painting by which it is illustrated.[5] Painting and kindred arts produce their effects by taking advantage of certain optical illusions ; the perception of the actual proportions of objects is kept in abeyance by the mere appearance, until corrected by scientific measurement. Similarly the poet takes advantage of illusions of feeling ;[6] the aspects of character which he likes to represent are not those where it is simple, quiet, consistent, and rational, but rather its emotional aspects, with their shifting lights and shadows, where the contrasts are strong and the transitions rapid ; and the element in his audience to which he appeals, and upon which he reckons for his success, is not the sober judgment which sees life in its true proportions, but the illusory feelings of the moment which care only for their immediate satisfaction. So that, judged by the worth

---

[1] 3. 397 d.   [2] 397 e—398 b.   [3] 10. 602 c—605 c.
[4] 605 c—606 d ; 605 b.   [5] 602 c-e.   [6] 604 d—605 e.

both of what it represents and of what it appeals to, dramatic poetry seems to condemn itself to inferiority. The second charge against it is an expansion of that made in the third book. Few people reflect that in putting themselves in the positions of others, they catch something which becomes their own.[1] Yet this is the case when, in seeing tragedy and comedy, we give unrestrained way to emotions which we should be ashamed to indulge in real life. We think it does not matter, because we stand outside the circumstances which call them forth; but when similar circumstances arise in our own experience we find that our will has been weakened and our self-respect undermined.

Two dominant ideas underlie all the objections urged by Plato against the dramatic element in literature: the duty of being true to ourselves, and the duty of being true to facts. The two were in his mind closely related. As the burden of his philosophy of knowledge was that we should learn to see things as they are, not as they appear to us to be, so the burden of his philosophy of conduct is that we should learn to be what we really are, and not what our fancy makes us. And as the belief in an objective world of reality, an order of existence which we do not create, but which we find and must recognise, pervades his logical speculation, so it is the corresponding conviction that the rational self in man is his most real self, and that life in accordance with the rational order of the world is his truest life, which gives nerve and consistency to his theories of morality. We have already seen expressions of this conviction in the denial of the possibility of change in the divine nature, and in the condemnation of excessive indulgence of emotion. Order and immutability seemed to Plato the attributes of what is best and highest both in the physical and in the moral world, and it is just these attributes which he missed in the capricious current of feeling. The lower he went in human nature or in human society, the more did he seem to find men the creatures of their sentiment, and the less purpose or law did he discern in their lives.[2] And art, especially dramatic art, seemed to him to pander to this natural fickleness. It had

---

[1] 606 b.   [2] 4. 431 c; 3. 397 d; 10. 604 e; 608 a.

no principle of selection, no law of better and worse;[1] wherever it could raise a laugh, or draw a sigh, or tickle an appetite, there it was ready with its phantasmagoria of life. It had a direct interest in "watering and nourishing"[2] the lower and more trivial impulses which reason calls upon us "to dry up," and it stimulated the already too great tendency in us to do everybody's business except our own, to be actors instead of citizens, to play at life instead of living it. The words of Bacon, in which he gives the reason why poetry "was ever thought to have some participation of divineness," might have been used by Plato in another sense to express why it is so far from being divine; "poetry doth raise and erect the mind, by submitting the shows of things to the desires of the mind, whereas reason doth buckle and bow the mind unto the nature of things."

The very emphasis and fulness of Plato's polemic against dramatic literature must make us feel that he was writing in a different atmosphere from our own. Few modern writers on education in England would reckon the stage amongst the most powerful agents, whether for good or bad ; few too would regard a tendency to theatricality and effusiveness as one of the most serious dangers to the English character. Not the most extravagant admirer of our dramatists would claim for them what Plato heard men claim for Homer, that they have "educated their country, and deserve to be read over and over again as authorities on human conduct and education, and as models on which men may order the whole of their lives."[3] Nor is the average Englishman likely to be too "imitative" in the sense which alarmed Plato. The suppleness of nature which made it hard for the Athenian to be "one man and not many," is generally replaced in us by a sturdiness and concentration, of which consistency and self-respect, self-consciousness and selfishness, are respectively the good and the bad developments. Yet it must be admitted that these qualities are not incompatible with illusions and extravagances of feeling, none the less dangerous because outwardly repressed ; and though we are not, on the whole, a nation of theatre-goers, we are undoubtedly a nation of novel-readers, and may find there the dramatic

---

[1] 605 a-c.   [2] 10. 606 d.   [3] 10. 606 e.

stimulants against which Plato protested. It must be borne in mind, in comparing any ethical influence of literature in ancient and modern times, that what in Greece was mainly a public of spectators and listeners is now mainly a public of readers. It is true that in the pulpit we have a medium of oral communication which they had not, but, speaking generally, it is not now in the open places of the theatre, the camp, the law-courts, and the marketplace, that the uttered word most circulates and works; it is rather in silence or in solitude, through the newspaper on the family table, the periodical at the club, the poem or novel in the bedroom, that the modern writer speaks to his fellow-men. And the difference in the medium goes along with a difference in the effect. Instead of the noisy publicity in which contagious feeling grows as it spreads from man to man, till the individual is "borne helplessly along the stream,"[1] and loses himself in an indiscriminate froth of exaggerated feeling, we brood over books in the heated cells of our own imagination, build castles of the fumes of our own emotions, and come forth to measure the world by the mock-heroic standard of our own littleness. But the craving for change and excitement, the desire to escape from our own true selves with the responsibilities which they entail, are not the less strong in us because we are not born actors or mimics; the mind can make its own stage and act upon it, while the body remains immobile and unexpressive. Nor does the modern demand exceed the modern supply. The novel, which absorbs so much of our dramatic talent, lends itself with fatal ease to the promiscuous photography of situations and feelings. The increased sense of the importance of human life and of the inexhaustibleness of its problems supplies a ready argument to those who find anything and everything "interesting;" and there are still writers of whom we might say metaphorically what Plato intended literally, "that there is nothing which they will not imitate, thunder and wind, trumpets and whistles, dogs and sheep."[2]

The same principles which guided Plato in his conception of the educational function of literature guided him also in his treatment of the other constituents of "musical" education, and

---

[1] 6. 492 c.   [2] 3. 397 a.

led him to conclusions still more at variance with modern practice and theory. That poetry and literature, which express definite ideas, should be made to serve the interests of society, is an intelligible if surprising proposal; but that music, painting, and sculpture should be pressed into the same service, will seem to many a vague fancy, impracticable in education, and destructive of art. Let us then see what Plato's idea of the use of the arts in education precisely was. "Music," he says,[1] "involves three elements, words, harmony, rhythm," or, as we may say, to bring his meaning nearer home, without pretending to give it an exact modern equivalent, words, key, and time. As to the words, they must conform to the same canons as the words of other poetry, and the character of the two remaining elements must be determined by that of the words. Those "harmonies" and "rhythms" then must be employed in musical composition which will express the qualities which we wish to develop in the soul. What these are we already know. They are the qualities which result from the right nurture of the two higher psychological elements in human nature, the "spirited" and the "philosophic." We must therefore have a music of corresponding character, a music of war and a music of peace,[2] a "harmony" of violence and effort, and a "harmony" of conciliation and calm, a "harmony" to represent the daring of the soldier and the endurance of the martyr, and a "harmony" to express the accents of entreaty or persuasion, of submission or acquiescence. Other kinds than these, and other instruments than these require, are superfluous luxuries which must be "purged away"[3] in a healthy state, whose object is not to stimulate every feverish craving of its citizens, but to weave strongly those vital strains of character which sustain the fabric of society. The same principle will apply to the "rhythms"[4] and measures of music and dance, as to the "harmonies" in which they are composed; they must not develop in lawless independence, but must be such as will express "the orderly and brave life."

There is then, according to Plato, a right and a wrong in the musical relations of pitch and time, and this right and wrong

---

[1] 3. 398 d.   [2] 3. 399 a-c.   [3] 399 e.   [4] 399 e—400 c.

is in some sense akin to the right and wrong in human
nature and conduct. Goodness and badness of form, he says,
follow goodness and badness of rhythm, and goodness and badness of rhythm follow goodness and badness of language, and
these again depend upon goodness and badness of character.[1]
Nor is it only in the movements of dance and song that there
is this correspondence; in all sensuous material there is a similar
capability of expression;[2] it is present in the forms of painting
and sculpture, of weaving and embroidery, of building and
manufacture, of animal and vegetable life; " in all of these
there is shapeliness or unshapeliness, and unshapeliness and unrhythmicalness and inharmoniousness are the kindred of badness
of language and badness of character, while the opposites are
kindred and imitations of the opposite character, the chastened
and the good." The poets then are not the only artists over
whom the state should exercise control;[3] attention must be
given to the whole body of craftsmen, and they must be prevented from expressing what is vicious and unchastened, mean
and unshapely, whether in the figures of living things or in
buildings or in any other work of art. The artists who should
be encouraged by the state must be " those who have the
genius to track out the nature of what is fair and shapely "[4] and
to embody it anew in their works. For the young citizens must
not be allowed to grow up amongst images of evil, lest their
souls by daily contact gradually and unconsciously assimilate
the ugliness of their surroundings.[5] Rather they should be
like men living in a beautiful and healthy place; from everything that they see and hear, loveliness, like a breeze, should
pass into their souls, and teach them without their knowing
it the truth of which it is a manifestation. In such an
atmosphere they will not only acquire a natural grace and
proportion of bearing and character, but an instinctive sense of
what is fair and what is foul in nature and in art; and this
instinctive sense is a kind of anticipation of a rational understanding of the nature of good and evil; for the reason which
is now presented to them in forms of sense, and calls forth
sensuous delight, is the same reason which they will afterwards

---

[1] 3. 400 c-d.   [2] 401 a.   [3] 401 b.   [4] 401 c.   [5] 401 c-d.

learn to know in its own form as an intelligible principle, and which they will then recognise as an old friend with a new face.[1]

Such is the nature and such are the limits of the education of "music." It has a more intellectual and a more emotional aspect. From the former point of view, it is completed when we have "learned to read"[2] the world of sights and sounds which is about us. That world is like a language which we have got to master; the sensible forms of good and evil pass and repass before us in an infinite variety of combinations, like the letters of an alphabet which combine into an infinity of words, great and small. No form can be disregarded; acts and speeches which seem trivial, like the little words in a book, may contain a world of meaning and be the key to a character. And the true function of the artist is to help us to learn this language of life; he is the man who knows the shapes of the letters and the laws of their combinations. In the "mirror" which he holds up we may see reflected the images of courage, temperance, generosity, and their opposites, and thus learn to know the realities when we see them. Thus art should find its fulfilment in life; and he may most truly be said to be "musically" educated, whose eye and ear are trained to detect what is right and wrong, not only in the creations of art, but also, so far as it can be apprehended by the senses, in the actual world of which art is the reflection.

If, on the other hand, we regard the emotional effects of "musical" education, they may be summed up in two, that it infuses a spirit of order,[3] and that it develops the "true love" of beauty,[4] the former being the more passive condition of which the latter is the more active expression. To Plato, most of the evils of sensual passion fall under one of two heads, unregulated variety or unregulated intensity. He considered passion to be essentially "many-headed," and capable of indefinite multiplication and expansion; and one of his chief charges against the art of his time was that it fostered and satisfied the indiscriminate craving for emotional excitement. In contrast with it,

---

[1] 3. 402 a.   [2] 402 a-c.
[3] 3. 404 e, σωφροσύνην; 4. 424 e, ἐννομωτέρου παιδιᾶς; 425 a, εὐνομίαν : cf. 413 e.   [4] 3. 402 d—403 c.

he demanded an art which should not merely stimulate, but should also discipline, the feelings ; which should not follow but lead them ; which should chasten their disorder and brace their indolence by making them move in the delicate lines of proportion and beauty, and respond to the quiet emphasis of harmony and rhythm. For the balance and symmetry which are essential to good artistic work are also, he conceived, essential to true artistic feeling. Love is the typical feeling awakened by sensuous beauty, and the genuine love of genuine beauty is incompatible with ungoverned emotion. The mere "mad"[1] intensity of animal appetite has nothing to do with such love, which is not for the body except so far as it is the expression of soul. "Where beauty of inward character meets with beauty of outward form, each corresponding and harmonising with the other, and cast in a common mould, there is the fairest sight to a man who has the eyes to see it. And what is most fair is also most loveable."[2] It is this perfect accord of the inward and the outward which the truly "musical" man seeks and delights in ; but if it cannot be realised, if one or the other element must be imperfect, he will surrender the outward, and while no perfection of form will atone to him for defect of soul, he "will not refuse to take pleasure in" a fair soul even though it appear in an "inharmonious" body.[3]

Before considering the general view here given of the functions of art in education, a word must be said about the relative position which Plato assigns to the various specific arts. We are at once struck by the great prominence given to music as compared with painting, sculpture, and architecture ; and this may seem the more surprising when we remember the excellence attained by the Greeks in the last two and the rudimentary character of their achievements in the first. It may be that Plato did not see in the sculptors and architects of his time the signs of degeneracy which drew his attention to the poets and musicians ; but more probably he estimated the practical influence of the former upon the national character as less important than that of the latter. The frame of mind in which pictures and statues, and still more buildings, are most appre-

---

[1] 3. 403 a.   [2] 402 d.   [3] 402 d.

ciated and enjoyed, is rather one of open and undisturbed receptivity than of active emotion, and to most temperaments the burning word and the stirring melody have far more effect upon action than brilliancy of colouring or majesty of form. But whatever may be the cause, it is a fact worthy of attention that a philosophical iconoclast like Plato, in attacking the idols of sensationalism both in knowledge and morality, should have almost ignored the painters and sculptors, and confined his assaults to the musicians and still more to the poets. Another noticeable point is the simplicity and uniformity of the criteria which Plato applies to the several arts. Proportion, in one form or another, is the single source to which he refers all artistic excellence, in the musical relations of time and tone no less than in those of space in the arts of form and construction. And this leads us lastly to remark how extremely rudimentary must have been the music of which he was speaking. He assumes throughout that music always implies words, and the whole subject of harmony, in its modern sense, is absent from his consideration. The truth seems to be, paradoxical as it may sound, that it was the very simplicity of Greek music which led Greek writers to assign to it such a direct and important educational influence. As in the early days of sculpture or painting, the crudeness and symbolism makes the meaning of the artist more clear, when compared with the subtle design and colouring of great masters, so when music was chiefly limited to an accompaniment giving emphasis or precision to a recitation or a dance, its effect would be more strongly recognised in proportion as it was more simple. Even now there are dancing and marching melodies which exercise a direct and almost physical influence on a susceptible hearer, just because there is nothing but the simple act of dancing or marching which they suggest; and if music generally were intimately associated with a few elementary acts and feelings, its power, being more easily expressible, would be also more reducible to rule and to practice, than when it has developed into a vast and independent growth, speaking in its own language and obeying its own laws, of which it is itself the sole interpreter.

This difference, however, great as it is, and much as it increases the difficulty of applying Plato's ideas to modern music, does not except it from the general scope of his theory concerning the educational use of art, the main features of which we may now proceed to consider. Of these the central and most characteristic one is undoubtedly the idea that art may have, and ought to have, a definite function in the development of character; and we have to ask how Plato conceived this function to be exercised. "Education in music," he says, "is so telling, because rhythm and harmony sink so deeply into the inward part of the soul, and take hold of it so strongly, and make it graceful with the grace which they bring with them."[1] And again, "Gracefulness and ungracefulness go along with rhythmicalness and unrhythmicalness, and rhythmicalness and unrhythmicalness follow and resemble goodness of language, or the reverse; the style of language, again, follows the character of soul, and thus goodness of language, of harmony, of form, and of rhythm go along with goodness of character."[2] "Are the gestures and accents of a brave soul in trouble the same as those of a cowardly one?" he asks in a closely analogous passage of the *Laws;* "surely not; the very colours of the two men are different."[3] From these few passages, which could easily be multiplied, so much is clear, that Plato was in earnest with the idea that there is some real connection between character and artistic form, and that the common element in both is found in the rightness of proportion which is essential alike to beauty in art and to goodness in conduct. We shall perhaps understand him better if we reflect (what the passages above will suggest) that in the early stages of civilisation the whole of life tends to be more symbolical, and the connection between mental states and their physical expression more immediate. In such stages speech has something of the crudity of a language of signs, while gesture and sound approach the delicacy and articulateness of words. With the progress of civilisation the symbolism of sense does not, as is sometimes supposed, disappear, but it gets infinitely more complex and subtle; colours and lines, tones and measures, instead of being like letters of an alphabet with fixed and uniform values, be-

---

[1] 3. 401 d.   [2] 3. 400 c-e.   [3] *Laws,* 2. 654 e.

come fitful centres of multitudinous associations, so various to different sensibilities, and so remote from their primitive significance, that men are tempted to deny their validity or to relegate them to the sphere of individual caprice. It is curious to see the human mind thus refusing to recognise, or to be recognised by, its own offspring as they grow up. In the infancy of art, nobody doubts but that it has a meaning, that mind speaks to mind in it. Only when it has ceased to lisp and to point, when the simple singer has grown into a "mighty-mouthed inventor of harmonies," and the sculptor's one poor thought has made way for

> "The thousand sounds and sights that broke
> In on him at the chisel's stroke,"

only then do men begin to question whether what they have created is really their own, and to explain it away by chance, by convention, by mechanics, by anything but mind. Yet this is not really to be wondered at ; for as soon as we try to account for any but the simplest effects of art, they escape us, the truth being that "accounting for" them merely means translating one medium of expression into another and less perfect one. Language and music and painting are all significant, but the significance of one is not convertible with that of another. We cannot listen to the meaning of colour and form, we must see it ; we cannot make music speak in words without its ceasing to be music, any more than we can resolve a poem into sound and rhythm without its poetry evaporating. And if the relationship of the arts to one another is so difficult to express, much more so is the relationship of art in general to other modes of human activity. Few people, indeed, can seriously doubt that the character of an imaginative man is ultimately affected by what he habitually sees and hears ; or, again, that what one person apprehends as right or expedient, another person may apprehend as beautiful ; or, once more, that devotion, similar in effect to that of the saint for the being whom he worships, may be felt by the man of science for the truth which he pursues. But when we have made a few general statements such as these, we are brought to a standstill by the intricacy of the subject and the limitations of our analysis. The fact remains irrefragable that to the vast majority of mankind art and conduct, religion and science, are very different things, with little or nothing in common; and that the attempt to fuse them generally results in sermonising pictures, rose-water morality, and unctuous sciolism. And as, at most times and for most purposes, it is of more practical importance to realise proximate differences than fundamental unities, the world at large instinctively looks with suspicion upon those who, in trying to see through the ordinary distinctions of life, appear to be removing its ordinary land-marks. No one has insisted more strongly than Plato himself upon the dangers of passing too hastily " from the many to the one ; " but for that very reason we need not be afraid to follow him, when, with the courage of his conviction that reason is one in its essence, he leads us now and again to " a high rock " from which we may see that it is one also in its manifestations. To Plato the laws of proportion, which are the condition of beauty in art, seemed to betoken the presence of the same mind as is revealed in the immutable order of the universe, and more imperfectly in the moral order of human life.[1] He was very far from identifying or confusing artistic beauty with moral goodness; but, believing, as he did, that the whole physical world is " the image of its maker, God manifest to sense," [2] he could not but believe that in all things sensible, and therefore in the relations of figure, time, and tone, there is a right and a wrong, a good and a bad, according as they do or do not express and obey intelligence. And since bodily movement and sight and hearing are among the most prominent and important of our vital activities, especially in early life, he drew the natural conclusion that it must make a difference to the growth of the human soul and character, how, and upon what occasions, those activities are exercised, and that it is the function of the arts to provide for their exercise in the best way and upon the best objects. It is, in fact, rather the real simplicity than the sup-posed vagueness of Plato's ideas which makes them embarrass-ing. The luxuriant development of the arts in modern times, in independence both of one another and of the other elements of human life, makes it difficult to apply to them conceptions formed at a time when they were modest and business-like

[1] *Timaeus,* 47 b-d. [2] *Timaeus,* 92 b.

appendages of religion, war, or public amusement; almost as difficult as it would be to transfer the lessons learnt on a school drilling-ground to the evolutions of a modern army on the battle-field.

Plato would have his young citizens, who are one day to govern and protect the state, nerved and inspirited, soothed and softened, by warlike and peaceful songs; he would have them disciplined to order by the precision of time and tune, of movement and voice; he would remind them of their duties by the sculpturesque embodiments of undying types of true manhood; he would make grace and dignity as natural to them as the air which they breathe, and lead them to bear themselves unconsciously as if they were in the presence of others. In all this there is nothing strange. But from the austere beauty of the conception of the Greek philosopher to the confused jargon of modern æsthetic culture, is a bewildering and unwelcome step. Our masterpieces of art are mostly foreign, and speak a language unintelligible to the ordinary English mind. Even if it were otherwise, they are meaninglessly arranged in galleries, cut adrift from the surroundings for which they were made, but which they can never recover. Our greatest artists are going back to an unreal or unnational past, or "are making the public their master more than necessity requires."[1] Where are we to look for the "breeze of beauty and health," for the craftsmen who "can track out the nature of loveliness and grace"? We may collect engravings, and photographs, and china, and make ourselves learned in the history of art; we may found museums and institutes, and spread casts of Venus and Apollo through the land; we may give thousands of pounds for pieces of clever vulgarity; but we shall not make English life much more beautiful or more joyous, unless we can produce art which will educate the nation to see with its eyes and to hear with its ears the country in which it dwells and the history which it inherits. It is in music perhaps that the outlook is the least discouraging. Here there is a possibility of acting upon large masses with some effect; here social distinctions are less felt; here too the English nature seems to show more aptitude and susceptibility. We can hardly hope to make our great

---

[1] 6. 493 d.

towns beautiful, but it is not chimerical to look forward to a time when they may each have their orchestra and chorus, and adequate provision for hearing them. There is no need to quarrel about the precise educational effect which modern music has or may have. That it has some such effect will not be denied except by those who wish to keep it to themselves, or by those who are irritated at the stupidity of its would-be advocates. The apparent vagueness of its influence, arising from the difficulty of formulating it, is neither a proof of its unreality nor an argument against utilising it. Everybody who is at all susceptible to music knows that he is better for having it, and worse for being without it; he also probably knows that the composers whom the world has agreed to call great are, some, or all of them, those to whose music he most likes to listen; more than this he need not be able to say, for a fact is not made more of a fact by being talked or written about. If it be once fully recognised that music has a great emotional power over a considerable proportion of English people, the proper application of the power becomes a public duty, and it is only a question of time to discover the best ways of doing it.

We have thus far considered Plato's conception of the education in " music," mainly in its ethical and psychological aspect, but we should represent him very imperfectly if we omitted to mention the importance which he attaches to it on social and political grounds. The often-quoted text, that " the fashions of music are never changed without changes in the most important laws of the commonwealth,"[1] may serve here as a point of departure. It is difficult for us to understand the concern with which Plato urges the importance of permanence and continuity in the system of " musical" education. " It is in music," he says,[2] " that the guardians of our state must build their guardhouse; for it is here that lawlessness easily creeps in unperceived. People think that it is only play, and does no harm. And what harm does it do? Little by little it gets a footing, and spreads gently and silently into the habits and arrangements of life; from these it passes, gathering force as it goes, into the transactions of business, and from business it gets to

---

[1] 4. 424 c. "Music" is here used in its modern sense.　　　[2] 424 d-e.

the laws and the constitution, with licence full-grown in its train, until it ends by ruining everything, both public and private." On the other hand, "when the play of children is good from the first, and they take in a spirit of law through their music, then it has just the opposite effect, attending them at every step in life, making it grow, and building it up where it had fallen down."[1] And as in the other case the spirit of lawlessness, beginning at the trifles of education, ends by overthrowing law itself, so the law-loving temper, fostered from childhood, is the pregnant germ of the full insight of the legislator and statesman.[2] If it only be started well, it will assimilate nourishment and grow by its own inherent vitality. To people who have thus lived in an atmosphere of order, the details of legislation will offer no difficulty; with an instinctive and inherited tact they will regulate their life wisely and well, whether it be in the lesser matters of social behaviour and usage, or in the greater ones of business, commerce, and trade.

We have had occasion before to remark on the difference between the small and simple civic communities of Greece and the complex masses of modern nations, in regard to the directness and rapidity of the transmission of social and political changes. The passage just quoted brings that difference again vividly before us. To Plato, with the restlessness and instability of Greek political life before his eyes, the one thing needful seemed to be to establish in society a permanent "ethos," a traditional character, which should be able to resist the shocks of party-spirit and individual caprice. And if this could only be done by a system of education, which should receive each citizen at birth and retain its hold upon him through life, it was no mere fancy to watch with a jealous eye the first symptoms of innovation in the system, even in matters so apparently trivial as popular songs. To us, with our national gift for forming and carrying on traditional modes of life and thought, it will often seem that in education we need more exhortation to adopt new ideas than to remain faithful to old ones. Our great schools and universities are typical instances of the way in which prejudice and tradition may uphold

---

[1] 4. 425 a.

[2] 424 a; 425 a-e.

methods of teaching and social habits which have ceased
to have a reason for existence. As regards the other part of
Plato's opinion, that for men who are going to serve their
country in government and legislation the early formation of a
" constitutional" character is of much more importance than a
study of written systems or codes, we are more nearly at one
with him. If the Duke of Wellington could say that the
battle of Waterloo was won on the playing-fields at Eton, we
need not be surprised at Plato when he speaks of children
" receiving the spirit of law through their music," [1] or when he
says that " one of the greatest tests of a man's character is the
show which he makes in his gymnastics." [2]   The distrust in
" technical" education for the higher spheres of public life, and
the belief in the efficacy of a " liberal culture," which glories in
having nothing directly to do with a profession, are both strong,
sometimes perhaps too strong, in the English mind. Even if
the theory itself were in no danger of being overdriven, the
poverty of the culture which we provide on the strength of it
might give us some qualms. The principle of our system, put
at its best, is that by taking the mind through the greatest
works of classical literature, we both train it to habits of
exactitude and observation, and cultivate the taste, imagination,
and judgment with the finest and wisest thought of antiquity.
We inherit the system from an age when the language and
literature of modern Europe had only just begun to exist, and
when great thoughts adequately expressed could only be found
in classical writers. The value of the intellectual discipline
gained in the curriculum cannot seriously be disputed; but
whether, as it is at present worked, even when supplemented by
the teaching of parts of the Bible, it supplies the best and most
natural food to the " philosophic" element in the English mind,
is extremely doubtful. It is not indeed upon this ground, of
inadequacy for its professed purpose, that the system is generally attacked; its assailants are more often persons who are
crying out for " practical" education, and who, if they had their
way, would eliminate from the culture of the human mind the
study of its own greatest works. But it is just this which

---

[1] 4. 425 a.   [2] 7. 537 b.

makes the question a serious one. For if the position of the higher education is assailed from without by misguided or mercenary ignorance, while its natural defenders are beginning to doubt whether they have anything to defend, we may well fear for its future. In the confusion and din which surrounds the subject, nothing seems so important as to come to a clear understanding of the point at issue. It should be seen that convenient catch-words like "supply" and "demand," or well-sounding oppositions like "words" and "things," tell us absolutely nothing unless we realise first by what the "demand" is made, and what "things" are. It should be understood that the primary question is, not whether to refine the taste, or to produce a gentleman, or to teach useful knowledge, is the end of education; but, before all, how the whole man is to be made the best of; and that whether it be nature and her works, or man and his works which are studied (and neither can rightly be neglected), it is ultimately mind in some form or another which we have to educate, and mind in some form or another through which alone it can be educated. The representatives of religion, literature, and science might then join hands over their common subject-matter, instead of snatching at it by turns, and trying each to undo the work of his supposed rival. In the meantime, until we are nearer to such a result, two lesser and more practicable things may be done by the teachers of language; they may try to make classical education less a matter of mere grammatical discipline or of imitative ingenuity, and more a study of human thought and character; and they may try to rescue our own English literature from its present neglect, to treat it in the spirit of the great men who have created scholarship, not on methods combining the worst features of the traditional classical curriculum, and, by making it speak to the youth of the nation, give it a systematic place in the development of the national character.

We may conclude Plato's representation of the political and social importance of "musical" education by looking with him for a moment at some of the consequences of its neglect. In the eighth and ninth books of the *Republic*, Plato has given us in a series of pictures an ideal history of the fall of the human soul, both in the individual and in society. He had previously shown us what he conceived that the life of man might be if it were allowed to follow the highest law of its development; he now shows us to what lowest depths it might be supposed to sink if the logical principle of degeneration were allowed to work unchecked. He had followed man up to the point at which he is nearest to God; he now traces his descent to the point when he is on the verge of passing into a beast. In this picture of the progress of evil a strikingly prominent place is assigned to the gradually increasing neglect of "music;" and nowhere does Plato express more clearly his sense of the vital importance, social and political, of a thing apparently so far removed from society and politics as the early culture of the higher side of human nature. The ideally best condition of life, individual and social, had been represented by him as resulting from the harmonious and normal development and operation of certain psychical forces. In accordance with this view, the gradual declension from such a condition is represented as a continually increasing discord in the vital faculties, beginning with the failure of the highest to perform their proper functions, and the usurpation of their place by lower ones, and ending with the complete inversion of the true psychological relations, and the absolute dominion of those activities which have no right even to exist in the organism. And as the ideally best conditions were conceived by Plato to depend upon a right system of education, maintaining and transmitting a certain character, so the typical forms of evil or imperfection in the world are pictured by him as resulting from the abandonment or perversion of such a system, the soul being thereby deprived of its proper nourishment, and left a victim to the bad influences of its environment and its own lower nature.

The first effect of the neglect of "music" is a certain loss of elevation in the general aim of life.[1] The "philosophic" faculties, deprived of their true object, find exercise in calculating means to lower ends, and in this unnatural service lose that simplicity and directness which are alone compatible with the pursuit of truth in the interests of society. The element of "spirit" rises into the place thus left vacant, and makes the

---

[1] Cf. 8. 546 e ; 548 b-c ; 549 b ; 547 d-e.

desire for distinction the ruling principle of life. But the falseness of its position reacts upon it; deprived of the higher inspiration which its nature requires, it sinks itself into mere personal ambition, while the meaner desires, which it should have joined with reason to regulate or repress, begin to lift up their heads. Such is Plato's psychological diagnosis of certain well-known social phenomena. When the best intellects in the community begin to be suspected of being "too clever," and are kept out of high places in favour of "honest and down-right" men; when self-respect tends to degenerate into self-will, and the desire for personal distinction becomes a passion; when moral rectitude is upheld more by fear of disgrace than by inward conviction, and a chivalrous bearing in public is compatible with the pursuit of money and pleasure "in the dark;"[1] then we may suspect that "the Muses are beginning to be neglected,"[2] and that "reason tempered with music, which is the only guardian-angel of virtue,"[3] is being driven from its natural home in the souls of men.

The continued neglect of education brings with it more aggravated results.[4] As the eye of the mind grows more and more unaccustomed to the vision of beauty and truth, its sight gets more and more narrowed to the objects nearest to it, and the "blind god" of wealth becomes the leader of the "blind" soul. And the fresh downward step of the higher self is accompanied by a fresh rise in the lower; the animal appetites, which ambition had affected to despise and repress, now no longer "tamed" by reason or swayed by high purpose, become noisy and importunate; and though respectability and self-interest may still keep them down, "want of education" leaves them free to engender a brood of "drone-like" passions, unproductive and inorganic, the paupers and criminals of the soul. The same "want of education," operating over a wider area, produces analogous conditions in a state, where the neglected and unnurtured children of the upper classes first sink into unproductive spendthrifts, and then swell the useless and dangerous elements of the society which, in its blind devotion to money, had helped to impoverish them.

[1] Cf. 8. 547 d-e; 549 a; 548 a-b. [2] 8. 546 d.
[3] 8. 549 b. [4] 554, b-d; 552 e.

It is a further stage in decline 'when the comparative respectability and consistency of the pursuit of wealth gives way to the mere restlessness of indiscriminate impulse, and the satisfaction of the passing moment is erected into a principle of life. Here, again, it is the " uneducated "[1] soul which falls a victim. A father, who believes in nothing that does not pay, gives his son a cheap education.[2] The son gets into fast society; its flashiness dazzles his eyes, which have never learnt to look at anything but the ground ; after a struggle perhaps he temporarily recovers his hereditary steadiness, but his soul is still empty and barren, and weeds, both native and exotic, have full liberty to grow there. The " words of truth and beauty, which are the best garrison of souls whom God loves,"[3] have never been allowed to hold their rightful citadel, and their vacant place is gradually occupied by the " false and swaggering "[4] theories, which promise " initiation " into the " mysterious " knowledge of the world.[5] Their key to the mystery is simple, and consists in " calling insolence good breeding, anarchy freedom, prodigality magnificence, and shamelessness manhood."[6] For a soul so circumstanced, the best chance is that it may stop in its career of licence before it has become the victim of any one dominant passion, and arrive at a sort of equilibrium in its desires, satisfying them each in turn, and living that life of so-called " freedom " which consists in being the creature of the moment.[7] But if circumstances are not so favourable to it,[8] the trembling balance of discordant appetites is sure to be overset, the irresistible impulse of passion to absorb everything unless it be itself absorbed will assert itself, and the easy-going " liberty and equality " of many-coloured caprice will settle down into the cruel and sombre " tyranny " of lust.

These meagre fragments, from what forms perhaps the most powerfully written section of the *Republic*, will suffice to illustrate Plato's conception of the consequences of neglecting the education of the reason through the imagination and the emotions. They will show how strongly he felt the truth which we are sometimes in danger of forgetting, that the evil in human life

---

[1] 8. 559 d. [2] 559 d—560 a. [3] 560 b. [4] 560 c.
[5] 560 e. [6] 560 e. [7] 561 a-e. [8] 9. 572 e—573 c.

is quite as much due to negative as to positive conditions ; that
it is the absence of healthy and bright surroundings, the want of
healthy and interesting employments, the abeyance of healthy
and inspiring emotions, which drag so many men down.   We
cannot help seeing this in the case of the lower strata of
society, where the pressure of circumstances is so gross and
palpable ; but if we agree with Plato, we shall feel that the
more richly endowed and the more delicately organised human
nature is, the more important and also the more difficult it is to
educate it well, and the more fatal are the consequences, both
to itself and to society, of educating it badly or not at all.   And
what is true of different natures compared with one another, is
true also of the different elements in the same nature.   Good,
like evil, begins at the top and radiates downwards.   If we can
secure that the highest faculties, intellectual and emotional, are
at their highest activity, the lower ones will not probably be
seriously disorganised ; but no amount of decent regularity in
the working of the lower will guarantee the vitality of the
higher.   " When the whole soul follows the philosophic element,
and there is no faction in it, the justice of each separate part is
secured, and each does its own work and reaps its own pleasures
too, the best pleasures, and also up to its measure the truest.
But when any of the other elements dominates, it not only fails
to find its own pleasure itself, but it compels the other elements
to pursue a pleasure which is not their own nor true."[1]

The evils arising from the neglect of " music" are not the
only evils which Plato describes in connection with it ; we have
already seen what he considered to be the psychological effects
of its excessive or exclusive study.   To obviate these effects is,
as we also saw, the proper function of gymnastic ; and we have
now to complete our account of Plato's conception of that
branch of education.   Of this, as of music, he only lays down
certain general " outlines" or principles, leaving the details to be
filled in by those who have to apply them.   The most important
of these principles, which we have already had occasion to notice,
is that gymnastic, though concerned primarily with the body,[2]
is to be considered as ultimately affecting the soul and the

---

[1] 9. 586 e.   [2] 3. 410 c.

character, and owes to this fact its educational importance. This principle at once determines the general aim of bodily exercises ; they should aim " not so much at producing mere strength, as at awakening the spirited element in human nature."[1] It is the fault of the professional trainers that they ignore the educational side of their business, and attend only to developing the muscles. And their system not only fails in an ethical point of view, but even where it might be expected to succeed, it does not really do so. " The athletic habit of body is a sleepy sort of habit, and is liable to upset the health. We see how the professional athletes doze away their life, and how, if they deviate a little from their prescribed diet, they get serious and violent diseases."[2] A " finer kind of training" is wanted for a man who is to serve his country as a soldier ;[3] he must have his wits wide awake, be quick of sight and hearing, and able to endure changes of food and weather without breaking down. Of the two elements in such a training, diet and exercise, Plato, in the *Republic*, devotes much more consideration to the former. The most characteristic point in what he says of the latter is, that for a certain period physical exercise should be pursued alone, to the exclusion of all serious mental work.[4] This period would apparently be from two to three years,[5] between the ages of seventeen and twenty. Two reasons are given for this view : that " hard work and sleep are enemies to study," and that " the figure which a man makes in his gymnastic is one of the greatest tests of his character."[6] Every one who knows anything of English school-life will be ready to indorse both these statements ; but he will not probably consider the truth of them a reason for making two years and a half of exclusive athletic exercises a necessary part of education. We must remember, however, that Plato was thinking of something more analogous to an incipient military service than to the games of our schools. The exercises upon which so long a time was to be spent would aim principally at disciplining the body for the work of a soldier, and would include, if practicable, some actual " taste of blood " on the battle-field.[7] Still,

---

[1] 3. 410 b. [2] 3. 404 a. [3] 404 a-b.
[4] 7. 537 b. [5] Cf. 7. 537 b ; 539 e. [6] 7. 537 b.
[7] 5. 466 e—467 e ; cf. 7. 537 a ; 3. 404 a-b.

even with this explanation, it is curious that his belief in the importance of " specialising" work should have so far over-ruled his consciousness of the dangers of one-sided develop-ment.

Plato has more to say on the other branch of gymnastic, the system of diet and general management of the body ; for he is here brought into contact with the medical practice of his day, and about this he held some strong opinions. Impressed with the want of principle and purpose, of simplicity and concentra-tion, in all departments of Greek life, he saw in the recent growth of luxury, with its attendant crop of new diseases, and its new methods of medical treatment, an analogous phenomenon to that which he observed in the sphere of art. While the artists seemed to him to be mainly engaged in catering for a morbid appetite for emotional stimulants,[1] helping to enervate morality and to fill the law-courts with litigants, instead of to make men a law to themselves, the doctors, he thought, were pampering a luxurious valetudinarianism, and flattering the whims of rich voluptuaries whose disorders were the result of their own mismanagement.[2] The simplicity for which he had cried aloud in art, he now demanded in living, and upon the same grounds. In a well-ordered society, every man ought to have his work to do ; and if he has work to do, he must make himself fit to do it.[3] The spiced luxuries of a feverish civilisa-tion, with its "sauces from Sicily," its " grisettes from Corinth," its " Athenian confectionery," have no more place in his life than they would have if he were training for a race.[4] Most of the long names which recent medicine has given to diseases are, in Plato's opinion, the polite inventions of doctors who will not offend their rich patients by telling them the truth, that they have worked too little and eaten too much.[5] A man who is always wanting to see a physician, except in case of accidents or epidemics, ought to be as much ashamed of himself as a man who is always going into court to get justice, because he has none of his own.[6] We might learn a lesson here from the de-spised artisan.[7] He cannot afford to be long in bed ; his work

---

[1] 3. 404 e—405 a.   [2] 3. 405 c—408 b.   [3] 3. 406 c.
[4] 404 d ; cf. 2. 373 a, where ἑταῖραι are similarly inserted between ὄψα and πέμματα.   [5] 3. 405 d.   [6] 3. 405 a-d.   [7] 406 c-d.

will not wait for him; and if he cannot be cured soon, he dies. But the rich man is supposed to have no work to do, abstention from which would make life not worth living.[1] He is to be allowed to give up his duties as a householder or a citizen, or to let his brain lie fallow as long as he likes, whenever he fancies that he has a sick headache.

Modern life would have supplied Plato with close analogies to the evils which he saw in the gymnastics and dietetics of his own day. Our public schools and universities have no lack of the sleepy and brutalised athlete, who has not an idea of doing anything except by force, whose perceptions are cloyed and dull, whose "life moves without grace or rhythm,"[2] and who yet probably could not serve on a campaign or a geographical expedition. Nor is the well-to-do valetudinarian an unfamiliar creature amongst us, the man who "suffers torments if he depart at all from his accustomed diet," and "is always in labour about his body."[3] Both phenomena may be said to represent the bad sides of something which is intrinsically good; the exaggerated interest taken in athletic exercises, while it partly defeats its own aim by artificialising school life, and making games into professions, is nevertheless the outcome of a genuine desire to broaden the basis of education, and to lose no chance of developing character out of strong national tendencies. So, too, the attention given to diet and the less serious forms of ailment, though it may sometimes result in making a man "profitable neither to himself or society,"[4] is a symptom of the higher and more intelligent value which is set upon human life. Every real advance in civilisation, along with the higher responsibilities and the more delicate public conscience which it brings with it, entails also fresh forms of abuse and greater necessity for taking trouble; but the best modern minds will not agree with Plato that it is the duty of society to let anybody die who can be kept alive. If, however, we have advanced upon his ideas in this point, we are still far from having realised them in others. We have not yet found the best way " to blend music with gymnastic and apply them proportionately to the soul" of the average schoolboy; and we have scarcely

---

[1] 3. 407 a-c.   [2] 3. 411 e.   [3] 3. 406 b and 407 c.   [4] 407 e.

begun to entertain the idea that a man is as much bound to manage his health properly as he is to manage his morals, much less to diffuse the knowledge which would enable him to do it.

Let us now gather up briefly the main threads in Plato's account of "musical" education, which, in its wider sense, as implying the harmonious development of the whole nature, includes "gymnastic" as well as "music." Its function is to provide nurture for the soul from childhood to youth. Upon the lower or "appetitive" element its action is more indirect than direct; it tames, regulates, or represses its various manifestations, by encouraging interests and emotions by which they are absorbed, or with which they are incompatible, as the case may require. Upon the "spirited" and "philosophic" elements it acts directly, by compelling and encouraging their normal activity through the bodily limbs and senses. The means which it employs for the former are diet and exercise, for the latter they are poetry and the arts. These last are the appropriate nurture of the "philosophic" nature, not in its entirety, but in that phase of its growth in which it is mainly imaginative and emotional, not logical and reflective. By presenting to the soul the true principles of human life in the sensuous material which it is able to assimilate, they prepare it unconsciously for assimilating them when presented at a later stage in a more rational form. They teach it how to live by telling how divine beings and great men live and have lived; they teach it what to love by surrounding it with what is really loveable; they foster its acquisitive instincts by encouraging the quick and accurate use of the senses; they develop its tendency to order and law by accustoming it to recognise severe symmetries of sound and form; and, finally, they introduce it to manhood endowed with an instinctive capacity of doing and saying the right thing at the right time, and with an instinctive perception of what is right and wrong in the deeds and words of others. In calling the capacity and perception thus acquired "instinctive," it is not intended that Plato conceived them to be received at birth or got by natural selection. No doubt Plato did attach immense importance to natural endowment; no doubt also he believed that there was some natural tendency in human nature towards what was good for it; but we have abundantly seen that this belief was more than counterbalanced by a conviction that mere natural endowment may be simply destructive, and that a mere tendency to what is good may ultimately tend to what is bad.[1] By "instinctive" then is meant that the substance of the education of "music" is appropriated and held by the soul without real reflection; that, in Greek phraseology, it feels neither the need nor the capacity to "give an account of" it; that it is conscious of it only as part and parcel of itself, not as an object which it can hold apart, look at, and criticise. Such a condition of mind is not of course unreflective in the sense of implying any capriciousness or instability; on the contrary, the imperceptible degrees by which it has been formed guarantee its depth and fixity. And, accordingly, when Plato wishes to describe finally the effects of "music" upon the character, he can find no better metaphor than one taken from the process of dyeing. The dyers, he says,[2] when they want to dye wool a fine purple, first select white wool from amongst the various colours; then they prepare it very carefully to receive the bloom, and then at last they dye it; a dye put in in this way is fast for ever, whereas if otherwise treated it washes out in a ridiculous manner. "This then was what we were trying to do when we selected our citizen-soldiers, and educated them by music and gymnastic; our whole object was that by obedience they should take in the laws like a dye, so that their belief about danger and all other things might become fast, through their having both the proper nature and the proper nurture, and thus the influences of pleasure, pain, fear, and appetite, which are more potent than all the soaps and solvents in the world, might never be able to wash it out."

The question now arises, Is education so conceived complete? Is the soul, when nurtured up to this point, full-grown as far as education can make it? At one time Plato seems to have thought that it was;[3] that at about twenty a man must cease learning in the narrower sense of the word, and get the rest of his knowledge in the practical life of a citizen, and that it rested with those in authority to watch his development and regulate his career accordingly. But we have also seen that

---

[1] 6. 491 b.   [2] 4. 429 c—430 b.   [3] 3. 413 e—414 a.

in the second section of the *Republic*, he clearly expresses his
feeling of the imperfection of the education of "music," and
assigns to it a subordinate and preparatory function in a more
elaborate system.[1] There are two main points in which Plato
finds it imperfect: subjectively, from the side of the soul, it
leaves important capacities undeveloped; objectively, regarding
the matter which it imparts and the form in which it imparts
it, it stops short of the requirements of knowledge. On the
one hand, it teaches the "philosophic" nature to love what is
beautiful, but not to understand what is true;[2] it makes it
quick to recognise the forms of goodness presented to sense or
imagination, but not to see with the mind's eye the essential
principles which those forms imperfectly express;[3] it infuses
into it indelible beliefs and convictions, attaching to the particular characters and actions which have come before it in the
course of education, but it does not satisfy the desire to know
the laws to which those beliefs can be referred.[4] On the other
hand, if we regard the matter which it teaches, this consists
mainly of ideas embodied in sensible forms; the characters
and deeds of individual men are described in poetry or suggested in music or pictured in painting and sculpture, with the
view of stimulating imitation and educating the sense for the
corresponding realities in life. The ideas thus imparted carry
conviction to the soul, not through their logical consistency and
irrefragability, but through their familiarity; they are apprehended, not in the systematic form of science in which each
part is seen to be connected with every other, but as a multitude of isolated instances, each complete in itself, and containing its own justification.[5] A person in this mental condition
does not satisfy the requirements of what Plato understands by
knowledge; and here few thoughtful people would disagree
with him; where he differs from most of the world is in thinking that the further mental progress, instead of being left to the
circumstances and choice of the individual, should be systematically provided for by a continued education. He seems to have
been led to this idea by reflecting upon the consequences which

---

[1] 7. 522 a; 6. 503 e ff.   [2] Cf. 3. 402 d and 403 c, with 5. 475 d-e.
[3] Cf. 3. 402 b-c with 5. 476 a-d.   [4] Cf. 3. 412 d—414 a with 6. 503 a-e.
[5] See the account of δόξα and its objects, 4. 477 a—480 a.

seemed to him to follow from the neglect of it. He was persuaded that the evils of human life had their root in ignorance, and that if men could once realise what their true interests required them to do, they would do it. He did not expect that mankind at large should ever have such a keen and profound perception of the truth, but it seemed to him not impossible that a few exceptional persons might arrive at it, and that society might allow itself to be governed by them; at any rate he was convinced that this sovereignty of true knowledge was the ideal to be aimed at, convinced that there is an intelligible principle pervading and connecting not only the life of men but the life of the whole universe, convinced that to discern this principle and to conform to it is the highest achievement of knowledge and of conduct, and that to " rise by stepping-stones " towards this height is the true education both of the individual and of the human race. Of such a principle the education of " music " had nothing to tell;[1] it showed examples and types of courage, temperance, justice, but it did not show " wherein they are good,"[2] what is the end to which they all converge, and which gives unity and meaning to their variety; and without some such perception how can we be said to " know " justice, or even to possess it? We may know it in one form, but we might mistake it in another; we may think we have got hold of it at one moment, in one place, under one set of circumstances, but it may escape us when we have changed our point of view. This is why the results of the first education are " sketchy " and "inexact," and require " filling up " and completing by a further education.[3]

But there was another consideration which led Plato to the same conclusion. It has already been shown how the conception of what he called the " philosophic " nature grows under his hands in the *Republic,* and how from being a complementary psychological element it comes ultimately to be represented as the germ of complete manhood. Though, however, it has in it this inherent capability, like other germs it depends for its development upon its environment, and Plato is the first

---

[1] 7. 522 a.   [2] 6. 506 a.
[3] 6. 504 b, ἀκριβείας ἐλλιπῇ ; *ib.* d, ὑπογραφήν . . . ἀπεργασίαν, κ.τ.λ.

to admit, and even to insist upon, the fact, that this richly-endowed " philosophic " nature, which might be the cause of the greatest good to mankind, is generally the cause of the greatest evils.[1] The reason of this strange phenomenon is found, partly in the very gifts of the nature itself, partly in the external advantages, so called, which it usually commands.[2] Driven by the native force of genius, it cannot rest in the narrow conventionalities of common opinion.[3] But its un-quenchable thirst for what is real, its far-reaching vision, its magnificent aspirations, find no true satisfaction or guidance. The atmosphere in which it lives is public opinion, speaking through its hired mouth-pieces, who think themselves its leaders; loud, exaggerated, irresistible, intolerant of principles, and confident in facts, which are really nothing but the dictates of its own caprice.[4] What can save a great nature in such an atmosphere, especially if his force of mind be supplemented by beauty and strength, wealth and connections ?   His power is flattered by venal servility, his ambition spoiled by easy triumphs; he feels the world within his grasp.   And if some wiser man whisper in his ear the hard truth that he is living the life of a fool, how should he listen ?   Or if his better genius chance to make him listen, how should he escape the clutches of the parasites, who had looked forward to living upon his success ? So it is that the philosophic nature is corrupted, and sinks to a life unworthy of itself, while philosophy, deserted by her true kinsmen, falls a victim to any jackanapes who can afford to de-spise his own profession, and bears in this enforced and unnatural union the wretched bastards who go about the world bearing her name, and bringing shame upon their mother.[5] Only here and there, by some exceptional circumstance, ill-health perhaps, or banishment, or pride, or possibly an inward and inexplicable monition, a man of the true stuff is kept back from public life and saved for philosophy ; and those poor few can do nothing better than stand aside out of the storm of the world, happy if they can live without sin and die in hope.[6] Such is Plato's

---

[1] 6. 487 e.   [2] 6. 491 b-c.
[3] 6. 490 a, οὐκ ἐπιμένοι ἐπὶ τοῖς δοξαζομένοις εἶναι πολλοῖς ἑκάστοις.
[4] 6. 491 d—495 c.   [5] 6. 495 c—496 a.   [6] 6. 496 a—497 a.

indictment against the society in which he was living. "No one of the forms of constitution now existing is worthy of the philosophic nature. Therefore it is changed and distorted, and as a seed sown in a strange soil will lose its virtue and become a victim to the influences amongst which it lives, so in the present state of things this kind of soul does not keep its force, but falls away to a nature not its own. But if it can find a form of society good enough for it, then men will see that it was always really divine, and that all else in their nature and ways of life is human only."[1]

It is then in the interests of society, whether we regard them as endangered by want of real knowledge, or by the neglect and corruption of its noblest natures, that Plato finds a further education to be necessary; and the question is, firstly, How did he conceive of the higher kind of apprehension which he called knowledge and the higher form of object which he called truth, and by what means did he think that the mind might be educated to the knowledge of such truth? and secondly, How did he hope to avoid the dangers attendant on the philosophic nature, and to make it an instrument of salvation instead of destruction to society? These two questions were to Plato really one; for in his view the dominant impulse of the philosophic nature is the impulse to know the truth, and to know the truth of things is to know the reason of them, and to know their reason completely would be to see them as convergent parts in a whole governed by a single end, or, in Platonic language, a single "good;" so that ultimately to know the truth of the world would be to know "the good" of the world, or the "reason why" of its existence, and to understand human life thoroughly would be to see the end or purpose which governs it in the light of that larger end or purpose which makes the whole universe luminous and intelligible. Thus the true interests of society coincide with those of its highest natures; for the study of what the good of man is and requires, is the best way of satisfying the best impulse of those natures, and the same process which develops the philosophic mind to its highest pitch, and makes a man a true philosopher,

---

[1] 6. 497 b-c.

will bring it also to the knowledge of the principles which should guide human conduct, and will make a man a true statesman. Thus the question with Plato comes to be, What is the education by which the human mind may be brought nearer to that truth which is at once the keystone of knowledge and the pole-star of conduct? And this question is most instructively treated under three heads, firstly, What is the nature of intellectual progress? the answer to which will give us a scale of knowledge and truth up which education should lead the mind; secondly, What is the nature and cause of human ignorance, which keeps the mind from thus advancing? and thirdly, What are the specific means by which this ignorance may be removed, and the inherent capacity of the mind developed and regulated? The last only of these questions concerns education directly; but just as in the case of the earlier education of character it was impossible to understand Plato without considering the constituent elements out of which the character had to be formed, so in order to make intelligible his account of the later education of reason, it is indispensable to consider in a general way how he conceived the activity and sphere of reason, in other words, knowledge and truth. And further, as Plato's manner of developing a view by antagonism to an existing state of things is nowhere more forcibly illustrated than in his treatment of this part of his subject, we should be throwing away the half of our information if, in examining the ideal of knowledge at which he aimed, we neglected his picture of the ignorance from which he wished to escape.

At the end of the sixth book of the *Republic*[1] Plato gives us, under the figure of a line divided into four parts, a series of the objects of mental apprehension, and of the mental operations which correspond to them, arranged in an ascending order of clearness and truth. At the bottom of the scale of objects he places what he calls " images," and at the bottom of the scale of mental activities the " perception of images." By " images " he understands primarily shadows and reflections, but he seems also to include under the term any perceivable object which

---

[1] 6. 509 d—511 e.

reproduces or suggests another in the same kind of way that shadows and reflections suggest and reproduce the things which occasion them. Thus all works of art may be called, more or less appropriately, "images," for it is common to them all to represent how things appear, or what they suggest to sense or imagination, by means of words, sounds, colour, or form, which, however directly related to the things, cannot be identified with them.[1] This is of course far from being a full account of what the arts do ; but they all do at least this, and Plato, for reasons which we shall presently see, chose to emphasise this characteristic of artistic representation, and to class together indiscriminately all objects of perception to which it is common. Judged then by the standard of clearness and truth, the lowest kind of perception is that which perceives merely shadows, reflections, or analogous images, of things, whatever the medium through which the image is conveyed. The Greek substantive (εἰκασία) used by Plato to describe this " perception of images," means literally the act of making one thing like another. The corresponding verb, besides the corresponding sense of copying or imitating, is commonly used in the sense of " conjecturing," apparently because one of the most obvious forms of conjecture is an inference drawn from comparing, that is, mentally " making like," one thing to another. No doubt this double association of the verb recommended the substantive to Plato's use; for it enabled him conveniently to characterise the lowest stage of perception, not merely as a perception of " images," but also as having only a " conjectural " certitude.[2] It is obvious that if we compare the knowledge about an object or an event derived from a picture or a description, with the knowledge of a person who has seen the object or been present at the event, the former is not only more indirect and superficial than the latter, but the certainty which we are justified in feeling about it is also less.

It would seem to be in relation to the last-mentioned sense

---

[1] Cf. 10. 599 a ; 605 c ; 3. 402 b-c ; 7. 517 d, where the "shadows of images " would be, *e.g.*, the representation or misrepresentation of the existing laws (themselves only " images " of justice) by a rhetorician or pleader.

[2] See 7. 516 c-d, for an application of εἰκασία in the sense of " conjecture."

of εἰκασία that Plato calls the next stage in the scale of know-ledge πίστις, "belief" or "conviction." Here, as in the former case, when the word has so many associations, it is important to seize the particular one which Plato apparently intended to convey. The objects of "belief," he says, are the things of which the images of the first stage are resemblances, in other words, what are ordinarily understood by "real things." The differences in the mental state of a man whose knowledge con-sists in "images" and that of one whose knowledge is derived from personal contact are many, but the one which is emphasised by Plato for his present purpose is that the latter, besides being more clear and true, is also more certain.[1]

The two kinds of mental objects and operations just described, while they differ from one another in important respects, have certain other important points in common when both compared with a higher stage of knowledge; and they are accordingly comprised by Plato under the single generic name of δόξα, or, as it is usually translated, "opinion."[2] Neither the Greek word nor its English equivalent, in their ordinary usage, gives any indication of the special meaning which Plato here intended to express. The characteristic marks of what he chooses to call "opinion" are the following: subjectively, it is a state of mind which carries with it no guarantee either of truth or per-manence; it may be either true or false[3] (whereas what we understand by "knowledge" must be true), and it is liable to be changed or lost[4] (whereas when we really know a truth once we know it always); objectively, it relates to a matter which is given in forms of sense, and which is manifold, particular, and relative.[5] An illustration will best explain Plato's meaning. A man has "opinion" about justice or beauty or weight or size; that is, he "thinks" that certain things are just or beauti-ful, heavy or large. His thought may be more or less positive according to his nature and circumstances, but however posi-tive he may feel, he cannot use "thinking" as equivalent to "knowing." If asked, What is justice? What is heaviness? he will probably answer by pointing to this or that instance of

---

[1] Cf. 10. 601 e—602 b.   [2] 7. 534 a.   [3] 5. 477 e ; cf. *Theaetetus*, 187 b.
[4] 3. 412 e ; cf. 6. 508 d ; and *Meno*, 97 e—98 a.   [5] 5. 476 a—480 a.

what he means ; justice perhaps will be to him bound up with certain particular laws, actions, or persons, heaviness with certain particular materials. The respective aggregates of these particular instances will make up his conceptions; justice *is* to him this aggregate, and nothing more. But now, suppose the actions or institutions in which his conception of justice was embodied to be done under different circumstances or worked under different conditions, they may very likely appear to be unjust instead of just. And similarly the materials with which alone he associated heaviness will seem light and not heavy when put alongside of materials which are heavier. The matter of " opinion," then, whether it be moral or æsthetic, mathematical or physical (for in this respect there is no difference), is, firstly, " manifold," consisting of a number of sensible or imaginable objects; and secondly, it is " particular" and " relative," for each of its constituents depends for its character upon its own particular position, and changes its character as its relative position changes. And it is clear that these characteristics belong equally to the matter in question, whether it be apprehended directly in actual sensible experience, or indirectly through an artistic or other medium. The condition of mind thus characterised is that of the majority of people on most subjects, and of all people on many subjects.[1] What we commonly call our knowledge, except where we may have made a special study in a special direction, is either derived from the representation of other men, or from our own casual and limited observation of the particular objects with which we happen to have come in contact. On the other hand, though the mind is for the most part content to remain in this condition, there are occasions on which it is conscious of its unsatisfactoriness. This must be the case, for instance, as soon as it begins to see that the sensible qualities of things, which it supposed to be fixed and absolute, are after all variable and relative, and that the same thing seems to have opposite attributes according as its position is changed. This relativity, which is inherent in the matter of sensation, whether in the physical or moral world, is one of the first difficulties which stimulates thought or

---

[1] 5. 479 d, τὰ τῶν πολλῶν πολλὰ νόμιμα.

reflection.[1] The same thing seems to be both light and heavy, both just and unjust; how can this be? Are then lightness and heaviness, justice and injustice, one and the same? To suppose this is to give the lie to one's own consciousness. The dilemma forces the mind to advance and to analyse further this perplexing matter of sensation, which, instead of the clear and permanent thing which it seemed to be, has become a "confused" centre of contradictory and fluctuating attributes.[2] To detect distinctions in this confusion, to ask, What then really *is* weight? What then really *is* justice? and to distinguish finally the object of sense, with its capacity of developing contradictions and of "playing double,"[3] from the object of thought which can be fixed and defined, these are the further steps which reflection takes, and with these we have left the domain of "opinion" and entered upon that of science. And this brings us to the next stage in the Platonic scale of mental objects and activities.

When we reflect upon the meaning of "knowledge" or "science" (for the Greek word is the same for both), it seems incongruous to apply it to a state of mind which is liable to error, or to an object-matter which is liable to change. We cannot say that we "know" what justice is, if the embodiments of our conception may become unjust by a change of relations, any more than we could say that we "knew" what a triangle was, supposing that we found that the properties of triangles as such varied with the size, colour, or position of the particular figures of which we demonstrated them. This, however, is just what we do not find; we conceive that a triangle is always and everywhere a triangle, that once known it is always known: and in this belief we speak of geometrical science or knowledge, which we distinguish from our ordinary state of mind on ordinary subjects. What we only "think" or "believe" is scattered about in a number of separate objects; what we "know" is one, and only one, however many may be the instances in which we perceive its truth. What we only "think," depends for its character or validity upon its particular form or environment, and changes with them; what we "know" is independent of its particular presentation, and remains true under all apparent

---

[1] 7. 523 a—524 d.   [2] συγκεχυμένον τι, 524 c.   [3] ἐπαμφοτερίζειν, 5. 479 c.

changes. The state of mind thus distinguished from "opinion" is what is commonly understood by "scientific," and as the only sciences which could be said to exist in Plato's time were mathematical, he took mathematics as the type of the third stage in his scale of knowledge, though his characterisation of them would equally apply to all sciences ordinarily so called. The geometrician, Plato says,[1] uses sensible figures in his reasoning, but does not really think of them. What he really has in his thought is not the particular triangle which he draws on paper, but the "triangle itself," which the one on paper "is like" or "is an image of." Similarly we might say of the botanist or political economist, that in proportion as their subject-matter has reached a scientific stage, they ignore the particular modifications under which it is presented to them, and see through these to the essential forms or laws of which they are symbols. In doing this they have no more doubt than has the geometrician, that they are nearer to the truth than if they allowed themselves to attend to nothing but the particular circumstances of the place or the moment. Whatever popular prejudices may be violated by the scientific mode of thought, and whatever metaphysical difficulties may be raised by the assumption of degrees of reality, the best minds are practically, if not theoretically, convinced that there is a difference between "thinking" and "knowing," and that in the latter they are more in conformity with what is real than in the former.

The word διάνοια, which Plato[2] appropriated to the form of mental activity just described, had no more fixed connotation in ordinary Greek usage than such English words as "thought," "intellect," "understanding." We have seen what was the particular meaning which he wished to convey by it, namely, that the next step in the scale of clearness and truth above the mere certainty of opinion, is that in which the mind, while employing sensible objects, is really occupied with something of which they are only symbols or images. It is necessary to dwell at a little more length upon Plato's conception of the distinction here involved, which plays such a vital part in his theory of education and knowledge. The opposition between sense and

---

[1] 6. 510 d-e.   [2] 6. 511 d ; 7. 534 a.

thought in various forms had attracted the attention of Greek thinkers from the earliest times. The apparent arbitrariness and fluctuation, both of our physical sensations and of our moral ideas, were continually contrasting themselves with the fixity and substantiality which the simplest conception of knowledge and the most rudimentary moral distinctions alike seem to presuppose. The necessity for immutable principles, if the world of nature and human life is to be explained, impressed itself upon Plato with all the greater force that he seems to have realised with peculiar vividness the mutability of much which ordinary experience pronounces permanent. To the element of reality which his mind discovered or surmised everywhere behind the appearance and change which sensation shows us, he gave the name of "form." It is a curious instance of the changes of fortune in the life of language, that the Greek word "idea," which Plato chose to express what is most profoundly real, and least dependent on the human mind for its reality, should have come to be used for a mere mental creation or fiction, and that its English equivalent "form" is now mainly suggestive of what is superficial and unsubstantial. The history of the word in Greek speculation before its employment by Plato is very slight; we can only conjecture that to a Greek, peculiarly organised for the perception of shape, and accustomed to find significant and typical lines in all that he saw, it was a natural transition from what is outwardly and visibly characteristic to what is inwardly and theoretically essential. Every people, like every individual thinker, has its favourite metaphors for expressing ultimate philosophical conceptions. In the phraseology of Greek philosophy there is no phenomenon of which we are more constantly reminded than that of vision, and the use of the word "form" by Plato is only the most pregnant and far-reaching instance of a metaphor which, in the way of analogy, simile, or suggestion, pervades his speculation. We have here only to indicate in the briefest and most general way the meaning of the Platonic conception of "form," so far as it enters into the theory of knowledge and education. It may be said to combine elements of all the modern conceptions of essence, law, and ideal. Those qualities or characteristics in a thing which most make it what it is, and which contrast with others that are casual and separable, are the "form" which characterises and individualises the thing. That principle which gives consistency and continuity to changing manifestations of activity, is the "form" which works itself out in a plastic material. And once more: the aim or mark to which the various steps in a process converge is the "form" to which the agent in the process looks, and which he strives to attain. So that alike in art, in science, in morality, it is the "form" which is essential and important, the "form" which the imagination discerns through the chaos of sense-impressions, the "form" which the reason separates from the accidental conditions of time and place, and the "form" in which the moral consciousness finds rest and guidance amidst the distractions and contradictions of experience.

Plato has various ways of expressing the mode in which the "form" exists, and is apprehended. It is that which really "is," as opposed to that which "seems;" that which is "one," as opposed to that which is "many;" that which is self-identical and permanent, as opposed to that which is always becoming something else. Or, again, the sensible world is only the "appearance" of the intelligible; the things which we see and hear are "images," that only "resemble" and suggest something which we cannot see or hear; and each of these images or resemblances only "participates in," but does not adequately embody, the reality which is grasped in and over it. The vivid and sometimes crude manner in which Plato represents the relationship between what is and what is not "form," has given rise to much misunderstanding of him as well as to many real difficulties, and has left a doubt whether he had himself clearly apprehended what he was endeavouring to express. The truth seems to be that no great genius, "stung by the splendour of a sudden thought," can ever work out or even conceive his idea with the coolness and completeness which are necessary to make it consistently intelligible and to guard it from misinterpretation. But we are here concerned, not with the exaggerations and confusions, real or supposed, to which Plato fell a victim, but with the central truth which he saw clearly, and to which he held tenaciously.

Returning now to the scale of knowledge, we see that

whether we regard the sense of unsatisfactoriness which impels the mind to advance upon sensible opinion, or the intellectual condition in which that impulse results, it is what Plato understands by " forms," for which the mind is looking, and in which it rests. The mathematical sciences, which spring from, and are the answer to, questions raised by the mathematical properties of sensible objects, take account, not of the particular figures to which they refer, but of the " objects themselves," of which those figures are only the " images ;" these " objects themselves" are clearly what we have learnt to know as "forms." Though, however, it is about the " form " of the triangle or of unity that the geometrician and arithmetician really reason, not about the figures on the paper, they cannot dispense with those figures. They exercise intelligence, but intelligence which still has an appendage of sense, and is not therefore perfectly intelligent. And along with this imperfection in the knowledge of which mathematics are a type, goes another one which Plato expresses by saying that such knowledge is "assumptive" or "hypothetical." "Geometricians, arithmeticians, and the like, assume the odd, the even, the figures, the three kinds of angle, and other similar things, according to the particular branch of the science with which they are dealing ; these they assume themselves to know, and make them hypotheses, and do not think themselves bound to give any further account of them either to themselves or others ; they suppose every one to see the truth of them. From these hypotheses they start, and when they have got this start they go on through the remaining steps, and arrive conclusively at the result which was the original object of their inquiry." [1] Such a procedure does not satisfy the full conception of knowledge or science ; for "when the starting-point of the argument is something assumed and not known, and the end and intermediate steps depend for their connection upon this unknown starting-point, how can such a conclusion possibly constitute knowledge ?" [2] By "hypotheses," then, Plato understands, not assumptions temporarily made for certain definite purposes, but truths which, while really depending for their validity upon their connection

---

[1] 6. 510 c-d ; 511 d.   [2] 7. 533 c.

with higher truths, are treated as if they were independent of that connection, and self-proven. In this sense, each one of the "forms" of existence with which the special sciences are concerned, number, figure, motion, etc., is a "hypothesis;" the special sciences are scientific so far as they follow logically from these "hypotheses" which form their principles, but so far as those principles themselves are not, strictly speaking, "known," they do not satisfy the ideal requirements of science. For science to Plato means explanation and intelligibility; we "know" a truth when we can "give account of" it, and the way in which we give account of it is by showing its necessary connection with wider and more independent truths. Progress in science is progress from isolated to connected thought; and if we try to imagine such a progress consummated, we are led to the conception of a universal science, in which every part is seen in its relation to every other part, and of which the whole forms a perfect orb of truth, beginning and ending in itself. Of such a science, as it might be if the speculative impulse of the human mind were fully satisfied, Plato has given us a picture,[1] though he is conscious that it is only a picture, and that to realise what he is imagining is "a flight above"[2] both himself and his readers. The whole matter of knowledge is imaged as a perfectly graduated scale of the essential "forms" of existence; each "form" is seen to be, not an ultimate truth, but a "hypothesis," depending for its truth upon one above it; the mind mounts from "form" to "form," using each as a "point of departure" to the next, until it reaches the topmost "unhypothetical principle," upon which the whole chain hangs, and from which it can descend again securely down the ladder of intelligible reality. In such a perfect system of knowledge, as there would be nothing "hypothetical" or unproven, so there would be no element of sense or unintelligibility. The symbolism of sensible appearances, which suggest imperfectly something which they are not, and blur the intellectual vision with an unexplained residuum, would melt into the perfect transparency of reason, when mind met mind face to face.

We have thus reached the highest stage in the Platonic

---

[1] 6. 511 b-c.   [2] 6. 506 e; cf. 7. 532 e—533 a.

scale of mental development, that stage to which he applies emphatically the name of "knowledge," and the object-matter of which is the essential "forms" of existence without admixture of hypothesis or sense. Like the preceding stage, it represents an inherent impulse in the mind; but, unlike it, it leaves the impulse in the main unfulfilled. The different specific sciences owe their existence to the dissatisfaction occasioned to the mind by reflection upon its sensible experience. This dissatisfaction they remove by revealing permanent and consistent "forms" in what before seemed a fluctuating chaos; but it still survives in the sense of incompleteness and limitation which the mind feels, when it finds that each science rests upon an unproven basis and points beyond itself for the ultimate establishment of its conclusions. The force or faculty in virtue of which the mind is perpetually trying to rid itself of this dissatisfaction, to get out of the region of "hypotheses," and to see truth as a whole of parts, is called by Plato the "dialectical" faculty,[1] and the ideal science which the completed exercise of that faculty might be conceived to create, is the "science of dialectic," the only form of science or knowledge which seemed to him strictly to deserve the name.[2] The term "dialectic," which plays almost as conspicuous a part in the Platonic philosophy as "form," means originally nothing more than the process of oral discussion by question and answer. Naturally a prominent and familiar word among a people where ideas were communicated so much more by talking than by reading, and specially consecrated to Plato by the example of his master Socrates, it was adopted by him to describe the process by which the mind endeavours to arrive at true conceptions, whether by actual verbal discussion or by inward "dialogue with itself." And as Plato conceived that the truth exists in a certain form or order, and that the human mind in learning and apprehending it must conform to that order, he naturally used "dialectic" for that particular mode of manipulating language and thought which seemed to him most consonant with truth, and most fitted to lead to its discovery. What that mode must be we

---

[1] 7. 533 a; cf. *ib.* c, and 532 a.   [2] 7. 533 c-e.

have already had some indication. If the only conception of reality which satisfied Plato was that of a cosmos which is neither a vacant unity nor a crowded chaos, but a reasonable system of interrelated elements, the only true logic or method of knowledge must seem to him to be that which obeys the two-fold requirement arising from such a conception, a method which unifies without confounding, which specifies without separating, a method which does not "break the limbs" of truth,[1] but follows and reveals the natural articulations of its subject-matter till it has reached the perception of its organic unity. Such a method is the true "dialectic," the only true method of learning, teaching, and investigating, because the only method which is in agreement with the inherent constitution of the real world. And if the method be supposed to have been carried through to the utmost verge of truth, the moving process passes into a completed result, and dialectic, instead of a logic of discovery and definition, becomes the living expression of the truth itself, the embodied logic of reality. Plato has nowhere filled up the outline of his conception of "dialectic;" but the greater part of his dialogues are practical illustrations of the principle, and the suggestions of a theory which are scattered up and down them are often more instructive as well as more stimulating than the finished systems of other men.

We have now seen how Plato conceived the natural order in the ascent of the mind towards truth. It begins by seeing things "darkly," through the uncertain "glass" of fancy; it goes on to the certainty of direct sensible experience; from the objects of sense and opinion, with their local and temporal limitations, it advances to the perception of essential "forms" and principles, which those objects symbolise or suggest; and from the understanding of isolated principles and their conse-quences it passes to the apprehension of them as steps in a connected scale of existence. We have next to ask, How far does the human mind actually obey this principle of progress? What is the actual state and opinion of mankind as regards its "education," in the fuller sense in which we have now come to use the word? Plato has expressed his views upon this sub-

---

[1] *Phaedrus*, 265 e.

ject in the famous allegory of the cave, with which the seventh
book of the *Republic* opens.   The allegory to be understood
and appreciated must be studied in its entirety.   A few only
of its main features need be dwelt upon here.   Mankind in
general, Plato gives us to understand, so far from advancing up
the road which leads to truth and light, remain for the most
part during their whole life in the state of mind which is only
fit for children.   They are like men sitting bound at the bottom
of a cave, lit by a fire to which their backs are turned, able
only to look straight before them at the wall of their prison.
The living world of nature and man lies behind them, and all
that they know of it are its shadows and echoes, the hazy,
unsubstantial, artificial reproductions of the minds of other
men.   At this moving world of phantasms they stare, and
in its reality they believe, with all the fixity and fervour of
men who have done a thing from their childhood.   They watch
its vain shows as they pass and repass, observe the order of
their succession, and formulate a conjectural science which is
to enable them to predict the future.   From this condition
there is for most men no escape, for they do not know, and
therefore cannot desire, any other sort of existence.   Only now
and then, by some force of nature or circumstances, a prisoner
is set free from his chains, made to stand on his feet and look
round, to see with his own eyes, and hear with his own ears,
and step by step, perhaps, to make his way to the upper air
and the sunlight of knowledge.   But each stage in the process
is grievous to him ; the first experience of actual life confuses
him, and makes him wish for his old world of fancy again, and
the sudden revelation of scientific truth dazzles his mind,
which is only used to empirical certitude.   Only by slow
degrees he gets an insight into the principles which really
govern the world, and the supreme principle upon which they
all depend; and if in compassion for the ignorance of mankind he tries to teach them his new knowledge, he is received
with ridicule and opposition, which in the end may cost him
his life.

Philosophy, like religion, has often begun by calling upon
men to get rid of their prejudices and illusions.   It is customary, indeed, to look upon the two as antagonistic, and to con-

trast the humility required by the Gospel with the supposed arrogance and self-sufficiency of the philosophic spirit. Yet if we take men so different, and so representative in their differences, as Plato, Bacon, and Spinoza, we find them all agreeing, not in a glorification of the human mind, but in the imperative demand that it should shake off its " chains " and turn to receive the light, that it should surrender its " idols " and " become as a little child," that it should look at things " under the form of eternity," not through the vague confusion of its own imagination. To all alike, however different their phraseology and their motive, the conviction is common, that there is an order of existence or of nature which man does not make but finds, which he must wait upon and not forestall, if he would attain to the wellbeing, the power, or the freedom, of which he is capable.

Passing from these common features to the details of Plato's conception of human ignorance, we do not find him, like Bacon, giving any classification of the false " shadows and images," but we can gather many hints as to their nature. Primarily they are the dim, exaggerated, and shallow representations of things through the medium of art, literature, and rhetoric.[1] In explaining Plato's antipathy to dramatic representation, we have already had occasion to notice some of his attacks upon art in general. Those attacks seem to be valid if, and so far as, artistic representation produces actual illusion, and substitutes appearance for reality. To a mind which is really fitted by nature and education to receive art in the spirit of art, illusion, so far from being a necessary element in æsthetic enjoyment, is a distinct bar to it. A person who looks at a play exactly as if it were real life may be vehemently moved for a moment, but will eventually find the spectacle either so exciting or so wearisome that he will wish to interrupt it or to go away. It is essential to the perfect reception of artistic effect that the impulse to action should be in abeyance, and the theoretic faculties at their fullest activity. The after-effect may issue in acts, but at the moment of seeing, or hearing, or reading, the work of art, considered as such, demands that " wise passive-

---

[1] Cf. 7. 517 d-e ; 10. 600 e—602 b ; 605 c.

ness" which is only the other side of theoretic energy. But
there are comparatively few imaginative persons in whom the
double power of self-control and self-surrender, of entering in
and yet of standing outside, is so strong that they "cannot
choose but" hear or see. To most of us the message of art
awakens a cross echo in our own selves, and we go away with
the flattering feeling that the vapours or the rhetoric of egoism
are the universal types or tones of genius and truth. Then it is
that the artist, often without knowing it, and against his will,
becomes "a mimic and a juggler" to the public;[1] the spirit
distilled in the crucible of imagination gets cloyed with the
lees of prejudice or sentiment; and the "impassioned expression, which is in the countenance of all science," stiffens into a
masquerade which can "deceive children and fools."[2]

The "shadows and echoes" amongst which Plato's prisoners
live are not, however, only the illusions, intentional or un-
intentional, produced by art and literature; they are also the
illusions of our own passions. It would be a great mistake to
regard the darkness of the cave as a mere darkness of intellectual ignorance, or the escape from it as a mere intellectual
enlightenment. In the mind of Plato, reason is never for long
dissociated from emotion, or knowledge from purpose; the
highest impulse to him is the impulse towards truth, and the
highest knowledge is knowledge of the end of action. Thus
the great reason why the spark of "divine"[3] intelligence is so
nearly smothered in man is not primarily the difficulty of
learning or the mysteriousness of nature ; the fetters which
bind the men in the cave are those "leaden weights which the
pleasures of gluttony and the like gather round them, and
which turn the eye of the soul to the earth."[4] The "impulse"
which, if it had sway,[5] would carry the soul out of the "sea"
of earthly life, to union with "the divine, immortal, and
eternal" to which it is "akin," is checked and thwarted by no
irresistible necessity or power of evil, but by the "shells and
stones and tangle" with which the "delights of the table"
gradually incrust it. The "painted images of true pleasure,"[6]

---

[1] 10. 598 d.   [2] 10. 598 c.   [3] 7. 518 e.
[4] 7. 519 b.   [5] 10. 611 c—612 a.   [6] 9. 586 a c.

with which men choose to dwell, are the offspring of their own nature, which leads them about " like cattle, with their heads down and eyes fixed upon their dinners, feeding and breeding, and kicking and butting one another because they cannot get enough." It is not the thought of "this unsubstantial pageant" which leads Plato like Shakespeare to call human life a " dream ;"[1] rather it is the same feeling as that of Lucretius when he cries to man,

> " Qui somno partem majorem conteris aevi,
>   Et vigilans stertis nec somnia cernere cessas."

It is because men will not rouse themselves to the reality which is there if they had the eyes to see it, because they mistake the passing shows of sense for the eternal essence of which they are the mere outside, because they " fight about shadows" of power and clutch after " phantoms of good," that " before they are well awake in this world they find themselves in the other, sleeping the heavy sleep of death."[2]

" How then " (and this is the third and last part of our question) " are men to be led up to the light, as some are said to have gone up from Hades to dwell with the gods in heaven ?"[3] Or, as we may also put it (for it is upon progress in knowledge that the good of mankind depends), " what kind of studies and practice will produce the men who are to save society ?"[4] Or, once more (for the interest of society is ultimately identical with that of its noblest natures), " how is the commonwealth to handle philosophy so as not to be destroyed by it ?"[5] Clearly it is important that society should look to it ; that her greatest sons, instead of being criminals or outcasts, who owe their mother nothing for their bringing up, should be bound to her by ties of mutual obligation.[6] The principle of justice which regulates other spheres of life ought to hold good here too ; the man who has the philosophic faculty should not be allowed to do what he likes with it ;[7] he should be induced to contribute his share to the common good, and to help in " binding the commonwealth together," while his fellows should do for him

---

[1] 7. 520 c ; 5. 476 c-d ; cf. *Timaeus,* 52 b-c.
[2] 7. 534 c-d.   [3] 7. 521 c.   [4] 6. 502 d.
[5] 6. 497 d.   [6] 7. 520 b.   [7] 7. 519 e—520 a.

what he cannot do for himself, provide him with the necessary material of life and supply his soul with the nurture which it demands. The general character, then, of the duty of society is clear: it has to find a way for doing methodically and with the greatest possible ease what now takes place exceptionally by the force of circumstances and under almost insuperable obstacles. And the general character of the education which shall do this is also clear: it must be an education which will help the soul to " see " the truth, to penetrate the darkness which fancy and appetite spread between it and facts, to follow its own " divine impulse," and to shake off the fetters of its own forging. Some " professors of education,"[1] indeed, talk as if the soul were like a blind eye and teaching were " putting sight into it." But the truth is that the " eye of the soul," the " organ with which it learns and understands," is not like the eye of the body. The latter is more or less independent of the rest of the organism, and can be moved without it; but the former can only be " turned to the light " if the whole soul be turned with it. The soul is not in pieces, but continuous; knowledge in the highest sense is not an independent act of a part of the self, but that union of the whole with truth, in which the lower parts are taken up into the higher according to their capacities.[2] It is not possible to be habitually living the life of the lower elements, and to keep the higher at their greatest efficiency. Evil is the " disease " of the soul,[3] and to be or do evil and still expect to exercise the highest psychical activity is as reasonable as it would be, if body cured body by contact, to expect the most diseased body to be the best healer. It is from this point of view that Plato denies the possibility of getting to know the real nature of evil by personally experiencing it; the very experience which is to be the object of knowledge spoils the instrument by which it is to be known. The " whole " soul then must be turned to the light, for the " eye of the soul " is the highest element in it, and carries with it the other elements.

In another respect also the mental is unlike the bodily vision. The bodily eye may lose its power of sight and have it

---

[1] 7. 518 b-c.   [2] 9. 586 e.   [3] 4. 414 e—415 b; 3. 409 a-e.

restored to it again, but the analogous faculty in the mind can neither be created nor destroyed; "the other virtues of the soul, as they are called, seem to be nearly akin to those of the body, for they are not originally in existence, but are an after product of habit and practice; but the virtue of intelligence seems to belong to something altogether more divine, something which never loses its force, but is made serviceable or unserviceable, helpful or harmful, according as it is turned to the light or not."[1] The power of mental insight still remains active in the warped soul of the clever scoundrel; it is the divine and immortal part in the soul, that which makes it "capable of bearing all good things,"[2] but capable also of bearing "all evil things;" it may be "buried in the mud" of ignorance or overgrown with the "incrustations" of passion, but it is never so lost that it cannot be lifted up, purged, and re-illumined, or so negative that anything else can be substituted for it.

The general principle, then, of the higher education is expressed in the term "conversion."[3] How is this to be effected? Clearly the educational process must follow the true and natural order of mental development. If the scale of knowledge and truth is what it has been represented to be, education must be a method for leading the soul from the lowest stage, where it apprehends nothing but "images," through that of direct sensible experience, to the region of essential "forms" of existence, and so finally to that perception of the systematic unity of truth which is the ideal of science. The first two steps are provided for if the education in "music" be successfully carried through. Its function was precisely to obviate the possible perversion of the imagination and emotions, by training them rightly; to prevent people from being still children when they ought to be men, by making childhood the real precursor of manhood; to train the imagination so that it should not lead to an idolatry of sensible forms which the mind can only leave with pain and difficulty, but that "when reason comes" she may be "welcome" to the soul which has already learnt to know her unconsciously; to form habits which may not be mere habits, but the basis for fresh acquisitions of character, and convictions which shall

---

[1] 7. 518 d—519 a.   [2] 10. 621 c.   [3] 7. 518 d; 521 c.

not be merely fixed, but shall offer a ready material for receiving the form of principles. In a soul thus trained, with its imagination filled with fair sights and sounds, its emotions instinctively responsive to what is really loveable, its beliefs " dyed fast " with truth, the new structure of knowledge has to be reared. The steadfastness of opinion has to be translated into logical consistency; the quickness and exactness of perception and fancy into the power of abstraction and reasoning; the love of things and persons into the devotion to principles and ideas. What the first step in the new " conversion " will be we already know by anticipation. The mathematical sciences, which are at once the product and the type of the third stage in the scale of mental activity, are clearly marked out to be the instruments for stimulating and training that activity. Those sciences, as we saw, owe their existence to the difficulties which the soul experiences when it reflects upon the matter of sensuous opinion. It is in meeting those difficulties, in obedience to an inherent speculative impulse, that the soul passes from the supposed clearness and consistency of local and temporal truth to the more transparent clearness and the more rigorous consistency of a truth which is not sensible but intelligible. If, then, we could make the soul perform methodically and under guidance the process which it is its nature to perform imperfectly and at random, if the sciences could be utilised for training its scientific faculties as the arts were utilised for training its artistic faculties, we should be helping in the most effective, because the most natural, way to " make the work of conversion easy."

Plato complains[1] that the true educational function of the sciences has been ignored or neglected. Arithmetic has been studied so far as is useful for trade and commerce, geometry for the purposes of measurement, astronomy for its value in navigation, harmonics in the interest of the professional musician; but it is hard to make people believe the truth that each of these sciences may be made a means for " purging and rekindling an organ of the soul which would otherwise be spoiled and blinded, an organ more worth saving than ten

---

[1] 7. 525 c ; 527 a-b, d-e ; 531 a.

thousand eyes, for by it alone the truth is seen." He does not
of course deny the importance of such practical applications in
their proper sphere; on the contrary, he himself emphasises
the practical utility of arithmetic and geometry to a man who
is to be a soldier and tactician.[1] But he points out that for
such practical purposes a very slight amount of science is
necessary, and that the methods of study which serve for such
purposes are not the methods which serve for education.[2] The
mere empirical observation of objects, which is all that is
necessary for immediate utility, does not " lead the soul to
look upwards,"[3] whereas the study of the same objects in the
scientific spirit is just what is wanted to make " the natural
intelligence useful instead of useless."[4] For, as we have already
been told, the really scientific man, though he employs sensible
objects in his reasoning, does not " think of them." The numbers of the arithmetician are such as " can only be manipulated
by thought;"[5] and if we point out to him that the visible or
tangible object which represents his unit is not " one " at all,
but is divisible into infinite multiplicity, he will only laugh at
our simplicity, and will adhere to his assertion that one is one,
and never anything else, invariable and indivisible. Geometry,
too, so far as it is scientifically treated, relates to "what is
invisible and eternal,"[6] and not to the sensible figures which are
" becoming " something else at the very moment that we speak
of them. Nor will Plato admit that the case is really different
when we come to astronomy. Here indeed the splendour and
beauty of the visible objects with which the science is concerned, easily deceive us into thinking that this merely sensible
nature is in itself important and interesting. But gazing up
at the stars in open-mouthed wonderment will no more give us
knowledge than gazing at a very excellently constructed dia-
gram.[7] The whole celestial universe, so far as it " has body and
is visible," is subject to the same conditions as other material
things. It does not "admit of knowledge" in the strict sense;
it is a symbol, but not the truth symbolised. The material
heavenly bodies, as such, do not realise the relations of figure

---

[1] 7. 522 e; 526 d. [2] 7. 526 d. [3] 7. 529 a-b. [4] 7. 530 c.
[5] 7. 526 a. [6] 7. 527 b. [7] 529 c-e.

and motion which they suggest;[1] those relations "cannot be apprehended by sight, but by thought only;" and it is as figures and diagrams for the discovery and analysis of these intelligible relations that the visible bodies ought to be used, if we are really to study astronomy and thereby to educate the human intelligence. The methods adopted in harmonics, or the science of sound, admit of a similar reform; it too may be made to help in the work of "conversion" by revealing the abstract numerical conditions upon which musical harmony depends. But this is not understood either by the professional musicians who fight over the "smallest audible interval" and "set their ears before their minds,"[2] or even by the Pythagorean philosophers who,[3] though they appreciate the true interest of the subject, confine their investigations to what they can hear, and do not go on to ask what relations of number produce harmony and what do not, and what is the cause of each.

Plato's conception, then, of the educational function of the sciences is, primarily, that they may be used to teach men to think. This they do by presenting to the mind sensible objects, and at the same time compelling it to ignore or abstract from the particularity and limitation incident to sense-presentation, to fix its attention solely upon the essential and universal "forms" which are confusedly "imaged" to sense, and to deduce consistently the consequences which follow from them. The difficulties or misunderstandings to which he has given occasion in expressing this conception, seem mainly due to the embarrassing combination of an extremely limited and simple scientific experience with an almost prophetic power of advancing upon it, or divining its possibilities. In the childlike confidence inspired by the still fresh perception of the nature of arithmetical and geometrical truth, he leaps the barrier which modern thought has erected between deductive and experimental science, and boldly surmises a state of human knowledge in which the whole web of cosmic conditions should be as rigorously intelligible as the simplest relations of number and figure. He sees how the senses confuse the reason in its early reflections upon units and triangles, and how the reason

---

[1] 530 a-c.   [2] 531 a-b.   [3] 531 c.

sets the senses at defiance and goes on its own way securely, and at a stroke he pictures to himself the whole phenomenal world seen as the symbol of an intelligible order. He knows by experience how the study of mathematics quickens the mind and compels the practice of abstract thinking, and there seems to him to be no reason why the whole of human science should not be pressed into the same high service, the education of the human race.

We have however mentioned only one, and the lesser one, of the motives which led Plato to advocate the study of the sciences. The ten years between twenty and thirty, over which he would continue that study, would be a very long time to spend in the mere practice of logical thinking. But the study has to him a real as well as a formal significance. It serves not only as a mental gymnastic, helping the soul to reach the place where the truth is to be found,[1] but also as an actual introduction to the truth for which it is looking. That this is Plato's conception appears both from his enumeration of the sciences themselves, and, still more, from the principle upon which he directs that they should be studied. In his series of sciences, arithmetic, geometry, stereometry, astronomy, and harmonics, he is clearly following an order of progression in their respective subject-matters,[2]—number, planes, cubes, motion of cubes, motion of audible bodies. We need not suppose the series to be intended to be complete, even in the then condition of knowledge; we are expressly told that there are many other forms of motion which might be mentioned;[3] still it would seem that Plato meant to co-ordinate, in outline at least, those portions of the knowledge of his time which could pretend to the name of science. This appears more clearly from the passage in which he indicates the method upon which they should be studied. "If the pursuit of all these subjects which we have enumerated be carried on to the point where they communicate with and are related to one another, and their natural affinities be inferred, I think it is of some use for our present purpose, and not labour spent in vain, as it otherwise is."[4] And again,[5] when the age of twenty is reached,

---

[1] 7. 526 e.   [2] See, *e.g.* 7. 528 b.
[3] 530 c-d.   [4] 531 c-d.   [5] 537 c.

the branches of knowledge which have been placed before the
student in boyhood "promiscuously," to be picked up without
system or constraint, "are to be brought together, so that he
may have a comprehensive view of their relationship to one
another, and to the nature of being." From these passages we
see that Plato regarded the sciences which he had enumerated,
not as arbitrary and isolated pieces of knowledge, still less as
merely formal constructions, but as directly related to the sum
of being or reality, of which each one of them expresses a
particular aspect, and in which they all find a common meet-
ing-point. Number, extension, motion, are primary "forms"
of being; the first especially[1] is involved in the simplest acts of
thought, and underlies the processes of all the arts and sciences.
In learning to deal with them we are not only preparing ourselves for dealing with more important subjects, but we are
actually setting our foot upon that "ladder" of existence, the
ascent of which would be the summit of scientific attainment.
And here we are reminded of the language in which Plato
explains what he considers to be the imperfection or inadequacy
of the knowledge of which mathematics are a type. That
knowledge, we were told, is "hypothetical," that is, it rests
upon principles which are unproven, because they have not
yet been apprehended in all their relations to other principles.
In requiring, then, that the study of the sciences should be
constantly directed to the perception of their mutual relationships, Plato is clearly intending to remedy this characteristic
defect by pointing the way from the region of the "hypothetical" to that of a self-demonstrated system of knowledge.
To such a system Plato, as we saw, gave the name of "dialectic,"
and the impulse which leads, and the rules which guide, the
mind in the endeavour to realise it, are the "dialectical" faculty
and method. Accordingly we find, as we might expect, that
in the power of perceiving the mutual relationships of the
particular sciences, Plato finds "the greatest test of the presence or absence of a dialectical nature," for "the man who
can see things together is a dialectician, and he who cannot is
not."[2] And as to "see things together," or in their natural and

---

[1] 7. 522 c.   [2] 537 c.

necessary connection, is the same thing as to understand, explain, or account for them, the "dialectician" is also naturally described as the man who "can give account both to himself and others of the essential nature of any given thing."[1]

The sciences, then, "ordinarily so called,"[2] are the "prelude"[3] or the "propædeutic"[4] to "dialectical" science. The study of them, as usually conducted, is far from making a man a "dialectician," for it generally leaves him incapable of "giving any account of" his knowledge,[5] and knowledge thus unaccounted for is neither an intelligent nor a permanent acquisition. But if studied on the principles above suggested, they not only "purge and rekindle"[6] the mental vision, they are not only "fellow-labourers in the work of conversion,"[7] but they also directly prepare the way for a higher study, partly by discovering and developing the requisite faculty for it, partly by introducing the mind to the elementary basis in that structure of knowledge of which "dialectic" is "the coping-stone."[8]

The study of the sciences during the ten years between twenty and thirty is not, in Plato's plan, to claim the whole time and energy of the citizen who is admitted to it. He is to be at the same time serving his apprenticeship in military service, and testing the courage of his moral convictions under the various trials of pleasure and pain, fear and persuasion, which meet him in the course of his public duties.[9] The study of "dialectic," on the other hand, which is to go on from thirty to about thirty-five, is to concentrate the entire faculties of the student while it lasts.[10] Of the form and substance of this "dialectical" science we can only collect hints from Plato. And, firstly, as to its form. If we conceive "dialectic" as a body of scientific truth, it would be nothing less than a system of universal knowledge, in which not only the "hypothetical" principles of the mathematical and physical sciences, but those of all other branches of human inquiry, found their place and justification, and were seen to depend upon a single "unhypothetical principle." Plato was as conscious as we are that no

---

[1] 7. 533 b ; 534 b.   [2] 533 d.   [3] 531 d.   [4] 536 d.
[5] 531 e.   [6] 527 d.   [7] 533 d.   [8] 534 e.
[9] Cf. 6. 503 e ; 3. 412 e—413 e ; 7. 537 d ; 535 c.   [10] 539 d.

such universal science was in existence, but perhaps he felt more strongly than we do the importance of insisting upon its theoretical necessity, and of keeping the outlines of it before the mind. If, on the other hand, we think of the study of " dialectic " as an educational study of the true method or logic of thinking, the simplest account of it is that it is " that education which will enable the student to question and answer in the most scientific way."[1] This may seem to be a great fall from the height to which we are carried by the conception of a universal science, but this is mainly because we use oral discussion so comparatively little as a means for arriving at truth, and because our ideas of science and speculation are associated with printed books and systems, rather than with the living processes of thought which produce them. If we substitute for "the man who can question and answer in the most scientific way," "the man who can elicit, whether from his own mind or that of others, the truest thought on every subject which comes before him," we shall have a more adequate notion of what Plato meant. For if, as he conceived, truth is a system in which no part can be fully known until its connection with all other parts has been apprehended, it follows that in proportion as a man can "give and take account of" any subject, or part of a subject, he must have the system before his mind. We can therefore understand how Plato can say that "no other procedure can undertake to give a complete and methodical grasp of the essential nature of any given thing."[2] For what is the case in what is commonly called discussion? Generally we go no further with it than to produce a certain comfortable persuasion in our own minds or that of others; we appeal to no higher standard than the current opinions and desires of the public which we address;[3] we are satisfied when we have turned a smart phrase or won a verbal victory.[4] Even reasoning which aspires to be "philosophical" is often only an artificial arrangement of skilfully adjusted words, which seem to have admirable coherence, but bear no relation to facts.[5] But let us suppose a mind to which debate,

---

[1] 7. 534 e.   [2] 533 b.   [3] 533 b.
[4] 6. 499 a.   [5] 6. 498 e.

whether outward or inward, has no other object than the attainment of truth;[1] a mind bent upon arriving at and imparting conviction, and feeling that a lifetime is but a fragment in the eternity which such a work demands;[2] suppose it filled with an insatiate desire for reality,[3] which no fragment is so insignificant as to escape,[4] no objections so formidable as to deter,[5] no complexity so great as to confuse,[6] no hypothesis so ultimate as to satisfy;[7] suppose too that such a mind had been trained by many years' practice in the power of abstracting itself from the immediate presentations of time and place, so that it was able to "let go eyes and other senses, and make its way to the real truth;"[8] and suppose that there is present in it, not only the general desire for truth and the belief in the possibility of arriving at it, but also a conception, in outline only, but not therefore the less firm or definite, of the form in which the truth exists and in which it must be apprehended by the mind, a conception leading us to look everywhere for unity in multiplicity and differentiation in unity, so that while no piece of truth can be confounded with any other, no piece can be isolated from any other; and suppose, lastly, that this conception of the constitution of truth had borne fruit in an approximate systematisation of the existing sum of knowledge, a logic of truth as complete as the state of the human mind at the time admits, and that this logic had been studied and practised unremittingly for years: then we shall perhaps have some idea of what Plato intended by the true "dialectical" nature and the true "dialectical" education.

We shall probably feel that such an education must depend for its success more upon the spirit in which it is imparted and received than upon its particular form and matter. And certainly no one can be further than Plato from the idea that "dialectic" is a ready-made system of formulas to be swallowed whole by the mind. He is never tired of insisting upon the importance of choosing the right natures for the study of the

---

[1] 6. 499 a. [2] 498 d. [3] 5. 475 b-c. [4] 6. 485 b.
[5] ὥσπερ ἐν μάχῃ διὰ πάντων, κ.τ.λ., 7. 534 c.
[6] ἀπὸ τῶν ἄλλων πάντων ἀφελὼν, κ.τ.λ., 534 b. [7] 7. 533 c.
[8] 7. 537 d.

sciences, and still more for that of "dialectic." They must be, not "bastards," but "genuine" children of philosophy;[1] "sound in limb and sound in mind," well grown and developed, not one-sided "cripples."[2] They must not only be quick to learn, but must have also the qualities of intellectual retentiveness and endurance and love of work, "for hard study makes a craven of the soul much more than gymnastic; the work comes more home to it, for the soul has it all to itself, and does not share it with the body."[3] Above all, they should be of the proper age, and should have been "dyed" indelibly with the spirit of law and order, so that they may combine, what it is hard to find in combination, constancy and steadiness of character with speculative activity and aspiration.[4] Otherwise the study of dialectic will continue to bring upon philosophy the charge which is so often made against it, that it unsettles the mind and undermines morality.[5] For, as we have already heard,[6] philosophy is a double-edged instrument; the speculative spirit which demands to have its beliefs justified and its experience accounted for, may by a turn of the hand become the spirit of revolution, denying the validity of all beliefs and the reasonableness of any experience; and the same logical method which, when rightly handled, guides us through the maze of opinion and reveals the essential forms of truth, may be applied by the intellectual gladiator to show that one thing is no more true than another, and to confound real distinctions in a mist of words. The danger lies in the transition from the atmosphere of "opinion" to that of "knowledge." In the former we seem to be surrounded by a world of solid and permanent objects, each with a definite position and character of its own, with which our ideas are inseparably bound up. Our principles are materialised in particular persons and things, and these in their turn are invested with the sanctity of principles. Of the possible incongruity between an idea and its local and temporal embodiment we are as yet unconscious. But the mind has an inherent and a justifiable impulse to advance upon this state; for, as a matter of fact, truth is not

---

[1] 7. 535 c-d.   [2] 536 b.   [3] 535 b.
[4] 6. 503 c-e; cf. 7. 535 a; 539 d.   [5] 7. 537 e—539 d.   [6] 6. 497 d.

merely local or temporal, and however necessary it may be that our experience of it should be so, it will be continually, so to say, giving the lie to that experience and breaking the limitations imposed upon it. And in this capacity which the mind possesses of rising above itself,[1] asking itself questions, feeling dissatisfaction with its own results, lies the real condition and source of progress, intellectual and moral. But the difficulty is to regulate the capacity rightly, to awaken it at the right moment, and to exercise it in the right method. The power of logical manipulation in clever people is often far in advance of the strength of their character. The first sense of command over logical formulas, not unlike that of command over literary expression, is apt to upset the balance of the mind, which feels as if it had the world at its command, because it can set it up and knock it down again in syllogisms. Many of us must have observed, as Plato had done, " that schoolboys, when they get their first taste of logic, make free with it as if it were a game ; they are for ever using it to contradict people, and in imitation of those who confute them they go and confute others, as pleased as puppies to worry and tear every one who comes in their way."[2] But there is a more serious danger than that arising from the mere delight in the exercise of a new accomplishment. The " flattering "[3] voice of pleasure is always encouraging the intellect to find a flaw in the beliefs and institutions in which we have been brought up. The " questioning spirit"[4] comes to us and asks " What is honour ?" " What is justice ?" We answer by pointing to this and that belief, this and that course of action, according to what we have been taught. But logic has no difficulty in confuting us, in showing that this particular belief or action is in itself " no more right than wrong;"[5] for the particularity of the belief or the act is just what is unessential to their moral quality, as the particular colour or size is unessential to the mathematical quality of a triangle. It is only as " partaking in " or " imaging " something which cannot be apprehended in the limits of sensible experience, that the particular phenomenon has a moral value.

---

[1] 7. 524 a-b.   [2] 7. 539 b.   [3] 7. 538 d.
[4] 538 d.   [5] 538 e ; cf. 5. 479 a-b ; 7. 524 a.

But if the mind has not yet realised this,[1] if it has only realised the relativity of the particular form of presentation, it will probably identify the unessential and phenomenal conditions with this essential reality, and in ceasing to believe in them will cease to believe in anything at all. Against such a tragic result, which brings discredit on philosophy and turns into enemies of society men capable of being its saviours, Plato would guard by putting off real philosophical study till thirty, restricting it as far as possible to those characters which combine the requisite moral constancy with the requisite speculative interest and ability, and preparing for it by a long and severe discipline both in intellectual and practical work. In other words, he would not have " the question " asked until the mind is already on the way to answer it, or the " reason why " given until it merely means the throwing of a stronger light upon truth already seen. " Dialectic " should " destroy hypotheses,"[2] but only " in order to establish them ;" it should lead the mind to see through empirical facts, but not into a darkness or vacuum, only into a wider vista of clearer truth.[3]

A systematic study of philosophy, in the spirit and under the conditions suggested by Plato, is as remote from the modern theory and practice of education as a systematic employment of the arts. His account of what actually took place in his time might be applied with slight modifications to our own : " those who study philosophy at all, do it in this way : when they are just emerged from boyhood, in the intervals of business and money-making, they go into the most difficult part of the subject, I mean logic, and then they leave it ; I am speaking of those who become the greatest proficients ; and in after years, if they ever accept an invitation to listen to a philosophical discussion, they are quite proud of themselves, for they look upon it as a mere pastime ; and as they draw towards old age, their light goes out, all but that of a very few, and is never kindled again."[4] Philosophy in modern England has not even the advantage, a dubious advantage perhaps, of that conventional glory which attached to the word in the society of Plato's day, when a " philosopher " seems to have combined in himself

---

[1] τά τε ἀληθῆ μὴ εὑρίσκῃ, 7. 539 a.   [2] 7. 533 c.
[3] Cf. 7. 520 c, and 532 a.   [4] 6. 497 e—498 a.

the lofty associations of the " savant " with the social prestige of the " man of culture." It would hardly now be said of philosophy that it is " a place full of fair names and shows,"[1] into which the " escaped convicts " of other professions " are glad to take a leap." In the popular estimation, it is a cold and comfortless region, haunted mainly by the fancies of dreamers, the sneers of sceptics, and the formulas of pedants. Not, indeed, that it is looked upon with less suspicion on that account. The cry is as loud now as it was in Plato's time, that speculation unsettles and corrupts the mind of the young. And if we may retort with him that the so-called theories upon which society is so hard are often nothing but its own opinions articulately expressed,[2] and though we may not attach so much importance as he did to the love of speculative truth and the dangers of its perversion, we cannot deny that the forcible or adroit expression of what many men are dumbly feeling has in itself an incalculable power, and that not only are many honest minds needlessly perplexed by speculative writing and discussion, but that much real force of intellect and character is spoiled or frittered away by the want of method and management in the higher branches of our education. But though we may still feel the reality and presence of Plato's difficulties, we are as far as he could be from any prospect of applying his remedies. If the idea of concentrating the efforts of literary and artistic genius upon education seemed chimerical, what are we to think of the proposal that our best and ablest men should combine a severe course of scientific study with the first ten years of active life, and then give exclusive attention to logic and metaphysics for five years more ? Or, even if the proposal itself were more likely to find favour or attention, where is that co-ordination of the sciences, and, still more, where is that science of logic, which could, with any confidence, be set before an aspiring mind ? In the case of this, as of others of the most valuable ideas in the *Republic*, we are reduced to content ourselves with the crumbs which fall from the " feast of reason." In the way of its literal execution we can do hardly anything; but we might do a little towards carrying out some of its spirit. We

---

[1] 6. 495 c d.   [2] 6. 493 a.

might introduce more continuity into the curriculum of our schools and universities, trying to give the mind its natural food at the right times, and not letting it be still sprawling on the ground when it ought to be able to walk, nor asking it to climb a mountain before it can find its way about the house. The writers and supporters of our periodical literature might have more sense of the responsibility of their calling, and realise more fully that they spread truth or falsehood, as well as provide excitement or relaxation. Above all, we might convince ourselves that speculation, when it deserves the name, does not mean spinning cobwebs or playing with fireworks, but the finding of clews in the chaos of fact, and the letting in the daylight through the mist of prejudice ; and that the speculative spirit, though it may have many counterfeits, is a real element in human nature, and an element to which it owes both its most splendid achievements and its most disastrous failures. To discuss the details of any educational system, actual or possible, would be far beyond the scope of an essay, and would be especially fruitless when the position of the natural sciences in education and their relation to philosophy is still a subject of so much dispute. As long as the advocates of scientific education suppose themselves, or are supposed, to be in essential antagonism to those of a literary education, and as long as metaphysics is understood to mean a mass of exploded fancies, there can be no common ground between ourselves and Plato. His whole theory hangs upon the principle that the study of the sciences should be complementary to a previous training through literature and art, and should itself be supplemented in turn by a study of those universal logical principles to which it points, and in which its problems find solution. Amongst ourselves the educational use of science, apart from its teaching for practical application, can only be said to have just begun, and is still mostly confined to the popularisation of certain elementary truths with a view of stimulating early habits of observation and an interest in external nature. The idea of a systematic exhibition of the leading principles of the sciences, such as should not only train the mind to think, but should awaken its perception of the real nature of the world in which it lives, and " draw it gently out of the outlandish slough " in which it is half buried, is still only an idea. Nor can the existing teaching of philosophy be said to satisfy Plato's requirements any better than that of science. A not very profound knowledge of small portions of Plato and Aristotle, a smattering of the history of philosophy mainly derived from second-rate handbooks, or a familiarity with some generalised theory of evolution, represent the chief part of what we can point to as the results in this branch of education. Meantime the air teems with speculation and discussion ; questions are raised and answered in newspapers and periodicals which could hardly have been printed twenty years ago without raising an uproar; and there is no lack of those " young men of talent, able to skim the surface of everything that is said, and to draw inferences from it as to the best way of leading their lives,"[1] of whom Plato anxiously asked, " What are we to suppose that they will do ?" In the dearth of really original contemporary speculation, we seem to be driven back upon a work only less difficult than that of creation, the work of interpreting the past. The task of editing philosophical books for educational purposes requires, as much as any task, real editorial genius, and as yet it has scarcely been attempted ; nor have we any adequate collection of the most valuable parts of great philosophical writings, such as can be put into the hands of students. Perhaps, if the present interest in elementary education is ever followed by an equal interest in its higher grades, the expenditure of industry and ability upon primers and handbooks will be paralleled by an effort to make accessible to the more advanced minds of the community some of the original works which are now being made meat for the babes. We cannot expect to revive the days when truth was communicated by question and answer, though we may adopt some of their method on a humble scale ; but it is all the more important that the few men in each generation who might once have discussed philosophy in the streets of Athens or the gardens of the Academy should make the works of the great thinkers of the world not a dead letter, but a living voice, by entering into their spirit, interpreting their speech, and carrying on their thought.

---

[1] 2. 365 a.

We have been thus far considering the Platonic education in science and "dialectic" mainly in its formal aspect, and we have found in it a method for leading the soul from the stage in which its knowledge is held in the form of opinion and imagination to that in which it is held in the form of an intelligible system. But we have heard scarcely anything of the matter or substance of the education: much about the way in which it is to teach the mind to think, little of *what* it is to teach. And the question which now remains to be asked, and the answer to which puts the coping-stone to Plato's theory of education, is, What is the ultimate lesson which the human mind has got to learn, and for the sake of which all this elaborate apparatus has been put together? In the language of Plato's allegory, Where is the upper air to which the prisoners have to ascend, and what is the sun to which their eyes have to be turned? Or, in his technical phraseology, What is that unhypothetical first principle upon which the whole structure of truth depends, and to grasp which is the crowning act of knowledge? We have already seen (p. 137) briefly and by anticipation what is Plato's answer to these questions. It is "the form of the good" which is "the greatest of all studies;"[1] it is this which "comes last in the world of knowledge;"[2] it is this which is the end of the "dialectical" process,[3] the ultimate principle to which all the "hypotheses" of knowledge are to be referred.

The word "good" has so many meanings and associations in English, that it is important to be clear as to the particular sense in which its Greek equivalent was used by Plato. That sense is perhaps most simply and most clearly illustrated in the familiar expressions, "What is the good of a thing?" and "What is a thing good for?" The answers to both these questions will give us the use, purpose, or end, which the thing in question serves, and when we say a given thing is "good" in this sense, we can generally paraphrase the expression into "it does its work, or serves its purpose, well." From this sense is to be distinguished what would commonly be called the more "moral" sense of "good." It is indeed difficult to say how far the two uses have modified one another; but in the minds of

---

[1] 6. 505 a.   [2] 7. 517 b.   [3] Cf. 6. 511 b-c, and 7. 532 a-b.

most people there is a tolerably marked distinction between the sense in which they speak of "a good man" and that in which they speak of "a good horse" or "a good plough." In the former case they think primarily of a certain state of mind or character, secondarily of the end which it fulfils, or the work in which it is manifested ; in the latter, the work which the horse or plough does is the first consideration, the conditions of their doing it come second. We shall understand, not only Plato, but the whole of Greek moral philosophy, better, if we bear the second use of "good" in mind ; if we accustom ourselves to think of man as having a specific work to do, of morality as his doing that work well, of virtue or "goodness" as the quality which makes him do it well, and of "the good" as that which the work serves or realises, and in serving and realising which it is itself "good." Unfortunately the modern associations with the word "good" in this sense are somewhat narrow and mis-leading. When we ask, What is the "good" of a thing ? we are apt to think of the "good" in question as a purpose or end out-side the thing itself, to which it is made or supposed (perhaps only by ourselves) to contribute ; and it is to this perversion of a true idea that the doctrine of final causes owes much of its de-served disrepute. To conceive of a thing as good for something, or having some good, is, in the truest sense of the words, nothing more than to conceive of it as having a meaning or being intel-ligible ; for, strictly speaking, a thing of which the elements exist side by side in no connection or order whatever, or a thing which itself exists by the side of other things without standing in any expressible relation to them, is to our intelligence an inconceivable nonentity. And the moment that we mentally interpret a thing, or, in other words, understand it, we give it a reason for existing, whether that reason be a form which it assumes, a purpose which it serves, a function which it per-forms, or a substance which it is. We may protest as vigorously as we can against the utilitarian or pietistic applications of such a conception ; we may warn students of science against the dangerous tendency to anticipate nature, and to translate facts into the formulas of their own wish or fancy ; but such protests and warnings touch only the abuse, not the essence, of the conception, that the world is not an unmeaning chaos, but a something of which, however slowly and with however many mistakes, we are discovering, and not merely inventing, the significance.

It seemed necessary to make these few preliminary remarks in order to get a point of departure for considering Plato's account of "the good" in the *Republic*. That account may be treated conveniently under three heads, according as "the good" is regarded from an ethical, a logical, or a metaphysical and religious point of view. And firstly, "the good" is "that which every soul pursues, and for the sake of which it does all that it does ;"[1] it is the object in life which all men more or less feel themselves to have, but which very few clearly conceive or could clearly express ; it is that which makes everything which we do seem worth doing, and everything which we possess worth possessing ;[2] that about which no one would willingly deceive himself, but of which every one says or thinks, "this at least is something real, and this is what I really live for."[3] Theories of life apparently the most opposite imply the existence of this conception ; the man who lives for pleasure does not really live for pleasure pure and simple ;[4] he admits the distinction of "good" and "bad" pleasures, and he chooses the good ones, in other words, those which fall in with his general scheme of life, however fragmentary or dim that scheme may be. So, too, with those who live for knowledge ;[5] it is not mere intellectual insight which is their aim, but insight into something "good," something which they think worth knowing or having ; for what is all knowledge worth unless it have some relation to our life, unless it show us what is the good in our life, and in the world where it is lived ? And yet, though every one has, more or less consciously, some such ultimate object, something about which he would wish to be sure, something which makes things worth doing and having, it is here more than in any other point that the ignorance of mankind is most conspicuous. Most people "have no one mark in life at which to aim in all that they do,"[6] and are more sure about anything almost than about the real object of their desire. The

---

[1] 6. 505 e.   [2] 505 b.   [3] 505 d.
[4] 505 c.   [5] 505 b.   [6] 7. 519 c.

immediate steps which they take, the present means which they employ, seem to them much more clear than the ultimate goal to which they aspire. And this uncertainty of aim reacts upon the rest of their life; the proximate advantages which they grasp at elude them and turn out profitless, just because they have no connection, no pervading purpose, no whole in which they find a place.[1] It is the same want of unity and consistency which makes most of our moral ideas and character so vague and insecure. We talk of our principles of justice and honour, but how can we be said to understand, or even to possess, a principle or a virtue, unless we see "wherein they are good,"[2] unless we know what it is which gives them their value, unless they are not isolated fragments in a vague "sketch"[3] of life, but connected parts in a fully wrought design ? How can a man order his own life or that of others, if he has "no clear pattern in his soul"[4] to the ideal truth of which he can look for guidance ? How can he maintain existing laws or institutions, or reform them when they need it, if his acquaintance with them is the merely empirical familiarity which a blind man might have with things which he had often touched, or with a road along which he had learnt to walk straight ?[5] Such a man is only half awake;[6] the good things which he supposes himself to secure are only images and shadows of the truth; his mental grasp of them is conventional and unintelligent,[7] and is liable to be loosened by every logical objection. He can "give no account" of them to himself or others, can see no single "form" underlying their variety, but confuses what is essential in them with what is unessential, the fragment with the whole, the resemblance with the reality.

It is the perception of "the good," then, which is required to complete morality, to do away with the vagueness, the aimlessness, the blindness, the fragmentariness, of life, and to give it unity, completeness, and decision. But Plato sees in it the condition, not only of conduct, but of knowledge also. What the sun is in the world of visible objects, that he conceived " the

---

[1] 6. 505 e ; cf. 7. 534 c, οὔτε ἄλλο ἀγαθὸν οὐδέν.

[2] 6. 506 a.   [3] 6. 504 d, ὑπογραφὴν . . . τελεωτάτην ἀπεργασίαν.

[4] 6. 484 c.   [5] 6. 484 c-d ; 506 c ; cf. 493 b, χρόνου τριβῇ.

[6] 5. 476 c-d.   [7] 7. 534 c.

good " to be in the sphere of intelligence.[1] To the complete
fact of sight there are, in Plato's view, four factors necessary,
an eye capable of seeing, an object capable of being seen, light
in the eye and the object, and the sun of which the light is an
" effluence." The fact of knowledge may be analogously ana-
lysed : there must be a subject capable of knowing and an object capable of being known, there must be intelligence present
in both making the one intelligent and the other intelligible, and
there must be a source of intelligence from which it is diffused
through the twin world of subject and object, soul and being.
Such a source is " the good," which " supplies truth to the
object of knowledge, and gives to the subject the power of
knowing."[2] Nor is this all : as the sun is the condition not only
of vision and visibility, but also of birth, growth, and nurture
to visible things, so the objects of knowledge owe to " the
good," not only their truth, but also their very being and
essence.[3] And lastly, like the sun in the allegory of the cave,
" the good " is the crowning vision in the upward progress of
the soul from darkness to light ; or, speaking without metaphor,
if the soul, in the strength of the dialectical impulse, penetrates
right through the imagery of sense, and traverses the whole
chain of intelligible relations, the " end of the intelligible "[4] at
which it arrives, the " unhypothetical first principle," upon
which it sees the whole structure of knowledge to depend, is
again " the good." In Plato's mind then, the conception of
knowledge and truth, the conception of objective reality or
essence, and the conception of a systematic order or cosmos,
alike implied the conception of a " good," which cannot be
identified with any of them, but is the condition or logical
prius of them all.[5] Things are known and understood so far as
they are seen as elements in a rational order ; knowledge is the
perception of them as such, and things so perceived are truly
perceived. Again, a thing is what it is in virtue of its position
in such an order. As in the physical organism the character
of each organ depends upon its relation to the whole, and has
no existence apart from that relation ;[6] as in the larger whole

---

[1] 6. 507 b—509 b.   [2] 508 e.   [3] 509 b.   [4] 7. 532 a-b.
[5] πρεσβείᾳ καὶ δυνάμει ὑπερέχοντος, 6. 509 b.   [6] 4. 420 d.

of the state each member only preserves his true individuality so long as he takes his proper place in the organisation of labour, and loses it when he ceases to do so ;[1] so in the universal order of existence, each constituent not only is understood, but subsists, only so far as it remains true to its place in the order, and as that place is determined by the ruling principle, end, or " good," of the order, it is to this ultimately that it owes what it is. Lastly, as a life without purpose is blind, as qualities without unity and connection are sketchy and incomplete, so a system of truth without an unconditioned principle to depend on is baseless and " dreamy ;" and such an unconditioned principle Plato could only conceive in the form of an absolute end, which casts a light backward through the whole system of existence, but is itself above and beyond it. It thus becomes intelligible how he could speak of sciences so abstract as the mathematical as leading up to " the good,"[2] of geometry as "making us see the form of the good more easily,"[3] and of the study of harmony as "useful for the investigation of the beautiful and the good."[4] For, if each science deals with a particular "form" of universal being, and each "form" points to and connects with the "form" above it, and ultimately the highest "form," then even in the simple relations of number, figure, and sound, we may expect to hear the faint "prelude"[5] to the far-off "strain" of that fuller intelligence "whose voice is the harmony of the world."

From this conception of a logically implied condition or postulate of the world of knowledge, it was to Plato an easy step to the conception of a creative cause of the universe, both material and intelligible, and we are not surprised to hear the sun spoken of, not only as the "analogue," but as the " begotten child,"[6] of the good. Plato seems here to have combined the metaphysical conception which he expresses in the *Phaedo* with the more mythological ideas of the *Timaeus*. In the former dialogue,[7] the "choice of the good and the best" is represented as the essential characteristic of intelligence, and

---

[1] 4. 420 e—421 a ; cf. 3. 417 b ; 5. 466 b.   [2] 7. 532 b-c.
[3] 7. 526 e.   [4] 7. 531 c.   [5] 7. 531 d.
[6] 6. 508 c ; 7. 517 c.   [7] *Phaedo*, 99 a-c.

any one who holds that the universe is really the work of intelligence is bound to show that "it is the good and right which binds and holds it together;" for it is folly to think that we shall ever find "an Atlas" to support it "more mighty and more immortal and more sustaining" than this.   In the *Timaeus*,[1] "the maker and father of the universe," whom "it is hard to find out and impossible to declare to every one," being himself good, and therefore incapable of envy, creates the sensible world in all things as good, that is as like himself, as the conditions of sensible existence allow.   The whole material universe is thus the "image"[2] or expression to sense of an intelligible system, and though this intelligible system is sometimes spoken of as the "pattern"[3] upon which the Creator made the world, it seems to be practically absorbed in the Creator himself when, at the end of the work,[4] the visible cosmos is said to be "the image of its maker, God manifest to sense."   In the light of these passages we may interpret the account of the good in the *Republic*.   It is the final cause of the world; not that

> "far-off divine event
> To which the whole creation moves,"

but the immanent reason in things, in virtue of which each realises its own end in realising that of the whole.   It is also the eternally creative power which sustains existence; which imagination represents in [5] "picture-language" as a person making all things good, and which reason apprehends as the "unhypothetical principle" which all truth and goodness lead up to and imply.   Art, morality, and science have each something to tell of it, for it is "in a manner the cause of all that we know,"[6] whether in a more or a less perfect form.   It is foreshadowed in the child's story of the God who is perfectly good and unchangeable,[7] in the poem which presents the [8] "image of the good character" in its simplicity and integrity, in the beauty of line and melody which speak of "that beauty in which all things work and move."[9]   Or again, it is the divine beneficence

---

[1] *Timaeus*, 28 c—29 c.   [2] *Ib.* 30 c-d.   [3] *Ib.* 28 c—29 a.
[4] *Ib.* 92 b.   [5] *Ib.* 29 b-d, εἰκότας λόγους.   [6] 7. 516 c.
[7] 2. 380 b—383 a.   [8] 3. 397 d ; 401 b.   [9] *Timaeus*, 47 b-d.

which does no evil, the moral perfection in which our fragmentary virtues find their " filling up,"[1] the spirit of a world
where injustice is neither done nor suffered,[2] and which we may
look at until we become like it. Or, once more,[3] the sciences
put us on the ascent which leads to it, and surrender their
hypotheses to receive them from it again connected and established; philosophy teaches us to find the outlines and articulations of its presence under the motley confusion of appearances;[4]
and the working life of mature and educated manhood supplies
the rough material in which those who have mastered their
lesson in theory may learn to understand and work it out in
practice. For we must not forget that the fifteen years of
training in sciences and dialectic are to be followed, in Plato's
scheme, by fifteen more years of public service, " in order that
the citizen may not be behind the rest in experience;"[5] and
during all this time he is to be tested in the strength of his
mind and character, " whether he will stand being pulled about
this way and that, or will blench at all." Not till he has
" passed through this trial and shown himself foremost both in
action and in knowledge," is he to be made " to turn the eye
of his soul upward and look at the very good itself, which is
the universal source of light."[6] Then at last the world will lie
open before his mind, ordered and intelligible, connected and
pervaded by a single principle which he can trace in many
forms and combinations,[7] but can distinguish from them all.
Then the shadows and images of everyday life will acquire
their true meaning, for he will see through and over them to
the realities which they reflect.[8] The isolated and self-con-
tradictory maxims of popular morality will interpret themselves
into fragments of a single perfection, which human life suggests
though it does not realise it.[9] The separate sciences will cease
to talk " in dreams,"[10] and will point beyond themselves to the
waking vision of an absolute being. Philosophy will be, not a
cunning device of words or an occupation for a listless hour,

---

[1] 6. 504 d.
[2] 6. 500 c.
[3] 7. 533 c-d ; 517 b.
[4] 7. 534 b-c.
[5] 7. 539 e.
[6] 7. 540 a.
[7] 7. 534 c.; cf. 5. 476 a.
[8] 7. 520 c.
[9] 6. 501 b.
[10] 7. 533 c.

but the articulate language of truth which a lifetime is too short for learning. Only eternity can interpret that language fully,[1] but to understand it is the nearest approach to heaven upon earth, and to study it is true education.[2]

R. L. N.

---

[1] 6. 498 c-d.
[2] 7. 519 c, τοὺς ἐν παιδείᾳ ἑωμένους διατρίβειν . . . ἡγούμενοι ἐν μακάρων νήσοις ζῶντες ἔτι ἀπῳκίσθαι.

ARISTOTLE'S CONCEPTION OF THE STATE.

ARISTOTLE'S work on *Politics* has a twofold interest—historical and theoretical. If it does not add very materially to our knowledge of facts and events, it throws more light than any other writing, ancient or modern, on the constitutional forms and struggles of the Greek States. It is the result of the political experience of a people, reflected in the mind of one of its wisest men and reduced to theory. Aristotle wrote of a life that was going on around him, and the freshness of personal knowledge enlivens his coldest analysis. Thus, in spite of the scientific character of his theory, it is national. He does not write as though Greek civilisation were in his eyes something transitory, or a single stage in history. Though he had been tutor to Alexander, he seems unaware that the day of autonomous republics was passing, and that in the Macedonian monarchy a kind of government was arising hitherto unknown in the development of his race. On the other hand, the very fact that he stood on the confines of change gives him a peculiar advantage. His position is not midway in a political development, where the character of institutions and the meaning of movements is obscure. The strength and weakness of Greek society and of Greek civic virtue, the political structure which had protected that virtue and been upheld by it, the gradual decline of public spirit, the corruption of military aristocracy into an oligarchy of wealth at Sparta, of active free government into impotent ochlocracy at Athens, the war of classes which sprang from a social question and became a political one,—all this lay behind him. The prime of Greek life was nearly past when he wrote. What we miss in his work, what would have been of such great interest now, a description of military monarchy and of federal government, would not have touched the life which rises before our minds when we hear of Greek history. And what he *does* describe is fully developed, and therefore capable of adequate analysis.

But it is not merely our desire to understand the past which is satisfied by a treatise like the *Politics*. That which is true of the art and literature of the Greeks is only less true of their political creations. Their most intensely national products are at the same time " purely human." To apply to modern affairs conclusions drawn from Greek history is indeed hazardous, and such reasonings are often as futile theoretically as the imitations of Roman virtue in the French Revolution were practically hollow. The fate of Athenian democracy will not disclose to us the future of the American Republic, for the circumstances are radically different. But in spite of change there are permanent characteristics of social forces and of forms of government, of commerce and agriculture, wealth and poverty, true and false aristocracy, oligarchy and democracy. Not only this : among the subjects of which the *Politics* treats there is something even more permanent and universal, and that is the simple fact of political society. Let a State be the organisation of a nation or a city, it is still a State ; and what is true of its nature and objects in one case will, up to a certain point, be true of them in another and in every case. It is in the discovery of these truths and the investigation of such ideas as those of justice and right, that the primary business of philosophy in its application to politics consists ; and Aristotle is before all things a philosopher. These facts and ideas are so familiar to us that we take little account of them; they seem to us self-evident, and we prefer to deal with more concrete difficulties. But to philosophers the self-evident ceases to be so, and their effort is to know what everybody seemed to know before. Thus Aristotle makes these preliminary problems the basis of all further discussion. It would have seemed absurd to him to attempt the settlement of complex problems, when the elementary conceptions on which they depend have been subjected to no analysis ; to blame the State perhaps for overstepping its limits, when we do not know what the State is, and therefore cannot possibly tell what its limits are ; or to assert a right to share in government when we can attach no intelligible meaning to the word " right." The fault of reasoning on insufficient data has never been charged on Aristotle's *Politics;* every one knows that he founded his theory on researches into more than a hundred and fifty Greek constitutions, and that he even made a collection of the social and political usages of foreign tribes. But he is equally free from other defects more easily forgiven: he does not use criteria the value of which he has never questioned, nor try to account for one set of human phenomena in total isolation from the theory of all the rest. To him political science is founded on ethics, and ethics on psychology; and all these rest upon metaphysic and its application to nature.

In the following pages I propose to give a sketch of the views which Aristotle held on a few of these preliminary questions. In the nature of things, these questions are less affected than any others by historical changes; and an attempt to show their vital meaning through the forms of Greek thought may have an interest, although it can offer nothing to professed students of antiquity. But the differences which exist between Greek political conditions and those of our own time, and between the ideas associated with each, are so marked that they appear even in the most abstract discussions; and there are some of such importance that, unless they are constantly kept in sight, it is impossible rightly to appreciate Aristotle's views, or to separate what is essential in them from what is merely temporary. In spite of their familiarity, therefore, it will be as well to begin by recalling some of these points of difference to mind, and examining Aristotle's position in regard to them.

First of all, the Greek State was a city, not a nation. If we think of an English county with a single city and its surrounding territory, and imagine it to be independent and sovereign, we shall have more idea of one of the largest Greek States than if we compare it with a modern nation. Political life was concentrated in the capital to such an extent that the same word stands for city and State. In such a community public affairs were as much matters of every day as the municipal politics of an English town, and yet they had all the dignity of national decisions. The citizen, in a State like Athens, took part in politics personally, not through a representative; not once in four or five years, but habitually. His convictions or his catchwords were won not through the dull medium of the press, but from the mouths of practised orators. The statesmen of his time were familiar figures in his daily life. The opposite party to his own was not a vague collective name to him, but he rubbed shoulders with it in the streets. Thus political life was his occupation and acquired the intensity of a personal interest. The country and its welfare had a vivid meaning to him; he felt himself responsible for its action and directly involved in its good or evil fortune. Under these conditions, the rise and fall of a State visibly depended on the character of its citizens; its greatness was nothing but the outward sign of their energy and devotion; the failure of virtue in them acted immediately on it. Thus the bonds of reciprocal influence, which we can only believe in now, were palpable facts then; and the more direct danger of foreign attack or of civil war was seldom far distant. Hence the vital interest taken by the State in the character of its members and their education. Hence also an amount of governmental inspection and control of private affairs which, even if it suited modern ideas, would be scarcely possible in a nation. Such "interference with liberty" was then not felt to be an interference. In the best days of Greece, to participate in this rapid and ennobling public life was enough for the Greek citizen. If his country was independent and himself an active member of it, this community satisfied him too completely for him to think of " using his private house as a state"[1] or a castle. " To live as one likes,"—this is the idea of liberty which Aristotle connects first with the most primitive barbarism (*Eth.* 10. 9. 13), and then with that degraded ochlocracy which marked the decay of the free governments of Greece (179. 20; 185. 9; 216. 16).

The effects of this one difference on a political theory are incalculable. And Aristotle not only adopts the Greek idea of the State, and consequently thinks of it as a city, but he has expressly raised the question of its proper size. The discussion of this point in the account of the ideal State (101. 14 ff.) contains one or two chance remarks which throw a strong light on the Greek idea and its results. Aristotle mentions an opinion

---

[1] 73. 16. Here and throughout this Essay, where mere figures are given, they indicate the pages and lines of Bekker's small edition of the *Politics* (Berlin, 1855).

that the State or city should be large; and, while he admits
that largeness is an advantage so long as it involves no
diminution of that real energy of the State which makes it
great and not simply big, he insists that this proviso sets
definite limits to the increase of size or population. It is
essential that the State should be "easily overseen" (εὐσύνοπ-
τος, 103. 11). Just as a boat can no more be two furlongs
long than a span long, so a State can no more have 100,000
citizens than ten (*Eth.* 9. 10. 3). Such a number is possible
for a mere tribe (ἔθνος), but not for a political community.
And why not? The answer is in the highest degree characteristic. The State implies government; and the function of
the governor is to issue orders and to judge. "But if just
legal decisions are to be given, and if office is to be apportioned
to men according to merit, it is necessary for the citizens to
have a knowledge of each other's characters, since, where this
is not the case, things must needs go wrong with the appointment
of officials and the administration of the law; but it is not right to
act off-hand in either of these matters, and that is plainly what
happens where the population is over-large." In such a case,
again, it is impossible to prevent strangers from quietly obtaining the rights of citizens. And finally, who could be the one
general of such a multitude, and who, unless he had the voice
of Stentor, their one herald?[1]

A second fundamental distinction is to be found in the
social organisation of the Greek State. The political life of
Sparta or Athens rested on the basis of Slavery. The citizen-
body might trace its descent to a conquering race which had
reduced the original possessors of the country to a position of
more or less complete subjection, and lived upon their agricultural labour, as in the one case; or the slaves might be
procured through war and a slave-trade, as in the other. But
in both instances the bulk of the necessary work was performed by an unfree population, far outnumbering the select
aristocracy of free citizens. This institution and the contempt
even for free labour are the most striking proofs that the

---

[1] 102. 15 ff. In 62. 10 the size of Babylon is said to fit it for an ἔθνος
rather than a πόλις; cf. 33. 30.

Hellenic solution of social problems was inadequate; modern writers find in them the "dark side" of Greek life, or even the "blot upon their civilisation." But the latter expression at least is misleading, since it implies that such defects had no organic connection with the strength and beauty of this civilisation; whereas, in fact, the life of "leisure," devoted to politics and culture or to war, would have been impossible without them, and general conclusions drawn from Greek history which do not take them into account are inevitably vitiated.

On this point Aristotle shares the view common to his countrymen. He recommends that slaves should be kindly treated, and that good conduct on their part should be rewarded by their liberation. He does not admit that the slavery of men born to be free is justifiable, since, in his view, it is a violation of nature. But he definitely holds that there are men (apparently as a rule "barbarians") whose right and natural destination is servitude; and he adopts the institution in his ideal state. Into his analysis of slavery and his partial justification of it it is unnecessary to enter. Its chief interest is that he attempts to put the question on a moral ground, and therefore in his attempt to defend a bad cause falls into contradictions. He does not base slavery on political utility, nor fortunately has he Biblical arguments at hand which he can call religious. Its morality—and that to him was the deciding question—depends on the fact that some men are destitute of reason in the highest sense of the word; "those men who differ from others as widely as the body does from the soul, or a beast from a man (and men stand in such a relation when the use of their bodies is their function and the best thing that can be got out of them), are by nature slaves" (7. 15); and for them servitude is not merely a painful necessity, but their good. The problem is, then, to find men whose nature is of this kind, and who at the same time are capable of obeying and even anticipating orders (5. 21), of receiving rational instruction (22. 9), and of standing in the relation of friendship to their masters (*Eth.* 8. 10. 6). And this is a contradiction which cannot exist. The weakness of the position is brought out in the words which Aristotle adds to his assertion that friendship is possible between master and slave—"not as a slave, but as a man." In other words, to treat a man as a slave is to treat him as though he were not a man.

Another distinction which calls for some remark concerns religion. It would be superfluous to compare the doctrine and spirit of Christianity and Greek religion: superfluous, and perhaps misleading. For the vital differences which really exist between them are liable to be exaggerated by a statement of opposing principles, especially when it is assumed that the "ideal" morality which we describe as Christian is that by which modern Christians, for the most part, really live. But though the actual religious motives and practice of Greeks and Englishmen may be nearer to one another than we are apt to suppose, in the position of religion in the community there is a striking dissimilarity. Greek religion knew no recognised orthodox doctrine and no recognised expositor of that doctrine. A Greek had no church. Consequently one of the most fruitful sources of conflict in modern nations had no existence in Hellas. There is nothing in Greek history even analogous to the struggles of Church and Empire and Church and State, to the religious wars of Germany and France, or even to the semi-theological Great Rebellion, and in Aristotle's list of the causes of στάσις or civil discord religion is hardly mentioned. A second consequence is this, that the Greek knew little, either for good or evil, of the modern idea that the State is " profane." His religious feelings attached themselves to it. It was not merely the guardian of his property, but the source of right and goodness to him, the director of his worship and guarded by the gods he worshipped. He might not insult its gods, although within certain limits he was left to think and speak of them as he thought right. In the absence of a powerful priesthood, the natural development of the religious ideas of the people was unhampered and could pass easily into corresponding action; a vote of the Legislature might adopt a new deity into the number of those already recognised. Thus, but for the occasional influence of the Delphic oracle, we may say that to the Greek citizen his State was the moral and religious law in one.

It is easy for us to realise the defects of such a relation

and the want of truth in the religious ideas connected with
it.   But it had also a greatness of its own; and this we do not
feel so readily.   It fostered the social and political virtue of the
citizen; and in his devotion to his State, his perception of its
greatness and dignity, and the fusion of his reverence for it
with that which he felt for his gods, he possessed a spiritual
good which the modern world has known only in the scantiest
measure, and that only since the Reformation.   It is this spirit
which breathes throughout the *Politics*, the spirit which is
willing to be guided by the highest authority it knows; which
emphasises its duties to the community, and has not even a
word to signify its "rights" against it; which describes the
possession of property and the begetting of children not as the
private affair of individuals but as services to the State; [1] and
which finds in the law, not a restraint but the supremacy of
the divine element in human nature, "reason without desire."
For the rest, there is nothing specially noticeable in Aristotle's
remarks on the religious services of his ideal city.   He seems
to place this social function first in importance (108. 4).   It
is provided for from the proceeds of the state-lands (111. 28),
and performed by the oldest citizens, who are freed from the
duties of war and public life (109. 28).   It cannot be said
that Aristotle attributes to religion anything like the importance it has for us.   It is characteristic of him that though
he certainly did not believe the popular mythology, uses the
plainest language respecting it, and even thought that some of
it had been deliberately invented by rulers for political ends,[2]
he proposes no kind of change in the public worship, and
contents himself with trying to guard against the moral
dangers connected with the celebrations of some deities (128.
29).   What he would have thought of the use of this
mythology in education we can do no more than guess, for
the book which treats of that subject breaks off long before it
can be supposed to be complete.   But that his attitude was
not due to moral indifference is quite certain.   He probably
considered the common people incapable of any such exalted

---

[1] λειτουργεῖν τῇ πόλει, 126. 21, and 152. 10.   So also of government, 152. 11.
[2] *Met.* 1074 a 38.

monotheism as his own, and thought that their own creed had
the sanctity for them that in all cases belongs to the highest
form in which the truth is attainable.

It will be already apparent, lastly, that if Aristotle's views
represent Greek opinion, we must not expect to find in him our
own ideas of the individual. Roman law, with its presumption
that every one is a person and capable of being the subject of
rights ; Christianity, which asserts an identification of the
human and divine spirit capable of becoming actual in
the soul of the believer, and giving his existence an absolute
value ; the more popular caricature of this doctrine, which
places the end of this individual soul in the attainment of
perpetual private pleasure ; the romantic preference of personal
honour and loyalty to public spirit, and of purity and humility
to the social virtues ; the principles of the French Revolution
and of English liberalism,—all this lies between us and
Aristotle. It is natural to us to base our political theories on
individual liberty and rights. We look upon man as having a
nature of his own and objects of his own, independently of
society. We look upon the State as a contrivance for securing
to him the enjoyment of his liberty and the opportunity of
pursuing his ends, a contrivance which involves some limitation
of his rights and ought to involve as little as possible. Even
when reflection has shown us that there is something theoretically wrong with these ideas, we remain convinced that a
happiness or a morality which is imposed on us from without
loses half its value, and that there are spheres of our life and parts
of our inward experience into which no one ought to intrude.
And if we feel strongly our unity with others, and are willing
to admit that social and political institutions have a positive
object and not the merely negative one of protection, we
emphasise the fact that the character or happiness they are to
promote are those of individuals, and are often in danger of
falsifying our position by regarding the community and its
institutions as something separable from this individual welfare,
and a mere means to it. When we read Plato or Aristotle everything seems to be changed. The State is regarded not as a contrivance for making possible the objects of individuals, but as
a sun on which the lesser bodies of its system are absolutely

dependent, or rather as this system itself. It does not limit private existence; private existence derives its being, its welfare, and its rights from it. The community and even its institutions seem to be regarded as an end in which personal happiness has no necessary place, and to which the existence of any number of individuals is a mere means. We soon discover that the Greek philosophers held no such absurdity as this, that they regarded personal welfare in the highest sense as the sole object of the State, and that they were in far less danger than ourselves of seeking it in conquest or in wealth. But after this has been taken into account, and after we have realised that the modern citizen's patriotism and reverence for law seem to answer more to Greek ideas than to our own theories, there remains a decided difference both in fact and in feeling, a difference which appears again and again in political questions.

For a century or more before the *Politics* was written, the traditional Greek view had been called in question, and ideas had been opposed to it which strike us at once by their modern air. What is the State ? Is it something inevitably produced in the development of human nature, or an invention ? Is it a whole, the source of all freedom and morality to its members, or a contrivance of individuals, deriving its authority simply from their agreement and from enactment ? Is its object something common and equivalent to the end of human life, or is it a mere means to the attainment of the private objects of the individuals who combined to form it ? In some such way we may make explicit the questions which decide the character of Aristotle's theory. And they may be summed up in the single inquiry, started by the Sophists,—Is the State natural or conventional ?[1] If, with some of them, we hold that it is the latter, that it rests upon custom and enactment, the result seems at first sight to be that the reverence and devotion which it claims from the citizen are misplaced, and that its identifica-

---

[1] φύσει or νόμῳ. It is impossible to render νόμος by a single word, as it means both enactment and custom. The *Gorgias* and the first two books of the *Republic* contain full illustrations of the Sophistic views referred to.

tion with the moral law is absurd. Yet it is clearly dependent on man's will and intelligence, and neither fixed nor natural as the stars are. If then it is still to be regarded as an absolute moral power, and not the product of fear or force, we must find some way of reconciling this absoluteness with a recognition of the action of man's will in law or custom. Thus we shall find that Aristotle's position towards the question practically amounts to a denial of the antithesis between φύσις and νόμος, and an assertion that the State is at once due to man's will and the necessary or "natural" expression of his progress. This result Aristotle reaches not by a refutation of opposing theories, but by his own analysis and interpretation of facts. And the first question, on which all others depend, is : What does the fact of political community mean ? What is the State ?[1]

"Since all communities or associations are formed for the sake of some good, this must be especially true of that community which is the highest and includes all the rest, and it

[1] We use the word State in at least two different senses, and to prevent misapprehension it may be as well to define shortly the meaning attached to it in these pages. By State we seem to mean (1) such a community as possesses not only a social but also a political organisation, or, in the widest sense, a government. As a State the body politic is not merely a collection of individuals or classes, but is itself an individual or person ; as is especially evident in its relations with other States, and in the existence of a monarch or president. In the case of modern States, most of which are already founded upon nationality, the word "nation" expresses this idea ; and language which may seem overstrained when applied to the State sounds more natural if we substitute "nation." That word, however, is inappropriate to Greek politics ; and even if it were not it does not express clearly the fact that society has a political organisation : it is sometimes true to say "the nation does or wills" this or that, when it would not be true to say this of the State. It is in this first sense that I commonly use the expression State. But (2) as this expression lays stress on the organisation of the community in *government*, we come to use it as equivalent to government. Thus a single function of the State gets the name of the whole, and acquires a false isolation. Accordingly when language used of the State is understood to apply to the government, it becomes absurd, unless indeed the government is regarded as representing the State and, for the time being, equivalent to it. In such discussions as those on the end of the State, then, it is important to bear in mind that the State is distinct, on the one hand, from *government*, since it is the unity of which government is a single function, and that it is distinct, on the other hand, from *society*, because it is this unity as it expresses itself in political organisation and, through the fact of this organisation, acts as a person.

will clearly have for its object the highest and most commanding good. This community is the State." With some such
words the treatise opens.   Their simplicity conceals the extent
to which they define Aristotle's position, yet when they are
admitted some of the most vexed questions are settled beforehand.   In accordance with his fundamental idea that everything is defined by the end it is destined to attain, they lay it
down that there is a definite object for which the State exists;
that this object is not something accidental, suggested by the
chance desires of individuals; and that it is not the merely
relative end of making possible the attainment of other ends;
but that the State is the highest of human associations,
and, instead of being one among others, includes in itself all
other associations; and that, as the good at which it aims includes the subordinate objects of desire arrived at by the subordinate communities, this good is nothing short of the final
object of human life, the end which alone gives value to all
lesser ends and has no end beyond it.

Whatever this chief good which makes life worth living
may be, it is the end of *man* and not of an abstraction such as
the State is sometimes thought to be.   In other words, it is the
end of the citizens who compose the community; for the good
of the State and that of the individual are, according to
Aristotle, precisely the same, although, when we regard this
good in the first way, it has a greater perfection and grandeur
(*Eth.* 1. 2. 8; cf. 93-96).   But many men pursue a false end;
they give their lives to objects unworthy of a man, such as
mere pleasure, or to objects like wealth, which, though they are
really desirable, are so only as means to a good beyond them.
In the same way there are States which pursue unworthy aims,
and Aristotle finds opinions prevalent which either tacitly or
openly assign to the State ends which are really beneath it.
His opposition to these views brings out his own more distinctly.

There are, for example, certain oligarchic and democratic
arguments which assume that the possession of wealth and free
birth, respectively, forms such a contribution to the purposes of
the State as ought in justice to be rewarded by political privileges.   But these arguments, as Aristotle points out, really pre-

suppose that the end of the State is wealth or free birth, positions which he cannot for a moment admit. Not that these elements of life are without importance for the political community; they may even be means necessary to its welfare, but they do not on that account constitute its essence or end. The same is true of other necessary conditions. The State is not a defensive alliance, concluded by individuals who wish to pursue their various objects in security from hostile attacks. Nor is it a device they have adopted for facilitating trade with one another, and insuring themselves against force or fraud. If it were, its object would be (to borrow modern language) merely the protection of person and property; " the law," in Aristotle's own language, " would be a contract and, as Lycophron the Sophist says, a pledge of lawful dealing between man and man;" and two different nations which had formed a defensive alliance, and whose citizens, when their trading led to disputes, could sue and be sued in the courts of either State alike, would only be considered separate States because their territories happened to be distinct. But even if this difficulty were overcome, and to communion in all these points were added the right of legal intermarriage and the existence of societies for holding common festivals and joining in common amusements, the resulting association would still fall short of being " political." " All this must be there, if there is to be a State; but even if all this is there, there is not yet a State." For the members of the society would not only lack the single government which is essential to a State, but they would not necessarily have any share in that which alone gives a value to these subordinate bonds of union, the final end of human life (72. 4—74. 7).

What, then, is this final end or chief good, the pursuit of which and a common share in which is the essence of the State? What additional bond would make this imaginary society political? Aristotle has answered this question in the concrete in the passage before us. This society is a community in mere " living;" and a State is a community in " good living." These associates do not trouble themselves about each other's moral character or wellbeing; and the State aims at nothing short of that. The law to them is a mere contract, protecting their persons and property; but the real law, the law of the State,

aims at making the citizens good and just men. " Good living"
(3. 9; 72. 14), " noble actions" (74. 1), a " perfect and self-sufficing
life,"[1] " well-being " or happiness,—these are all various names
for the chief good of man. The full discussion of it is the
subject of the *Ethics;* and we have to do with it here only so far
as is necessary to bring out the positive character of the end at
which the State is said to aim. It is the full and harmonious
development of human nature in the citizen, or, in other words,
the unimpeded activity of his moral and intellectual " excellence" or virtue. In the freedom of this activity from
hindrances is implied a certain amount of " prosperity" or of
" external goods." But the goods of fortune are not goods at
all except to the man who can use them aright, and therefore
the essence of his wellbeing lies in the activity itself, or in his
character, not in what he has, but in what he is. The virtues
or excellences in which his true nature is developed are naturally
manifold; but in Aristotle's view they fall into two main
groups. The soul feels and desires; it thinks and it rules its
emotions. In so far as its desires are moulded by reason into
harmonious and controlled activities, the soul attains the
" moral" virtues in the narrower sense of the word; in the
employment of reason itself it reaches what Aristotle calls the
intellectual virtues. In both it feels that pleasure which
accompanies the free exercise of a function. That all these
functions are equally ends in themselves, Aristotle, of course,
no more believes than any one else : there is a higher and lower
in them, and a greater and less desirability in men's lives,
according as they develop one kind of excellence or another.
It is when the care and the necessary incompleteness of the
active citizen life are laid aside, and a man attains to speculative

---

[1] 73. 25 ff. ζωῆς τελείας καὶ αὐτάρκους. One idea connected with the latter
word is that of completeness. The chief good must lie in a life which leaves no
want of man unsatisfied, whether these wants be external or spiritual, a life in
which man's self (αὐτός) is fully realised, and which therefore attains his final
end (τέλος). " Self-sufficience " has already a meaning of its own in English,
and in many ways " freedom" seems to answer best to αὐτάρκεια : freedom
not in a merely negative sense, but in that in which it is said that the truth
makes men free ; or, as by Carlyle, that the object of all religion is to make
man free ; or, as by Hegel, that the idea of mind and the end of history is
freedom.

insight into the reason of the world, that the divine element in him approaches nearest to its source, and he touches that highest blessedness which all great philosophers, as well as religious men, have found in union with God. That a whole life of such activity and joy is more than human, and that it can be known only in moments, is no reason for falling back on Philistinism. " We ought not to listen to those who tell us that, since we are men, our thoughts should be those of men, and since we are mortal they should be mortal ; but, so far as in us lies, we ought to rid ourselves of our mortality and do all we can to live in accord with that which is noblest in us; for though in bulk it be a little thing, in power and preciousness it far surpasses all things" (*Eth.* 10. 7. 8). A life of such happy moral excellence and active " contemplation " is what Aristotle calls " good living." To attain and further this is the end of the State. This itself, community in this, *is* the State.

An inseparable connection of this kind between political society and man's chief good leaves only one possible answer to the question, Is the State natural or conventional ? It is man's destination, that in which and through which his end is realised. It is therefore " natural" in Aristotle's use of the word, at least in so far as man is concerned ; and if man's end is also an end in the system of the world, the State will be natural in a still further sense. The meaning of these ideas will be clearer if we first consider the steps by which man reaches the stage of political society, and thereby advances towards the goal of his progress. Aristotle's account of the origin of the State (2. 1—3. 9) sounds very meagre at the present time ; but, besides its historical interest, it contains a further refutation of the view that the relations which connect men with each other are accidental bonds of their own contriving. It destroys beforehand the various theories which found society on an explicit or implicit agreement.

The beginnings of the State, the final community, are to be sought in the most primitive forms of association. These are the unions, Aristotle tells us, of those " who cannot exist without one another;" man and woman, master and slave. Man and woman come together not from any rational resolve, but because in them, as in the other animals and in plants, there is a natural desire to reproduce themselves. Master and slave are united by the desire for security; the master being one whose superior intelligence enables him to foresee the future and fits him for rule, whereas the slave is naturally adapted for simple obedience, because he is only capable of carrying out the orders given him. Thus, we may say, he is a body of which his master is the soul; and owing to this natural division of functions the relation of slavery is for the interest of both parties.[1] It is of these two associations that the household or *family* consists; and Hesiod's verse, " first of all a house and a wife and an ox to plough " is true, since to the poor man the ox stands in stead of a servant. Thus the origin of the State is to be looked for in the Family. But there is an intermediate step between them—the stage of the *village*. The village consists of several families. Whether it is formed by the aggregation of independent households or by the expansion of a single one, Aristotle does not tell us; but the latter view seems to be favoured by the words, " it seems most naturally to be an offshoot or colony ($\dot{a}\pi o\iota\kappa\acute{\iota}a$) of the family ($o\dot{\iota}\kappa\acute{\iota}a$), and its members, being the sons and sons' sons [of the family], are called men of the same milk ($\dot{o}\mu o\gamma\acute{a}\lambda a\kappa\tau\epsilon\varsigma$)." In these first beginnings Aristotle finds the explanation of two interesting facts. They show us why the earliest form of political government, like the government of tribes not yet political, is monarchical; for the village from which the State springs is governed by its oldest member. And this explains why the same form of government is attributed to the gods; " for men imagine in their own likeness not only the shapes, but also the mode of life of the gods." Beyond this scanty notice, we have hardly any reference to the village in Aristotle's work. We do not know whether he connected it as a stage in the growth of society with the formation of the $\gamma\acute{\epsilon}\nu o\varsigma$ or clan, though the passage quoted above seems to make this probable; and there is a further one in which he speaks of the State first as a " a community of families and clans," and immediately afterwards as a " community of clans and villages " (73. 24 ff.). However this may be, and in whatever way he

---

[1] Later on (68. 20), though it is reiterated that " in reality the interests of the natural master and slave are identical," we are told that the master seeks properly his own good, and only accidentally that of the slave.

may have imagined the transition from village to city, he mentions no further stage between them. With the union of several villages we have the State.

Thus the individuals who became citizens of a State had already been members in two previous forms of community, each of which involved a definite organisation, and, what is more, a relation of government. And in the same way the son of a citizen has his individuality circumscribed or developed by his position not only in the city, but also in these subordinate spheres, which both preceded the State and continue to exist in it.[1] But this is not all. If we look closer, we shall see a deeper connection between the various stages. Each is a preparation for the next; each is produced by the effort of human nature to realise itself; it is because of the failure of each to satisfy this desire fully that a new form is created. And this process cannot cease until that kind of association is reached which gives man the attainment of his true end. Thus the two relations which compose the family are due to the necessity of mere existence; they are formed by those who simply cannot do without each other; and it is obvious that neither propagation nor mere preservation, which are their ends, is any complete realisation of human nature. Again, the end for which the family exists is defined as the satisfaction of daily wants. With the village a further advance is made; the needs which it aims at providing for are more than those of the day. But it is only in the State that the " limit of perfect self-sufficiency" is attained.[2] And if in this passage the imperfection of the lower stages is placed mainly in their failure to reach αὐταρκεία, and we are inclined to regard this αὐταρκεία as equivalent merely to a complete satisfaction of merely external wants, Aristotle makes his

---

[1] It should be noticed, accordingly, that what is said of the family, as a community *preceding* the State, is not intended to be a satisfactory account of it as a *part* of the State. When the State has come into being, its nature and object must affect its constituent elements ; and therefore Aristotle postpones the full discussion of the family until he has examined the political whole with reference to which its relations and education must be arranged (22, 12. ff.).

[2] In *Eth.* 8. 9. 5 the State is distinguished from other communities by its aiming at good " for the *whole* of life," which makes the series of the *Politics* complete.

meaning clear by at once adding—" and though the State comes into existence for the sake of mere life, it exists for the sake of good life." For man's end is not reached until his " wellbeing" or "good life" is reached ; and it is this which drives him on from stage to stage, and is both the aim and the cause of the whole process of his development.

This process, therefore, and most of all its completion, the State, is *natural*. To say that the State secures or is the end of man is with Aristotle not a *proof* that it is natural : it is simply equivalent to describing it as his nature. For the realisation of the nature of anything is its end : that which a thing is when its process of growth is complete, is its nature (3. 11). It is this that defines a thing, or is its formal cause or essence. It is this also that causes its existence, developing it from a merely potential condition to its full actuality. Thus if Aristotle's is a doctrine of final causes, it is not so in the ordinary sense. The final cause is not one imposed on the object from without, an end to which the object is a mere means ; it consists in the completed nature of the object itself. In so far as the given thing is " actual," it is equivalent to its final cause; in so far as it is only partially realised, its final cause or end is immanent in it and moves it to its perfection. Thus the final cause of man is realised when his "nature," in the sense of his mere potentiality, is developed into his " nature," in the sense of his end or good. His final cause is to be himself. As a child he is only potentially what he should be or is destined to be ; and therefore he grows. And so, as a master, a husband, a father, a member of a village, his possibilities are still in various degrees latent, only partially brought into life. It is only in the State that they come into full play, and therefore the State is " natural " to him.

And this, which is the law of man's being, is the law of the whole world. Throughout the universe this process of the realisation of ends is going on ; and, what is more, these ends or " natures " are not all of equal value, but form a series of grades of excellence. Thus a lower stage of existence is not merely " for its own sake," but it is also a step to the next highest ; and in this sense it is " for the sake of " another, and a means to it. Thus, we may say, to Aristotle all nature is a striving towards its highest form, and what we have seen in the development of man is true on this wider field. One principle, in its impulse to realise itself, produces those lower forms which are the necessary foundation for the higher, and passes beyond them to a less inadequate development, approaching more and more nearly to the divine actuality in which no imperfection remains. That man attains only for moments to some likeness of this divine perfection we have already seen ; but that he does so even for moments, and for a longer time can produce those activities of the moral life which are the victory of the divine element in him over his lower nature, is enough to place him at the head of earthly things. In him— not as a vegetable nor as an animal, but in so far as his true nature, his better self, is active—the highest existence of which the earth is capable is brought into being. In this sense the whole inorganic, vegetable, and animal kingdoms may be said to exist for his sake. And in this final and highest sense the State is natural, and man by nature a " political animal."

Such, in the barest outline, is Aristotle's answer to the Sophistic question. In substance it might almost be expressed by that startling formula of a modern philosopher, that the object of history is the State. This is not the place to criticise it ; but, in common with most other metaphysical theories of politics, it is easily misapprehended. Such theories are often accused of annihilating man's will before a spiritual fatality. It is true that Aristotle's ideas lose all their meaning if we suppose that human action is perfectly capricious, or that it is destitute of an " end," or that this end stands in no relation to the order of things. But they are not inconsistent with any sober notion of freedom. When Aristotle said that the State was by nature, he was not denying that it is due to human thoughts and resolutions, any more than Mr. Carlyle, when he speaks of an improvement in human affairs as an approach to obeying Nature, means that man would be perfect if he were law-abiding like a stone. To hold that there is within certain limits of deviation a fixed development of human nature—and is not so much as this implied in our calling one change a development or progress, and another the opposite ?—is not to hold that this development takes place in as involuntary a manner as does a flower's. And it is those very actions which most further this definite progress that are most free; since that which acts in them is in the fullest sense ourself, and not a distorted fraction of it. But just because they are not assertions of our separate existence, we are apt to speak of such actions as *least* our own. The same apparent contradiction meets us elsewhere. In the creations of art, or in the experience of religion, that which is the most perfect realisation of man's higher self abolishes this separate feeling; and so it is with moral action and its concrete products. Thus when we wish to express the freedom of such creations or experiences from our lower selves, or to contrast their absoluteness with the results of our shifting desires, we are apt to use language which takes no notice of the share our will has had in them. It is not the poet who creates, but an inspiration of which he is the mere vehicle; it is not I who act but Christ that dwelleth in me; and the State or justice are due to nature and not to enactment. When language of this kind is used, there is a temptation to fall under its influence, and to separate what we know to be really identical. It is such a separation that is expressed in the antithesis of φύσις and νόμος, or in the modern opposition of moral necessity to free-will. But the Greek rose superior to that antithesis; though he might be puzzled when it was put clearly before him, he felt no incompatibility between the origin of the law of his State in the human will and its absolute validity. And Aristotle is only giving a theoretical justification of the position which he could not justify for himself.[1]

It is perhaps hardly necessary to notice another possible misconception. If Aristotle is not abolishing man's will before the moral order of the world, still less does he mean by the "nature" which produces the State what we mean when we contrast the natural and the spiritual. It is true that he not unfrequently uses "nature" in this lower sense, as in the *Ethics*, where he is showing that virtue does not come by nature but through a discipline of the will (*Eth.* 2. 1). In this

---

[1] On the conception of Law compare K. F. Hermann, *Ueber Gesetz Gesetzgebung und gesetzgebende Gewalt im griechischen Alterthume.*

sense those elements of man's being which he shares with the other animals are more natural than his reason and rational desires. In this sense, again, man is by nature "rather a pairing animal than a political one" (*Eth.* 8. 12. 7). And the double use of the word may be charged with some of Aristotle's prejudices in questions of political economy. But in the doctrine before us nature has exactly the opposite meaning, and that which is most natural in the lower sense is furthest removed from that nature which is man's end. On the other hand, there is an essential connection between the two; and that connection is teleological. To Aristotle the higher is not so much the result of the lower, as the lower is a preparation and material for the higher. It would be misleading, on his view, to say that man produced the State because he wished to satisfy certain primary needs; those primary needs and instincts are the stirring in him of that immanent end or idea which is expressed in the State. "The impulse to political society exists by nature in all men" (4. 10); but the Aristotelian view is not that man invents the State to satisfy the impulse; he has the impulse because his destination is the State. Thus when it is said that Aristotle's is the first "scientific" view of politics, this assertion may be either true or false. If it means that he considered the laws and productions of human nature to be identical with those of physical nature, it possesses no foundation. It was not in that sense he asserted the unity of the world, for he never held the strange belief that we are to form an idea of nature in abstraction from her highest product, and then to expect no difference between that highest stage and this truncated "nature." If those who propose to treat the State exactly like the objects of physical science are to find an ally in Aristotle, they must adopt the unity of nature in *his* sense; they must admit not merely that man and his works are the *result* of her lower stages, but that the lower stages are (not in a metaphor, but really) the "potency" of man, and that the evolution is determined by its end. When this is admitted, it will be found that Aristotle is by no means averse to recognising the forms or laws common to man and the lower stages of existence, and that he has little sympathy with that idea of a total breach between the two, in the maintenance of which our spiritual interests have often been supposed to be involved.

Putting metaphysical questions aside, we have now to ask, What is Aristotle's *ground* for regarding the State as man's destination and good ? " Man is by nature a political animal," he tells us ; "and he who, owing to his nature and not to ill fortune, has no State, is either morally bad or something more than a man " (3. 16). And again : " He who cannot form one of a community, or who does not need to do so because he is already sufficient to himself, is no part of a State, and is therefore either a brute beast or a god " (4. 8). Here we have two characteristics of the State noticed, both of which we have met before ; it alone can supply αὐταρκεία, and in it alone is morality possible. The reason why it is necessary for morality lies in the imperfection of man, and in the fact that the State has might. " As man in his perfection is the best of animals, so when he is separated from law and justice he is the worst of all," the " unholiest, the most savage, and the most abandoned to gluttony and lust. And justice belongs to political society " (4. 12). At the end of the *Ethics*, again, Aristotle has explained how the State is directly involved in the attainment of morality. There are three ways, he tells us, in which men attain virtue. One of these, our natural endowment, is out of our power. Another, intellectual teaching, has little or no effect except on young men of a generous temper, or those who have been schooled in experience. For those who live by their feelings, obeying the dictates of pleasure and pain, it is useless. It is only by the third means, by habituation, that the impulses which lead away from virtue can be trained, and that men can by degrees acquire that love of the good and hatred of the bad without which mere instruction avails little. For the purpose of this habituation, especially if, as is necessary, it is to be exercised throughout the whole of life, we need an authority which must unite two requisites. It must itself be an expression of reason ; and it must have the fullest powers to compel and punish. And this union of right and might Aristotle finds only in the State. But it is not only by its direct action, by its compulsory education and its moral guardianship, that the State contributes to " good living." If we examine those

virtues in the exercise of which this good living consists, we
shall find that they all imply social relations or life in community, and one of the most important, that practical wisdom
the possession of which implies the presence of the rest (*Eth.*
6. 13. 6), has its sphere not only in private life, but also in the
ordering of State-affairs: and the *Politics* adds that the virtue
of the best man, the perfect virtue, is equivalent to the virtue
of the ruler (119. 22). Thus we find that the individual who
realises his chief good or happiness is necessarily a citizen.
And the strongest expression which Aristotle has given to this
view is to be found in his statement that the individual is
posterior to the State, and a part of it.

To say that the State is prior to the individual means
primarily no more than that his end is realised in it. By
"prior" Aristotle often means not anterior in time, but prior
in idea or, as he sometimes says, in nature. Thus in idea or
in nature the end is prior to the means, and the actuality to
the potentiality. But in the order of time, or again relatively
to our knowledge, the means may, and often do, precede the
end, and the potential existence is prior to the actual. In one
sense of the word, then, the family may be said to be earlier
than the State, and in another sense the opposite is true; and
in this latter meaning Aristotle might say that the individual
is "later" than political society. In the present case, however,
this dictum has a further meaning. The State is said to precede
the individual not merely as the actual precedes the potential,
but as a whole precedes its parts. The part is itself only in
relation to the whole, has no existence outside it, and is
intelligible only in reference to it. It is therefore said to be
posterior to it; for, to take the instance of a living body, "if
the whole is destroyed, there will no longer be a foot or a hand,
except in name, and as one may call a stone foot a foot; for
everything is defined by its function" (4. 1), and with the
dissolution of the body the functions of its members have
disappeared. Such is the relation of the individual to the
State.

Language like this at once recalls the current phrase, "the
body politic," and the theories which have attempted to make
it more than a phrase. Aristotle has nowhere called the State

an organism, and doubtless he did not explicitly connect that
idea with it. But, apart from the present passage, there is a
close connection between this idea and his view that political
society is natural, and he not unfrequently employs in his
consideration of it criteria gained from the study of living
beings. The use of such criteria no doubt requires caution,
and we are sometimes told that the conception of an organism
belongs only to the physical world and becomes a mere metaphor when applied to human society. But most of the ideas
we use in describing spiritual things are derived from the
world outside us, and it is not clear that the categories " thing,"
" collection," " mechanism," and the like, are any less metaphorically used of a State than the category of life. On
the other hand, reasons are not wanting for the view that the
latter idea is at least less inadequate than the others; and, if
this is the case, what we have to do is only to distinguish
in what respects the conception of an organism must differ
when it is applied to the animal body and to the political
body. It may be interesting, considering the present prominence of this conception in English philosophy, to notice some
passages in which Aristotle seems implicitly to regard the
State as an organism, and then to ask whether his doctrine
recognises those characteristics in which it differs from living
things.

That the State, in the sense of the political community, is a
totality or composition ($\sigma\acute{\upsilon}\nu\theta\epsilon\sigma\iota\varsigma$), admits of no question. Its
unity is formed of a multiplicity of parts; it is a number of
citizens (58. 31). But there is more than one kind of composition. For example, a heap of cannon-balls is a whole made
up of parts. But here the whole is made up by the mere
addition of unit to unit: it is a collection. In such a totality
the part does not get its existence or character from its relation to the other parts and to the whole; it is the same thing
in the pile that it was out of it, and has merely had a relation
added to it. If the State were a collection of individuals of
this kind it would be absurd to say of it that it was prior to
its parts; it would be absurd to compare one of these parts
with the hand or foot, which have no existence or function
apart from the body to which they belong. A composite body

of which this can be said is not formed by the addition of
units, and not even the category of whole and parts is in strict-
ness applicable to it. Its "parts" are members; it is a unity
which expresses itself in diverse members, functions and
organs, and the connection between these members is not
mechanical but organic. Apart from the decisive language
already quoted, Aristotle insists in more than one place on the
diversity of the parts of the State. He is especially emphatic
on this head, because he considers that Plato had neglected it
and, in his desire to attain a complete unity of the whole body,
had disregarded the necessary "differentiation" of its parts.
He had wished to see the principle of the whole clearly realised
in every member, and, in Aristotle's view, had failed to perceive that this result cannot be obtained by making all the
members alike. "The State does not consist simply of a
number of men, but of men specifically different from one
another;"—these are Aristotle's words,[1] and he at once illustrates his meaning by referring to the distinction between a
State and an alliance.[2] In the latter the mere addition of a
quantity of men of the same sort is a direct good; but in the
State, a community in the functions of good life, the unity to
be attained must issue from diversity. It is not true, he insists, that mere unity is its object: if it were, the State would
not exist. For the family is, in this sense, more one than the
State, and the individual than the family.

In other passages the dissimilar parts of the State are regarded as classes of society, not as mere individuals. These
classes are formed of groups of men performing separate "functions," or "works," in the whole. In the description of the ideal
constitution these works are enumerated as the agricultural food-
providing function, the technical or mechanical, the military,
the religious, the function of property, and that of government
in its two main branches, according as the decisions arrived at

---

[1] 24. 4. The same law which prevents a *commercial* κοινωνία between two
men of the same trade (*Eth.* 5. 5. 9) is active in the political κοινωνία.

[2] It will be remembered that Aristotle, in discussing the end of the State,
distinguished it from an alliance on the ground that an alliance has no common end, and its law is a mere contract. In other words, an alliance is a
collection of homogeneous units, not a unity in diversity.

concern the common interest or the administration of justice (107 and 108). In another passage (150-152) the list is repeated with some enlargements, and it is pointed out that the reason why different species and sub-species of constitution arise is that, though all these functions or social elements are necessary to a State, the particular forms which each of them takes may vary, and, further, the varieties of each may be combined with those of the rest in different ways. To illustrate his meaning Aristotle refers to the manner in which the various kinds of animals are distinguished. There too we find certain functions which are necessary to animal life, such as those of sense, nutrition and motion; and there are special organs appropriated to them. These appear in various forms, and the varieties of one may be found in combination with those of another. There are different shapes of the mouth, for example, and various developments of the organs of motion; and not only these varieties, but the different combinations in which they are found to coexist, may be made the ground for distinguishing species and sub-species of animals.

From this differentiation of functions it immediately follows that inequality among the parts of the State is regarded not as an imperfection, still less as an injustice, but as natural and necessary. And not merely inequality, but a relation of government; "for wherever a single common whole is formed out of a number of elements, a ruler and a ruled is to be found, whether these elements are continuous," as in a physical organism, " or discrete," as in the relation of master to slave, or in a political organism; and an analogue to this relation may be found even in "compositions" not organic (6. 21). But there is a still closer correspondence between the living body and the State in this point. We soon find in reading the *Politics* that all the "parts" or members of the State are not of equal importance; that some of them, as for example the agricultural and industrial functions, are mere means or necessary conditions to others; and that only those which are ends are properly called "parts" at all. Such are obviously those which really share in the life of the whole, or realise its end; in other words, those which are organs of "good living." Accordingly the real parts of the State are, to Aristotle, the citizens alone,

who exercise the functions of government and religion, defend
the State and possess its landed property. The rest of the
population are mere means, or *sine quibus non*. If we turn
to the account of the animal body, we come upon a precisely
similar distinction. There too the whole body and each of its
organs exists for the sake of a certain function or "action"
($\pi\rho\acute{a}\xi\iota\varsigma$), but only certain parts of the body are regarded as
ends. These are distinguished as the specially "organic"
parts, and among them are counted the hand and foot, to
which at the beginning of the *Politics* Aristotle compares the
citizen of the State. To these organic or heterogeneous parts
the rest, which are homogeneous,—such as the blood, flesh,
fat, bones, and sinews—merely serve as constituents or means.
"The living body is composed of both, but the homogeneous
are for the sake of the heterogeneous."[1] And so the State is
composed both of citizens and of a labouring population; but
the one is for the sake of the other.

In Aristotle's treatment of the State as something which
has laws of its growth and health, not reversible by man's will
except within certain limits, we may trace a further likeness
to the conception of an organism. This point of view is
especially evident in his remarks, already referred to, on the
magnitude of the city. It does not depend simply on the
arrangements which the citizens choose to make, how large
their State is to be. As a natural existence the State has a
definite function, and this function can only be exercised if a
certain limit of size is preserved. It is as much subject
to this law as other things,—animals, plants, or lifeless instruments (102. 13). A departure from the ideal standard in
either direction weakens its power to perform its function,
and therefore lessens its existence.[2] A still further departure
destroys its nature altogether, so that it ceases to be a State. If
it has too small a population, it ceases to be "self-sufficing;"
and if it has too large a one, it no longer admits of order.
But self-sufficience ($a\mathring{v}\tau a\rho\kappa\epsilon\acute{\iota}a$) is its essence ; and order ($\tau\acute{a}\xi\iota\varsigma$)
is implied in its very existence as a work of nature.

---

[1] *Part. an.* ii. 1 ; cf., in particular, 646 b 10.

[2] Hence, to Aristotle, a *great* State does not mean a large one, but one
which vigorously exercises its function.

The same point of view is apparent where Aristotle is treating of the necessary equilibrium of the various elements of society. It is only within certain bounds that this equilibrium will bear disturbance. The disproportionate development of one social function is hostile to the wellbeing of the whole, and may destroy the constitution (212. 1 ff.; 201. 2). The illustration is again taken from the living body. "A body is composed of parts, and they ought to grow proportionally, that its symmetry may be preserved; otherwise it perishes;" as it certainly would, if "the foot were six feet long and the rest of the body only two spans." So it is with the State. And as again a certain kind of disproportionate growth may result in one animal form actually passing into another, so one constitution may from the same cause pass into another, and the whole nature of the State be therefore changed (197. 30). The same idea lies at the root of Aristotle's advice to those who wish to preserve either of the two principal "perverted" forms of government, oligarchy or democracy. It is the essence of these constitutions that they represent the preponderance of one social element in the State, whether it be that of the few rich or the many poor, and that this class rules not for the common good but in its own interest. Even so perverted a State has a vital principle of its own. But this principle will not bear straining too far; and Aristotle points out that the worst friends of such constitutions are those who wish to develop their characteristics to the uttermost. "Many of those things that are counted democratic destroy democracies;" and the same is true of oligarchies. The governing class cannot really get on without the opposite element which it strives to suppress, and therefore the pursuance of its main principle beyond a certain point ends in its self-annihilation. "A nose," as Aristotle drily tells us, "may depart from the ideal straightness and tend to be either aquiline or snub, and yet it may still be beautiful and have a charm for the eyes; but if an artist were to push the deviation to excess, first of all the feature would lose its due measure of size, and at last it would not look like a nose at all" (214. 26). The principle of measure or the mean (τὸ μέσον) rules the State, as it does the moral character of the individual.

We may thus reach an important conclusion. That end of the State which is described as good living or happiness is also described as the common interest or good (τὸ κοινῇ συμφέρον, 68. 9), that noble living (καλῶς ζῆν) in which each shares according to his ability. In any whole that is "prior" to its parts, in any organism, there is an identity between the general welfare and the particular welfare of each part. It is in the healthy and harmonious development of its organs or functions that the health of the whole body lies, and the interest of the State is nothing but that of its citizens. And conversely, there is no part which really has a separate interest; for its essence and good lie in its function, and this is a function of the whole body. Thus if it appears to have a private interest which is thwarted by its membership in a system and sacrificed to that system, this appearance must be considered a delusion. The disproportionate growth of a single organ, for example, is its real misfortune; for its true nature is not developed, and it injures the whole on which its own health depends. And in the same way we may say that the dependence of one member on the rest is not a sign of bondage but its real liberty, if liberty means "self-sufficiency;" and the growing independence of the parts is equivalent to the loosening of that bond which is the life of the organism and only disappears in its decay.

Such are some of the points in which Aristotle seems to find the characteristics of animal life in the body politic. It is clear that they would not justify us in calling his conception of it organic; but perhaps they amount to something more than analogies, and they give a fuller meaning to his description of the State as a natural existence with laws of its own. If, however, we are to retain this idea at all, it is essential to realise how vitally a political organism differs from a merely physical one; and a few words will suffice to show that Aristotle's view does not obscure the distinction between the two.[1]

---

[1] In *Mot. an.* 703 a 29 there is an interesting comparison of the animal body to a State, and the fact that the "order" of the latter is due to the human will is pointed out. But it is doubtful whether this treatise is genuine.

"That man is a political animal in a higher sense than the bee or any other gregarious creature, is clear. For nature, as we say, makes nothing in vain; and man is the only living thing that possesses rational speech (λόγος). A mere voice (φωνή) serves to signify pleasure and pain, and therefore it is possessed by the other animals as well as by man; for their nature goes so far that they feel pain and pleasure, and signify these feelings to each other. But language has for its office to express what is helpful and hurtful, and therefore also what is right and wrong (τὸ δίκαιον καὶ τὸ ἄδικον). For this is peculiar to man, as compared with the other animals, that he alone has a perception of good and evil and of right and wrong. And it is community in good and right that constitutes a family and a State" (3. 20). Thus, in modern language, the State is more than an organism; it is a moral organism. The soul of man is not a mere principle of growth and nutrition, like that of plants. Its activity is not confined to sense and the desires which depend on sense, like that of the lower animals. It is intelligence and rational will. And therefore man not only has a law of his life, but is capable of knowing the law of his life: he not only knows it, but is capable of living by it. In him therefore appears the separation of what is and what might be, of good and evil, of right and wrong; in a word, morality. And this morality is not something which belongs to each man's private life. It is community in it which constitutes the State or political organism. But the consciousness of this organism, and therefore its morality, can exist nowhere but in its members. The principle of the whole is present in the parts. Its reason and morality are theirs; its end is theirs; it is in them that it feels, suffers and enjoys. And if the converse is not true, if the end of any particular member seems to be something else than the end of the whole, it is because this single function attempts to deny the relation in which it stands, and must stand, to the whole.

From what has been already said, it will be evident that Aristotle is in no danger of obliterating these distinctions. The citizen is related to the State as the hand is to the whole body. But the end of the State is happiness or noble action; the State itself is community in this good life, or in the right

which language only can express. If the whole then is
rational and moral, its highest functions must be rational and
moral. But these highest functions are those of its members; and for that very reason those of its parts which fulfil
no such function are not, properly speaking, members of it,
but merely necessary conditions of its life. For the same
reason, however, its true " parts " necessarily attain their
own ends in attaining the end of the whole. "Happiness is
not a·conception like that of evenness in number. That may
be predicated of the whole number" (say 10) "without being
predicated of its component parts" (say 3 and 7); "but this
is impossible with happiness" (32. 27). On the other hand,
the welfare of the citizen is not merely bound up with that
of the whole, but he is capable of realising this, and of either
devoting himself to the State or making his supposed private
advantage his end. His relation to the State is not, like that of
the hand to the body, one simply of *fact*, but also one of *duty*.
"No citizen ought to think that he is his own, but all that
they are the State's" (130. 15). And Aristotle does not suppose that, left. to himself, a man is likely to identify his good
with that of the whole organism in the manner of a healthy
animal organ. It is just because he is a

> "fool whose sense
> No more can feel but his own wringing,"

that the education of the State and the arm of the law are
required, to convert him from a life "according to passion" to
one of true citizenship and participation in happiness.

The functions of the body politic, then, are moral functions;
and the members which exercise these functions are consequently moral agents. It must be remembered, lastly, that the
virtue or happiness which is the end of State and citizen alike,
is not something distinct from the direct duties of citizenship,
but that these duties themselves play a large part in it. A
man is not a good citizen in order that he may gain something
by it. Happiness is the exercise of "virtue." In being brave
and self-controlled and liberal a man is attaining happiness,
and at the same time showing the virtues of citizenship. But
there are excellencies of a more commanding kind than these.

As we have already seen, the crowning talent of moral wisdom, with the possession of which all the virtues are given, has its sphere no less in affairs of State than in a man's own household. It is the virtue of government, the possession of which makes a " good citizen " and a "good man " equivalent terms, while the citizen-virtues of obedience would by themselves not amount to perfect goodness. The citizen must be free from the mere wants of life that he may have time for politics no less than for philosophy; for those are the two main forms of happiness. So far then from the growth or action of the political organism being merely natural, they are to be consciously guided by the most developed character and wisdom. It is as though a plant should be aware of the conditions on which its perfect growth depends, and, making this perfect growth its object, should consciously attempt to realise those conditions. Whether this conscious guidance is a characteristic of the State which renders the conception of an organism radically inapplicable to it, we need not stop to dispute. It certainly is at first sight more in accordance with our common view of government as a mechanism ; and to Aristotle it suggests the metaphor of the "ship of State" rather than that of the "body politic." He compares the citizens to sailors (63. 9), and (by implication) the citizen as ruler to the steersman (68. 31). And there is a psychological fitness in the comparison. For reason, which acts in government, is not in his view connected with the human organism in the same way as the inferior "faculties ;" and in the case of this psychical "part," he would have answered in the affirmative the question raised in *de Anima* (2. 1. 11), whether the soul is related to the body as " a sailor to his boat."

In any great political theory the comprehension of one main idea makes the rest comparatively obvious. The remaining conclusions on which our space allows us to touch, follow naturally from the general ideas already sketched, and will serve to give them a more substantial shape. With this purpose we may rapidly review Aristotle's teaching on the subjects of citizenship, State-education, the various forms of government, the meaning of political justice and political rights.

Aristotle's view of the nature of citizenship has been already indicated; but it can hardly fail to be misunderstood unless we take into account his judgment as to the political position of the labouring classes. From the conception of the State two main results directly follow: first, that citizenship can mean nothing less than the right or duty of exercising political functions; and, secondly, that this exercise is, in the true State, the activity of those higher virtues which make the good citizen identical with the good man. For practical purposes it may be, though it is not always, true to say that a citizen is one whose father and mother were both citizens. But this is a mere external mark, and does not tell us in what citizenship consists. In what does it consist? Not in the mere possession of civil rights. Just as the State is not merely a community in territory or in the legal protection of person and property, so a citizen does not mean one who resides in a certain city and can be sued in its law-courts. These are not functions of the State, and do not involve participation in its end. If the citizen is to be really a part of the State, he must live its life; and that in the concrete means that he must govern. Thus citizenship may be defined as "ruling and being ruled," and a citizen as one who shares, or has the right to share, in government, deliberative, executive and judicial. In so doing he uses not only the virtues of obedience, not only the common moral virtues, but also the excellencies of moral wisdom and command. His life is pre-eminently one of ἀρετή.

But the brain cannot think unless the heart beats; and society cannot exert its highest powers when its lowest needs are unsatisfied. The whole must exist before it can exist well; and it cannot exist well if the organs whose office is to think have to attend to mere living. A life of culture and political ἀρετή implies freedom in him who lives it from the necessity of looking after these lower wants (66. 22). It implies what Aristotle calls "leisure," and this leisure must be supported on some one's labour. The life of labour is a mere means to the higher life. It is not a participation in the State-life, but a condition of it, a *sine qua non.* It does not do what is noble, but provides what is necessary. It might produce a joint-stock company, but not a State. It creates mere material prosperity, and "no class has a share in the State which is not a producer of virtue" (109. 21).

The result of this hard and fast distinction is obvious. So far as ἀρετή is concerned, it makes no great difference whether the labourer is a slave or a free man. "Those who provide necessaries for an individual are slaves, and those who provide them for society are handicraftsmen and day-labourers" (66. 24 ; cf. 21. 32). And the labouring class includes not only peasants, but all βάναυσοι, a designation which covers artisans, professional singers and artists, and no doubt all persons engaged in trade. It is against βαναυσία that the reproach of ignobleness is especially directed ; and the word, like our "mechanical," has an ethical significance. "That," says Aristotle, "must be considered a mechanical practice or art or subject of study, which makes the body or the soul or the intellect of free men useless for the activities of virtue" (131. 7). *Βαναυσία* deforms the body (18. 8), and renders it unfit for military and political duties (140. 15). It accustoms a man's mind to low ideas, and absorbs him in the pursuit of the mere means of life. The βάναυσος seeks the satisfaction of other people's wishes, and not the improvement of his own character; and this is the mark of slavery. It is for this reason that the occupation of the professional musician is considered unworthy of a man (136. 18). He treats his art "technically" or professionally, practises "amazing and brilliant pieces" (140. 19), has to gratify an audience often of vulgar tastes, and therefore practises a kind of day-labour (141. 25).[1] If citizenship then means essentially the practice of

---

[1] It will be remembered that in Greece not only professional performers but even original artists were considered "mechanical." It is inconceivable that Aristotle, with his high view of art, should have considered his account of βαναυσία applicable to Phidias ; but probably the following typically antique passage would not have sounded so strange to him as it does to modern ears : "If a man applies himself to servile or mechanical employments, his industry in those things is a proof of his inattention to nobler studies. No young man of noble birth or liberal sentiments, from seeing the Jupiter at Pisa, would desire to be Phidias, or, from the sight of the Juno at Argos, to be Polycletus ; or Anacreon, or Philemon, or Archilochus, though delighted with their poems."—Plutarch's *Life of Pericles* (Langhorne's translation).

ἀρετή, there can be no question for Aristotle as to the admission of the βάναυσοι to political rights. In such perverted constitutions as "democracy" they might find a place, as they actually did; for the principle of that constitution is not the true principle of the State. And in an oligarchy, the "perversion" which substitutes wealth for political virtue, though a day-labourer could hardly attain the property-qualification necessary for citizenship, a βάναυσος might (67. 2). Accordingly at Thebes, we are told, a law was in force that a man could not take part in government until ten years after his retirement from the market. But in any true State, in any constitution in which "the honours of office go by excellence or merit," it is impossible that the βάναυσος should be a citizen. For his life is "ignoble and opposed to ἀρετή" (66. 31; 108. 32).

Aristotle's view is only the reproduction of current Greek ideas. At first sight it is so repulsive to us that we are tempted to condemn it wholesale. But it should be observed that it is due not only to a contempt of labour connected with the institution of slavery, but also to the height of the ideal with which the labouring life is compared. In this point it contrasts favourably with the modern upper-class sentiment which it seems at first to resemble. And it is worth while to ask where its falsity lies.

If we grant Aristotle's premises, no fault can be found with his exclusion of the labouring classes from political rights : their admission would have been a mere inconsistency. It is simply true that, as a body, they could not have possessed the qualities he demands in the citizen, even if they had found the leisure for military, political, and judicial duties. We have given up the idea of professedly apportioning shares in government according to merit, virtue, or culture (words which Aristotle uses interchangeably in this connection) ; all that we hope for is that, through a political machinery which assigns no superior rights to these qualities, they may yet find their way to the helm. But if we did accept Aristotle's principle in the matter, we should certainly arrive at his conclusion, and should wish to exclude from the suffrage the great majority of those who possess it. Nor again is the idea that this culture depends upon lower labour false. It is a fact which, however painful, cannot be too clearly recognised, that the existence of those excellencies in which Aristotle finds the end of life and the virtues of the citizen, rests upon a mass of mere work as its necessary condition.   And is there any modern society which can plume itself on the advances it has made in uniting these two elements, the end and the means, in the same persons or classes ?   If not, we must admit that, so far, Aristotle's view is not open to reproach.   Nor, lastly, will any honest observer deny that there is a moral βαναυσία which besets some of the occupations included under that term.

What is disputable in Aristotle's view is the too exalted idea of citizenship, an idea which, with the increase in the size of States, has ceased to be even plausible.   What is psychologically untrue is the pre-eminence given to intellect in the conception of man's end, and the hard and fast line drawn between the virtues of government and those of obedience.   What is morally repulsive is the consequent identification of the end and means of life with two separate portions of the community, and the feeling that moral lowness has anything to do with labour, as such, or with a professional occupation.   Modern civilisation, in its best aspects, tends to unite what is here separated.   The intellectual excellencies themselves have become the basis of professions.   Payment for performing the duties of government, in Greek democracy the symptom of decay, is the recognised rule of modern States, so far as administration is concerned.   Clergymen, artists, poets, authors, philosophers receive, or may receive, wages for their work, and it is not supposed that they necessarily work with a view to their wages.   We anxiously avoid even the semblance of contempt for the labouring classes ; not only out of deference to their political power, but from a conviction that there is no shame in labour.   It is felt that work, be it what it will, may be done in such a spirit that moral character may be developed by it ; and that in this character, in family affection, and in religion a happiness is attainable which contradicts the idea that in the mechanical life there can be no production of "virtue," and therefore nothing to make life worth having.   Some of our language would even imply that mere labour was the end of life, and not a means to something beyond itself ; but this piece of

cant is implicitly contradicted by efforts to educate the classes
engaged in manual work, and to put suitable "occupations of
leisure" within their power.

But it is easy to make too much of these differences, and to
imagine a correspondence between the facts of modern society
and its best tendencies which does not really exist. Prejudices,
resting on old custom and containing half a truth, repose com-
fortably in our minds side by side with ideas which, if we were
thoroughly awake, would destroy them. Aristotle himself has
laid down with the greatest clearness that even the most menial
services need not be ignoble, and that the slavishness of a pursuit lies not in the things that are done, but in the spirit in
which they are done, and in their object. And for this reason
he would have some of such services performed by the youthful
citizens (119. 17; 131. 16). And yet he seems hardly to ask
himself whether work which is rewarded in money may not be
done for its own sake; and, with ideas of art hardly less exalted
than Plato's, he utters no word of protest against the identification of the artist with the βάναυσος. Nor, again, can it be said
that these old prejudices are wanting in vitality at the present
day. If a good many "young men of liberal sentiments" would
so far differ from Plutarch that they would desire rather to be
Shakespeare than Pericles, most of their relations, and perhaps
all their mothers, would take quite another view; and they
themselves might not all persist in an ambition which would
involve their ceasing to be "gentlemen" and becoming common
actors. One of the wisest of Englishmen, when he heard a
compliment to the Queen, which Garrick had introduced into a
play, characterised as "mean and gross flattery," asked "(rising
into warmth): How is it mean in a player—a showman,—a
fellow who exhibits himself for a shilling, to flatter his Queen?"[1]
Yet Garrick was the greatest actor of the day, and Johnson's personal friend. Again, what does the respectable father of a family
think of the boy who turns painter or musician? What does the
respectable man of learning think of him? If we do not know
from experience how "society" looks upon artists, Thackeray
will tell us; what it thinks of "persons in trade," not to speak

---

[1] Boswell's *Life of Johnson*, vol. ii. p. 215 (edition of 1824 in 4 vols.).

of the "lower orders," no one can help knowing. But there is a difference between this sentiment and Aristotle's. If he shares our prejudice, he does not share our ideal. The leisure which he thought indispensable for a citizen was not leisure to be stupid, idle, or busy only in amusement. The notion that *that* was the end to which a thousand lives of toil were a mere means would have seemed an astounding one to him. The strenuous exercise of the highest powers of body and mind in defending and governing the State, and in striving to quicken the divine reason in the soul,—this is the kind of " high life " with which βαναυσία is contrasted, and the citizenship of which it is declared incapable.

If this life is man's personal ideal, there can be little question of the mode in which it is to be approached. Without the gifts of nature not much can be done, and Aristotle hardly seems to find the happy mixture of spirit and intelligence in any race except the Greek (105. 25).   But, given the good material, the rest is the work of *Education.* And Aristotle uses this word in its strict sense. The natural effects of climate, air, water, and the like, are important (112. 23 ff.). The unconscious influence of a moral atmosphere can do much. The direct action of the Legislature in arranging institutions has its effect. But it is not communism which will cure the moral diseases of society, but education (30. 30; 38. 6) : and when he is describing the ideal city Aristotle's interest in outward arrangements soon flags. He turns abruptly to the question, How shall we make our citizens good men ?—and answers, By education.

From the very beginning the child must be definitely trained and guided ; and this training has to follow its natural development.   Care can be taken of the body before the mind is active, and the desires are in full energy long before the intellect.   It is in this early time that the habituation, on which Aristotle lays so much stress, is possible. Pleasure and pain rule the first years of the soul, and the problem of education is to attach these feelings to the right objects; not to teach the reasons of good and evil, but to nurture a love of the one and a hatred of the other. If this has not been done, the cultivation of the intellect will have little moral result; and, if it has been done, reason will afterwards appeal not to a chaos of passions, but to emotions which have taken her own order and colour, and to habits which form a body pliant to her will. A nature which has gone through such a training has a chance of reaching that energy of the soul which is the main constituent of happiness.

To Aristotle then the fundamental problem of politics is one of education. And to him the practical conclusions are inevitable. Education must be *public* and *compulsory*. Aristotle is not blind to the advantages of private instruction, the system followed in most of the Greek States (129. 26). It has the same advantages which government by a person possesses over government by a fixed law; it can adapt itself to individual differences. But he cannot admit that the State should give up the training of its citizens. That it attended to it, in however narrow a spirit, at Sparta and Crete, was one of the chief claims of those communities to honour. Not only does the State possess a conception of the end which training is to attain, but it, and it alone, has power to enforce this training on unwilling subjects; and, owing to its impersonal character the compulsion it exercises is comparatively inoffensive (*Eth.* 10. 9. 12). Nor, even if it were possible, would it be right for the State to leave this duty to that private enterprise which means private opinion. It has an end and a moral character exactly as an individual has, and its responsibility is like his (130. 19). If the object it sets before it is not realised in the persons of its citizens, it is not realised at all. And this object is not something indefinite, but a fixed type of character, or ἦθος. The failure to produce it is the failure of the State, and may be its danger; for the ἦθος is that living spirit which keeps the political body healthy and united. "The greatest of all securities for the permanence of constitutions is what all men now neglect, an education in accordance with the constitution," and the best laws in the world are of no avail if men are not educated in the spirit of the State (215. 27; cf. 78. 7; 146. 17).

And this is not all. The same reasoning leads Aristotle to the further conclusion that education must be *uniform* and *universal.* The end of the whole State is one (130. 10), and its spirit must be one. Some of the imperfect constitutions might, and naturally would, depart from this rule; for in them the rulers and the ruled form two distinct classes, and would consequently require a different training. But in the true State every citizen at some period of his life takes part in government, and a common culture is the ideal to be sought. Whatever departure from this uniformity might be admitted would be due to that insistence on the absolute universality of education which is one of the most striking features of Aristotle's doctrine. The State is not to content itself with the training of its active citizens. That of its women is hardly less important. It was a fatal error in the Spartan constitution that it educated its men and left its women uncared for, a negligence which bitterly avenged itself in the effect they produced on the moral character of the whole State (45. 11). For the women "form half the free population" (22. 23), and where their condition is not what it should be, "half the State must be considered uncared for by the law." Doubtless, if Aristotle's promise to deal with this subject were fulfilled in the book, as we possess it, we should find that he gave very different regulations for the training of the two sexes; but the same law of conformity to the constitution is insisted on for both.

Nor can the State afford to relax its care with the manhood of its pupil. Its education, in the wider sense of the word, ought to last through life (*Eth.* 10. 9. 9; cf. 115. 11 ff.; 128. 22). For the mass of men, at least in ordinary States, can hardly be expected to live by the light of their own reason. Under the inferior forms of government it is of so great importance that men should live in accordance with the established constitution, that special officials ought to watch and control the lives of disaffected persons (212. 10); and the best of existing governments, we are told, have functionaries to guard the conduct of women (174. 21). If we turn from the adult years of the citizen to his very birth, we find the same point of view. If the contribution of nature to man's good lies in part beyond our power, it is only in part that it does so. And with a view to the production of the best material for education the whole arrangements of marriage are placed under the absolute control of government. It is at such points as these that we feel farthest removed from Greek ideas, and are surest of our progress. But there is at least nothing unworthy in the spirit which dictates such interferences with private life. We feel all the moral intensity as well as all the harshness of the ideal statesman (*Eth.* 1. 13. 2) in the rebuke with which Aristotle meets those who wish to live "after their own heart's desire." "But this is base : for one ought not to think it slavery to live in the spirit of the constitution" (216. 18) ; and, "No man ought to think that he is his own, but all that they are the State's" (130. 15).

Of the education which seemed to Aristotle ideal we have only a fragmentary sketch. Its spirit may be conjectured from the end at which it aims, but any account of it would lead us beyond our immediate subject. If we turn now to the perfect city for which this education is intended, a glance at the very scanty account of its political organisation will enable us to understand the imperfections of the other forms of government.

All the citizens of the ideal State have received the same education; they are "free and equal." Their education was designed to fit them not only for obedience, but also for government, and for the second by means of the first. Of the virtue implied in this function there is one indispensable condition, —freedom from the necessity of providing the means of life. Accordingly the property of the community is in the hands of the citizens ; and though they ought to some extent to permit a common use of it, they hold it as their own, and not in common.[1] Under these conditions what distribution of public rights or duties does justice demand ? In virtue of the equality of the citizens, it demands that *all* shall share in civic rights. Of these functions there are two main classes,

---

[1] One is tempted to suppose that by "property" is meant landed property ; since the βάναυσοι, who are not citizens, might possess wealth of another kind. But it is possible that Aristotle, who dislikes trade and manufactures, may have intended his State to be almost entirely agricultural. And the agricultural labourers would not be free men (112. 13).

military and political; and accordingly every one has to take part in each. But the equality of the citizens is not identity; they are unlike as well as like; and in the necessary distinction which nature makes between them Aristotle finds the ground for a difference in rights or duties. Various functions demand various capacities, and these capacities belong roughly to separate periods of man's life. Energy or force ($\delta\acute{v}\nu\alpha\mu\iota\varsigma$) is the gift of youth, and wisdom ($\phi\rho\acute{o}\nu\eta\sigma\iota\varsigma$) of riper years. In the ideal State, then, the citizen in his earlier manhood will perform the military duties, and will only take part in government when they are completed. The remaining function of citizenship, the care of religious worship, is assigned to those advanced years which relieve men from more active services. We shall see that, as in this distribution of work, so in other respects the ideal State is the image of that perfect justice which in Aristotle goes by a name afterwards applied to a very different conception—natural right.

That every constitution existing in Aristotle's time answered to his idea of the State no one could suppose. Not one fully corresponded to it, and the majority fell far short of it. In this, as in every other work of nature, there are variations and defects. Nature, as Aristotle mythologically says, aims at the best, but she cannot always attain it (cf. 7. 27; 9. 18). Her creation is arrested at some point, or it develops itself awry. Thus men do not always reach the stage of political society, and when they do they often form imperfect or even "perverted" States. They mistake the true end, or else they do not take the right means to reach it (116. 8). Yet the mere beginnings, or the deformed growths, are better than nothing. "Man is by nature so political an animal that, even when men need no assistance from each other, they none the less desire to live together;" and though the common good of a noble life is in the highest degree their end, yet "they come together for the sake of mere life, and form political communities even for it alone. For perhaps it has something of the noble in it" (68. 7). Thus subordinate ends which fall short of man's true development are raised into ultimate ones, and form the bases or fundamental principles ($\acute{v}\pi o\theta\acute{e}\sigma\epsilon\iota\varsigma$) of imperfect constitutions. On the "hypothesis" of wealth arises what Aristotle calls oligarchy, on that of mere freedom what he calls democracy. As we have seen, neither wealth nor freedom is the end for which the State exists ; but both are necessary to that end. Hence at once the existence and the weakness of such forms of government. They are States, and so far good ; and of neither of them does Aristotle use the language he applies to tyranny, which takes the pleasure of the tyrant for its object. On the other hand, in common with tyranny, they are perversions of the true idea, and therefore contrary to nature (92. 1). Each of them, if it pursues its " hypothesis" to the legitimate conclusion, destroys itself, whereas the true end cannot be pursued to excess. With every step in its development the chance of permanence for the constitution decreases ; the extreme forms live a hazardous life, and, like diseased organisms, perish of trifling ailments (187. 25). The reason is that they diverge from the idea of the State so far, they realise it so little, as hardly to be States at all. And we shall find that this is equivalent to saying that they pursue a false end, that they pervert justice, and that their government is selfish and not public.

When Aristotle thus distinguishes between an ideal State and various perversions of it, he is far from supposing that the existence of bad forms of government is avoidable. He does not dream of framing an ideal scheme of government, the adoption of which would turn a misshapen State into the image of his idea. To him the constitution ($\pi o\lambda\iota\tau\epsilon\acute{\iota}a$, a word which has a wider sense than its English equivalent) is inseparable from the nature of the people who live under it—as inseparable as any organisation is from the matter organised in it. It is the " order" of the citizens ($\tau\acute{a}\xi\iota s$, 58. 28). It is the " form" of the State, and constitutes its identity (62. 22 ff.) : and it is often spoken of as the State itself. But it is possible, and even necessary for our purpose, to draw a distinction between the two. To ask why an imperfect *State* exists is to enter at once on a metaphysical question, and comes at last to the problem of the existence of evil. But there is a more obvious meaning in the inquiry why an imperfect *constitution* exists, although this inquiry must ultimately merge in the other. It exists because it is the natural outcome of a given social condition.

Given a certain material, a population of a certain kind and in a definite degree of civilisation, and there is a form or order naturally fitted for it; and no other order, however superior it would be in better circumstances, is better for *it*. This fact Aristotle clearly recognises. There are populations, he tells us, naturally adapted to monarchy, aristocracy, and a constitutional republic (91. 31 ff.) ; and though he adds that all the perversions are unnatural, he does not mean by this that they do not naturally arise under the appropriate social conditions : on the contrary, this is true not only of oligarchy or democracy, but of the various sub-species of those forms (166. 14 ff.; 178. 22 ff.). Accordingly, when he is describing his own ideal State, Aristotle does not confine himself to the arrangements of government. He realises that, if his sketch is to have any verisimilitude, he must imagine also the population for which the constitution is intended, and even the physical conditions under which it lives. In other words, he describes an ideal State, and not merely an ideal constitution. In the same way he recognises that the approaches which can be made to the constitution of this ideal are very various in degree, and that it is essential for a political theorist to consider all of them. False simplicity he regards as the besetting sin of such theorists. Some of them investigate nothing but the one best constitution, in which things we wish for, and cannot insure, play so large a part ; others eulogise a single existing form, like the Spartan, and sweep all the rest out of sight. But it is necessary, Aristotle points out, not only to know what we wish for and to take care not to want impossibilities (34. 1), but also to find out what constitution suits any given population ; what is the best constitution that can be framed on a given " hypothesis ; " what form is the highest attainable by an average State ; and, instead of supposing that there is one oligarchy and one democracy, to study all the varieties of each (145 and 146). On the other hand, from the fact that for any given people that constitution is best which is fit for *it*, Aristotle does not draw the hasty inference that all constitutions stand on a level. If we consider that people which is fitted for free institutions more civilised than that which is fitted for despotism, we implicitly assert that one form of government is also superior to the other. This is the language which Aristotle commonly adopts : nor is there any objection to it, so long as we bear in mind, as he invariably does, that the constitution is the form of the State, and, considered apart from the State, is an abstraction.

Aristotle's main division of the forms of government is into six (69. 19 ff.). Of these three are good or right, and of each of the three there is a perverted form ($\pi\alpha\rho\acute{\epsilon}\kappa\beta\alpha\sigma\iota\varsigma$). The first set consists of Kingdom, Aristocracy, and Republic ($\pi o\lambda\iota\tau\epsilon\acute{\iota}\alpha$) ; the second of Tyranny, Oligarchy, and Democracy. And, according to some passages, the first three are placed in a descending order of goodness, and the second three in a descending order of badness, so that the corruption of the best (kingdom) is the worst (tyranny). But this division, probably suggested by Plato's *Statesman*, undergoes serious modifications in the course of the work. The historical forms of kingdom and aristocracy receive slight attention, mainly because in Aristotle's time they were of little importance. On the other hand, an ideal State, not identical with any of these historical forms, but regarded indifferently as either a kingdom or an aristocracy, though commonly as the latter, becomes a main subject of discussion. In accordance with this point of view, the main division into good and bad States loses its sharpness. The Republic or Politeia [1] is always regarded as markedly inferior to its two companions (cf. 70. 7 ; 92. 16 ; 158. 20), and is once roundly called a $\pi\alpha\rho\acute{\epsilon}\kappa\beta\alpha\sigma\iota\varsigma$ (149. 15). And there is another important change. The three constitutions in each set are at first distinguished according to the number of the government, which may consist of one man, a few or many. But Aristotle has no sooner adopted this principle than he points out that the distinction is in some cases illusory. The number of the governing body is a mere accident of oligarchy or democracy, which are really distinguished by the wealth or poverty of the ruling class (71. 8) ; and though in the later books Aristotle again modifies his new principle, he never deserts it. In the same way in

---

[1] This form of government is, as the reader will see, called simply Constitution. In English we have nothing that is even an apparent equivalent. So far as any Greek State can be called a republic, the Politeia may be called a republic of the middle classes. But there is no single case in all the six in which the use of the designations given to modern States is not misleading.

various passages various causes are assigned for the existence of different forms of government; and the truth is that there is no one principle of division in the *Politics*. This wavering procedure seems to be due in part to the recurrence, at various times, of two distinct points of view, and an indifference to their relation to each other. After what has been said, it will be obvious what these points of view are. At one time Aristotle's endeavour is to fix clearly in what the goodness or badness of a State consists; to discover the fundamental principle of each main form of government, and, by a comparison of it with the standard of the ideal State, to determine its value. At other times the fact that every actual constitution is the expression of a certain social order becomes prominent; and it is found that, though the previous distinction may determine the general goodness or badness of such a constitution, it does not really explain its concrete character. It will be best, without entering into any critical discussion, to separate these methods from each other, and to ask, first, what is the main external difference of constitutions, and afterwards to analyse those characteristics which distinguish any good government from any bad one.

The question what social condition is appropriate to each constitution lies beyond the scope of this Essay. Still less can we reproduce Aristotle's sketch of the order in which the main forms of government appeared (88. 8 ff.), or his explanation of the fact that some of them had ceased to answer to the needs of the time.[1] The doctrine which we have to notice is that the constitution is not merely in general the result of social conditions, but that it expresses the relative power of the different elements or sections of society. Every political community contains a variety of parts, elements, or functions. Translating this into the concrete, we may say that every society is divided into classes, although it does not necessarily happen, and, according to Aristotle, had better not happen, that every functio is allotted to a single class. Each of these elements or

---

[1] See, for example, on the disappearance of the kingly form of monarchy, 223. 3 ff.; and on the connection of democracy with the increased size of States, 88. 25; 188. 3; 186. 4.

classes—which are variously enumerated in different passages—contributes something to the State, and so has a certain claim to share in its life, or constitution,[1] or political rights. And, apart from the justice of these claims, as a matter of fact the relative strength of these elements determines the question where the supreme power or sovereignty lies in the community, and therefore settles what the constitution of the State shall be (*e.g.* 80. 20 ff.). Thus Aristotle tells us more than once that the variety of constitutions is due to the various ὑπεροχαὶ, or preponderances of the social parts (148. 7 ; 149. 1 ; 152. 29) ; and this must be regarded as his settled view of the existing States, although he does not admit the complete justice of the claim of any class to exclusive power (*e.g.* 81. 12). Thus again the true difference between oligarchy and democracy, the commonest actual forms of government, consists in this, that in the one the element of wealth, which naturally falls into a few hands, is supreme (κύριον) among the social elements, whereas in democracy the poor multitude has got the mastery. And in the same way the superiority of the Politeia to these two constitutions is that in it neither of these extremes has overpowered the other, but the middle class possesses a social force which results in political supremacy.

These distinctions of fact, however, are only the signs of a difference in moral value. The transition from one point of view to the other is facilitated by the haphazard way in which Aristotle uses abstract and concrete expressions. He speaks of a social element indifferently as wealth or the wealthy, freedom or the free, virtue or the good. Accordingly, instead of saying that one of the classes of society, say the wealthy, predominates in a State, he defines the constitution of that State as one which takes a single social element, wealth, for its standard (ὅρος). Thus, he tells us, of the qualifications which can claim to be such a standard there are on the whole three—free birth, wealth, and virtue (since a fourth, nobility, means ancestral wealth and virtue); and these are the standards respectively of democracy, oligarchy, and aristocracy (159. 15). From the notion of a standard to that of an end the step, especially in

---

[1] ἡ γὰρ πολιτεία βίος τίς ἐστι πόλεως.—163. 3.

Greek, is a short one. Accordingly, we are not surprised to find
Aristotle distinguishing constitutions by the *ends* they pursue.
And again, since the end or standard determines the rights
which are thought to belong in justice to the citizen, we are
told that the existence of certain constitutions is due to the
fact that men have not a right idea of *justice* (193. 28 ff.). But
when we come to divide States according to the ends they
pursue and the justice they realise, we have left the ground of
a mere analysis of social forces, and have entered the region of
moral judgment. If we add to these criteria the question what
kind of rule is exercised in a given State, we shall have found
the three tests by which the goodness or badness of a constitution may be tried.

The *first* of these criteria is obvious. The very definition
of the State places its whole nature in its end. To pursue a
false end is to be a bad State, or even (so far) to fail of being a
State at all. The true end, as we know, is that noble life which
is identical with happiness or the exercise of complete virtue.
But there are various subordinate constituents or various
necessary conditions of this end, which may be mistaken for
it. And just as a man may take as the object of his life
not real happiness, but wealth or pleasure, so may a State.
Thus the end of the good State is, as we may suppose, the true
end. That of the ideal State is this end in its perfection, so that,
in the aristocratic form of it which is really Aristotle's ideal,
the virtue of the good citizen is, as such, identical with the
virtue of the good man. In the same way the fact that the
Politeia is counted among the good States, must mean that its
end is virtue; but the virtue at which it aims is that imperfect ἀρετή of which a large number of men is capable, the
virtue of the citizen-soldier (70. 15).[1] On the other hand, the

---

[1] In this instance we have an example of the way in which the real conditions of a society are connected with the moral qualities of the constitution.
The possibility of attaining the true end depends on a limitation of the
number of the body which governs; even in the ideal States only some of the
citizens *actually* rule. If a large number are to govern, the end must be
lowered, and with it the standard for political rights. Thus the qualification
in the Politeia is the possession of arms, or (what comes to the same thing in
a Greek State) such a property-qualification as admits only the upper and
middle classes to power.

ends which define the perverted forms are not merely imperfect degrees of ἀρετή, but something subordinate to it. Thus we shall expect to find the object of oligarchy in wealth, and this is implicitly asserted by Aristotle (*e.g.* 218. 9). That of democracy must be freedom, since the other characteristics of that form, poverty, numbers, and low birth, are obviously incapable of being ends (159. 15; 179. 7; 180. 17). That of tyranny again is not the noble life on which pleasure necessarily follows, but pleasure itself and, with a view to pleasure, wealth (218. 4).

In the perversions, then, the government does not seek the good. But, *secondly*, it does not seek the *common* good (τὸ κοινῇ συμφέρον, 68. 5). It pursues the end for itself, and not for the whole State. Its rule therefore is not political but despotic; that is, a kind of rule applicable to the relation of master and slave, but not to the relation of citizens to each other. The welfare of the ruled is, like the slave's, only accidentally involved in that of the ruler, in the sense (apparently) that more than a certain amount of ill-treatment destroys the living material or instruments by which the master or tyrant obtains his own objects. Thus the subject, like the slave, is the means to another man's end; whereas it is the essence of political society to be a community of *free* men. In this sense democracy, oligarchy, and tyranny are alike despotic (69. 17). In other words, they are so far not States at all; they are insecure; their vital principle is self-destructive; and their safety lies in suppressing the full development of this principle, or in adopting for a bad end measures which, as a matter of fact, tend to the common good.

Each of these two moral characteristics is indispensable. To seek an end which is common to all the citizens will not make a government correct, if the end is false; and to seek the true end will not do so either, if this end is not sought for all. And Aristotle combines the two characteristics when he defines the common good as the share of noble life which falls to each citizen (68. 10). But beyond this mere *assertion* of their union he does not go; he does not attempt to prove that the pursuit of the true end is necessarily unselfish, whereas that of a false one is not. We may gather such a result

from his denial that a mere society of traders would constitute a State. The ground of this denial is, that such a
society has not a really "political" end; it seeks nothing more
than protection for the endeavour of each man to attain his
private end of wealth, an endeavour in which the welfare, and
even the wealth, of his fellows is involved, if at all, only
accidentally. And to this is opposed the interest of the citizen
in the moral character of others, that is, in the attainment of
the end of the State by others as well as himself. Or again, we
may infer that the true end of the State is necessarily a *common*
good, from the account of justice in *Ethics* v. 1. In that passage justice is identified with virtue, when virtue is regarded
in its relation to other men; and the virtue of the citizen is,
as we know, the end of the State. But to seek this justice must
be to seek the good of *all* the citizens; for, owing to its relation to others, it may be defined, Aristotle says, as the "good
of others" (ἀλλότριον ἀγαθὸν), and not merely of the just man
himself. But we have to find such indications for ourselves.
The antithesis of selfishness and disinterested action, which
suggests the difficulty, had no such prominence in Greek Ethics
as it possesses for good and evil now. Aristotle never explicitly raises the question, so obvious to us, in what relation
a man's happiness stands to the realisation of the same end in
others, and whether it is possible for one to be attained without the other, and, therefore, to be preferred or sacrificed to
the other. And in the same way here, there is no attempt to
show that the pursuit of the real end is in its nature public-
spirited, and that of wealth or mere freedom or pleasure *necessarily* the subordination of the public good to a private or class
interest.

We have to ask, *thirdly*, in what way is the State a realisation of justice or right.[1] It is so, first of all, in this general
sense, that it produces in its citizens that virtue for which,
as we have seen, justice is another name. But there is also
a more special principle of right in political society. This is

---

[1] On this subject H. A. Fechner's tract, *Ueber den Gerechtigkeitsbegriff des
Aristoteles* may be compared. The corresponding passages in the *Politics* and
Ethics are fully pointed out in the notes to Mr. H. Jackson's edition of the
fifth book of the *Ethics*.

what Aristotle calls *distributive* justice; and its law is that
public honours, advantages, or rights, are distributed among
the citizens, not arbitrarily, but in proportion to their contribution to the end of the State, or, in other words, according to
their worth (ἀξία). Thus this justice may be defined in modern
language as the correspondence of rights and duties. A right
given, which does not answer, and answer proportionately, to
a duty done, is a violation of justice. A duty done, a contribution to the State, which does not meet with its proportionate
return in the shape of a right, is equally a violation of justice.
Or, again, this justice may be represented as a geometrical proportion. If A and B are two citizens whose worths differ, the
rights a, which go to A, ought to differ in amount from the
rights b, which go to B, proportionately to the difference in
worth between A and B; or, $A : B :: A + a : B + b$. In the same
way Aristotle calls political justice a principle of *equality*. And
by this he means not absolute equality, but equality of ratios.
Thus if A gets the amount of rights which answer to his
worth, and B does the same, they are treated justly; and,
although they receive unequal rights, they are treated equally.
To give equal rights to unequal worths, or unequal rights
to equal worths, is to violate equality. In so far then as a
State applies this law of proportion, it realises distributive
justice. On the other hand, although it fairly distributes
rights according to worth, it may in reality violate justice by
using a false or one-sided standard of worth. Instead of rating
the citizen by his capacity of exercising true citizen functions,
it may adopt a criterion answering to its own false end. In
this case, among others, the justice of the State will, in a
higher sense, be unjust. And it is only when this positive
justice corresponds to, or expresses, *natural* justice, that the
State can be said to be a full realisation of right.

This is not the case with the perverted States. Plainly,
none of them is likely to produce justice in its citizens. None
of them, again, fully satisfies distributive justice. Though all
—except, we may suppose, the tyrant—admit that justice
means proportionate equality (193. 29; 195. 14), in no State
except the ideal is political right wholly coincident with
natural (*Eth.* 5. 7. 5). The departure from natural justice in

oligarchy and democracy is represented by Aristotle in two
different ways. A partial equality or inequality is taken as
absolute, and a false standard of worth is adopted. Thus in
the oligarchy an inequality in one respect is considered a just
ground for the exclusive possession of power; and political
rights are restricted to those who are superior to their fellow-
citizens in one particular, viz., wealth. Here is already an injustice; but it is heightened by the fact that the measure of
worth is itself a false one. " What is a man worth?" means
in an oligarchy not " What is his *merit*, his contribution to the
true end of the State?" but " How much *money* is he worth?"
The injustice of democracy, though it leads to very different
outward results, is in principle the same. Grasping the fact
that in one point, freedom, all its citizens are on a level, it
takes this partial equality for an absolute one, and gives equal
rights to everybody. In other words, it gives equals to un-
equals, and thereby violates justice. And again, though
according to the standard of worth it has adopted it may
apportion fairly, this standard is not merit but the imperfect
one of free birth. Hence Aristotle can at one time insist that
equality is justice, and at another condemn democracy on
account of its passion for equality, since the equality it realises
is not proportionate but absolute or numerical.[1] So it comes
about that there is an " oligarchical right " and a " democratic
right." They are not, in the highest sense, right at all. But
to a certain extent they are so; partly because the ἀξία which
they take as the qualification for political power, although not
the true one, still has a subordinate importance for the State;
and partly because, on the basis of this standard, they do distribute public advantages and honours according to a fixed law.
Thus, though Aristotle does not trace the gradual decline of
justice in the various stages of these παρεκβάσεις, it is not an
accident that those extreme forms of oligarchy and democracy,
which are furthest removed from right and almost on a level
with tyranny, are characterised in his view by contempt of the

---

[1] Hence also Aristotle sometimes says (*e.g.* 188. 4) that democracy is opposed
to "justice according to worth (ἀξία)." Its standard of worth is mere freedom, and, therefore, scarcely a standard at all.

law, and the substitution for it of the mere will of "dynastic"
plutocrats (157. 16) and the momentary decrees of the despot
mob (154. 15).

Aristotle's application of these ideas to the various grounds
on which political power may be claimed is, in the main, very
simple.   The nearest approach to our modern notion of a "right"
is to be found in his discussion of this subject; and, like him,
we seem to use this word, as well as "justice," in a double sense.
Let us take, as an example of political rights, the suffrage.   The
poor man, then, claims this privilege as his right; and he bases
his claim on the ground that he is equal to, or as good as, those
who possess it.   The rich man claims a greater or unequal
share of power, on the ground that he is superior or unequal
to his poorer fellow-citizens.   The idea underlying each
argument is that of distributive justice, and it is a sound one.
If the poor man *is* equal to the rich, he *has* a right to equal
powers; and if not, not.   But the real question is, What does
the equality or inequality of men mean in this connection?
In *what* are they equal or unequal? (78. 19 ff.)   It is evident
that equality or inequality in any quality whatever which we
choose to take will not give a right to equal or unequal
political power.   If it did, a man might claim the suffrage
because he was the same colour or the same size as those who
possess it.   An illustration from another field will guide us to
the true conclusion.   Suppose we had certain flutes to distribute.
We should scarcely give the best of them to those players who
happened to be of the highest birth; "for they will not play
better than other people on that account."   And even if the
superiority of one man to another in wealth or birth far
exceeded his inferiority to him in flute-playing, we should still
give the best flute to the poor and low-born proficient.   "For
it is to the function or work in question that the superiority
in birth or wealth ought to contribute; and it contributes
nothing."   The same principle will apply to politics; and it
will not justify either of the claims in question.   It is not unjust that a real inequality, a superior contribution to the end
of the State, should be rewarded by a superior share in the
function.   But against the favour shown to *irrelevant* in-
equalities the democrat rightly protests.   On the other hand,

the point in which he is equal to every other citizen is not that which ought to settle his political ἀξία. The end of the State is no more free birth than wealth; and absolute justice belongs in reality only to claims based on the equal or superior possession of intelligence and moral character. Suppose, however, that a given State pursues a false end, and accordingly adopts a false standard of worth. In this case, whatever the standard may be, he who contributes to it equally with other men may truly be said to have an equal right to political power with other men, although his right would in an ideal State be none. So, again, in an oligarchy a wealthy man has a right to greater privileges than others; and his superior in ἀρετὴ, or the real capacity for government, might be legally treated as inferior to him. In such a case, in one sense the poor man of ability would have no right to the power refused to him, and yet, in another sense, he might be said to have an absolute right to it. Obvious as these distinctions appear, any controversy on the suffrage will show how easily they may still be confused, and that the twofold idea of "rights" is still current. When we say that a man has a right to the franchise, what do we mean? We may mean that according to the constitution, the English political δίκαιον, he can claim it, because he satisfies the conditions laid down by the law as necessary to the possession of it. But when the franchise is claimed as a right by those who do not satisfy these conditions, this cannot be the meaning. They really affirm that the actual law, the English δίκαιον, is not properly or absolutely just, and does not express "natural right;" that, according to real justice, they ought to have the suffrage, and that, if they had it, the State would be less of a παρέκβασις and nearer to the ideal. And if the further question were asked, *why* true justice demands the change, would not the answer (unless it were a piece of mere clap-trap) involve the notion that equal rights ought in justice to follow equal duties to the State, and the assertion that those who claim the suffrage contribute equally to the State with those who already possess it?

The result of these principles for Aristotle would seem to be clear; and to a certain extent it is so. That the only true standard of worth for distributive justice is merit, or virtue, or

education (παιδεία, "culture"), is obvious. But in the immediate application of this doctrine uncertainties arise. First of
all, there is one limitation on all governments, a limitation
which has, fortunately for us, become almost too obvious to be
worth mentioning. The rule of those who possess *any*
superiority, even that of virtue, is to be considered inferior to
the rule of law. It is only because the law is too general to
meet all the particular cases that arise, that a government is
necessary to supplement as well as execute it; and therefore,
with one exception to be noticed later, the rule that all governments ought to be subject to it is absolute (*e.g.* 77. 30).
Secondly, an element of doubt is introduced by the true perception that, though wealth or free birth are not direct contributions to the end of the State, they yet constitute elements
necessary to its existence (79. 22). There is consequently a
certain amount of justice in the demand that the possession of
them should be followed by some share in public rights. But
what share this should be, and in what rights it should be a
share, are questions which Aristotle does not discuss. Lastly,
his view of the claims of individuals to political power receive
an important modification in the account of the imperfect
States. Aristotle tells us (166. 6 ff.) that we have to consider
not only quality, but quantity; that is, not only the element or
quality on which a claim to rule is based, but also the *number*
of those who possess it. It is the comparative power of these
factors which settles the constitution of a State. Thus
oligarchy means the preponderance of the quality of wealth
over the superior quantity of the poor, and democracy [1] the
opposite. It is the tendency of either government to push its
principle to an extreme. Oligarchy heightens the amount of
the "quality" of wealth necessary for political rights, and
thereby increases the numbers opposed to it. Democracy

---

[1] Obviously, according to Aristotle, democracy is absolute government of
a quality, viz. free birth, and the oligarchs make up a quantity of men.
But then free birth is common to rich and poor, the noble by nature and the
noble by birth alike. Accordingly he sometimes speaks as if the essence of
democracy were *mere* number, *i.e.* mere quantity, or this united with
poverty and low birth, *i.e.* the *absence* of certain qualities. In the same
way, as we saw, he speaks as though democracy recognised *no* ἀξία, because
its ἀξία is so slight a one.

extends the franchise more and more, and with its increase of
quantity loses more and more all distinctive quality.   The
further this development goes, and the further these factors
are separated, the worse the State becomes, and the nearer it
approaches to an internecine struggle between them.   Accordingly, it is the characteristic of the Politeia, which is distinguished for its stability, that it combines these elements;
and it is in this connection that Aristotle's celebrated eulogium
on the middle classes occurs.   But it is clear that the application of this idea to the question of political rights will make
our previous results uncertain.   For those results are based
simply on an inquiry into the *quality* which any individual
can allege as a claim to power: this doctrine, on the contrary,
touches the rights not of an individual, as such, but of a
number, or possibly a class, and it expressly admits that their
quantity must be considered.

A consideration not quite identical with this, but closely
allied to it, is applied even to the good States; and it has a
special interest, because it leads Aristotle to discuss the rights
of the mass or people ($\pi\lambda\hat{\eta}\theta os$, the whole body of citizens).
Let us assume,—so we may state his results (75. 6—77. 30),—
that wealth is the standard by which rights are apportioned.
Still, it will not follow that "the rich" should rule.   The mass
might justly dispute their claim; for although the wealth of any
rich man might far exceed that of any poor one, yet the collective wealth of the people might exceed that of the wealthy
class.   Again, even if we admit that the true standard of
justice is $\dot{a}\rho\epsilon\tau\dot{\eta}$, it is not certain that the best and ablest man
in the State, nor the few best and ablest men, have a right to
hold the reins · of government.   It is possible that the
aggregate $\dot{a}\rho\epsilon\tau\dot{\eta}$ of the people might outweigh that of this
individual or class; and then the very arguments on which the
latter claim to govern might be turned against them.   The
man of distinguished $\dot{a}\rho\epsilon\tau\dot{\eta}$, we might say, is like the ideal
portrait.   In it are united the various beauties which in life
are distributed among different men, and it is therefore more
beautiful than the average man.   Yet if we take a crowd, we
may find in it here a mouth, and there eyes, and there again
another feature, still more beautiful than are the features of the

portrait. And so, although each individual of the πλῆθυς may be far inferior in political merit to the aristocrat, yet if we take the whole mass, it may contain an aggregate of merit exceeding his. Each member of it brings a contribution to the one vast man, who has many feet and hands and senses. In the same way we find that the judgment of the mass on poetry and music is better than that of a single critic; for one man appreciates one excellence, and another another, whereas the taste of an individual is necessarily one-sided. And again, as a large quantity of water is less easily defiled than a small, so it is harder to corrupt a whole people than an individual; and "it is not easy for them all to be enraged or mistaken at once." For these reasons it may be just to give such powers as those of election and the scrutiny of official actions to the whole people. And if the objection be raised that, if they are not fit to hold office themselves, they cannot be fit to choose officials and judge their conduct, the answer is that in many cases it is not necessary to know how a thing is made in order to judge of it. The head of a household, who could not have built the house, is a better judge of the product than the builder, the man who eats a dinner than the cook who prepared it.

This is Aristotle's version of "the sovereignty of the people;" and his arguments, whether wholly sound or not, have a permanent value. But it is important to recognise clearly on what basis they rest, and to what conclusion they are supposed to lead. We have to remember, first, that the "people," here as everywhere, is not equivalent to the whole male population, and does not include the enormous body of slaves and aliens. Nor does Aristotle suppose that his arguments will apply to any and every mass; for, "by heaven, in some cases this is clearly impossible." And, further, the sovereignty of the people to whom they do apply is doubly limited. It is subject to the ultimate supremacy of the law; and even under the law it is not complete. The very reasons which establish it restrict it to those cases in which the people can act *en masse*, and not individually. In other words, the functions of government in which the πλῆθος can claim a share are the general ones of deliberation and decision, which constitute the definition of citizenship, and not the highest executive offices, for which special ability is required. Lastly, it will be observed that the ground on which these claims are based by Aristotle is not that of simple quantity as opposed to quality. It is a claim based on the superior quantity of a quality. It is not because "all government rests on the consent of the governed," nor because one man is as good as another, nor because the people is a majority, that it has a right to rule; but because, in the case of a high level of civilisation, its rule is more likely to realise the government of intelligence and character than any other arrangement. Number stands on no higher level, or even on a lower level, than money or birth. Whatever rights belong to it, belong to it as the sign of something beyond itself.

Partly on account of this discussion, partly through the mis-interpretation of various passages in the *Politics*, some readers of the work have identified the Politeia with Aristotle's ideal State. But it is quite impossible to maintain this view. It is true that in both the suffrage is widely extended. But the Politeia is only the practical ideal. It is the constitution adapted to an average good State. It is a government of ἀρετὴ, but of imperfect ἀρετή. The whole people does not rule; there is a strict qualification for political rights, and, with a view to obtaining a rule of fair ἀρετὴ, the qualification fixed is one of moderate wealth. The ideal State, on the other hand, is the true aristocracy; a government of *complete ἀρετὴ*, a government of the best men (ἄριστοι) for the best end (ἄριστον), (70. 1). In the form which Aristotle has given to it the whole body of citizens bears rule. But then he is constructing a State according to his wishes; he supposes all the citizens to be men of high excellence; and even then he does not give the actual functions of government to them until they have reached a certain age. If his "wish" should not be fulfilled, justice would demand a different constitution. A population, in which a small band of men were distinguished to such a degree that their ἀρετὴ surpassed that of the remaining πλῆθος, would, on Aristotle's principle, be governed by that select few. And a still stranger case is not inconceivable to him. It might happen that a man appeared in the State, gifted with a great-ness of soul which raised him far above all his fellows. In such an event no love of his own ideal will deter Aristotle from the consistent result of his principles. If the great man really has a spirit so exalted in energy and virtue that these gifts exceed in quantity those of the whole body of his fellow-countrymen, justice demands that he should be held for what he is, "a god among men" (82. 6). The conditions of common political life cease to be applicable. He is not an equal among equals, to be bound by equal rules. In this single case even the supremacy of law must be abandoned. He is to be recognised as of right an absolute king, governing for the common good. That Aristotle considered such an occurrence extremely improbable is obvious. But that it was conceivable is the reason why he describes the ideal State as either monarchy or aristocracy (147. 1). And as in the *Ethics* (8. 10. 2), so in the *Politics* he has even given the first place to the former (147. 10).[1]

The true State may take various forms; but, whatever form it takes, these two requirements are absolute: it must strive to realise perfect justice by giving power to the natural sovereignty of intelligence and virtue, and it must seek the common good. The Greek constitutions have no more than a historical interest for us now. Our monarchy, our feudal aristocracy, our representative government, were things unknown to them, and the most democratic of their democracies we should call an oligarchy. But these principles remain. The first of them modern States attempt to carry out in various ways. From the very force of circumstances we are even less tempted than the Greeks to translate the truth that reason alone has a "divine right" to rule, into the dictum that philosophers should be kings; but it is still possible to forget that wealth and numbers have no political value except as symbols, and that political machinery is very far from being an end in

---

[1] The absolute kingship described above is of course the exact opposite of tyranny. It has been supposed that, in speaking of it, Aristotle was thinking of Alexander, and the enthusiasm of his language is certainly striking. But it is almost incredible that such an opinion of the new military monarchy should have left so little trace on the structure of his whole political theory. And it should be observed that the comparison of the rule of law and of an absolute king has throughout a reference to Plato's *Statesman*, and that Aristotle makes use even of Plato's illustrations.

itself. The second of these principles may be thought, fortunately for us, to have lost the pressing importance it had to Aristotle. For him the ruin of the Greek States was the witness of its violation.[1] The organisation of the State, instead of representing the common good and standing above the strife of social parties, had become in many cases the prize for which they fought, and a means which the victorious party used for its own exclusive advantage. Cities were divided into two hostile camps of the rich and poor. In this immediate dependence of the State on society we have one of the most marked characteristics of Greek politics. In modern nations the struggle of classes for political power does not, as a rule, rise prominently to the surface; and, though a change in social conditions—such as the decay of a landed aristocracy, or the rise of the commercial or the labouring classes,—inevitably expresses itself in politics, it commonly does so slowly and, so to speak, unintentionally. The State has a fixity and power such as the Greeks—in spite of the far greater part played by government in their lives—never knew; and, where the opposition of classes begins to pass from the social sphere and to take an openly political form, we recognise a peril to the national welfare and morality which to the Greek, instead of being a rarity, was ever at the doors. But it is impossible to say how far this supremacy of the State is connected with the modern institution of monarchy, and to what extent more popular forms of government, by whatever name they go, may be able to preserve it. That it needs no preservation, that great nations can do without it, and can subsist on nothing but the natural competition of interests modified by public opinion, is a hope which underlies some forms of the democratic faith, and seems to be implicitly adopted by many who have no theoretic convictions on the subject. Yet it seems too probable that, in more than one European country, the irruption of an exasperated social strife into the political arena would follow any weakening of the central power; and it would be a poor change which freed men from the burden of that power only to bring

---

[1] Cf. L. v. Stein in the *Zeitschrift für die gesammte Staatswissenschaft* for 1853, pp. 115-182.

it back in its least beneficent and progressive form, that of military force. Nor is it possible to confine these doubts to the great continental States. In more than one of the English colonies, unless they are maligned, the interest of a class is predominant in politics, and is susceptible of scarcely any check from above. And if representative institutions are not in other cases to be misused for the same "despotic" purposes, if they are not to produce, instead of the public good and the rule of ἀρετή, class-government and the supremacy of the dema- gogue and the wire-puller, it may be that the sluggish action of public opinion will need to be reinforced by some strengthen- ing of the State and some counterpoise to those tendencies which characterised the extreme democracy described by Aris- totle, the gradual weakening of the executive and the grasping of all the powers of government by the popular assembly (154. 26; 170. 12; 174. 16; 179. 25—180. 11).

There is no fear that modern civilisation will abandon the ideas which mark its progress. Unless some gigantic calamity were to overtake it, men who have once conceived of God as identical with the inmost spirit of humanity and bound by no limits of race or nation, who have realised that the breath of morality is freedom, and that voluntary association may be almost as powerful a force as the State, are never likely to find their ideal in the Greek city. The dangers are still on the other side. The process through which those ideas gained strength involved serious losses, and the false antitheses to which it gave rise have not yet ceased to rule our thoughts. To them the spirit of Aristotle's conception may still serve as a corrective. With every step in the moralising of politics and the socialising of morals, something of Greek excellence is won back. That goodness is not abstinence but action; that egoism, to however future a life it postpones its satisfaction, is still nothing but selfishness; that a man does not belong to himself, but to the State and to mankind; that to be free is not merely to do what one likes, but to like what one ought; and that blindness to the glory of "the world," and irreverence towards its spiritual forces, are the worst of passports to any "church" worthy of the name,—every new conviction of such truths is an advance towards filling up the gulf between religion and reality, and restoring, in a higher shape, that unity of life which the Greeks knew.

So far as opinions have weight, there are not many which more retard this advance than the idea that the State is a mere organ of "secular" force. That it is so seems to be the theoretical, though not the practical, belief of most Englishmen; and Aristotle's fundamental position, that its object is nothing short of "noble living," seems to separate his view decisively from ours. The partial truths that the law takes no account of moral character, and that Government ought not to enforce morality or interfere with private life, seem to be the main expressions of this apparent separation. But, to say nothing of the fact that legal punishments do in some cases habitually consider a man's moral guilt as well as his illegal act, it is forgotten that the reason why this is not the rule is itself a moral reason, and that if, by making it the rule, the good life of the community were likely to be furthered, it would be made the rule. And in the same way the reason why the State does not to any large extent aim at a directly moral result, is not that morality is something indifferent to it, but that it believes it will help morality most by not trying to enforce it. If we hold to Aristotle's definition, it does not follow that we are to pass sumptuary laws and force men to say their prayers. Every argument that is brought against the action of Government may (so far as it does not rest on a supposed right of the individual) be applied, with whatever truth it possesses, under that definition; and if, in the pursuit of its final object, the State, with a view to that final object, refrains from directly seeking that final object, that does not show that the immediate ends which it pursues are its ultimate and only end. But, apart from this, it is not true that in our own day the State has ceased actively to aim at a positive good, and has restricted itself to the duty of protecting men's lives and property. If the theory that its duty should be so restricted were carried out, it would lead to strange results and would abolish public laws and acts which few would be willing to surrender. We need go for a proof no further than our own country, where the action of Government is certainly not overvalued. A State which, in however slight a degree, supports science, art, learning, and religion; which enforces education, and compels the well-to-do to maintain the helpless; which, for the good of the poor and weak, interferes with the "natural" relations of employer and employed, and regulates, only too laxly, a traffic which joins gigantic evil to its somewhat scanty good; a State which forbids or punishes suicide, self-maiming, the voluntary dissolution of marriage, cruelty to animals, offences against decency, and sexual crimes which, if any act could be so, are the private affair of the persons who commit them,—a State which does all this and much more of the same kind, cannot, without an unnatural straining of language, be denied to exercise, in the broad sense, a moral function. It still seeks not merely "life," but "good life." It is still, within the sphere appropriate to force, a spiritual power,—not only the guardian of the peace and a security for the free pursuit of private ends, but the armed conscience of the community.

A. C. B.

EPICURUS.

In the year 1752, certain workmen, who were excavating the soil of the modern Portici, which covers the ancient Herculaneum, struck upon a small chamber or cell belonging apparently to a country house which in former times looked over the sea. Round the walls of this little chamber were arranged, on a pavement of mosaic, chests and cupboards of marqueterie, and standing on one of these, in the middle of the room, were seen busts of Demosthenes, Epicurus, Zeno, and Hermarchus. It was almost the first discovery of real importance which had rewarded the patience of the explorers.[1] Some ancient statues had indeed been unearthed in 1713, during the excavations carried on by the Prince d'Elbœuf, and again in 1737 under the orders of Charles III.: but the discovery of Pompeii in 1748, and the superior facility with which excavations could be carried on in the "passamonte" (light cinders) which covered the ruins of the sister town, had diverted attention for a while from Herculaneum. Yet the soil beneath Portici and Resina offered relics of far greater value. On the shelves of the cupboards found in the room of the buried villa lay little rolls, about two or three inches in diameter and a palm in length, the appearance of which gave

---

[1] Perhaps the Emperor Titus was anxious to restore the city, which had been ruined in A.D. 79 ; cf. Suetonius, *Tit.* 8 : "Bona oppressorum in Vesevo, quorum heredes non exstabant, restitutioni afflictarum civitatum attribuit." Winckelmann is supposed to be wrong in saying (*Werke*, ii. p. 23), on the strength of an inscription containing the words "signa translata ex abditis locis," that the Romans carried on excavations.

the workmen the notion that they were in the shop of a charcoal or coal merchant. An accidental fall revealed the fact that they were covered with decipherable letters,—that in reality the charcoal-rolls were nothing but rolls of papyrus, charred with the action of fire.[1]

So startling a discovery was not long in engaging the attention of savants. A certain Camillo Paderni, who was superintending the excavations in 1752, was the first to make an attempt to open the volumes. Despairing of success in other ways, he adopted the barbarous plan of cutting the volume in half longitudinally, and was quite satisfied, if the result of his labours revealed the language in which the manuscripts were written. By this means, no less than 337 Greek volumes and eighteen Latin were destroyed in a few months. Fortunately his successors in inquiry were neither so impatient nor so unfortunate, and something was done to repair his ravages as well as to carry on his original object. A series of investigators since 1752 have worked with admirable devotion to recover the manuscripts, amongst whom the important names are those of Piaggio in 1754, Mazocchi, Lapira in 1786, Hayter at the commencement of the nineteenth century, Sickler in 1814, and Davy in 1819 and 1820. Every kind of plan has been tried, —fumigation, exposure under glass to the sun, and different modes of chemical treatment; but it has had in the long-run to be confessed that the plan which Piaggio invented is on the whole the most successful. It is an infinitely slow and laborious

---

[1] What this villa was, and to whom it belonged, forms an interesting matter for speculation. According to Prof. Comparetti, whose name is honourably known in connection with explorations at Herculaneum, the villa belonged to Calpurnius Piso, the colleague of Gabinius in the consulship (58 B.C.) The majority of the charred scrolls found there are the works of Philodemus, a late Epicurean, of no particular merits as a philosopher. Philodemus was unlikely to have a villa of such pretensions belonging to himself; and he might have been a sort of superior secretary and philosophical instructor to Piso. Comparetti further supposes that two bronze busts, which have been sometimes called Seneca and Berenice, represent in reality Piso and Gabinius, the latter of whom Cicero calls effeminate. See the essay furnished by Comparetti to the volume of articles published on the occasion of the eighteen-hundredth anniversary of the destruction of Pompeii and Herculaneum. ("*La villa dei Pisoni in Ercolano e la sua Biblioteca,*" published in "*Pompei e la Regione sotterata dal Vesuvio nell' anno* LXXIX." Napoli; Giannini, 1879.

process. The first task is to discover the margin of the paper, which is by no means always easy. Then the roll is hung on two ribbons and rests on wool, spread on a piece of card. This card is held on leather supports, which can be raised or lowered by a screw. After all this preliminary work, the real process begins. Small portions of goldbeaters' skin are glued to the paper by means of isinglass, and, when the back of the paper is thus strengthened, threads of silk are attached to it, fastened to a cylinder. The cylinder is slowly turned, while other workmen open out the leaf with the point of a needle; and in this manner, in the course of four or five hours, a single inch is unrolled. The portions thus opened are laid on linen, copied and engraved, and the engravings form the collection now known as the "Volumina Herculanensia," brought out under the authority of the *Academia Ercolanese.*[1]

Such is a brief history of the discovery which will in time give us, in all probability, a fuller acquaintance with the Epicurean philosophy. For of the unearthed fragments, the great majority belong either to Epicurus himself, or to Philodemus, an Epicurean contemporary of Cicero. Hitherto we have learnt much of Epicureanism from the mouths of its adversaries: from the professed sceptic, Sextus Empiricus—from Plutarch, who wrote against an influential Epicurean named Colotes—from Seneca, who was a Stoic—from Cicero, above all, in most cases a most unfriendly and even contemptuous critic of Epicureanism. Of the positive tenets of Epicurus we learn most from the tenth book of Diogenes Laertius, to whose recital we must, of course, add the testimony of the eloquent Epicurean poet Lucretius. Of all the 300 rolls of Epicurus's own writings, the scant remains we possess are his will, a few epistles and letters, and a philosophical epitome, entitled κύριαι δόξαι, preserved by Diogenes: some individual expressions which we find in Seneca, Plutarch, and others: and fragments of Books ii. and xi., and portions of a few other books of his large

---

[1] See the account given by Dr. J. C. G. Boot in his *Notice sur les manuscrits trouvés à Herculanum* (Amsterdam, 1841), and also the report of Mr. Hayter, who was sent by the Prince Regent to Naples.

work " on Nature," which form part of the Volumina Herculanensia.[1]

To recast for ourselves, however, the society of Epicurus
in its main features is no difficult task. There is hardly any
other ancient philosopher whose personality comes before us
with such strikingly clear and definite traits. His was essentially a simple character, with none of the profundity of the
student, or the exclusiveness which marks the expounder of a
singular and isolated system. It was indeed the adaptability
of his doctrines to general life—to the ordinary pursuits of
ordinary people—which gave them such an unique charm in
the eyes of his contemporaries, and made his school flourish
from the third century before Christ to the third or fourth
century after.[2] Nor were the characteristics essentially changed
in this long life of 700 years, for there was no school which
was more careful to preserve the actual words of the founder.
Epicurus had not the obtrusive idiosyncrasy of the Cynic, nor
the severe and strict austerity of the Stoic. Philosophy with
him did not mean speculation, nor yet an isolated seclusion :
neither was its effect to be seen in the outward clothing, or
want of clothing, of a Diogenes. Philosophy was " a daily
business of speech and thought, to secure a happy life," ἐνέργεια

---

[1] The following, according to Professor Gomperz, is a table of fragments
belonging to Epicurus from Herculaneum :—

1. 2. } περὶ φύσεως	Bk. ii.	
3. 4. }	Bk. xi. Bk. xi. }	On μετέωρα.
5.	Bk. xiv.	
6.	Bk. xv.	
7.	Bk. xxviii.	On Causes of Error.
8. 9. }	? ?	{ Fragments on the Freedom of { the Will.
10.	?	On Error.
11.	?	On Life after Death.
12.	?	

The treatise was originally in thirty-seven books. Facsimiles of 1 and 3-10 are
preserved in the Bodleian Library at Oxford. In 2 occurs a curious word,
ἐξωστικός. Is this the right reading of the word in Diog. L. x. 143, which
usually stands ἐξοριστικῇ (al. ἐξεριστικῇ, ἐξαιρετικῇ) ?

[2] Epicurus was born in the year 342 or 341 B.C. Came to Athens in 306
B.C. (Diog. x. 2). Died 270 B.C. (Diog. x. 15). That the school lasted to at
least the third century after Christ is proved by what Diogenes says (§ 9),
writing in the first half of the third century, according to Zeller.

λόγοις καὶ διαλογισμοῖς τὸν εὐδαίμονα βίον περιποιοῦσα. It was
not necessary to have read deeply or thought profoundly :
indeed, literature and education were often more of a hindrance
than otherwise. " My good sirs, leave all culture alone" (παιδείαν
πᾶσαν, μακάριοι, φεύγετε) writes Epicurus in his letter to
Pythocles.[1] It need not trouble any one, says Metrodorus, his
pupil, if he had never read a line of Homer, and did not
know whether Hector was a Trojan or a Greek. And Cicero[2]
adds his testimony, "nihil opus esse eum, philosophus qui
futurus sit, scire literas." One study, however, for a philosopher
was absolutely necessary, the study of nature, and that for
the reason that a man cannot be happy unless he discard
superstition. "A man cannot be released from his fear on
matters of highest import, unless he knows the nature of the
universe and discards mythical superstition, so that without
physical science our very pleasures are tainted " (ὥστε οὐκ ἦν
ἄνευ φυσιολογίας ἀκεραίας τὰς ἡδονὰς ἀπολαμβάνειν).[3] For the
rest, a simple life without ostentation, without meanness, not
pharisaically temperate, nor yet too liberally self-indulgent,
was the ideal of Epicurus. " For myself, I can be pleased
with bread and water," he says, "yet send me a little cheese,
in order that when I want to be extravagant, I may be." [4]
This was the man, Diogenes pithily adds, whose doctrine was
that pleasure was the end of life.

Not less clearly stand out the personal kindliness, the sympathy, the generosity, the sweetness of Epicurus's character.
In the little circle which surrounded the philosopher in his
famous gardens were Polyaenus, Hermarchus his future successor, Colotes, possibly Leonteus and his wife Themista,
Leontion, and a beloved disciple, Metrodorus. Metrodorus,
who from the time of his first acquaintance with Epicurus
only left his side for six months, died before his master,
leaving two children. For these Epicurus seems to have
had an especial tenderness, leaving many injunctions about
them in his will. "Let my heirs watch over the daughter of
Metrodorus," he writes, "and when she grows up, let them

---

[1] Diog. x. 6 ; cf. § 121 : "The wise man lives poems, and does not make
them"—ποιήματά τε ἐνεργεῖν, οὐκ ἂν ποιῆσαι. Also § 87.

[2] Cic. *de Fin.* ii. 4. 12.   [3] Diog. x. 143.   [4] *Ibid.* 11.

give her in marriage to whomsoever Hermarchus shall choose,
if she be modest and obedient." Among the Herculanean
remains there is a letter of Epicurus to a little child, who may
possibly be this daughter of Metrodorus. The letter runs
thus: "We came to Lampsacus, Pythocles, Hermarchus,
Ctesippus and myself, and we are quite well. We found there
Themista and our other friends, and they are quite well. I
hope you are well too, and your mamma, and that you obey her
and papa and Matron in everything, as you used to do. For
you know quite well, my pet, that I and all the others love
you very much, because you are obedient to them in everything."[1] The use of the very words of childhood (" papa " and
" mamma "), the tender little expression, ναπία (though why
Doric in form it is hard to say), the travelling with a sort of
retinue, all seem to mark this letter as genuine. But if so,
what an admirable comment it forms on the encomiums in the
9th and 10th sections of Diogenes's history !—on the man who
could keep about him, " held prisoners by the siren-charms of
his teaching" (ταῖς δογματικαῖς αὐτοῦ σειρῆσι προκατασχεθέντες),
such a host of followers " that whole cities could not contain
them," who counted in his school men and women alike, and
could enlist in the number of his disciples even his slaves, one
of whom, named Mus, attained some celebrity as a philosopher !
And in this context we may perhaps read his dying words to

---

[1] Cf. Gomperz's "Ein brief Epikurs an ein kind " in *Hermes*, vol. v. (1871)
pp. 386-395.
    According to the arrangement of Gomperz the fragment is as follows :—

ἀφείγμεθα εἰς Λάμψακον ὑ-
γιαίνοντες, ἐγὼ καὶ Πυθο-
κλῆς καὶ Ἕρμαρχος καὶ Κτή-
σιππος, καὶ ἐκεῖ κατειλήφα-
μεν ὑγιαίνοντας Θεμίσ-
ταν καὶ τοὺς λοιποὺς φίλους.
εὖ δε ποιεῖς καὶ εἰ σὺ ὑγι-
αίνεις, καὶ ἡ μάμμη, καὐτῇ (?)
καὶ πάπᾳ καὶ Μάτρωνι πάν-
τα πείθῃ, ὥσπερ καὶ ἔμ-
προσθεν· εὖ γὰρ ἴσθι, ναπία,
ὅτι καὶ ἐγὼ καὶ οἱ λοιποὶ
πάντες σε μέγα φιλοῦμεν
ὅτι τούτοις πείθη(ι) πάντα.

Idomeneus,[1] which though they contain possibly a note of
exaggerated rhetoric, yet bear a last testimony to the quiet
happy life among friends, which his philosophy recommended.
" On this last, yet blessed, day of my life, I write to you.　Pains
and tortures of body I have to the full, but there is set over
against these the joy of my heart at the memory of our happy
conversations in the past.　Do you, if you would be worthy of
your devotion to me and philosophy, take care of the children
of Metrodorus." Ἐπιμελοῦ τῶν παίδων Μητροδώρου were the
last words he wrote.

If this is not the ordinary notion which is held about
Epicurus, the reason is that his philosophy is more studied
than his life, and there are many points of view from which his
philosophy seems to invite criticism and disparagement.　With
some critics, the fundamental idea of Epicurus—the value of
human happiness—is not one which enlists their sympathies ;
by others an unconscious comparison is drawn between Epicureanism and the magnificent systems which preceded it—very
much of course to the detriment of the former ; by others, again,
that notorious dislike of culture, which the founder of the
school not only felt but was proud of, is considered fatal to his
philosophic fame.　And in these ways Epicureanism is undoubtedly open to blame ; to which must also be added a
certain logical weakness and inconsistency of thought which is
not surprising in one who thought so lightly of logic as a study.
The poverty of the theory of knowledge and truth, the inconsistency between a systematic incuriousness about astronomy,[2]
and the acknowledgment of the necessity of physics, the flat
contradiction between the reign of Law in Nature and the
Freedom of Will in Man, the difficulty of understanding how a
purely selfish theory of life could not only extol disinterested
friendship, but even worship gods from whom nothing could
be obtained,—all these points, and many others beside, must
tend to lower our admiration for Epicurus as a philosopher,

---

[1] Diog. x. 22.　The power and influence of Epicurus over his disciples is
acknowledged by Lucian : *Alex. Pseud.* caps. 17, 25, and 61 (Jacobitz).

[2] Cf. the astonishing assertions in Diog. x. 91, 92 ff.,—Epicurus thought that
the sun was about the same size as it appears to be, etc. etc.

however attractive a character may belong to Epicurus as a man.

But the historical circumstances of the time, which perhaps promoted individual virtues, were fatal to the elaboration of a systematic philosophy. It was a time of weariness and exhaustion—a weariness of metaphysical abstraction, a weariness of sophistical ingenuity and rhetoric, a weariness of political activity. At the time when Epicurus was living at Athens, at the close of the fourth century B.C., the Grecian world had seen the downfall of Thebes, the exile of Demosthenes, the shipwreck of the Hellenic state-system. The death of Alexander at Babylon had led to the fruitless struggle for independence in the Lamian war; the conquest of Antipater had crushed out the last efforts of Greek spirit. Aristotle, accused of atheism, had left the city of Socrates and Plato, and had died at Chalcis. In the misery and repression of the time, men did not want far-reaching theory or elaborate system, but something definite, precise, concrete : some ideal of existence which would suit those who had given up politics and had become isolated and self-centred, a theory of individual life, not a compendium of cosmical knowledge. The philosophy of Epicurus was the most effectual answer to the needs of the age. While Stoicism preached heroic fortitude, and had to be transformed in a century and a half, Epicureanism in the fourth century after Christ remained essentially the same system which had been promulgated by the son of Neocles.

" The aim and end of all action," says Epicurus, " is that we may neither suffer nor fear,"—τούτου γὰρ χάριν ἅπαντα πράττομεν ὅπως μήτε ἀλγῶμεν μήτε ταρβῶμεν [1]— " when once this end is realised, all the tempest of the soul subsides, for animal nature has then no need to satisfy, nothing is wanting to the full completion of good, whether of body or soul. For we want pleasure when we feel pain at its absence ; when we feel no pain, we want no pleasure. It is for this reason that we say that pleasure is the beginning and end of a happy life." Here at least there is a concrete and definite answer to men's demands. " Who will show us any good ? " was the pressing

---

[1] Diog. x. 128.

question asked amid the ruins of Hellenism. The good
is pleasure, and pleasure is the good, is the answer of Epicurus. Nor will he have any mistake as to his meaning.
"I can conceive of no good remaining," he says, "if you
take from me the pleasures of taste, the pleasures of love,
and the pleasures of ear and eye."[1] And Metrodorus, the
disciple, exaggerating, as is the wont of disciples, the teaching
of his master, says boldly: "It is in the belly that the natural
reason of man finds the chief object of his care."[2] The brother
of Metrodorus, a certain Timocrates, who was a renegade from
Epicurus's school, found in this and other texts plenty of matter
for scandal. He had had hard work, he said, to get away from
his nightly revels and all his mystic confraternity. As to
Epicurus δὶς τῆς ἡμέρας ἐμεῖν ὑπὸ τρυφῆς·—συνεῖναί τε αὐτῷ τε
καὶ Μητροδώρῳ ἑταίρας καὶ ἄλλας· Μαρμάριον καὶ Ἡδεῖαν καὶ
Ἐρώτιον καὶ Νικίδιον.[3] "Notum inter accolas odium," and
Epicurus's name was the subject of many attributes, of which
κιναιδολογός was by no means the worst.

But Epicurus was not such a tiro in pleasures as to suppose that a life of sensual enjoyment was a life of happiness.
A man of fierce, sensual nature like Aristippus, with the hot
blood of Africa in his veins, might indeed think so, and make
moments of pleasurable emotion (μονόχρονος ἡδονή) the motto
of his school. But a man who lived no tempestuous life like
the Cyrenaic, but taught in his garden at Athens, who expressly
recommended his pupils to live in the country,[4] was not likely
to be a libertine and a voluptuary. Does pleasure only consist
in motion and restlessness? Can indiscriminate indulgence in
pleasures secure happiness, not only for the present, but for
life? Do pleasures differ only in quantity and not in kind?
and is not the pleasure of the mind higher than the pleasure of
the body? Does not man, as rational, look before and after,
and is not therefore the future and the past, as well as the
present, matter of concern for him? Such were the questions
which naturally presented themselves to Epicurus, and mate-

[1] Diog. x. 6.
[2] Ap. Athen. vii. ii., περὶ γαστέρα ὁ κατὰ φύσιν βαδίζων λόγος τὴν ἅπασαν ἔχει
σπουδήν. Cf. Eur. *Cyclops*, 335 (Paley), καὶ τῇ μεγίστῃ γαστρὶ τῇδε δαιμόνων.
[3] Diog. x. 6, 7.   [4] [τὸν σόφον] φιλαγρήσειν.—*Ibid.* 120.

rially qualified his views on pleasure. "We do not choose every pleasure: there are times when we relinquish many pleasures, when the consequent inconveniences are greater, and we hold many pains to be more choiceworthy than pleasures, when, after much endurance of pain, we are rewarded by a higher pleasure. Every pleasure is in its essential nature a good, but not every pleasure is choiceworthy, just as every pain is an evil, but is not therefore always to be avoided."[1] And again, very explicitly: "When we say that pleasure is the end, we do not mean the pleasures of the libertine and the pleasures of mere enjoyment, as some critics, either ignorant, or antagonistic, or unfriendly, suppose; but the absence of pain in the body and trouble in the mind."[2] Hence the necessity of prudence and self-control in the direction of life— a prudence which is only to be taught by philosophy. "For it is not drinkings and revellings, nor the pleasures of love, nor tables loaded with dainties, which beget the happy life, but sober reasoning (νήφων λογισμός), to discover what must be sought or avoided, and why, and to banish the fancies which have most power to distract men's souls. Philosophy has no more priceless element than prudence, from which all the other virtues flow, teaching us that it is not possible to live pleasantly without also living sensibly, honourably, and justly: nor yet to live sensibly, honourably, and justly without living pleasantly."[3] Therefore says Epicurus, "Let not the young man delay to learn philosophy, neither let the old man weary of philosophy: for no one is either under age or over age to secure his soul's health."[4] In point of fact, the end of a wise man's life is not pleasure in the ordinary sense, but health, ease, serenity (ὑγίεια, ἀπονία, ἀταραξία).[5]

To the realisation of this serenity many things appear as obstacles. Nature seems against a man, fate crushes him in its grasp, the gods are not always his friends, death comes at the last to end all his hopes and energies. Epicurus saw

---

[1] Diog. 129.   [2] *Ibid*. x. 131.   [3] *Ibid*. 132.   [4] *Ibid*. 122.
[5] Cf. Lucian, *Bis accusatus*, cap. 22.   *Parasitus*, ch. 11. The former passage is a dialogue between the Στοά and Epicurus himself; the latter is concerned with the Epicurean idea of felicity.

clearly enough that these impediments must be removed out of
the path of men's happiness, although, unfortunately, in nearly
each case, the removal is effected at the expense of his logic.
The whole of the superstructure which he builds on the foundations of Hedonism and Sensationalism is an interesting attempt
to go beyond his ground-plan, to find room for the complexity
and the many-sidedness of life on the narrow platform of what
is called Individualism. Most of the miseries of life are caused
by superstition, and the first effort of the wise man must consequently be to oppose science to religion, a knowledge of
nature to an imaginative mythology. Science, says Epicurus,
is freedom; mental serenity means enfranchisement from all
mythical opinions, and the constant memory of the main facts
of nature. "For if we study those events whence arise our
anxiety and fear, we shall find their true causes and be free."[1]
Here is the first breach made in that theory of unintellectual-
ism with which Epicurus started. It is all very well to tell
men to eschew culture and be happy; but it is impossible at
the same time to tell them to be sages. However much it may
be true in some given point that ignorance is bliss, it is not a
good maxim for a life which aims at being continuously happy.
The theory breaks down at the outset, directly it is discovered
that happiness means at least freedom from fear, and that fear-
lessness is not attainable without knowledge. Some of the
elements of culture may indeed be abandoned; a man need
not know literature, he may "act poems and not make them;" a
Polyaenus may, on his entrance to the Epicurean ranks, abjure
the higher mathematics which made him famous; and Epicurus
himself might declare the knowledge of celestial phenomena to
be either useless or unattainable a few years before Archimedes
and Hipparchus measured the volume of the earth and the
approximate distance of the moon;[2] but yet a certain amount
of science is indispensable, so as to make head against foolish
superstition. Almost the chief endowment of the Epicurean
sage must be a knowledge of nature, for "without physical

---

[1] Diog. x. 82.

[2] Cf. M. Guyau's *La Morale d'Épicure*, p. 185. He there compares
Epicurus's incuriousness with that of Auguste Comte. Cf. too Cic. *Acad.* ii.
33. 106; *Fin.* i. 6. 20.

knowledge our very pleasures are tainted." Religion has been, as Lucretius afterwards said, the chief cause of the greatest evils; and it is only possible to checkmate religion by science.

What then is to be our view of natural operations? what is the character of this saving and enfranchising physics? Epicurus's scheme is a strictly materialistic one, for the details of which he is mainly indebted to Democritus. All life is material, some form of body being at the base of all existence. The ultimate elements of nature are not the so-called elements which Empedocles made his στοιχεῖα. Fire, earth, air, and water are, in fact, not simple bodies at all, but complex aggregates, which can be divided into something more primordial and original. At the base of things scientific analysis reveals two elements, atoms and void, both of which are infinite; and the beginnings of creation are due to the infinite atoms falling through infinite space, collecting and aggregating themselves here and there and forming worlds, life meaning the collection of atoms, death their dispersion.[1] Even the soul is really material, formed out of atoms which are indeed finer and rarer than those which go to the creation of other substances, but still essentially material in their structure.[2] Atoms have only primary qualities, shape, size, and weight; other qualities of taste or colour are only subjective and secondary.[3]

But before we get so far as this, the question naturally occurs as to the capacities of the human mind for ascertaining the truth about nature. What is the criterion of truth? Sensation, αἴσθησις, is the answer of Epicurus. In that part of his philosophy which answers to Logic, and which in his terminology is τὸ κανονικόν, he is very explicit on this matter. " The criteria of Truth are sensations:—There is nothing which can convict sensations of error; neither a similar sensation, for similar sensations have an equal value; nor yet different sensations, for they refer to different objects; nor yet reason, for reason itself is constructed out of, depends upon, sense (πᾶς γὰρ λόγος ἀπὸ τῶν αἰσθήσεων ἤρτηται)."[4] How then does error arise, for it is obvious that hallucinations, for instance, and dreams, are real? It arises, not in the sensation itself, but

---

[1] Diog. x. 39, 40, 41.　　[2] *Ibid.* 63.　　[3] *Ibid.* 44.　　[4] *Ibid.* 31, 32.

in our inference from the sensation. The actual sensation of a ghost which a nervous man sees is real and indubitable; the mistake arises when he draws the inference that what he sees has a real existence outside him. Yet go beyond mere sensation we must; for how else are we even to attempt to interpret for ourselves the constitution of nature? Epicurus feels the necessity, but is not very scientific in his theory of the processes founded on sensation. There are προλήψεις, he says, which are notions founded on repeated sensations, and δόξαι, which are opinions, and λόγος, which is ratiocination. The whole process seems to go on naturally, without any idea of the activity of mental construction. Every body throws out εἴδωλα, images of itself, and these images may come differently to different men—not that the thing itself changes, but that the images, which men see of it, are different. Hence, as Protagoras said, what seems to a man to be true is true for him, and yet there is a real objective truth, as well as subjective opinions. But how in any given case are we to know that we have got hold of the true image? Here Epicurus fails us; whether he falls back upon the Democritean dogma that there is a true knowledge of the intelligence, as well as a false knowledge of mere sense-impression, or whether he cuts the knot by the assertion that the images of the wise man are always true. In each case the solution is more than unsatisfactory; and in this failure, the whole theory of nature, so far transcending the mere impressions of sense, is involved in uncertainty and doubt.

But this is after all a logical or metaphysical difficulty, antecedent to the study of nature. There is, however, another of a more practical nature which the Epicurean system of physics has to meet. If everything in nature goes by fixed and unalterable laws, is not man too bound in the links of an iron fate? For man is, according to the materialistic position, part of nature, his body formed of the grosser atoms and his soul of the finer. And if so, what becomes of human happiness before the rigid laws of Necessity? For Fate, too, as well as superstition, is a stern schoolmaster, driving us in ways which do not make for our peace. How can man's freedom, on which his happiness seems to depend, be secured side by side

with that regularity of natural law which is to banish superstition ? Here Epicurus's theory, judged by a modern standard,
becomes almost puerile. The atoms, according to him, have a
certain wilful spontaneity of their own ; they do not descend
in parallel lines : they swerve aside, self-moved, and in this
power of the atoms to deviate from the perpendicular, Epicurus
finds the origin of human free-will.[1] This is the celebrated
doctrine of the " clinamen," which Lucretius expounds at
length, and which Cicero covers with ridicule.[2] It may be,
of course,. that we have not as yet got the theory in its true
outlines. Recent fragments from Herculaneum throw, according to Professor Gomperz of Vienna, clearer light upon this
much-vexed question. " From these fragments there arises a
series of deductions which, it seems to me, are indubitable.
Epicurus was not, as has been hitherto supposed, an Indeter-
minist : he was an opponent of Fatalism, not of Determinism :
he did not believe in the causelessness of human acts of will ;
for, like Voltaire and others, he believed that man to be morally
free whose actions were determined by his own opinions : he
avoided, like the best thinkers of our day (like Mill, Grote, or
Bain), the use of the word Necessity in the processes of the
will, as a misleading expression. Like these philosophers, he
held that it was unsuitable to denote the efficacy of irresistible
causes, and the efficacy of all causes generally by one and the
same expression. Finally, his theory of the will was coloured
by that doctrine of knowledge which was peculiar to him and
to Democritus. The problem evidently culminates with him
in the question—How can an act of will through an image
($\epsilon\check{\iota}\delta\omega\lambda o\nu$) from without (the antecedent of every perception
and mental representation) be excited and determined by the
collection of our convictions, *i.e.* (in his sense) our whole
personality."[3] Whatever may be the exact opinions of Epicurus
on this matter, two things are clear—First, that he declared (as
against the Stoics) that such a thing as Fate did not exist ($\tau\grave{\eta}\nu$

---

[1] Plutarch, *de Solert. Anim.* 7, ὅπως τὸ ἐφ' ἡμῖν μὴ ἀπόληται.

[2] M. Guyau, in his *La Morale d'Epicure*, defends the doctrine. See pp.
71-103.

[3] *Neue Bruchstücke Epikur's insbesondere über die Willensfrage*, von Th.
Gomperz (Wien, 1876), pp. 9-11. The fragments in question are those marked

εἱμαρμένην ὑπό τινων δεσπότιν εἰσαγομένην πάντων μὴ εἶναι) ;
secondly, that freewill in man was necessary to insure the
validity of moral distinctions (τὸ δὲ παρ' ἡμῶν ἀδέσποτον· ᾧ καὶ
τὸ μεμπτὸν καὶ τὸ ἐναντίον παρακολουθεῖν πέφυκεν).[1]

Even though a man should disbelieve in Fate, he yet may
believe in the influence of the Divinity upon human affairs, and
the Divine influence may chance to be malevolent. In the
thoughts of many of the Greeks, the godhead was not free from
envy; and human happiness, if prolonged for many years, was
sure to bring down the gods' displeasure. Even though such
definite maleficent purpose were wanting, yet in the action of
the godhead there was something at once irresponsible and
incalculable, which would make the Epicurean "serenity"
difficult to realise. What then does Epicurus bid his followers
think about the gods ? "In the first place," he says in the
letter to Menoeceus, "you must think the god to be a being
incorruptible and blessed, according to ordinary notions on the
subject : attribute to him nothing which is inconsistent with
his incorruptibility, or inappropriate to his blessedness, but
think about him everything which is true to that union of
happiness and immortality which he enjoys. For gods there
veritably are, because our idea of them is clear. But they
are not what most people think them to be; and the atheist
is not he who destroys the gods of the people, but he who
attributes the fancies of the people to gods." [2] And again :

---

8 and 9 in the list given above. [Pap. 1056 ; Coll. prior x. 697 ; Coll. alt.
vi. 55 *seq.*] Here is a fragment tolerably easy to follow, as restored
by Professor Gomperz :—

οὐ (δὲ ἀπ)ολείπει τὰ πάθη τοῦ γίν(εσθαι) νουθε(τ)‖εῖν
τε ἀλλήλους καὶ (μ)άχ(εσ)θαι καὶ μεταρυθμίζειν (sic)
ὡς ἔχοντας καὶ ἐν ἑα(υ)τοῖς τὴν αἰ(τ)ίαν καὶ οὐχὶ
ἐν τῇ ἐξ ἀρχῆς μόνον συστάσει καὶ ἐν τῇ τοῦ
περιέχοντος καὶ ἐπεισιόντος κατὰ τὸ αὐτόματον
ἀνάγκη(ι). εἰ γὰρ τις καὶ τῷ νουθετεῖν καὶ τῷ
νουθετεῖσθαι τὴν κατὰ τὸ αὐ(τό)μα(τ)ον ἀνάγκην
πρ(οσ)ν(έμοι).—Pap. 1056, 21, and Pap. 697, D, 1.
Cf. too *Die Ueberreste eines Buches von Epikur* περὶ φύσεως (Gomperz, Wien,
1879), which adds to the foregoing. Also Fr. Bahnsch (*Philolog. Anzeiger*
1878, Nr. 5, Art. 73.)

[1] Diog. x. 133.

[2] *Ibid.* 123, ἀσεβὴς δὲ, οὐχ ὁ τοὺς τῶν πολλῶν θεοὺς ἀναιρῶν, ἀλλ' ὁ τὰς τῶν
πολλῶν δόξας θεοῖς προσάπτων.

" The blessed and immortal deity neither feels trouble nor causes trouble : he feels no anger, nor is he moved by flattery : for all such feelings indicate weakness " (ἐν ἀσθενεῖ γὰρ πᾶν τὸ τοιοῦτον).[1] ` On the one hand, then, if the gods are really happy, they can have nothing to do with the troubles of the world; on the other hand, if they have nothing to do with human affairs, men need not be afraid of their interference. Thus the very condition of happiness in the gods secures the inviolability of human happiness. The gods, infinite in number, live in happy ease in the intervals which separate the infinite worlds.[2] They are in stature like men, composed of very fine atoms ; they eat food, and thus repair the ravages of time ; they are male and female ; and Philodemus, according to a Herculanean fragment, has the hardihood to assert that they speak something like the Greek language.

It is at the least doubtful how far Epicurus himself would assent to all these predications about the godhead which were certainly rife in his school. It would savour too much of that " attributing of the fancies of the people to gods," which, in his own fine phrase, constituted the character of the real atheist. But, whatever may be the mental reservations or *nuances* of thought involved, Epicurus undoubtedly asserted that the gods exist, for the notions we have of them (based on sensations) are clear, and clearness is to him, as well as to Descartes, the test of truth. Perhaps the images of them which are found . in men's minds are due, as Democritus thought, to the fact that while all objects, distant as well as near, send off εἴδωλα of themselves, the intervening medium of air distorts and magnifies the images received by the senses. Perhaps they were mere ideals of human life and happiness, for Epicurus in one passage declares that they were only to be apprehended by reason—λόγῳ θεωρη- τοὺς εἶναι.[3] Perhaps Epicurus was after all, in this respect, somewhat of a hypocrite, according to the judgment of Posi- donius. This much at least is certain, that, whatever the gods were, they were not to be allowed to interfere either with the reign of law in the natural world, or with the happiness of the

---

[1] Diog. x. 139.　　　　　　　[2] τὰ μετακόσμια, intermundia.

[3] Diog. x. 139. Lucian makes Epicurus an atheist ; cf. the *Bis accusatus, Zeus Tragoedus,* 22, and *Icaromenippus,* 32.

Epicurean wise man. The Epicureans might worship at the temples, and a Diocles might feel the grandeur of Zeus himself increased by the sight of an Epicurus on his knees;[1] but Zeus was no longer to be the cloud-compeller, the lord of heaven and earth: he might retain his majesty, but he must lose his terrors.

Yet, even so, the possibility of worshipping such gods demands greater self-forgetfulness in the wise man than Epicurus allows him. It is a remark of Seneca, that although Epicurus banished disinterestedness from morality, he yet allowed it a place in the worship of the gods.[2] What reason could induce a man who was persuaded that his own pleasure was his only object in life, to worship gods who had nothing to do with the course of the world? What good could he get from them? what evil could he avert by his bended knees? And if nothing could be gained from such an act, what inducement was there for a man to perform it? The same difficulty occurs in the Epicurean theory of friendship. Friendship, like every other external relation, must in such a system be ultimately based on its advantages. Ἡ φιλία διὰ τὰς χρείας, says Epicurus, although he adds that a great part of the resulting advantage is the sense of community in enjoyment. Yet, however selfish in origin, friendship appears eventually to figure as a highly disinterested virtue—Epicurus in this view of the subject resembling the ordinary modern Utilitarian. Hardly any friendships, moreover, were more celebrated than the Epicurean, as Cicero remarks; and hardly any words were too strong to recommend it. "Of all the things which wisdom provides for the happiness of a lifetime by far the greatest is friendship."[3] And so high a view has Epicurus of the society of friends, that he expressly discountenances the Pythagorean formula of friendly communism. A professed communism argues distrust, and distrust is the ruin of friendship.[4] When

---

[1] Acc. to M. Guyau, *La Morale d'Epicure*, p. 178.
[2] Senec. *de Benef.* IV. xix.
[3] Cic. *Fin.* i. 20, 65; *ibid.* ii. 25, 80.
[4] τόν τε Ἐπίκουρον μὴ ἀξιοῦν εἰς τὸ κοινὸν κατατίθεσθαι τὰς οὐσίας, καθάπερ τὸν Πυθαγόραν, κοινὰ τὰ τῶν φίλων λέγοντα· ἀπιστούντων γὰρ εἶναι τὸ τοιοῦτον· εἰ δ' ἀπίστων, οὐδὲ φίλων.—Diog. x. 11; cf. *ibid.* 148.

we consider the selfish origin of friendship, it is not surprising
to learn that the later Epicureans were much exercised with
regard to the proper interpretation of the phenomenon.

One more obstacle to happiness remains, the most difficult
yet the most necessary to remove. The awful shadow of death
lies across men's lives, quenching not only enthusiasm but
serenity in the fear of impending pain and perfect annihilation.
How is a man to bear up against so inevitable a future? How
is the delicate plant of human happiness to thrive in such an
undermined soil? Some of Epicurus's best sayings have reference to death. " Accustom yourself," he tells Menoeceus, " to
think that death has nothing to do with us, since every good
and every evil depends on sensation, and death is the absence
of sensation. Whence it comes that the true knowledge that
death has nothing to do with us makes what is mortal in life
really enjoyable, not because it adds to life immortality, but
because it takes away our longing for immortality. For there
is nothing which can terrify a man in life, when he is assured
that there is nothing terrible in the absence of life. So that he
is a fool who tells us to fear death, not because its presence
will torment us, but that its anticipation torments us. For
that which troubles us not when it is come, has but vain
terrors when it is looked forward to. Death, then, the most
awful of ills, is nothing in our eyes; for when we are, death is
not, and when death is, we are not."[1] But fear is not to be
exorcised by sophisms, and the question still presses for an
answer, Are not our pleasures ruined by the prospect of death?
No, answers Epicurus, for pleasure is not made pleasure by
continuance, it is whole and entire in every pleasurable
moment. Pleasure is still pleasure, happiness is yet happiness,
even though it be doomed to an inevitable death. "Time,
whether limited or unlimited, involves an equal amount of
pleasure, if a man measures it by reason."[2] Can this consideration, then, help the Epicurean, that pleasure is pleasure,
whether it is fleeting or permanent, whether it comes once or
lasts a lifetime? Yet, when we remember that it was only by
means of the idea of continuance that Epicurus overcame the

---

[1] Diog. x. 124.   [2] *Ibid.* 145.

μονόχρονος ἡδονή of the Cyrenaics, that the pleasure he recommended was precisely not the pleasure of any given moment, but that pleasure which could last and become a permanent possession, even this consolation breaks down. Here once more, in the case of death, as in the case of fate, freewill, and the gods, the higher philosophy of Epicurus is found too wide for his foundation, and mental serenity, the Epicurean ideal of life, can only be gained at the expense of Epicurean logic.

After all, one has to turn away from the system, in order to reconstitute one's notion of the man. We think rather of the kindly and genial teacher, realising the "rus in urbe" in his Athenian garden, and surrounded by his friends, the faithful Metrodorus, Polyaenus the converted mathematician, Hermarchus the future successor, above all, the little Epicurus and his sister, Metrodorus's children. There are no asperities about Epicurus, no angular points of chagrin or disappointment or baffled hopes. He is as much above his professed opinions as the ordinary man is below them. His system may require a selfish account of friendship, yet he can say, " It is more blessed to give than to receive."[1] His theoretic view of death forces him to deny it any terrors ; yet he knows the full value of life, and can administer a stern rebuke to the pessimist (perhaps Hegesias, ὁ πεισιθάνατος) of his own day. " He who admonishes a youth to live well, and an old man to die well, is a fool; but far worse is the man who says, ' It is well not to have been born, and, when born, it is best to die.' For if he means what he says, why not die at once ? It is quite open to him to do so. But if he is jesting at us, he is frivolous on subjects which do not admit of jest." [2] Epicurus might despise superstition, yet he felt that fatalism was more morally ruinous. " It were better to follow the myths about the gods than be a slave to the fate of the physicists." [3] Seneca, who felt all the attractions of the Epicurean system, has preserved for us another saying of

---

[1] τὸ εὖ ποιεῖν ἥδιόν ἐστι τοῦ πάσχειν.—Plut. *Non posse suav. viv.* 15. 4.

[2] Diog. x. 126, 127 ; cf. Soph. *Œd. Col.* 1225.

[3] *Ibid.* 134. So again a man's happiness is not to be imperilled by a belief in luck and chance. " Little indeed is the power which fortune has over a wise man, for the main interests of life have been, are, and will be ordered by Reason" (c. 144). And again : "Chance does not give us good and ill, but only the beginnings whence good or ill may come " (c. 134).

Epicurus, which has quite a modern sound : " Initium salutis est notitia peccati "—the knowledge of sin is the first step in reform.[1] Indeed, there is much modern quality in Epicurus. Besides that doctrine of Utilitarianism, which fathers so much modern philosophical thought, there is his belief in progress and the slow results of Time. " We must admit," he says, " that the nature of man is in many respects forced and schooled (διδαχ-θῆναι τε καὶ ἀναγκασθῆναι) by circumstances. Reasoning after-wards perfects nature's lessons, and adds thereto new discoveries, sometimes quickly, sometimes slowly, sometimes in long periods of time, practically infinite."[2] It is difficult to find in any other Greek writer so explicit a statement as this of the effects of Time on human development. Or again, there is his theory of justice, which anticipates Hobbes and Locke and Rousseau : " Justice is nothing in itself, apart from human societies :— Justice is the token of a common interest, a contract not to wrong or to be wronged."[3] Or, once more, there is the natural origin attributed to Language (by no means the ordinary Greek idea), which is said to be neither a divine creation nor an artificial product, but which both Epicurus and Lucretius explain as due to the natural emission of sounds expressive of sensations and ideas.[4]

But Epicurus's chief merit is undoubtedly found in the simple, practical, and unaffected morality which he inculcated both by precept and example. As a summary of the philo-sophy of life the following maxims are not unworthy to be reckoned with the thoughts of greater men than the Gargettian sage :—" The injuries which come to men either through hatred or envy or pride, the wise man will conquer by reason. He will acknowledge the power of feelings and passions, but will not thereby be hindered in his wisdom. Even though he be tortured, he is yet happy, albeit that at times in his torture he will moan and groan.[5] It is the wise man only who can feel

---

[1] Senec. *Ep.* 28, 9.
[2] Diog. x. 75 ; cf. Lucret. v. 1452 :—

> Usus et impigrae simul experientia mentis
> Paulatim docuit pedetemtim progredientes.

[3] Diog. x. 150.   [4] Diog. x. 75 ; Lucret. v. 1027.
[5] As against the Stoical endurance of pain.

affection for his friends, whether present or absent. He will
not punish his servants, but will be compassionate, and pardon
those who are worthy. No wise man will fall in love, nor
believe that Eros is heaven-sent. Nor will he be a good
orator. At times a sage will marry and beget children; at
times, if circumstances be adverse, he will not marry, and will
try to dissuade others. He will neither cherish wrath in drunkenness, nor will he engage in politics, nor become a tyrant, nor
yet flatter. Neither will he beg. Even though bereft of eyes,
the wise man will still have a hold on life. He will feel grief:
he will think about property, he will provide for the future.
He will be fond of a country life, and bear a stout front against
fortune. Only so far will he think of repute amongst men,
that he be not contemned. More than others he will feel
delight at the theatre. It is only the wise man who will have
a right opinion on music and poetry; yet the sage lives poems,
and does not make them. Money he will make, yet only in
wisdom, if he be in want. He will court a monarch at the
proper moment; he will humour a man, in order to correct
him. He will found a school, but not to gain crowds of
scholars. He will give his opinion freely, and never be at a
loss; in his dreams he will be true to himself. And sometimes he will die for his friend."[1]

Epicurus has had many resurrections; his spirit has lived
again in Gassendi, in La Rochefoucauld, in Saint-Evremond, in
Helvetius, and in Jeremy Bentham. Perhaps this fragment
from Saint-Evremond may be most fitly compared with the
summary of virtue just quoted from Epicurus :—

" He is a philosopher who keeps aloof alike from superstition
and from impiety; an Epicurean, whose distaste for debauchery
is as strong as his appetite for pleasure; a man who has never
known want, but at the same time has never enjoyed affluence.
He lives in a manner which is despised by those who have
everything, envied by those who have nothing, appreciated by
those who make their happiness and their reason agree. In his
youth he hated waste, being persuaded that property was
necessary to make a long life comfortable. In his age he cares

---

[1] Diog. x. 117-121.

not for economy, feeling that want is little to be feared, when one has but a little time left to want in. He is grateful for the gifts of nature, and finds no fault with those of fortune; he hates crime, endures error, and pities misfortune. He does not try to find out the bad points of men in order to decry them, but he looks for their foibles in order to give himself amusement; is secretly rejoiced at the knowledge of these foibles, and would be still more pleased to make them known to others, did not his discretion forbid. Life is to his mind too short to read all sorts of books, and to load one's memory with all sorts of things at the risk of one's judgment. He devotes himself not to the most learned writings, so as to acquire knowledge, but to the most sensible, so as to strengthen his understanding. At one time he seeks the most elegant to refine his taste, at another the most amusing to refresh his spirits. As for friendship, he has more constancy than might be expected from a philosopher, and more heartiness than could be looked for even in a younger and less experienced man. As for religion, he thinks justice, charity, and trust in the goodness of God of more importance than sorrow for past offences."[1]

Such too was the Epicurean sage; not a hero, not a statesman, not even a philosopher, but a quiet, humane, and prudent man, —"a hero," as Seneca says, "disguised as a woman." Epicureanism was undoubtedly not a speculative success, but as a practical code of life it suited the world far more than its rival, Stoicism, and lasted longer. It could not produce martyrs,[2] or satisfy the highest aspirations of mankind, but it made men fall back on themselves, and find contentment and serenity in a life at once natural and controlled. *Λάθε βιώσας,* Live in secret, was the Epicurean watchword. "Keep my words," said Epicurus, "and meditate on them day and night, by yourself or with your friend, and you shall live as a god amongst men. For there is nothing mortal about a man who lives in the midst of immortal good." **W. L. C.**

---

[1] Quoted in George Saintsbury's article on Saint-Evremond, *Fortnightly Review*, July 1879.

[2] M. Guyau, however, says that Vanini, who had his tongue cut out, and was burnt at Toulouse in 1619, was a martyr for the sake of Epicureanism.— *La Morale d'Épicure*, p. 192. He is usually called a Peripatetic.

THE SPEECHES OF THUCYDIDES.[1]

§ 1. THE famous phrase in which Thucydides claims a
lasting value for his work has had the fate of many striking
expressions : it is often quoted apart from the words which
explain it. "A possession for ever," not "the rhetorical
triumph of an hour:" taken by itself this has a ring of exultation, noble perhaps, yet personal, as if the grave self-mastery
of the historian had permitted this one utterance in the tone of
the Roman poet's confident retrospect or the English poet's
loftier hope, speaking of a monument more enduring than brass,
of things so written that men should not willingly let them die.
It is the context that reduces the meaning to a passionless precision. "The absence of fable in the History," he says, "will
perhaps make it less attractive to hearers ; but it will be enough
if it is found profitable by those who desire an exact knowledge
of the past as a key to the future, which in all human probability
will repeat or resemble the past. The work is meant to be a
possession for ever, not the rhetorical triumph of an hour." [2]
That the intention of Thucydides has been fulfilled in his own
sense is due largely to the speeches which form between a
fourth and fifth of the whole work. It is chiefly by these that
the facts of the Peloponnesian war are transformed into typical
examples of universal laws and illuminated with a practical
significance for the students of politics in every age and country.

---

[1] A table of the Speeches will be found at page 322.
[2] i. 22. The τε after κτῆμα in the original marks the connection of the
thought : "and so." Cp. i. 4, Μίνως . . . ἐκράτησε . . . τό τε λῃστικόν,
ὡς εἰκός, καθῄρει : so 5, τό τε σιδηροφορεῖσθαι : 6, ἐγυμνώθησάν τε : 9, Ἀγα-
μέμνων τε.

The scope of the speeches is seen best if we consider what the History would be without them. The narrative would remain, with a few brief comments on great characters or events, and those two passages in which Thucydides describes the moral effects of pestilence and of party-strife. But there would be little or no light on the inner workings of the Greek political mind, on the courses of reasoning which determined the action, on the whole play of feeling and opinion which lay behind the facts.

§ 2. The introduction of speeches became a regular part of ancient historiography, and came in again at the revival of literature, not quite going out, in Italy and France at least, till the end of the last century. But the followers of Thucydides were obeying an established tradition; he was the writer who had done most to establish it; indeed, he might properly be called its founder. The place of the speeches in his design was due to special influences of the age as well as to the peculiar bent of his mind; we have to consider what had been done before him, and the plan on which he went to work.

At the beginning of the Peloponnesian war a Greek prose literature scarcely yet existed. The Ionian prose-writers before Herodotus, or contemporary with him, are known to us only from scanty fragments. But the Augustan age possessed all, or nearly all, their writings; and Dionysius of Halicarnassus has described their general characteristics, comparing them collectively with Herodotus and Thucydides.[1] These Ionian writers, he says, treat the annals of cities and people separately,[2]—not combining them into a large picture, as Herodotus does. Their common object was to diffuse a knowledge

---

[1] Dionys. *de Thuc.* c. 5. Dionysius concedes the more dignified name of συγγραφεῖς to the Ionian logographers. He names, (1) as anterior to the age of Thucydides,—Eugaeon of Samos, Deiochos of Proconnesos, Eudemos of Paros, Democles of Phigaleia, Hecataeus of Miletus, Acusilaus of Argos, Charon of Lampsacus, Amelesagoras of Chalcedon; (2) as elder contemporaries of Thucydides,—Hellanicus of Lesbos, Damastes of Sigeion, Xenomedes of Chios, Xanthos of Lydia. His words imply that these, "and many more" (ἄλλοι συχνοί), were then extant.

[2] *Ib.* οὐ συνάπτοντες ἀλλήλαις (τὰς ἱστορίας), ἀλλὰ κατ' ἔθνη καὶ κατὰ πόλεις διαιροῦντες : whereas Herodotus is said πολλὰς καὶ διαφόρους πράξεις ἐς μίαν περιγραφὴν πραγματείας ἀγαγεῖν.

of the legends which lived in oral tradition (ὅσαι διεσώζοντο μνῆμαι), and of the written records (γραφαί) preserved in temples or state-archives; and to publish these "such as they received them," without adding anything, and on the other hand without omitting "myths" and 'theatrical episodes" which appear childish to a more critical age.[1] As to style, it is much the same for all of them,—plain, concise, "strictly to the point," [2] without artificial display; but with a certain freshness, he adds, and some degree of charm, which has been the secret of their survival. The meagre fragments which remain, such as those of Xanthus and Charon, Hecataeus and Hellanicus, consist chiefly of short, jerky sentences, strung together in the baldest possible fashion.[3] If these Ionian writers introduced dialogues or speeches—as the example of the epic poets might have led them to do—it may be conjectured that these were of the simplest kind. There is one, indeed, who has left proof that he could write dialogue with the ease and grace of Herodotus himself.[4] But Ion of Chios was a poet as well as a chronicler; he knew the

---

[1] Dionys. de Thuc. c. 5, ἐν αἷς καὶ μῦθοί τινες ἐνῆσαν ὑπὸ τοῦ πολλοῦ πεπιστευμένοι χρόνου (cp. Thuc. i. 21, of the stories told by the logographers, ὑπὸ χρόνου . . . ἐπὶ τὸ μυθῶδες ἐκνενικηκότα) καὶ θεατρικαί τινες περιπέτειαι, πολὺ τὸ ἡλίθιον ἔχειν τοῖς νῦν δοκοῦσαι.

[2] Ib. τοῖς πράγμασι προσφυῆ. In Herodotus (i. 27, etc.) προσφυέως λέγειν is simply "to speak pertinently." But the phrase of Dionysius seems to mean, not merely "adapted to the subject," but closely adhering to the facts of the story (whether mythical or not), without attempt at verbal embellishment. It is illustrated by the dry and absolutely matter-of-fact style of the extant fragments.

[3] Müller, Fragm. Histor. Graec. i. 1-68. The longest fragment of Hecataeus may serve as a specimen :—"Orestheus, son of Deucalion, arrived in Aetolia in search of a kingdom ; and a dog produced him a green plant ; and he ordered the dog to be buried in the earth ; and from it sprang a vine fertile in grapes. Wherefore he called his son Phytius. Now the son of Phytius was Oeneus, so named after the vine-plant ; for the ancient Greeks called the vine Oena : and the son of Oeneus was Aetolus." (Frag. 341, p. 26.)

[4] The story of the poet Sophocles defending the phrase ἐπὶ πορφυρέαις παρῇσιν against the criticisms of a learned guest at a supper-party in Chios. (Müller, Fragm. Hist. vol. ii. p. 46.) The Ἐπιδημίαι, in which it occurred, seem to have been Ion's account of his own " visits " to Athens and other cities. (Ibid. p. 45.)

Athens of Pericles; and his memoirs, with their sprightly gossip, must have been very unlike the normal type of Ionian chronicle.

Herodotus is distinguished from his predecessors, first of all, by an epic unity of plan. It is hard to say exactly how far he was superior to them in his method of verifying facts his diligence and his honesty are both unquestionable, and we know that he attempted—not very scientifically, perhaps—to decide between conflicting versions of the same story. But in the dramatic element of his narrative he shows the true freedom of an epic poet. In his History, as in the *Iliad* and the *Odyssey*, the author seldom speaks when there is a fair pretext for making the characters speak. The habitual use of " direct speech," or easy dialogue, is evidently a different thing from the insertion of set speeches : there is nothing necessarily rhetorical about it. It is merely the vivid way of describing thought and motive, the way natural to a simple age; and in the case of a work meant to be heard rather than to be read, like the early Greek prose works, it has the obvious recommendation of helping to keep the attention alive. Even the longer speeches in Herodotus have usually the conversational tone rather than the rhetorical.[1] On the other hand, there are a few which may be considered as properly rhetorical, that is, as efforts by Herodotus to work up a vague tradition in the most effective form. The debate in the Persian cabinet on the invasion of Greece [2] is a case in point. The speeches of

---

[1] *E.g.* the speech in which Aristagoras of Miletus appeals for aid to Cleomenes, king of Sparta (Herod. v. 49), and that of Sosicles at Sparta (v. 92), which is simply a plain sketch of the Corinthian tyrannies, put into the mouth of a Corinthian speaker.

[2] Her. vii. 8-11. The council is called σύλλογος ἐπίκλητος Περσέων τῶν ἀρίστων : as in viii. 101 Xerxes ἐβουλεύετο ἅμα Περσέων τοῖσι ἐπικλήτοισι : *i.e.* with his "privy-councillors." Later writers went at least as far as Herodotus in reporting speeches made on occasions which presuppose privacy ; as when Dionysius, Livy, and Plutarch give the expostulations of Veturia (or Volumnia) with Coriolanus,—when Sallust is present in imagination at a debate of Catiline's conspirators,—or when Livy transcribes the brilliant, but domestic, remonstrances of Pacuvius Calavius with his son Perolla, offered with a view of dissuading the young man from murdering Hannibal at Capua. Thucydides never violates dramatic probability in this particular way.

Xerxes, Mardonius, and Artabanus have been carefully elaborated, and have the elementary dramatic merit of expressing
views which Persian speakers could conceivably have taken.
Another example is the debate of the Persian conspirators
after the death of the false Smerdis.   Otanes argues for
democracy, Megabyzus for oligarchy, Darius for monarchy;
but here the points of view seem purely Hellenic.[1]   Herodotus
prefaces his report of the discussion by saying, "Speeches
were made which some of the Greeks refuse to credit; but
made they were:"[2] and elsewhere[3] he remarks with triumph
that "those Greeks who do not believe" in Otanes having
advocated democracy will be surprised to hear that Mardonius
established democracies in the Ionian cities.   The ground of
this dramatic episode, then, was a story current among the
Greeks of Ionia, but rejected by some of them as manifestly
inconsistent with Persian ideas.   The spirit of rhetorical
dialectic may be traced again very clearly in the conversation between Solon and Croesus, where Solon refines on
the distinction between wealth, good fortune, and happiness.[4]   Still, it cannot be said that Herodotus had much
love for set rhetorical display: his taste was for conversation—lively, ingenious, argumentative it might be, but still
mainly in the colloquial key.[5]   A good instance of the

---

[1] Her. iii. 80-82.   Similarly in Her. iii. 36 the Lydian Croesus utters
Hellenic thoughts.

[2] Her. iii. 80, ἐλέχθησαν λόγοι ἄπιστοι μὲν ἐνίοισι Ἑλλήνων, ἐλέχθησαν δ' ὦν.

[3] Her. vi. 43, ἐνθαῦτα μέγιστον θῶυμα ἐρέω τοῖσι μὴ ἀποδεκομένοισι Ἑλλήνων
Περσέων τοῖσι ἑπτὰ Ὀτάνεα γνώμην ἀποδέξασθαι, ὡς χρεὼν εἴη δημοκρατέεσθαι
Πέρσας : where μὴ ἀποδεκομένοισι implies more than μὴ πιστεύουσι would have
implied,—viz. that the statement was offered for acceptance, not simply
by Herodotus himself, but by a widely-spread rumour.

[4] Her. i. 32.   The question of Croesus to Solon had been—τίνα ἤδη πάντων
εἶδες ὀλβιώτατον ; Solon answers, in effect, that πλοῦτος is certainly an
element of ὄλβος, but that complete ὄλβος requires εὐτυχία also, and that
a man's life cannot be called εὐτυχής unreservedly until we have seen it
to the end.   Dean Blakesley observes (on Her. i. 32), that this "might
have proceeded from the mouth of Protagoras, or Hippias, or any other
of the μεριμνηταὶ λόγων alluded to by Euripides" (in Medea 1225 f.).   If it
has not the matured subtlety of the rhetorical dialectic, it may certainly
be said to anticipate its spirit.

[5] Dionysius says most truly of Herodotus that he has almost all the
excellences of style except the ἐναγώνιοι ἀρεταί—the combative excellences,—

way in which he passes by an opportunity for oratory is his
brief notice of the speech made by Themistocles just before the
battle of Salamis :[1] " His theme was the contrast between all
that is worthy and all that is base. He exhorted them to
choose the better part in all that men's nature and condition
permit; and then, having wound up his discourse, he ordered
them to embark." The true rhetorician would have developed
the topic which Herodotus barely indicates.[2] It may be
noticed, too, that the ornament of the speeches in Herodotus is
sometimes distinctly Homeric—illustrating his nearer affinity
to epos than to rhetoric. Thus the Corinthian Sosicles, in
the debate at Sparta, begins with truly epic force : " Verily
now the sky shall be under the earth, and the earth shall
hang above the sky, men shall have their pastures in the
sea, and fish upon land," if Spartans become the friends of
tyranny.[3]

§ 3. Thucydides has stated the general principles on which
he composed the speeches in his History. The precise interpretation of that statement depends, however, partly on the question
—How far is it probable that Thucydides is there instituting
a tacit comparison between his own method and that of Herodotus ? So far as we know, the work of Herodotus was the
only prose work in which Thucydides could have found a pre-

---

such as were afterwards developed by strenuous controversy, political or
forensic. οὐδὲ γὰρ δημηγορίαις πολλαῖς ὁ ἀνὴρ οὐδ' ἐναγωνίοις κέχρηται λόγοις, οὐδ'
ἐν τῷ παθαίνειν καὶ δεινοποιεῖν τὰ πράγματα τὴν ἀλκὴν ἔχει (*de Thuc.* c. 23).

[1] Her. viii. 83, τὰ δὲ ἔπεα ἦν πάντα κρέσσω τοῖσι ἕσσοσι ἀντιτιθέμενα. ὅσα
δὲ ἐν ἀνθρώπου φύσι καὶ καταστάσι ἐγγίνεται, παραινέσας δὴ τούτων τὰ κρέσσω
αἱρέεσθαι καὶ καταπλέξας τὴν ῥῆσιν ἐσβαίνειν ἐκέλευε ἐς τὰς νῆας.

[2] Cp. Plato, *Hippias Major*, p. 286, where the sophist Hippias tells
Socrates that he has composed " an admirable discourse " on the theme of a
question supposed to be put by Neoptolemus to Nestor after the taking of
Troy—What are καλὰ ἐπιτηδεύματα ? The phrase of Herodotus, καταπλέξας
τὴν ῥῆσιν, reminds us of the tone in which the speakers of Thucydides sometimes decline to develop commonplaces.

[3] Her. v. 92, ᾗ δὴ ὅ τε οὐρανὸς ἔσται ἔνερθε τῆς γῆς καὶ ἡ γῆ μετέωρος ὑπὲρ τοῦ
οὐρανοῦ καὶ οἱ ἄνθρωποι νομὸν ἐν θαλάσσῃ ἕξουσι καὶ οἱ ἰχθύες τὸν πρότερον ἄνθρωποι,
ὅτε γε ὑμεῖς, ὦ Λακεδαιμόνιοι, ἰσοκρατίας καταλύοντες τυραννίδας ἐς τὰς πόλις κατά-
γειν παρασκευάζεσθε. Compare the epic phrase which closes the spirited
oration of Dareius in the debate of the conspirators—οὐ γὰρ ἄμεινον (Her. iii.
83 ; *Iliad* xxiv. 52, οὐ μήν οἱ τό γε κάλλιον οὐδέ τ' ἄμεινον, etc.).

cedent for dramatic treatment applied to history. If Thucydides knew that work, it would naturally be present to his mind at the moment when he was stating the rules of his own practice. It can be shown almost certainly that a period of at least twenty years must have elapsed between the time at which Herodotus ceased to write and the time at which the History of Thucydides received the form in which it has come down to us.[1] It was possible, then, for Thucydides

---

[1] Herodotus alludes to no event later than 425 B.C., the latest mark of time being a *doubtful* reference to the death of Artaxerxes in 425 (vi. 98). And there are instances in which his silence affords presumptive proof that later events were unknown to him. (1) In 437 B.C. Athenian colonists founded a city on the spot formerly called Ennea Hodoi, and their leader Hagnon named it Amphipolis, because the Strymon flowed on both sides of it. Herodotus mentions Ennea Hodoi (vii. 114), but nowhere speaks of Amphipolis. Had he been writing after the new colony had become important, he would naturally have mentioned it in this connection ; he could scarcely have failed to do so after the battle of Amphipolis in 422 B.C. had made the place famous. (2) Demaratus tells Xerxes that Spartans never yield : it is their fixed law to conquer or die (Her. vii. 104 ; cf. 209). This passage would have been singularly infelicitous if it had been written after the surrender of the Lacedaemonians at Pylos in 425 B.C., when 120 Spartan prisoners were brought to Athens ; an event which, as Thucydides expressly says (iv. 40), astounded the Greeks, precisely because their belief had been that which Herodotus expresses. (3) Demaratus advises Xerxes to detach 200 ships from his fleet, for the purpose of occupying the island of Cythera, and quotes the saying of Cheilon, that it would be well for Sparta if Cythera were sunk in the sea (Her. vii. 235). Xerxes neglected the advice. But in 424 B.C. the Athenians actually occupied Cythera, and the damage thence inflicted on Laconia was one of the causes which disposed the Spartans to conclude peace. Herodotus would not have omitted, if he had known, so forcible an illustration of Cheilon's saying. And there are indications that Herodotus did not live to give the last touches to his work : thus a promise made in vii. 213 is left unfulfilled. [The revolt of the Medes "from Dareius" (Her. i. 130), which Dahlmann identified with the revolt of 408 B.C. (Xen. *H.* i. 2. 19), has been shown by the Behistun inscription to belong to the reign of Dareius Hystaspes.]

F. W. Ullrich (*Beiträge zur Erklärung des Thukydides ;* Hamburg, 1846) has ingeniously argued that Thucydides composed his first three Books, and Book IV. as far as ch. 48, in exile (about 421-413 B.C.) ; and the rest of the work, as a continuation, after the final close of the war. This view rests mainly on the alleged existence of passages in Books i.—iv. 48 which imply ignorance of later events. Classen has examined these passages in detail (*Einleitung*, xxxii.—liv.), and has, I think, shown that they are insufficient to support the theory built upon them. My opinion has not been altered by reading a learned essay in favour of Ullrich's hypothesis, which has appeared

to know the work of Herodotus; that he actually knew it, and that he pointedly alludes to it in several places, cannot be doubted by any one who weighs the whole evidence.[1]

In the view of Thucydides there had hitherto been two classes of writers concerned with the recording of events. First, there were the poets, especially the epic poets, of whom Homer is the type, whose characteristic tendency, in the eyes of Thucydides, is to exaggerate the greatness or splendour of

---

since Classen's Introduction was published (*Ueber die successive Entstehung des Thucydideischen Geschichtswerkes*, by Julius Helmbold; Colmar, 1876). But for the present purpose it is enough to assume, what even the supporters of Ullrich's view would allow, viz. that the whole work was at least revised by Thucydides after the end of the war. (See Thuc. i. 13. 18; ii. 65.) The probable influence of Herodotus is here being estimated in relation to those parts of the work of Thucydides which would have been the last to receive his finishing touches—the speeches.

[1] That Thucydides knew the work of Herodotus is assumed by Lucian (*de cons. hist.* § 42), Marcellinus (*vit. Thuc.* 54), Suidas (s.v. ὀργᾶν), Photius (*cod.* 60), and the Scholiast on Thuc. i. 22, etc. In modern times it has been denied or questioned by F. C. Dahlmann (*Herodot.* p. 214), K. O. Müller (*Hist. Gk. Lit.* c. xxxiv. § 2, and *Dorians*, ii. 98, § 2), by J. C. F. Bähr (in his edition of Herodotus), and in an essay *De plurimis Thuc. Herodotique locis*, by H. Fütterer (Heiligenstadt, 1843). The proofs that Thucydides knew the works of Herodotus have been brought together by Mure (*Hist. Gk. Lit.* Bk. iv. ch. 8), and more recently by H. Lemcke, in an essay entitled *Hat Thuc. das Werk des Herod. gekannt?* (Stettin, 1873.) The crucial texts are (1.) Thuc. i. 20, on the common errors regarding the vote of the Spartan kings and the Pitanate company, compared with Her. vi. 57 and ix. 53; (2.) Thuc. ii. 97, on the Thracians and Scythians—tacitly correcting what Herodotus says of the Thracians (v. 3) and of the Scythians (iv. 46); (3.) Thuc. i. 126, on Cylon's conspiracy, compared with Her. v. 71; Thuc. vi. 4 on Zankle (Messene) compared with Her. vi. 23; Thuc. ii. 8, on the earthquake at Delos (cf. i. 23) compared with Her. vi. 98. In view of all these passages, it seems impossible to doubt that in i. 97 Thucydides includes or specially designates Herodotus among those who ἢ τὰ πρὸ τῶν Μηδικῶν Ἑλληνικὰ ξυνετίθεσαν ἢ αὐτὰ τὰ Μηδικά.

I must add a word on the vexed interpretation of Her. vi. 57, τοὺς μάλιστά σφι τῶν γερόντων προσήκοντας ἔχειν τὰ τῶν βασιλέων γέρεα, δύο ψήφους τιθεμένους, τρίτην δὲ τὴν ἑωυτῶν. The question is, Does Herodotus mean τιθεμένους δύο ψήφους ἑκάτερον, τρίτην δὲ τὴν ἑωυτοῦ? Shilleto (Thuc. i. 20) thinks that this is not *certain*, suggesting that τοὺς προσήκοντας might mean τὸν ἀεὶ προσήκοντα, and comparing Her. iv. 62, τοῖσδε = τῷ ἐν ἑκάστῳ ἀρχηΐῳ, but he sees the difficulty of supposing the same person to be nearest of kin to both kings. Failing this resource, we must surely allow that Herodotus means δύο ψήφους ἑκάτερον, for else how could he possibly have written τρίτην δὲ τὴν ἑωυτῶν? Would he not have written δευτέρας δὲ τὰς ἑωυτῶν?

things past.[1] Secondly, there were the prose writers whom he
calls chroniclers (λογογράφοι); and .these he characterises by
saying that they " compiled "[2] their works with a view to
attracting audiences at a recitation, rather than to truth ; dealing largely, as they did, with traditions which could no longer be
verified, but had passed into the region of myth. Now with
such chroniclers Herodotus was undoubtedly classed by Thucydides. The traits common to Herodotus and the other chroniclers, as Thucydides viewed them, were (1) the omission of
really accurate research—the tendency to take what lay ready
to the writer's hand (τὰ ἑτοῖμα, i. 20) ; (2) the mixture of a
fabulous element with history ; (3) the pursuit of effect in the
first place, and of truth only in the second. Probably Thucydides would have said that Herodotus was more critically
painstaking and less indiscriminately tolerant of fable than
most of the other chroniclers, but that his study of effect was
more systematic and more ambitious. The imaginary dialogues
and speeches in Herodotus would be the most conspicuous
illustrations of this desire for effect. If they were not absolute
novelties in the chronicler's art, at least we may be sure that
they had never before been used in such large measure, or
with such success.

The first aim of Thucydides in his introduction is to show
that the Peloponnesian war is more important than any event
of which the Greeks have record. He then states the principles
on which his History of the War has been composed. " As to
the various speeches made on the eve of the war, or in its
course, I have found it difficult to retain a memory of the
precise words which I had heard spoken ; and so it was with
those who brought me reports. But I have made the persons
say what it seemed to me most opportune for them to say in
view of each situation ; at the same time, I have adhered as
closely as possible to the general sense of what was actually
said. As to the deeds done in the war, I have not thought
myself at liberty to record them on hearsay from the first in-

---

[1] Thuc. i. 10, εἰκὸς ἐπὶ τὸ μεῖζον μὲν ποιητὴν ὄντα κοσμῆσαι : 21, ὡς ποιηταὶ
ὑμνήκασιν ἐπὶ τὸ μεῖζον κοσμοῦντες.

[2] Thuc. i. 21, ξυνέθεσαν, as again 97, ξυνετίθεσαν, implying a process more
external and mechanical than ξυγγράφειν.

formant, or on arbitrary conjecture. My account rests either on personal knowledge, or on the closest possible scrutiny of each statement made by others. The process of research was laborious, because conflicting accounts were given by those who had witnessed the several events, as partiality swayed or memory served them."[1]

The phenomena of the war, then, as materials for history are classed by Thucydides under two heads—λόγοι, things said, and ἔργα, things done. These are the two elements of human agency.[2] As regards the ἔργα, the deeds, he is evidently contrasting his own practice with that of the chroniclers generally. He has not taken his facts, as they did, without careful sifting (ἀβασανίστως): he had formed a higher conception of his task (ἠξίωσα). In regard to the words, the λόγοι, he is tacitly contrasting his own practice with that of Herodotus, the only conspicuous example in this department. If his statement were developed in this light, it might be paraphrased thus:— Thucydides says: (1) I have not introduced a speech except when I had reason to know that a speech was actually made: unlike Herodotus, when he reports the conversation between Croesus and Solon, the debate of the Persian conspirators, the discussion in the cabinet of Xerxes. (2) I do not pretend to give the exact form of the speeches made: as a writer implies that he does when, without warning the reader, he introduces a speech with the formula, "He said these things" (ἔλεγε τάδε),[3] instead of "He spoke to this effect" (ἔλεγε τοιάδε).

---

[1] Thuc. i. 22.

[2] Shilleto remarks (on i. 21 § 2): "τὰ δ' ἔργα τῶν πραχθέντων is a somewhat bold expression for τὰ δ' ἔργα τὰ πραχθέντα." It may be added that the phrase has the special effect of bringing out the antithesis between *facts of speech* and *facts of action.*

[3] Cp. Her. iii. 80, where the speeches of Otanes, Megabyzus and Dareius are introduced by λέγων τάδε . . . λέγων τάδε . . . ἔλεξε τάδε: so v. 91, ἔλεγον τάδε . . . εἶπον ταῦτα: 92, ἔλεξε τάδε (Sosicles): vii. 8, ἔλεξε Ξέρξης τάδε: and so usually. Thucydides nearly always has ἔλεξαν or ἔλεγον τοιάδε, with τοιαῦτα (or τοσαῦτα) at the end. In i. 85 (of Sthenelaidas), ἔλεξεν ὧδε ("in this manner," not = τάδε). In iv. 58 the speech of Hermocrates is introduced by τοιούτους δὴ λόγους εἶπεν, where δή appears to mean "as we may presume;" *i.e.* he spoke "to this general effect"—the phrase intimating somewhat more plainly than the usual τοιάδε that Thucydides had only a very general notion of the ξύμπασα γνώμη.

(3) On the other hand, I have faithfully reproduced the speaker's general line of argument, the purport and substance of his speech, so far as it could be ascertained. Herodotus disregards this principle when he makes Otanes, Megabyzus and Dareius support democracy, oligarchy and monarchy by arguments which no Persian could have used. And in filling up such outlines, my aim has been to make the speaker say what, under the circumstances, seemed most opportune (τὰ δέοντα μάλιστα).

The last phrase is noticeable as marking a limit of dramatic purpose. According to the regular usage of the words[1] (τὰ δέοντα) in Thucydides, it can mean only "what the occasion required"—not necessarily what was most suitable to the character of the speaker. The latter idea would have been expressed by a different phrase (τὰ προσήκοντα). That is, in filling up the framework supplied by the reported "general sense" of a speech, Thucydides has freely exercised his own judgment on the situation. Suppose a report to have reached him in this shape: "Hermocrates spoke in the congress at Gela, urging the Sicilian cities to lay aside their feuds and unite against Athens." In composing on this theme, the first thought of Thucydides would be, "What were the best arguments available?" rather than, "What arguments would Hermocrates have used?" This general rule would, of course, be liable to various degrees of modification in cases where the speaker was well known to the historian as having marked traits of character, opinion or style.

§ 4. "Set speeches," says Voltaire, "are a sort of oratorical lie, which the historian used to allow himself in old times. He used to make his heroes say what they might have said. . . . At the present day these fictions are no longer tolerated. If one put into the mouth of a prince a speech which he had never made, the historian would be regarded as a rhetorician."[2] How did it happen that Thucydides allowed himself this "oratorical lie,"—Thucydides, whose strongest characteristic is

---

[1] Thuc. i. 70, τὸ τὰ δέοντα πρᾶξαι : 138, αὐτοσχεδιάζειν τὰ δέοντα : ii. 43, γιγνώσκοντες τὰ δέοντα : ii. 60, γνῶναί τε τὰ δέοντα καὶ ἑρμηνεῦσαι ταῦτα.

[2] Preface to the *Hist. of Russia*, § 7.

devotion to the truth, impatience of every inroad which fiction makes into the province of history, laborious persistence in the task of separating fact from fable; Thucydides, who was not constrained, like later writers of the old world, by an established literary tradition; who had no Greek predecessors in the field of history, except those chroniclers whom he despised precisely because they sacrificed truth to effect? Thucydides might rather have been expected to express himself on this wise: "The chroniclers have sometimes pleased their hearers by reporting the very words spoken. But, as I could not give the words, I have been content to give the substance, when I could learn it."

In order to find the point of view at which Thucydides stood, we must remember, first of all, the power which epic poetry had then for centuries exercised over the Greek mind. The same love of the concrete and comprehensible which moved the early Greeks to clothe abstract conceptions of a superhuman power in the forms of men and women, "strangers to death and old age for ever," led them also to represent the energy of the human spirit as much as possible in the form of speech. The Homeric ideal of excellence is the man of brave deeds and wise words. The Homeric debates are not merely brilliant, but also thoroughly dramatic in their way of characterising the speakers.[1] The *Iliad* and *Odyssey* accustomed the Greeks to expect two elements in every vivid presentation of an action—first, the proofs of bodily prowess, the account of what men did; and then, as the image of their minds, a report of what they said. Political causes strengthened this feeling. Public speech played a much larger part in the affairs of States than it now does. Envoys spoke before an assembly or a council on business which would now be transacted by the written correspondence of statesmen or diplomatists. Every adult citizen of a Greek democracy had his vote in the assembly which finally decided great issues.

---

[1] Sir G. C. Lewis, in illustrating this point, instances the embassies from Corcyra and Corinth to Athens (Thuc. i. 68), from Mitylene to Olympia (iii. 9), and from the Athenians and Syracusans to Camarina (vi. 76). (*Methods of Observation and Reasoning in Politics*, vol. i. p. 232.)

To such a citizen the written history of political events would appear strangely insipid if it did not give at least some image of those debates which imparted the chief zest to civic life and by which political events were chiefly controlled. He was one who (in modern phrase) had held a safe seat in Parliament from the time when he came of age; who had lived in the atmosphere of political debate until it had become to him an almost indispensable excitement; and who would feel comparatively little interest in hearing the result of a Parliamentary division unless he was enabled to form some idea of the process by which the result had been reached. Such a man would not have been satisfied with the meagre information that the Athenian Ecclesia had discussed the fate of Mitylene, that Cleon had advocated a massacre, that Diodotus had opposed it, and that the view of Diodotus had prevailed by a narrow majority. His imagination would at once transport him to the scene of the parliamentary combat. He would listen in fancy, as he had so often listened in reality, to the eloquence of antagonistic orators, he would balance the possible arguments for severity or clemency, he would conceive himself present at the moment when one uplifted hand might incline the scale of life or death, and he would feel the thrill of relief with which those who supported Diodotus found that Athens was saved at the eleventh hour—saved, if the bearers of the respite, rowing night and day, could reach Lesbos in time—from the infamy of devoting a population to the sword. When Thucydides gave in full the speeches made by Cleon and Diodotus, he was helping his reader, the average citizen of a Greek republic, to do on more accurate lines that which the reader would otherwise have tried to do for himself. Thucydides was writing for men who knew Greek politics from within, and he knew that, if they were to follow him with satisfied attention, he must place them at their accustomed point of view. The literary influences of the age set in the same direction. At the beginning of the war the Attic drama had been in vigour for more than forty years. The fame of Aeschylus was a youthful memory to men who had passed middle life; Sophocles was sixty-four, Euripides was forty-nine. Each had given great works to Athens, and was yet to give more. An age of vivid energy had found the poetry most congenial to it in the noblest type of tragedy, and this, in turn, fed the Greek desire to know character through deed and word. In the hands of Euripides tragedy further became the vehicle of dialectical subtleties and the dramatic mirror of public debate. At the same time Attic oratory was being prepared by two currents of influence which converged on Athens—the practical culture of Ionia, represented by the Sophists, and the Sicilian art of rhetoric.[1]

§ 5. If the speeches in Thucydides were brought under a technical classification, the Funeral Oration would be the only example of the " panegyrical" or epideictic class ; the pleading of the Plataeans and Thebans before the Spartan Commissioners might possibly be called " forensic ;" and all the other speeches would be in some sense " deliberative."[2] But such a classification, besides being rather forced, does not correspond to any real differences of structure or form. If the speeches are to be viewed in their literary relation to the History, it is enough to observe that the addresses of leaders to their troops may be regarded as practically forming a class apart.[3]

The right of an adult citizen to attend the debates of the Ecclesia must have been acquired by Thucydides many years[4] before the war began. From its very commencement, as he says, he had formed the purpose of writing its history. There is every probability that he had heard most or all of the important discussions which took place in the Ecclesia between 433 and 424 B.C. It was in 423 B.C., or at the end of the year before, that his exile of twenty years from Athens began. Thence we can name some at least of the speeches to which he probably refers as heard by himself ($a\mathit{v}\tau\grave{o}\varsigma$

---

[1] The early history of Greek oratory, and the various influences which contributed to mould it during the fifth century B.C., have been traced by the writer in the *Attic Orators from Antiphon to Isaeos*, vol. i. Introduction, pp. xciii-cxxxvii.

[2] *I.e.* in the largest sense of συμβουλευτικοί, under which the addresses of leaders to troops would be included as προτρεπτικοί—the speeches in political debate being δημηγορίαι in the proper sense.

[3] See the table at the end ; and below § 7.

[4] Probably from 451 B.C., if his birth may be placed in 471 B.C. Cp. K. F, Hermann, *Antiq.* i. § 121 ; Xen. *Mem. Socr.* iii. 6. 1.

ἤκουσα), and not merely reported to him. Such would be the
addresses of the Corcyrean and Corinthian envoys, when they
were rival suitors for the Athenian alliance in 433 B.C.; the
speeches of Pericles; the debate on Mitylene in 427 B.C.; and the
speech of the Lacedaemonian envoys in 425 B.C., making overtures of peace to Athens. If he was not present on all these
occasions, still, as a resident citizen, he would have exceptional
facilities for obtaining a full and accurate account. Taking this
group of speeches first, then, we may consider how far they are
apparently historical in substance, or show traces of artificial
treatment.

After giving the addresses of the envoys from Corcyra and
Corinth in 433 B.C., Thucydides notices the course of the debate
in the Ecclesia. Two sittings were held. At the first, he says,
the Athenians inclined to the arguments of the Corcyreans, and
were disposed to conclude an alliance both offensive and
defensive; at the second they repented of this, but decided to
conclude a defensive alliance. The considerations which prevailed with them were, that war was unavoidable in any case;
that the Corcyrean navy must not be allowed to pass into the
hands of the Corinthians; and that Corcyra was a useful
station for coasting voyages.[1] These three arguments are just
those on which the Corcyrean speech, as given by Thucydides,
chiefly turns.[2] The circumstantial account of the debate in the
Ecclesia cannot be treated as fictitious. Either, then, Thucydides has given the substance of the arguments really used by
the Corcyreans, or he has ascribed to them arguments used on
their side by Athenian speakers in the Ecclesia. Now the
speech of the Corinthian envoys has at least one mark of
substantial authenticity: the references to benefits conferred
on Athens by Corinth in the matters of Samos and Aegina [3]
would certainly have occurred to a Corinthian envoy more
readily than to an Athenian writer. In both the Corcyrean
and the Corinthian speech it seems probable that Thucydides
has given the substance of what was really said, though he may
have added touches from his recollections of the subsequent
debate in the assembly. Similar is the case of the speech

---

[1] Thuc. i. 44.   [2] i. 32-36.   [3] i. 42.

made by the Lacedaemonian envoys at Athens in 425 B.C.[1] The historian's comment on it is as follows : " The Lacedaemonians spoke at such length[2] [*i.e.* for Spartans], in the belief that the Athenians had previously desired a truce, and had been hindered only by Spartan opposition; so that, when peace was offered, they would gladly accept it, and restore the men." This clearly implies that the speech ascribed to the envoys— which Thucydides may well have heard—is historical in substance.

The Thucydidean speeches of Pericles raise three distinct questions:—How far do they preserve the form and style of the statesman's oratory? how far do they express the ruling ideas of his policy? and how far do they severally represent what he said on the several occasions?

As Thucydides must have repeatedly heard Pericles[3]— whom he describes as the first of Athenians, most powerful in action and in speech,[4]—it would be strange if he had not endeavoured to give at least some traits of the eloquence which so uniquely impressed contemporaries. Pericles is said to have left nothing written :[5] but Aristotle and Plutarch have preserved a few of the bold images or striking phrases which tradition attributed to him.[6] Several examples of such bold imagery occur in the Thucydidean speeches of Pericles,[7] and it

---

[1] Thuc. iv. 17-20.

[2] By τοσαῦτα in such a context Thucydides usually means "*only* thus much," as ii. 72, τοσαῦτα εἰπόντων Πλαταιῶν. But in iv. 21, τοσαῦτα εἶπον refers back to iv. 17 § 2, τοὺς δὲ λόγους μακροτέρους οὐ παρὰ τὸ εἰωθὸς μηκυνοῦμεν.

[3] See *e.g.* ii. 13, ἔλεγε δὲ καὶ ἄλλα οἷάπερ εἰώθει Περικλῆς.

[4] i. 139.

[5] Plutarch, *Pericl.* c. 8 : ἔγγραφον μὲν οὐδὲν ἀπολέλοιπε πλὴν τῶν ψηφισμάτων, ἀπομνημονεύεται δὲ ὀλίγα παντάπασιν.

[6] Arist. *Rhet.* iii. 10 § 7 : ὥσπερ Περικλῆς ἔφη τὴν νεότητα τὴν ἀπολομένην ἐν τῷ πολέμῳ οὕτως ἠφανίσθαι ἐκ τῆς πόλεως, ὥσπερ εἴ τις τὸ ἔαρ ἐκ τοῦ ἐνιαυτοῦ ἐξέλοι: *ib.* τὴν Ἄιγιναν ἀφελεῖν ἐκέλευσε τὴν λήμην τοῦ Πειραιέως. Plut. *Per.* 8 § 5 quotes his saying, τὸν πόλεμον ἤδη καθορᾶν ἀπὸ Πελοποννήσου προσφερόμενον : and of those who fell at Samos, ἐγκωμιάζων ἐπὶ τοῦ βήματος ἀθανάτους ἔλεγε γεγονέναι καθάπερ τοὺς θεούς· οὐ γὰρ ἐκείνους αὐτοὺς ὁρῶμεν, ἀλλὰ ταῖς τιμαῖς ἃς ἔχουσι καὶ τοῖς ἀγαθοῖς ἃ παρέχουσιν ἀθανάτους εἶναι τεκμαιρόμεθα.

[7] *E.g.* ii. 43, τὸν ἀγήρων ἔπαινον κάλλιστον ἔρανον προϊέμενοι . . . : 41, μνημεῖα κακῶν κἀγαθῶν ἀΐδια ξυγκατοικίσαντες . . . : 43, ἀνδρῶν ἐπιφανῶν πᾶσα γῆ τάφος . . ., and others *passim* in the ἐπιτάφιος : in ii. 62, κηπίον καὶ

can hardly be doubted that they are phrases which have lived
in the historian's memory. But the echo is not heard in single
phrases only. Every reader of the Funeral Oration must be
aware of a majesty in the rhythm of the whole, a certain
union of impetuous movement with lofty grandeur, which
Thucydides has given to Pericles alone. There is a large
alloy, doubtless, of rhetorical ornament in the new manner
of overstrained antithesis:[1] but the voice of the Olympian[2]
Pericles is not wholly lost in it. There can be no question,
again, that the speeches of Pericles in the Ecclesia accurately
represent the characteristic features of his policy at the
time.[3] But how far do they severally represent what Pericles
said on the several occasions? Thucydides makes Pericles
use different topics of encouragement at three successive
stages.

In 432 B.C. Pericles emboldens the Athenians to reject
the Peloponnesian demands by a general comparison of the
resources and prospects on either side.[4] In 431 B.C., when
Archidamus is about to invade Attica, Pericles repeats his
former exhortations, but supplements them by a detailed
exposition of Athenian resources, financial and military.[5] In

---

ἐγκαλλώπισμα πλούτου, and many more. Bold imagery of this kind was
characteristic of the elder school of oratory, and generally of what Dionysius
calls the αὐστηρὰ ἁρμονία: cp. *Attic Orators*, vol. i. p. 27.

[1] The most glaring example is the reiterated contrast of "word" and
"deed," which occurs some eighteen times in the Funeral Oration, and is
parodied (as Mr. H. M. Wilkins observes, *Introduction to the Speeches*, p.
xxv) in the Platonic *Menexenus* [*Menex.* p. 236 D, Ἔργῳ μὲν ἡμῖν οἵδε ἔχουσι
τὰ προσήκοντα σφίσιν αὐτοῖς, ὧν τυχόντες πορεύονται τὴν εἱμαρμένην πορείαν,
προπεμφθέντες κοινῇ μὲν ὑπὸ τῆς πόλεως, ἰδίᾳ δὲ ὑπὸ τῶν οἰκείων· λόγῳ δὲ δὴ,
κ.τ.λ. And immediately afterwards, ἔργων εὖ πραχθέντων . . . λόγῳ καλῶς
ῥηθέντι.]

[2] Περικλέης οὐλύμπιος, Ar. *Acharn.* 530. Eupolis notices the *rapidity*, the
charm, and the *sting* of his eloquence (Δῆμοι, *Frag. Com.* i. 162); cp. *Attic
Orators*, i. p. cxxx.

[3] Viz., to make no derogatory concessions, but to accept the war; to wage
it, however, mainly on the defensive, allowing the enemy to ravage their
lands, but guarding their possession of the city and the sea; to rely chiefly
on their navy, and to retain a firm hold upon the allies, whose tribute gave
the financial superiority to Athens.

[4] i. 140-144.   [5] ii. 13.

430 B.C., after the second invasion of Attica, when the land had been devastated and while the plague was raging, Pericles convened a special meeting of the Ecclesia,[1] with the twofold purpose of reassuring his countrymen and of allaying their resentment against himself. " As to the prospects of the war, you may rest satisfied," he says, " with the arguments by which I have proved to you on many other occasions that you have no cause of uneasiness. But I must notice a special advantage which the scale of your empire confers,—one, I think, which has never occurred to you,—which I have not mentioned in addressing you before, and which I should not have noticed now —as the claim implied might seem too arrogant—did I not see you unreasonably dejected. You think that you rule your allies alone. I tell you that of the two fields open to human action, land and sea, the latter is under your absolute dominion, not merely to the extent of your actual empire, but as much further as you please. While you hold the sea in your present naval strength, you cannot be resisted by the Persian king, or by any nation on earth."[2] Thus, as the pressure on the Athenian spirit becomes more and more severe, the exhortations of Pericles go on from strength to strength, until, at the darkest hour of all, they culminate in a triumphant avowal that the naval empire of Athens is not relative but absolute, is not an empire over a limited confederacy but a boundless supremacy on the sea. If this ascending scale, so fitly graduated, was due to the invention or arrangement of Thucydides, it was a dramatic conception. But it seems more probable that the topics really used by Pericles on these three occasions were substantially those given by the historian. It is difficult otherwise to justify the emphatic clearness with which the special theme of the second speech is distinguished from that of the first, and that of the third, again, from both.[3] On the

---

[1] ii. 59, ξύλλογον ποιήσας, *i.e.* ξύγκλητον ἐκκλησίαν, which Pericles could convene as one of the Ten Generals (ἔτι δ' ἐστρατήγει).

[2] ii. 62 § 2.

[3] Compare ii. 13 § 2, παρῄνει δὲ καὶ περὶ τῶν παρόντων ἅπερ καὶ πρότερον (referring to i. 140-144) . . . θαρσεῖν τε ἐκέλευε, κ.τ.λ. (introducing the special subject of the second speech), with ii. 62 § 1, introducing the special subject of the third.

other hand, the first speech of Pericles betrays some remarkable traces of manipulation by the writer. Earlier in the same year the Corinthian envoy at the Peloponnesian congress had given several reasons for believing that the Peloponnesians were likely to prevail in the war. With help from the sacred treasuries of Delphi and Olympia, he had said, they might lure away the foreign seamen of Athens by offering higher pay. They could acquire naval skill by practice. And among the possibilities of the war he suggests the occupation of a fortress in the enemy's country.[1] The speech of Pericles answers these arguments point by point. But the correspondence is not merely in the topics. The very phrases of the Corinthian speech are repeated by Pericles in his reply.[2] Similar parallelisms may be traced between the Corinthian speech and that delivered by the Spartan Archidamus on the occasion of the former congress : one with which the Corinthians cannot be supposed to be acquainted in detail, since it was made to the Spartans only, after strangers had withdrawn.[3] The fact is that the eight[4] speeches recorded by Thucydides as delivered at Athens or Sparta before the commencement of the war form, for his purpose, a group by themselves. In these he has worked up the chief arguments and calculations which were current on either side. Collectively, they are his dramatic presentation of the motives at work, the grievances on each side, the hopes and fears, based on a comparison of resources, with which the combatants entered on the struggle. At the end of his first speech Pericles says : "I have many other reasons to give for hoping that we shall prevail; but these shall be given hereafter as the events arise ($ἄμα$ $τοῖς$ $ἔργοις$) " —thus foreshadowing the speech of which an abstract is given

---

[1] i. 121 §§ 3-4 ; 122 § 1.

[2] Compare (1) Pericles, i. 143 § 1, $εἴ$ $τε$ $καὶ$ $κινήσαντες$ $τῶν$ $Ὀλυμπίασιν$ $ἢ$ $Δελφοῖς$ $χρημάτων$ $μισθῷ$ $μείζονι$ . . . $ὑπολαβεῖν$ $τοὺς$ $ξένους$ $τῶν$ $ναυτῶν$, with the Corinthian speech, i. 121 § 3, $ἀπὸ$ $τῶν$ $ἐν$ $Δελφοῖς$ $καὶ$ $Ὀλυμπίᾳ$ $χρημά$-$των$ . . . $ὑπολαβεῖν$ $μισθῷ$ $μείζονι$ $τοὺς$ $ξένους$ $αὐτῶν$ $ναυβάτας$: (2) Pericles, i. 142 § 6, with Corinthian, i. 121 § 4 ; (3) Pericles, i. 142 § 2, with Corinthian, i. 122 § 1.

[3] Compare i. 120-4 with i. 80-85.

[4] See the Table at page 322 ; cp. i. 21, $ὅσα$ $εἶπον$ $μέλλοντες$ $πολεμήσειν$.

on a subsequent occasion.[1] In this particular case, as we have
seen, the disposition of topics may well be authentic in the
main. But the composer's phrase is significant. It suggests
the habit of selecting from a certain stock of available material
and disposing the extracts with something of a dramatist's
freedom.

In the Funeral Oration there is nothing, apart from the
diction, which distinctly shows the invention of Thucydides.
At first sight there is some plausibility in the view that such
an oration would probably have contained allusions to the
heroic legends of Attica, and that the mind of Thucydides is to be
traced in their suppression.[2] But the argument may be turned
the other way. The very absence of mythical embellishment,
it might be urged, is rather a proof of the fidelity with which
Thucydides has reported a speaker who, regardless of the
vulgar taste, was resolved to treat a well-worn theme in a new
and higher strain. One or two passages, indeed, have been
supposed to hint at the moral deterioration of the Athenian
democracy in the years which followed the death of Pericles;[3]
but the supposition seems gratuitous.

It remains to notice the debate in the Ecclesia on the
punishment of Mitylene. Cleon urges a massacre, Diodotus
opposes it. "These views," says Thucydides, "having been
stated with nearly balanced effect, the assembly came after all
to a division; and on a show of hands the parties proved nearly
equal, but the view of Diodotus prevailed." The words can
only mean that, in the speeches of Cleon and Diodotus, Thucydides has given the real substance of the arguments which were

---

[1] i. 144 § 2, ἀλλ᾽ ἐκεῖνα μὲν καὶ ἐν ἄλλῳ λόγῳ ἅμα τοῖς ἔργοις δηλωθήσεται. The
promise is fulfilled by the speech of which an abstract is given in ii. 13, and
by that reported in the direct form in ii. 60-64.

[2] The suggestion of F. C. Dahlmann (*Hist. Forschungen*, i. 23), to which
Grote justly opposes the μακρηγορεῖν ἐν εἰδόσιν οὐ βουλόμενος ἐάσω (Thuc. ii. 36).
The analogy of similar extant pieces (the *Menexenus*, the ἐπιτάφιοι falsely
ascribed to Lysias and Demosthenes, the *Panathenaicus* of Isocrates, etc.)
justifies Dahlmann's major premiss, but does not support his conclusion.

[3] Viz. (1) ii. 37 § 3, the reference to a restraining δέος, and to those laws,
ὅσοι ἄγραφοι ὄντες αἰσχύνην ὁμολογουμένην φέρουσι : (2) 40 § 1, φιλοκαλοῦμεν μετ᾽
εὐτελείας καὶ φιλοσοφοῦμεν ἄνευ μαλακίας. I cannot assume the allusions which
Classen finds here to a subsequent and opposite state of society.

found to be so "nearly balanced," and which led to so close a division. Cleon's speech has one striking characteristic. In several places it echoes phrases which occur in the speeches of Pericles.[1] But, with these verbal parallelisms, there is a pointed contrast of spirit. As Pericles describes the good side of the intellectual Athenian nature, Cleon brings out its weak side. As Pericles insists on the Athenian combination of intelligence with courage, Cleon declares that this intelligence leads men to despise the laws, and prefers ignorance combined with moderation.[2] Pericles is gone: Cleon echoes the words of the statesman as whose successor he poses, at the very moment when he is contradicting his principles. It may be observed that when Thucydides reports the speech of the Syracusan demagogue Athenagoras, he marks his manner by a certain violence of expression.[3] Cleon, whom Thucydides calls "most violent," has no violence of expression. Probably this abstention from vehemence of the demagogic type, this superficial imitation of Pericles, are traits in which the Cleon of Thucydides is historical.

This closes the series of those seven speeches, delivered at Athens, for which Thucydides probably derived the "general

---

[1] Compare (1) Cleon, iii. 37 § 2, τυραννίδα ἔχετε τὴν ἀρχήν, with Pericles, ii. 63 § 2, ὡς τυραννίδα γὰρ ἤδη ἔχετε τὴν ἀρχήν : (2) Cleon, iii. 40 § 4, ἐκ τοῦ ἀκινδύνου ἀνδραγαθίζεσθαι, with Pericles, ii. 63 § 2, εἴ τις καὶ τόδε ἐν τῷ παρόντι δεδιὼς ἀπραγμοσύνη ἀνδραγαθίζεται : (3) Cleon, iii. 38 § 1, ἐγὼ μὲν οὖν ὁ αὐτός εἰμι τῇ γνώμῃ, with Pericles, ii. 61 § 2, καὶ ἐγὼ μὲν ὁ αὐτός εἰμι καὶ οὐκ ἐξίσταμαι. Compare also Cleon's notice (iii. 37 § 2) of τὸ καθ' ἡμέραν ἀδεές in Athenian life, with what Pericles says of τὰ καθ' ἡμέραν ἐπιτηδεύματα, ii. 37 § 2.

[2] Cleon, iii. 37 § 3, ἀμαθία τε μετὰ σωφροσύνης ὠφελιμώτερον ἢ δεξιότης μετὰ ἀκολασίας, κ.τ.λ., contrasted with Pericles, ii. 40 § 2, οὐ τοὺς λόγους τοῖς ἔργοις βλάβην ἡγούμενοι, κ.τ.λ., and ii. 62 § 5, τὴν τόλμαν . . . ἡ ξύνεσις . . . ἐχυρωτέραν παρέχεται.

[3] E.g. vi. 40, ἀλλ' ἔτι καὶ νῦν, ὦ πάντων ἀξυνετώτατοι, εἰ μὴ μανθάνετε κακὰ σπεύδοντες, ἢ ἀμαθέστατοί ἐστε ὧν ἐγὼ οἶδα Ἑλλήνων, ἢ ἀδικώτατοι, εἰ εἰδότες τολμᾶτε.

In a Mémoire sur Thucydide, by M. Meierotto (in the Memoirs of the Berlin Academy for 1790-91, p. 530), the writer observes, with reference to the discrimination of character in the speeches : "Cléon et Athénagore parlent ordinairement d'un ton dur, offensant et grossier, dont pourtant ils s'écartent quelquefois." We have only one speech of Cleon and one of Athenagoras ; so far as these go, however, the striking thing, it seems to me, is not the resemblance, but the contrast.

sense" either from his own recollection or from the sources accessible to a resident citizen. The only one of these which exhibits distinct traces of artificial dealing with subject-matter is the first speech of Pericles. And in this the only traces are, first, a certain adjustment of the language to that of the Corinthian speech made earlier in the same year;[1] and, secondly, a phrase by which the composer prepares the reader for a subsequent speech of Pericles.

§ 6. We now come to the speeches made elsewhere than at Athens from 432 B.C. onwards, or made at Athens later than 424 B.C. In regard to all or most of these, Thucydides must have relied on reports of the "general sense" brought to him by others (τοῖς ἄλλοθέν ποθεν ἐμοὶ ἀπαγγέλλουσιν).[2] The first general characteristic which claims notice is the occurrence of passages certainly, or almost certainly, written with a consciousness of later events. These passages may be cast into three groups, according as they relate to (I.) the affairs of

---

[1] As the Corinthian speech contains a prophecy (after the event) of the occupation of Deceleia (ἐπιτειχισμός, i. 122 § 1), so the corresponding passage of Pericles contains what *may* be a reference to the Athenian occupation of Pylos and of Cythera (i. 140 § 3, ἐπιτειχίζειν . . . πλεύσαντας ἐς τὴν ἐκείνων).

[2] Thuc. v. 26 : "It befell me to live in exile for twenty years [423-403 B.C., or nearly so] after my command at Amphipolis. I thus became conversant with both parties—indeed, as an exile, I saw most of the Peloponnesians—and was enabled to study the events more at my leisure." The phrase here—καὶ γενομένῳ παρ' ἀμφοτέροις τοῖς πράγμασι—certainly implies more than that Thucydides was *in the countries* which were the theatre of the war. It implies that he was *in intercourse with the actors.* The words καθ' ἡσυχίαν denote the "ease" or "leisure" of one who had no official status, political or military. Hitherto Thucydides had been himself an actor in the war (in the Ecclesia or as στρατηγός) ; *now* he was only a thoughtful spectator. During his exile Thucydides certainly spent some time in Italy and Sicily. Marcellinus quotes (§ 25) the statement ὡς φυγὼν ᾤκησεν ἐν Ἰταλίᾳ, and there was even a tradition of his burial there (§ 33). There are traces, I think, of Thucydides' personal knowledge of Sicily in the speech of Alcibiades (vi. 17 § 3). Niebuhr conjectured, and E. Wölfflin has shown (*Antiochus v. Syrakus u. Coelius Antipater*, Winterthur, 1872), that Thucydides (vi. 2 ff.) used the Σικελιῶτις συγγραφή which Antiochus of Syracuse brought down to 424 B.C. These are the chief data for conjecturing the general nature of the materials which Thucydides may have had for the speeches subsequent to 425 B.C. In many cases, probably, he had good sources of information, though it is hardly likely that the words ὧν αὐτὸς ἤκουσα can include any speeches except those made at Athens before his exile.

Sicily, (II.) the Deceleian war, (III.) the final defeat of Athens.[1]

(I.) 1. Speaking in the congress at Gela in 424 B.C., Hermocrates warns his hearers against the designs of Athens. The Athenians, he says, are now on our coast with a few ships; but some day they will come with a larger fleet, and endeavour to reduce the whole island.[2] The Athenian fleet on the Sicilian coast at this time must have numbered some fifty or sixty triremes.[3] Hermocrates, speaking in 424 B.C., certainly would not have spoken of these as " a few ships," least of all when it was his object to show that Athens was formidable.[4] But Thucydides, when he composed the speech, had in view the vast fleet—at least thrice as numerous[5]—sent to Sicily in 415 B.C.

2. Nicias, in his second speech dissuading the Athenians from the expedition to Sicily, says that the only Sicilian cities likely to join the invaders are Naxos and Catana.[6] Both Naxos and Catana did, in fact, join the Athenians. But the Athenians, when they opened the campaign in Sicily, had hopes of other cities also. The alliance of Messene[7] was solicited by Alcibiades, though without success. Both Athenian and Syracusan envoys were sent to Camarina, and it was not without much hesitation that Camarina resolved to remain neutral.[8] The

---

[1] In the list of nine passages noticed here, I have not included any in which the suggestion of acquaintance with subsequent events did not seem to me tolerably strong and clear. Thus I have purposely omitted the passage in which Archidamus says (432 B.C.) of the war, δέδοικα δὲ μᾶλλον μὴ καὶ τοῖς παισὶν αὐτὸν ὑπολίπωμεν (i. 81 § 6), in which some find a knowledge of its actual duration; a passage in vi. 11 (in the speech of Nicias), which might possibly be regarded as foreshadowing the aid actually lent by Sicily to Sparta at a later time (viii. 26); and a reference by Hermocrates to future feuds and reconciliations between the Sicilian cities (iv. 64).

Five of these passages have been noticed by previous writers, viz. Nos. 1, 5, 6, 7, 9; the others—Nos. 2, 3, 4, 8—have not, to my knowledge, been considered in this light before.

[2] iv. 60, ὀλίγαις ναυσὶ παρόντες . . . πλέονί ποτε στόλῳ ἐλθόντας.

[3] Twenty triremes had been sent in 427 B.C. under Laches (iii. 88), whom Pythodorus had superseded; forty more were afterwards sent under Eurymedon (iii. 115), and these had now joined the first detachment (iv. 48).

[4] As Grote remarks, vii. 189, n.

[5] Thuc. vi. 31.   [6] vi. 20.   [7] vi. 50.   [8] vi. 88.

precision of the forecast made by Nicias betrays knowledge of the event.

3. Again, when the Athenian attack on Sicily is imminent, Hermocrates, in his speech at Syracuse, gives reasons for thinking that it will fail. Numerous as the Athenians are, he says, they cannot outnumber the united forces of Sicily. "And if they should fail from want of supplies in a foreign country, they will still leave glory to those against whom their design was laid, even though they should be ruined mainly by their own errors."[1] Thucydides elsewhere expresses his own view of the Sicilian disaster. The primary cause of the failure was not, he thinks, a miscalculation of forces, but rather the neglect of the Athenians at home—distracted as they were by faction—to support the army in Sicily, a neglect which blunted the zeal of those engaged in the campaign.[2] The words ascribed to Hermocrates were written by Thucydides in retrospective view of the Athenian errors which had led to the Athenian defeat.

4. The speech of Euphemus, the Athenian envoy at Camarina, offers another example. Urging the people of Camarina to join the Athenians rather than the Syracusans, he reminds them that they will not often have an opportunity of securing such powerful auxiliaries. And if, he says, you dismiss them now, "one day yet you will long to see even the least part of them, when their succour can no more avail you."[3] A few years later (405 B.C.), the Carthaginians, already victorious over Selinus, Himera, and Agrigentum, advanced against Gela and Camarina. Dionysius, who had become tyrant of Syracuse, failed to relieve Gela. The inhabitants of Camarina, like those of Gela, were forced to abandon their city; and when the conclusion of peace between Dionysius and the invaders allowed them to return, they returned as tributaries of Carthage.[4] The protection of Syracuse, in which Camarina had

---

[1] vi. 33. [2] ii. 65.

[3] vi. 86, ἢν εἰ τῷ ὑπόπτῳ ἢ ἄπρακτον ἐάσετε ἀπελθεῖν ἢ καὶ σφαλεῖσαν, ἔτι βουλήσεσθε καὶ πολλοστὸν μόριον αὐτῆς ἰδεῖν, ὅτε οὐδὲν ἔτι περανεῖ παραγενόμενον ὑμῖν. (For ἔτι thus used in menace or presage, cf. Soph. *El.* 471. In Aesch. *Eum.* 812, Shilleto conjectured ὑμεῖς δ' ἔτ' [for ἐς] ἀλλόφυλον ἐλθοῦσαι χθόνα | γῆς τῆσδ' ἐρασθήσεσθε.) [4] Diod. xiii. 108-114; Xen. *Hellen.* ii. 3.

trusted, proved a broken reed. Thucydides must have been at work on his History for some years after the end of the Peloponnesian war, perhaps as late as 396 B.C.[1] When he put that emphatic menace into the mouth of Euphemus, the fate which actually overtook Camarina soon afterwards was surely present to his mind.

(II.) 5. The Corinthian speaker at Sparta in 432 B.C. alludes to the establishment of a fort in Attica as one of the possibilities of the war;[2] and Pericles, in the parallel passage of his first speech, admits that the construction of a hostile fort might do harm by facilitating raids and by tempting slaves to desert.[3]

6. Alcibiades, speaking at Sparta in 415 B.C., urges the occupation of Deceleia. "It will benefit you," he says, "and will embarrass the enemy in many ways. I will briefly notice the chief of these. Most of the property in the country will become yours by capture or surrender. The Athenians will forthwith lose their revenues from the silver mines of Laurium, and all their present gains from the land and the law-courts. Above all, they will suffer by the irregular transmission of tribute from their allies, who, when satisfied that you are making war in earnest, will slight their demands."[4] These predictions accurately correspond with the effects of the occupation as afterwards described in the historian's own words.[5] The temporary presence of the invading enemy had not hitherto hindered the Athenians from reaping the fruits of the soil; but now "they were deprived of their whole land"—including, of course, the mines at Laurium. "More than twenty thousand slaves had deserted to the enemy." All their sheep and oxen

---

[1] Thucydides mentions an eruption of Aetna in 426 B.C. as the third on record (iii. 116)—implying ignorance of that in 396 B.C., noticed by Diodorus, xiv. 59. On the probability that Thucydides was at work on his History for at least some years after 403, cp. Classen, *Einl.* xxx. I cannot, however, accept Ullrich's ingenious suggestion that the reference to Antiphon—ἄριστα τῶν μέχρι ἐμοῦ θανάτου δίκην ἀπολογησάμενος (viii. 68)—points to a tacit comparison with the defence of Socrates (399 B.C.).

[2] Thuc. i. 122 § 1.   [3] i. 142 § 2.

[4] vi. 91 § 7. In the sentence, οἷς . . . ἡ χώρα κατεσκεύασται, τὰ πολλὰ πρὸς ὑμᾶς τὰ μὲν ληφθέντα, τὰ δ' αὐτόματα ἥξει, the word αὐτόματα, as commentators have seen, refers to the desertion of slaves, included in the κατασκευαί as household chattels or "live stock."

[5] vii. 27-28. On the αὐτομολίαι of slaves, cf. viii. 40.

were lost. The whole number of adult male citizens was required for military duty on the walls or in the field, a necessity which would suspend the sitting of the law-courts and, as Alcibiades foretold, close that source of profit.[1] The expenses of the State were heavily increased, its revenues were perishing. Alcibiades might easily have foreseen the importance of occupying Deceleia. But the minute correspondence between the special results which he is made to predict and those which Thucydides relates in his own person indicates that the prophecy followed the event.

(III.) 7. The Athenian speaker at Sparta in 432 B.C. says to the Spartans : " If you were to overthrow our empire and establish your own, you would soon alienate the good-will which you have gained because we are feared,—if you are to continue the policy of which you gave a specimen during your brief leadership of Greece against Persia. The usages of your community preclude intercourse with others, and moreover a Spartan citizen on foreign service observes these usages as little as those of Hellas at large."[2] There is a manifest reference here to the period after the close of the war, when the Spartan promises of " liberating Greece" were falsified. And the reference to the misconduct of the Spartan citizen abroad was certainly not suggested by the case of Pausanias alone. The war had furnished two signal instances. Gylippus had been convicted by the Ephors of appropriating part of the treasure taken after the capture of Athens.[3] Lysander—the first Greek who received divine honours from Greeks—had surpassed the arrogance of Pausanias.[4]

---

[1] The reference of Alcibiades in the words ὅσα . . . ἀπὸ τῶν δικαστηρίων νῦν ὠφελοῦνται is to the income which the State derived from court-fees of various kinds, especially the deposits (πρυτανεῖα) made by parties to a law-suit, as well as from pecuniary fines, confiscations, etc. Böckh (*Publ. Econ.* i. 461) understands the passage thus, following the scholiast. Meineke (*Hermes* iii. 359) and Madvig (*Adv.* i. 328) conjecture δεκατευτηρίων, "places where public tithes and taxes were taken"—objecting, as against the vulgate, that it does not appear why even a virtual state of siege should suspend the sitting of the law-courts. Thucydides, vii. 28 § 2, gives the plain answer—all the citizens were required for military duty.

[2] Thuc. i. 77 § 6.

[3] Plut. *Lys.* 16-17, *Nic.* 28, cf. Diod. xiii. 106.

[4] With Plut. *Lys.* 18 cf. Paus. vi. 3 §§ 14-15, Athen. xv. 696.

8. The striking speech of Brasidas to the Acanthians (424 B.C.) deserves to be considered in this connection. It is throughout an emphatic assertion that the cause in which Sparta fights is the cause of Greek liberty. " I have not come," he says, "to support a party. I do not consider that I should be bringing you freedom in any real sense if I should disregard your constitution, and enslave the many to the few, or the few to the many. Such freedom would be harder than a foreign yoke : and we, the Lacedaemonians, should reap no thanks for our pains, but rather blame instead of honour and renown."[1] Now, what Brasidas protests that Sparta will not do, is precisely what Sparta actually did at the end of the war, with the result which he anticipates. Oligarchies of the narrowest type—boards of ten—were established by Lysander in most of the cities, with a Spartan governor and garrison in each to repress the popular party.[2] The many were literally enslaved to the few, and they found the freedom which Sparta had given them harder indeed than any foreign rule. It can scarcely be doubted that this speech of Brasidas—composed by Thucydides after the close of the war—was inserted by him here, just at the moment when Sparta was making the first advances to the democratic cities of Northern Greece, for the purpose of bringing out the glaring contrast between Spartan promise and Spartan performance.

9. In the conference between the Athenian and Melian negotiators, the Athenians remark that, in the event of Athens being vanquished, they would have less to fear from the vengeance of Sparta than from the vindictiveness of smaller States.[3] The reference here is unmistakable. After the surrender of Athens in 404 B.C., a congress was held at Sparta

---

[1] Thuc. iv. 86 § 3. In § 4 there is no doubt to my mind that οὐδ' ἂν σαφῆ [for οὐδὲ ἀσαφῆ] is the right reading, ἂν ἐπιφέρειν being the oblique of ἂν ἐπιφέροιμι.

[2] See Isocr. *Panegyricus*, §§ 110-114, where he denounces the partisans of the narrow Lacedaemonian oligarchies in the several States—οἱ τῶν δεκαρχιῶν κοινωνήσαντες—and speaks of the miseries which they inflicted on their own cities by "choosing to be enslaved to a Helot" (*i.e.* to the μόθαξ Lysander : ἡροῦντο δὲ τῶν. Εἱλώτων ἑνὶ δουλεύειν). The passage is a striking commentary on the Acanthian speech of Brasidas.

[3] Thuc. v. 91.

in which the destruction of the defeated city was advocated, according to Xenophon, "by the Corinthians and Thebans chiefly, but by many other Greeks too." It was by the Spartan vote that Athens was saved.[1]

The effect of such touches as these—suggested by a knowledge of occurrences subsequent to the dramatic date—may be compared with that produced in a Greek tragedy when one of the persons unconsciously utters a word or phrase which foreshadows the catastrophe. The spectator who knows the destined end of the drama is affected in the same manner as the reader who knows the sequel of the history. In using such touches, however, Thucydides was probably thinking more of logical than of artistic effect. His mind, with its strong concentration, grasped the whole series of arguments or illustrations which the experience of the war could yield; and he brought the most forcible of these to bear on his point without caring whether the facts which suggested them were earlier or later than the supposed date.

§ 7. It has already been remarked that the addresses of leaders to their troops may be considered as forming a class apart from the rest. These military harangues, of which there are twelve in all, are usually short. The object is always the same—to bring out vividly the essential points of a strategical situation; and the historian has been less uniformly attentive here to the details of dramatic probability.[2] A modern writer

---

[1] Xen. *Hellen.* ii. 2, §§ 19-20..

[2] Thus (1) the harangue is sometimes ascribed to several leaders collectively ; *e.g.* vii. 65, παρεκελεύσαντο ἐκείνοις οἵ τε στρατηγοὶ καὶ Γύλιππος καὶ ἔλεξαν τοιάδε. So ii. 86, ὁ Κνῆμος καὶ ὁ Βρασίδας καὶ οἱ ἄλλοι τῶν Πελοποννησίων στρατηγοί . . παρεκελεύσαντο καὶ ἔλεξαν τοιάδε. In the case of the political speeches, the only similar instance is when a single speech is given as made by the two spokesmen of the Plataeans (προτάξαντες σφῶν αὐτῶν Ἀστύμαχόν τε . . καὶ Λάκωνα). It is obviously a different case when a speech is assigned to envoys collectively (i. 32, οἱ Κερκυραῖοι ἔλεξαν τοιάδε, etc.), when one would speak for the rest. (2) The military harangue is sometimes introduced in words which imply that it was made several times over ; thus iv. 91 (Pagondas), προσκαλῶν ἑκάστους κατὰ λόχους, ὅπως μὴ ἀθρόοι ἐκλίποιεν τὰ ὅπλα, ἔπειθε . . λέγων τοιάδε. Cf. vi. 68 (Nicias), κατά τε ἔθνη ἐπιπαριὼν ἕκαστα καὶ ξύμπασι τοιάδε παρεκελεύετο. (Cf. ἐπιπαριὼν τὸ στρατόπεδον παρεκελεύετο, iv. 94.) In vii. 76 Nicias ἐπιπαριὼν ἐθάρσυνέ τε καὶ παρεμυθεῖτο, βοῇ τε χρώμενος ἔτι μᾶλλον ἑκάστοις καθ᾽ οὓς γίγνοιτο, καὶ βουλόμενος ὡς ἐπὶ πλεῖστον γεγωνίσκων ὠφελεῖν.

would have attained the object by comments prefixed or added
to his narrative of the operations.   Thus Archidamus, addressing the Peloponnesian officers before the first invasion of Attica,
dwells on the certainty of the Athenians being stung into
giving battle when they see their lands ravaged.[1]   This serves
to heighten the reader's sense of the provocation offered, and
of the difficulty which Pericles must have had in restraining his
fellow-citizens.[2]   Sometimes the speech of the general on one
side is as distinctly a reply to the general on the other as if it
had been delivered in debate.   The Peloponnesian captains,
exhorting their men before the action in the Corinthian Gulf,
tell them that, though naval skill is much, it cannot avail
against courage.[3]   Phormio, exhorting the Athenian crews,
tells them, as if in retort, that though courage is invaluable,
their decisive advantage is in their naval skill.[4]   Pagondas,
before the battle of Delium, tells the Boeotians that they must
fight, even beyond their own border, for the safety of Boeotia,
and reminds them that their fathers secured it for a time by
defeating the Athenians at Coroneia.[5]   Demosthenes tells the
Athenians that they must fight, even on Boeotian ground, to
protect Attica, and reminds them of the Athenian victory over
the Boeotians at Oenophyta.[6]   The speech of Brasidas to his men
on his Illyrian expedition is intended to bring out the contrast
between Hellenic and barbarian warfare;[7] his speech at
Amphipolis serves to explain his tactics.[8]   The harangue of
Nicias before the last sea-fight at Syracuse marks the peculiar
character of the action as " a land-battle on board ship "
($\pi\epsilon\zeta o\mu\alpha\chi\acute{\iota}\alpha$ $\dot{\alpha}\pi\grave{o}$ $\nu\epsilon\hat{\omega}\nu$), and at the same time sums up for the
reader the whole meaning of that supreme crisis, when, as
Nicias reminds the men about to embark, the fleet is all that
remains of Athens and her great name.[9]   This, and the corresponding speech of Gylippus on the Syracusan side,[10] are in a
high degree powerful and pathetic; so, above all, is the last

---

[1] Thuc. ii. 11.   [2] ii. 59 f.   [3] ii. 87.
[4] ii. 89.   [5] iv. 92.   [6] iv. 95.
[7] iv. 126.   [8] $\tau\grave{\eta}\nu$ $\dot{\epsilon}\pi\acute{\iota}\nu o\iota a\nu$ $\phi\rho\acute{a}\sigma a\iota$, v. 9.
[9] vii. 61-64, $\dot{\eta}$ $\dot{\upsilon}\pi\acute{o}\lambda o\iota\pi os$ $\pi\acute{o}\lambda\iota s$ $\kappa a\grave{\iota}$ $\tau\grave{o}$ $\mu\acute{\epsilon}\gamma a$ $\check{o}\nu o\mu a$ $\tau\hat{\omega}\nu$ $'A\theta\eta\nu\hat{\omega}\nu$.
[10] vii. 65.

speech of Nicias before the retreat.[1] Nowhere else, perhaps, has Thucydides given so free a scope to his own rhetorical power; yet even here it is strictly subordinated to his primary purpose—that of faithfully presenting the cardinal facts of the situation as he conceived them.

§ 8. The expression of character in the Thucydidean speeches has the same kind of limitation which was generally observed in Attic tragedy. It is rather typical than individual. Thucydides seizes the broad and essential characteristics of the speaker, and is content with marking these. We are sometimes reminded of the direct simplicity with which the epic or tragic heroes introduce themselves : " I am Odysseus, the marvel of men for all wiles, and my fame goes up to heaven." " I am pious Aeneas, renowned above the stars."[2] " You voted for war," says Pericles, " and now you are angry with me,—a man who deems himself second to none in discerning and expounding the right course,—a man devoted to his country and proof against corruption."[3] These were salient points in the public character of Pericles as conceived by the historian,[4] and accordingly Pericles is made to say so. The fate of Nicias seemed to Thucydides a signal example of unmerited misfortune, since Nicias had been remarkable throughout life for the practice of orthodox virtue.[5] And so, in his speech before the retreat from Syracuse, Nicias says, " The tenor of my life has been loyal to the gods, just and without offence among men."[6]

---

[1] vii. 76. The two last military speeches of Nicias take something of the political character from the fact that, as he says in both, the army *is* now the city : ἄνδρες γὰρ πόλις—a striking illustration of Sophocles, *Oed. Tyr.* 56.

[2] *Od.* ix. 19 ; *Aen.* i. 379 ; cf. Soph. *Oed. Tyr.* 8, αὐτὸς ὧδ᾽ ἐλήλυθα, | ὁ πᾶσι κλεινὸς Οἰδίπους καλούμενος.

[3] Thuc. ii. 60.　　　　　　　　　　　　　　　　　　　　[4] ii. 65.

[5] vii. 86, ἥκιστα δὴ ἄξιος ὢν τῶν γε ἐπ᾽ ἐμοῦ Ἑλλήνων ἐς τοῦτο δυστυχίας ἀφικέσθαι διὰ τὴν πᾶσαν ἐς ἀρετὴν νενομισμένην ἐπιτήδευσιν : *i.e.* lit., his whole course of life, regulated by law and tradition (νενομισμένη) in the direction of virtue. The ἀρετή of Nicias was that which consists in fidelity to the established observances of religion and to received notions of duty—as distinguished from the ἀρετή, less in conformity with popular conceptions, which Thucydides can still recognise in such a man as Antiphon (viii. 68).

[6] Thuc. vii. 77, πολλὰ μὲν ἐς θεοὺς νόμιμα δεδιήτημαι, πολλὰ δὲ ἐς ἀνθρώπους δίκαια καὶ ἀνεπίφθονα. As to the Letter of Nicias (vii. 11-15), its *substantial*

In the debate at Athens on the Sicilian expedition Alcibiades
is introduced by a prefatory sketch of his position and character.
Thucydides notices his ambition, his magnificence, especially
in the matter of horses and chariots, the licence of his private
life, his insolence, his public efficiency, his personal unpopularity.[1] Then Alcibiades speaks, and begins by saying in so
many words that he has a better right than others to high
command; he boasts of having entered seven chariots at
Olympia; he avows that he does not regard his fellow-citizens
as his equals; he asks whether his personal unpopularity interferes with his administrative capacity.[2] The speech is merely
the sketch developed. It is the character of Alcibiades, as
Thucydides saw its salient points, condensed in a dramatic
form; but it is not such a speech as Alcibiades could conceivably have made on this occasion, or indeed on any. Thucydides has given us distinct portraits of the chief actors in the
Peloponnesian war, but these portraits are to be found in the
clearly narrated actions of the men; the words ascribed to
them rarely do more than mark the stronger lines of character;
they seldom reveal new traits of a subtler kind. The tendency
of Thucydides was less to analyse individual character than to
study human nature in its general or typical phenomena. His
observation was directed, first, towards motives and passions
which may be considered, in regard to practical politics, as
universal influences:[3] next, towards the collective attributes
which distinguish whole communities from each other. Thus
the normal Spartan character is exhibited in its merits and its
defects.[4] The political character of the Athenians is arraigned
and defended;[5] their intellectual character is illustrated in its
strength and its weakness.[6] And Thucydides shows a desire
to comprehend these conceptions of national character in formulas, which he gives as epigrams to his speakers. The

genuineness might perhaps be argued from the fact that, while it dwells on
the wear and tear of the armament, there is no attempt to excuse his own
delay and his failure to prepare for the coming of Gylippus ; but the manner
of its introduction (δηλοῦσαν τοιάδε) seems to indicate the *composition* of
Thucydides.

[1] vi. 15.   [2] vi. 16.
[3] iii. 82 § 2, γιγνόμενα μὲν καὶ ἀεὶ ἐσόμενα ἕως ἂν ἡ αὐτὴ φύσις τῶν ἀνθρώπων ᾖ.
[4] i. 68-72, 80-85.   [5] i. 68-72, 73-78.   [6] ii. 37 f. ; iii. 37-40.

Spartan disposition, says an Athenian, might be described as one which regards everything that is pleasant as honourable, and everything that is expedient as just.[1] The Athenians, says a Corinthian, are, in brief, men who will neither rest nor allow others to rest.[2] Athens, says Pericles, might be described as the school of Greece, and the Athenian nature as the most gracefully versatile in the world.[3]

§ 9. Those cases in which Thucydides · gives merely a brief summary[4] of a speech or debate suggest how slight the materials may often have been which he worked up in the oratorical form. The political or ethical reflections with which the meagre outlines were filled up were doubtless supplied in large measure by Thucydides himself. The speeches, taken altogether, are pervaded by certain general conceptions, expressed in formulas more or less constant, which indicate unity of authorship. But it cannot be said, in the same sense, that they bear the stamp of one mind. They do, indeed, suggest certain intellectual habits, but it is seldom possible to distinguish between opinions or modes of thought which were in the air, and such as may have been proper to Thucydides. Nor would much be gained if we could. The real interest of the speeches in this aspect is something more than biographical; it is their interest as a contribution to the intellectual history of a transitional period in an age of singular mental energy. The age of faith was passing by, and a rational basis for ethics—which were then included in politics —was only in process of being sought. Thucydides is here the representative of a time which, for the most part, could no longer believe with Herodotus, but which had not yet learned

---

[1] v. 105.   [2] i. 70.

[3] ii. 41. I regard the Melian dialogue as neither less nor more historical than those speeches in which Thucydides had to rely on a slight knowledge of the ξύμπασα γνώμη. I cannot suppose, with Classen, that Thucydides had any written documents to go upon. The frankness of the Athenians, which Grote finds startling, is Thucydidean : his wish to portray ruling motives is stronger than his regard for dramatic nicety.

[4] *E.g.* i. 72 (where the general lines of the discourse in 73-78 are indicated) ; iv. 21 (the general sense of Cleon's answer to the Spartan envoys); iv. 58 and vi. 32 (debates at Gela and Syracuse); viii. 53 (debate at Athens in 411 B.C.), etc.

to bring a Socratic method to bear on generalisations. He appears—so far as he is revealed at all—as a thinker of intense earnestness, with a firm and subtle apprehension of his chosen subject, alike in its widest bearings and in its minutest details ; and of profound sensibility in regard to the larger practical aspects, that is the political aspects, of human destiny. He has neither a dogmatic religion nor a system of ethics. He cleaves to positive fact ; his generalisations rarely involve a speculative element, but are usually confined to registering the aggregate results of observation upon human conduct in given circumstances. In the spirit of a sceptical age he makes his speakers debate questions of political or personal morality to which no definite answer is offered. In Plato's *Gorgias* Callicles distinguishes between "natural" and "conventional" justice, contending that "natural justice" entitles the strong to oppress the weak, and that "conventional justice" is merely a device of the weak for their own protection.[1] In the *Republic* Thrasymachus defends a similar doctrine, namely, that "justice is another's good and the interest of the stronger, and that injustice is a man's own profit and interest, though injurious to the weaker." [2] The sophist Hippias, in Xenophon's *Memorabilia,* argues in a like strain that justice and law are merely arbitrary and conventional.[3] This, no doubt, was one of the commonplaces of sophistical dialectic in the time of Thucydides. The Athenian speakers in his History defend the aggressive policy of Athens by arguments which rest on substantially the same basis as those of the Platonic Callicles and Thrasymachus.[4] But the historian is content to state their case from their own point of view ; he does not challenge the doctrine—as the Platonic Socrates does—by comments of his own. The victims of aggression, indeed, the Plataeans or Melians, appeal to a higher justice than the right of might, and Thucydides hints that his sympathies are with them ; [5] but that is all. The abstention is characteristic. On the whole, it may be said that he evinces a

---

[1] Plato, *Gorgias,* p. 482, c. 38.   [2] *Rep.* p. 367 c.
[3] Xen. *Mem.* iv. 4. 14.   [4] Thuc. v. 105 ; vi. 82-87.
[5] Not expressly, but by the naked repulsiveness in which he exhibits the "right of might."

personal liking for moral nobleness,[1] but refrains from deliver-
ing moral judgments,[2] as if these would imply laws which he
was not prepared to affirm or deny. But he insists on discovering a rational basis for action. If a man or a State pursues
a certain line of policy, there must be some intelligible reasons,
he feels, which can be urged for it. This desire to enter into
the mind of the actors—to find the motive behind the deed,
and to state it with all possible logical force—is the mainspring
of the oratory in Thucydides, in so far as this is his own
creation. It is an element of dramatic vividness; sometimes
also of dramatic untruth, when the reasonings supplied by the
historian to his actors are subtler than would probably have
occurred to the speakers or commended themselves to the
hearers. Thucydides is a philosophical historian, in the sense
that he wishes to record the exact truth, in a form which
may be serviceable for the political instruction of mankind.
But he has not, in the sense of Plato or Aristotle, a theory of
ethics or politics. Thucydides groups the observed facts of
practical politics, but without attempting to analyse their
ultimate laws. It might be possible to piece together Thucydidean texts and, by filling up a few gaps, to form a tolerably
coherent system of doctrine; but the process would be artificial
and delusive. Possibly a Shakespeare might re-create Thucydides from the fragments of his personal thought, but the breath
of life would be the poet's gift; the broken lights are all
that really remain. The paradoxes of one age are said to
be the truisms of the next, but the violent contrast suggested by the epigram is hardly the important point to seize
if we desire to trace the growth of opinion. There was a
moment when the so-called paradoxes were neither paradoxes
nor as yet truisms, but only rather new and intelligent opinions,
seen to be such against the foil of notions which were de-

---

[1] As Professor Sellar says ("Characteristics of Thucydides," *Oxford Essays*,
1857): "His own feeling shines out in such expressions as this,—'Simple-
mindedness, which is mostly an ingredient in noble natures' (iii. 83). The
speeches attributed to Pericles are especially expressive of generous ideas of
man."

[2] It is enough to instance the manner in which he relates without comment
the treachery of Paches to Hippias (iii. 54), and the assassination of two
thousand Helots by the Spartans (iv. 80).

caying, but had not quite gone out. For instance, when Thucydides makes his speakers say, as he so often does, that the future is uncertain,[1] we do more justice to the originality of the remark if we remember that in the time of Thucydides there were those who thought that the future was very frequently indicated, at great moments, by signs from the gods. Herodotus, for example, would have disputed the statement that the future is uncertain, if it had been placed before him as an unlimited proposition covering such crises as the Peloponnesian war.[2] The same consideration applies to many of the political or moral aphorisms, which may be regarded as those of Thucydides himself. They are in silent controversy with some unexpressed dissidence of contemporaries. The principle of tacit contrast pervades the whole History, as in the Funeral Oration the picture of Athens requires to be supplemented by a mental picture of the Sparta to which it is opposed.[3] This was of the inmost nature of Thucydides: the reluctance "to speak at superfluous length"[4] was deep in him. His general views must be measured both by the credulity and by the higher scepticism of a naïve age; so gauged, they are never commonplaces, but, at the least, hints for a part of the history which he has not told in words, because he did not distinctly conceive that it could ever need to be told. "Fortune," τύχη, is the name by which he usually designates the incalculable element in human life; but this "fortune" is no blind chance; it is, as he once explains it, "the fortune given by heaven" (ἡ τύχη ἐκ τοῦ θείου), the inscrutable dispensation of a divine Providence.[5] The course of this fortune not only baffles prediction, but is sometimes directly opposed to the reasonable beliefs of men concerning the source which dispenses it. Thrice only in the long tragedy of the war, as Thucydides unfolds it, do men appeal expressly to the gods, invoking the

---

[1] E.g. iv. 62, τὸ ἀστάθμητον τοῦ μέλλοντος ὡς ἐπὶ πλεῖστον κρατεῖ : vi. 9, περὶ τῶν ἀφανῶν καὶ μελλόντων κινδυνεύειν : ii. 42, τὸ ἀφανὲς τοῦ κατορθώματος : ii. 87, νομίσαι ταῖς τύχαις ἐνδέχεσθαι σφάλλεσθαι τοὺς ἀνθρώπους, etc.

[2] See e.g. Her. i. 45, θεῶν τις μοι . . . προεσήμαινε τὰ μέλλοντα ἔσεσθαι : vi. 37, φιλέει δέ κως προσημαίνειν ὁ θεός, κ.τ.λ. On the omens, prodigies, dreams, etc., in Herodotus, see Mure, Bk. iv. ch. 6, § 3, and Rawlinson, i. 71 f.

[3] Esp. ii. 37 and 39.

[4] μακρηγορεῖν : i. 68, ii. 36, iv. 59.　　　　[5] v. 104.

name of religion, in their agony, against tyrannous strength;
thrice the power behind the veil is deaf, thrice the hand of the
avenger is withheld, and the miserable suppliant is struck
down by the secure malignity of man. The Plataeans appeal to
the altars which had witnessed the consecration of Greek
liberty,[1] and the Spartans kill them in cold blood. The
Melians are confident against the Athenians as the righteous
against the unjust;[2] their city is sacked, their men are slain,
their women and children enslaved. Nicias, after the great
defeat at Syracuse, believes that the jealousy of the gods must
now be exhausted, and has a firm hope, based on a good life,
for himself and his followers;[3] but the wretched remnant of
his defeated army are in great part butchered as they slake
their thirst with the bloody water of the Assinarus; he himself
is put to death lest he should tell tales under torture, and the
survivors pass into a horrible slavery. Thucydides feels that
the ways of Heaven are hard to understand, but he does not
complain of them; they are matters not for reasoning but for
resignation.[4] He regards the fear of the gods as a potent check
on the bad impulses of men, and notices the loss of this fear[5]
as a grave symptom of moral anarchy. As to omens, oracles,
and similar modes of seeking miraculous light or aid, he nowhere denies the possibility of such light or aid being occasionally given, though his contempt is excited by the frequency of
imposture;[6] this, however, he would affirm—that such resources are not to be tried until all resources within human
control have been tried in vain.[7] There is one way only,
Thucydides holds, by which man can certainly influence his
own destiny, and that is by bringing an intelligent judgment
(γνώμη) to bear on facts. Some have traced the influence of
Anaxagoras in the prominence which Thucydides gives to the
intellectual principle; but no such prompting was needed
by a strong understanding of sceptical bent, and it may

---

[1] iii. 59 § 2. [2] v. 104, ὅσιοι πρὸς οὐ δικαίους.

[3] vii. 77 § 4, καὶ ἡμᾶς εἰκὸς νῦν τά τε ἀπὸ τοῦ θεοῦ ἐλπίζειν ἠπιώτερα ἕξειν.
οἴκτου γὰρ ἀπ᾽ αὐτῶν ἀξιώτεροι ἤδη ἐσμὲν ἢ φθόνου.

[4] ii. 64, φέρειν τε χρὴ τά τε δαιμόνια ἀναγκαίως τά τε ἀπὸ τῶν πολεμίων
ἀνδρείως. [5] ii. 53; iii. 82.

[6] E.g. ii. 21; v. 26, 103; vii. 50 (of Nicias), ἦν καὶ ἄγαν θειασμῷ τε καὶ τῷ
τοιούτῳ προσκείμενος. [7] v. 103.

be observed that Thucydides has at least not adopted the language of Anaxagoras.[1] It is the peculiar merit of the Athenian character, as portrayed in Thucydides, to recognise intelligence as the true basis of action and the true root of courage,[2] instead of regarding mental culture as adverse to civic loyalty and warlike spirit.[3] If soothsayers cannot give us prescience, reason well used can enable such a man as Themistocles at least to conjecture the future.[4] In a trial of human forces the chances baffle prediction, but superiority in ideas (διάνοιαι) is a sure ground of confidence.[5] Yet the man of sound judgment will not presume on this confidence, for he will remember that the other element, "fortune," is beyond his control.[6] Justice, rightly understood, is the "common good,"[7] and is identical with true self-interest.[8] As the remorseless exaction of an extreme penalty, "justice" may be opposed to "equity;"[9] or as a moral standard, it may be opposed to "self-interest" in the lower sense.[10] And self-interest, when thus opposed to justice, can appeal to "the immemorial usage,"[11] believed to obtain among the gods, and so certainly established among men that it may plausibly be called a sort of natural necessity,[12]—that the stronger shall rule the weaker. No speaker in Thucydides goes quite so far as Callicles in the *Gorgias*, or proclaims this to be "natural" as distinguished from "conventional" justice. It is not said to be just, but only natural and not unreasonable.[13] The argument against capital punishment, which is put into the mouth of Diodotus, rests on the observation that no restraints have yet been devised which can be trusted to keep human passions in check.

---

[1] νοῦς, in Thucydides, occurs only in the phrases ἐν νῷ ἔχειν (to intend), τὸν νοῦν ἔχειν πρός τι, or προσέχειν, and κατὰ νοῦν,· "to one's mind." The general term for the power of the intellect is γνώμη, with which διάνοια and σύνεσις are sometimes nearly synonymous.

[2] ii. 40 § 2 ; 62, § 5.

[3] As Archidamus does (i. 84), and Cleon (iii. 37).

[4] i. 138, τῶν μελλόντων ἐπὶ πλεῖστον τοῦ γενησομένου ἄριστος εἰκαστής.

[5] i. 84 § 3 ; vi. 11 § 6.　　　　[6] iv. 64.

[7] τὸ κοινὸν ἀγαθόν, v. 90.　　[8] i. 41.　　　[9] iii. 40 ; iv. 19.

[10] i. 76, 79 ; iii. 56 ; v. 90 ; iv. 61.　　[11] i. 76, τὸ ἀεὶ καθεστός.

[12] v. 105, ἡγούμεθα γὰρ τό τε θεῖον δόξῃ τὸ ἀνθρώπειόν τε σαφῶς διὰ παντὸς ὑπὸ φύσεως ἀναγκαίας, οὗ ἂν κρατῇ, ἄρχειν. Cf. iv. 61, vi. 87.

[13] vi. 85, οὐδὲν ἄλογον ὅτι καὶ ξυμφέρον.

Legislators have gone through the whole list of possible penalties, and even the prospect of death is found insufficient to
deter those who are goaded by want or ambition, and tempted
by opportunity.[1] The friendship of men and of communities
must be founded in the first place on a persuasion of mutual
benevolence, and on some congeniality of character;[2] but in
the long-run the only sure bond between States is identity of
interests.[3] The Peloponnesian league is loose just because the
interests diverge.[4] In default of a common interest, the only
guarantee for an alliance is balanced fear.[5] Similarly, in the
relation of the citizen to the State, patriotism is enforced by
the dependence of private on public welfare.[6] Pericles even
says that no fair or just legislation can be expected from
citizens who have not such a stake in the country as is represented by the lives of children.[7] The distinctive merits of an
oligarchy—always provided that it is constitutional, and not of
the narrow type which Thucydides calls a "dynasty"[8]—are
fairly recognised in the History. Archidamus and Brasidas
claim stability, moderation and disciplined loyalty for the
Spartan State.[9] A true democracy is pictured as one in which
three elements work together for the common good : the rich
are the guardians of property, the able men offer counsel,
and the mass of the citizens decide on the opinions laid before
them.[10] Democracy was the form of government under which
Athens had been greatest and most free :[11] and the best phase of
the Athenian democracy in his recollection, Thucydides says,
was just after the Revolution of the Four Hundred, since then
the oligarchic and popular elements were judiciously tempered.[12]
Destiny may alter the part which a State is called upon to
perform, and its institutions may require to be modified
accordingly. Thus the Corinthians say to the Spartans, " Your

---

[1] iii. 45 § 3. [2] iii. 10. [3] i. 124. [4] i. 141.

[5] τὸ ἀντίπαλον δέος, iii. 11 ; cf. iv. 92. [6] ii. 60. [7] ii. 44.

[8] The δυναστεία (οὐ μετὰ νόμων, unconstitutional) of Thebes in the Persian
wars is opposed to the later ὀλιγαρχία ἰσόνομος, iii. 62.

[9] i. 84 ; iv. 126 § 4.

[10] vi. 39 (Hermocrates) ; cf. ii. 37 (Pericles). It is only Alcibiades (at
Sparta) who uses δημοκρατία in a narrow and bad sense, as a synonym for
ἀκολασία πλήθους (vi. 89).

[11] vi. 89 § 6. [12] viii. 97.

system is out of date if you are to cope with Athens. In politics, as in art, improvements must prevail. Fixed institutions are best for a city at peace. . But the call to manifold enterprise imposes the need of manifold development. Hence —owing to their varied experience—the Athenians have been ' greater' innovators than you."[1] The analogy suggested here between politics and a progressive art[2] is the more significant when it is remembered what the historian's age had seen accomplished in sculpture, architecture and drama. It is also worthy of remark that the only unqualified censures of democracy which occur in Thucydides, and the only protests against change as such, are ascribed to the " violent " Cleon and the " licentious " Alcibiades.[3]

§ 10. The choice of moments for the introduction of speeches is not, with Thucydides, a matter of rhetorical caprice, but has an intelligible relation to the general plan of his work. A speech or debate reported in the direct form always signalises a noteworthy point in the inner or mental history of the war, as distinguished from the narrative of its external facts: it announces thoughts and arguments which exercised an important influence, and which therefore require to be apprehended with the utmost possible distinctness. The event which furnishes the occasion for inserting a speech need not be of first-rate importance in itself, if only it is typical of its kind, and therefore suitable for the dramatic exhibition of reasonings which applied to several similar cases. The destruction of Plataea by Sparta was an impressive event; but its effect on the general course of the war would scarcely have warranted the amount of space devoted to the Plataean and Theban pleadings,[4] if the occasion had not been a typical illustration of Spartan and Theban policy. Such, again, is the case of Mitylene, viewed as exemplifying the relation between

---

[1] i. 71.

[2] " Among early inquirers into the nature of human action the arts helped to fill up the void of speculation." (Prof. Jowett, Introduction to *Plato's Republic.*)

[3] iii. 37 § 3 ; vi. 18 § 7. Thucydides speaks of the οὐ δημοτικὴ παρανομία of Alcibiades in vi. 28 ; cf. vi. 15, where the same term is applied to him as in i. 132 to Pausanias.

[4] iii. 53-59, 61-67.

Athens and her subject allies ; and the dramatic form is given accordingly, not merely to the Athenian debate on Mitylene, but also to the appeal of the Mityleneans at Olympia.[1] The speech of Brasidas at Acanthus is given in the direct form as a specimen of his persuasive diplomacy in dealing with the cities of the Chalcidic peninsula.[2] The rival overtures of Athens and Syracuse to Camarina have a similarly representative character in relation to the wavering neutrality of the Sicilian cities, and accordingly the direct form is given to the arguments of Euphemus and of Hermocrates.[3] The absence of speeches in the Eighth Book has been reckoned among the proofs that this book had not received the author's last touches. There can be no doubt that Thucydides was prevented by death from completing or revising the Eighth Book :[4] but if his general practice is considered, the argument from the absence of speeches will appear questionable. Much of the Eighth Book is occupied with negotiations, either clandestine or indecisive, or both ; and in a period of similar character which fills the greater part of the Fifth Book Thucydides nowhere employs the dramatic form.[5] It cannot surprise us that Thucydides has not given a dramatic emphasis to the mere misrepresentations by which Alcibiades and Chalcideus prevailed on the Chians to revolt.[6] The Revolution

---

[1] iii. 9-14. [2] iv. 85-87. [3] v. 76-80 ; 82-86.

[4] Classen examines the evidence in his *Vorbemerkungen* to Book viii., with these results :—(1) Book viii. was left unrevised, owing to the author's death while he was engaged upon it, and hence several inaccuracies of expression or statement remain [cf. *e.g.* cc. 8 § 3-4 : the notice of the βραχεῖα ναυμαχία in c. 80, compared with c. 102 : c. 89 § 2 (τῶν πάνυ στρατηγῶν, κ.τ.λ.) : c. 90, § 1, where σφῶν recurs four times in a few lines : c. 101 § 3, where the geographical details are obscure]. (2) Such defects of the text were early recognised, but for a long time no attempt was made to remedy them. (3) In the Alexandrian or Roman age a recension of the whole History was made, of which codex Vaticanus 126 is the representative. For Books i.—vi. the cases in which the codex Vaticanus *alone* has the true reading are not numerous : in vii. they are more so: in viii. they are so frequent that here the Vaticanus, as compared with all the other MSS., assumes the character of a revised text.

[5] Thuc. v. 14-83 (422-416 B.C.). In Book v. the direct form of speech occurs only in the harangue of Brasidas (v. 9) and the Melian dialogue (85-116).

[6] viii. 14.

of the Four Hundred certainly afforded opportunities for the insertion of speeches made in debate. But that Revolution was primarily concerned with the form of the Athenian constitution; its special importance for the history of the war lay in the use which Alcibiades was making of it to procure his own recall. This is perhaps the only point in the extant part of the Eighth Book at which the usual practice of Thucydides would lead us to expect the dramatic emphasis; and just here it is found. Peisander brings his opponents to admit that the case of Athens is desperate without the help of Persia. "This, then," he says, "we cannot get, unless we adopt a more temperate policy, and concentrate the administration in fewer hands, so as to secure the confidence of the king, . . . and recall Alcibiades, the only man living who can gain our end." [1] In a revision of the book Thucydides would possibly have worked up the speech of Peisander at greater length.[2]

§ 11. As regards the language of the speeches, Thucydides plainly avows that it is chiefly or wholly his own.[3] The dramatic truth, so far as it goes, is in the matter, not in the form. He may sometimes indicate such broad characteristics as the curt bluntness of the ephor Sthenelaidas [4] or the insolent vehemence of Alcibiades.[5] But, as a rule, there is little discrimination of style. In all that concerns expression, the speeches are essentially the oratorical essays of the historian himself. At the end of the war, when he composed or revised them, the art of Rhetoric was thoroughly established at Athens. The popular dialectic of the Sophists had been combined with

---

[1] viii. 53.

[2] The absence of military harangues, too, in Book viii. is sufficiently explained by the absence of any good occasion for them. The sea-fights at Euboea (95) and Cyzicus were hardly such : and the narrative breaks off before the more decisive actions of Cynossema and Aegospotami. The question has been discussed lately in an essay, *De Thucydidei Operis Libri viii. indole ac natura*, by Paul Hellwig (Halle, 1876).

[3] i. 22, where the ἀκρίβεια αὐτὴ τῶν λεχθέντων is opposed to the ξύμπασα γνώμη.

[4] i. 86, τοὺς μὲν λόγους τοὺς πολλοὺς τῶν Ἀθηναίων οὐ γιγνώσκω, κ.τ.λ.

[5] vi. 18 § 3, ταμιεύεσθαι ἐς ὅσον βουλόμεθα ἄρχειν : § 4, στορέσωμεν τὸ φρόνημα, etc., where the scholiast remarks that this is the harshest (σκληρότατον) of the metaphors in Thucydides, ἀλλὰ κατὰ Ἀλκιβιάδην.

lessons in the minute proprieties of language. Protagoras taught correctness in grammatical forms,[1] Prodicus in the use of synonyms.[2] The Sicilian Rhetoric had familiarised Athenian speakers with principles of division and arrangement.[3] Gorgias, with his brilliant gift of expression,[4] had for a while set the fashion of strained antithesis and tawdry splendour. It might have been expected from the character of his mind that Thucydides would be keenly alive to what was hollow and false in the new rhetoric. Several touches in the History show that he was so. Citizens in grave debate are contrasted with men who play audience to the empty displays of sophists.[5] A contempt for rhetorical commonplace is frequently indicated. Thus Pericles declines to dilate on the legendary glories of Athens[6] or on the advantages of patriotic fortitude,[7] and Hermocrates begs to be excused from enlarging on the hardships of war[8] or the blessings of peace.[9] On the technical side, however, Thucydides shows the influence of the new art. This often appears in his method of marshalling topics and in his organisation of the more elaborate speeches.[10] It is seen still more clearly if his style is compared with that of the orator Antiphon. The extant work of Antiphon as a writer of speeches for the law-

---

[1] ὀρθοέπεια, Plat. *Phaedr.* 267 c.

[2] ὀρθότης ὀνομάτων, Plat. *Euthyd.* p. 277 E.

[3] The two things which the early Sicilian Rhetoric most sought to teach were skill in marshalling facts and skill in arguing probabilities: cp. *Attic Orators*, vol. i. p. cxviii f.

[4] Cp. *ib.* i. cxxiii. Gorgias was not properly either a student of technical rhetoric or a sophist.

[5] Thuc. iii. 38 § 7. σοφιστῶν [the word only here in Thuc.] θεαταῖς ἐοικότες καθημένοις μᾶλλον ἢ περὶ πόλεως βουλευομένοις. Cf. § 5, μετὰ καινότητος λόγου ἀπατᾶσθαι ἄριστοι. Thucydides thrice uses ἐπίδειξις, but only once in reference to oratory, and then in a general, not in a technical sense (iii. 42). The regular speakers in the Ecclesia are thrice spoken of as ῥήτορες, and always in a more or less unfavourable tone (iii. 40 ; vi. 29 ; viii. 1).

[6] ii. 36.   [7] ii. 43.   [8] iv. 59.

[9] iv. 62. Compare what Alcibiades says at Sparta in declining to dwell on the evils of democracy—ἀλλὰ περὶ ὁμολογουμένης ἀνοίας οὐδὲν ἂν καινὸν λέγοιτο.

[10] As in the Plataean and Theban speeches to the Spartan judges (iii. 53-59, 61-67), in the speeches of Hermocrates and Athenagoras to the Syracusan assembly (vi. 33-34, 36-40), and in the Funeral Oration. We can recognise a conscious partition, more or less complete, into προοίμιον, πρόθεσις (or προκατασκευή), διήγησις, πίστεις, ἐπίλογος. Cp. *Attic Orators*, vol. i. pp. 36, 181 ; ii. 422.

courts falls in the years 421-411 B.C.[1] The warmth of the
terms in which Thucydides describes him as " a master of device
and of expression," [2]—a phrase identical with that which is
ascribed, as a definition of statesman-like ability, to Pericles—
testifies at least to an intellectual sympathy. There is, however, no evidence for the ancient tradition that the historian
was the pupil of the orator.[3] Thucydides and Antiphon belong
to the same rhetorical school, and represent the same early stage
in the development of Attic prose. Both writers admit words
of an antique or a decidedly poetical cast.[4] Both delight in
verbal contrasts, pointed by insisting on the precise difference
between terms of similar import.[5] Both use metaphors rather
bolder than Greek prose easily tolerated in its riper age.[6] On
the other hand, there are three respects in which the composition
of Thucydides may be contrasted with that of Antiphon. First,
Thucydides has a pregnant brevity which would not have been
possible in such measure for a practical orator, since no ordinary

---

[1] Of his extant works, Or. v., περὶ τοῦ Ἡρώδου φόνου, may be referred to about
417 B.C., and Or. vi., περὶ τοῦ χορευτοῦ, to about 412 B.C. Cp. Attic Orators,
i. 34, 58, 63.

[2] viii. 68, κράτιστος ἐνθυμηθῆναι . . . καὶ ἃ γνοίη εἰπεῖν. Cf. ii. 60, ὃς οὐδενὸς
οἴομαι ἥσσων εἶναι γνῶναί τε τὰ δέοντα καὶ ἑρμηνεῦσαι ταῦτα.

[3] Caecilius of Calacte, in the Augustan age, conjectured that Thucydides had
been the pupil of Antiphon (Vitt. x. Oratt.); Hermogenes (περὶ ἰδ. ii. 497)
notices the belief as current, but rejects it. It seems to have been a mere
guess, resting on resemblance of style. See Attic Orators, i. p. 4.

[4] E.g. Antiphon : ἀλιτήριος—ποινή—προστρόπαιος—ἐνθύμιος—ἀσπαίρω (ii. δ. 5)
—ἀνθρώπινον φῦλον (iv. a. 2)—εὐδία (ii. β. 1)—χωροφιλεῖν (v. 78)—φιλοθύτης (ii.
β. 12). Thucydides : περιωπή (=σκοπία, iv. 86)—ἀχθηδών (ii. 37)—ναυβάτης
(i. 121; cf. Pollux i. 95, τὸ ναυβάτας ὀνομάζειν (τοὺς ναύτας) τραγικώτερον—ἐσθή-
ματα (iii. 58)—ἐσσαμένων (=ἱδρυσαμένων, ib.)—κεκμηῶτες (iii. 59)—περίρρυτος
(iv. 64)—φυλοκρινεῖν (vi. 18)—ἐπηλυγάζεσθαι (vi. 36), and many more.

[5] E.g. Antiphon: γνωρισταί—δικασταί—δοξασταί—κριταί (v. 94): the πράκτορες
τῶν ἀκουσίων distinguished from the αἴτιοι τῶν παθημάτων (ii. β. § 6) : τὰ παρῳχη-
μένα σημείοις πιστῶσαι, τὰ δὲ μέλλοντα τεκμηρίοις (ap. Ammon. 127). Thucydides :
αἰτία—κατηγορία (i. 68) : φρόνημα—καταφρόνημα—αὔχημα—καταφρόνησις (ii. 62) :
ἐπανάστησαν—ἀπέστησαν (iii. 39)—οὐκ ἀξυνετωτέρου, κακοξυνετωτέρου δέ (vi. 76) :
κατοικίσαι—ἐξοικίσαι (ib.)—παραίνεσις—ἀξίωσις (i. 41)—δοκοῦσα—φαινομένη (i. 32)
—προεπιβουλεύειν—ἀντεπιβουλεύειν (i. 33): δικασταί . . . σωφρονισταί (vi. 87).

[6] E.g. Antiphon: τὰ ἴχνη τῆς ὑποψίας εἰς τοῦτον φέροντα (ii. γ. 10): ἰατροὺς τῆς
ἀτυχίας (ii. β. 13); cf. i. γ. 1 and ii. β. 10. Thucydides: ἡ ἐπιστήμη ἐγγηράσεται
(vi. 18)—ἰατρὸς τῆς πόλεως (vi. 14)—δουλοῖ τὸ φρόνημα τὸ αἰφνίδιον (ii. 61)—πόλεμος
βίαιος διδάσκαλος (iii. 82)—ἐπικλασθῆναι (iii. 59), etc.

hearer could have followed his meaning with full comprehension.[1] Secondly, Thucydides often departs not only from the natural but from the rhetorical order of words, in order to throw a stronger emphasis on the word which is the key-note to the thought; and in this again he is seen to be writing for readers, not for hearers.[2] Thirdly, the strings of clauses, forming periods of a somewhat loose and inartistic kind, are longer with Thucydides than with Antiphon, and this because Thucydides is striving to express ideas of a more complex nature.[3] The originality and the striking interest of the historian's style consists, in fact, in this, that we see a vigorous mind in the very act of struggling to mould a language of magnificent but immature capabilities. Sometimes the direction of the thought changes in the moment that it is being uttered.[4] Then arise obscurities which have their source in the intense effort of Thucydides to be clear at each successive moment—to say exactly what he means at that moment. The strong consciousness of logical coherence then makes him heedless of formal coherence. The student of Thucydides has one consolation which is not always present to the student of a difficult writer. He knows that he is not engaged in the hopeless or thankless

---

[1] This brevity appears (1) in such constructions as γυναικείας ἀρετῆς, ὅσαι. . . ἔσονται (ii. 45), or τῶν μὲν ἄρχειν τῶν δὲ διανοεῖσθαι (sc. ἄρχειν, i. 124) ; (2) in the suppression of a clause which can be supplied mentally, as often before a sentence introduced by γάρ (cf. i. 120 *ad init.*) : (3) in the pregnant use of words, as vi. 11, ὅπερ ἡμᾶς ἐκφοβοῦσι (=ἐκφοβοῦντες λέγουσι). Cic. *de Orat.* ii. 22, sententiis magis abundat quam verbis . . . ; 13, ita verbis aptus et pressus est, etc. Quint. x. 1, densus et brevis et semper sibi instans. Dionys., p. 792, says that it belongs to Thucydides πειρᾶσθαι δι' ἐλαχίστων ὀνομάτων πλεῖστα σημαίνειν, and Marcellinus, § 50, speaks of his θαυμασταὶ βραχύτητες.

[2] *E.g.* iii. 39, μετὰ τῶν πολεμιωτάτων ἡμᾶς στάντες διαφθεῖραι : i. 33, γενήσεται δὲ . . . καλὴ ἡ ξυντυχία κατὰ πολλὰ τῆς ἡμετέρας χρείας : vi. 82, οὓς ξυγγενεῖς φασιν ὄντας ἡμᾶς Συρακόσιοι δεδουλῶσθαι : v. 91, ἐπὶ σωτηρίᾳ νῦν τοὺς λόγους ἐροῦμεν τῆς ὑμετέρας πόλεως.

[3] *E.g.* Such a sentence as that in Antiphon v. 21, ἡ μὲν πρόφασις ἑκατέρῳ—ἀποθανεῖν αὐτὸν τὸν Ἡρώδην, may be compared in general structure with Thuc. vi. 82, ἡμεῖς γὰρ Ἴωνες ὄντες . . . Συρακόσιοι δεδουλῶσθαι, but the latter has a much longer series of clauses. In Thucydides the transition from a simple string of clauses to a period properly so called is commonly made by the insertion of explanatory parentheses introduced with γάρ.

[4] *E.g.* vii. 42, τοῖς Συρακουσίοις . . . κατάπληξις ἐγένετο . . . ὁρῶντες, κ.τ.λ. Cp. iii. 36, vi. 24, iv. 108, etc.

task of unravelling a mere rhetorical tangle. Every new light on the thought is sure to be a new light on the words.[1]

§ 12. The practice of introducing speeches was continued through the whole series of Greek and Roman historians, and, owing to its classical prestige, even maintained itself for a time in modern literature. But it is curious to trace the process by which it was gradually estranged from the spirit and significance of its origin. For Xenophon, the idea of portraying character in deed and in word was as natural as for Thucydides. Herodotus, Thucydides, and Xenophon, with all their differences, alike belong to an age in which the historian draws from life and for life, setting forth what has been done and said, but rarely theorising or commenting. In the political life which Thucydides and Xenophon represent, public speech wielded the decisive force; but while the main purpose of Thucydides is political, that of Xenophon is rather ethical. Xenophon introduces direct speech or dialogue chiefly to enforce the moral lessons of individual character. The colloquial tone prevails even in political debate,[2] and there is rarely any attempt at condensed reasoning of the Thucydidean type. In the course of the fourth century B.C. the school of Isocrates developed a normal literary prose, and such writers as Ephorus and Theopompus applied a rhetoric more florid than their master's to the misplaced embellishment of history.[3] At the same time the political life of Greece was decaying, and with it

---

[1] Jelf (following Kühner) rightly classes Thucydides with those writers who, "engrossed with the subject, were overpowered by their flow of thought, and endeavouring to concentrate these notions in all their fulness in as few words as possible, passed from thought to thought, without taking much care that the several parts of the whole sentence should be connected together with a strict grammatical accuracy." The constructions of Thucydides, he adds, "in spite of, or perhaps because of, their grammatical inaccuracy, have a power and depth of expression which perhaps no other prose writer ever attained." (*Greek Grammar*, ii. 593.)—Thucydides wishes his *thought* to be what Aristotle requires in the period (*Rhet.* iii. 9)—εὐσύνοπτον. Cp. *Attic Orators*, i. 35.

[2] See *e.g.* the speeches of Critias and Theramenes in Xen. *Hellen.* ii. 3. This colloquial tone is one element of the quality in Xenophon which Quintilian (x. 1) calls "iucunditas inaffectata."

[3] On the rhetorical historians of the Isocratic school, see *Attic Orators* ii. 48 and 427.

the instinct which in earlier days would have been offended by the obtrusion of false ornament on a narrative of civic action. Then came the age of the Alexandrian erudition, and history was made a province of learned research. Polybius is a learned historian with a theory, but he is also a practical statesman and soldier. He is utterly opposed to the rhetorical treatment of historical subjects. He expressly condemns the sensational writers who confound the scope of history with that of tragedy. Tragedy, he says, may stir the emotions by any fiction which is not too improbable : the part of history is to teach lessons of permanent worth " by means of real deeds and words."[1] At the same time, he is keenly alive to the power of oratory. He observes how a single weighty speaker may turn the tide at a crisis,[2] and he apparently feels bound to make some attempt at representing oratorical effect. When he makes his persons speak, he does so much in the spirit of Thucydides, though less elaborately : that is, he has some definite points or arguments which he wishes to present in the most vivid form at a critical moment. Like Thucydides, he sometimes balances the harangues of generals on opposite sides.[3] Sometimes he begins to give merely the purport of what was said, and then passes from the oblique to direct speech,[4] as Thucydides occasionally does. And it may be concluded that, like Thucydides, he gave the " general sense " faithfully whenever it could be ascertained.[5] But Polybius stands alone in this respect among the historical writers after Xenophon. In the period between Alexander and Augustus the rhetorical school of history prevailed. Diodorus Siculus

---

[1] Polyb. ii. 56 : ἐκεῖ μὲν γὰρ (*i.e.* in Tragedy) δεῖ διὰ τῶν πιθανωτάτων λόγων ἐκπλῆξαι καὶ ψυχαγωγῆσαι κατὰ τὸ παρὸν τοὺς ἀκούοντας, ἐνθάδε δὲ (in History) διὰ τῶν ἀληθινῶν ἔργων καὶ λόγων εἰς τὸν πάντα χρόνον διδάξαι καὶ πεῖσαι τοὺς φιλομαθοῦντας.

[2] Polyb. xi. 10 : οὕτως εἷς λόγος, εὐκαίρως ῥηθεὶς ὑπ᾽ ἀνδρὸς ἀξιοπίστου, πολλάκις οὐ μόνον ἀποτρέπει τῶν χειρίστων ἀλλὰ καὶ παρορμᾷ πρὸς τὰ κάλλιστα τοὺς ἀνθρώπους.

[3] *E.g.* of Hannibal and Scipio, Polyb. iii. 108-111.

[4] Polyb. xi. 28 ; xxii. 14.

[5] See Polyb. xxx. 4 : ἦν δ᾽ ὁ νοῦς τῆς ἀποκρίσεως τοιοῦτος,—the ξύμπασα γνώμη of Thuc. i. 22.

and Dionysius of Halicarnassus[1] are both rhetoricians, the
rhetoric of Diodorus being combined with a quasi-philosophical
bent, and that of Dionysius with æsthetic criticism. Diodorus,
indeed, has some quaintly judicious remarks on the introduction
of long speeches into history. They interrupt the story, he
says, and distract the reader: writers who wish to show their
eloquence should do so somewhere else. A history should be
an organic whole; a speech which is inserted amiss cannot
have vital grace.[2] Still, speeches are sometimes desirable,
Diodorus adds, for the sake of variety (ποικιλία). When
circumstances require that an envoy or senator should speak,
the historian must gallantly accompany his personages into
the arena of debate.[3] Diodorus appears to recognise, as he
certainly used, the free licence of invention.[4] His view is substantially that of Plutarch[5] and Lucian.[6] They demand that the
speech shall be appropriate to the speaker and to the occasion,
but the same conditions are equally binding on an epic poet.
Among the Roman historians of the first rank, Livy is the one
who has made the largest use of this freedom. He once says,
in reference to a speech of Cato's, that, as the real text is extant in Cato's *Origines*, he will not give the reader a pale copy

---

[1] I have purposely abstained from examining the criticisms of Dionysius on
the speeches in Thucydides, since he regards them exclusively from the point
of view of contemporary rhetoric, not at all from the historian's. His
criticisms on Thucydides are, for this very reason, immeasurably inferior to
those in his excellent essays on the orators. The lengthy speech of Veturia
to Coriolanus (Dionys. *Ant. Rom.* viii. 46-53) is a fair specimen of his own
practice in the rhetorical embellishment of history.

[2] ἐστέρηται τῆς ψυχικῆς χάριτος, Diod. xx. 2.

[3] Diod. xx. 2, ὁ μὴ τεθαρρηκότως συγκαταβαίνων πρὸς τοὺς ἐν τοῖς λόγοις ἀγῶνας
καὶ αὐτὸς ὑπαίτιος ἂν εἴη.

[4] Thus he says, *ib.*, μεγάλων καὶ λαμπρῶν τῶν ὑποθέσεων οὐσῶν, οὐ περιο-
ατέον ἐλάττονα τῶν ἔργων φανῆναι τὸν λόγον.

[5] Plut., *praecept. ger. Reipubl.* 6, where he objects to long speeches before
battles as out of place. The speeches, often happily dramatic, in his own
biographies are the best comment on his remark (*de glor. Athen.* p. 346), τῶν
ἱστορικῶν κράτιστος ὁ τὴν διήγησιν ὥσπερ γραφὴν πάθεσι καὶ προσώποις εἰδωλο-
ποιήσας.

[6] Lucian, *de conscrib. hist.* 58, ἢν δέ ποτε . . . δεινότητα : "And if it should
ever be necessary to introduce a person speaking, first of all let the speech be
suitable to the person and the matter ; next let it be as clear as possible :
then, however, you are at liberty to declaim (ῥητορεῦσαι) and to show your
oratorical power."

of that rich eloquence.[1]   It might have been inferred that Livy
was careful in his speeches to represent individual character
and manner.[2]   But the inference is scarcely supported by the
extant portion of his work, though it is possible that his
portraits may have become more accurate in this respect as he
came to later times and ampler materials.   The speeches are
sometimes of great power and beauty, but the rhetorical colour
is uniform, and there is sometimes an absolute disregard of
dramatic probability.[3]   Sallust has higher merit in this department.   The war of Jugurtha and the conspiracy of Catiline
were, when Sallust wrote, events of recent memory, and each
had been illustrated by striking contrasts of character.   According to Plutarch, the employment of shorthand writers[4] to
report debates in the Roman Senate began in 63 B.C.; it was
certainly well established in the closing years of the Republic.
Sallust had some advantages for the presentation of character
in a manner at once dramatic and historical, and he seems to
have used them well.   There is no reason to doubt that Caesar's
speech in the debate on the punishment of the conspirators
was substantially such as Sallust reports;[5] and his way of
introducing a discourse of Memmius in the Jugurthine War
implies that it is true not only to the substance but to the
manner.[6]   Tacitus uses the dramatic form more variously than

---

[1] "Simulacrum viri copiosi," Liv. xlv. 25.

[2] As Quintilian says of Livy, "ita dicuntur omnia, cum rebus tum per-
sonis accommodata," x. 1.

[3] *E.g.* Liv. ii. 40; xxiii. 8, 9.   Livy seems sometimes to have taken hints
from Polybius or Thucydides ; cp. xxx. 30 with Polyb. xv. 6, and vii. 30 with
Thuc. i. 32.

[4] Plut. (*Cat. min.* 23) says that the speech of Cato in the debate on the conspiracy of Catiline is believed to be the only one of his preserved—Cicero
having taught some of the most rapid writers the use of a shorthand (σημεῖα
προδιδάξαντος ἐν μικροῖς καὶ βραχέσι τύποις πολλῶν γραμμάτων ἔχοντα δύναμιν), and
having distributed these writers through the Senate-house.   For the Romans,
Plutarch adds, did not yet possess τοὺς καλουμένους σημειογράφους : this was
the beginning of it.   Suetonius mentions a speech of Julius Cæsar which,
Augustus thought, must have been imperfectly taken down by the *actuarii*
(*Caes.* 55).   The usual Roman word was *notarius*.   Martial has an epigram on
a shorthand writer, .xiv. 208.

[5] Sallust, *Catil.* 51, 52.

[6] *Bellum Jugurth.* 31—a striking illustration of the Roman feeling that
oratory, for its own sake, deserved a place in history.

Sallust, but with a stricter historical conscience than Livy. He ·resembles Thucydides and Polybius in never introducing a speech merely for oratorical effect, but always for the purpose of illustrating a political situation or character.[1] There is a well-known instance—the only one in ancient literature—in which the discourse given by the historian can be compared with an official record of the discourse really delivered. In the Eleventh Book of the *Annals* the Emperor Claudius addresses the Senate in support of a proposal for imparting the Roman franchise to the provincials of Gallia Comata.[2] The bronze tablets found at Lyons in the sixteenth century, and now in the Museum there, give what purports to be the real speech of Claudius on this occasion. Tacitus and the tablets disagree hopelessly in language and in nearly all the detail, but agree in the general line of argument.[3] Knowing the antiquarian turn of Claudius, Tacitus might easily have concluded that the Emperor's speech would dwell largely on historical precedents; but it seems more likely that he knew, from oral or written report, the substance of what Claudius had said, and worked up this in his own way. Here, then, is a rough gauge of the approximation which might be made to the truth by a historian who composed a speech based on "the general sense of what was really said." Thucydides and Polybius, Sallust and Tacitus, are widely removed from writers who introduce harangues merely as opportunities of display.[4] The latter tendency prevailed in

---

[1] Ulrici, indeed (*Charakteristik der antiken Historiographie*, p. 148) regards some of the speeches in Tacitus as inserted merely for dramatic ornament; *e.g. Ann.* i. 17, 22, 42, 43, 58, 59 ; ii. 14, 45, 46 ; iii. 16, 61 ; iv. 34, 35 ; xii. 10. But in all such cases, I think, it will be found that a more serious motive is also present.

[2] Tac. *Ann.* xi. 24.

[3] The text of the two bronze tablets, found in 1524, has been edited by A. de Boissieu in his *Inscriptions antiques de Lyons*. It is printed in Orelli's edition of Tacitus at the end of Book xi. of the *Annals*, p. 342.

[4] As they are introduced, for example, by Quintus Curtius, who gives the speech of the Scythian ambassadors to Alexander (vii. 8), and an impossible harangue of Dareius to his army before the battle of Arbela (iv. 14).

what Gibbon calls "the elaborate and often empty speeches of the Byzantine historians."[1] The Latin chroniclers of the middle ages rarely ventured on such ambitious efforts. But at the revival of letters the classical practice of inserting speeches was revived by historical writers, whether they wrote in Latin[2] or in their vernacular.[3] M. Daunou[4] quotes some curious examples from the French literature of the three centuries before our own. Thus Vertot, in his *Révolutions romaines,* entered into competition with Dionysius, Livy and Plutarch, by inventing a fourth version of the appeal made to Coriolanus by his mother in the Volscian camp. Mézerai could make Joan of Arc address her executioners in a harangue full of violent invective and sinister prediction; and this when the contemporary record of her trial existed, with its notice of the rare and broken utterances which belonged to her last hours.[5] By degrees a controversy arose on the question whether a historian is entitled to invent speeches for his persons, and the literary world was long divided upon it. Isaac Voss[6] and Mably[7] were among the more distinguished champions of the oratorical licence; among its opponents were Voltaire—whose opinion has been quoted already—and D'Alembert. The latter declared, in 1761, that a historian who filled his work with

---

[1] *Decline and Fall*, ch. 43. It is difficult to believe, with Gibbon, that the speech of Attila to his soldiers before the battle of Chalons—as given in Cassiodorus—can rest on any basis of fact (ch. 35); however it may be with the letter of Belisarius to Justinian given by Procopius, which Gibbon thinks "genuine and original" (ch. 43).

[2] *E.g.* Paulus Aemilius, Strada Mariana, Buchanan, Grotius, De Thou.

[3] *E.g.* Machiavelli, Guicciardini, Mézerai.

[4] *Cours d'Études Historiques*, vol. vii. p. 466 ff.

[5] As M. Daunou gravely observes : "La plus simple réflexion suffit pour concevoir que les Anglais, tenant en leur pouvoir la malheureuse Jeanne, ne lui auraient pas permis, à sa dernière heure, de débiter publiquement toutes ces sottises" (p. 476). The authentic records of her trial and execution are contained, he adds, in vol. iii. of the *Notices et Extraits des Manuscrits de la Bibliothèque du Roi.* It is an extraordinary example of the rhetorical taste of the age that Mézerai should have preferred to declaim, when he might have told a true story of the deepest pathos.

[6] *Ars Historica*, 20.

[7] *De la manière d'écrire l'Histoire*, Works, vol. xii. 452-461.

speeches would be sent back to college.[1] But the practice
lingered on a little longer, being commonly defended by the
plea that it was enlivening, and that it could not be really
deceptive.[2] The spirit of scientific criticism has now banished
it for ever from history, and has relegated it to its proper
sphere in the province of historical romance.

§ 13. Thucydides set the first great example of making
historical persons say what they might have said. The basis
of his conception was common to the whole ancient world : it
was the sovereign importance of speech in political and civic
life. But in Thucydides the use of the licence is dramatic—
that is, conducive to the truthful and vivid presentment of
action. In most of the later Greek and Roman historians it is
either rhetorical—that is, subservient to the display of the
writer's style—or partly dramatic and partly rhetorical. The
art of rhetoric passed through two stages of educational significance in the ancient world. In the first stage, with which
Thucydides was contemporary, rhetoric meant a training for
real debate in the assembly or the law-courts. Then, as Greek
political life died down, rhetoric came to mean the art of
writing or declaiming.[3] The speeches in Thucydides have the
dramatic spirit, and not the rhetorical, because, although the
art of rhetoric has helped to make them, they are in direct
relation with real action and real life. The rhetorical historians
of the ancient world represent the second stage of rhetoric :

---

[1] "Tranchons le mot, aujourd'hui l'on renverrait aux amplifications de
collége un historien qui remplirait son ouvrage de harangues :" quoted by
Daunou (vii. 472) from a paper on the art of writing history, read by D'Alembert to the French Academy (*ib.* p. 115).

[2] Thus Gaillard, in his History of Francis I., published in 1766, answers the
charge of a "petite infidélité" by saying : "Je réponds que je ne puis voir
une infidélité réelle où d'un côté personne ne veut tromper, et où d'un autre
côté personne ne peut-être trompé" (Daunou, p. 458). This is much the same
as the apology for Livy's speeches made by Crevier in the preface to his
edition : "Quasi vero cuiquam innocens ille dolus imponat." Botta's History
of Italy from 1780 to 1814 contains one of the latest examples, perhaps, of the
licence, when he gives (Book iii.) the speeches of Pesaro and Vallaresso in the
debate of the Venetian Senate on the French invasion of Italy (1793), and
(Book v.) a debate in the Piedmontese Council. The practice was thoroughly
suited to the Italian genius, and maintained itself longest in Italy.

[3] The process of this change has been sketched in the *Attic Orators.* vol. ii.
ch. xxiv.

their speeches are only more or less possible declamations. The modern writers who attempted to revive the practice were in a lower deep still, since for them rhetoric was not even a living element of culture.[1] But it may be well to consider a little more closely how far and in what sense Thucydides can be called dramatic. The epithet "dramatic" is sometimes applied to narrative when no more is apparently meant than that it is vivid or graphic. In the proper sense, however, a narrative is dramatic only when it elicits the inherent eloquence of facts. Thucydides is dramatic, for instance, when he places the Melian dialogue[2] immediately before the Sicilian expedition. The simple juxtaposition of insolence and ruin is more effective than comment. The bare recital, thus ordered, makes the same kind of impression which the actions themselves would have made if one had immediately succeeded the other before our eyes. It might not be difficult, with a little adroitness, to represent Thucydides as a conscious dramatic artist throughout his work; and an ingenious writer has actually shown how his History may be conceived as a tragedy cast into five acts.[3]

---

[1] The Roman historical writers of the Empire were under the influence of the recitations (cp. Mayor on Juvenal iii.; and Heitland and Raven, in the Introduction to their extracts from Quintus Curtius, in the Pitt Press Series, p. 12). Prejudicial to history as this influence was, it yet gave a special interest to the speeches, regarded as exercises in a familiar art.

[2] In the remarkable speech of the Athenian envoy Euphemus at Camarina (vi. 82-86, 415 B.C.), the dramatic purpose of the Melian dialogue is continued and completed. The plain avowal of Athenian motives is reiterated, and their bearing on the Sicilian expedition is explicitly stated. See vi. 83, τήν τε γὰρ ἐκεῖ ἀρχὴν (in Greece) εἰρήκαμεν διὰ δέος ἔχειν, καὶ τὰ ἐνθάδε (in Sicily) διὰ τὸ αὐτὸ ἥκειν μετὰ τῶν φίλων ἀσφαλῶς καταστησόμενοι. 85, ὥστε καὶ τἀνθάδε εἰκὸς πρὸς τ λυσιτελοῦν καί, ὃ λέγομεν, ἐς Συρακοσίους δέος καθίστασθαι.

[3] Ulrici, *Charakteristik der antiken Historiographie*, p. 313. Book i. is a prologue, he says, which acquaints the reader with the immediate antecedents of the drama and the relative positions of the chief actors. The First Act comprises the plague at Athens, the supreme efforts of Pericles and his death, the destruction of Plataea by Sparta, the overthrow of Mitylene by Athens (ii. 1—iii. 68). The Second Act presents the typical party-strife at Corcyra; fortune wavers; the Athenians are defeated by the Aetolians, but blockade the Spartans in Sphacteria (iii. 69—iv. 36). The Third Act opens with the surrender of the Spartans; the Athenians occupy Cythera; both sides are weary of the struggle, and at length a peace is concluded. But there are signs that it cannot last, and now Alcibiades comes forward to

But it would perhaps be truer to say that the war itself presented striking contrasts, analogous to those which a dramatic
poet contrives: the dullest writer could not have wholly
missed these contrasts; and if Diodorus had been the historian,
his work, too, might have revealed the five acts; but Thucydides was peculiarly well fitted to bring out these contrasts
with the most complete effect. He was so, because he felt
the whole moment and pathos of the events themselves;
because he saw them with the distinctness of intense concentration; and because, partly under the influence of language,[1]
he had even more than the ordinary Greek love of antithesis.
It is obvious that the Peloponnesian war, as a subject for
history, may be said to have dramatic unity in the sense that
it is a single great action: as, by an analogous metaphor, the
subject of Herodotus may be said to have epic unity, because
the various parts, though they cannot be brought within the
compass of one action,[2] can be brought within the compass of
one narrative. And, apart from this rudimentary dramatic
unity, the Peloponnesian war has a further analogy to a drama
in presenting a definite moment at which the cardinal situation
is decisively reversed—as it is reversed in the *Oedipus
Tyrannus,* for instance, when the king discovers that he is an
incestuous parricide. That moment is the Sicilian expedition.
The supreme test of "dramatic" quality in a history of the
Peloponnesian war must be the power with which the historian

---

advocate the Sicilian expedition (iv. 37—vi. 23). The Fourth Act is the
crisis—the Sicilian expedition, ending in the Athenian defeat (vi. 24—vii.). In
the Fifth Act the catastrophe is delayed for a moment by the recall of
Alcibiades. He brings back a gleam of prosperity with him. But he is
again dismissed; and then comes the final ruin of Athens (viii.).

[1] The Greek instinct for symmetry and just measure sharpened the perception of contrast, and the desire of vividly expressing contrast helped to mould
the language. Thus when it is said of Antigone, πασῶν γυναικῶν ὡς ἀναξιω-
τάτη | κάκιστ᾽ ἀπ᾽ ἔργων εὐκλεεστάτων φθίνει (694), it is the keenly felt opposition
of things that is striving to utter itself in the forcible opposition of words.
Then Rhetoric arose, with its opposition of words even where there was
no commensurate opposition of things. Thucydides was partly under
this influence of Rhetoric: witness his ἔργον and λόγος, etc.; but, by a
reversal of the natural process, the very habit of verbal antithesis tended to
quicken the observation of opportunities for its effective employment.

[2] *I.e.* no drama on the Persian wars could have included (*e.g.*) the Egyptian
and Scythian episodes of Herodotus.

has marked the significance of the Sicilian expedition as the
tragic "revolution" (*peripeteia*), the climax of pity and terror,
the decisive reversal. Thucydides has devoted the whole of
his Sixth and Seventh Books to the events of those two years,
thus at once marking the significance of the expedition as the
turning-point of the war. And every reader knows with what
tremendous effect he has traced its course, from the moment when
the whole population of Athens was gathered at the Peiraeus
in the early midsummer morning to see the splendid fleet sail
for Sicily, and the trumpet commanded silence while the whole
multitude joined in prayer, and wine was poured from vessels
of silver and gold as the pæan [1] arose, down to that overthrow of
which he writes that they were destroyed with utter destruction,
and that few out of many came home.[2] Here, at the point in
his story which supplies the crucial test, Thucydides shows
that he possesses true dramatic power. By the direct presentment of the facts, not by reflections upon them, he makes us
feel all that is tragic in the Sicilian disaster itself, and also all
that it means in relation to the larger tragedy of the war. The
same power is seen in many particular episodes of the History :
for example, in the self-restrained majesty of Pericles, the great
protagonist of the opening war, whose courage, amidst havoc
and pestilence, ever rises as the Athenian courage declines; or
in the first appearance of Alcibiades on the scene, with his
brilliant versatility and his profound lack of loyalty, with his
unmeasured possibilities for good or evil, just when the Sicilian
project is trembling in the balance. Without pressing the
parallel between the History and a work of dramatic art to
any fanciful length, it may be said with a definite meaning
that Thucydides has not merely the inspiration of action, but
often also the spirit of the noblest tragic drama.

It is natural to regret his silence in regard to the social and
intellectual life of his age.[3] The simplest explanation of it is

---

[1] vi. 30.   [2] vii. 87.

[3] The names of Aeschylus, Sophocles (the poet), Euripides (the poet),
Aristophanes, Pheidias, Ictinus, Anaxagoras, Socrates, are among those which
Thucydides nowhere mentions. In addition to Helen (i. 9) and Procne
(ii. 29), only four women are named in the whole History, and not one of
them has the slightest human interest in reference to the war—Chrysis and
Phaeinis, successively priestesses of the Argive Hera (ii. 1, iv. 133) ; Strato-

that he did not conceive such details as requisite for the illustration of his purely political subject. The art and poetry of the day, the philosophy and the society, were perhaps in his view merely the decorations of the theatre in which the great tragedy of the war was being played. Though he wrote for all time, he did not conceive of an audience who would have to reconstruct this theatre before they could fully comprehend his drama.[1] No writer has ever been at once so anxiously careful and so haughtily improvident of the future. His characteristic dislike of superfluous detail seems to have been allied with a certain hardness of temperament, such as is indicated by the tone of his reference to the poets.[2] His banishment may also have infused something of bitterness[3]

---

nice, the sister of Perdiccas (ii. 101) ; and Archedice, the daughter of Hippias (vi. 59). The Parthenon is alluded to as a treasury ; and the Propylaea are noticed—as a work which had reduced the balance in it (ii. 13, § 3, where ἐν τῇ ἀκροπόλει = ἐν τῷ ὀπισθοδόμῳ).

[1] Thucydides can, indeed, imagine a time when Sparta shall be desolate, and only the ruins of Athens shall remain ; i. 10 § 2, Λακεδαιμονίων γὰρ εἰ ἡ πόλις ἐρημωθείη . . . ᾿Αθηναίων δὲ τὸ αὐτὸ τοῦτο παθόντων, κ.τ.λ. But he has no conception of a time when the Hellenic civilisation that he knew should have passed away. Thus Pericles says that Athens (unlike Troy or Mycenae, he means) needs no Homer to persuade posterity of her greatness : she has established on every shore *imperishable monuments* of her power for evil or good, where the ἀΐδια μνημεῖα are the Athenian settlements on conquered or on friendly soil. Cf. ii. 64, ἢν καὶ νῦν ὑπενδῶμέν ποτε . . . μνήμη καταλελείψεται, κ.τ.λ.—where the μνήμη assumes a purely Hellenic standard.

[2] He cites them simply as authorities for facts, whose statements often require to be modified : i. 21 § 1. Thus he makes a sort of apology for quoting so equivocal an authority as Homer respecting the power of Agamemnon (i. 9 § 4), and the size of the Greek fleet (10 § 3). His extracts from the fine passage in the Hymn to the Delian Apollo are the briefest which could establish his two points—that there *was* an Ionian festival at Delos, and that it included a musical contest (iii. 104).

[3] There is a singular suggestiveness in the speech which the exile Thucydides attributes to the exile Alcibiades (at Sparta in 415 B.C., vi. 92). It is the historian's way of showing how the pain which he himself had known might work in a disloyal character. "My patriotism," says Alcibiades, "is not for a country that wrongs me ; it was given to a country that protected my rights. . . . The true patriot is not he who abstains from moving against the country from which he has been unjustly banished, but he who, in his passionate love for her, strives by all means to regain her."

May not these words—καὶ φιλόπολις οὗτος ὀρθῶς, οὐχ ὃς ἂν τὴν ἑαυτοῦ ἀδίκως ἀπολέσας μὴ ἐπίῃ—have a reference to Thrasybulus and the patriotic exiles who marched from Phyle upon Athens? Just after the restoration of the democracy the point would have been peculiarly effective.

into his recollections of the Athenian life, with all its gracious surroundings, with all its social and intellectual delights, from which he was suddenly cut off, so that he should know them no more until he came back in his old age and found them changed. No one can tell now how the memories of early sympathies may have grouped themselves in his mind as he looked out in later years from his home in Thrace on the sea over which he had sailed on the long-past day when he failed to save Amphipolis; but at least there is a twofold suggestiveness in those passages[1] which touch on the glories of Athens. There is the feeling of the man who has never lost his love and admiration for the Athenian ideal; and there is also a certain reluctance to translate this ideal into concrete images,[2] as if, in the words of Oedipus after his ruin, it were sweet for thought to dwell beyond the sphere of griefs.[3] Perhaps in this very reticence the modern world may find a gain when it views his work from the artistic side. Thucydides must always hold his fame by a double right; not only as a thinker who, in an age of transitional scepticism, clearly apprehended the value of disciplined intelligence as a permanent force in practical politics, but also as a writer who knew how to make great events tell their own story greatly; and the dramatic power of the immortal History is heightened by its dramatic reserve.

R. C. J.

---

[1] Most striking of all these, perhaps, is one in the speech of Nicias to the army before the retreat from Syracuse (vii. 63, § 3), where, addressing the *non*-Athenians, he reminds them of the pleasure (ἡδονή) which they have derived from *passing for* Athenians—through their knowledge of the Attic dialect, and their imitation of Attic manners—and so being admired throughout Greece : Ἀθηναῖοι νομιζόμενοι καὶ μὴ ὄντες . . . τῆς τε φωνῆς ἐπιστήμῃ καὶ τῶν τρόπων τῇ μιμήσει ἐθαυμάζεσθε κατὰ τὴν Ἑλλάδα. Among Peloponnesians, Italians or Siceliots, the Athenian exile had ever carried about with him the consciousness of belonging to that city which was the παίδευσις Ἑλλάδος.

[2] Even in the Funeral Oration—that splendid monument of his grave enthusiasm for Athens—Thucydides has been restrained, whether by fidelity to the original or by his own feeling, from exceeding the limit of such abstract expressions as τὰ καθ᾽ ἡμέραν ἐπιτηδεύματα, πόνων ἀναπαῦλαι, ἀγῶνες, θυσίαι, φιλοκαλεῖν, φιλοσοφεῖν.

[3] τὸ γὰρ | τὴν φροντίδ᾽ ἔξω τῶν κακῶν οἰκεῖν γλυκύ, *Oed. Tyr.* 1390.

TABLE OF THE SPEECHES.

[Asterisks mark those delivered at Athens before the exile of Thucydides.]

Book.   Date B.C.

I. 32-36   433 Corcyrean ⎞ Envoys to the Athenian Ecclesia.*
,, 37-43   ,,   Corinthian ⎠

,, 68-72   432 Corinthian ⎞ Envoys in the first Congress at Sparta.
,, 73-78   ,,   Athenian ⎠

,, 80-85   ,,   King Archidamus   ⎞ to the Spartan Assembly.
,, 86   ,,   The Ephor Sthenelaidas ⎠

,, 120-24   ,,   Corinthian Envoys in the second Congress at Sparta.
,, 140-44   ,,   Pericles to the Athenian Ecclesia.*

II. 35-46   431 Funeral Oration of Pericles.*
,,   60-64   430 Pericles to the Athenian Ecclesia.*

III. 9-14   428 Mitylenean Envoys to the Peloponnesians at Olympia.

,, 37-40   427 Cleon   ⎞ to the Athenian Ecclesia.*
,, 42-48   ,,   Diodotus ⎠

,, 53-59   ,,   Plataeans ⎞ to the Spartan Judges.
,, 61-67   ,,   Thebans   ⎠

IV. 17-20   425 Lacedaemonian Envoys to the Athenian Ecclesia.*
,,   59-64   424 Hermocrates in the Sicilian Congress at Gela.
,,   85-87   ,,   Brasidas to the Acanthians.

V. 85-116   416 Conference between Athenian and Melian negotiators.

VI. 9-14   415 Nicias   ⎞
,, 16-18   ,,   Alcibiades ⎬ to the Athenian Ecclesia.
,, 20-23   ,,   Nicias   ⎠

,, 33-34   ,,   Hermocrates   ⎞
,, 36-40   ,,   Athenagoras   ⎬ to the Syracusan Assembly.
,, 41   ,,   A Syracusan General ⎠

,, 76-80   ,,   Hermocrates as Envoy of Syracuse ⎞ at Camarina.
,, 82-86   ,,   Euphemus as Envoy of Athens   ⎠

,, 89-92   ,,   Alcibiades at Sparta.

Military Harangues.

II. 11   431 Archidamus to the Peloponnesian Officers before invad-
                ing Attica.

,, 87   429 Peloponnesian Commanders to their ⎞ before an action
                crews   ⎬ in the Corinthian
,, 89   ,,   Phormio to the men of the Athenian ⎠ Gulf.
                Fleet

IV. 10   425 Demosthenes to his troops at Pylos.
,, 92   424 Pagondas to the Boeotian troops ⎞ before the battle
,, 95   ,,   Hippocrates to the Athenian troops ⎠ of Delium.

Book.		Date B.C.	
IV.	126	423	Brasidas to his troops on the campaign against Arrhibaeus.
V.	9	422	Brasidas to his troops before the battle at Amphipolis.
VI.	68	415	Nicias to his troops before the first battle at Syracuse.
VII.	61-64	413	Nicias to the Athenian troops ⎱ before the last sea-
,,	66-68	,,	Gylippus to the Syracusan troops ⎰ fight.
,,	77	,,	Nicias to his troops before the retreat from Syracuse.

The short speech of the Elean Teutiaplus to Alcidas and the Peloponnesian leaders at Embaton (iii. 30, 427 B.C.) is virtually of this class.

From the set speeches are to be distinguished a few shorter utterances in the direct form, but of a more colloquial character, viz. the dialogue between Archidamus and the Plataeans (ii. 71-74, 429 B.C.) ; the conversation with the Ambracian herald and an Athenian (iii. 113, 426 B.C.) ; and the words of Peisander in the Athenian Ecclesia (viii. 53, 411 B.C.) The letter of Nicias (vii. 11-15, 414 B.C.) would be classed by some with the speeches composed by Thucydides, by others as an authentic document. Cp. p. 98, note 6.

XENOPHON.

"The sage and heroic Xenophon."—GIBBON.

IF the learning of Gibbon had chanced or chosen to add another epithet to the two in which he has justly commemorated the virtues of Xenophon, perhaps with the σοφὸς and ἥρως of Plutarch and Longinus he would have coupled the λογιώτατος of Polybius; for the companion of Cyrus, who tramped or galloped over the sandy plains of Mesopotamia seven centuries and a half before the fatal march of Julian, in the end proved himself no less an adept in the art of words than of warfare, and lived to display to after-time, as the outcome of multiform gifts, a triad of interblending qualities as a man, philosopher, and stylist.

It is under this threefold embodiment that an attempt is here made, in some sort briefly, to estimate the genius of Xenophon. But intentionally, the scope of this Essay is confined to an appreciation of the more salient characteristics of the writer. What was the main drift of his talents? How was he placed with regard to the times at which he lived? In what relation does he stand to our own? The answer, or some answer, to these questions may well present itself as a quite sufficient object without plunging into polemic, even where the views maintained run counter to those of higher authority. On the same principle, it seems right to avoid all detailed discussion of the various 'vexed questions' and perplexities familiar to the student of the life and literature before us.

Some of these have the abstract interest of problems proper, in which the balance of argument in favour of this conclusion or the other is so evenly poised, that a tremor of the investigator's hand will turn the scale, and the work will need to be recommenced; as, for instance, the time-honoured inquiry, "de simultate Platonis cum Xenophonte," or the question whether he fought at Delium and was carried off the field on the shoulders of Socrates; or, again, in what year he was born. Of these, some, it is felt, are comparatively otiose, others lure the searcher on, in hopes of a discovery, where perhaps discovery is impossible. Thus we may ask, What light does 'the *Anabasis*' throw upon the question of Xenophon's age at the date of the matters there recorded (B.C. 401)? Let us suppose, for the moment, that the book itself is simply a splendid work of imagination, of the Robinson Crusoe type, based upon the verisimilitude of thrilling incidents such as might have occurred during the actual advance and retreat, and in which a 'well-girt' Athenian volunteer might have played a conspicuous part, but which were really the clever invention of some Hellenic Defoe:[1] would such a work fix with certainty the age of this ideal Xenophon, as under thirty-five rather than over forty? Or, on the counter supposition that the tale itself is a *vera narratio*, not more coloured than would be the contributions of a fairly accurate military correspondent to a modern newspaper, who should find himself actively employed in command of a Russian column in Central Asia:—in this case, do any expressions used—οὐδὲν προφασίζομαι τὴν ἡλικίαν, "my age shall not stand between me and your orders," etc., settle the question?[2]

Another class of difficulties has this special attractiveness, that—being involved with more vital points of interest which lie still in a haze of uncertainty—with the elucidation of the one will come, perhaps, an inpouring of light upon the others. What, for instance, was the date of Xenophon's banishment from Athens? What was the cause of it? Supposing him to have been sentenced ἐπὶ Λακωνισμῷ,[3] " on the ground of ' *Laconism*,' " in what way were these objectionable or culpable proclivities exhibited? Was it through attachment to

---

[1] To this inventive personage, possibly named Themistogenes, but more probably Xenophon himself, Xenophon is an ideal being. The stone of stumbling, perhaps intentionally placed, is the passage in *Hellen*. iii. 1. 2. ὡς μὲν οὖν Κῦρος στράτευμά τε συνέλεξε καὶ τοῦτ' ἔχων ἀνέβη ἐπὶ τὸν ἀδελφὸν, καὶ ὡς ἡ μάχη ἐγένετο, καὶ ὡς ἀπέθανε, καὶ ὡς ἐκ τούτου ἀπεσώθησαν οἱ Ἕλληνες ἐπὶ θάλατταν, Θεμιστογένει τῷ Συρακοσίῳ γέγραπται. *Vide infra*, p. 352, for further problems connected with the person of Themistogenes.

[2] Xen. *Anab*. iii. 1. 14 and 25 ; compare Thirlwall, *Xenophon, Niebuhr, and Delbrueck*, Philol. Mus. vol. i. p. 510.

[3] Diog. Laert. ii. 7. 15.

Cyrus? or coquettings with Spartan Harmosts, the admirals
and governors-general of Byzantium? or were these at worst
forgotten bygones? Was it his new friendship with Agesilaus, or his presence at Coroneia, or something altogether
different, which brought about the sentence? Again, was
Xenophon present at Coroneia? If present, was he there in a
private capacity, as a mere spectator conceivably? or was he,
necessarily, personally engaged? Or, given that he was present
on the field, does it remain important whether he fought or
not? Again, assuming that he was not only there, but fought
beside Agesilaus, can his conduct be explained or justified on
general grounds? or by application of any ethical standard
suited to the peculiar political situation? This standard may
either be normal,[1] that is to say, in accordance with the more
or less fixed Hellenic 'interpolitical' morality; or abnormal,[2]
the outcome of a temporary confusion of ideas. It is clear
that such confusion was inevitable, in the struggle between
incipient Panhellenism, and a belief in the 'natural' claims
of Sparta to hegemony, which is *Laconism*, coupled possibly
with anti-Theban jealousy? It is no less clear that these
currents and cross-currents must set more or less in a direction
contrary to the old customary and sacred separate-State
doctrine, which would usually, and more properly, be distinguished by the name of 'patriotism.' Nor is it to be denied that
a right answer to these and other similar questions would lead
directly to the better understanding either of Hellenic history
as a whole, or of the Socratic and Sophistic era in particular;
of the times or personality of Xenophon; of his political stand-
point or his military and literary genius. Hence their fascina-
tion—here to be resisted.

A third class of difficulties, however, intermediate between
these latter and the problem proper, may not be so easily

---

[1] *Normal.* It must be borne in mind that 'the opposition' were in all
Greek states (even tolerant Athens) liable to find themselves outside the walls
of their πόλις, and then civic duties became hazy and ambiguous. Cf.
Alcibiades.

[2] *Abnormal.* The opinions of Isocrates, only a stage later than Xenophon,
throw much light on this matter. *Vide* Jebb, *Orators*, vol. ii. ch. xii. for his
Philippising Panhellenism. Panhellenism in itself is the prototype of modern
cosmopolitan morality.

avoided, for they run up into the substance of any general appreciation; yet, even so, they can be only dealt with indirectly in this essay. They cluster chiefly round the *Memorabilia*, or else round the *Hellenica*. Of the first, these are samples: What is Xenophon's estimate of Socrates worth? Is he unworthy the name of a philosopher, if only as being unintelligent of his great associate? Of the second, these: Why is his History so one-sided? Why these astonishing gaps? Why no mention of Pelopidas in the recapture of the Cadmeia, nor of Epaminondas at Leuctra? Not a word of the re-establishment of Messene on Mount Ithomé, or of the founding of Panarcadian Megalopolis. What, on the other hand, is the meaning of the encomium passed upon the historian by Lucian,[1] for honesty and impartiality? It cannot be alleged of these questions, as of others possibly, that they are either insoluble or of no deep biographical interest; yet, to rivet attention, in a sketch, to the difficulties rather than the patent characteristics of a period in the life of a people or an individual; to arrange the materials before us so as to constitute a series of diverting or discouraging riddles, may be the worst mode of distorting the truth; and, in a rapid survey, it would seem better to allow the lights and shadows to arrange themselves, than microscopically to examine the obscurer portions. The former at any rate is the method adopted here.

But there is yet another class of questions, which, although individually included in one or other of the above divisions, might better be treated separately. I refer to the whole topic of the canon. Which of the works attributed to Xenophon are genuine? and, amongst those regarded as genuine, which, if any, are suspected portions? However formidable this group of ἀπορίαι, its discussion is inadmissible here; and in lieu of which, it may be deemed sufficient to append a list of works accepted as, for the most part, genuine. Nor does this solution seem objectionable, if, in so doing, we conscientiously refrain from colouring our judgment on any essential point by data drawn from those works, or portions of a work, the genuineness of which we more than half suspect. The list itself, appropriated bodily from Sauppe's stereotyped edition in five volumes,

---

[1] Lucian, πῶς δεῖ ἱστορίαν συγγράφειν; 39.

will serve to draw attention to a point of some importance, not unfrequently forgotten while we are thinking of Xenophon's talents as pre-eminently embodied in this or the other of his larger works; as the author of the *Anabasis,* or the *Cyropaedia,* of the *Hellenica,* or the *Memorabilia.* The point referred to is the versatility and productiveness, and, as a closer consideration reveals, the inventiveness of this writer's genius; while the titles themselves, and still more the subject-matter, show that these qualities are not literary simply, but part of the underlying capacity of the man.

Lastly, and as might *a priori* have been expected in the case of so 'vocal' an actor, the writer, it will be admitted, has not failed to reveal either himself, or the stage on which he moved, and this to a quite unprecedented degree. These works [1] (with their approximate dates) are rich with the best autobiographic matter, and burn brightly with the spirit of the times. But what is meant by biographic, or autobiographic, matter? I would fain use the words in only the higher sense, and exclude a particular kind of 'inferential' biography of a type with which the so-called lives of certain saints or sinners have made us in our childhood familiar. We are content to know that Proxenus was a time-honoured friend, and can gather food for reflection from the description of the after-supper walk in the camp, in front of the *place d'armes,* where the two friends paced together a few days before the youthful Boeotian general was murdered. [2] We

---

[1] [*The Polity of Athens,* probably not by Xenophon, written about B.C. 426]

Hiero,	written after	,,	394
Memorabilia (or *Recollections*),	written about	,,	390
Treatise on Hunting,	written after	,,	389
Hellenica, Part I.,	written before	,,	387
The Symposium,	written before	,,	385
The Economist,	written not before	,,	383
The Anabasis (or the *Advance on Susa and the Retreat*),	written after	,,	380
The Polity of the Lacedaemonians,	written about	,,	369
A Cavalry General's Manual,	written about	,,	363
A Treatise on Horsemanship,	written about	,,	362
The Cyropaedia (or the *Education of Cyrus*),	not finished before	,,	361
Agesilaus (a panegyric on),	written about	,,	360
Hellenica, Part II.,	written about	,,	357
A Pamphlet on Revenues,	written about	,,	356

[2] *Anab.* ii. iv. 15.

can almost overhear the words they said together. So again
the delineation of his friend's character, in juxtaposition with
those of Clearchus and Menon, is speakingly suggestive. But
we do not care to make this biographic incident a ground for
concluding that the early years of Xenophon were spent in
captivity at Thebes; where, with Proxenus, who learnt wisdom
as we know from Gorgias, he may have listened to Prodicus
expounding the choice of Heracles; where also he doubtless
contracted that general antipathy to Thebans, of which his
exceptional affection for Proxenus gives a kind of proof. So
again the picture of his life at Skillus, drawn by himself, suffices.
Here we see him offering daily sacrifice to his patron goddess
Artemis,[1] or worshipping in the miniature model of the temple
of the great goddess of the Ephesians at Ephesus by the banks
of the miniature Selinus, or hunting antelopes and boars
with his sons and friends on the slopes of Pholoe. Nor is
any strong desire aroused in us to ascertain what really
happened eventually; whether or not the Eleians restored the
recaptured farm, or whether the wanderer was driven to retire
to Corinth, where he ended his days. In truth, a question of
deeper interest does arise: whether the περὶ προσόδων was, as
we incline to believe, a work of his old age, and, not improbably,
written in requital to Eubulus for the kindly service of his
restoration; but whether he actually ended his days at Athens
or Corinth, or elsewhere, is not in itself a fact which we ought
to jump at inferentially; or need unduly lament as still relegated to the region of open surmise.

It is, however, not to be denied that within the biography of
inference lurk also the germs of better things; ceasing to deal
with trivialities and the more mundane materials, it rises at
once in validity and in dignity: so that, instead of a tissue
of external 'facts' whose objectivity is questionable,' we get,
in some sort of matter-of-fact setting, a group of rational inferences, drawn from the cognition of real and truly apprehended
qualities. In such or such way must this man, being of this
sort, have behaved in these circumstances. The qualities of
the individual and the circumstances being given, the inference
of any sympathetic and intelligent biographer will probably

---

[1] *Anab.* v. 3. 5-12.

be worth recording ; or, in the case of a tradition, the subjective
summing up of a whole cluster of unconscious biographers—
to wit, the age which records it—may have the further charm
of contributing to the autobiography of humanity itself.   This
high order of conjectural biography, doubtless, deserves to be
called 'ideal' rather than inferential.   Such is its true nature,
and it is generally interesting as throwing light on the mind
of others quite as much as on his who is the subject of the narrative.   Hence the charm and interest of Plutarch's *Lives*, which
may be spoken of as chapters from the autobiography of Greece
and Rome.   In them there is still a contribution from the
actual life, it may be of a Pompey or an Alcibiades, the rest
being the offerings of contemporaries, or posterity constructing
inferentially, and only half-consciously, the two lives as they
should, nay must, have shaped themselves.   In other words,
they were sentences of activity or inaction, spoken by twin
guardian divinities, to be graven by the fingers of a mortal upon
the hearts of men.   A stage further, and a whole people writes
its own "phase of faith" in the life of its greatest religious
teacher, the facts being of the flimsiest historic validity, but the
idea stamped as genuine gold with the impress of eternity.
When this happens to humanity as a whole, there is only one
title to be given to these self-delineations.   They are the everlasting portraitures of man, the express image of the offspring
of divinity.   Apart from this, it would seem better to be represented by no biography of the mundane sort, or next to none—
as is the case with Shakespeare,—but to live by works in the
faithful hearts of posterity.

In more self-conscious times, however, the impulse to conscious self-revelation has produced another type, and, with the
growth of science and regard for "objective" truth, perhaps in
this direction may be expected the happiest results : when the
writer is content to set forth his life simply as it lies spread
out before the all-seeing, neither despising the physical and
material side of his nature, nor taking part for or against his
spiritual self; pending which, we are grateful to those who
have written, whether consciously or unconsciously, the history
of their religious opinions or their intellectual growth.

In the particular case before us the inferior inferential bio-

graphies are chiefly of modern manufacture; but the ancients
themselves are not altogether guiltless: and, not to speak of mere
gossips, the statement of Plutarch, that Xenophon was actually
present at Coroneia, has commonly been accepted as of equal
authenticity with the remark of Xenophon[1] upon which it
doubtless was based. Strabo also, Athenaeus, Diodorus, and
Diogenes Laertius, have all more or less interpreted the Xenophontine tradition inferentially, but the last named has, at the
beginning and end of his life of Xenophon, incorporated two
stories which, on ideal grounds, bear the stamp of validity,
being not only beautiful in themselves, but as striking the key-
note to what we are to discover about him from himself.
The one illustrates the hero, the other anticipates the sage, or,
more correctly, it has a whisper of the religious nature within,
which was the soul's soul. For our purposes let us invert
them, and let us first listen to the tale of his old age. His
son Gryllus, serving in the Athenian cavalry at Mantinea,
fought with might and main, and met his end; but at that
instant fell also Epaminondas, so that afterwards he was said
to have fallen by the hand of Gryllus, the son of Xenophon
the Athenian. Meanwhile, as the story goes, the father was
engaged in offering sacrifice; the chaplet was upon his brow,
when they brought him news saying, "Thy son has fallen,"
whereupon he removed the chaplet; but as the messengers
added 'nobly' he replaced it on his head, shedding, as others
have mentioned, no tear, but only uttering the words, ᾔδειν
θνητὸν γεγεννηκώς, "I knew my child was mortal." The
other tale has fully as clear a ring of spiritual truth, though
the particular circumstances need never have taken place. It
is a tale of boyhood, but its note is a rhythm of the melody
of the man. "Xenophon was the son of Gryllus: he was
an Athenian, of the dême Erchia; modest of demeanour
was he, fair also to look upon beyond description. Tradition
tells how Socrates met him in a narrow way, and, stretching
his staff athwart him, so as to bar his passage, plied him with
inquiries as to where this or that commodity was to be pur-
chased, to all which the boy answered fluently: when the

---

[1] *Anab.* v. 3. 6; Plutarch's *Lives*, Clough, vol. iv. p. 21 : *Agesilaus.*

sage at length put to him a final question, 'And where are the
fair and noble to be found?' The boy shook his head in
perplexity; then, said he, 'Follow me, and be taught.' So he
followed him, and thereafter became his 'hearer.'" The date of
Diogenes is scarcely ascertained, but we may suppose that the
above anecdote represents a tradition of perhaps six hundred
years; and, skipping twice that period of time to the date of
Raphael and "*The School of Athens*" (1510 A.D.),[1] we shall find it
still fresh: fresh, doubtless, in the mind of Fabio Calvi, who supplied the youthful painter with the hint of information which he
needed. The rest was supplied by the spirit of the time, speaking through the prophetic soul of the artist. Among the six or
seven figures which compose the Socratic group (Socrates
himself being so truly depicted as to form a companion to the
portrait drawn by Alcibiades in Plato), none are more truthful to the imagination than those of Alcibiades and Xenophon.
The helmeted, mail-clad warrior facing the philosopher with
exquisite proud poise, indicative of a graceful self-confidence on
the very verge of ὕβρις, is unmistakable; but beside the talker,
with back-turned face, hanging on his lips, is a youth with rosy
cheeks, auburn-haired, leaning on one arm, in a brooding
attitude of deep, earnest, religious gaze:—that is Xenophon,
the future apologist of the life of Socrates, treasuring one of the
recollections of the *Memorabilia.*

Pre-eminently among the old writers has Xenophon written
a sort of *apologia pro vita sua*, a many-sided life indeed, as an
artist, a citizen, *émigré*, philosopher, householder, public man
or private friend; and that not only in the most admissibly
autobiographic of his works, the *Anabasis*, but unconsciously
throughout. This also he has done with so naïve a trans-
parency that he cannot escape the good or the evil of such self-
delineation. Only, it should be borne in mind that at one time
it is his artistic self that speaks, at another it is to the political
man that we are listening; now we catch the undertone of self-
defensive diurnal combativeness, and again predominates the
clear voice of single-sighted Hellenic objectivity. The only
guide and clew to a fair interpretation is the reader's sympa-

---

[1] *Vide* Symonds, *The Fine Arts*, p. 335, for the notes on Greek philosophy
which Fabio Calvi may have supplied to the painter.

thetic intelligence; nought else will avail to arouse and
attune our modern minds or feelings to a wakeful harmony,
in response with the pulses of old days : the world of Hellas
at a crisis of spiritual turmoil; the ἀρχὴ ὠδίνων of thought
in the person of Socrates, whose issues are eternal; the
quickening of a politico-ethnic consummation, ere long to spring
to life in the person of Alexander, with consequences by nature
temporal, but on a scale colossal.   Portions, indeed, of this self-
revelation of the man or of his times a later age may, through
its own defects, or even merits, fail duly to appreciate; or
again, in other cases, we may withhold our moral while according our intellectual sympathy, and this from some moral progress or regress of to-day in which we share.   But in the main,
to the scientifically trained mind it will seem sufficient to
understand the time, neither praising nor blaming over greatly;
and Xenophon is qualified to help us to this scientific, or, if we
please to call it so, this optimistic apprehension.

   To science and to the God of natural laws, as to the God of
Paradise, everything is '*wie am ersten Tag*,'—very good.   How
can we, therefore, trained in this school, and considering the
progressive tendency of human nature, which is our faith, and
which gives an optimistic colour to our ἀπομνημονεύματα,—how
can we, as a whole, do other than sympathise with the past,
out of which that which is ideal in us has grown, and in which
it is rooted?   This or that thing we may turn our backs upon
in scorn or disgust, but, calmly considering, the whole substratum of ourselves seems excellent,—it has played its part
well enough.   What seems less good and more doubtful is
ourselves, as the substratum of the future.   Here our verdict
swings round self-accusingly, but not of necessity unscientifically, unless indeed the principle of progress 'I count not myself
to have apprehended' is psychologically false.   Here, at the
same time, let us guard against a misconception.   However high
and optimistic our appreciation of Xenophon, to intercede as
his apologist would be impertinent.   Inevitably, in the case
of so transparent a human being, tenets and points of view
revealed in naked simplicity present themselves, with which it
is hard if one man in a thousand will feel more than the
scantiest sympathy.   His views about the democracy, about

the political problems of the day, about war or the chase, are
not as our views; if we had lived then, we trust we should
have been differently disposed. But is not all this, in the
language of Xenophon or Socrates, to stamp ourselves as " busy-
bodies and vain fellows"? Why not take Xenophon as we find
him, and make the best of him ? We shall not find him so very
bad ; nor his times. Even where we dissent, as children of a
democratic age, perhaps, from his prejudices in favour of οἱ
βέλτιστοι, "the *better* classes;" as befrienders of animals from
his inveterate love of hunting ; or, again, as British sportsmen,
from his methods of snaring hares ; or, on general grounds, from
this, that, or the other limitation of his horizon, we may still to
ourselves seem to see how this partial view and these *arriéré*
tenets were natural and appropriate to him.

Neither impelled by any prejudice as against any past phase
of humanity, nor furnished with any critical apparatus of art, or
philosophy, or religion, by which to bind or loose the men of
old, we may take an acquiescent joy in contemplating the great
art products of a world which is past, but, like the scenes of our
childhood, still abides closer to us, in a sense, than our present
surroundings. Not indeed that such criteria of art, religion, and
philosophy as will square with science are wanting. Hegel's,[1]
for instance, in the well-known passage where he bids us take,
as a key to the understanding of Greece, " an insight into the
ideal forms of sculpture," instructing us that " the images of
statesmen and philosophers, as well as epic and dramatic
heroes, must be regarded from the point of view of plastic
art, for that is the character of all, actors, poets, thinkers,
alike; great and free they have grown up on the soil of
their own individuality, creating themselves out of themselves, and moulding themselves to what they were and willed
to be. The age of Perikles is specially rich in them. Perikles
himself, Phidias, Plato, above all Sophocles : Thucydides also,
Xenophon and Socrates, each in his own department : none
greater or less than another : ideal artists of themselves ; cast
in flawless mould : works of art which stand before us as an
immortal presentment of the gods." Such is the sentence of

---

[1] Hegel, *Æsthetik*, 3. 2. 3, translated in Pater's *Studies in the History of the
Renaissance*, pp. 192, 193, *Winckelmann*.

art, a sentence of salvation and security against the finger of
corruption and temporal decay, wherewith the verdict also of
Religion and Philosophy accords. "But the souls of the righteous are in the hand of God. There shall no torment touch
them. But they are in peace."

> "Then all this earthly grossness quit,
>   Attired with stars, we shall for ever sit,
>   Triumphing over Death, and Chance, and thee, O Time."

To the profound antique philosophy the modern deep makes
answer, "Notre nature a besoin d'être épurée par la mort, pour que
ses meilleurs attributs puissent assez ressortir en surmontant les
grossières nécessités qui d'abord les dominent. C'est uniquement
ainsi que peut s'accomplir la sublime inversion où tend l'anima-
lité ;" while to narrow-souled censure of ever-shifting *Sittlichkeiten* the old rebuke suffices: διὸ ἀναπολόγητος εἶ, ὦ ἄνθρωπε πᾶς
ὁ κρίνων. Let Xenophon and the rest be judged by their own
συνείδησις, not by another, alien to ourselves and everything
except the particular historical instant, or temporary moral need,
from which it was abstracted for illegitimate and unseasonable
application elsewhere. Let us not do this ; which is to do
violence to the historic sense, and in so far to dull the best
and most precious gift of progressive humanity.[1] Lastly, the
attitude here pleaded for is not more in agreement with the
spirit of art and religion than consonant with the scientific
movement of the day. If in one sense the Græco-Roman world
seems less important to us than to the humanists of the Renaissance ; " if the first enthusiasm for antiquity shall never be
restored, nor the classics yield that vital nourishment they
offered in the spring-time of the modern era," [2] still there is a
charm in the lengthening shadows ; or, more truly, we seem to
be cresting to-day the last high-tidal waves of a rediscovery,
which confronts us face to face with the very soul of past
humanity, and scientifically we are nearer than when we en-
thusiastically believed. To the half-appeased hunger of a
passionate curiosity it is as if their secret would soon be out,
and we should know them 'even as we are known.'

---

[1] An intelligent respect for the *Sittlichkeiten* of the moment, past and
present, seems essential for the preservation of the spiritual continuity no
less than the solidarity of our race.

[2] Symonds, *Revival of Learning*, p. 539.

But, for the present, the question of the συνείδησις of the Socratic age of Greece claims our attention: What was the relation of Xenophon to his era ? It does not concern us whether his birth falls about the date of the thirty years' truce (445 B.C.), or only somewhere near the commencement of the Peloponnesian war (in 431 B.C.) ; nor again is the actual date of his death, between 359[1] and 355, or 354 B.C. in all probability, of any serious importance. In any case we shall be right in regarding the adult Xenophon as a representative pre-eminently of the period from 411 (at which point he takes up the History of Thucydides) to 359, the first year of Philip of Macedon. Thanks to the genius and "good fortune" of the Athenian people, it was not possible or conceivable that this century of time should pass unchronicled. Hence it is that Thucydides appears as the historian of the great war; and when his voice is hushed, a most vocal witness and participator of the subsequent events presents himself in the person of Xenophon. It is thus that we also assist at the uncoiling, as it were, of two mighty lengths of Hellenic history : the thread of the first being the conflict between Athens and Sparta, fully unwound at the taking of Athens by Lysander (in 404) ; the second representing the struggle for hegemony between Sparta and the rival powers, with the momentary supremacy of Thebes and the apotheosis of Epaminondas at Mantinea, which form the last links of a chain of closely connected incident.

Of this later period Xenophon is at once the mouthpiece and a product. In him we have a witness whose combined qualities as a thinker, writer, and man of action make him, even where he is defective or incomplete in his character and views of existence, pre-eminently representative. Briefly stated, what we find is that certain features of an interesting time are in this individual written large, so that he who runs may read ; though others doubtless are less apparent or altogether absent. What then are these characteristic features, " the signs of the times " ?

---

[1] The assassination of Alexander of Pherae, mentioned by Xenophon, *Hellen.* vi. 4. 35-37, took place between 359 B.C. and 357 B.C. The date of the περὶ προσόδων, or *de Reditibus* (if correctly ascribed to Xenophon), extends the life of its author four or five years longer than the earlier of these two dates.

In the spiritual world they are the emergence of " subjectivity," of self-examination and self-expression of all sorts,
the awakening of self-consciousness, the earnest application
to one's-self and others of the Delphic injunction Γνῶθι
σεαυτόν with a view to self-culture, which is an epitome
of the Socratic method, the spiritually-minded sophistry.
Parallel with this is the development of dialectic, the art
of words and of conduct, the sharpening of the instrument
of mind, and the working up of the raw material of subtle
thought as a power in itself, to be wielded irrespectively of the
moral guidance of the Νόμος, and the limited requirements of the
public weal, but so as to suit the taste and exigencies of the
thought-emancipated individual with a view to personal success,
which is an epitome of the carnally-minded sophistry. " The pre-
Socratic thinkers," it has been said,[1] " from Thales downwards,
were all primarily devoted to ontological research, but by the
middle of the fifth century B.C. the clash and conflict of their
dogmatic[2] systems had led some of the keenest minds to doubt the
possibility of penetrating the secret of the universe. This doubt
found expression in the reasoned scepticism of Gorgias, and produced the famous doctrine of Protagoras, that the human apprehension is the only standard of what is and what is not. A
similar view of the natural limits of the human intellect repelled
the philosophic ardour of Socrates from physico-metaphysical
inquiries." Again the same writer says, " This emergence of an
art of conduct with professional teachers cannot thoroughly be
understood, unless it is viewed as a crowning result of a general
tendency at this stage of Greek civilisation to substitute
technical skill for traditional procedure and empirically developed faculty. In the age of the Sophists we find, wherever
we turn, the same eager pursuit of knowledge and the same
eager effort to apply it directly to practice. The method of
earth-measurement was rapidly becoming a science ; the astro-

---

[1] *Ethics*, Encyc. Metrop. pp. 576-7, but I think the writer of the article himself would state the matter differently. The antithesis might be put thus : In
one aspect, an age of Doubt, of emancipation of the questioning subject from
Tradition and Custom. In another, an age of Faith, of belief in the largest
possibilities of Art, Science, Method. This last is Mr. Sidgwick's point.

[2] Cf. Xen. *Mem.* i. 1. 14.

nomy of Meton was introducing precision into the computation of time; Hippodamus was revolutionising architecture by building towns with straight broad streets; old-fashioned soldiers were grumbling at the new pedantries of tactics and 'hoplitics;' the art of music had recently received a great technical development; and a still greater change had been effected in that training of the body which constituted the other half of ordinary Greek education. If bodily vigour was no longer to be left to nature and spontaneous exercise, but was to be attained by the systematic observance of rules laid down by professional trainers, it was natural to think that the same might be the case with mental excellences." Briefly, this was an age stamped, as we might say, 'internationally,' with the conflict or contrast of rival νόμοι, of 'creeds' and national political theories; in private life, with the escape from νόμος of the individual, with 'atheism,' as it was called, in the wake of physics.[1]

In the world of politics, the 'signs of the times' are the red and lowering clouds which betoken a new and turbulent day. These are, the accentuated antithesis of stable (or relatively stable) rule, and the liberty of anarchic minorities or majorities. At Athens are to be seen the confronting idols of *Laconism* and *the Demos*; at Thebes, of autonomy and pan-Bœotarchy; in Peloponnese there are symptoms of anti-Spartan Argolism;[2] north of the isthmus, of embryo empires in Thessaly or Thrace. Everywhere miso-Persian Hellenism is confronted with the incompatible desire for hegemony, only to be obtained at the price of Persian assistance; everywhere, also, the hand of the ἰδιώτης is against the hand of the πολίτης, or that

---

[1] *Physics* = a sort of physico-metaphysical philosophy, running inevitably counter to theology, or possibly theoseby, "theology and even religious feeling." [Cf. Aristoph. *Clouds*, 380. Not God, but *Vortex* reigns, according to Anaxagoras.] It is true, physical science, in the stricter sense, was silently working in the direction of real discovery, and, as the Comtists say, encyclopædic knowledge. Not to speak of numerical and geometrical conceptions carried up to the point of their application to astronomy, to Thales and Democritus are already due the sphericity of the earth and the "atomic" theory. Hippocrates also should be coupled with Meton and Hippodamus.

[2] *Hellen.* iv. 8. 34, ἐπεὶ γὰρ οἱ Ἀργεῖοι τὴν Κόρινθον Ἄργος ἐπεποίηντο, κ.τ.λ.; cf. *ibid.* v. 2. 6.

of the State against society ;[1] everywhere there is a bourgeoning
of Panhellenic vitality at the expense of (state) patriotism.

Of some of these propensities, the evidence of a disjointed
world, Xenophon is either the victim or the scarcely unwilling
tool, of others he is the censor and the antagonist, and in all cases
(consciously or unconsciously) the exponent and interpreter;
while (which is only tantamount to realising the completeness of
his assimilation) through good report and evil report his voice is
not only a witness to the present but a prediction of the future.
To quite a startling extent, perhaps only in a chance word or a
cherished aspiration, we discover in him an earnest of things
which are yet to be. For if the political world was out of joint,
he that was destined to set it for a season right was nigh at hand ;
if, in a deeper sense also, the age itself was travailing and heavy-
laden, the times of refreshing were not far distant ; nor was their
labour destined to be in vain, but rather rich with the fruitage
of intellectual achievement ; of the consummation and world-
wide diffusion of the gifts of Hellenism. The era of Aristotle and
of Alexander was speedily approaching. Under this head Xenophon is wonderfully typical. As a man of action, and personally
mixed up with the incidents of the day, and tossed on a sea of
political troubles, he is individually and conjointly with others
of a kindred spirit (as Alcibiades perhaps, certainly Agesilaus[2]
and Jason of Pherae[3]), anticipative of Alexander the Great. As
a thinker he is symptomatic of the approach of Aristotle.[4] As
a stylist and part-inventor of the κοινὴ διάλεκτος, he is one of
the fountain-heads of the great common literature of the Eastern
empire, the lineal ancestor of the Septuagint, of Lucian, and
perhaps of the best style of modern Greek to-day.

---

[1] Not unfrequently. Cf. the two famous occasions on which Socrates found
himself in isolated opposition to the government of the day, *Mem.* i. 1. 18 ;
iv. 4. 3 ; *Hellen.* ii. 3. 39, and, generally speaking, many an *émigré* doubtless
was the victim of State oppression. Cf. *Hellen.* v. 4. 2.

[2] *Hellen.* iv. 2. 3.   [3] *Ibid.* vi. 1. 12.

[4] Xenophon, the σοφὸς or σοφιστὴς, seems to some extent to have anticipated,
from a common-sense point of view, the *Ethics* of Aristotle ; while, as a
ῥήτωρ, and author of such treatises as the *Polity of the Lacedaemonians*, he
foreshadows the *Politics*. This view might be pushed further in reference
to the more technical treatises on *Hunting, Horsemanship,* etc. But in the
pamphlet on *Revenues,* or the panegyric of *Agesilaus,* the reader's thought is
carried forward no further than Isocrates. In other ways also he is an ἀρραβὼν
τῆς κληρονομίας.

Nor, if we now turn to the second question raised above, and ask ourselves, What is the closest bond of intimacy between us ?—what is there common to our mental and spiritual horizon and that of Xenophon ?—shall we find him barren or devoid of interest. Indeed, that we have one such link of connection of a firm sort will appear obvious to him who recognises that the underlying personal quality of the man, the primitive substratum of his character, is nothing more nor less than his piety and devotion (τὸ εὐσεβές and θεοσέβεια). His motto, many times repeated, and oftener implied, is not to be mistaken : Σὺν τοῖς Θεοῖς παντὸς ἄρχεσθαι ἔργου (Ask the blessing of Heaven upon all thy purposes) is the daily and hourly watchword of his soul.[1] It is true that this δεισιδαι-μονία[2] is a quality not peculiar to Xenophon, but one which he holds largely in common with his fellow-countrymen; which endears the Hellenic world to us, and the existence of which it would be foolish in us to ignore. Possibly, in the case of Xenophon, his natural piety was refined and even crystal-lised in what we must call his second nature, as a loyal "listener" to Socrates. But if the "theoseby" of the natural man brings him close to us on grounds of common humanity and common needs, so also is Xenophon 'after the (Socratic) spirit' welcome as a personal friend, on grounds of transmitted inherited philosophy. Without here entering into the question of supposed metaphysical or philosophic deficiencies, it is clear that the disciple was largely appre-ciative of the master's ethical stand-point; neither blind to his originality as "the inventor of morals," nor throughout a long life forgetful of the painstaking self-command and improve-ment which was the practical side of the teaching which he reverenced. But (1) Εὐσέβεια is a quality suited to all times, and not less interwoven with the texture of humanity to-day than with the life of ancient Hellas; in spite of many external and some intrinsic differences in the attempt to deal with that most real world beyond, which, with all reverence, we formulate as GOD. Also, (2) at the basis of our own popular or quasi-

---

[1] Cf. *Agesilaus*, i. 27.

[2] Acts xvii. 22, and Mr. Ruskin's comment on the mistranslation in his pre-face to *The Economist of Xenophon* in the *Bibl. Pastorum*, vol. i. p. xxv.

philosophic moral theology lies the "teleology" of Socrates.[1]
To this twofold extent Xenophon appears as the clear-toned
ἐξηγητὴς of his times—and not of his times only, but in some
sense also of Hellas as a whole.

Of this general thesis we may find ample illustration, either
in the main characteristics of his writings, however rapidly sur-
veyed, or by direct handling of the matter in answer to the question, What are the various personal or professional, philosophical
or literary, qualities of the author ? Let us then, in pursuance
of such an object, review these various qualities. Those which
we call personal would seem to depend chiefly on a certain
healthiness of body and brain (εὐεξία); original probably, and
emphasised by the regular gymnastic of the city, which we
are aware was indorsed by Socrates.[2] Tradition tells us that
Xenophon was καλὸς and εὐειδέστατος, and conjecture adds that
he must have possessed great bodily strength and endurance.
Indeed, with the exception of his piety and affectionate remembrance of Socrates, nothing is more pronounced in him than his
devotion to γυμναστική : field-sports and field-work, being a sort
of duty to one's-self and to the State, so that the bodily frame
may be inured "by toils and sweat" to the more serious business of life and war. "Agriculture, devotion to the tillage of
the soil, has this high praise, that it implies a training of the
limbs till they are capable of performing everything that a freeman should. Though earth gives of her abundance, yet her
blessings are not showered on the lap of laziness; but in hus-
bandry she inures her servitors to suffer gladly summer's heat
and winter's cold. Those that labour with their very hands,
the actual delvers of the soil, she trains in a wrestling ground
of her own, giving them strength for strength ; while those
others whose devotion is confined to the overseeing eye and to
studious thought she makes more manly, rousing them with

---

[1] The distinctive teaching of our Lord, taken in the deepest modern sense,
as the gospel of human fraternity and love, being either ignored or non-
assimilated (cf. the unchristian acceptance of much needless war) ; and regarded practically as a quite separate inner and independent principle of
action, or else added as the graceful coping-stone and crown of the pagan
morality of Greece and Rome.

[2] Cf. *Mem.* iii. xii. ; also Socrates' humorous defence of dancing, *Symp.*
ii. 15-18.

the crowing of the cock, and compelling them to be up and
doing betimes in many a long day's march."[1] In these and
similar passages the scent of the morning air is so keen and in-
vigorating, and the play of the limbs so joyous and godlike,
that we catch the hunter's or the husbandman's enthusiasm;
riding with Ischomachus cross country over his estates, or
running a novel 'lampadephoria' with the soldiers after wild
asses in the desert of Arabia; or coursing hares and shouting to
the dogs with the old Athenian *émigré* and his sons and friends
on the farm at Skillus; or now with Astyages, smiling a proud
smile at sight of his grandson, about fifteen years old, and
allowed, after much supplication, to hunt large game for the
first time. "The heart of the old man was overjoyed to see his
grandson, unable to keep silence in the excess of his delight,
but 'baying' with excitement like a well-bred whelp whenever
he came to close quarters with a beast, and shouting to his
fellows by name." But the fullest gospel of Ὑγίεια or Εὐεξία
is to be found in the treatise on hunting, in the prefatory chapter,
and again later near the suspected attack on the Sophists: " My
word of exhortation to the young is: do not despise hunting or
the other training of your boyhood, if you desire to grow up to
be good men—good not only in war, but in all else of which
the issue is perfection in thought, word, and deed." "Those
that make this their passionate pursuit will reap their reward
in the health which will accrue to their bodily frames—the
quickening of the eye and the ear—the postponement of old
age; not to speak of the warlike training which is given, so
that long marches under arms will seem mere child's play."
This bodily training is, in fact, the keystone to Xenophon's
theory of education. He seems to have said to himself: "Here
is the one great pleasure which is harmless in itself; whereas
all the other rival pleasures, either in themselves or incidentally,
may become ruinous to health of body and soul; but this is
innocuous, and in its consequences most useful, as a training in
virtue and good habit." These warning voices to the young
have a genial cheery ring in them, like the voice of the Δικαῖος
Λόγος in Aristophanes,[2] expounding to us the old theory of

---

[1] *Oecon.* v. 4.

[2] Arist. *Clouds*, 961, etc., and cf. Symonds, *Greek Poets*, vol. i. p. 280.

education in that blissful time "when he flourished, and modesty and temperance were practised :"—"If you do what I tell you, and apply your mind moreover, you will have big brawny shoulders and a polished chest, with the fair white complexion of health." Indeed, taken *in extenso*, the Xenophontine passage reads much like a prose version of the Aristophanic moral. If we are also curiously reminded of educational doctrines in vogue in our own particular polity of modern Europe, that is only another instance of what may be called a modern element in our author, which seems to make us, even in education, more akin to the ancients than we might suppose.[1]

Even while we confine our attention to this matter of health and educational training, two other traits silently obtrude themselves, and may conveniently be dealt with at this point. In the first place, there is the amiable air of didactic teaching, which we should now-a-days call "moralising"—a touch of the doctrinaire, short of pedantry certainly, and dulness, but still noticeable and truly Xenophontine. The minor works on hunting and horsemanship are full of this, as also is the *Cavalry General's Manual* (a work which the inferential biographer shall be allowed to consider as addressed by the old philosopher soldier in his declining years to his son Gryllus, the same who fought in the Athenian squadron at Mantinea, and fell face to face with Epaminondas). In these it was natural perhaps to fall into a didactic vein, and to speak as one of 'those who know.' But the opening paragraphs of the *Cyropaedia*, and other passages interspersed in the larger and probably more youthful compositions, testify to the same propensity. We seem at times to be listening to a sweet-tongued talker, a wise man and a good, whose style reminds us of the Vicar of Wakefield. In spite of his sage talk he presents to us the appearance

---

[1] It is interesting to compare the elaborate Spartan education, with its proud motto, τῷ ταπεινοὶ εἶναι μεγαλύνονται (*Lac Pol.* viii. 2): "*The Spartans manifest a lordly pride in submissiveness:*" *vide* Müller's *Dorians*, vol. ii. p. 309. "During the progress from the condition of an ephebus to manhood, the young Spartans were called *Sphaereis*, probably because their chief exercise was football, which game was carried on with great emulation, and indeed resembled a battle rather than a diversion. In their nineteenth year they were sent out on the crypteia," etc. To such training, as tradition tells us, were the sons of Xenophon submitted.

of a practical man who has seen men and manners, and tasted wisdom at the fountain-head. Nothing is pleasanter than to sit by and listen to his reflections somewhat loosely and yet pretentiously delivered.

The other something referred to is easier to feel than to define in words, yet it is absolutely Xenophontine; being neither more nor less than the consciousness of the man himself—his personalism or individualism, or by whatever name we are to name it, which probably owes its origin to the general subjectivity of the age, in the spirit of which he so largely shares; to the Socratic training and the lessons in self-knowledge which that implied when faithfully carried out. It is a self-consciousness, enhanced conceivably in this case by the isolation of exile, and the sharp differentiation of the personal against the impersonal element within; as if the ἰδιώτης rose in judgment against the πολίτης, and the πολίτης against the ἰδιώτης, and the one self accused or else excused the other, with the result at last of a novel and, for a Greek, curiously modern egoism.[1]　Hence these phrases: ἐμοὶ μὲν δοκεῖ—"I should say," or "if you ask my opinion," or "my observation tells me;" and these first personal beginnings, ἤκουσα δέ ποτε —οἶδα μὲν, ὅτι—πολλάκις ἐθαύμασα; or the personal pronouns anticipative of the pleonastic usage of a later day, which again give a modern feeling to this subjective artist. Connected with this is a higher personal quality, or, in other words, the same quality when brought into grander relations with the world beyond man's control and knowledge— "the region of obscurity, the home of things about which we cannot say whether they will turn out thus or otherwise; which really includes the most important elements even of things that lie within the circumscribed region of our own knowledge and activity; where we are bound to reflect and exert ourselves without superstitiously turning for querulous help to heaven."[2]

---

[1] The naïveté of the egoism of Herodotus is childlike, suggestive of wonderment at once and a desire to speak the truth : that of Xenophon has a touching parental gravity.

[2] *Mem.* i. 8. Doubtless the ἄδηλα ὅπως ἀποβήσεται here are things mundane and practical ;˙but Xenophon would almost have applied the term to the larger issues of life, and the general government of the world.

This, which the hearer has shown us to have been his teacher's creed, was certainly his own also ; and no heart can fail to be touched by the utterance of so genuine a faith, as profound as it is simple, in which he has chronicled their common conduct as a self-annihilating trust in the goodness of God. "He prayed to the gods simply to give him what was good for him ; for they know best what good things are." "To pray for gold and silver or a despotism is no better than to make a particular throw at dice or a battle the subject of prayer, when no man can prophesy what the consequences of one or other will be."[1] Here indeed we have reached the most central and vital thing in all Xenophon, his devoutness or holiness; it cannot help bringing him close to us, and otherwise doubtless has a direct bearing upon ourselves. But as it would be a mistake to exaggerate the matter in his favour, as if he only and Socrates,[2] and a few other exceptional specimens of that people, were capable of pure and lofty religious feelings, so also we ought not to overlook something which is original and idiosyncratic in the 'religiosity' of this particular follower of the unique teacher. It is, to begin with, to some extent an accident that we hear so much of *piety ;* that *devotion* is so prominent a virtue on his lips—devotion especially as shown in prayer and μαντική. Why, for instance, is no light thrown on that other large department of Greek religious feeling which found satisfaction in the *Mysteries ?* The explanation of this outspokenness in particular directions, this insistance on the necessity of prayer, etc., seems to be that the moment required it. We gather our views largely from *The Recollections of Socrates,*—a work written under certain self-imposed limitations —in a truthful, loving, but 'apologetic' strain, and for a distinct object, viz., to set his 'master's' reputation right in the eyes of the Athenian people. Now an indictment against his friend was, that he refused to acknowledge and believe in

---

[1] *Mem.* i. 3. 2.

[2] The commentators compare the poet's prayer in Plato, *Alcib.* ii. 143 A :

Ζεῦ βασιλεῦ, τὰ μὲν ἐσθλὰ καὶ εὐχομένοις καὶ ἀνεύκτοις

Ἄμμι δίδου, τὰ δὲ δεινὰ καὶ εὐχομένοις ἀπαλέξειν.

"O King Zeus, grant to us all blessings, whether we pray for them or not, and deliver us from evil, even to the denial of our prayers."

the gods of the state, preferring to introduce new divinities of
his own. These charges were contrary to the patent everyday
witness of the philosopher's life, who came not to destroy but
to fulfil, and was particularly punctual and conservative in all
acts of worship—in prayer and sacrifice—in what may with
reverence be called the machinery of daily worship; while as
to the introduction of new divinities, if by these δαιμόνια was
meant the divine whisper, which checked or propelled his
' master's ' action, was not that simply a form of μαντική like
any other admonition howsoever vouchsafed to man from
heaven, whether by flight of birds, or a voice heard, or a sound
uttered, or something crossing the path ?

But with regard to the Mysteries, whatever we are to think
of them in our present imperfect knowledge, we must hold that
they were not " generally necessary to salvation:" we may
indeed speculate as to whether they were the relics of some
primitive worship—" ancient foreign rudiments containing no
greater wisdom than already existed in the consciousness of
the Greeks "—which is Hegel's view,[1] and introduces his remark that " all Athenians were initiated in the Mysteries—
Socrates excepted, who refused initiation, because he knew
well that science and art are not the product of mysteries;
that wisdom never lies among arcana." Or, our opinion may
incline us to believe with others that, even so, there was
a deep underlying meaning in the scenic representation of
old Chthonian creeds, calculated to work powerfully upon
the spiritual emotions of the beholder: some steeping in the
blackest gloom of a night of sorrow and bereavement—suddenly, in the twinkling of an eye, relieved by an inrush of
light and joy and rejuvenescence; the renewing, with the
passion of early spring, of wintry weeds outworn. In any
case, this side of the religious life of their times is not divulged
to us by either Plato or Xenophon. So far as the age of Pericles goes, the least faint echo of what it betokened is to be
got from the parody of Aristophanes in the *Frogs;* while the
deep implication of religious feeling in the name is sufficiently

---

[1] Hegel's *Phil. of Hist.*, Engl. transl. p. 248, also 257, 258; compare
Hausrath, *Neutest. Zeitgesch., Die Mysterien,* p. 68, etc.

attested by the description in Thucydides of the mutilation of the Hermae.[1]

It also appears that apart from 'apologetically' explaining the tenets of Socrates, Xenophon—a man of culture as well as of action—was satisfied to follow that leading; holding the hand of his guide with confidence, and following in his path, *haud passibus aequis.* In illustration of which there is the famous story of his going against the wise elder friend's advice to his cost—in the matter of accepting Proxenus's invitation to join Cyrus.[2] The sage has an instinct (possibly the voice of the δαιμόνιον) that no good will come of this, but he advises his associate to ask the will of God at Delphi. From whatever cause, Xenophon asks, not "Shall I go?" but "To which god should I sacrifice on this journey?" The answer is given accordingly: but the rebuke of Socrates is too late now: and there is nothing for it but to do as the oracle has said—and go. In the *Recollections* Xenophon[3] tells us "that so strong a faith had Socrates in the intimations vouchsafed to him by heaven, that without a moment's apprehension of writing himself down 'fool or impostor,' he would freely, and on the authority of the divine voice alone, tender advice to his friends to do this, or to abstain from doing that; and so with those who followed his injunctions it went well, while those who lent a deaf ear lived to repent of their obstinacy." Thus it requires all the childlike religious trust, reconciling contraries, on the part of Xenophon, to discover how in the end—after the pains and perplexities of the advance and retreat—the ways of God were finally justified, and the promised help of Zeus, whose name is kindness, literally fulfilled. This touch of superstition in him has Xenophon by comparison with the pure faith of Socrates. But σὺν θεοῖς πράττειν, trust in heaven, has become to him so emphatically a part of his theory of life and practice, that in one of the works, probably of his old age, the *Hipparchicos*, he touchingly apologises for the reiteration of the phrase in such a context; not as though he used it as a mere phrase, but as an English colonel

---

[1] Thuc. vi. 28. 1, καὶ τὰ μυστήρια ἅμα ὡς ποιεῖται ἐν οἰκίαις ἐφ' ὕβρει.
[2] *Anab.* iii. 1. 4-8.   [3] *Mem.* i. 1.

might apologise, so to speak, for some custom in his regiment of
prayer-meetings or reading of the Bible : " If the repetition of
the phrase throughout this treatise, 'act with God,' surprises
any one, he may take my word for it, that with the daily or
hourly recurrence of perils which must betide him, his wonderment will diminish ; as also with the clearer recognition of the
fact that, in a time of war, the antagonists are full of designs
against each other; but the precise issue of these plots and
counterplots is rarely known: to what counsellor then can a
man apply for advice in his extremity save only to the gods,
who know all things, and forewarn whomsoever they list by
victims, or by omens, by voice or vision ? And is it not rational
to suppose that they will prefer to help in their need, not those
who merely seek them in time of momentary stress and trouble,
but who in the halcyon days of their prosperity make a practice of
rendering to heaven the service of heart and soul?"[1] The sentiment, it may be retorted, is the sentiment of Christian times,
but the means are the measure of a creed that is past: which
is so far true that the ἱερὰ and φῆμαι, the οἰωνοὶ and ὀνείρατα,
take us out of ourselves into a pre-scientific world ; but to insist
further is neither fair nor rational.   The question of the relative
value of creeds must be discussed with less prominence given
to a machinery common to the whole ancient world, Jewish and
Gentile alike, and more in reference to the spirit which animates
the worshipper; when the gain will not all be on the side of later
times or ' purer' beliefs.

To test this matter fairly then, to escape purblindness
so as to see clearly into the Xenophontine heart at any
rate, we must, without laying sacrilegious hands on our own
sacred things, " not to speak it profanely," mentally remove
the religious machinery of to-day,—our sacramental feasts,
our prayer and thanksgivings, our devotional musings ;
replacing these by the secret rites of Demetêr and Iacchos,
—by all that is comprehended under μαντική, from the roll of
thunder, or the dream or chance word of good or evil import,
down to the still small voice, not refused to Socrates, which was
the oracle of " private judgment,"—by the public oracles, by

---

[1] *Hipparch.* ix. 8, 9.

prayer for prayer, by faces veiled in sorrow and beaten breasts in lieu of bent knees and contrite hearts, by lifted hands and chanted pæans of the Adorante in lieu of jubilates and choral hallelujahs. ·Some of these cover the same ground, however different in outward appearance or construction ; others point to real chasms between the ancient Hellenic spirit and that which is the breath of our life to-day. But just as in the origin of species, the very progress in and through the continuity may, if we neglect the true links, seem to imply a gap which does not really exist, so here; and what is of equal importance, we may fail to notice the solidarity of the advanced peoples of ancient times as regards the machinery of their worship, however divergent their creeds. It seems the *mécanique céleste* of the soul of man is the same for long ages together; and thus in the Acts of the Apostles,[1] when St. Peter is quoting the prophet Joel, the ὁράσεις, ἐνύπνια, τέρατα, σημεῖα all occur in a perfectly rational and natural way, as judged by the common mind of the time. " Φήμη—a voice from heaven,"—" Bath Kol," one calls it; " An angel spake to him," says another ; " it thundered," to a third; but thunder in a clear sky—that is a word of warning. These strange coincidences between the world beyond myself and what is thrilling me must be ' symbolic ' of the divine will.

It is not easy for the scientifically trained mind to go out of itself, reverting to the every-day surroundings, the scenery of a religion that is past. The demarking barrier between *then* and *now* (or *there* and *here*, this very day) is hard to cross ; yet it is science—at least the supreme science—which bids this to be done. Nor, even for sympathetic natures, is it easy to revive and realise the diffused condition of religion in a world, or among peoples, in which sanctity is conterminous with existence, and the godhead peers through every cranny of nature: the days when baptisms were not so much a type of the spirit, as literally spiritual ; when every fountain was sacred, and the huntsman is enjoined not to interfere with springs and streams, τὰ νάματα καὶ τὰ ῥεῖθρα ἐᾶν, for to meddle with these is ugly and base—τὸ γὰρ ἅπτεσθαι τούτων αἰσχρὸν καὶ κακόν: not

---

[1] Acts ii. 16-22.

to speak of the bad example of lawlessness set to the beholder—*καὶ ἱνὰ μὴ τῷ νόμῳ ἐναντίοι ὦσιν οἱ ἰδόντες.*[1] Some
dim intelligence of these things we may get from the reminiscences of childhood and the natural sacraments of inventive
innocence; when our nurse blessed us if we sneezed; and we
held in secret silence commemorative feasts. Such is the
simple-minded, extended religiousness of early days, not subtle
indeed nor intense, but more thoroughly permeating every
hour and movement of existence—religion interblent with life.

As to Xenophon personally, only a Hellene among Hellenes,
a specimen of a particular race, the product of a period interesting but transient, we can see that he was doubly conditioned
by these circumstances,—in the direction of superstition
" naturally," in the direction of monotheism through Socratic
training,[2] or something infectious in the great searcher's faith.
On the other hand, oracles and omens, prayers and *μαντική*
generally, are his essentials (for he is at one with the
kindly race of man), and his theology revealed to him in the
' cities and tribes of men ' a region of rational common-sense
religion, God-fearing in the appointed ways ; but at either limit
of this religious world he beheld two " maniacal " extremes—
here the worshippers of stocks and stones,[3] or again of animals
—and *there* those who contrived to pass through life without
God or gods at all. Probably he had as little intellectual
sympathy with a fetichist or animal-worshipper, a mad Mossyn-
oecian[4] turning all customs upside down, as with a civilised
non-barbarian atheist like Aristodemus the little, who figures in
the memorable conversation with Socrates on the omnipresence
of God. But if (and it is an open question only, an inference,
in fact) Xenophon was so far narrow in his sympathies, or, as
we may say, unscientifically disposed, we must do him the
justice to admit that he is also in advance of his times in his
theologic views. It is to him we owe the clear appreciation of

---

[1] *Cyn.* v. 34.

[2] Cf. Cicero's very interesting criticism, *de Nat. Deorum*, ii. v. 18. An
argument is drawn from the mind in man to establish a directing principle
in the universe, *τὸ ἡγεμονικόν*, taken from Plato and the Xenophontine
Socrates.

[3] Cf. *Mem.* i. 1. 14, and i. 4. 19.　　　　　　　[4] *Vide infra*, p. 365.

some of the most important of his master's tenets : his natural
theology, his 'teleologic' proofs of a beneficent Providence,
his speculations on immortality. These are not only conveyed in
reported conversations of the teacher, but they interpenetrate the
writings of the disciple. Once and again we listen to them in the
conversations, and they fall in most clear accents from the lips
of the dying Cyrus.[1] Nor, once propounded, have they been
allowed to die away. We do not compare them with the
argument of a later lover of mankind in 1 Corinthians xv.,
but handed on from age to age through the Stoics, through
Plutarch, through Cicero (through the Fathers surely and the
schools), we hear a ring of them in the Evidences and sermons
of to-day : and of these Socratic "mysteries" the hierophant
is Xenophon.

Let us, however, abandoning "the things concerning the
gods," turn and consider the bent of our author's mind towards
his fellow-men. His φιλανθρωπία and his appreciation of human-
heartedness in others are remarkable. Here again the words
which he applies to Socrates, "that he was perpetually trying
to be of service to those with whom he was brought in contact,"
may with certain restrictions be applied to himself ; for in the
main, and in spite of strong political bias, and the prejudices of
"a beautiful and good" but still circumscribed nature, he is full
of loving-kindness, and of a friendly disposition to his fellow-
men, Hellenes and barbarians alike. He bears no spite or
grudge against humanity, being devoid, as far as we can discover, of any deep-seated selfishness or *arrière pensée.* Of
Socrates he says :[2] "If his friends were ever in difficulties,
where ignorance was the cause, he tried to heal the trouble by
a dose of wisdom ; or where want and poverty were to blame,
by lessoning them that they should assist one another as far as
in them lay." And of Cyrus, whom he selects to represent the
ideal ruler, he says : "In legend and song he is still commemorated by the Eastern world as of bodily shape most fair to
look upon, but in soul so replete with the threefold love of
man, of knowledge, and of honour, that there was no toil he
would not suffer, or danger incur, to win the praise and admira-

---

[1] *Cyropaed.* viii. 7. 17-19. [2] *Mem.* vii. 7.

tion of mankind." With the "philanthropic" type of character, and for true friendship with its duties, the writer has evidently the deepest sympathy and concern; but his personal possession of the quality is proved rather by the manifest warmth of his affection for many personal friends, etc. It is an admiration reaching the point of 'hero-worship' in the case of Socrates, and perhaps Agesilaus; but not less genuinely exhibited, after humble human fashion, in the tender panegyrics or criticisms of Proxenus, his "ancient friend," or of the younger Cyrus. "Among those who were brought into communion with Socrates, and recognised his greatness, all true lovers of virtue still to this day cease not to lament his incomparable loss with the bitterest regret, as for him who, as none else could, helped them in the pursuit of perfection. For my part, when I think of his qualities . . ."[1] Part of the brightness of the *Anabasis* and *Hellenica* is due to his warm-hearted sympathy with this or that human being; sometimes a friend and companion, like Teleutias the Spartan admiral, brother of Agesilaus;[2] sometimes a stranger associate, like Seuthes;[3] or only some distant hero whose splendidly shining life has caught the historian's attention, and still gleams upon his page, like Pasimachus.[4] But their name is legion. Others are nameless heroes, like the two whose καλοκαγαθία and needless sacrifice during the Retreat have touched his heart, and whose epitaph he writes: "See, they have died thus, these 'galant-uomini,' and we were not able to remove their bodies or bury them."[5]

It would be safe to conjecture that this generosity of disposition must find vent for itself in all natural and orderly ways; that the broad-souled philanthropist and staunch friend would also prove, under the right circumstances, a passionate lover—husband—father; but for proof we are not left to surmise or even inferential biography or tradition. To the old grammarian Tzetzes, indeed, Themistogenes appears as Shakespeare's Mr. W. H.; and he regards him as in a special sense "the only

---

[1] *Mem.* iv. 8. 11, τῶν δὲ Σωκράτην γιγνωσκόντων οἷος ἦν, κ.τ.λ.

[2] *Hellen.* iv. 4. 19.　　　　　　　　[3] *Anab.* vii. 6. 43.

[4] *Hellen.* iv. 10.　　　　　　　　　[5] *Anab.* iv. 1. 19.

begetter" of the *Anabasis.* " As Phidias made statues for the
Eleian Pantarces—inscribing the name—so did Xenophon
with regard to his '*Advance of Cyrus,*' setting a certain name
to the work to please him whom he loved." Who can contradict this ? A similar tale in Diogenes Laertius[1] contradicts itself.
That writer first tells us that Aristippus relates in Book iv. of
his treatise περὶ παλαιᾶς τρυφῆς that Xenophon loved Cleinias,
whom he apostrophises thus, νῦν γὰρ ἐγὼ Κλεινίαν ἥδιον μὲν
θεῶμαι ἢ τἄλλα πάντα τὰ ἐν ἀνθρώποις καλά, quoting *totidem
verbis* from a speech of Critobulus, one of the interlocutors in the
Symposium, a work which later on he justly assigns to Xenophon. To Critobulus (the real lover of Cleinias) the time has
come, according to the rules of the after-supper entertainment,
to defend as his thesis " that on which I pride myself most is—
my beauty." This he does in the broadly humorous but still
delicately ironic style suited to the occasion and the author,
who at will infuses a touch of bombast. " ' It is now my turn,
I think, to state to you the grounds on which I pride myself
on beauty.' A chorus of voices rejoined, ' Say on.' ' To
begin with, if I am not beautiful, as methinks I be, you will
bring on your own heads the penalty of perjury one and all:
for, without waiting to have the oath administered to you,
you are always taking the gods to witness that you find me
beautiful : and I must needs believe you—are you not all
honourable men ? If then I be so beautiful, and affect you
even as I also am affected by him whose fair face here attracts
me, I swear by all the company of heaven, I would not choose
the Great King's empire in exchange for what I am, the
beauty of the world, the paragon of animals ; and at this
instant I feast my eyes on Cleinias gladlier than on all other
sights which men deem fair. Joyfully will I welcome blindness to all else, if but these eyes may still behold him, and
him only. With sleep and night I am sore vexed, which rob
me of his sight, but to daylight and the sun I owe eternal
thanks, for they restore him to me, my heart's joy, Cleinias.' "
Unauthentic, as that of Tzetzes was apocryphal, this tale
proves nothing which we did not perceive already. Xeno-

[1] Diog. Laert. *Xenophon.*

phon, like Socrates, understood the influence of the masculine
ἔρως. This to him is the highest type of passionate affection.[1] Nor need we further witness than his own words to put
us at the right point of view with regard to him:—" The men
of old, Achilles, Heracles, and the rest, learnt at the feet of
the Centaur Cheiron many a noble art, and they began with
the chase. From these they attained to great virtue, and
became men of renown, and are admired even to this day for
their goodness,—goodness, who numbers all men as her lovers,
as is very plain; only, because of the pains they must take to
win her many fall away, for the achievement of her is hid
in obscurity, but the pains that cleave to her are manifest.
Perchance, if only she were endowed with a visible bodily
frame, men would less have neglected her, knowing that even as
she is visible to them, so they also are not hid from her eyes.
For is it not so, that when a man moves in the presence of him
whom he dearly loves, he rises to a height above himself,
being incapable of aught base or foul, in word or deed, in sight
of him? but, fondly dreaming that the eye of virtue is closed
to them, they are guilty of many a base thing and foul before
her very face, who is hidden from their eyes. Yet she is present everywhere, being dowered with immortality; and those
who are perfect in goodness she honours, but the wicked
she thrusts aside from honour. If only men could know that
she regards them, how eagerly would they rush to the embrace
of toilful training and tribulation, by which alone she is hardly
taken; and so should they gain the mastery over her, and she
should be laid captive at their feet."

More striking perhaps, as being possibly more exceptional, is
his guardedness. He is so fully aware of the danger which
lurks in the things of Ἀφροδίτη and ἔρως that his mature creed
is almost puritanic. Unconscious carelessness, followed by
a storm of personal struggles to end in eventual calm, may possibly be pointed at in the biographic passage of the *Recollections*,
à propos of the same Critobulus and Cleinias:[2] " A touch of the
lips" in certain temperaments may be " the poisonous bite of
the tarantula; nay, this creature is less deadly, for it must cling

---

[1] *Cyn.* xii. 18-21.　　　　[2] *Mem.* i. 3. 8-14.

to its victim in order to inject its poison; but do you not know that this wild beast which men call beauty is so much more terrible than the tarantula, that, by a mere glance, it will inject something into you yards away which will drive you mad? . . . My advice to you, Xenophon, is, 'Whenever you set eyes on any fair face or form, to run helter-skelter without casting a glance behind you;' and to you, Critobulus, my advice is, 'Go abroad for a year; so long will it take you to be healed of this wound.'" "Such," adds the biographer, "in the affairs of Aphrodite, should be the attitude of those who do not stand firm as a rock." But perhaps Xenophon was not more distinguished from other Hellenes of this date in this than in the kindred subject of intersexual or domestic relations, and the state of marriage. The dignity of the wife, the education of women, the humane treatment of slaves, are matters in which he is for some reason (perhaps the Socratic self-discipline of a naturally philanthropic disposition) in advance of his compeers; or, if that seems too partial a statement, to his art of words, at any rate, we owe the revelation of the most pleasing pictures of inner life and *ménage* in contrast with that of the reigning beauty of the day; and to the same gift we owe a series of portraits of great women, which, for truth of delineation and inventiveness of design, would alone mark this writer as a great artist of a noble school of realism.

In reference to tenderness and the topic now before us, it is sufficient to record an interview of Socrates with Theodote [1] in the *Recollections,* and to compare it with the conversation between Ischomachus, an Athenian country gentleman, and his young wife, in the *Economist.* Theodote is probably painted from life, and nothing certainly could be more life-like, while round all objects, and the persons present with the two that are speaking, and the words and manner of their speech, plays a delicate air of Hellenic grace, and the irony of Socrates stings innocuously; so that he also who, to-day, has surreptitiously listened, departs wiser and more tender-hearted than when he entered. Perhaps it is base to unveil a portion of so charming a scene. The lady says, at last: "'Oh! why, Socrates,

---

[1] *Mem.* iii. 11. 1.

why are you not at my side (like the huntsman's assistant) to help me snare my friends and lovers?' 'That will I be,' he answered, 'if only you can woo and win me.' 'How shall I woo and win you?' she asked. 'Seek and you will find means, if you truly need me.' 'Then come and visit me often,' she said. And Socrates, poking sly fun at his own lack of business occupation, answered, 'Nay, Theodote, leisure is not a commodity in which I largely deal. I have a hundred affairs of my own to attend to; and then there are my lady-loves—my dear friends —who will not suffer me day or night to leave them, for ever studying to learn love-charms and incantations at my lips.' 'Why! are you really versed in those things, Socrates?' 'Of course, or else how is it, do you suppose, that Apollodorus here and Antisthenes never leave me, and why have Cebes and Simmias come all the way from Thebes to stay with me? Be assured, these things cannot happen without divine love-charms and incantations and magic wheels.'[1] 'I wish you would lend me your magic wheel then,' she said, 'and I will set it spinning for you first.' 'Ah, but,' he answered, 'I do not wish to be drawn to you. I wish you to come to me.' 'Then I will come,' she answered, 'only will you be " at home " to me?' 'Yes,' he answered, 'unless I am already engaged.'"

Let us turn to a scene in domestic life: Socrates is interrogating the "husband who had received into his arms his young wife of fifteen, absolutely ignorant of the world and its ways," as Mr. Lecky tells us.[2] "'Then all else,' said I, 'you taught your wife yourself, Ischomachus, until you had made her proficient in careful attention to her appointed duties?' 'That did I not,' replied he, 'until I had first offered sacrifice and prayed, that I might teach and she might learn all that could conduce to the happiness of us twain.' 'And did your wife join in sacrifice and prayer to that effect?' 'Most certainly, with many a vow registered to heaven to become all she ought to be; giving plain proof that, if the teaching failed, it should not be from want of due attention on her part.' 'Pray narrate to me what you first essayed to teach her; to hear that

---

[1] Cf. Theocr. ii. 17.
[2] *History of European Morals*, vol. ii. 305 ; Xenophon, *Oecon.* vii.

story would please me more than any description of the most splendid gymnic contest or horse-race you could give me.'" As soon as the fluttering fawn-like little creature had become accustomed to her husband's hand, and was now sufficiently trained to bear the effort of discussion, he commenced by asking: "Did it ever strike you to consider what led me to choose you as my wife among all women, or your parents to intrust you to me of all men?" Gently and gradually, drop by drop, with infinite tact and delicacy, the questions and answers come, until the girlish wife is led to realise her position clearly; and the *raison d'être*, practical and spiritual alike, of matrimony, with its providentially devised scheme of manifold co-operation, is revealed. She is to be the Queen-bee in her hive; and the works and duties, for which her woman's nature is so well adapted, will not be of trifling importance. For God, perceiving that a fearful spirit would be no detriment to guardianship, has endowed her with a larger measure of timidity than he bestowed on man. She must receive and register the products of their joint estate, apportioning part for daily and current use, and making provision to garner and guard the rest, so that the outgoings destined for a year may not be expended within a month. "'There is just one of the occupations which devolve upon you,' says the husband, 'that you may find not altogether pleasing: when any member of our household falls sick, it will be your care to see and tend them to the recovery of their health.' 'Nay,' replies the wife, 'that will be my pleasantest of tasks, if careful nursing may touch the springs of gratitude and leave them friendlier than heretofore.'" We are reminded of the Euripidean Alkestis parting with her slaves:—

> " All of the household servants wept as well,
> Moved to compassion for their mistress ; she
> Extended her right hand to all and each,
> And there was no one of such low degree
> She spoke not to, nor had an answer from." [1]

"With a very tender and delicate care to avoid everything resembling a reproach, the husband persuades his wife to give up the habits of wearing high-heeled boots in order

---

[1] Browning, *Balaustion's Adventure*, p. 38.

to appear tall, and of colouring her face with vermilion and white-lead. He promises her that if she faithfully performs her duties he will himself be the first and most devoted of her slaves. He assured Socrates that when any domestic dispute arose, he could extricate himself admirably if he was in the right, but that whenever he was in the wrong he found it impossible to convince his wife that it was otherwise."[1] Let us once more overhear the last few words of this dialogue. Ischomachus is speaking and says: "'Things have indeed now got so far, that it has happened to me to be taken apart and to have judgment passed upon me,—what penalty I must pay or what requital I must make.' 'And at whose bar,' I asked, 'is the sentence given? I cannot guess.' 'Whose but my own wife's?' he answered. 'And pray how do you conduct your own case?' 'Not so badly—when truth and interest are on one and the same side; but when these are opposed—indeed, Socrates, I have no skill to make the worse appear the better argument.' To which I: 'No, in truth, Ischomachus, black cannot be made to look white.'"[2]

But, for the light which it throws on this matter, let us turn to another discourse quoted by Cicero from the Socratic Aeschines, as a specimen of the "inductive" method.[3] The interlocutors are Aspasia, Xenophon's wife, and Xenophon himself. Aspasia asks, "'Tell me, wife of Xenophon, if your neighbour possesses better jewellery than you, would you rather have hers or yours?' 'Hers.' 'If her dresses, etc., are better and costlier, would you rather have your own or hers?' 'Hers, I suppose.' 'Well! well! and if she has a better husband than yours, which would you rather have, hers or your own?' A blush suffused the lady's cheeks; and Aspasia turned to Xenophon: 'Tell me, Xenophon, if your neighbour rides a better horse than yours, would you rather have his or yours?' 'His.' 'Well, if he owns a better farm than yours, would you rather have his farm or yours?' 'The better one, of course.' 'Well! but if he has a better wife than yours, which would you choose?' Silence sealed his lips. Then Aspasia:

---

[1] Lecky, *ibid. l.c.*
[2] *Oecon.* xi. 25.
[3] *De Invent.* l. xxxi. 51 *et seq.*

' Very well ! since you will neither of you tell me the only thing I wished to hear, let me interpret to you your thoughts. You, lady, wish to have the best of husbands, and you, Xenophon, the queen of wives; but if you fall short of a perfection that lies in your own hands, you will feel an aching void which nought else can supply since you both covet earnestly this best possession.' They assented." This tale, which has a dramatic truth about it, is not, of course, to be used for purposes of biography, and we need not speculate whether the lady's name was Soteira or Philesia; but for the uses of ideal biography we shall, with a good conscience, let it throw what light it can upon the matrimonial happiness of our author; and if we feel inclined we shall say that Philesia or Soteira or some other real woman, " better than any portrait by Zeuxis," was the prototype, in some sort, of the wife of Ischomachus, the Portia at whose judgment-seat we have lately sat; or of Panthea—that fairest lady in all the land, and most loyal of wives—the wife of Abradatas; or of the wife of Tigranes ;[1] and the other Xenophontine women, worthy to rank, not with Antigone perhaps, but with many of the women of Euripides.

As to Panthea, for her at least have our hearts melted ' with the droppings of warm tears;' like Araspas we have been made unawares captive in love, and at the hands of the wicked sophist ῎Ερως have been taught wisdom ; to know that we have two souls, and that when the good and lovely soul prevails, all lovely and good things are wrought, but the villain soul lays to her hand to work things base and ugly.[2] But this whole story, " perhaps the most pathetic recital embodied in the works of Hellenic antiquity,"[3] is too good and sacred to spoil by breaking up into fragments. For the present let us only recognise that it is a tale of conjugal love, which we keep among the eternal κτήματα owing to the inventive genius of Xenophon. Less tragical, but much to the point, is the narrative of Tigranes, the son of the king of Armenia, and the Armenian princess his wife, in Book iii. of the *Cyropaedia*, of whom Heywoode writes : " The

---

[1] Heywoode has put these two deservedly into his Γυναικεῖον (1624), pp. 126, 245.

[2] *Cyr.* vi. 1. 41. [3] Grote, *Plato*, chap. xxxix. vol. iii., *Xenophon.*

wife of Tygranes having been with her husband at a sumptuous banquet made by King Cyrus in his Pallace Royall, when every one extold the majestie and applauded the goodlinesse of the King's person; at length Tygranes askt his queen what her opinion was of his magnitude and person. She answered: ' I can say nothing, sir, for all the time of the feaste mine eyes were stedfastle fixed upon you, my deare husband; for what other mens beauties are it becomes not a married wife to inquire.' " That is graceful, but the original is more graceful and simpler than the Elizabethan reflection. The father of Tigranes, also called Tigranes, beleaguered in a fastness with his wives and daughters and all that he had, has been forced to come down and submit to be tried by the conqueror Cyrus. At that crisis the eldest son of the Armenian monarch Tigranes, an old hunting companion of Cyrus, was returning home after a long journey, and when he heard what was done he presented himself to Cyrus even as he was; but when he saw his father and his mother, his brethren, yea, and his own wife also, that were made prisoners, he could not refrain himself from tears. Constrained by Cyrus, he assists at the trial of his father. There is just that tinge of Oriental feeling which gives the *Cyropaedia* part of its charm; as of the meeting of Hellenism and the Eastern world. Is this the court of Solomon? or are we in a sort of philosophic *dicasterion* of the Elect, such as might be found in Plato's ideal state? It is hard to say; we seem to be in two places at once, yet there is no confusion, so great is the potency of the poetry of this master: behind the Socratic dialogue and the Spartan character of the Ruler and true Prince we are made aware of the parabolic wisdom of Nathan, and the king of kings.[1] The Armenian monarch is forced to pass a sentence of death upon himself; but the son pleads for the father, and the conqueror, who is as clement as he is politic and princely, yields. " But when they were gotten home they talked of Cyrus—one praising his wisdom, another his endurance, and a third the gentleness of his nature, and a fourth his beauty and magnificent stature. Then Tigranes turned to his wife and asked: ' Did Cyrus seem beautiful in thine eyes also?' To whom

---

[1] Cf. Sidney's *An Apologie for Poetrie*, 1595: "So right a prince as *Xenophon's Cyrus*," p. 25.

he answered: ' Nay, my lord, for I set not mine eyes upon him.' ' But on whom then?' asked Tigranes. ' On him who, to free me from slavery, offered his own life.' For that proposal had the husband made. . . ." The next day it is a question whether the son or father shall command the Armenian contingent. The father says: " He of us twain upon whom thou shalt lay this injunction." But the son says: " Nay, Cyrus, if I must even follow as one of your baggage-bearers, I will never leave you." Then with an arch smile Cyrus asked: " And what will you take that your wife should learn of you that you are become a baggage-bearer?" " She will not need to learn the fact from others, for I shall take her with me, and she can see for herself with her own eyes all that I do." " It is time then you two got your ' kit' together." So the wife followed her husband on the campaign; and when the empire of Cyrus was established, and the rewards of valour were to be distributed at Heywoode's " sumptuous banquet," he brought out and gave to Tigranes a woman's attire and adornment, bidding him bestow it on his wife—ὅτι ἀνδρείως συνεστρατεύετο τῷ ἀνδρί—" for that she manfully followed her own man to war."

Side by side with these pictures of fair women and good wives ought to be placed, not only on artistic grounds, but as throwing a clear light on a leading portion of our author's human-heartedness, the boyhood of Cyrus; and if Philesia may have been the model for the wife of Tigranes, so certainly may the childhood of Cyrus have been studied from one or other of Xenophon's sons. Xenophon is a true artist, and, without possessing the chief distinguishing Euripidean qualities, curiously witnesses to the realism of his time, coming to much the same point as the great poet analyst, by opposite means. He sees the character or object or personage he wishes to describe, *en bloc,* but with the clear-sighted precision of a photographer's lens; and his hand hardly falters in the delineation; his ' negatives' are generally good; in the case of this young boy, perhaps, exceptionally perfect;—but what purges the artist's vision here is the philanthropy of the father and the man. Throughout a long sustained account, extending over several quarto pages, the relations of the boy to his mother;

his school-fellows, his grandfather, his uncle, his admirers, the chief butler, etc., are all exquisitely and inimitably drawn, and preserved without perhaps one false note. We have seen Cyrus hunting to the admiration of his grandfather; and if space permitted, we might see him slay his stag and boar, even as his great historic compeer, the ideal monarch of a neighbouring people, slew a lion and a bear. We might represent scene upon scene—some of proverbial notoriety : the judgment of the coat, and the whipping consequent; the exclamation at sight of his grandly-attired Median grandfather, ὡς καλός μοι ὁ πάππος; his overflow of animal spirits ; the stirrings of his soul by affection ; the light-as-air whispers of the divine ἔρως in his ear; the heavy-hearted contritions and short, sharp pangs of boyish remorse, etc. etc., and we should at no moment doubt but that the delineator had a true and loving conception of boyish nature, as being the "programme of all good."

But this topic has detained us long enough ; only, in kindred connection, and before we turn to consider qualifying points, let us in a series of pictures appreciate that most untranslatable of all qualities—the humour and geniality, without which a man is scarcely a man, and to which the healthy irony of the Greeks gives so rare and intellectual a beauty. We will let our minds revert freely to the *Anabasis*, though the special quality in question is not confined to that buoyant work, but is everywhere, and is made the staple of the broader fun of the *Symposium*, which holds its sides and 'guffaws,' like a Brobdingnagian expansion of the gossamer wit of Lilliputia.

Bacon has recounted to us in vivid style the humorous interview, after Cunaxa, between the generals and Phalinus, the agent of the Great King, himself a Greek and a sort of professor of strategics at the Persian court. Bacon was not troubled by any manuscript reading Theopompus for Xenophon, nor disturbed by doubts as to the absolute authenticity of so graphic a history.[1] Therefore the passage which is here quoted, for the humour of the situation, is also an epitaph engraven with the high encomium of "the young scholar or philo-

---

[1] *Advancement of Learning,* I. vii. 30. Lord Bacon's *Works,* vol. iii. p. 313. (Spedding and Ellis.)

sopher:"—" The message imported that they should deliver up their arms, and submit themselves to the king's mercy. To which message, before answer was made, divers of the army conferred familiarly with Falinus, and amongst the rest Xenophon happened to say, ' Why, Falinus, we have now but these two things left, our arms and our virtue; and if we yield up our arms, how shall we make use of our virtue ?' Whereto Falinus, smiling on him, said, ' If I be not deceived, young gentleman, you are an Athenian, and I believe you study philosophy, and it is pretty that you say ; but you are much abused if you think your virtue can withstand the king's power.' Here was the scorn; the wonder followed : which was that this young scholar or philosopher, after all the captains were murdered in parley by treason, conducted those ten thousand foot through the heart of all the king's high countries, from Babylon to Grecia, in safety, in despite of all the king's forces, to the astonishment of the world, and the encouragement of the Grecians in times succeeding to make invasion upon the kings of Persia; as was afterwards proposed by Jason the Thessalian, attempted by Agesilaus the Spartan, and achieved by Alexander the Macedonian,—all upon the ground of the act of that young scholar." But while considering his heroism, let us not forget the humour of Xenophon.[2] On the night after the murder of the generals we are fairly resolved on the march ; our wagons and tents are burnt; we have shared with each other what we need from our superfluities, and thrown the rest into our watch-fires ; and with a good conscience we betake ourselves to breakfast. Just then up rides Mithridates with about thirty horsemen. Summoning the generals to within earshot, he makes us a fine long speech: ' Men of Hellas,—I was faithful to Cyrus, and I am well-disposed to you, and now I am here ' living in great dread. What are you going to do ? If it seems rational, I am disposed to join you with my retainers,' etc. etc. This sounds promising, but after various consultations out it comes. In the style of a preacher the excellent Asiatic tries to persuade us

---

[1] Grote is still at Bacon's point of view ; and seems hardly sufficiently to recognise the colouring element of Xenophon's strong subjectivity.

[2] *Anab.* iii. 3.

that without the good graces of the Great King our salvation is
hopeless. We part friends. After the mid-day meal we cross
the great Zab, and are jogging along in regular marching
order. But before we have got very far, lo and behold, ἐπι-
φαίνεται πάλιν ὁ Μιθριδάτης,[1] there he is again. Yes, surely,
that's he—Mithridates with a couple of hundred horse at his
back this time, and twice as many bowmen and slingers; and
in another five minutes we are in the thick of a pelt of arrows
and stones. The cavalry of this false friend, whose appearance we shall never forget, dog us all day. The scene changes:
—We are on the edge of a river with beetling Carduchian
crags hemming us in. We sound the depth of the river. We
can't bottom it with our long spears. In the midst of our perplexities a Rhodian comes up with a proposal:[2] 'I am ready,
sirs, to carry you across 4000 heavy infantry at a time, if you
will furnish me with what I need, and give me a talent for my
services.' 'What will you need?' 'Only 2000 wineskins.
I see there are multitudes of sheep and goats and asses.
They have only to be flayed and their skins inflated, and they
will readily give us a passage. I shall want also the straps you
use for the baggage-animals. With these I shall couple the
skins to one another, and then I shall moor each skin, by
attaching stones and letting them down like anchors into the
water. Then I shall carry them across, and when I have fastened the links at both ends, I shall place layers of wood on
them and a coating of earth on the top of that. You will see
in a minute that there is no danger of your drowning, for every
skin will be able to support a couple of men without sinking;
and the wood and earth will prevent your slipping off.' This
seems a pretty invention enough; but the generals think it
not altogether practicable in the face of cavalry on the other
side, etc. Every now and again the march is enlivened
by 'chaff' and repartee between the quick-witted Athenian
and the respectable Laconian Cheirisophus. Views of education are compared.[3] The Athenian suggests, *à propos* of steal-
ing a march upon the enemy, that the Spartan training will

---

[1] *Anab.* iii. 3. 6.   [2] *Ibid.* iii. 5.
[3] *Ibid.* iv. 6. 14-16.

now be of use. The Spartan mutters something in the nature of a *tu quoque*, about those who are taught to filch the public moneys in a democratic state, of which he has heard. On the slopes above Trebizond there is a great sacrifice and games.[1] The master of the ceremonies, a Spartan, Dracontius by name, is asked to conduct them to the course. He merely waved his hand, pointing to where they were standing, and said : ' There, this ridge is just the place for running—anywhere, everywhere.' ' But how will they manage to wrestle on the hard scrubby ground ?' ' Oh ! worse knocks for those who are thrown.' There was horse-racing also. The riders had to gallop down a steep incline to the sea, and then turn and come up again to the altar; and on the descent more than half rolled head over heels, and then back they came toiling up the tremendous steep, scarcely out of a walking pace. Loud were the shouts, the laughter, and the cheers.—The quaint customs of semi-barbaric tribes in matters of eating and drinking are a constant source of mirth, as we sit imbibing beer through long reeds;[2] or, in Thrace, Seuthes throws us junks of meat; or the wine-cup is handed, and we must get up and make speeches and promise gifts.[3] Again, no one who ever visited the Mossynoecians, *i.e.* the wooden-tower dwellers, will ever forget them. Transported suddenly into the world of Sir John Mandeville, he feels as if μανία were only next door; but there is a comical method in this madness. The customs of these people were the customs of civilised folk turned inside out. They do in a crowd what *nous autres* do in private, and *vice versa*.[4] There they go, talking and laughing to themselves, standing and capering about, as if their sole business were to show off to the rest of the world. They are very white-skinned, the men as well as the women. One of their entertainments consists of an exhibition of fatted children belonging to the wealthy classes, fed up on boiled chestnuts until they are as white as white can be, and very nearly as broad as they are long." But these humorous situations are endless.

---

[1] *Anab.* iv. 8. 26.
[2] *Ibid.* iv. 5. 26.
[3] *Ibid.* vii. 3. 22, 26 *et seq.*
[4] *Ibid.* v. 4. 32-34.

Xenophon then is, without exception, a type of the φιλάν-θρωπος, but of course it is a φιλανθρωπία conditioned by his age and " political " circumstances, neither of which does he transcend to any miraculous extent. His world is peopled, somewhat unduly to our democratic minds, with οἱ βέλτιστοι and οἱ καλοὶ κἀγαθοί. The *better classes* and the *people of culture* limit or confine the horizon of his sympathies ; even as now-a-days, when caste prejudices are clearly decadent, the garb or general appearance of a man may impose on the imagination of a Christian, or as the philosophy of some thinkers seems to be warped by contact with coloured races and less advanced civilisations. The eye of Xenophon may similarly have looked askance at some one whose political or social setting was not to his taste ; but this προσωποληψία does not render him less graphic, nor, in any deep sense, poison the springs of his phil-anthropy. Indeed his sympathy is so akin to clear-sightedness, and in keeping with the bright keen atmosphere and sunny *Heiterkeit* of his native olive-clad hills and vales, that nothing, not even anti-Theban political partisanship, can dull its trans-parency ; and so, whatever he may have thought of the two heroes who slipped through the fingers of Agesilaus from the closely-watched citadel of Phlius, his description of them lives in our memory, through the vividness of his style.[1] " Agesilaus granted a truce for the embassy, but at the same time he was so angry at their setting his personal authority aside that he sent to his friends at home, and arranged that the fate of the little township should be left to his discretion, and meanwhile proceeded to tighten the cordon of investment, so as to render it impossible that a single soul should escape." In spite of which he was not clever enough for Delphion. " This brilliant organiser of the defence, with a single comrade (στιγ-ματίας τις), a branded dare-devil, who had already shown great dexterity in relieving the besieging parties of their arms, escaped in the night."

In close connection with the healthy humanity of our author (which in reference to others is φιλία, to one's-self εὐεξία, and negatively implies an absence of πλεονεξία and ὕβρις),

---

[1] *Hellen.* v. 3. 22-24.

are to be ranged his favourite virtues : the special 'rule of life,' to which his nature was doubtless prone; but with the emphasising of which 'the great companion' must surely be largely credited, though to what extent we can only dimly conjecture. For undoubtedly on many important moral questions or (to speak correctly) ethical theories, the disciple differed largely from his master, and was, so far, nearer to the average mind of even later ages.[1] Thus, according to Xenophon, who is interpreting the Socratic mind to 'the Athenians,' *i.e.* to a general audience, and in a somewhat apologetic style, in keeping with the mental vernacular,—to Xenophon virtue is a branch of μάθησις (learning) indeed, and so far a thing to be taught; but then ἄσκησις, discipline (including objective discipline of the individual and subjective self-discipline), is a means of teaching. Again, ἐπιστήμη, the highest type of intellectual knowledge (science), readily transforms itself into σοφία, the highest sort of wisdom. Possibly the transformation, so far as Xenophon himself is concerned, takes place through some such train of thought as the following, taken from a conversation between Socrates and Euthydemus : [2]—

Question. And what shall we say of wisdom ? Tell me : do the wise seem to you to be wise in things they know, or are there, who are wise in what they know not ?

Answer. Clearly in what they know ; for how should a man have wisdom in what he knows not ?

Quest. The wise, in fact, are wise in knowledge ?

Ans. Why, in what else could a man be wise, save only in knowledge ?

Quest. And wisdom ! is it aught else, think you, than that wherein men are wise ?

Ans. Certainly not.

Quest. It seems, knowledge is wisdom ?

Ans. I think so.

---

[1] I do not mean, contrariwise, to imply that the true Socrates is to be found in Plato rather than in Xenophon (*vide* note [1] next page, and note [1] page 369), but rather, that the Aristotelian theory of virtue was latent in the common-sense views of the moralist. What the profound identification of σοφία with ἐπιστήμη was in the mind of Socrates, lies beyond the present discussion.

[2] *Mem.* iv. 6. 7.

Quest. Do you think that a man is capable of knowing all the things that are ?

Ans. I should say he cannot know even the millionth part of them.

Quest. It seems a human being cannot be all-wise?

Ans. Certainly not.

Quest. The conclusion is, the wisdom of each man is limited to that which he knows.

This is by no means tantamount to saying that σοφία = ἐπιστημη : but one sees that wisdom and knowledge might easily come to be convertible, in inexact thought or expression ; and the practical loss (or gain) is the same.[1] On the other hand, σοφία is apt to fade away, and to transform itself into σωφροσύνη (an untranslatable "mixed mode"— temperance, modesty, sobriety, and rhythmical self-completion and adjustment).[2] " Now wisdom and σωρφοσύνη he did not distinguish, his verdict being that the one thing needful was that a man should make himself acquainted with ' the beautiful and the good,' and practise them ; or, again, he should learn to know the ugly and base, and avoid it. Such a man was σοφός and σώφρων, wise and well-regulated. For justice (or uprightness) and all things that are wrought with virtue are beautiful and good.".[3] And, again, " justice and all the rest of virtue are wisdom."

Whether, then, in these kaleidoscopic views Xenophon is only expressing his own reading of the philosopher's mind, or whether he has also the mind of the philosopher, which, thirdly, he may be translating into language to be understood of the mass of men,—is a most serious investigation, raising as it does

---

[1] It may be urged that, as far as this passage goes, the disciple is truly, if perhaps crudely, intelligent of his master ; for, admittedly, the identification of knowledge, wisdom, and virtue is the most characteristic of Socratic doctrines ; while the scope and intention of the *Recollections* exclude severe philosophising. But, even so, the impression left upon the mind is that Xenophon himself took merely a *common-sense* view of the subtleties of the spirit, in which the teacher dealt ; and, except as a moralist and sympathiser, failed to fathom the distinctive doctrine. Nor does it appear that Plato, from another side, was more successful.

[2] Cf. J. S. Mill, *Dissertations and Discussions*, vol. iii. 326, 327.

[3] *Mem.* iii. 9. 4, 5.

the whole question of the philosophic value of the *Recollections.*
But its pursuit would lead us too far afield, and it seems sufficient to get an insight into the mind of the *Hearer* rather than
of the *Inspirer*; for if we find it next to impossible to separate
the chaff of Xenophon[1] from the wheat of Socrates, we have no
similar difficulty in detecting the idiosyncratic virtues of this
particular Hellene. We have only to carve them out of the
whole assemblage of moral qualities which make up the ἀρετή
of man; and the "virtues," which constitute the sum of ethical
principle, whether of the unwritten code, the ἄγραφοι νόμοι[2]
(with which Socrates confutes the scepticism of Hippias), or
that wherein the law of the State is embodied, are for the
main easily enumerated. Often hard, or even impossible, to
represent by any one equivalent or string of half-equivalents in
English, they are not hard to realise with tolerable definiteness.
The names of several occur in *Mem.* iv. 6, and are so current
indeed in all Greek literature that if Plato and Xenophon and
Aristotle were destroyed we still should possess or re-discover
them. The four 'cardinal' virtues are[3]—(1) σοφία; (2) δικαιοσύνη; (3) ἀνδρεία; (4) σωφροσύνη—(1) wisdom; (2) justice or
social uprightness (in New Testament "righteousness"); (3)
courage; (4) temperance.[4] Akin to σωφροσύνη is ἐγκρατεία
(self-control), and in the same breath with σοφία must be
mentioned φρόνησις (prudence or practical wisdom) and ἐπι-

---

[1] Again, by this expression I do not wish to suggest that the Socrates of
Xenophon is more (or less) real or true than that of Plato. Personally, I
regard these portraitures as both true, both defective. They are single-sided
and opposite ideals; and, *pro tanto,* caricatures in part of the actual being,
whose real self was not truly depicted by any mortal. Whose has been?
The Xenophontine Socrates (of the *Recollections*) is drawn to suit the every-
day spectator, and possesses a certain precious, if limited, "historic" truth.
The limitations of the Platonic draught are of a different kind. The theorist
and philosopher needs the high-aiming, unselfish *eristic* inspirer and searcher,
as the most important of his *dramatis personœ.* Plato also is a poet; and
will 'poetise' the real man to the same extent that the historian 'historicises'
him—askew. Yet both are good and noble portraits.

[2] *Mem.* v. 4. 19.

[3] *Ibid.* iv. 6: §§ 2-4, Piety (εὐσεβεία); 5-6, Justice (δικαιοσύνη); 7, Wisdom
(σοφία); 8-9, le Beau (τὸ καλόν); 10-11, Courage (ἀνδρεία).

[4] "'Temperance,' while corresponding to a part of the word, is ridiculously
inadequate to the whole."—J. S. Mill, on "Mixed Modes," different from
or corresponding to our use.—*Diss. and Disc.* vol. iii. 328.

στήμη. These, with others, constitute the full perfection of man: they are virtue. But roaming among these the soul of Xenophon was chiefly enamoured of εὐσεβεία, of ἀνδρεία, and of σωφροσύνη in its kinship to ἐγκρατεία rather than σοφία; *i.e.* on the moral and emotional rather than the intellectual side; but as a follower of Socrates it is sufficient for him to put consciously into the foreground growth in καλοκἀγαθία, as the chief aim and rule of life. For the religious, temperate, self-controlled, rhythmically attuned, just, righteous, prudent, scientific, wise, and good man is he who has absorbed into himself the καλὰ κἀγαθά, the whole list of beautiful and noble things; or, in the language of Lycurgean training, τὰ καλά simply, the chivalrous "code of honour" at Sparta. In a less formal way, but with a still more penetrative persistence, as of a man who knows that he has no better gospel of salvation to give, he insists on a still unmentioned virtue which must be regarded as highly idiosyncratic: to wit, ἐπιμέλεια, painstaking care. Possibly there is the slightest aristocratic tinge to this excellence; perhaps a touch of superiority in its possessor is implied as of the *overseer's* care; but however incompatible with things low and sordid (τὰ βαναυσικά), the doctrine is the same: οὐδὲν ἄνευ πόνου καὶ ἐπιμελείας—γυμναστέον σὺν πόνοις καὶ ἱδρῶτι, which Cicero would turn "nihil sine sudore et studio," nothing without painstaking care, and trouble;[1] and this it is which, with (εὐσεβείὰ) his piety, endears Xenophon to the heart of Mr. Ruskin, and most deservedly, for when it enters in and dwells with a man, out of his heart perishes all ἀλαζονεία and ματαιότης, all moral thinness and quackery; and it is therefore quite comprehensible how, to a practical temperament, such as Xenophon's, the problem, Can virtue be taught? resolves itself for the most part into an affair of training (ἄσκησις).

With regard to "King Νόμος," his bias is strongly Athenian, or else Laconian. "The laws" of Thebans or Eleians shock or revolt him, or are beyond even his stricture as something alien —much as a good English Protestant not so long ago might have been scandalised by the beliefs and customs of the Parisians or

---

[1] *Mem.* ii. 1. 28.

Catholics, and as for the political or religious views of Turks or Russians, would not reckon them as within the pale of his observation. This analogue, if not pressed too far, throws some faint light on Xenophon's limitations, which are 'national,' nothing more.[1]

Orderliness, not to speak of piety, economy, self-cultivation—these lead to success in life, but also to the highest perfection of the Hellenic soul. By comparison with these, even φιλοτιμία, that first and last infirmity of noble-minded citizens, ambition and the love of honour, ranks nowhere; and it is easy to see how closely connected with this somewhat Spartan (or Socratic?) self-supervision is what we venture to call the Puritanism, or even Calvinism, of his soul. Over and over again we seem to hear a prophecy of language which we think appropriate enough on the lips of St. Paul, but which startles us some four hundred odd years before those birth-throes of our spirit. "The majority of pleasures are bad," says Xenophon,[2] and hence an argument in favour of the healthy excitement and the joyous discipline of the chase; for, of course, the pains and pleasures of animals are ignored then as now. If he has said, or rather has introduced Simonides as saying to Hieron, "All the troubles which you 'tyrants' endure are well repaid, since in the end you receive more abundant honour than the rest of mankind; and no pleasure which men can enjoy approaches nearer to the divine than the delight in being honoured;" he has also written this apostolic passage:[3] "Where, then, is the difficulty of supposing that a man may be virtuous and temperate to-day, and to-morrow the reverse; or that he who once has had it in his power to do what is right, may not quite lose that power? No; if I may venture to express an opinion of my own, I would say that all beautiful and noble things are a matter of constant practice and training; and this applies pre-eminently to the virtue of temperance,

---

[1] Socrates, in his famous speech in the *Symposium,* viii. 34, argues against Pausanias's theory of the invincibility of a sacred band of lovers, and as to the customs of Elis and Thebes adduced in support of his view,—"that," says Socrates, "is a one-legged proof at best, for what they accept as highly proper we regard as simply scandalous." The point to bear in mind is that NOMOI correspond to our CREEDS pretty much.

[2] *Cyn.* xii. 12.   [3] *Mem.* i. 2. 23.

seeing that in one and the same bodily frame pleasures are planted and spring up side by side with the soul, ever whispering in her ear, ' have done with self-restraint, make haste to gratify us and the body (our common lord).'"

In these last considerations we seem to have been exploring a mind partly 'Socratic,' partly independent of Socrates; and at length when we come to the writer's philosophic self, the σοφισ-τής, or σοφός, or φιλόσοφος, as we may term it, within him, this ambiguity is intensified. We find ourselves fully launched indeed into ' Socratic' influence, with all the external apparatus of method, the *elenchos*, the dialectic process, the cut and parry and thrust of *eristic* argumentation, the *epaktic* or inductive reasoning, the arrangement of what we talk about by " families," *i.e.* " generalisation;" but while caught into this wise man's debating ground, we seem to be in it, and not of it. To say that our feelings resemble those of the poor old Athenian country gentleman in the *Thinkery*, φροντιστήριον, would be libellous, because the μαθητὴς, Xenophon, is at anyrate quite at home. Possibly he is hardly aware of the gap which separates him from the philosophy of him at whose feet he sat ; even as Aristippus, Antisthenes, Euclides, and the rest, may have regarded their own fragments over fondly as the keystone of the palace of thought. Here the distinction seems not difficult to grasp.

Between the world of the wise man and that region which is inhabited by the οἱ πολλοί, the children of everyday life, there is a gulf fixed, but there is no want of intercommunication ; there is what may be termed the Xenophontine bridge, and on this, which is neutral ground for the philosopher and the mass of men to meet, there are no hostile catchwords ; " the stock argument and the ready-to-hand reproaches " are in abeyance. On the far side is the most original of men seeking as an absolutely lofty and philanthropic object to awaken self-consciousness in his fellows or in himself ; this is the noble, nay sublime, Hellenic effort for " the salvation of souls." [1] As Mr. Sidgwick in the treatise already quoted says :[2] " The radical and most impressive article of his creed was constituted by his

---

[1] " Socrates, the Jesus Christ of Greece."—SHELLEY.
[2] *Ethics*, Ency. Metrop. p. 576.

exalted estimate of this knowledge that was so hard to find, his conviction that ignorance of the good and evil in human life was the source of all practical error." "Take heed," he was always saying in his own language, "take heed, therefore, that the light which is in thee be not darkness." This enlightenment is at once knowledge and goodness and moral attainment. When shall we attain to Socratic wisdom? when, in Xenophontine hunting metaphor, shall virtue be laid captive at our feet? These are the questions we ask, as we take our stand on the hither side with the ordinary Hellene, bent upon self-culture.[1] From this point of view we persuade ourselves that Socrates did really care less for his method, his elenchos, his induction, his novel class or clan system of arrangement (τὸ κατὰ γένη διαλέγειν), than for benefiting, by hook or by crook, the interlocutor (or possibly some other at his expense), but with infinite "philanthropy" in all cases. As performing a solemn and charitable duty, he sought to awaken self-consciousness, to throw a stream of light into a dark place, and to convict of ignorance, confusion and obscurity of thought and behaviour, for the sake of clearer intelligence and a firmer moral foothold. The machinery was the whole "maieutic" apparatus of the new method: so important indeed in the history of philosophy, that Aristotle can sum up his great discovery thus: "he sought the abstract (τὸ καθόλου),[2] and was the first who thought of giving definitions." But to himself neither the method nor any part of the machinery was of vital necessity, only these were the natural handiest instruments for his purposes. (If 'anæsthetics' would have served, he would have applied them.) The important point was, not the intellectual or metaphysical training, or the philosophising even by a better method—though "to make his associates more dialectic," to sharpen and keep bright their lancets, was in its due place part of his daily business,[3]—but better philosophising as a step forward in the direction of manly virtue and human completeness, which is happiness.

In some such light we may imagine that Socrates revealed

---

[1] σωφροσύνη περὶ τοὺς Θεούς, περὶ τήν δικαιοσύνην—a rhythmical self-completion and adjustment towards God and the righteousness of man (social uprightness).

[2] Arist. *Metaph*. xiii. 4.   [3] *Mem*. iv. 6. 1.

himself to the concrete mind of Xenophon. Some of his doctrines may have been absorbed at once; others, really put forward tentatively for the awakening of another soul, Xenophon may have assimilated in the half-ripe condition; hence the rounded teleology and the views about immortality (in the *Memorabilia* and *Cyropaedia*). In other cases, he gives rein to his own philosophic propensities, and in the satisfaction of his own highest nature, attempts to answer various questions, which he had often heard raised for the twofold purpose of getting a clear concept, and of creating a thorough moral awakening. The result of this fashion of his own is some of the most beautiful pieces of Greek literature: the *Economist,* the *Hieron,* the *Cyropaedia.* He asks, Who is the economic man? Who is the despot? Who is the kingly personage with the gift of ruling? and with some semblance of the Socratic "induction," his own thoughts the while working along the "epaktic" grooves, he comes to a conclusion which is, if you like, a generalisation, but is nevertheless embodied in a concrete shape; he has, in fact, drawn upon his canvas, as an answer to the philosophic inquiry, with which we started, a Cyrus or a Hiero, or an Ischomachus. That which might have ended in metaphysics turns out to be an exquisite work of art, carefully elaborated line for line, but at the same time not devoid of ethic and allegoric import.

Here, however, we will be quit of the σοφιστής and turn to interrogate the ῥήτωρ, the political reformer, and professor of strategics, the author; not indeed of the earliest political brochure, for we are agreed to exclude from our canon that "oldest extant specimen of literary Attic prose," and otherwise remarkable work, the essay *On the Athenian Polity;*[1] but—of the *Laconian Polity,* the *Hipparchicos,* the pamphlet *on Revenues.* We will confront the artist, who has skilfully worked into the texture of his larger works much that belongs to the statist and the tactician; and this to so great an extent that in the eyes of the modern military historian "tactics" seem to form the main thread of the *Cyropaedia,* and the chief point of interest of the *Anabasis* (or *Hellenica*).[2]

---

[1] 420 B.C., Jebb, *Greek Literature Primer,* and *vide supra,* p. 328, note.

[2] *Vide* Rüstow and Köchly *passim,* also the former's *Militärische Biographieen.*

To speak of these "political" and professional gifts in a breath is not easy, though there is a marked 'solidarity' between the diverse selves of the man whom we are cross-questioning; and the native rhythm of even so many-sided and Odyssean a character predominates. Under favourable circumstances it is quite likely that Xenophon might have appeared in history as another Iphicrates,[1] a μορμὼ and bugbear[2] to Spartan allies or Boeotians, or as a second Chabrias or Charidemus, a higher type of military reformer or captain of mercenaries than the Cœratidases and Phalinuses whose features he has so indelibly imprinted on our minds.[3] His interest at any rate in military matters is obvious;[4] and, if sentiment is to weigh, the *Hipparchicos*, addressed to a commandant of cavalry for the benefit possibly of his own son, and as a seal of reconciliation to his fatherland, has a special interest for us: a remark applicable also to the latest work of his old age, written as tradition infers for Eubulus, the finance minister of Athens, who had been instrumental in rescinding the vote of banishment, and in that case doubly, for the sake of peace. As practical works the value of these political tracts would probably be as great in the eyes of the modern reader as the companion treatises on Hunting and Horses, if only the species of things with which they deal were of a type as fixed as horses and grooms, dogs and hares. Dealing with the more shifting or evanescent topics of cavalry tactics, and of Athenian finance, they may easily be misjudged. For instance, as far as the military manual goes, we ought not to allow mere change in numbers or equipment to affect our judgment, if, as regards evolutional and other efficiency, the precepts appear to possess a more permanent value. A fairer difficulty, the insertion of pompous regulations which would have no parallel in a similar modern treatise, is to be explained by the close connection in a Greek city community between the citizen soldier's service as a defender of his country in war,

---

[1] Xenophon's Seuthes' experiences present a strong family likeness to those of Iphicrates and Cotys.

[2] *Hell.* iv. 4. 17.   [3] *Anab.* vii. 1. 21-25 ; *ibid.* ii. 1. 6-15.

[4] Plutarch says Xenophon taught Agesilaus. Cicero tells us Scipio Africanus carried a copy of the *Cyropaedia* about in his breast pocket.

and his employment in religious processions during peace.[1]
Her Majesty's household troops throw little light on this side
of the matter, which, however, in Xenophon's time could hardly
have been omitted. So, again, our more advanced views of
political economy—our intelligent appreciation of the application of "*the law of diminishing returns*" to mineral products,
ought not to lead us to laugh at the fundamental hypothesis of
the *de Reditibus* that the silver mines of Laurium were inexhaustible. Better economised labour, and more of it, would
probably have rendered them more lucrative. Besides which,
they were as inexhaustible for the Athenians, at any rate, as
the coal-fields of Great Britain are for the people of England;
nor is there anything in the rest of the scheme to stamp its
author as an unpractical politician.

Of course it is not pretended that these treatises have, or
ever had, any claim to rank highly among the πολιτικοὶ λόγοι,
the production of which, in the eyes of Isocrates, guarantees to
the author the title of philosopher refused to the verbose or
disputatious professor of wisdom; moreover, we have hardly
the means of gauging the value attached by his contemporaries to any of these minor works. The fact that they were
written by Xenophon would have preserved them; and what is
more profitable here is to discover in the mature treatise the
floating schemes and enthusiastic aspirations of youth or middle
age. In the nonagenarian Nestor, of the *Revenues*, devising
means to counteract pauperism and turn exceptional wealth to
account, while adding honour to the state, we hear the voice of
the youthful and athletic captain of the Retreat, brimming
with an Odyssean joy in experience and irrepressible good-
humour. Our minds revert to the fatal night of the murder of
the generals; the dream and the resolution are past, the first
hurried meetings have taken place, the new generals have been
appointed. The council is held as day breaks; the speeches
follow: Cheirisophus' laconic, as it ought to be; Cleanor's
of Orchomenus artistically suited; then Xenophon rose—he
was arrayed for war in all his finery.[2] If the gods grant us
victory, thought he, the finest attire will accord with the event;

---

[1] *Hipparch.* iii.   [2] *Anab.* iii. 2. 7.

XENOPHON. 377

or, if death is our doom, then for him who has claimed the finest it is as well there should be some correspondence between the expectation and the end.[1] . . . "But perhaps," he urged, "it is well· we did not stop, for I fear that if we once learn to live in idleness and luxuriously to batten, in intercourse with these tall and handsome Median and Persian women and maidens, we shall be like the lotos-eaters, and forget the road home altogether. It seems to me it is only rational and right, in the first instance, to make an effort to return to Hellas and to revisit our hearths and homes, if only to prove to our countrymen that it is their ówn fault that they are poor and needy, seeing it is in their power to give to those now living a pauper life at home a free passage hither, and to convert them into well-to-do burghers at once." Here seems to be the germ of the colonisation scheme, of which we hear again and again, whether in the shape of a project of forming a settlement at Cotyora,[2] or of sailing off for a similar purpose to the mouth of the Phasis, or of establishing a new " politeuma" on the auspicious promontory of Calpe. The scheme of the *de Reditibus* half a century later is more elaborate, but is marked by the same philanthropic *savoir faire*.[3]

The special evils of a still later date have been described as, " 1. The accumulation of wealth in the hands of the rich, and the corresponding growth of rapacity on the part of the poor. 2. The growth of egotism and unprincipled ambition since the rupture between society and the state.   3. The swarms of men without cities, paupers, political exiles, malefactors, for ever moving over the face of Greece, ready for mercenary service, and ripe for mischief."[4] Of all these things we are aware from the pages of Xenophon, who lived, indeed, down to the days of Philip, but is representative of a generation earlier.   Still stronger light is thrown on the underlying causes of this " political decomposition " and increasing chaos, by a great modern thinker.[5] The philosopher has done speaking of the " diversion of Greek

---

[1] *Anab.* iii. 2. 25.   [2] *Ibid.* v. 6. 15.
[3] *De Redit.* i., διὰ δὲ τὴν τοῦ πλήθους πενίαν ἀναγκάζεσθαι ἔφασαν ἀδικώτεροι εἶναι περὶ τὰς πόλεις; also vi., καὶ ὁ μὲν δῆμος τροφῆς εὐπορήσει, οἱ δὲ πλούσιοι, κ.τ.λ.   [4] Jebb, *Orators, Isocrates*, ch. xii. p. 15.
[5] Comte, vol. iii. of *Pos. Polit.* p. 245, Engl. transl. (Beesly.)

intellect from politics," and is concerned with the spectacle of independent states united by common sentiments and beliefs. "The political decomposition served as a new impelling force, for it kept before men's eyes the continual spectacle of an intellectual and moral association between states independent of each other. That spontaneous church, even then as much a reality as the cities composing it, could by no territorial restriction be hindered from arousing in those whose qualities of heart and mind inclined them towards social generalisations, an unmistakable desire for a universal communion." [1] In other words, the reign of the Νόμος dynasty in the different states was tottering to its fall, and out of the void (no real vacuum, but the abiding-place of the ἄγραφοι νόμοι), was fast shaping itself the new law, whose best name in history is "the scientific conscience," the heirloom of Hellenic intellect. To this chaos and decomposition Xenophon, amongst others, has borne testimony; for better or for worse he is a veritable "enfant du siècle," and that is his high praise; but we ought not to restrict our regard for him to that view. By a kind of accident, owing to the preservation of the diverse products of his fertility, and because his genius is that of the universally representative rather than exceptionally original artist in some one department of things—the child of Thalia or Calliope or Melpomene; for these reasons, and for others which go deeper, to wit his humanity, his moral earnestness, his appreciation of Socrates, he has always, even when his fame suffered declension, been honoured as the foreordained depositary of precious information about the ancient Greeks, which, but for him, would certainly have perished. This, then, is a high prestige, but it is one which a man has to share with the Moabitish Stone, the obelisks, or the ruins of Nineveh. Not "half-sunk," indeed, or "shattered is the visage" of this ancient Hellene, but rather he is a "pyramid built up by renewed might of all Time's

---

[1] To understand "Laconism," we ought to go to a somewhat analogous period —the Italy of the Republics, where Venice with her relative stability and oligarchical government = Sparta; Florence with her intellectual turmoil and political self-consciousness = Athens. The comparison would be worth working out in detail. *Vide* Symonds, *Age of Despots*, chap. iii. *passim*, and ch. iv. p. 236; also Freeman, *Historical Essays*, 2d series, p. 32.

artificers," by Plutarch, by Cicero, by Alberti, Sidney, Bacon, down to the warm-hearted and broad-souled exponent of the great Athenian Demos, of whom we have all been ' hearers.'[1]

But for Xenophon one may claim a more than monumental title. He is also essentially a stylist, the forerunner of the masters of *belle lettere.* Like Herodotus, like Pindar, like his other literary compeers, he has, if in a less degree, some claim to the additional meed of absolute originality, not only as the inventor of a style of literature, but of many of its minor subdivisions. "For Xenophon, who did imitate so excellently, as to give us *effigiem justi imperii,* the portraiture of a just empire under the name of Cyrus (as Cicero saith of him) made therein an absolute heroicall poem."[2] And there are poems within the poem. How novel must have appeared this Eastern version of King Arthur, this premonition of the Table Round, written in the choicest "euphuism" of that day; in which, round[3] the blameless king, are grouped a dozen lesser characters, whose action harmoniously adjusts itself to the main thesis, enlivening and assisting its development. While there is room, in a natural way, also, for disquisitions on military matters, for moral delineations and the growth of character, for pathetic tales and skilfully interwoven episodes, like that of Gobryas and Gadatas, or of Panthea and Abradatas—"the earliest prose love-story in European literature;" where a place, too, is found for comic supper-parties and interludes, in which the fun is of a robust, broad type, contrasting with the delicately ironic humour which ripples through the *Anabasis,* but helping, and helped by, our appreciation of the Aristophanic vein of the *Symposium;* in both, the breadth of the jocularity being redeemed, as in Shakespeare, by truth to nature and grace of style. Scarcely behind the *Cyropaedia* in inventiveness, and its superior in a certain quality of opaline beauty, ranks the *Economist.* It is full of the Xenophontine limpidity, the little bells of alliteration, the graceful antithetic balance; the sweet

[1] Grote, *Hist.* vol. viii. *passim,* compared with his *Plato,* vol. iii. ch. xxxix.
[2] Sir Philip Sidney, *An Apologie for Poetrie,* p. 28.
[3] Compare the ψυχρὸς βασιλεὺς with Tennyson's King Arthur, Araspas with Lancelot or Sir Bedivere, etc.

sounds helping out the healthy sense, as of a fragrant air breathed upon us from fresh and well-worked fields, where we cherish content in winter by a blazing fire, or in summer lulled by a trio of babbling streams, soft airs, and tender shades.[1] This is a work the careful thoroughness of which, and its praise of Masserizia, found great favour with the Italians of the Renaissance, so that Alberti, or some other, speaks of imitating[2] "quel Greco dolcissimo e soavissimo scrittore Senophonte."

This Cicero indeed had done before,[3] whose remarks upon the style of Xenophon are worth remembering.[4] "The Muses they say spoke by the lips of Xenophon." "I have come across students of forensic oratory who wished to take Xenophon as their model, cujus sermo est ille quidem *melle dulcior, sed a forensi strepitu remotissimus;*"[5] and in praise of his portrait of Agesilaus, "Xenophon's one little book, as a panegyric, is better than all the pictures and statues put together," "in eo rege laudando facile omnes imagines omnium statuasque superavit;"[6] or again, in an interesting discussion of the qualities requisite for writing history, in which we get a comparison of Roman and Greek standards with criticisms of different historians, Xenophon and Callisthenes, two "philosophic" historians, emanating respectively from Socrates and Aristotle, are contrasted. The Aristotelian wrote "rhetorico paene more;" the Socratic "leniore quidem sono est usus, et qui illum impetum oratoris non habeat, vehemens fortasse minus, sed aliquanto tamen est, ut mihi quidem videtur, dulcior."[7] Reference has already been made to Cicero's translations of Xenophon, and the rendering by this great monotheistic Latin of Cyrus's dying speech on immortality was nothing less than a handing on of the torch to after times, a torch not yet quite antiquated in pattern.[8] His estimate of the work itself is nearly

---

[1] *Oecon.* v. 7. The 'horizontal' structure of the Xenophontine sentence is conspicuous in this work ; the members balancing with a tender minuet-like movement.   [2] Opere volgari di Leon Battista Alberti.
[3] Fragments of Cicero's translation of the *Economist* remain.
[4] Cic. *Or.* xix. 62.
[5] *Ibid.* ix. 32, and on this point cf. Jebb, ii. ch. xxiv. p. 449.
[6] Cic. *Ep. ad Div.* v. 12. 7.   [7] Cic. *de Orat.* ii. xiv. 58.
[8] Cicero's monotheism is felt to be more consistent and defined than Plato's or Xenophon's ; *de Nat. Deorum*, i. xii. 31.

that of Sir Philip Sidney, as above recorded. The letter to his brother Quintus,[1] in which he recommends him to follow the example of Africanus, and make its chapters his constant companions, as containing "the whole duty of government," " nullum est enim praetermissum in his officium diligentis et moderati imperii," shows the practical value attached to so poetical a work. And later criticism, while ready to assign greater historical importance,[2] retains the idea of a philosophic and poetic treatise on *the ideal monarchy*, as of a work written (*caeteris paribus*) with an object similar to that of Tacitus's *Germania*.

The *Anabasis* is so well-known a book, and has been so universally appreciated, that to add even a few words seems an impertinence ; as if to whole generations of schoolboys tied down to fragments of the classics for many years, in this book at any rate had not come an " apocalypse " of Greek life ; or as if its more essential, epic and Homeric, qualities had not been fully and affectionately enough insisted on in the pages of Grote (and his followers) ; yet the topic of its literary merits is by no means exhausted. Like the *Hellenica*, it seems to hinge on a kind of unconscious "peripety ;" also, like the *Hellenica*, read as a whole work, it contains what we may call a double (Euripidean) plot. In the *Anabasis* the battle is the crisis, and Trebizond the solution of the first plot ; then comes the really tragic, swinging round of Fate, the true " peripeteia." Just when the situation becomes so dramatic that the joyous cry from the hill-top, " The sea ! the sea !" has become a proverb, and their final escape is accomplished out of the jaws of death into the bosom of that friendly sea which girds their islanded home ; then as a matter of fact, and perhaps in the mind of the narrator, the too cruel reversal of good fortune. Persians and savage tribes, and the inclemencies of Armenian snows, or the intricacies of Kurdistan defiles, are nothing which stout hearts cannot without too great strain surmount ; but at the instant at which the ingenuous grumbler, with Homer on his lips, sighs to give up all this forced marching and

---

[1] *Ep. ad Qu. Fratr.* 1. 1. viii. 23.

[2] Xenophon clearly was working upon legendary accounts ; *vide* Duncker, Breitenbach, etc.

picket duty, preferring to tumble into a hammock and sail away home like Odysseus,[1] the real troubles of the heroic little band are about to commence—troubles chiefly of their own countrymen. Cheirisophus goes to fetch ships from his friend the Spartan admiral, but his absence is interminable; when after various vicissitudes they eventually reach Europe, they are regarded, as what indeed they partly are, a wolfish rabble, barely to be trusted if not tearing barbaric sheep or turning their teeth against one another. The Spartan governor-general in Byzantium by a *ruse* succeeds in kidnapping and knocking down to the hammer as slaves about 600 of the band. The semi-barbarian Thracian Seuthes is no better than the civilised Greek. Dissension too has broken up their ranks, and it requires all the piety of Xenophon to sustain him until the finger of Zeus Meilichios is plainly visible at Pergamus,[2] when "the Lacedæmonians, the captains and the rest of the generals, and the soldiers generally, united to give him the pick of horses and cattle and other spoil, so that now he could do a friend a good turn; and meanwhile Thimbron arrived, and he received the Cyreians, whom he incorporated with the rest of his Hellenic forces, and proceeded to prosecute a war against Tissaphernes and Pharnabazus."

In the *Hellenica* there is a similar twofold climax corresponding to the well-known division of the work: the first attained in the reconciliation of the Demos and the Eleusinian supporters of the Thirty is the finale of the work of Thucydides.[3] The second and larger volume has been described as *The Epic of Agesilaus*, who is certainly to some extent the protagonist; but the pivot of the piece, the peripety, is the turn of the tide of Laconian prosperity, consequent, in the eyes of Xenophon, upon the lawless seizure of the Theban citadel by the Spartan general Phaebidas. "I do not think it would be necessary to ransack either Hellenic or foreign history in proof of the proposition that the divine powers are extreme to mark what is

---

[1] *Odyssey*, xiii. : "Then they alighted from the benched ship upon the land, and first they lifted Odysseus from out the hollow ship, all as he was in the sheet of linen and the bright rug, and laid him yet heavy with slumber on the land."—Butcher and Lang.

[2] *Anab.* vii. 8.　　　　　　　　[3] *Hellen.* ii. 4. 43.

done amiss, winking not either at impiety or the commission of unhallowed acts; but at present it is my duty to confine myself to the facts before me."[1] When the end draws nigh—not too soon indeed, but with a certain dimly realised dramatic effect, owing to the long-sustained silence—in praise and blame alike, the fire of the old soldier burns; and the historian's tongue is loosed in a panegyric of the strategy of Epaminondas, and the pall descends upon the great Theban, but upon Sparta herself the penumbra of total eclipse. Nor is there wanting a touch of pathos in the half-baffled realisation of the beginning of the end. As to Guicciardini, reviewing the posture of affairs after the peace of Cambray,[2] things seem pretty much unaltered; so to Xenophon after Mantinea the old balance is renewed, or rather, in the language of the Greek, "Where it was expected that one or other of these fell combatants would rule an empire, there set in once more confusion worse confounded (not an ἀρχή, but worse anarchy)." In the one case really the knell of Venice was sounded; in the other the prestige of humbled Sparta fled with the triumphant spirit of her mighty rival. The other questions connected with the *Hellenica* do not fall within the scope of this Essay, nor is any attempt to harmonise the antique acceptance and the modern mistrust of the historian here offered. Only it is well to bear in mind that the title of a δίκαιος συγγραφεύς—a just historian [3]—has been accorded to Xenophon; and, apart from the omissions extraordinary to a modern reader, it is plain that the quality of transparency which belongs to all his writings holds here even in the moral import of the word; so that his demerits, if demerits they be, amount to nothing worse than a species of colour-blindness. We know and he does not attempt to conceal, the point of view from which he writes; moreover, as a philosopher, he has a right to his philosophy, however defective it may render him as a philosophic historian, and he makes no secret of his sympathy with the ideal of Sparta and Lycurgus (his Laconism), or for the "aristocratic" sections of society. But the quality which, like the vigour and the humour and the

[1] *Hellen.* v. 4. [2] Symonds, *Age of Despots*, iv. p. 232.
[3] Lucian, *vide supra*, p. 327.

healthy, joyous youthfulness of the *Anabasis,* permeates this
sadder and more sober production, is a certain vividness
and brightness of delineation suited to the clear skies of
Hellas and Asia Minor, and the sparkling waves of the Aegean
and the Straits. What M. Renan has said of the Acts of the
Apostles may be almost verbatim applied to this work:—
" Une brise matinale, une odeur de mer, si j'ose le dire, in-
spirant quelque chose d'allègre et de fort, pénètre tout le livre et
en fait un excellent compagnon de voyage ; le bréviaire exquis
de celui qui poursuit des traces antiques sur les mers du midi." [1]
The *Hellenica* is not a dull book, and the period with which it
is concerned—however sad in part and disheartening—is never
tedious. With it in our hands we bound over the glancing
waves in rhythmical obedience to our beloved Keleustes, [2] or scale
the heights of besieged citadels, or for the moment are friends
with the living personalities of a tumultuous time. We have
been Spartans and tramped along by forced marches in the
night, after the destruction of a whole army corps, on its road
to Amyclae : [3] thus we proudly sneaked, for fear, not so much of
the jeers of lukewarm friends or half foes, as of ourselves and
the evil that might come of it. We have crossed the heights at
Creusis between Attica and Boeotia, and our shields have been
snatched by a violent tornado from us and whirled into the
abyss. [4] We have watched the deadlock at Coroneia, and seen the
slain with their shields battered, their swords snapt off at the
hilt, their daggers still clutched between their fingers, etc. ; [5] and
all these things, page after page, has Xenophon by his photo-
graphic art and his Euripidean or Zeuxis-like skill, [6] wrought for
us ; so that the feeling left on our minds is one of exhilaration
and content. Of course, if we had had the making of those
days and persons, we should have provided that the hero friend
of Xenophon should be Epaminondas not Agesilaus ; but the
gods, it seems, willed it otherwise, and so this matter has
issued thus.

---

[1] Renan, *St. Paul,* pp. 12, 13.　　　　[2] Cf. *Oecon.* xxi. 3. 4.
[3] *Hellen.* iv. 5.　　　[4] *Ibid.* v. 4. 17.　　　[5] *Ibid.* iv. 3. 19 ; *Agesil.* ii. 14.
[6] Three instances, at least, of what may be called Euripidean art, may be
mentioned, how (*Anab.* ii. 5. 33) after the generals were seized and the
army waited in expectation, suddenly sight was caught of a man galloping

Before we part with our author, let us briefly summarise certain things in which, ceasing to be merely representative of his days, he seems to utter things to come. His pregnancy in a variety of departments is remarkable, and to be traced probably to the underlying subjectivity of his disposition, which takes him as it were out of the ordinary objective setting of his fellows. Hence his colonisation schemes and higher speculations on the conquest of the east already mentioned,—the prophecy here pointing through Agesilaus and the rest to the times of Alexander,—but as yet there are many years to run, and Xenophon will not live to see that day. Again, in his quasi-philosophical and political pamphlets he may be said to be pointing through Isocrates and his school to Aristotle. In his high standard of moral self-culture, in the καρτερία of his women, he is anticipative of stoicism. In just that faint touch of orientalism, the unnameable somewhat reminding us of Mithra worship in the east; possibly also in his admiration of the same Cyrus who restored the Jews, he is anticipative of the interblending of two worlds—of Semitic monotheism and Greek science. In his purity and mistrust of pleasures which seduce the soul, and in his religiousness generally, he makes us realise how the earth prepared herself for the seed of Pauline Christianity; nay, in a certain sense we seem to be aware of something which we held to be peculiar to Protestantism. Is this a Hellenic Havelock? But not least of all this pregnancy belongs to his style, the antithesis and grace of which have a ring of Italian or Elizabethan " euphuism."[1] The love-story of Panthea, and the whole court and courtesy

---

wildly—the Arcadian Nicarchus who had escaped with a wound in the belly —he rode into camp holding his entrails in—to tell the news ; or, again, how (*Cyr.* vi. 4. 9) Panthea bade sad but stout-hearted farewell to her husband whom she was not to see alive again, and ran to give a last kiss unperceived to the chariot which held him. Abradatas turned and looked upon her and said, " Be strong and of a good courage, Panthea, and hie thee home." And how (*Cyr.* vii. 3. 9) the same lady tenderly kissed and replaced the poor dismembered right hand of her dead lord, which Cyrus, unwitting of what was done, had grasped in friendly sorrow. With Cyrus we also weep for some time in sorrow.

[1] The ancients fully appreciated the γοητεία or witchery of his style ; a quality not to be discerned in translations offered only as reminiscences of the writer's thought.

of the prince, are as near the romance of chivalry as aught
Hellenic can be ; while last of all, in the mere lucidity and
" plainness " of his Attic, not excluding foreign and poetic words,
he is the author of what must always from the first have been,
and in modern Hellas is probably destined in a still higher
degree to become, the model of expression, a transcendental
κοινὴ διάλεκτος.

Is the fame of Xenophon decreasing ?   That is scarcely cred-
ible.   At various periods he has stood high in the appreciation
of mankind, and for various reasons ; nor is it likely that any
partial obscuration of his brightness will last long.   The modern
historic sense will assuredly remove the scales from our eyes.
Nor though it has chanced to Xenophon, because he wrote
history, to be weighed in the balances against Thucydides, and
condemned ; though it has also befallen him, on the ground of
his delineation of Socrates, to be compared with Plato and
voted no philosopher ; though it has been his paradoxical fate
to have stood somewhat in his own light, and, as the author of
the *Anabasis*, partly to have effaced his own reputation as the
author of less appreciated works,—none of these mishaps are
real misfortunes.   The " chef-d'œuvre," Victor Hugo has said,
" is on a par with the chef-d'œuvre," or, as a more ancient
prophet words it, " One star differeth from another star in glory."
The glory of philosophic history is one ; the glory of Platonic philosophy is another ; and there is a third glory of the
" fair and gentle "—" beautiful and brave " Hellenic culture,
which is Xenophon.   If pallid, the light of this genius has a
lustre of its own, once discerned, not soon to be lost sight of,—
a potency of tender, transparent brightness, which invites the
gaze, undimmed by the fiercer rays, or more mystic brilliancy,
of larger luminaries blazing in envious proximity.   But to the
scientific student the spectrum yielded by this planet is of even
weightier importance.

H. G. D.

POLYBIUS.

No ancient writer of equal interest and importance finds fewer readers than Polybius. It is probable that for a hundred Englishmen familiar with Herodotus and Thucydides not more than three or four would be found who had made the acquaintance of the third great Greek historian. The struggle between Rome and Carthage for the foremost place in the world, and its result in the establishment of Roman domination over the whole circle of the Mediterranean States, present a topic unsurpassed in history; and in knowledge, in industry, and in candour, Polybius is not unworthy of his subject. His own life and fortunes are intimately involved in the great events which he records. The Roman conquest bore away the Achæan statesman, brought up at the feet of Philopœmen, to be a prisoner in Italy, a man of literary leisure, and a cosmopolitan student of politics; it sent him back to his native land as the mouthpiece of the conquering power; above all, it bound him in ties of the closest intimacy to a Roman friend. His life seems framed as of set purpose to mould the historian who was to bridge over for us the interval between the Greek and the Roman world. With all his excellences, it is not probable that Polybius will ever be widely read. He cannot command the tones to sway or impress the mind. His book remains a storehouse from which the historian and the antiquary may draw, rather than a possession to enrich the mind of the ordinary reader. The neglect which he has experienced leaves a wide choice of comparatively fresh and unknown material, and may justify the endeavour to give a short account of Polybius and his work, with some attempts at criticism, and some elements of a judgment on his qualifications as a writer of history.

Polybius was by birth a citizen of Megalopolis in Arcadia, the most vigorous and uncompromising member of the Achæan

League. He tells us with pride how Megalopolis and Stym-
phalus were the only cities in which Cleomenes of Sparta
could not find a partisan or a traitor.[1] Cleomenes, with the
aid of some Messenians, to whom Megalopolis had given hos-
pitable shelter, finally succeeded in surprising and capturing
the town (223 B.C.) The inhabitants for the most part escaped
and retired into Messenia. There a message reached them
from the Spartan king, with offers to restore their town and
territory uninjured, if only they would separate themselves
from the Achæan Federation. The refugees refused to hear
the letter to the end. "They chose," says their countryman,[2]
"to be deprived of their lands, their graves, their country, and
their goods, of everything, in a word, that men hold dearest,
rather than flinch from their good faith to their allies." The
full wrath of Cleomenes now fell on the town itself: "he laid
it waste so savagely and vindictively, that no one supposed it
could ever be made habitable again."[3]

The victory of Antigonus and the Macedonians, and the
extinction of the power of Sparta after its brief flicker of
renewed life under Cleomenes, restored the people of Megalopolis to their ruined home. What followed is known to us by
Polybius's account of a commission granted by the Achæan
League to their President, Aratus, four years later, to settle
the discords of Megalopolis; the passage may be worth quoting
as an illustration of the sort of difficulties which beset the
internal politics of a Greek State :—

"Their spirit was unbroken, but they were crippled by want
of means, public or private. And, as usual, when means are
deficient, controversies and jealousies and quarrels were rife
amongst them. The first subject of dispute was about the
fortifications; some thought they ought to contract them to a
size which would enable them to make an end of the business
of building at once, and also to man them in any sudden
emergency; and they attributed their present disaster to the
extent of the works and the difficulty of guarding the whole
line. Besides, it was held by some that the landowners ought
to contribute a third of their possessions, so as to fill up the

[1] ii. 55.   [2] ii. 61.   [3] ii. 55.

ranks by addition of fresh citizens. The other party would neither submit to make the city smaller, nor consent to contribute a third of their land. But the chief cause of contention was the constitution drawn up by Prytanis. He was one of the leaders of the Peripatetic sect, and had been nominated to legislate for them by Antigonus."[1]

The Achæan arbitrator seems to have been more successful than the Aristotelian philosopher. The difficulties were at length settled, and the city took its old place in the League. Aratus himself was a native of Sikyon. But the other great men whose policy gave dignity to the last years of Greek freedom, Philopœmen, Lycortas, and Polybius, all sprang from Megalopolis :—

"The League," after years of modest obscurity, "at last found leaders worthy to represent it, and then it quickly manifested its power by accomplishing the noblest of tasks, the concord of Peloponnesus. The credit of being the originator and pioneer of this policy must be assigned to Aratus of Sikyon; Philopœmen of Megalopolis was its champion, and consummated it in action ; and its consolidation and subsistence, up to the present time, is due to Lycortas and those who followed his lead."[2]

Philopœmen served as a young man under Antigonus in the decisive battle with Cleomenes (221 B.C.), and on the death of Aratus, in 213 B.C., succeeded to the position of foremost man of the League. Lycortas first appears in the narrative in 186 B.C.,[3] and must have been many years junior to Philopœmen. Polybius was the son of Lycortas.

Our historian was thus brought up in the midst of the circle of Greek statesmen who staked their hopes upon the Achæan League, and who, while anxious above all things to avoid collision with the overpowering strength of Rome, and willing to appear as her ally in all her contests in the East, nevertheless strove to maintain an attitude of independence, and to manage the affairs of Greece without Roman intervention. Their policy is summed up in the rebuke which Philopœmen administered to Aristænus, the leader of the Roman party :

---

[1] v. 93.   [2] ii. 40.   [3] xxiii. 1.

" Man, why are you in such haste to behold the fate that waits for Greece ?"

Polybius was selected as the youth who was to bear the urn containing the ashes of Philopœmen to the tomb (183 B.C.). The first reference in his History[1] to his own personal recollection is the record of a political conversation held by Philopœmen two years before his death, in the presence of Polybius, in which the young man silently disapproved the conclusions of the President. Polybius afterwards wrote a biography of Philopœmen, which has not been preserved. In his History, while freely criticising some of Philopœmen's actions, he always shows a loyal respect and affection for the memory of his leader.

We next find Polybius, three years later (180 B.C.), selected as one of the ambassadors who were to renew the alliance of the Achæans with Ptolemy Epiphanes, king of Egypt. He tells us[2] that at this time he was too young to be legally qualified for the post, but was nevertheless chosen on account of the friendly relations existing between his father, Lycortas, and the Egyptian Court. The death of Ptolemy rendered this mission abortive.

We now pass on to the year 169 B.C. The great struggle between Perseus and the Romans was at its height. Lycortas, Polybius, and Archon had succeeded Philopœmen as leaders of the moderate party among the Achæans, which had to steer a difficult and dangerous course between the servile tools of Rome on the one hand, and the reckless partisans of Macedon on the other. Their attitude of neutrality had caused offence at Rome, and the Roman commissioners sent by Mancinus, the consul of the previous year, are said to have intended to denounce them all as secret supporters of Macedon, but to have been deterred by the utter lack of evidence against them.[3]

Polybius, convinced that action was necessary, now separated from the policy of his father, who still counselled neutrality, and declared, along with Archon, for an alliance with Rome. Archon was thereupon elected President for the year, with Polybius for Master of the Horse.[4]

---

[1] xxiii. 10 *a.*   [2] xxv. 7.

[3] xxviii. 3.   [4] xxviii. 6.

It was now formally resolved to raise a general levy of the Achæan forces, to assist the Romans against Macedon; and while his chief was collecting the troops, Polybius was despatched into Thessaly to inform the consul, Marcius Philippus, of their approach. Marcius, while thanking the Achæans, declined the proffered assistance. The levy was countermanded, but Polybius remained in the Roman camp, and took part in the campaign. Afterwards, by direction of the consul, he returned home to relieve the Achæans from the burden of a requisition of 5000 troops which had been made on them by a subordinate Roman officer who had the command in Epirus.[1]

It was probably about this time that Polybius introduced a system of telegraphy for use in war. Preconcerted fire-signals had long been used. We hear of "hostile" and "friendly" signals, *i.e.* "danger," and "all's well;"[2] and this principle had been elaborated by ingenious contrivances which enabled a longer or shorter display of the light to indicate this or that message;[3] but its use was necessarily limited to the conveyance of information that was expected, and for which the signals could be arranged beforehand. The new system was to telegraph single letters instead of sentences. The idea was due, says Polybius,[4] to Cleoxenus and Democleitus; but he himself was the first to work it out in practice. The alphabet was written out on five tablets, each containing five letters. The signal-station consisted of two beacon-towers. The number of lamps displayed on the left-hand beacon showed the tablet to be referred to; that on the right showed the number of the letter signalled in its own tablet. Thus, one lamp to the left and three to the right indicates the third letter in the first tablet, γ. Two lamps displayed to the left and one to the right means the first letter on the second tablet, ζ. In this way letter after letter might be telegraphed, until a complete message was conveyed.

Next year we find Polybius nominated as lieutenant to his

---

[1] xxviii. 11.   [2] xii. 12 a.

[3] In the system described in x. 44, this was managed by a sort of water-clock set running at each station so long as the light was displayed.

[4] x. 45-47.

father, who was to lead a small Achæan contingent to Egypt at the request of the sons of the late king, to aid in protecting them against the Syrians. It may seem strange that those who aspired to the position of the leading statesmen of Peloponnesus should have been content to become the captains of a body of twelve hundred men who were to serve as mercenaries in a foreign country. But such an adventure was quite in character with the habits of the Greek statesmen of the day. Even Philopœmen more than once employed an interval of leisure from Peloponnesian politics, by serving as a soldier of fortune in the constant wars between the petty townships of Crete. In the present case, Lycortas and his son doubtless felt that their game was played out in Greece. The fate of the Macedonian monarchy could no longer be doubtful to such keen observers; and with the complete victory of Rome would come the domination in Greece of the party which had thrown away all regard for right and patriotism, and resolved to know no rule of conduct except the rule of subserviency to every whim of a Roman commissioner. Thus the prospect of an honourable exile, with some chance of glory and booty, was not unacceptable to the Achæan chiefs. Their rival Callicrates urged that there was no occasion for an armed contingent, and that it would be enough to send an embassy to mediate between the belligerents. The matter was on the point of being decided in favour of Lycortas, when a letter was brought into the assembly from Marcius Philippus, requesting that the Achæans would support a mission of mediation which the Romans were sending to Egypt. The request was taken as a command, and the proposal for an armed expedition was withdrawn.[1]

These instances of compliance did not serve to avert the impending danger. Perseus was defeated and made prisoner, and ten commissioners were sent by the Senate to arrange, in concert with the victorious general, Æmilius Paullus, the affairs of the peninsula (167-165 B.C.). This was the opportunity of Callicrates and the so-called " Roman party." They denounced all their opponents as enemies of Rome, and the commissioners were only too ready to lend an ear to their calumnies. Æmilius Paullus himself disapproved the action

---

[1] xxix. 8-10.

of the commission.[1] The papers of Perseus were ransacked in vain for proofs of complicity. But the judges had made up their minds beforehand. We are not informed of the fate of Lycortas; but Polybius was one of a thousand of the leading men of the Achæans who were deported to Italy, nominally to await a trial before the Senate on the charges brought against them. No trial ever took place: the suspected persons were detained year after year in Italy, and the Senate put aside every petition either for the investigation of their guilt or for leave to return to their country. In Greece the popular indignation against the sycophants who had procured their ruin was intense. The children as they came from school used the privilege of infancy to shout " traitor " after them in the street. If one of them gained a prize in the public games, the announcement of his name was greeted with storms of hissing. If one of them used the public baths, no one else would enter until the bath-man had let out all the water and put in fresh; " for every one thought he would be polluted by washing in the water which Callicrates or Andronidas had touched."[2]

At length, after seventeen years, when death had thinned the ranks of the exiles, and it became evident that, as Cato said, " the only question that remained was whether the under-takers of Italy or of Greece were to have the burying of them," the remnant, to the number of three hundred, were released. Meanwhile their native land, stripped of its best citizens, had been torn by factions. Servility had been followed by reaction. In their despair men plunged into wild schemes of resistance to Rome, and of savage vengeance on their domestic enemies. Rome was in no temper to pardon; her sentences were harsh and humiliating; the party of revolt got the upper hand, and a hopeless war followed (146 B.C.).

" Fortune," Polybius says,[3] " strove to save Greece; but the folly of the rulers trampled all her gifts underfoot. At last, as the only means of salvation, she granted a complete and speedy defeat, before the Romans had time to be exasperated by resistance, or the revolutionists to be encouraged to fresh excesses by a momentary triumph."

His exile in Italy was the turning-point of the life of

---

[1] xxx. 10.   [2] xxx. 20.   [3] xl. 5 (abridged).

Polybius. It removed him from political conflicts; it gave him at once leisure for his great work, and rare opportunities for observing events and collecting information. He became the friend of the most eminent Romans of the day. We find him accompanying Scipio in Africa, and Mummius in Greece. His influence at Rome is illustrated by the fact that he had interest enough to procure for the Locrians of Italy a much-coveted exemption from service in the Spanish and Dalmatian wars.[1]

Apart from his labours as a historian, the interest of Polybius's life henceforth centres round two points: first, his position as mediator between his countrymen and the conquerors; and secondly, the romantic friendship which united him to the younger Scipio.

Polybius returned to Greece to see the political ideal of his youth rudely shattered. Corinth, the capital of the Achæans, was destroyed under his eyes, and he records how he saw the choicest pictures of Greece lying on the ground, and the Roman soldiers using them as boards to play dice on.[2] Polybius had the satisfaction of pleading with success for the preservation of the statues of Aratus and Philopœmen, which some of the more brutal of the Romans wished to destroy.[3] But the Achæan League, their true monument, was swept away beyond all hope of restitution. In the bitterness of his heart Polybius exclaims that it would be better to be even as Carthage:—

"Though the fate of Carthage might seem to be the greatest of all possible calamities, yet one may well regard that which then befel Greece as not less, or even in some respects greater. For the former, their end is their plea with posterity,[4] but the latter have left not so much as a plausible excuse for those who would fain plead their cause. The Carthaginians, at the moment of their fall, perished from off the face of the earth, and were thenceforth insensible of their misfortunes: but the Greeks look on at their own calamities, and hand down their losses as an inheritance to their children's children; so that just as we count those who live on under torture more wretched

---

[1] xii. 5.   [2] xl. 7.   [3] xl. 8.

[4] Τόπον ἔσχατον ἀπολογίας γε πρὸς τοὺς ἐπιγιγνομένους περὶ σφῶν ἀπέλιπον. Compare Shakespeare's "If not, the end of life cancels all bonds."

than those who expire under their torments, so we should esteem the fate of the Greeks yet more pitiable than that which befel the Carthaginians."[1]

Worse than all, Polybius felt that his countrymen had brought their fate on themselves, and that it was his duty as a historian to expose their faults, and to give his verdict against them. There is something pathetic in the contrast between his feelings as a Greek and the sternness of his historical judgment :—

"Some perhaps will blame me and think that I write in a hostile spirit, I who ought of all men to palliate the errors of the Greeks. But I hold that men of sense will never esteem him a true friend who shrinks through fear from downright speaking, nor him a good citizen who deserts the truth because of any offence it may give at the moment. It is unpardonable for the historian to set anything whatever above the truth. A record handed down to posterity extends to more persons and to a further time than words uttered for a present purpose; and bearing this in mind, the writer ought to make truth his first object, and his hearers to welcome this disposition. At the time of these disasters it was my part, as a Greek for the Greeks, to give them my aid in all ways, defending them, palliating their faults, deprecating the anger of the conquerors ; and this I did then and there with all sincerity. But I here record for posterity the memory of the events, untinged with any animosity, not seeking to please for the moment the ears of my readers, but to edify their minds and save them from committing the same faults again. And so I leave this subject." [2]

It is characteristic of Polybius that he threw himself with all his might into the task of making the best of the disastrous circumstances, and of alleviating as far as possible the subjection of his countrymen. He had thoroughly won the confidence of the Romans, and was now selected by them as the representative of the Imperial power in Greece during the period of transition. Polybius's own opinions were democratic, and his party had always rested on popular support; but now he was

---

[1] xxxviii. 1 a.   [2] xxxviii. 1 d.

constrained to arrange the affairs of each state in accordance with the oligarchical models which their Roman masters preferred. We subjoin his own account of this painful but necessary and honourable task:—

" The ten commissioners having completed these arrangements sailed for Italy early in the spring, leaving behind in view of all Greece an honourable specimen of Roman policy. At their departure they instructed Polybius to make a progress through the various states, and to clear up any points about which people were in uncertainty, until they should get accustomed to the constitution and the laws. And this charge he fulfilled in process of time, so that men acquiesced in the constitution which had been given them, and no obscurity remained about any point of law, public or private." [1]

Polybius regarded this labour as the most useful and important of his life. His countrymen recognised his services with gratitude, and set up his statue where he would be best pleased to have it, side by side with those of Aratus and Philopœmen.[2]

We turn with relief from the melancholy spectacle of the enslavement of Greece to the story of the friendship of Polybius and Scipio Æmilianus.

Scipio was by birth the son of Æmilius Paullus, but was adopted when a child by the son of Scipio Africanus the elder, the conqueror of Hannibal. The early death of his adoptive father left young Scipio the possessor of a great fortune, and the inheritor of the first name in Rome. He was hardly more than a boy when he accompanied Paullus in the war against Perseus. After the victory his father gave him the free run of the royal forests of Macedon. These had been jealously preserved for years ; the sport they afforded was the finest then to be found in the world, and young Scipio was happy as a king [3] in his magnificent playground. When he returned to Italy he shunned the morning calls and the practice in the law-courts, which occupied the time of other young nobles. They strove, says Polybius, to keep themselves before the eye of the world by

---

[1] xl. 10.   [2] xl. 8.
[3] νομίσας οἷον εἰ βασιλεύειν.

being constantly in the Forum. Scipio found in his friend[1]
Polybius a passionate lover of sport, and the two spent their
days together in the chase. Scipio's daring exploits in the
hunting-field passed from mouth to mouth. " Before long he
outstripped all his contemporaries, and gained an unprecedented
reputation, though the way he took to acquire it ran counter to
all the habits and customs of the Romans." [2]

The beginning of their intimacy must be told in Polybius's
words.[3]

" As the process of our story and the period of events bring
us to this family, I wish now to fulfil, for the benefit of the curious,
the promise I held out in the last book. I undertook to relate
why and how the reputation of Scipio in Rome rose to such a
height and burst forth into such unexpected lustre ; and further,
how the affection and the intimacy between him and Polybius
became so strong, that not only did the fame of it reach throughout Italy and Greece, but even distant nations heard the story of
their friendship and association. I have already stated that
their first relations arose out of reading books together and
literary conversation. As their intimacy advanced, Fabius and
Scipio, the sons of Paullus, begged of the prætor to have Polybius remain at Rome, when the other Achæans who were under
detention were interned in the country towns of Italy. After
this they were constantly in one another's society. One day
the three walked together out of the house of Fabius, and Fabius
took the turn towards the Forum, while Polybius and Scipio
went in the other direction. As they walked, Scipio, blushing
scarlet, and in subdued and gentle tones spoke thus :—' How is
it, Polybius, we have been dining, two brothers together, and
yet you always talk to Fabius, and put your questions and
address your remarks to him and set me aside ? It is clear that
you share the opinion which I hear my fellow-citizens have of
me : they think me tame and dull, unlike a Roman in character
and action because I do not choose to speak in the courts ; and
they say that I am not the stuff for the head of such a house as
I am sprung from ; and this grieves me to the heart.' Polybius

---

[1] προσλαβὼν τὸν τοῦ Πολυβίου πρὸς τοῦτο τὸ μέρος ἐνθουσιασμόν.
[2] xxxii. 15,   [3] xxxii. 9.

was astounded to hear the lad (for he was not more than eighteen years old at the time) begin the conversation in this strain, and he replied, 'For heaven's sake, Scipio, do not speak so, or let such notions enter your head. I am not despising you or set-ting you aside; far from it, but as your brother is the elder, when we are in company I begin with him, and refer my remarks and plans to his decision, and lean on his judgment, assuming that you share his views. But you astonish me when you say that you are too gentle for the son of such a house; this reserve is the best evidence of force of character. For my part I would gladly devote myself as your fellow-worker to make you in speech and action worthy of your ancestors. For in the studies, into which you now throw your interests and your efforts, neither you nor your brother will have any lack of ready helpers; for I see that a throng of such persons is pouring over from Greece. But in the matters which now distress you, as you say, I think you will not find any fitter companion and fellow-worker than myself.' Before Polybius had done speak-ing, Scipio seized his hand with both his own, and pressing it fervently, exclaimed—' Would that I might see the day when you will make me your first interest and be my comrade. From that day forth I shall feel that I am not unworthy of my house and my ancestors.' Polybius was charmed with the fervour and open-heartedness of the lad, but was not without misgiving as he thought of the greatness of his house and the wealth and station of its members. But from the time of this compact young Scipio would never part from Polybius, and preferred his society to everything else. And as time went on, and the friends found each other faithful through the course of an un-broken intimacy, they conceived for one another an affection and devotion as of kindred or brethren."

Apart from its interest as an account of this notable friend-ship, the passage is instructive as showing that Scipio, like most great orators, was a man of nervous and sensitive tempera-ment. In later years, when he had overcome his reserve and shyness, he was a master of impassioned outbursts of invective. When the Roman mob, swollen with a motley throng of en-franchised slaves, tried to shout him down whilst speaking, he exclaimed, "Silence, you to whom Italy is not mother but step-mother ; " and as the clamour rose again, " Do you think I will fear those let loose, whom I brought in chains to the slave-market ?"

Another anecdote of Polybius's life in Rome shows the historian in a somewhat unexpected light, as a man with a love for an adventure, and ready to run a considerable risk from a good-natured wish to help an acquaintance in difficulty. Demetrius, a grandson of Antiochus the Great, had been shamefully treated by the Roman senate. He had been sent to Rome when a child, as a hostage on behalf of his father, Seleucus, who was then king of Syria. Seleucus died, and was succeeded by his brother, Antiochus Epiphanes. Demetrius now claimed release ; for he was no sort of hostage for the behaviour of his uncle, who would have been glad enough to see him out of the way. The Senate refused his petition. In process of time Antiochus died, and Demetrius, as the eldest member of the family, was the lawful heir to the throne. The Senate, however, preferred to acknowledge the young son of Antiochus, and sent commissioners, nominally to act as guardians to the infant prince. These commissioners, acting on instructions from Rome, proceeded to burn the ships of their ward, to hamstring his elephants, and to weaken the kingdom by every means in their power. The ministers whom they set up were notorious for misgovernment, and were hated by the people ; and there was no doubt that if Demetrius could once set foot in Syria he would be received with acclamation. The pretender was jealously detained in Italy, where he consoled himself with wine and hunting. This last amusement brought him into contact with Polybius : he confided his troubles to him, and Polybius resolved to plan his escape. He persuaded a Greek friend, who was at Rome on a mission from Ptolemy, to charter a vessel as if for his own return to Egypt. At the last moment the Alexandrine envoy sent word to the captain of the vessel that business detained him in Rome, and that he would send in his stead some friends with important letters for home. Demetrius, to avoid suspicion, sent out his servants with dogs and nets, instructing them to meet him at Circeii for a hunting party. He then went to dinner at the house of a friend. Polybius was at the time confined to his bed by illness, and was uneasy for fear that Demetrius should spoil everything by getting drunk at his dinner-party. He therefore sent one of his slaves with a sealed packet which was to be silently placed in Demetrius's hand at the dinner-table. The letter when opened contained no signature, but only a string of wise sayings extracted from the poets about the virtues of sobriety, resolution, and prompt action. Demetrius took the hint and retired from table. He left Rome, as if to join the hunters at Circeii, and hurried on board the ship which was moored at Ostia. The captain had not the least suspicion who was his passenger, and set sail immediately. It was not till the fourth day that Demetrius's retinue, uneasy at his breaking his appointment at Circeii, returned to Rome and gave the alarm ; and by the time the matter came to the ears of the government, Demetrius was beyond the Straits of Messina. He recovered his kingdom without much difficulty ; but the maxims on sobriety, which Polybius had been so careful to copy out for him, failed to impress him permanently, and hard drinking soon put an end to his life. The plans of his Greek friends were so well laid, that no suspicion seems to have been aroused as to their part in the escape, till Polybius himself told the story years after in the course of his narrative.[1]

The great business of Polybius's life was the collection of materials for his History. He had the advantage of living at the capital, in the very centre of political events, yet with the leisure and impartiality of a spectator. He was the most unwearied and conscientious collector of information. He knew that his work would be read by Roman critics, and he specially appeals to them to confirm the accuracy of his account of Roman institutions. He has the true instinct of a great historian in dealing with original documents. He does not load his pages with references to petty inscriptions, and he laughs good-humouredly at Timæus,[2] a sort of Dryasdust, who would pounce with delight on an error of three months in the synchronism of Athenian archons and Argive priestesses, and " who pried into what was written on the columns in the back premises of temples and the compacts of hospitality on the

---

door-posts." But where inscriptions will throw light on any questions that lie along the main lines of the history, he spares no trouble to avail himself of them. Finding contradictory accounts of the various treaties between Rome and Carthage, he studied and translated the originals, some of them written in language so archaic as to be almost unintelligible to the Romans of his day.[1] If he gives the numbers of Hannibal's army at different dates, it is always on the authority of an inscription set up by Hannibal himself at the Lacinian promontory before he left Italy.[2] For events before his time, or out of the reach of his personal knowledge, Polybius hunted up the evidence of eye-witnesses. He still found men alive who remembered the passage of Hannibal over the Alps.[3] He checked the Roman accounts of the Punic Wars by cross-questioning Carthaginians, and he refers especially to the information given him by Massinissa, the veteran king of Numidia, who had fought under the first Scipio, and who lived to see the beginning of the Third Punic War.[4] In his account of the obscure negotiations of Perseus and Eumenes (a matter in regard to which modern historians have been inclined to throw doubt on the veracity of Polybius), we find that he gathered his information from the Macedonian courtiers who were privy to the transaction.[5]

Polybius travelled far and wide to see with his own eyes the scenes of the events he describes. He points out most fairly the disadvantages under which previous writers had lain in their geographical descriptions. Eye-witnesses of distant countries were rare; and even these were hampered by the difficulties of language and the dangers of savage lands, and had every temptation to eke out their scanty information by the invention of mere travellers' stories. So far, then, from blaming his predecessors for their mistakes, he would rather give them all credit for any advance in knowledge which they effected.

"But in our day Asia, by the conquests of Alexander, and the rest of the world, by the supremacy of the Romans, have become almost everywhere accessible by sea and by land; and the same events, by withdrawing from men of energy all objects

---

[1] iii. 22 *seq.*   [2] iii. 33.   [3] iii. 48.
[4] ix. 25.   [5] xxix. 1 e.

of ambition in war and politics, have given occasion to great interest and curiosity about those other subjects; and thus it is incumbent on us to acquire better and more accurate knowledge of what was before obscure. This it shall be my endeavour to set forth in its place, and this was my chief incentive to undergo the dangers and hardships of journeys in Libya, Spain, and Gaul, and on the sea that forms the further boundary of these countries." [1]

He is thus able to speak from personal measurements of the plan of the city of Carthagena; [2] and he followed the footsteps of Hannibal across the Alps that he might be the better qualified to write the history of his passage. [3] Unfortunately, Polybius's power of graphic delineation of localities is not equal to his industry, and his account of Hannibal's route falls far short of the clear and exact description which he is careful to promise his readers.

Polybius makes use of his notes of travel to enrich his book with much curious information about the countries through which he passed. The fertility of Spain, for instance, is illustrated by elaborate statistics of the price of commodities, evidently gained from personal experience. [4] The natural history of the island of Corsica gives him an opportunity of correcting his rival Timæus, on whose blunders he always comments with satisfaction.

"His assertions about the island of Corsica are on a level with his random talk about Libya. He states, in his account of Corsica, in the second book, that it contains numbers of wild goats, sheep, and oxen; and likewise deer, hares, wolves, and other game; and that the inhabitants employ themselves in hunting these, and make the chase the business of their lives. Now, in that island, far from there being wild goats or oxen, there is not so much as a hare, a wolf, or a stag, nor any other animals of the sort, excepting only foxes, rabbits, and wild sheep. The rabbit at a distance looks like a small hare; but when you come to handle it, it is quite distinct both in form and in the taste of its flesh, and it generally lives under ground. The fact is, that the animals of the country have the

---

[1] iii. 59.   [2] x. 11.   [3] iii. 48.   [4] xxxiv. 8.

appearance of being wild, for the following reason. The herdsmen are not able to follow their beasts about on the pastures, owing to the wooded, steep, and rocky nature of the ground. But when they wish to collect them, they post themselves at convenient stations, and sound a call with the trumpet to their animals, who come running together without fail, each to its own trumpet-call. The consequence is, that when persons coasting along the island see goats and oxen pasturing untended, and wish to catch them, the animals will not suffer the strangers to approach them, but run away ; and when the herdsman sees them making off, he blows his trumpet, and immediately they hurry headlong in a drove, congregating towards the call. This gives them the appearance of wildness ; and thus Timæus is led into his random statement by careless and insufficient inquiry. As for their obedience to the trumpet, there is nothing to wonder at in that ; for in Italy, likewise, the owners adopt the same plan in pasturing swine. The swineherds do not follow at the heels of their beasts, as among the Greeks, but walk in front, blowing the horn at intervals, and the beasts follow behind, and run together towards the note ; and the familiarity which each shows with his proper horn is so remarkable, that those who hear of it for the first time are astonished and inclined to be sceptical."[1]

Another extract from Polybius's travelling note-book gives us a glimpse of the cost of board and lodging in Cisalpine Gaul, a land which must have been in those days a very Paradise for an economically-minded tourist.

" As to the details of the produce of wine, and of the plenty of the means of subsistence, we may best form a notion of them from the following fact. When persons travelling through the country put up at an inn, they do not bargain with the landlord as to the price of each article, but ask how much he charges to receive a guest ; and the innkeeper as a general rule admits his lodgers, undertaking to provide them with all they want, at the rate of half an as (that is a quarter of an obol) for each day ; and this charge is rarely exceeded."[2]

The *as*, when Polybius wrote, was equal in value to the

---

[1] xii. 3. [2] ii. 15.

sixteenth part of the denarius, and a denarius contains silver to the amount of about eightpence-halfpenny: it follows that a man could live *en pension* in the valley of the Po for a fraction over one farthing per diem. Two hundred years later, wine was still so cheap in this district, that the jest ran that pure water was a more costly liquor to drink; and Martial could complain that he was cheated by the tavern-keeper, who, when he called for wine and water, served him the wine neat.[1]

The plan of Polybius's History was altered and extended during the course of its composition. His original scheme is explained in the first book, and recapitulated at the beginning of the third. After two preliminary books—in which are narrated the events of the First Punic War, the revolt of the Carthaginian mercenaries, the war between Rome and the Cisalpine Gauls, and the affairs of Greece in the age of Cleomenes and Aratus, all as preliminary to the main subject—the body of the work commences with the third book, and is to comprise the period of fifty-three years, from the commencement of the Second Punic War down to the destruction of the kingdom of Macedon after the war with Perseus. Within it fall the wars with Philip of Macedon and with Antiochus, king of Syria. It is the history of the steps by which Rome attained the position of the dominant power in the world.

" This is the conclusion of our fifty-three years' period, and within this the growth and advancement of the Roman domination was accomplished; and further, it seemed agreed and forced on the conviction of all men, that all that remains to the world is to submit to the Romans, and to perform whatever they shall enjoin."[2]

But as early as the time when Polybius published his third book he had come to feel that this was insufficient. He must also show how the Romans used their supremacy, what view they took of their rights and duties as the rulers of the world, what was the political and social condition of the subjects, and what was their state of feeling towards their masters.

---

[1] Book iii. Ep. 56 and 57.

[2] iii. 4. The fifty-three years are counted (inclusively) from 219 B.C., the year of Hannibal's attack on Saguntum, to 167 B.C., the year of the settlement of Macdonia after Paullus's victory.

" For it is obvious that it is by considering these points that we must instruct our contemporaries whether the supremacy of the Romans is a thing to be abhorred or to be accepted, and form the judgment of future generations whether they are to praise and imitate the Romans, or to condemn them."[1]

He will therefore make a fresh start, and relate the events which succeeded the establishment of the Roman dominion, down to the time when fresh wars led to the revelation of the full results of the new system in the overthrow of Carthage and of Greece. This adds another period of twenty-one years (167-146 B.C.) to the subject-matter of his History. He is urged, he says, " partly by the greatness of the events, partly by the astounding nature of their consequences, but most of all because he was himself so largely not only a spectator but an actor in them."[2]

With reference to this last point it may be noticed that Polybius adopted the very strictest views as to the limits of historical credibility. In the two preliminary books he does not claim to be an original historian, but founds on the works of his predecessors, Aratus, Philinus, and Fabius. But for the main body of his work he chooses a period within the reach of his own personal inquiries.

" The period which follows this date (219 B.C.), and forms the subject of our History, corresponds partly with our own days and partly with those of our fathers; and from this it results that some of the events happened before our eyes, and of the rest we heard from those who had seen. For to stretch into earlier times so as to write down a report of a report appeared to us to give no security either for conclusions or assertions."[3]

The traces of a change in the point of view of the writer are left here and there on his work. Take, for instance, the following account of the Achæan League in the second book.[4]

" Concerning the Achæan nation and concerning the house of Macedon, it will not be out of the way to indulge in a short retrospect, seeing that our generation has witnessed the complete annihilation of the one and the marvellous growth and unity of the other. Many have attempted in past times to

---

[1] iii. 4.   [2] iii. 4.   [3] iv. 2.   [4] ii. 37.

lead the Peloponnesians to an appreciation of their common interests, and none have succeeded, because they were anxious rather for their own supremacy than for a liberty in which all should share. But in our time this undertaking has attained such a success and consummation, that not only is there an association for political purposes as of friends and allies, but they all have the same laws, the same weights, measures, and coins, the same magistrates, senators, and judges; and, in a word, the whole of Peloponnesus differs in construction from a single state only in this, that the inhabitants do not live within the same walls."

It is obvious that these words were written after the war with Perseus, and before the destruction of the Achæan League (*i.e.* between 167 B.C. and 146 B.C.). The writer either did not foresee, or with a natural and patriotic optimism refused to recognise, the ruin that was coming on his country.

The explanation no doubt is, that the two preliminary books were published before the final catastrophe had taken place. It was one effect of the transmission of books by manuscript copies, that it was impossible to correct what had once got abroad. The *Littera scripta manet* was strictly true. The author had none of the opportunities of the "new and revised edition" of modern times. We find this amusingly illustrated in the case of a Rhodian historian named Zeno, who had shocked Polybius by describing a Spartan expedition as passing through Sellasia on its way to Thalamæ and Pharæ; whereas Sellasia lay to the north-east of Sparta, and the other places to the south-west.[1] Polybius wrote off in hot haste to Zeno, but the book was already published, and correction was impossible. "Zeno was as vexed as could be, but the thing was beyond remedy: however, he acknowledged my efforts in the most friendly terms." [2]

Only the first five books of Polybius's History are preserved to us entire. The third book carries the history of the Second Punic War down to the battle of Cannæ, while the

---

[1] xvi. 16. Modern maps represent Sellasia as due north, and Thalamæ and Pharæ as south, or a point to the south-east of Sparta.

[2] xvi. 20.

fourth and fifth books deal with the contemporary history of Greece and Asia. The remaining thirty-five books are known to us by fragments. By far the longest is the account of the Roman constitution and military system, from the sixth book. This comprises fifty-eight chapters, probably about half the original book. The lost portion doubtless described the civil administration and financial system of Rome. "One may with justice reproach Fortune" (to borrow a phrase of our historian) for having preserved in the fourth and fifth books so much that is petty and off the main lines of the history, while withholding from us the light which would have been shed on some of the most difficult and interesting questions of ancient politics, if the sixth book had come to us unmutilated.[1]

Besides the usual sources of fragments in the quotations and allusions of other ancient writers, we have in the case of Polybius the help of volumes of compiled extracts which have survived the destruction of the complete works from which they were drawn.

A volume of Epitomes (so the MS. calls them) was known as early as the year 1549. These are really not epitomes in our sense of the word, but extracts tolerably copious from Books I.–XVIII. The earlier editors amused themselves with the fancy that they had in their hands the work on which, as Plutarch tells us,[2] Brutus was engaged on the eve of the battle of Pharsalia. Schweighäuser points out[3] that a much later date is determined for these extracts by comparing those of them which are taken from the first five books with the continuous manuscripts of these books. All our copies of the extracts conform, he says, exclusively to the readings of that family of manuscripts of which the Vatican is the chief, ignoring those of the other group on which the earlier editors framed the *textus receptus*. This seems to prove that the compilation was effected after the divergence of the two types which are respectively followed by these two classes of manuscripts. It is probably safest to attribute this collection to Byzantine compilers of a comparatively recent date.

---

[1] See Marquardt, *Römische Staats-Verwaltung*, vol. ii. p. 76.
[2] ἔγραφε συντάττων ἐπιτομὴν Πολυβίου. Plutarch, *Brutus*, 4.
[3] Preface, p. civ.

Of a second, and scarcely less important, compilation we have fuller information.[1] Constantine Porphyrogenitus, a Byzantine Emperor of the tenth century, ordered the formation of a sort of Digest of Historical writers for the use of persons who found the complete works too long and wearisome to study. Extracts from them were selected and arranged under different headings according to their subjects. He claimed to have included everything which was important in the Greek historians within the limits of his fifty-three volumes. Two of the fifty-three survive nearly complete, the one entitled *Embassies* (περὶ Πρεσβειῶν), the other *Virtue and Vice* (περὶ 'Αρετῆς καὶ Κακίας). Both draw largely from Polybius; they were first printed in 1582 and 1584 respectively, and Casaubon included the extracts from both in his great edition of Polybius. In the present century fragments of another volume, *Maxims* (περὶ Γνωμῶν), have been discovered in the Vatican Library by Cardinal Mai, and later editors have incorporated in the text many fresh extracts from Polybius drawn from this source.

The extracts and fragments preserved are longer by nearly a half than the five complete books, and they are also, taking them as a whole, far more interesting and valuable. The most striking passages were naturally selected for the compilations; and though we have to look elsewhere for the continuous history, and though we feel that the silence on particular points of interest is vexatious, yet in what remains we have evidently the pith of the work, and can find the picture of the age and its great events as the historian wished to portray them.

The task which Polybius proposed to himself was to write the history of the world during the period he had chosen for his subject. Such a universal history was demanded, so he thought, by the appearance of a universal Empire.

" Now in the times preceding this period, the events of the world's history may be said to have happened in a state of isolation, because each action, both in its inception and in its development, was disconnected with all others by time or

---

[1] See Schweighäuser's Preface, p. cxxxix.

place. But from this period we find that the history has become an organic whole, and the affairs of Italy and Libya are bound up with those of Asia and Greece, and the general current of events sets to one fixed point." [1]

" The distinctive feature of our work corresponds with the marvellous characteristic of our times; for as Fortune has swayed almost all the affairs of the world to one centre, and compelled every force to set in one and the same direction, so we would by means of our History bring under a common view, for the benefit of our readers, the operations which Fortune has employed for the completion of a combined system of the world. Indeed it was this above everything that incited and urged us to attempt the writing of history, and an additional incentive was the consideration that none of our contemporaries have attempted to construct a universal history; otherwise for my own part I should have been much less eager to occupy this ground. But now, seeing that many writers employ themselves on individual wars, and on some of the actions associated with them, but that the universal and connected disposition of events, when and from what causes they took their rise, and how they reached their full development, are questions which no one of them, so far as I know, even attempts to analyse, I conceived that it was absolutely necessary not to omit nor let pass without recognition this which is at once the noblest and most instructive of all the operations of Fortune. For while she is for ever working revolutions, and for ever busying herself over the lives of men, she never yet accomplished such a task, nor fought through such a struggle as has been exhibited in our day. But of this it is impossible to gain a clear conception from those who write history in isolated segments.

" It is by gaining a view of the connection and relationship of all events to each other, and of their resemblances and differences, that alone we càn reach the goal, and be enabled to get both profit and pleasure out of history." [2]

Polybius is thoroughly impressed with the majesty of his subject. In this conception of a systematic whole, and in the recognition that he must search for the hidden threads of reason

[1] i. 3.   [2] i. 4.

which bind events together, he finds an informing principle for his work. He gains from it the support of a duty clearly apprehended and loyally adhered to, and it supplies a certain elevation and dignity which would otherwise be wanting both to his thought and writing. It sets him in a sphere removed above the temptations of the rhetorician and the pamphleteer, and makes him the most trustworthy of historians. Polybius is an enthusiast for the truth wherever he finds it. He shows throughout a calm determination to probe to the bottom the conditions of the time with which men had to deal: what is inevitable he will accept without murmuring: he will state for his contemporaries the facts, whether agreeable or not, to which their conduct must be suited. Neither fear nor favour, he contends, must tempt the historian to waver for a moment in his allegiance to the truth. In this spirit he criticises the rival histories of Fabius and Philinus for their partisan accounts of the First Punic War.

"Now in most affairs of life, perhaps, a man would do ill to divest himself of such a fellow-feeling. For a good man should be attached to his friend and to his country, and out of sympathy for these should hate their enemies and love their friends. But when a man assumes the attitude of mind that is proper to history, he is bound to leave out of sight all such considerations, and he must often speak well of his enemies and adorn them with the highest praises when the facts demand this; and again he must often blame his nearest friends, and bring their faults home to them whenever their conduct requires it. For just as, if the eyes of a living animal are put out, the whole creature becomes maimed and helpless, so, if you take away the truth out of history, what is left is merely an unprofitable tale."[1]

Polybius's own practice shows that this homage to the truth is not merely a lip-service. We have seen how all his political hopes and aspirations were bound up with the Achæan League. Of all men of his age, Aratus, the founder of Achæan greatness, might seem to claim from him indulgent treatment, while Cleomenes, whose whole life was a struggle against the

---

[1] i. 14.

Achæans, and who had dealt a deadly blow at Megalopolis, Polybius's native town, might seem a natural mark for enmity and detraction. Yet he is careful to point out the great defects of Aratus, his want of skill and energy in the field of battle, and the numerous disasters which his incapacity inflicted on his countrymen. " All Peloponnesus was full," he says, " of the trophies which had been erected for victories over Aratus." On the other hand, when he comes to describe the death of Cleomenes, though it does not fall within his province to give the picturesque details which we learn from Plutarch, he fully recognises the dignity and heroism of his end. When all their efforts had failed, he and his companions " killed themselves bravely and as became Spartans : and this was the end of Cleomenes, a man of winning manners towards his fellows, and of ability in the affairs of State, and, in a word, framed by nature to be a leader and a king."[1]

To pass to the next generation : his character of the last Philip of Macedon leaves nothing to be desired in discrimination and soundness of moral judgment. He does equal justice to the courage, prudence, and self-restraint of his youth ; to the reckless vice and tyranny of his middle life ; and to the splendid resolution with which the old man, braced and sobered by misfortune, bent himself to the tremendous task of retrieving his shattered fortune, and reviving his country after the shock of its first great calamity.

Or again, let us consider Polybius's picture of Rome. Rome is the triumphant hero of his story. The object of his book is to show that the success of the Romans was not an accident, but the natural result of their character and their institutions. He accepts the supremacy of Rome as the voice of fate, and urges submission on the world. Yet he is never tempted by the desire for a false consistency to slur over the unjust, cruel, or mean actions of the Romans. Their conduct to Demetrius and to the kingdom of Syria is only a specimen of many discreditable deeds recorded by their historian : he tells of each occurrence in its place calmly and judicially, without fear or favour.

---

[1] v. 39.

With this absorbing passion for truth, Polybius has the "defects of his qualities" in a certain unfortunate contempt for the artistic presentation of the truth. The following is his criticism on his Rhodian friend :—

"What shall we say, then, is the defect of Zeno? That he is anxious, not so much about inquiring into his facts and dealing with his subject, as about perfecting his style; and it is clear from many passages that this is what he prides himself on, as is the case with many other distinguished historians. Now I hold that a man should by all means take pains and exert himself about the fitting presentation of what he has to say, for it is manifest that this contributes greatly to the effect of the narrative; but men of sound sense should not set up this as their first and leading object. Far from it; there are other nobler elements of history on which a statesmanlike historian would rather pride himself."[1]

The doctrine, as it stands, is of course indisputable; but Polybius in practice allowed his scrupulous performance of the first duty of a historian to serve him as an excuse for wholly neglecting the second. His style must, indeed, be acquitted of the very worst faults, those which spring from conceited pedantry and laborious folly. It is not vicious, nor forced, nor inflated, nor false. You listen to a man of sense telling his story in a way that is natural to him. Thus, whenever the events he is describing are in themselves sufficiently exciting to fix the attention of the reader by their intrinsic interest, he does not throw away the advantage, nor spoil the narrative by tinsel ornament. Some of the battle-scenes, for instance, in which Polybius's own bent towards military pursuits furnished a stimulus to his mind, are really well described. Perhaps the passages where one feels least the defects of the writer are the description of the revolt of the Carthaginian mercenaries in the first book, and that of the capture and death of Achæus in a fragment of the eighth.

Carthage had collected into her mercenary army a throng of Libyans, Celts, bastard Greeks, runaway slaves, and deserters from all parts of the world. These burst into mutiny after

---

[1] xvi. 17.

their return to Africa at the end of the First Punic War (241 B.C.). The long-suppressed hatred of the African population towards their Carthaginian tyrants assisted them in their revolt, and stimulated them to wild orgies of cruelty and destructiveness. They had no common language, and the only word they all understood was the Greek βάλλε, "pelt him." The leaders of the mutineers had only to raise this cry against any one who opposed them, and it was taken up from mouth to mouth, and the designated victim was stoned to death as a supposed spy or traitor. A reign of terror ensued, founded on mutual suspicion; no one was trusted unless he had given security for his fidelity by unpardonable crimes. The whole nature of these men became brutalised and poisoned with malignant passions; they tortured or mutilated every prisoner: Gesco, their favourite general, was seized when he came at their own request to treat with them in the camp, and put to death with horrible torments. Driven to bay, they resorted to cannibalism in their despair, and were at length either exterminated on the field, or else crucified or trodden under the feet of elephants by their conquerors.[1] It has been said by one who first read this description at the time when news was being brought by every mail of the events of the Indian Mutiny, that it was the story told by Polybius which best enabled him to enter into the spirit of what was passing in the East, and which brought most vividly before his mind the horrors of the armed rebellion of a savage race.

Not less striking is the story of the unfortunate pretender Achæus, besieged in the fortress of Sardis by King Antiochus.[2] He was enticed out by night by a traitorous Cretan named Bolis, who, having received a great sum of money to effect his escape, sold him to Antiochus. Achæus, who had doubts of the fidelity of his guide, had disguised himself, and instructed the leader of his party to tell the Cretan that Achæus had remained behind, and would content himself with sending three or four friends as messengers to his partisans outside. Bolis, now utterly puzzled, accompanied them through the darkness; but he soon noticed that there was one of the party to whom

---

[1] i. 66-88. [2] viii. 17-23.

the others seemed to show deference, taking care of him and helping him over rough and dangerous places. This, he rightly concluded, must be the prince; he suddenly flung his arms round him, the attendants were cut down by armed men who were lying in wait, and the Cretan, marching in the dead of night into the tent where Antiochus sat anxiously awaiting the issue of the plot, flung down the rebel, bound hand and foot, before the king.

In such passages as these, we feel that it is the thrilling character of the events described which gives power and interest to the description. Where Polybius lacks the stimulus of such a topic, and has to depend on his own skill for the artistic presentation of his subject, he fails from sheer carelessness and slovenliness. His sentences trail along without beginning, middle, or end. His remarks fall out pell-mell, without any regard to their suiting the tone or spirit of the context. As long as he can say what he wants to say, the manner has to take care of itself. He writes, indeed, not so much in a bad style, as with no style at all. The result is that, although hardly any writer has said more interesting things than Polybius, he is tedious and uninteresting as a whole. It is characteristic of the man that the fragments should be the most valuable part of his work. The extant portions of his writings occupy altogether nearly 1200 octavo pages of Bekker's edition. We may almost apply to him what Macaulay says of Spenser—that if the whole forty books, printed on some 4000 octavo pages, had remained to us, " we doubt if any heart less stout than that of a commentator would have held out to the end."

The Nemesis of his contempt for the form and style of his writing has come on Polybius in the neglect which he has experienced at the hands of the modern world. He can hardly have a place in the regular educational curriculum, for there could not be a worse book from which to teach boys Greek. His language lacks all the subtlety and depth of classical Greek, and has the indescribable flavour of a modern language, such as we find about the Dog-Latin of the Middle Ages. It is a cosmopolitan language, without character and without idiom, fitted only to serve as a medium of communication for the dead and colourless civilisation which remained to the Hellenised East under the crushing power of Rome.

In arrangement and choice of materials, we find in Polybius the same want of artistic sense. His proper subject is so vast, and embraces such a multiplicity of details, that, with all his anxious care for truth, he despairs of attaining absolute accuracy;[1] but, not content with this, he can never resist the temptation of talking and arguing about other matters. He cannot let his History speak for itself, but is always trying to justify his method, or his style, or his arrangement; if he introduces a new subject, he wastes time over an apology, and an attempt to show that the discussion is to the point; if he decides to omit something, still he cannot be silent about it, but must explain, generally at very unnecessary length, why it is not convenient to enter on this or that subject at present. He will not say a thing once and have done with it, but keeps harping on the same topics. It was useful and proper that he should point out the difference between his subject-matter and that of the writers of " special histories ;" but, from mere want of literary skill and critical sense, he insists on the theme till the reader is weary of it.

It is interesting to notice in this connection the different effects of the conditions of composition among the ancients on the form of their writings. The footnote, the reference, the appendix, the magazine criticism, are all modern inventions, and by their means the modern writer may purge his text. Whatever the ancient historian wished to say, he must introduce into the body of his work. Polybius sets no limits to this licence of forcing in extraneous matter. Side by side with the record of great events we find in him elaborate criticisms of rival historians—the fragments of that on Timæus alone occupy forty octavo pages—apologies, answers to objections, and even a sort of publisher's advertisement, which explains that the public are not to be alarmed at the size and price of his work, for that his forty books are really cheaper to buy and easier to read, in comparison of the ground they cover, than the works of the "special historians."[2] By such indiscriminate loquacity

---

[1] xxix. 6 a.　　　　　　　　　　[2] iii. 32.

the dignity and beauty of the History is seriously impaired; and the fault appears the greater, if we contrast the effect of the same conditions of writing upon the great masters of historical style. The responsibility of choice seems to strengthen and brace them; their taste and judgment are polished till they attain an almost unerring instinct of when to speak and when to keep silence. Polybius claims a place in the highest rank of ancient historians, and such a claim challenges a comparison with the greatest names—with the severe and stately thought and diction of Thucydides; with Tacitus, who carries the art of writing to its highest pitch, in whom no expression, no turn of a sentence, no hint, no digression, fails to heighten the effect of the whole; with Herodotus, who, whether by the simplicity of genius, or by art so consummate that the observer cannot distinguish it from nature, delights generation after generation of readers with a tale that leaves nothing to be desired in finish and beauty. Would it be well for ordinary classical students to give up any one of these to spend the time over Polybius? It must be confessed that Polybius as a writer cannot stand for a moment in the light of such a comparison. If "the style is the man," Polybius has no place in the first rank. He has not the genius, and will not take the trouble to acquire the trained sensitiveness of art which might have supplied its place; and thus his writing has no distinction and no charm, and we miss in reading him what gives half their value to great writers— the consciousness that we are in the hands of a master.

It is more difficult to come to a correct judgment as to the moral side of Polybius's writings. Mommsen, in his generally judicious criticism, lays down that "his treatment of all questions in which right, honour, religion are involved, is not only shallow but radically false."[1] This seems a harsh and unfair sentence. To judge Polybius rightly, we must take account of the experiences which formed his character. The life which he had led, and the events which he had witnessed, were not calculated to develop in a man the highest moral capabilities— self-sacrifice, devotion to a great cause, faith in an ideal, sympathy with great currents of human feeling. High hopes

---

[1] *Hist. of Rome*, vol. iii. p. 467 (English translation).

and sentiments, however delusive, are a necessary element in the lives of the deepest human interest, and such hopes and sentiments the triumph of Rome had crushed out except in the narrow circle of her own republican liberty. The spectacle of a heróic life like that of Hannibal, struggling against this terrible nation, is a tragedy for all time. But for those who saw the drama played out, the obvious moral was that such a life was an anachronism and a failure. Polybius has a hearty admiration for Hannibal; but he must have felt that his fate and the fate of his country decided once for all the question whether the struggle was worth continuing—

"si Pergama dextrâ
Defendi possent, etiam hâc defensa fuissent."

Polybius could not but be a "disillusionised man;" religion was dead to all reasonable men in his day, and patriotism, as it had been hitherto understood in the world, hopelessly wrecked. We have no right to blame Polybius for being a sceptic, and it should be put to his credit that he was not a cynic, that he kept his moral judgment of men and things clear, that he still believed in justice and right, and had the courage to speak his mind in praise or censure with a single eye to truth. What was an honest Greek to do in such a time? Mommsen sneers alike at Philopœmen, who hoped against hope for liberty and independence, and at Polybius, who, when this last chance was obviously and completely lost, resolved to accept what was inevitable, and to accommodate both his conduct and his counsels to that which history had decreed. It seems more rational to esteem both of them as men who with true wisdom and sincerity of purpose strove to do their best for their country and for the world under most difficult or even desperate circumstances. One article of faith remained to Polybius, and to this he clung with unswerving loyalty.

"I believe," he says,[1] "that nature has given to man Truth as the greatest deity, and has endued her with strength above everything. Sometimes when every one unites to beat her down, and when every plausibility is ranged on the side of falsehood, yet one way or other, by virtue of her own nature,

---

[1] xiii. 5.

she penetrates into the souls of men, sometimes revealing her might at once, sometimes after long eclipse, winning her way at last and fighting down falsehood."

He saw that it was his duty to look every fact in the face, to clear away every illusion, to conceal nothing and extenuate nothing; and he believed that the truth thus studied cannot but have its practical lessons, and that reality once fairly grasped and accepted must contain the germs of a policy which can secure a tolerable, if not a desirable, solution of the problems of the time.

Polybius's attitude towards religion deserves a more special notice. We see in it the strong effort of the man towards fairness and candour. Obviously an unbeliever himself, he is eager to recognise the good moral effect of the continuance of religious belief among the Romans.

"The most salutary feature of the Roman constitution is the belief it inculcates in the gods. And I think that the Roman state is held together by a quality which is a reproach among other men—I mean by superstition. For this motive is heightened in effect and enters into the life of the people and into public affairs to an almost incredible extent. This may seem astonishing to some, but I think that the Romans have acted thus out of regard to the multitude. For if it were possible to collect a nation of wise men, such a practice would perhaps be unnecessary. But since every multitude is fickle and full of lawless desires, of unreasonable anger, and of violent passions, it only remains to curb them with invisible terrors and such-like machinery. For this reason I think that the notions about the gods, and the belief in a future world, were not introduced by our fathers carelessly or at random, but that the recklessness and folly is rather on the side of this generation who reject them. And so amongst public officers in Greece, if a single talent be intrusted to their care, they have ten indorsers and as many seals and two witnesses to each signature, and with all this they cheat; while the Romans, as commissioners, pass great sums of money through their hands and never transgress, by virtue of the mere sanctity of their oath."[1]

---

[1] vi. 56.

To maintain this wholesome spirit he is willing to make some allowance for the introduction of myths and legends into history, though it is a liberty which he will grant to others but not use himself. Only the stories must be such as tend to keep up the reverence of the people for the gods, and must confine themselves within the limits of the possible, if not of the probable. This requisition leads him to reject peremptorily a fragment of primitive folk-lore, which lingered in his native Arcadia. We know from Plato[1] that the belief in were-wolves was localised in the temple of the Arcadian Zeus, and here we find another superstition which we are accustomed to think of as purely medieval, that of the "man without a shadow," attaching to the same spot.

"To say that some bodies when placed in the light cast no shadow, marks a mind beyond the influence of sense; and this is what Theopompus does when he says that those who enter into the forbidden precinct of Zeus in Arcadia lose their shadows."[2]

Polybius, however tolerant of religion in its proper place, is indignant when the credit which statesmen and generals deserve for wisdom or courage is taken from them by ascribing their success to providence or inspiration. The elder Scipio claimed to be a special object of the favour of the gods, and allowed his most successful enterprises to be attributed to divine admonition. It is amusing to see Polybius's anxiety to clear his hero from the suspicion of having sincerely believed any such nonsense. Scipio did not rely on dreams or mysterious voices for the measures by which he founded the greatness of his country; but he, like Lycurgus, perceived "that the masses will not accept any policy which is strange to them, nor meet danger with courage unless they hope for some assistance from heaven," and therefore "he inculcated the belief that his plans were suggested by inspiration, and thus put his men in good heart against danger. But that each of his actions was really done by calculation and foresight, and that his success was the legitimate issue of his plans, will be clear from the subsequent narrative."[3] The best example

---

[1] *Rep.* viii. 16. Also frequently in Polybius.   [2] xvi. 12.   [3] x. 2.

perhaps is the siege of Carthagena. Scipio, after a careful study of the habits of the tidal water in the harbour, timed his assault to coincide with an unusually low tide, and informed his troops that Neptune had promised him notable assistance at the crisis of the battle.[1] When the soldiers saw the water fall so as to permit of a party fording the harbour and attacking the fortress in flank, their enthusiasm at the divine interposition made their onset irresistible.

In another passage[2] Polybius attempts to establish a *modus vivendi* between religion and reason, by dividing the field of human life between them.

"Whenever it is difficult or impossible for human power to apprehend causes, we may fairly in our uncertainty refer such things to God or to Fortune; as, for instance, a continuance of storms and violent rainfall, or of droughts and frosts, and the loss of crops resulting from these, and in the same way, unhealthy states of atmosphere, and other things of the same kind, whose causes are not easy to discover. Therefore, in our uncertainty about such cases, we naturally conform to the opinions of the multitude, and propitiate heaven by supplications and offerings, and send to inquire of the gods what we are to do or say to obtain a blessing and a relief from the ills that beset us. But where it is possible to discover the originating and efficient cause of what has occurred, in such cases I think it wrong to refer it to the will of heaven. To take an instance :—In our time all Greece has been smitten with childlessness and deficient population, by which the cities are desolated, and sterility reigns, although no long wars nor unhealthy seasons have occurred. Supposing, then, that any one should advise us to send and inquire of the gods what we are to say and do to become more numerous and replenish our cities,—would not this be manifestly silly, when the cause is evident and the correction lies in our own hands? For men have fallen into habits of ostentation and greed and indolence, and they will neither marry nor bring up the children who are born to them out of wedlock, or else they rear one or two at the most, in order to leave these rich and luxurious, and the

---

[1] x. 11. [2] xxxvii. 4.

mischief, though not much noticed, has grown rapidly. For if this only child, or one of the two, is carried off by war or disease, it is manifest that houses must needs be left desolate, and before long the cities too become weak from lack of men, like a hive without bees.[1] And in all this there is not the least occasion to ask the gods how we may be released from such a calamity; for any man of ordinary intelligence will tell us that we can apply the remedy ourselves by reforming the objects of our ambition, or if this be impossible, then by making laws to provide for the rearing of all children born."

The reader can hardly fail to notice a peculiar modern tone in Polybius's manner of dealing with such questions; and this modern tone is the prevalent one throughout his work. The great difficulty in understanding classical writers is that they seem, almost all of them, to move and work in a different plane of thought from ourselves. It is probably this newness and freshness of the world they open out to us that constitutes the chief value of the classics in education. But it is not to be wondered at if, until the mind is thoroughly imbued with classical culture, a sense of bewilderment and impatience is produced. The schoolboy generally believes in his heart that there is no nonsense so enormous that it may not be a probable translation of a passage of Greek. Sometimes this strangeness in the tone of thought of ancient books to that of the every-day world leads men to desire to reject the first altogether, and to prefer the political wisdom of the *Times* to that of Thucydides. If there are any who seriously feel this often-quoted preference, they should be sent to make their peace with the ancients by reading Polybius. No effort is required to get at his point of view. Whatever question he starts, his attitude of mind towards it is such as to appeal to the sympathy, if not to the conviction, of the average modern reader. His remarks are always full of an obvious good sense, always enlightened, candid, and judicious, and, it must be added, rather commonplace.

Polybius is never so happy as when he is correcting a

---

[1] καθάπερ ἐπὶ τῶν μελιττῶν τὰ σμήνη. The sentence is obviously imperfect, and the text is faulty throughout the fragment.

popular error, or explaining and analysing what may appear at
first sight a paradox. A few characteristic specimens may
serve to complete the picture of our author. The first is a
curious instance of accurate observation conveyed in a somewhat pedagogic tone :—

"Most men suppose that cities which contain hills and
sloping-ground will hold more houses than those of the same
circumference built on a plain. But this is entirely wrong,
because the houses must be built perpendicular, not to the
slopes, but to the level below, on which the hills themselves
are planted. One may prove this from what is manifest to any
child, as the saying is. For if we conceive the houses on the
slopes built up until they are all the same height, it is clear
that the roofs of the houses will form a single plane, and that
this plane will of necessity be parallel and equal to the plane
on which the foundations of the walls and the hills themselves
rest."[1]

Mention has been already made of Polybius's discriminat-
ing account of Aratus. He lays down clearly the merits and
defects of the man,—an excellent organiser, and unsurpassed
in careful preparation and wise laying of plans, but destitute
of energy, courage, and resource, at the moment of action. The
spectacle of these discordant qualities in the same person leads
Polybius to generalise on the different grooves in which courage
and capacity run with different men.

"This is no paradox, but a familiar phenomenon, accepted
by judicious observers. Sometimes you have men courageous
in hunting, who will face wild beasts with boldness, and yet
these same men will be cowards when set in arms against the
enemy ; or again, some who are skilful and successful in single
combat, but useless when drawn up in line of battle. Then
there is the Thessalian cavalry, whose shock is irresistible when
they charge by troop or squadron, but they are slow and of no
avail for risking themselves in hand-to-hand conflict as place
and occasion serve, while just the contrary is true of the
Ætolians. The Cretans, both by land and sea, are invincible

---

[1] ix. 21. Modern land-surveyors apply Polybius's principle to vegetable
growths as well as to buildings, and estimate the acreage of hilly ground for
agricultural purposes in accordance with it.

in ambushes and marauding expeditions, and in kidnapping enemies, and in night attacks, and in all such individual services where cunning is required; but when the phalanx charges face to face on fair ground they turn cowardly and unsteady. The Achæans and Macedonians exhibit just the opposite temper."[1]

Another interesting passage in the same tone is where he defends the Greeks from the charge of fickleness and ingratitude in giving some sympathy to Perseus in his struggle against Rome.

"I think that the disposition of their minds is to be accounted for in this way. The phenomenon is the same as that which one often sees in athletic contests. For when a distinguished and seemingly invincible champion is opposed by an obscure and inferior antagonist, the multitude at once gives its good-will to the weaker man, and cheers him on and sympathises with his efforts; and if he touch his adversary's face and leave some mark of the blow, the spectators feel as if they had a share in the struggle, and sometimes they begin to clamour against his opponent—not that they dislike him or wish for his disgrace, but because they are carried away by sympathy, and so favour the weaker side. But if any one administers a timely rebuke, they soon repent and check their indiscretion."

After illustrating this by the case of a notable athlete, Clitomachus, who had thus recalled the sympathies of the spectators to an old and tried favourite, he proceeds:—

"The popular feeling towards Perseus is a parallel case. For if any one had withstood them, and asked them frankly if they desired to see such a supremacy fall into the hands of a single man, and to feel the weight of a monarchical power absolutely irresponsible, I conceive that they would soon have recanted and gone over to the other side; and still more if the speaker had briefly reminded them of all the injuries which the Greeks had experienced at the hands of the house of Macedon, and of all the benefits which they had received from the supremacy of Rome, I think that the revolution in their senti-

---

[1] iv. 8.

ments would have been complete and immediate. But under the irresistible influence of the first wave of opinion, the multitude betrayed its satisfaction at the news, being flattered by the unexpected appearance of a champion able to stand face to face with Rome. And so I close this discussion, the object of which has been to show that it is only a thoughtless judgment, and one ignorant of human nature, which will cast the reproach of ingratitude on the temper which the Greeks showed on this occasion."[1]

In the selection of these and the other pieces quoted in this paper the object has been to give passages illustrative of Polybius as a man and a writer, rather than those which are of intrinsic historical importance. The latter class of extracts would find their place in a picture of the Greek and Roman world in Polybius's time, which is a task too long to be attempted within the limits of this essay. For the present it must suffice to have placed before the reader materials for a judgment on the merits and the limitations of the Historian of the Roman Conquest.

It will be difficult, perhaps, to arrive at a more judicious verdict than that in which Mommsen sums up his criticism:—

"Polybius is not an attractive author; but as truth and truthfulness are of more value than all ornament and elegance, no other author of antiquity, perhaps, can be named to whom we are indebted for so much real instruction. His books are like the sun in Roman history; at the point where they begin, the mist which still envelopes the Samnite and Pyrrhic wars is raised; and at the point where they end, a new and, if possible, still more vexatious twilight begins."[2]

J. L. S. D.

---

[1] xxvii. 7 a. [2] *Hist. of Rome*, vol. iii. p. 468 (English translation).

GREEK ORACLES.

PREFATORY NOTE.

AMONG the sources to which I have been indebted in the composition of the following Essay, my first acknowledgments are due to the works of Mr. Tylor, Sir John Lubbock, and other ethnologists, whose labours in the comparative study of primitive beliefs and customs are perhaps even more important for the history of religion than were the great philological generalisations which immediately preceded them. On Greek religion, and Greek oracles in particular, I have consulted, among others, the following authors : —Becker and Marquardt, Bötticher, Bouché-Leclercq,[1] Bowen, Cox, Creuzer and Guigniaut, Curtius, Decharme, Fontenelle, Götte, Hendess, Hermann, Hoffmann, Hüllmann, Klausen, Lloyd, Lobeck, Maury, August Mommsen, Nägelsbach, Preller, Rödiger, St. Hilaire, Tzschirner, Vacherot, Van Dale, Wachsmuth, Welcker, F. A. Wolf, G. Wolff, Zander ; and the important monographs of Carapanos on Dodona, Foucart on Delphi, and Lebègue and Homolle on Delos. I owe special obligations to Maury's *Religions de la Grèce*, which contains an excellent collection of references to ancient authors, and to G. Wolff's two tracts *Porphyrii de Philosophia ex Oraculis haurienda Reliquiae*, and *De Novissima Oraculorum Aetate*, from which many of my later references are derived. In a subject which has been so often discussed it is no longer possible to lay claim to originality of citation, though much significance remains to be educed from the texts already known. And in fact, as will be seen by persons familiar with the literature of the subject, my treatment of the history of Greek oracles in some places differs widely from that adopted by my predecessors. While suggesting my own views with much diffidence, and venturing on very few definite conclusions, I cannot but feel that the difficulties of this manifold subject have hardly received adequate attention from scholars, and are as yet to a great extent unsolved. It would be tedious to specify the ancient writers consulted. Herodotus and Eusebius are the most important, but there is scarcely a Greek author, from Homer to Zosimus, from whom some illustration may not be drawn, and the range of such illustrations has been limited in the following Essay by the defect, not of applicable material, but of erudition, of space, and of time.

---

[1] Only the first volume of M. Bouché-Leclercq's *Histoire de la Divination dans l'Antiquité* has as yet appeared (July 1879). The third volume is to treat of Delphi and other Greek oracles, and is likely to form one of the most important works on the subject. Unfortunately, however, the lessons and methods of comparative ethnology are expressly excluded from M. Bouché-Leclercq's plan (Preface, p. 2).

Οὐ μέν πως νῦν ἔστιν ἀπὸ δρυὸς οὐδ' ἀπὸ πέτρης
τῷ ὀαριζέμεναι, ἅ τε παρθένος ἠΐθεός τε,
παρθένος ἠΐθεός τ' ὀαρίζετον ἀλλήλοιιν.

I.

IT is not only in the domain of physical inquiry that the advance of knowledge is self-accelerated at every step, and the very excellence of any given work insures its own speedier supersession. All those studies which bear upon the past of mankind are every year more fully satisfying this test of the genuinely scientific character of the plan on which they are pursued. The old conception of the world's history as a collection of stories, each admitting of a complete and definitive recital, is giving way to a conception which would compare it rather with a series of imperfectly-read inscriptions, the sense of each of which is modified by the interpretations which we gradually find for its predecessors.

And of no department is this truer than of the comparative history of religion. The very idea of such a study is of recent growth, and no sooner is the attempt made to colligate by general laws the enormous mass of the religious phenomena of the world than we find that the growing science is in danger of being choked by its own luxuriance—that each conflicting hypothesis in turn seems to draw superabundant proof from the myriad beliefs and practices of men. We may, indeed, smile at the extravagances of one-sided upholders of each successive system. We need not believe with Bishop Huet[1] that Moses was the archetype both of Adonis and of Priapus. Nor, on the other hand, need we suppose with Pierson[2] that Abraham

---

[1] *Demonstr. Evang.* iii. 3, viii. 5.   [2] Ap. Kuenen, *Religion of Israel*, i. 390.

himself was originally a stone god. We may leave Dozy[1] to pursue his own conjecture, and deduce the strange story of the Hebrew race from their worship of the planet Saturn. Nor need the authority of Anonymus *de Rebus Incredibilibus*[2] constrain us to accept his view that Paris was a young man who wrote essays on goddesses, and Phaethon an unsuccessful astronomer.

But it is far from easy to determine the relative validity of the theories of which these are exaggerated expressions,—to decide (for instance) what place is to be given to the direct transference of beliefs from nation to nation, to fetish-worship, to the worship of the heavenly bodies, to the deification of dead men. In an essay like the present, dealing only with a fragment of this great inquiry, it will be safest to take the most general view, and to say that man's fear and wonder invest every object, real or imaginary, which strongly impresses him,— beasts or stones, or souls and spirits, or fire and the sun in heaven,—with an intelligence and a power darkly resembling his own ; and, moreover, that certain phenomena, real or supposed,—dreams and epilepsy, eclipse and thunder, sorceries and the uprising of the dead,—recur from time to time to supply him with apparent proof of the validity of his beliefs, and to modify those beliefs according to the nature of his country and his daily life. Equally natural is it that, as his social instincts develop and his power of generalisation begins, he will form such conceptions as those of a moral government of the world, of a retributory hereafter, of a single Power from which all others emanate, or into which they disappear.

Avoiding, therefore, any attempt to take a side among conflicting theories, I will draw from the considerations which follow no further moral than one which is wellnigh a truism, though too often forgotten in the heat of debate, namely, that we are assuredly not as yet in a position to pass a final judgment on the forms which religion has assumed in the past ; we have traversed too small a part of the curve of human progress to determine its true character ; even yet, in fact, " we are ancients of the earth, and in the morning of the times." The

---

[1] Ap. Kuenen, i. 262.   [2] *Opuscula Mythologica* (Amst. 1688).

difficulty of bearing this clearly in mind, great in every age, becomes greater as each age advances more rapidly in knowledge and critical power. In this respect the eighteenth century teaches us an obvious lesson. That century witnessed a marked rise in the standard of historical evidence, a marked enlightenment in dealing with the falsities and superstitions of the past. The consequence was that all things seemed explicable; that whatever could not be reduced to ordinary rules seemed only worthy of being brushed aside. Since that day the standard of evidence in history has not declined,—it has become stricter still; but at the same time the need of sympathy and insight, if we would comprehend the past, has become strongly felt, and has modified or suspended countless judgments which the philosophers of the last century delivered without misgiving. The difference between the two great critics and philosophers of France, at that day and in our own, shows at a glance the whole gulf between the two points of view. How little could the readers of Voltaire have anticipated Renan! How little could they have imagined that their master's trenchant arguments would so soon have fallen to the level of half-educated classes and half-civilised nations, —would have been formidable only in sixpenny editions, or when translated into Hindostani for the confutation of missionary zeal!

What philosophical enlightenment was in the last century, science, physical or historical, is in our own. Science is the power to which we make our first and undoubting appeal, and we run a corresponding risk of assuming that she can already solve problems wholly, which as yet she can solve only in part, —of adopting under her supposed guidance explanations which may hereafter be seen to have the crudity and one-sidedness of Voltaire's treatment of Biblical history.

The old school of theologians were apt to assume that because all men—or all men whom they chose to count—had held a certain belief, that belief must be true. Our danger lies rather in being too ready to take for granted that when we have explained how a belief arose we have done with it altogether; that because a tenet is of savage parentage it hardly needs formal disproof. In this view the wide diffusion of a belief serves only to stamp its connection with uncivilised thought, and "quod semper, quod ubique, quod ab omnibus" has become to many minds rather the badge of superstition than the test of catholic truth. That any one but ourselves should have held a creed seems to lower the average intelligence of its adherents.

Yet, on behalf of savages, and our ancestors in general, there may be room for some apology. If we reflect how large a part of human knowledge consists of human emotion, we may even say that they possessed some forms of knowledge which we have since lost. The mind of man (it has been well said), like the earth on which he walks, undergoes perpetual processes of denudation as well as of deposit. We ourselves, as children, did in a sense know much which we know no more; our picture of the universe, incomplete and erroneous as it was, wore some true colours which we cannot now recall. The child's vivid sensibility, reflected in his vivifying imagination, is as veritably an inlet of truth as if it were an added clearness of physical vision; and though the child himself has not judgment enough to use his sensibilities aright, yet if the man is to discern the poetic truth about Nature, he will need to recall to memory his impressions as a child.

Now, in this way too, the savage is a kind of child; his beliefs are not always to be summarily referred to his ignorance; there may be something in them which we must realise in imagination before we venture to explain it away. Ethnologists have recognised the need of this difficult self-identification with the remote past, and have sometimes remarked, with a kind of envy, how much nearer the poet is than the philosopher to the savage habit of mind.

There is, however, one ancient people in whose case much of this difficulty disappears, whose religion may be traced backwards through many phases into primitive forms, while yet it is easy to study its records with a fellow-feeling which grows with our knowledge till it may approach almost to an identity of spirit. Such is the ascendency which the great works of the Greek imagination have established over the mind of man, that it is no paradox to say that the student's danger lies often in excess rather than in defect of sympathy.

He is tempted to ignore the real superiority of our own religion, morality, civilisation, and to re-shape in fancy an adult world on an adolescent ideal. But the remedy for over-estimates, as well as for under-estimates, lies in an increased definiteness of knowledge, an ever-clearer perception of the exact place in the chain of development which Greek thought and worship hold. The whole story of Greek mythology must ere long be retold in a form as deeply modified by comparative ethnology as our existing treatises have been modified by comparative philology. Such a task would be beyond my powers; but while awaiting some more comprehensive treatment of the subject by a better-qualified hand, I have in this Essay endeavoured to trace,—by suggestion rather than in detail, but with constant reference to the results of recent science,—the development and career in Greece of one remarkable class of religious phenomena which admits to some extent of separate treatment.

Greek oracles reflect for a thousand years[1] the spiritual needs of a great people. They draw their origin from an Animism[2] which almost all races share, and in their early and inarticulate forms they contain a record of most of the main currents in which primitive beliefs are wont to run. After-wards—closely connected both with the idea of supernatural possession and with the name of the sun-god Apollo—they exhibit a singular fusion of nature-worship with Shahmanism or sorcery. Then, as the non-moral and naturalistic conception of the deity yields to the moral conception of him as an idealised man, the oracles reflect the change, and the Delphian god becomes in a certain sense the conscience of Greece.

A period of decline follows; due, as it would seem, partly to the depopulation and political ruin of Greece, but partly

---

[1] Roughly speaking, from 700 B.C. to 300 A.D., but the earliest oracles probably date much further back.

[2] It is hardly necessary to say that by Animism is meant a belief in the existence around us of souls or spirits, whether disembodied, as ghosts, or embodied in fetishes, animals, etc. Shahmanism is a word derived from the title of the Siberian wizards, who procure by agitated trance some manifestation from their gods.

also to the indifference or scepticism of her dominant schools of philosophy. But this decline is followed by a revival which forms one of the most singular of those apparent checks which complicate the onward movement of thought by ever new modifications of the beliefs of the remote past. So far as this complex movement can be at present understood, it seems to have been connected among the mass of the people with the widespread religious upheaval of the first Christian centuries, and to have been at last put an end to by Christian baptism or sword. Among the higher minds it seems to have rested partly on a perplexed admission of certain phenomena, partly on the strongly-felt need of a permanent and elevated revelation, which yet should draw its origin from the Hellenic rather than the Hebrew past. And the story reaches a typical conclusion in the ultimate disengagement of the highest natures of declining Greece from mythology and ceremonial, and the absorption of definite dogma into an overwhelming ecstasy.

II.

The attempt to define the word "oracle" confronts us at once with the difficulties of the subject. The Latin term, indeed, which we are forced to employ, points specially to cases where the voice of God or spirit was actually heard, whether directly or through some human intermediary. But the corresponding Greek term (μαντεῖον) merely signifies a seat of soothsaying, a place where divinations are obtained by whatever means. And we must not regard the oracles of Greece as rare and majestic phenomena, shrines founded by a full-grown mythology for the direct habitation of a god. Rather they are the products of a long process of evolution, the modified survivals from among countless holy places of a primitive race.

Greek literature has preserved to us abundant traces of the various causes which led to the ascription of sanctity to some particular locality. Oftenest it is some chasm or cleft in the ground, filled, perhaps, with mephitic vapours, or with the mist of a subterranean stream, or merely opening in its dark obscurity an inlet into the mysteries of the underworld. Such was the chasm of the Clarian,[1] the Delian,[2] the Delphian Apollo; and such the oracle of the prophesying nymphs on Cithaeron.[3] Such was Trophonius' cave,[4] and his own name perhaps is only a synonym for the Mother Earth, "in many names the one identity," who nourishes at once and reveals.[5]

Sometimes—as for instance at Megara,[6] Sicyon, Orchomenus, Laodicea—the sanctity gathers around some βαίτυλος or fetish-stone, fashioned, it may be, into a column or pyramid, and probably in most cases identified at first with the god himself, though, after the invention of statuary, its significance might be obscured or forgotten. Such stones outlast all religions, and remain for us in their rude shapelessness the oldest memorial of the aspirations or the fears of man.

Sometimes the sacred place was merely some favourite post of observation of the flight of birds, or of lightning, like Teiresias' "ancient seat of augury,"[7] or the hearth[8] from which, before the sacred embassy might start for Delphi, the Pythaists watched above the crest of Parnes for the summons of the heavenly flame.

Or it might be merely some spot where the divination from burnt-offerings seemed unusually true and plain,—at Olympia, for instance, where, as Pindar tells us, "soothsayers divining from sacrifice make trial of Zeus who lightens clear." It is needless to speak at length of groves and streams and mountain-summits, which in every region of the world have seemed to bring the unseen close to man by waving mystery, or by rushing murmur, or

---

[1] Iambl. de Myst. p. 74.

[2] Lebègue, Recherches sur Délos, p. 89.

[3] Paus. ix. 3. See also Paus. v. 14 for a legend of an oracle of Earth herself at Olympia.

[4] Paus. ix. 39.

[5] Τροφώνιος from τρέφω. The visitor, who lay a long time, οὐ μάλα συμφρονῶν ἐναργῶς εἴτ᾽ ἐγρήγορεν εἴτ᾽ ὠνειροπόλει (Plut. de Genio Socratis, 22), had doubtless been partially asphyxiated. St. Patrick's Purgatory was perhaps conducted on the same plan.

[6] Paus. i. 43, and for further references on baetyls see Lebègue, p. 85. See also Lubbock, Origin of Civilisation, p. 225.

[7] Soph. Ant. 1001 ; Paus. ix. 16 ; and cf. Eur. Phoen. 841.

[8] Strabo, ix. p. 619. They watched ἀπὸ τῆς ἐσχάρας τοῦ ἀστραπαίου Διός. Even a place where lots were customarily drawn might become a seat of oracle.—Paus. vii. 25.

by nearness to the height of heaven.[1] . It is enough to understand that in Greece, as in other countries over which successive
waves of immigration have passed, the sacred places were for
the most part selected for primitive reasons, and in primitive
times; then as more civilised races succeeded and Apollo
came,—whence or in what guise cannot here be discussed,—the
old shrines were dedicated to new divinities, the old symbols
were metamorphosed or disappeared. The fetish-stones were
crowned by statues, or replaced by statues and buried in the
earth.[2] The Sibyls—symbol of the divinations that issue
·from chasms—died in the temples, and the sun-god's island
holds the sepulchre of the moon-maidens of the northern
sky.[3]

It is impossible to arrange in quite logical order phenomena
which touch each other at so many points, but in making our
transition from these impersonal or hardly personal oracles of
divination to the "voice-oracles"[4] of classical times, we may
first mention the well-known Voice or Rumour which as
early as Homer runs heaven-sent through the multitude of
men, or sometimes prompts to revolution by "the word of
Zeus."[5]

To this we may add the belief that words spoken at some
critical and culminant, or even at some arbitrarily-chosen
moment, have a divine significance. We find some trace of

---

[1] There is little trace in Greece of "weather-oracles,"—such as the Blocks-
berg,—hills deriving a prophetic reputation from the indications of coming
rain, etc., drawn from clouds on their summits. The sanctity of Olympus, as
is well known, is connected with a supposed elevation above all elemental
disturbances.

[2] Pind. *Ol.* viii. 3, and for further references see Hermann, *Griech. Ant.* ii.
247. Maury (ii. 447) seems to deny this localisation on insufficient grounds.

[3] The Hyperboreæ, see Reff. ap. Lebègue, p. 69. See also Klausen, *Aeneas
und die Penaten*, p. 207 foll., on the connection of Sibyls and χάσματα. Hero-
phile had herself prophesied from the Delphian baetyl, but in her epitaph
she thanks Apollo and complains of nobody but Fate. The bones of the
oracular Demo also were interred in a water-pot in the temple of Apollo at
Cumae.—Paus. x. 12.

[4] Χρησμοὶ φθεγματικοί.

[5] ὄσσα, φήμη, κληδών, ὀμφή—*Il.* ii. 93 ; Herod. ix. 100 ; *Od.* iii. 215, etc.
These words are probably used sometimes for regular oracular communications.

this in the oracle of Teiresias,[1] and it appears in a strange form
in an old oracle said to have been given to Homer, which tells
him to beware of the moment when some young children shall
ask him a riddle which he is unable to answer.[2] Cases of
omens given by a chance word in classical times are too familiar
to need further reference.[3] What we have to notice here is
that this casual method of learning the will of heaven was
systematised into a practice at certain oracular temples, where
the applicant made his sacrifice, stopped his ears, went into the
market-place, and accepted the first words he happened to hear
as a divine intimation. We hear of oracles on this pattern at
Memphis,[4] and at Pharae in Achaea.[5]

From these voices, which, though clearly audible, are, as it
were, unowned and impersonal, we may pass to voices which
have a distinct personality but are heard only by the sleeping
ear. Dreams of departed friends are likely to be the first
phenomenon which inspires mankind with the idea that they
can hold converse with a spiritual world. We find dreams at
the very threshold of the theology of almost all nations, and
accordingly it does not surprise us to find Homer asserting
that dreams come from Zeus,[6] or painting, with a pathos which
later literature has never surpassed, the strange vividness
and agonising insufficiency of these fugitive visions of the
night.[7]

And throughout Greek literature presaging dreams which
form, as Plutarch says, "an unfixed and wandering oracle

---

[1] *Od.* xi. 126.

[2] ἀλλὰ νέων παίδων αἴνιγμα φύλαξαι. Paus. x. 24 ; Anth. Pal. xiv. 66. This
conundrum, when it was at length put to Homer, was of so vulgar a
character that no discredit is reflected on the Father of Poetry by his perplexity as to its solution. (Homeri et Hesiodi certamen, *ad fin.*)

[3] Herodotus ix. 90 may be selected as an example of a happy chance in
forcing an omen.

[4] Dio Chrys. *ad Alex.* 32. 13, παῖδες ἀπαγγέλλουσι παίζοντες τὸ δοκοῦν τῷ θεῷ.

[5] Paus. vii. 22.

[6] *Il.* i. 63. Or from Hermes, or earth, or the gods below.

[7] *Il.* xxiii. 97. If we accept the theory of an older Achilleid we find the
importance of augury proper decreasing, of dreams increasing, in the Homeric
poems themselves. Geddes, *Hom. Probl.* p. 186 ; cf. Mure, *Hist. Gr. Lit.* i.
492. Similarly Apollo's darts grow more gentle, and his visitations more
benign.—Geddes, p. 140.

of Night and Moon,[1]" are abundant in every form, from the high behest laid on Bellerophon "when in the dark of night stood by him the shadowy-shielded maid, and from a dream, suddenly, a waking vision she became,"[2] down to the dreams in the temples of Serapis or of Aesculapius which Aristides the Rhetorician has embalmed for us in his Sacred Orations,—the dream which " seemed to indicate a bath, yet not without a certain ambiguity," or the dream which left him in distressing uncertainty whether he were to take an emetic or no.[3]

And just as we have seen that the custom of observing birds, or of noting the omens of casual speech, tended to fix itself permanently in certain shrines, so also dream-oracles, or temples where the inquirer slept in the hope of obtaining an answer from the god seen in vision, or from some other vision sent by him, were one of the oldest forms of oracular seats. Brizo, a dream-prophetess, preceded Apollo at Delos.[4] A similar legend contrasts " the divination of darkness " at Delphi with Apollo's clear prophetic song.[5] Night herself was believed to send visions at Megara,[6] and coins of Commodus still show us her erect and shrouded figure, the torches that glimmer in her shade. Amphiaraus,[7] Amphilochus,[8] Charon,[9] Pasiphae,[10] Herakles,[11] Dionysus,[12] and above all Aesculapius,[13] gave answers after this fashion, mainly, but not entirely, in cases of sickness. The prevalence of heroes, rather than gods, as the

---

[1] Plut. *Ser. Num. Vind.* 22.   [2] Pind. *Ol.* xiii. 100.

[3] Ar. Rhet. vol. i. p. 275 (Dind.), ἔχον μέν τινα ἔννοιαν λούτρου, οὐ μέντοι χωρίς γε ὑπονοίας, and i. 285.

[4] Athen. viii. 2, and see Lebègue, p. 218 ; comp. Aesch. *Ag.* 275.

[5] Eur. *Iph. Taur.* 1234 foll.   [6] Paus. i. 40.

[7] Paus. i. 34.   [8] Dio Cass. lxxii. 7.

[9] Eustath. *Schol. ad Dionys. Perieg.* 1153.

[10] Cic. *de Div.* i. 43 ; Plut. *Agis.* 9, and cf. Maury, ii. 453.

[11] Paus. ix. 24, comp. inscr. ap. G. Wolff, *de Noviss.* p. 29, and see Plut. *de Malign. Herod.* 31 for the dream of Leonidas in Herakles' temple.

[12] Paus. x. 33.

[13] Ar. Rhet. *passim* ; Iambl. *Myst.* 3. 3, etc. See also Val. Max. i. 7 ; Diod. Sic. v. 62 ; Ar. Rhet. *Sacr. Serm.* iii. 311, for dreams sent by Athene, the Soteres, Hemithea. Further references will be found in Maury, iii. 456, and for the relation of Apollo to dreams see Bouché-Leclercq, *Hist. de la Divination,* i. 204.

givers of oracles in dreams seems still further to indicate the immediate derivation of this form of revelation from the accustomed appearance of departed friends in sleep.

The next step takes us to the most celebrated class of oracles, —those in which the prophetess, or more rarely the prophet, gives vent in agitated trance to the words which she is inspired to utter. We encounter here the phenomena of possession, so familiar to us in the Bible, and of which theology still maintains the genuineness, while science would explain them by delirium, hysteria, or epilepsy. It was this phenomenon, connected first, as Pausanias tells us,[1] with the Apolline oracles, which gave a wholly new impressiveness to oracular replies. No longer confined to simple affirmation and negation, or to the subjective and ill-remembered utterances of a dream, they were now capable of embracing all topics, and of being preserved in writing as a revelation of general applicability. These oracles of inspiration,—taken in connection with the oracles uttered by visible phantoms, which become prominent at a later era,—may be considered as marking the highest point of development to which Greek oracles attained. It will be convenient to defer our consideration of some of these phenomena till we come to the great controversy between Porphyry and Eusebius, in which they were for the first time fully discussed. · But there is one early oracle of the dead, different in some respects from any that succeeded it,[2] which presents so many points for notice that a few reflections on the state of

---

[1] Paus. i. 34.

[2] The distinction drawn by Nägelsbach between this and other "Todtenorakeln" (*Nachhom. Theologie*, p. 189) is surely exaggerated. See Klausen, *Aeneas und die Penaten*, p. 129 foll., for other legends connecting Odysseus with early necromancy, and on this general subject see Herod. v. 92 ; Eur. *Alc.* 1131 ; Plat. *Leg.* x. 909 ; Plut. *Cim.* 6, *de Ser. Num. Vind.* 17 ; Tylor, *Prim. Cult.* ii. 41. The fact, on which Nägelsbach dwells, that Odysseus, after consulting Teiresias, satisfied his affection and his curiosity by interviews with other ghosts in no way alters the original injunction laid on him, the purport of his journey—ψυχῇ χρησόμενον Θηβαίου Τειρεσίαο. Nägelsbach's other argument, that in later times we hear only of a dream-oracle, not an apparition-oracle, of Teiresias seems to me equally weak. Readers of Pausanias must surely feel what a chance it is which has determined the oracles of which we *have* heard.

belief which it indicates will assist us in comprehending the nature of the elevation of Greek faith which was afterwards effected under the influence of Delphi.

For this,—the first oracle of which we have a full account,— the descent of Odysseus to the underworld, "to consult the soul of the Theban Teiresias," shows in a way which it would be hard to parallel elsewhere the possible co-existence in the same mind of the creed and practices of the lowest races with a majesty, a pathos, a power, which human genius has never yet overpassed. The eleventh book of the Odyssey is steeped in the Animism of barbarous peoples. The Cimmerian entrance to the world of souls is the close parallel (to take an instance among many) of the extreme western cape of Vanua Levi, a calm and solemn place of cliff and forest, where the souls of the Fijian dead embark for the judgment-seat of Ndengei, and whither the living come on pilgrimage, thinking to see ghosts and gods.[1] Homer's ghosts cheep and twitter precisely as the shadow-souls of the Algonquin Indians chirp like crickets, and Polynesian spirits speak in squeaking tones, and the accent of the ancestral Zulu, when he reappears on earth, has earned for him the name of Whistler.[2] The expedition of Odysseus is itself paralleled by the exploit of Ojibwa, the eponymous hero of the Ojibbeways, of the Finnish hero Wainamoinen, and of many another savage chief. The revival of the ghosts with blood, itself closely paralleled in old Teutonic mythologies,[3] speaks of the time when the soul is conceived as feeding on the fumes and shadows of earthly food, as when the Chinese beat the drum which summons ancestral souls to supper, and provide a pail of gruel and a spoon for the greater convenience of any ancestor who may unfortunately have been deprived of his head.[4]

Nay, even the inhabitants of that underworld are only the semblances of once living men. "They themselves," in the terrible words of the opening sentence of the Iliad, " have been left a prey to dogs and every bird." Human thought has not

---

[1] *Prim. Cult.* i. 408.
[3] *Ibid.* ii. 346.
[2] *Ibid.* ii. 42.
[4] *Ibid.* ii. 30.

yet reached a point at which spirit could be conceived of as more than the shadow of matter.

And if further evidence were needed, the oracle of Teiresias himself—opening like a chasm into Hades through the sunlit soil of Greece—reveals unwittingly all the sadness which underlies that freshness and power, the misgiving which so often unites the savage and the philosopher, the man who comes before religions and the man who comes after them, in the gloom of the same despair. Himself alone in his wisdom among the ineffectual shades, Teiresias offers to Odysseus, in the face of all his unjust afflictions, no prevention and no cure ; " of honey-sweet return thou askest, but by God's will bitter shall it be ; "—for life's struggle he has no remedy but to struggle to the end, and for the wandering hero he has no deeper promise than the serenity of a gentle death.

And yet Homer "made the theogony of the Greeks."[1] And Homer, through the great ages which followed him, not only retained, but deepened his hold on the Hellenic spirit. It was no mere tradition, it was the ascendency of that essential truth and greatness in Homer, which we still so strongly feel, which was the reason why he was clung to and invoked and explained and allegorised by the loftiest minds of Greece in each successive age ; why he was transformed by Polygnotus, transformed by Plato, transformed by Porphyry. Nay, even in our own day,—and this is not the least significant fact in religious history,—we have seen one of the most dominant, one of the most religious intellects of our century, falling under the same spell, and extracting from Homer's almost savage animism the full-grown mysteries of the Christian faith.

So dangerous would it be to assume such a congruence throughout the whole mass of the thought of any epoch, however barbarous, that the baseness or falsity of some of its tenets should be enough to condemn the rest unheard. So ancient, so innate in man is the power of apprehending by emotion and imagination aspects of reality for which a deliberate

---

[1] Herod. ii. 53, οὗτοι δέ (Homer and Hesiod) εἰσι οἱ ποιήσαντες θεογονίην Ἕλλησι, κ.τ.λ.

culture might often look in vain. To the dictum,—so true though apparently so paradoxical,—which asserts "that the mental condition of the lower races is the key to poetry," we may reply with another apparent paradox,—that poetry is the only thing which every age is certain to recognise as truth.

Having thus briefly considered the nature of each of the main classes of oracular response, it is natural to go on to some inquiry into the history of the leading shrines where these responses were given. The scope of this Essay does not admit of a detailed notice of each of the very numerous oracular seats of which some record has reached us.[1] But before passing on to Delphi, I must dwell on two cases of special interest, where recent explorations have brought us nearer than elsewhere to what may be called the private business of an oracle, or to the actual structure of an Apolline sanctuary.

The oracle of Zeus at Dodona takes the highest place among all the oracles which answered by signs rather than by inspired speech.[2] It claimed to be the eldest of all, and we need not therefore wonder that its phenomena present an unusual confluence of streams of primitive belief. The first mention of Dodona,[3]—in that great invocation of Achilles which is one of the glimpses which Homer gives us of a world far earlier than his own,—seems to indicate that it was then a seat of dream-oracles, where the rude Selloi perhaps drew from the earth on which they slept such visions as she sends among men. But in the Odyssey[4] and in Hesiod[5] the oracle is spoken of as having its seat among the leaves, or in the hollow or base of an oak, and this is the idea which prevailed in classical times.[6] The doves,[7]—if doves there were, and not merely priestesses, whose name, Peleiades, may be derived from

---

[1] The number of Greek oracular seats, with the Barbarian seats known to the Greeks, has been estimated at 260, or an even larger number ; but of very many of these we know no more than the name.

[2] Strab. viii. *Fragm.* ἐχρησμῴδει δ' οὐ διὰ λόγων ἀλλὰ διά τινων συμβόλων, ὥσπερ τὸ ἐν Λιβύῃ Ἀμμωνιακόν. So Suid. *in voc.* Δωδώνη, etc.

[3] *Il.* xvi. 233.

[4] *Od.* xiv. 327, xix. 296.

[5] Hes. *Fr.* 39. 7, ναιόν τ' ἐν πυθμένι φηγοῦ. See Plat. *Phaedr.* 275.

[6] Aesch. *Prom.* 832 ; Soph. *Trach.* 172 and 1167.

[7] See Herod. ii. 54, and comp. *Od.* xii. 63.

some other root,[1]—introduce another element of complexity. Oracles were also given at Dodona by means of lots,[2] and by the falling of water.[3] Moreover, German industry has established the fact, that at Dodona it thunders on more days than anywhere else in Europe, and that no peals are louder anywhere than those which echo among the Acroceraunian mountains. It is tempting to derive the word Dodona from the sound of a thunderclap, and to associate this old Pelasgic sanctuary with the propitiation of elemental deities in their angered hour.[4] But the notices of the oracle in later days are perplexingly at variance with all these views. They speak mainly of oracles given by the sound of caldrons,—struck, according to Strabo,[5] by knucklebones attached to a wand held by a statue. The temple is even said to have 'been *made* of caldrons,[6] or at least they were so arranged, as a certain Demon tells us,[7] that "all in turn, when one was smitten, the caldrons of Dodona rang." The perpetual sound thus caused is alluded to in a triumphant tone by other writers,[8] but it is the more

---

[1] On the Priestesses, see references in Herm. *Griech. Antiq.* ii. 250.

[2] Cic. *de Div.* ii. 32.

[3] Serv. *ad Aen.* iii. 466.

[4] I do not think that we can get beyond some such vague conjecture as this, and A. Mommsen and Schmidt's elaborate calculations as to months of maximum frequency of thunderclaps and centres of maximum frequency of earthquakes, as determining the time of festivals or the situation of oracular temples, seem to me to be quite out of place. If a savage possessed the methodical patience of a German observer, he would be a savage no more. *Savants* must be content to leave Aristotle's τύχη καὶ τὸ αὐτόματον,—chance and spontaneity,—as causes of a large part of the action of primitive men.

The dictum of Götte (*Delphische Orakel*, p. 13) seems to me equally unproveable : "Dodona, wohin die schwarzen aegyptischen Tauben geflogen kamen, ist wohl unbestreitbar eine aegyptische Cultstätte, die Schwesteranstalt von Ammonium, beide Thebens Töchter." The geographical position of Dodona is much against this view, the doves are very problematical, and the possible existence of a primitive priesthood in the Selloi is no proof of an Egyptian influence.

[5] Strab. lib. vii. *Fragm.* ap. Hermann, *Griech. Ant.* ii. 251, where see further citations.

[6] Steph. Byz. *s. voc.* Δωδώνη, quoted by Carapanos, in whose monograph on Dodona citations on all these points will be found.

[7] Müller, *Fragm. Hist. Gr.* iii. 125.

[8] Callim. *Hymn. in Del.* 286 ; Philostr. *Imag.* ii. 33 (a slightly different account).

difficult to determine in what precise way the will of Zeus was understood.

Among such a mass of traditions, it is of course easy to find analogies. The doves may be compared to the hissing ducks of the Abipones, which were connected with the souls of the dead,[1] or with the doves in Popayan, which are spared as inspired by departed souls. The tree-worship opens up lines of thought too well known for repetition. We may liken the Dodonaean "voiceful oak" to the tamarisks of Beersheba, and the oak of Shechem,—its whisper to the "sound of a going in the tops of the mulberry-trees," which prompted Israel to war,[2] and so on down the long train of memories to Joan of Arc hanging with garlands the fairies' beech beside her father's door at Domremy, and telling her persecutors that if they would set her in a wood once more she would hear the heavenly voices plain.[3] Or we may prefer, with another school, to trace this tree also back to the legendary Ygdrassil, "the celestial tree of the Aryan family," with its spreading branches of the stratified clouds of heaven. One legend at least points to the former interpretation as the more natural.

---

[1] *Prim. Cult.* ii. 6. The traces of animal-worship in Greece are many and interesting, but are not closely enough connected with our present subject to be discussed at length. Apollo's possible characters, as the Wolf, the Locust, or the Fieldmouse (or the Slayer of wolves, of locusts, or of field-mice), have not perceptibly affected his oracles. Still less need we be detained by the fish-tailed Eurynome, or the horse-faced Demeter (Paus. viii. 41, 42). And although from the time when the boy-prophet Iamus lay among the wallflowers, and "the two bright-eyed serpents fed him with the harmless poison of the bee" (Pind. *Ol.* vi. 28), snakes appear frequently in connection with prophetic power, their worship falls under the head of divination rather than of oracles. The same remark may be made of ants, cats, and cows. The bull Apis occupies a more definite position, but though he was visited by Greeks, his worship was not a product of Greek thought. The nearest Greek approach, perhaps, to an animal-oracle was at the fount of Myræ in Cilicia (Plin. *H.N.* xxxii. 2), where fish swam up to eat or reject the food thrown to them. "Diripere eos carnes objectas laetum est consultantibus," says Pliny, "caudis abigere dirum." And it appears that live snakes were kept in the cave of Trophonius (Philostr. *Vit. Apoll.* viii. 19), in order to inspire terror in visitors, who were instructed to appease them with cakes (Suid. *s. v. μελιτοῦττα*).

[2] 2 Sam. v. 24.

[3] "Dixit quod si esset in uno nemore bene audiret voces venientes ad eam." —On Tree-worship see Lubbock, *Origin of Civilisation*, p. 206 foll.

For just as a part of the ship Argo, keel or prow, was made of the Dodonaean oak, and Argo's crew heard with astonishment the ship herself prophesy to them on the sea :—

> " But Jason and the builder, Argus, knew
> Whereby the prow foretold things strange and new ;
> Nor wondered aught, but thanked the gods therefore,
> As far astern they left the Mysian shore," [1]—

so do we find a close parallel to this among the Siamese,[2] who believe that the inhabiting nymphs of trees pass into the guardian spirits of boats built with their wood, to which they continue to sacrifice.

Passing on to the answers which were given at this shrine, we find that at Dodona,[3] as well as at Delphi,[4] human sacrifice is to be discerned in the background. But in the form in which the legend reaches us, its horror has been sublimed into pathos. Coresus, priest of Bacchus at Calydon, loved the maiden Callirhoe in vain. Bacchus, indignant at his servant's repulse, sent madness and death on Calydon. The oracle of Dodona announced that Coresus must sacrifice Callirhoe, or some one who would die for her. No one was willing to die for her, and she stood up beside the altar to be slain. But when Coresus looked on her his love overcame his anger, and he slew himself in her stead. Then her heart turned to him, and beside the fountain to which her name was given she died by her own hand, and followed him to the underworld.

There is another legend of Dodona [5] to which the student of oracles may turn with a certain grim satisfaction at the thought that the ambiguity of style which has so often baffled him did once at least carry its own penalty with it. Certain Boeotian envoys, so the story runs, were told by Myrtile, the priestess of Dodona, " that it would be best for them to do the most impious thing possible." The Boeotians

---

[1] Morris's *Life and Death of Jason*, Book iv. *ad fin.*
[2] *Prim. Cult.* ii. 198.   [3] Paus. vii. 21.
[4] Eus. *Pr. Ev.* v. 27, παρθένον Αἰπυτίδαν κλῆρος καλεῖ, etc. See also the romantic story of Melanippus and Comoetho, Paus. vii. 19.
[5] Ephor. ad Strab. ix. 2 ; Heracl. Pont. *Fragm. Hist. Gr.* ii. 198 ; Proclus, *Chrest.* ii. 248, and see Carapanos.

immediately threw the priestess into a caldron of boiling water, remarking that they could not think of anything much more impious than *that.*

The ordinary business of Dodona, however, was of a less exciting character. M. Carapanos has discovered many tablets on which the inquiries of visitors to the oracle were inscribed, and these give a picture, sometimes grotesque, but oftener pathetic, of the simple faith of the rude Epirots who dwelt round about the shrine. The statuette of an acrobat hanging to a rope shows that the "Dodonaean Pelasgian Zeus" did not disdain to lend his protection to the least dignified forms of jeopardy to life and limb. A certain Agis asks "whether he has lost his blankets and pillows himself, or some one outside has stolen them." An unknown woman asks simply how she may be healed of her disease. Lysanias asks if he is indeed the father of the child which his wife Nyla is soon to bear. Evandrus and his wife, in broken dialect, seek to know "by what prayer or worship they may fare best now and for ever." And there is something strangely pathetic in finding on a broken plate of lead the imploring inquiry of the fierce and factious Corcyreans,—made, alas! in vain,—" to what god or hero offering prayer and sacrifice they might live together in unity?"[1] "For the men of that time," says Plato,[2] "since they were not wise as ye are nowadays, it was enough in their simplicity to listen to oak or rock, if only these told them true." To those rude tribes, indeed, their voiceful trees were the one influence which lifted them above barbarism and into contact with the surrounding world. Again and again Dodona was ravaged,[3] but so long as the oak was standing the temple rose anew. When at last an Illyrian bandit cut down the oak [4] the presence of Zeus was gone, and the desolate Thesprotian valley has known since then no other sanctity, and has found no other voice.

I proceed to another oracular seat, of great mythical celebrity, though seldom alluded to in classical times, to which

---

[1] Τίνι κα θεῶν ἢ ἡρώων θύοντες καὶ ὠχόμενοι ὁμονοοῖεν ἐπὶ τἀγαθόν.

[2] Phaedr. 275. *Recherches sur Délos*, par J. A. Lebègue, 1876.

[3] Strab. vii. 6 ; Polyb. ix. 67, and cf. Wolff, *de Noviss.* p. 13.

[4] Serv. *ad Aen.* iii. 466.

a recent exploration has given a striking interest, bringing us, as it were, into direct connection across so many ages with the birth and advent of a god.

On the slope of Cynthus, near the mid-point of the Isle of Delos, ten gigantic blocks of granite, covered with loose stones and the débris of ages, form a rude vault, half hidden in the hill. The islanders call it the "dragon's cave;" travellers had taken it for the remains of a fortress or of a reservoir. It was reserved for two French savants to show how much knowledge the most familiar texts have yet to yield when they are meditated on by minds prepared to compare and to comprehend. A familiar passage in Homer,[1] illustrated by much ancient learning and many calculations of his own, suggested to M. Burnouf, Director of the French School of Archæology at Athens, that near this point had been a primitive post of observation of the heavens; nay, that prehistoric men had perhaps measured their seasons by the aid of some rude instrument in this very cave. An equally familiar line of Virgil,[2] supported by some expressions in a Homeric hymn, led M. Lebègue to the converging conjecture that at this spot the Delian oracle had its seat; that here it was that Leto's long wanderings ended, and Apollo and Artemis were born. Every schoolboy has learnt by heart the sounding lines which tell how Aeneas "venerated the temple built of ancient stone," and how at the god's unseen coming "threshold and laurel trembled, and all the mountain round about was moved." But M. Lebègue was the first to argue hence with confidence that the oracle must have been upon the mountain and not on the coast, and that those ancient stones, like the Cyclopean treasure-house of Mycenae, might be found and venerated still. So far as a reader can judge without personal survey, these expectations have been amply fulfilled.[3] At each step M. Lebegue's

---

[1] *Od.* xv. 403. Em. Burnouf, *Revue Archéologique*, Aug. 8, 1873.

[2] *Aen.* iii. 84 ; Hom. *Hymn.*, *Del.* 15-18, and 79-81.

[3] M. Homolle (*Fouilles de Délos*, 1879) gives no direct opinion on the matter, but his researches indirectly confirm M. Lebègue's view, in so far as that among the numerous inscriptions, etc., which he has found among the ruins of the temple of Apollo on the coast, there seems to be no trace of oracular response or inquiry.

researches revealed some characteristic of an oracular shrine. In a walled external space were the remains of a marble base on which a three-legged instrument had been fixed by metal claws. Then came a transverse wall, shutting off the temple within, which looks westward, so that the worshipper, as he approaches, may face the east. The floor of this temple is reft by a chasm,—the continuation of a ravine which runs down the hill, and across which the sanctuary has been intentionally built. And in the inner recess is a rough block of granite, smoothed on the top, where a statue has stood. The statue has probably been knocked into the chasm by a rock falling through the partly-open roof. Its few fragments show that it represented a young god. The stone itself is probably a fetish, surviving, with the Cyclopean stones which make the vault above it, from a date perhaps many centuries before the Apolline religion came. This is all, but this is enough. For we have here in narrow compass all the elements of an oracular shrine ; the westward aspect, the sacred enclosure, the tripod, the sanctuary, the chasm, the fetish-stone, the statue of a youthful god. And when the situation is taken into account, the correspondence with the words both of Virgil and of the Homerid becomes so close as to be practically convincing. It is true that the smallness of scale,—the sanctuary measures some twenty feet by ten,—and the remote archaism of the structure, from which all that was beautiful, almost all that was Hellenic, has long since disappeared, cause at first a shock of disappointment like that inspired by the size of the citadel, and the character of the remains, at Hissarlik. Yet, on reflection, this seeming incongruity is an additional element of proof. There is something impressive in the thought that amidst all the marble splendour which made Delos like a jewel in the sea, it was this cavernous and prehistoric sanctuary, as mysterious to Greek eyes as to our own, which their imagination identified with that earliest temple which Leto promised, in her hour of trial, that Apollo's hands should build. This, the one remaining seat of oracle out of the hundreds which Greece contained, was the one sanctuary which the Far-darter himself had wrought ;—no wonder that his mighty workmanship has outlasted the designs of men !

All else is gone. The temples, the amphitheatres, the colonnades, which glittered on every crest and coign of the holy island, have sunk into decay. But he who sails among the isles of Greece may still note around sea-girt Delos "the dark wave welling shoreward beneath the shrill and breezy air;"[1] he may still note at sunrise, as on that sunrise when the god was born, "the whole island abloom with shafts of gold, as a hill's crested summit blooms with woodland flowers."[2] "And thou thyself, lord of the silver bow," he may exclaim with the Homerid in that burst of exultation in which the uniting Ionian race seems to leap to the consciousness of all its glory in an hour,—"thou walkedst here in very presence, on Cynthus' leafy crown!"

> " Ah, many a forest, many a peak is thine,
>   On many a promontory stands thy shrine,
>   But best and first thy love, thy home, is here;
>   Of all thine isles thy Delian isle most dear ;—
>   There the long-robed Ionians, man and maid,
>   Press to thy feast in all their pomp arrayed,—
>   To thee, to Artemis, to Leto pay
>   The heartfelt honour on thy natal day ;—
>   Immortal would he deem them, ever young,
>   Who then should walk the Ionian folk among,
>   Should those tall men, those stately wives behold,
>   Swift ships seafaring and long-garnered gold :—
>   But chiefliest far his eyes and ears would meet
>   Of sights, of sounds most marvellously sweet,
>   The Delian girls amid the thronging stir,
>   The loved hand-maidens of the Far-darter ;
>   The Delian girls, whose chorus, long and long,
>   Chants to the god his strange, his ancient song,—
>   Till whoso hears it deems his own voice sent
>   Thro' the azure air that music softly blent,
>   So close it comes to each man's heart, and so
>   His own soul feels it and his glad tears flow."

Such was the legend of the indigenous, the Hellenic Apollo. But the sun does not rise over one horizon alone, and the glory of Delos was not left uncontested or unshared. Another hymn, of inferior poetical beauty, but of equal, if not greater, authority among the Greeks, relates how Apollo descended from the Thessalian Olympus, and sought a place where he

---

[1] *Hymn. Del.* 27.   [2] *Ibid.* 138-164.

might found his temple: how he was refused by Tilphussa, and selected Delphi; and how, in the guise of a dolphin, he led thither a crew of Cretans to be the servants of his shrine. With this hymn, so full of meaning for the comparative mythologist, we are here only concerned as introducing us to Apollo in the aspect in which we know him best, "giving his answers from the laurel-wood, beneath the hollows of Parnassus' hill." [1]

At Delphi, as at Dodona, we seem to trace the relics of many a form of worship and divination which we cannot now distinctly recall. From that deep cleft "in rocky Pytho," Earth, the first prophetess, gave her earliest oracle,[2] in days which were already a forgotten antiquity to the heroic age of Greece. The maddening vapour, which was supposed to rise from the chasm,[3] belongs to nymph-inspiration rather than to the inspiration of Apollo. At Delphi too was the most famous of all fetish-stones, believed in later times to be the centre of the earth.[4] At Delphi divination from the sacrifice of goats reached an immemorial antiquity.[5] Delphi too was an ancient centre of divination by fire, a tradition which survived in the name of Pyrcon,[6] given to Hephaestus's minister, while Hephaestus shared with Earth the possession of the shrine, and in the mystic title of the Flame-kindlers,[7] assigned in oracular utterances to the Delphian folk. At Delphi too, in ancient days, the self-moved lots sprang in the goblet in obedience to Apollo's will.[8] The waving of the Delphic laurel,[9] which in later times seemed no more than a token of the wind and

---

[1] *Hymn. Pyth.* 214.

[2] Aesch. *Eum.* 2 ; Paus. x. 5 ; cf. Eur. *Iph. Taur.* 1225 *sqq.*

[3] Strabo, ix. p. 419, etc. In a paper read before the British Archæological Association, March 5, 1879, Dr. Phenè has given an interesting account of subterranean chambers at Delphi, which seem to indicate that gases from the subterranean Castalia were received in a chamber where the Pythia may have sat. But in the absence of direct experiment this whole question is physiologically very obscure.

[4] Paus. x. 16, etc.

[5] Diod. Sic. xvi. 26. Pliny (*Hist. Nat.* vii. 56) ascribes the invention of this mode of divination to Delphos, a son of Apollo.

[6] Paus. x. 5.   [7] Plut. *Pyth.* 24.

[8] Suidas, iii. p. 237 ; cf. Callim. *Hymn. in Apoll.* 45, etc.

[9] Ar. *Plut.* 213 ; Callim. *Hymn. in Apoll.* 1, etc.

spiritual stirring which announced the advent of the god, was probably the relic of an ancient tree-worship, like that of Dodona,[1] and Daphne, priestess of Delphi's primeval Earth-oracle,[2] is but one more of the old symbolical figures that have melted back again into impersonal nature at the appearing of the God of Day. Lastly, at Delphi is laid the scene of the sharpest conflict between the old gods and the new. Whatever may have been the meaning of the Python,—whether he were a survival of snake-worship, or a winding stream which the sun's rays dry into rotting marsh, or only an emblem of the cloud which trails across the sunlit heaven,—his slaughter by Apollo was an integral part of the early legend, and at the Delphian festivals the changes of the " Pythian strain " commemorated for many a year that perilous encounter,—the god's descent into the battle-field, his shout of summons, his cry of conflict, his paean of victory, and then the gnashing of the dragon's teeth in his fury, the hiss of his despair.[3] And the mythology of a later age has connected with this struggle the first ideas of moral conflict and expiation which the new religion had to teach ; has told us that the victor needed purification after his victory ; that he endured and was forgiven ; and that the god himself first wore his laurel-wreath as a token of supplication, and not of song.[4]

With a similar ethical purpose the simple narrative of the Homerid has been transformed into a legend [5] of a type which meets us often in the middle ages, but which wears a deeper pathos when it occurs in the midst of Hellenic gladness and youth,—the legend of Trophonius and Agamedes, the arti-

---

[1] I cannot, however, follow M. Maury (ii. 442) in supposing (as he does in the case of the Delian laurel, *Aen.* iii. 73) that such tree-movements need indicate an ancient habit of divining from their sound. The idea of a wind accompanying divine manifestations seems more widely diffused in Greece than the Dodonaean idea of vocal trees. Cf. (for instance) Plut. *De Def. orac.* of the Delphian adytum, εὐωδίας ἀναπίμπλαται καὶ πνεύματος.

[2] Paus. x. 5.

[3] ἄμπειρα, κατακελευσμός, σάλπιγξ, δάκτυλοι, ὀδοντισμός, σύριγγες. See August Mommsen's *Delphika* on this topic.

[4] Bötticher, *Baumcultus*, p. 353 ; and see reff. ap. Herm. *Griech. Ant.* ii. 127. Cf. Eur. *Ion*, 114 *sqq.*

[5] Cic. *Tusc.* i. 47 ; cf. Plut. *De Consol. ad Apollon.* 14.

ficers who built the god's home after his heart's desire, and whom he rewarded with the guerdon that is above all recompense, a speedy and a gentle death.

In the new temple at any rate, as rebuilt in historic times, the moral significance of the Apolline religion was expressed in unmistakable imagery. Even as "four great zones of sculpture" girded the hall of Camelot, the centre of the faith which was civilising Britain, "with many a mystic symbol" of the victory of man, so over the portico of the Delphian god were painted or sculptured such scenes as told of the triumph of an ideal humanity over the monstrous deities which are the offspring of savage fear.[1]

There was "the light from the eyes of the twin faces" of Leto's children; there was Herakles with golden sickle, Iolaus with burning brand, withering the heads of the dying Hydra,— "the story," says the girl in the *Ion* who looks thereon, "which is sung beside my loom;" there was the rider of the winged steed slaying the fire-breathing Chimaera; there was the tumult of the giants' war; Pallas lifting the aegis against Enceladus; Zeus crushing Mimas with the great bolt fringed with flame, and Bacchus "with his unwarlike ivy-wand laying another of Earth's children low."

It is important thus to dwell on some of the indications, and there are many of them, which point to the conviction entertained in Greece as to the ethical and civilising influence of Delphi, inasmuch as the responses which have actually been preserved to us, though sufficient, when attentively considered, to support this view, are hardly such as would at once have suggested it. The set collections of oracles, which no doubt contained those of most ethical importance, have perished; of all the " dark-written tablets, groaning with many an utterance of Loxias," [2] none remain to us except such frag-

---

[1] The passage in the *Ion*, 190-218, no doubt describes either the portico which the Athenians dedicated at Delphi about 426 B.C. (Paus. x. 11), or (as the words of the play, if taken strictly, would indicate) the façade of the temple itself.

[2] Eur. *Fr.* 625. Collections of oracles continued to be referred to till the Turks took Constantinople, *i.e.* for about 2000 years. See reff. ap. Wolff, *de Noviss.* p. 48.

ments of Porphyry's treatise as Eusebius has embodied in his refutation. And many of the oracles which we do possess owe their preservation to the most trivial causes,—to their connection with some striking anecdote, or to something quaint in their phraseology which has helped to make them proverbial. The reader, therefore, who passes from the majestic descriptions of the *Ion* or the *Eumenides* to the actual study of the existing oracles will at first run much risk of disappointment. Both style and subject will often seem unworthy of these lofty claims. He will come, for instance, on such oracles as that which orders Temenus to seek as guide of the army a man with three eyes, who turns out (according to different legends) to be either a one-eyed man on a two-eyed horse, or a two-eyed man on a one-eyed mule.[1] This oracle is composed precisely on the model of the primitive riddles of the Aztec and the Zulu, and is almost repeated in Scandinavian legend, where Odin's single eye gives point to the enigma.[2] Again, the student's ear will often be offended by roughnesses of rhythm which seem unworthy of the divine inventor of the hexameter.[3] And the constantly recurring prophecies are, for the most part, uninteresting and valueless, as the date of their composition cannot be proved, nor their genuineness in any way tested. As an illustration of the kind of difficulties which we here encounter, we may select one remarkable oracle,[4] of immense celebrity in antiquity, which certainly suggests more questions than we can readily answer. The outline of the familiar story is as follows:—Croesus wished to make war on Cyrus, but was afraid to do so without express sanction from heaven. It was therefore all-important to him to test the veracity of the oracles, and his character, as the most religious man of his time, enabled him to do so systematically without risk of incurring the charge of impiety. He sent messages to the six best-known

---

[1] Apollod. ii. 8 ; Paus. v. 3. [2] *Prim. Cult.* i. 85.

[3] Bald though the god's style may often be, he possesses at any rate a sounder notion of metre than some of his German critics. Lobeck (*Aglaophamus*, p. 852), attempting to restore a lost response, suggests the line

στενυγρὴν δ'ἐνοεῦν εὐρυγάστορα οὐ κατὰ γαῖαν,

He apologises for the quantity of the first syllable of εὐρυγαστορα, but seems to think that no further remark is needed.

[4] Herod. i. 47.

oracles then existing,—to Delphi, to Dodona, to Branchidae, to the oracles of Zeus Ammon, of Trophonius, of Amphiaraus. On the hundredth day from leaving Sardis, his envoys were to ask what Croesus was at that moment doing. Four oracles failed; Amphiaraus was nearly right; Apollo at Delphi entirely succeeded. For the Pythia answered, with exact truth, that Croesus was engaged in boiling a lamb and a tortoise together in a copper vessel with a copper lid. The messengers, who had not themselves known what Croesus was going to do, returned to Sardis and reported, and were then once more despatched to Delphi, with gifts so splendid that in the days of Herodotus they were still the glory of the sanctuary. They now asked the practically important question as to going to war, and received a quibbling answer which, in effect, lured on Croesus to his destruction.

Now here the two things certain are that Croesus did send these gifts to Delphi, and did go to war with Cyrus. Beyond these facts there is no sure footing. Short and pithy fragments of poetry, like the oracles on which the story hangs, are generally among the earliest and most enduring fragments of genuine history. On the other hand, they are just the utterances which later story-tellers are most eager to invent. Nor must we argue from their characteristic diction, for the pseudo-oracular is a style which has in all ages been cultivated with success. The fact which it is hardest to dispose of is the existence of the prodigious, the unrivalled offerings of Croesus at Delphi. Why were they sent there, unless for some such reason as Herodotus gives? Or are they sufficiently explained by a mere reference to that almost superstitious deference with which the Mermnadae seem to have regarded the whole religion and civilisation of Greece? With our imperfect data, we can perhaps hardly go with safety beyond the remark that, granting the genuineness of the oracle about the tortoise, and the substantial truth of Herodotus's account, there will still be no reason to suppose that the god had any foreknowledge as to the result of Croesus's war. The story itself, in fact, contains almost a proof to the contrary. We cannot suppose that the god, in saying, "Croesus, if he cross the Halys, shall undo a mighty realm," was intentionally inciting his favoured servant to his ruin. It is obvious that he was sheltering his ignorance behind a calculated ambiguity. And the only intelligence to which he or his priestess could, on any hypothesis, fairly lay claim, would be of the kind commonly described as " second-sight," a problem with which ethnologists have already to deal all over the world, from the Hebrides to the Coppermine River.

It is obvious that the documents before us are far from enabling us to prove even this hypothesis. And we are further still from any evidence for actual prophecy which can stand a critical investigation. Hundreds of such cases are indeed reported to us, and it was on a conviction that Apollo did indeed foretell the future that the .authority of Delphi mainly depended. But when we have said this, we have said all ;· no case is so reported as to enable us altogether to exclude the possibility of coincidence, or of the fabrication of the prophecy after the event. But, on the other hand,—and this is a more surprising circumstance,—it is equally difficult to get together any satisfactory evidence for the conjecture which the parallel between Delphi and the Papacy so readily suggests,—that the power of the oracle was due to the machinations of a priestly aristocracy, with widely-scattered agents, who insinuated themselves into the confidence, and traded on the credulity, of mankind. We cannot but suppose that, to some extent at least, this must have been the case, that when " the Pythia philippised," she reflected the fears of a knot of Delphian proprietors ; that the unerring counsel given to private persons, on which Plutarch insists, must have rested, in part at least, on a secret acquaintance with their affairs, possibly acquired in some cases under the seal of confession. In the paucity, however, of direct evidence to this effect, our estimate of the amount of pressure exercised by a deliberate human agency in determining the policy of Delphi must rest mainly on our antecedent view of what is likely to have been the case, where the interests involved were of such wide importance.[1]

---

[1] For this view of the subject, see Hüllmann, *Würdigung des Delphischen Orakels* ; Götte, *Das Delphische Orakel*, and Mr. Justice Bowen's Essay on " Delphi." August Mommsen (*Delphika*) takes a somewhat similar view, and

For indeed the political influence of the Delphian oracle, however inspired or guided,—the value to Hellas of this one unquestioned centre of national counsel and national unity,— has always formed one of the most impressive topics with which the historian of Greece has had to deal. And I shall pass this part of my subject rapidly by, as already familiar to most readers, and shall not repeat at length the well-known stories,—the god's persistent command to expel the Peisistratids from Athens, his partiality for Sparta, as shown both in encouragement and warning,[1] or the attempts, successful[2] and unsuccessful,[3] to bribe his priestess. Nor shall I do more than allude to the encouragement of colonisation, counsel of great wisdom, which the god lost no opportunity of enforcing both on the Dorian and Ionian stocks. He sent the Cretans to Sicily,[4] and Alcmaeon to the Echinades;[5] he ordered the foundation of Byzantium[6] " over against the city of the blind;" he sent Archias to Ortygia to found Syracuse,[7] the Boeotians to Heraclea at Pratos,[8] and the Spartans to Heraclea in Thessaly.[9] And in the story which Herodotus[10] and Pindar[11] alike have made renowned, he singled out Battus,—anxious merely to learn a cure for his stammer, but type of the man with a destiny higher than he knows,—to found at Cyrene "a charioteering city upon the silvern bosom of the hill." And, as has often been remarked, this function of colonisation had a religious as well as a political import. The colonists, before whose adventurous armaments Apollo, graven on many a gem, still hovers over the sea, carried with them the civilising

---

calls the Pythia a "blosse Figurantin," but his erudition has added little to the scanty store of texts on which Hüllmann, etc., depend. I may mention here that Hendess has collected most of the existing oracles (except those quoted by Eusebius) in a tract, *Oracula quae supersunt*, etc., which is convenient for reference.

[1] Herod. vi. 52 ; Thuc. i. 118, 123 ; ii. 54. Warnings, ap. Paus. iii. 8 ; ix. 32 ; Diod. Sic. xi. 50 ; xv. 54. Plut. *Lys.* 22 ; *Agesil.* 3.

[2] Cleisthenes, Herod. v. 63, 66 ; Pleistoanax, Thuc. v. 16.

[3] Cleomenes (Cobon and Perialla) Herod. vi. 66 ; Lysander ; Plut. *Lys.* 26 ; Ephor. *Fr.* 127 ; Nep. *Lys.* 3.

[4] Herod. vii. 170.   [5] Thuc. ii. 102.

[6] Strab. vii. 320; Tac. *Ann.* xii. 63 ; but see Herod. iv. 144.

[7] Paus. v. 7.   [8] Justin. xvi. 3.   [9] Thuc. iii. 29.

[10] Herod. iv. 155.   [11] *Pyth.* iv.

maxims of the "just-judging"[1] sanctuary as well as the brand kindled on the world's central altar-stone from that pine-fed[2] and eternal fire. Yet more distinctly can we trace the response of the god to each successive stage of ethical progress to which the evolution of Greek thought attains.

The moralising Hesiod is honoured at Delphi in preference to Homer himself. The Seven Wise Men, the next examples of a deliberate effort after ethical rules, are connected closely with the Pythian shrine. Above the portal is inscribed that first condition of all moral progress, "Know Thyself;" nor does the god refuse to encourage the sages whose inferior ethical elevation suggests to them only such maxims as, "Most men are bad," or "Never go bail."[3]

Solon and Lycurgus, the spiritual ancestors of the Athenian and the Spartan types of virtue, receive the emphatic approval of Delphi, and the "Theban eagle," the first great exponent of the developed faith of Greece, already siding with the spirit against the letter, and refusing to ascribe to a divinity any immoral act, already preaching the rewards and punishments of a future state in strains of impassioned revelation,—this great poet is dear above all men to Apollo during his life, and is honoured for centuries after his death by the priest's nightly summons, "Let Pindar the poet come in to the supper of the god."[4] It is from Delphi that reverence for oaths, respect for the life of slaves, of women, of suppliants, derive in great measure their sanction and strength.[5] I need only allude to the well-known story of Glaucus, who consulted the god to know whether he should deny having received the gold in deposit from his friend, and who was warned in lines which sounded from end to end of Greece of the nameless Avenger of the broken oath,—whose wish was punished like a deed, and whose family was blotted out. The numerous responses

---

[1] *Pyth.* xi. 9.

[2] Plut. *de EI apud Delphos.* Cf. Aesch. *Eum.* 40 ; *Choeph.* 1036.

[3] I say nothing, *de EI apud Delphos*, about the mystic word which five of the wise men, or perhaps all seven together, put up in wooden letters at Delphi, for their wisdom has in this instance wholly transcended our interpretation.

[4] Paus. ix. 23.　　　　　　　　　　　　[5] Herod. ii. 134 ; vi. 139, etc.

of which this is the type brought home to men's minds the notion of right and wrong, of reward and punishment, with a force and impressiveness which was still new to the Grecian world.

More surprising, perhaps, at so early a stage of moral thought, is the catholicity of the Delphian god, his indulgence towards ceremonial differences or ceremonial offences, his reference of casuistical problems to the test of the inward rightness of the heart.[1] It was the Pythian Apollo who replied to the inquiry, " How best are we to worship the gods?" by the philosophic answer, " After the custom of your country,"[2] and who, if those customs varied, would only bid men choose " the best." It was Apollo who rebuked the pompous sacrifice of the rich Magnesian by declaring his preference for the cake and frankincense which the pious Achæan offered in humbleness of heart.[3] It was Apollo who warned the Greeks not to make superstition an excuse for cruelty, who testified, by his commanding interference, his compassion for human infirmities, for the irresistible heaviness of sleep,[4] for the thoughtlessness of childhood,[5] for the bewilderment of the whirling brain.[6]

Yet the impression which the Delphian oracles make on the modern reader will depend less on isolated anecdotes like these than on something of the style and temper which appears especially in those responses which Herodotus has preserved,— something of that delightful mingling of *naïveté* with greatness,

---

[1] See, for instance, the story of the young man and the brigands, Ael. *Hist. Var.* iii. 4. 3.

[2] Xen. *Mem.* iv. 3. ἥ τε γὰρ Πυθία νόμῳ πόλεως ἀναιρεῖ ποιοῦντας εὐσεβῶς ἂν ποιεῖν. The Pythia often urged the maintenance or renewal of ancestral rites. Paus. viii. 24, etc.

[3] Theopomp. *Fr.* 283 ; cf. Sopater, *Prolegg. in Aristid. Panath.* p. 740, εὔαδέ μοι χθιζὸς λίβανος, κ.τ.λ. (Wolff, *de Noviss.* p. 5 ; Lob. *Agl.* 1006), and compare the story of Poseidon (Plut. *de Prof. in Virt.* 12), who first reproached Stilpon in a dream for the cheapness of his offerings, but on learning that he could afford nothing better, smiled, and promised to send abundant anchovies. ، For the Delphian god's respect for honest poverty, see Plin. *H. N.* vii. 47.　　　　　　　　　　　　　　[4] Evenius. Herod. ix. 93.

[5] Paus viii. 23. This is the case of the Arcadian children who hung the goddess in play.

[6] Paus. vi. 9 ; Plut. *Romul.* 28 (Cleomedes). For further instances of the inculcation of mercy, see Thuc. ii. 102 ; Athen. xi. p. 504.

which was the world's irrecoverable bloom. What scholar has not smiled over the god's answer [1] to the colonists who had gone to a barren island in mistake for Libya, and came back complaining that Libya was unfit to live in? He told them that "if they who had never visited the sheep-bearing Libya knew it better than he who *had*, he greatly admired their cleverness." Who has not felt the majesty of the lines which usher in the test-oracle of Croesus with the lofty assertion of the omniscience of heaven? [2] lines which deeply impressed the Greek mind, and whose graven record, two thousand years afterwards, was among the last relics which were found among the ruins of Delphi.[3]

It is Herodotus, if any one, who has caught for us the expression on the living face of Hellas. It is Herodotus whose pencil has perpetuated that flying moment of young unconsciousness when evil itself seemed as if it could leave no stain on her expanding soul, when all her faults were reparable, and all her wounds benign, when we can still feel that in her upward progress all these and more might be forgiven and pass harmless away—

for the time
Was May-time, and as yet no sin was dreamed.

And through all this vivid and golden scene the Pythian Apollo—" the god," as he is termed with a sort of familar affection—is the never-failing counsellor and friend. His providence is all the divinity which the growing nation needs. His wisdom is not inscrutable and absolute, but it is near and kind ; it is like the counsel of a young father to his eager boy. To strip the oracles from Herodotus's history would be to deprive it of its deepest unity and its most characteristic charm.

---

[1] Herod. iv. 157. There seems some analogy between this story and the Norse legend of second-sight, which narrates how " Mgimund shut up three Finns in a hut for three nights that they might visit Iceland and inform him of the lie of the country where he was to settle. Their bodies became rigid, they sent their souls on the errand, and awakening after three days, they gave a description of the Vatnsdael."—*Prim. Cult.* i. 396.

[2] Herod. i. 47.

[2] Cyriac of Ancona, in the sixteenth century, found a slab of marble with the couplet οἶδα τ' ἐγώ, etc., inscribed on it. See Foucart, p. 139.

And in that culminating struggle with the barbarians, when the young nation rose, as it were, to knightly manhood through one great ordeal, how moving—I had almost said how human —was the attitude of the god ! We may wish, indeed, that he had taken a firmer tone, that he had not trembled before the oncoming host, nor needed men's utmost supplications before he would give a word of hope. But this is a later view; it is the view of Oenomaus and Eusebius, rather than of Aeschylus or Herodotus.[1] To the contemporary Greeks it seemed no shame nor wonder that the national protector, benignant but not omnipotent, should tremble with the fortunes of the nation, that all his strength should scarcely suffice for a conflict in which every fibre of the forces of Hellas was strained, " as though men fought upon the earth and gods in upper air."

And seldom indeed has history shown a scene so strangely dramatic, never has poetry entered so deeply into human fates, as in that council at Athens[2] when the question of absolute surrender or desperate resistance turned on the interpretation which was to be given to the dark utterance of the god. It was an epithet which saved civilisation ; it was the one word which blessed the famous islet instead of cursing it altogether, which gave courage for that most fateful battle which the world has known—

> " Thou, holy Salamis, sons of men shalt slay,
> Or on earth's scattering or ingathering day."

After the great crisis of the Persian war Apollo is at rest.[3] In the tragedians he has risen high above the attitude of a struggling tribal god. Worshippers surround him, as in the *Ion*, in the spirit of glad self-dedication and holy service; his priestess speaks as in the opening of the *Eumenides*, where the settled majesty of godhead breathes through the awful calm. And now, more magnificent though more transitory than the poet's song, a famous symbolical picture embodies for the

---

[1] Herod. vii. 139 seems hardly meant to blame the god, though it praises the Athenians for hoping against hope.

[2] Herod. vii. 143.

[3] It is noticeable that the god three times defended his own shrine,— against Xerxes (Herod. viii. 36), Jason of Pherae (Xen. *Hell.* vi. 4), Brennus (Paus. x. 23).

remaining generations of Greeks the culminant conception of the religion of Apollo's shrine.

"Not all the treasures," as Homer has it, "which the stone threshold of the Far-darter holds safe within" would now be so precious to us as the power of looking for one hour on the greatest work of the greatest painter of antiquity, the picture by Polygnotus in the Hall of the Cnidians at Delphi, of the descent of Odysseus among the dead.[1] For as it was with the oracle of Teiresias that the roll of responses began, so it is the picture of that same scene which shows us, even through the meagre description of Pausanias, how great a space had been traversed between the horizon and the zenith of the Hellenic faith. "The ethical painter," as Aristotle calls him,[2] the man on whose works it ennobled a city to gaze, the painter whose figures were superior to nature as the characters of Homer were greater than the greatness of men, had spent on this altar-piece, if I may so term it, of the Hellenic race his truest devotion and his utmost skill. The world to which he introduces us is Homer's shadow-world, but it reminds us also of a very different scene. It recalls the visions of that Sacred Field on whose walls an unknown painter has set down with so startling a reality the faith of medieval Christendom as to death and the hereafter.

In place of Death with her vampire aspect and wiry wings, we have the fiend Eurynomus, "painted of the blue-black colour of flesh-flies," and battening on the corpses of the slain. In place of the kings and ladies, who tell us in the rude Pisan epigraph how

> Ischermo di savere e di richezza
> Di nobiltate ancora e di prodezza
> Vale niente ai colpi de costei,—

it is Theseus and Sisyphus and Eriphyle who teach us that

---

[1] For this picture see Paus. x. 28-31 ; also Welcker (*Kleine Schriften*), and W. W. Lloyd in the Classical Museum, who both give Riepenhausen's restoration. While differing from much in Welcker's view of the picture, I have followed him in supposing that a vase figured in his *Alte Denkmäler*, vol. iii. plate 29, represents at any rate the figure and expression of Polygnotus's *Odysseus*. The rest of my description can, I think, be justified from Pausanias.

[2] Ar. *Pol.* viii. 8 ; *Poet.* ii. 2.

might and wealth and wisdom "against those blows are of no avail." And Tityus, whose scarce imaginable outrage in the Pythian valley upon the mother of Apollo herself carries back his crime and his penalty into an immeasurable past,—Tityus lay huge and prone upon the pictured field,—but the image of him (and whether this were by chance or art Pausanias could not say) seemed melting into cloud and nothingness through the infinity of his woe. But there also were heroes and heroines of a loftier fate,—Memnon and Sarpedon, Tyro and Penthesilea, in attitudes that told of " calm pleasures and majestic pains ; " —Achilles, with Patroclus at his right hand, and near Achilles Protesilaus, fit mate in valour and in constancy for that type of generous friendship and passionate woe. And there was Odysseus, still a breathing man, but with no trace of terror in his earnest and solemn gaze, demanding from Teiresias, as Dante from Virgil, all that that strange world could show ; while near him a woman's figure stood, his mother Anticleia, waiting to call to him in those words which in Homer's song seem to strike at once to the very innermost of all love and all regret. And where the medieval painter had set hermits praying as the type of souls made safe through their piety and their knowledge of the divine, the Greek had told the same parable after another fashion. For in Polygnotus' picture it was Tellis and Cleoboia, a young man and a maid, who were crossing Acheron together with hearts at peace ; and amid all those legendary heroes these figures alone were real and true, and of a youth and a maiden who not long since had passed away, and they were at peace because they had themselves been initiated, and Cleoboia had taught the mysteries of Demeter to her people and her father's house. And was there, we may ask, in that great company, any heathen form which we may liken, however distantly, to the Figure who, throned among the clouds on the glowing Pisan wall marshals the blessed to their home in light ? Almost in the centre, as it would seem, of Polygnotus' picture was introduced a mysterious personality who found no place in Homer's poem, —a name round which had grown a web of hopes and emotions which no hand can disentangle now,—" The minstrel sire of song, Orpheus the well-beloved, was there."

It may be that the myth of Orpheus was at first nothing more than another version of the world-old story of the Sun; that his descent and resurrection were but the symbols of the night and the day; that Eurydice was but an emblem of the lovely rose-clouds which sink back from his touch into the darkness of evening only to enfold him brightlier in the dawn. But be this as it may, the name of Orpheus[1] had become the centre of the most aspiring and the deepest thoughts of Greece; the lyre which he held, the willow-tree on which in the picture his hand was laid, were symbols of mystic meaning, and he himself was the type of the man "who has descended and ascended"— who walks the earth with a heart that turns continually towards his treasure in a world unseen.

When this great picture was painted, the sanctuary and the religion of Delphi might well seem indestructible and eternal. But the name of Orpheus, introduced here perhaps for the first time into the centre of the Apolline faith, brings with it a hint of that spirit of mysticism which has acted as a solvent, —sometimes more powerful even than criticism, as the sun in the fable of Aesop was more powerful than the wind,—upon the dogmas of every religion in turn. And it suggests a forward glance to an oracle given at Delphi on a later day,[2] and cited by Porphyry to illustrate the necessary evanescence and imperfection of whatsoever image of spiritual things can be made visible on earth. A time shall come when even Delphi's mission shall have been fulfilled; and the god himself has predicted without despair the destruction of his holiest shrine—

> " Ay, if ye bear it, if ye endure to know
> That Delphi's self with all things gone must go,
> Hear with strong heart the unfaltering song divine
> Peal from the laurelled porch and shadowy shrine.
> High in Jove's home the battling winds are torn,
> From battling winds the bolts of Jove are born ;
> These as he will on trees and towers he flings,
> And quells the heart of lions or of kings ;

---

[1] See, for instance, Maury, *Religions de la Grèce*, chap. xviii. Aelius Lampridius (*Alex. Sev. Vita*, 29) says—"In Larario et Apollonium et Christum, Abraham et Orpheum, et hujusmodi deos habebat."

[2] Eus. *Pr. Ev.* vi. 3.

> A thousand crags those flying flames confound,
> A thousand navies in the deep are drowned,
> And ocean's roaring billows, cloven apart,
> Bear the bright death to Amphitrite's heart.
> And thus, even thus, on some long-destined day,
> Shall Delphi's beauty shrivel and burn away,—
> Shall Delphi's fame and fane from earth expire
> At that bright bidding of celestial fire."

The ruin has been accomplished. All is gone, save such cyclopean walls as date from days before Apollo, such ineffaceable memories as Nature herself has kept of the vanished shrine.[1] Only the Corycian cave still shows, with its gleaming stalagmites, as though the nymphs to whom it was hallowed were sleeping there yet in stone; the Phaedriades or Shining Crags still flash the sunlight from their streams that scatter into air; and dwellers at Castri still swear that they have heard the rushing Thyiades keep their rout upon Parnassus' brow.

III.

Even while Polygnotus was painting the Lesche of the Cnidians at Delphi a man was talking in the Athenian market-place, from whose powerful individuality, the most impressive which Greece had ever known, were destined to flow streams of influence which should transform every department of belief and thought. In tracing the history of oracles we shall feel the influence of Socrates mainly in two directions; in his assertion of a personal and spiritual relation between man and the unseen world, an oracle not without us but within; and in his origination of the idea of science, of a habit of mind which should refuse to accept any explanation of phenomena which failed to confer the power of predicting those phenomena or producing them anew. We shall find that, instead of the old acceptance of the responses as heaven-sent mysteries, and the old demands for prophetic knowledge or for guidance in the affairs of life, men are

---

[1] See Mr. Aubrey de Vere's *Picturesque Sketches in Greece and Turkey* for a striking description of Delphian scenery. Other details will be found in Foucart, pp. 113, 114; and cf. Paus. x. 33.

more and more concerned with the questions : How can oracles be practically produced ? and what relation between God and man do they imply ? But first of all, the oracle which concerned Socrates himself, which declared him to be the wisest of mankind, is certainly one of the most noticeable ever uttered at Delphi. The fact that the man on whom the god had bestowed this extreme laudation, a laudation paralleled only by the mythical words addressed to Lycurgus, should a few years afterwards have been put to death for impiety, is surely one of a deeper significance than has been often observed. It forms an overt and impressive instance of that divergence between the law and the prophets, between the letter and the spirit, which is sure to occur in the history of all religions, and on the manner of whose settlement the destiny of each religion in turn depends. In this case the conditions of the conflict are striking and unusual.[1] Socrates is accused of failing to honour the gods of the State, and of introducing new gods under the name of demons, or spirits, as we must translate the word, since the title of demon has acquired in the mouths of the Fathers a bad signification. He replies that he *does* honour the gods of the State, as he understands them, and that the spirit who speaks with him is an agency which he cannot disavow.

The first count of the indictment brings into prominence an obvious defect in the Greek religion, the absence of any inspired text to which the orthodox could refer. Homer and Hesiod, men like ourselves, were the acknowledged authors of the theology of Greece ; and when Homer and Hesiod were respectfully received, but interpreted with rationalising freedom, it was hard to know by what canons to judge the interpreter. The second count opens questions which go deeper still. It was indeed true, though how far Anytus and Meletus perceived it we cannot now know, that the demon of Socrates indicated a recurrence to a wholly different conception of the unseen world, a conception before which Zeus and Apollo, heaven-god and sun-god, were one day to disappear. But who, except Apollo himself, was to pronounce on such

---

[1] On the trial of Socrates and kindred points see, besides Plato (*Apol., Phaed., Euthyphr.*) and Xenophon (*Mem., Apol.*), Diog. Laert. ii. 40, Diod. Sic. xiv. 37, Plut. *de genio Socratis.*

a question? It was he who was for the Hellenic race the source of continuous revelation; his utterances were a sanction or a condemnation from which there was no appeal. And in this debate his verdict for the defendant had been already given. We have heard of Christian theologians who are "more orthodox than the Evangelists." In this case the Athenian jurymen showed themselves more jealous for the gods' honour than were the gods themselves.

To us, indeed, Socrates stands as the example of the truest religious conservatism, of the temper of mind which is able to cast its own original convictions in an ancestral mould, and to find the last outcome of speculation in the humility of a trustful faith. No man, as is well known, ever professed a more childlike confidence in the Delphian god than he, and many a reader through many a century has been moved to a smile which was not far from tears at his account of his own mixture of conscientious belief and blank bewilderment when the infallible deity pronounced that Socrates was the wisest of mankind.

A spirit balanced like that of Socrates could hardly recur, and the impulse given to philosophical inquiry was certain to lead to many questionings as to the true authority of the Delphic precepts. But before we enter upon such controversies, let us trace through some further phases the influence of the oracles on public and private life.

For it does not appear that Delphi ceased to give utterances on the public affairs of Greece so long as Greece had public affairs worthy the notice of a god. Oracles occur, with a less natural look than when we met them in Herodotus, inserted as a kind of unearthly evidence in the speeches of Aeschines and Demosthenes.[1] Hyperides confidently recommends his audience to check the account which a messenger had brought of an oracle of Amphiaraus by despatching another messenger with the same question to Delphi.[2] Oracles, as we are informed, foretold the battle of Leuctra,[3] the battle of Chaeronea,[4] the destruction of Thebes by Alexander.[5] Alexander himself consulted Zeus Ammon not only on his own

[1] *e.g.* Dem. *Meid.* 53 :—τῷ δήμῳ τῶν Ἀθηναίων ὁ τοῦ Διὸς σημαίνει, etc.

[2] Hyper. *Euxen.* p. 8.   [3] Paus. ix. 14.

[4] Plut. *Dem.* 19.   [5] Diod. xvii. 10.

parentage but as to the sources of the Nile, and an ingenuous author regrets that, instead of seeking information on this purely geographical problem, which divided with Homer's birthplace the curiosity of antiquity, Alexander did not employ his prestige and his opportunities to get the question of the origin of evil set at rest for ever.[1] We hear of oracles given to Epaminondas,[2] to the orator Callistratus,[3] and to Philip of Macedon.[4] To Cicero the god gave advice which that sensitive statesman would have done well to follow,—to take his own character and not the opinion of the multitude as his guide in life.[5]

Nero, too, consulted the Delphian oracle, which pleased him by telling him to "beware of seventy-three,"[6] for he supposed that he was to reign till he reached that year. The god, however, alluded to the age of his successor Galba. Afterwards Nero,—grown to an overweening presumption which could brook no rival worship, and become, as we may say, Antapollo as well as Antichrist,—murdered certain men and cast them into the cleft of Delphi, thus extinguishing for a time the oracular power.[7] Plutarch, who was a contemporary of Nero's, describes in several essays this lowest point of oracular fortunes. Not Delphi alone, but the great majority of Greek oracles, were at that time hushed, a silence which Plutarch ascribes partly to the tranquillity and depopulation of Greece, partly to a casual deficiency of Demons,—the immanent spirits who gave inspiration to the shrines, but who are themselves liable to change of circumstances, or even to death.[8]

Whatever may have been the cause of this oracular eclipse, it was of no long duration. The oracle of Delphi seems to have been restored in the reign of Trajan, and in Hadrian's

---

[1] Max. Tyr. *Diss.* 25.　　　[2] Paus. viii. 11.　　　[3] Lycurg. *Leocr.* 160.
[2] Diod. xvi. 91.　　　[5] Plut. *Cic.* 5.　　　[6] Suet. *Nero*, 38.

[7] Dio Cass. lxiii. 14. Suetonius and Dio Cassius do not know why Nero destroyed Delphi ; but some such view as that given in the text seems the only conceivable one.

[8] Plut. *de Defect. orac.* 11. We may compare the way in which Heliogabalus put an end to the oracle of the celestial goddess of the Carthaginians, by insisting on marrying her statue, on the ground that she was the Moon and he was the Sun.—Herodian, v. 6.

days a characteristic story shows that it had again become a centre of distant inquirers. The main preoccupation of that imperial scholar was the determination of Homer's birthplace, and he put the question in person to the Pythian priestess. The question had naturally been asked before, and an old reply, purporting to have been given to Homer himself, had already been engraved on Homer's statue in the sacred precinct. But on the inquiry of the sumptuous emperor the priestess changed her tone, described Homer as "an immortal siren," and very handsomely made him out to be the grandson both of Nestor and of Odysseus.[1] It was Hadrian, too, who dropped a laurel-leaf at Antioch into Daphne's stream, and when he drew it out there was writ thereon a promise of his imperial power. He choked up the fountain, that no man might draw from its prophecy such a hope again.[2] But Hadrian's strangest achievement was to found an oracle himself. The worshippers of Antinous at Antinoe were taught to expect answers from the deified boy : "They imagine," says the scornful Origen, "that there breathes from Antinous a breath divine."[3]

For some time after Hadrian we hear little of Delphi. But, on the other hand, stories of oracles of varied character come to us from all parts of the Roman world. The bull Apis, "trampling the unshowered grass with lowings loud," refused food from the hand of Germanicus, and thus predicted his approaching death.[4] Germanicus, too, drew the same dark presage from the oracle at Colophon of the Clarian Apollo.[5] And few oracular answers have been more impressively recounted than that which was given to Vespasian by the god Carmel, upon Carmel, while the Roman's dreams of empire were still hidden in his heart. "Whatsoever it be, Vespasian, that thou preparest now, whether to build a house or to enlarge thy fields, or to get thee servants for thy need, there is

---

[1] Anth. Pal. xiv. 102 :—ἄγνωστον μ' ἐρέεις γενεῆς καὶ πατρίδος αἴης
ἀμβροσίου Σειρῆνος, etc.

[2] Sozomen, *Hist. Eccl.* v. 19.

[3] Orig. *ad. Cels.* ap. Wolff, *de Noviss.* p. 43, where see other citations.

[4] Plin. viii. 46.

[5] Tac. *Ann.* ii. 54.

given unto thee a mighty home, and far-reaching borders, and a multitude of men." [1]

The same strange mingling of classic and Hebrew memories, which the name of Carmel in this connection suggests, meets us when we find the god Bel at Apamea,—that same Baal " by whom the prophets prophesied and walked after things that do not profit " in Jeremiah's day,—answering a Roman emperor in words drawn from Homer's song. For it was thus that the struggling Macrinus received the signal of his last and irretrievable defeat : [2]—

> " Ah, king outworn ! young warriors press thee sore,
> And age is on thee, and thou thyself no more."

In the private oracles, too, of these post-classical times there is sometimes a touch of romance which reminds us how much human emotion there has been in generations which we pass rapidly by ; how earnest and great a thing many a man's mission has seemed to him, which to us is merged in the dulness and littleness of a declining age. There is something of this pathos in the Pythia's message to the wandering preacher,[3] " Do as thou now doest, until thou reach the end of the world," and in the dream which came to the weary statesman in Apollo Grannus' shrine,[4] and bade him write at the end of his life's long labour Homer's words—

> " But Hector Zeus took forth and bare him far
> From dust, and dying, and the storm of war."

And in the records of these last centuries of paganism we notice that the established oracles, the orthodox forms of inquiry, are no longer enough to satisfy the eagerness of men. In that upheaval of the human spirit which bore to the surface so much of falsehood and so much of truth,—the religion of Mithra,

---

[1] Tac. *Hist.* ii. 78. Suetonius, *Vesp.* 5, speaks of Carmel's *oracle*, though it seems that the answer was given after a simple *extispicium.*

[2] Dio Cass. lxxviii. 40 ; Hom. *Il.* viii. 103. Capitolinus, in his life of Macrinus (c. 3), shows incidentally that under the Antonines it was customary for the Roman proconsul of Africa to consult the oracle of the Dea Caelestis Carthaginiensium.

[3] Dio Chrysostom, περὶ φυγῆς, p. 255.

[4] Dio Cassius, *ad fin.;* Hom. *Il.* xi. 163.

the religion of Serapis, the religion of Christ,—questions are asked from whatever source, glimpses are sought through whatsoever in nature has been deemed transparent to the influences of an encompassing Power. It was in this age[1] that at Hierapolis the "clear round stone of the onyx kind," which Damascius describes, showed in its mirroring depths letters which changed and came, or sometimes emitted that "thin and thrilling sound,"[2] which was interpreted into the message of a slowly-uttering Power. It was in this age that Chosroes drew his divinations from the flickering of an eternal fire.[3] It was in this age that the luminous meteor would fall from the temple of Uranian Venus upon Lebanon into her sacred lake beneath, and declare her presence and promise her consenting grace.[4] It was in this age that sealed letters containing numbered questions were sent to the temple of the sun at Hierapolis, and answers were returned in order, while the seals remained still intact.[5] It was in this age that the famous oracle which predicted the death of Valens was obtained by certain men who sat round a table and noted letters of the alphabet which were spelt out for them by some automatic agency after a fashion which from the description of Ammianus we cannot precisely determine.[6] This oracle, construed into a menace against a Christian Emperor, gave rise to a persecution of paganism of so severe a character that, inasmuch as philosophers were believed especially to affect the forbidden practice, the very repute or aspect of a philosopher, as Sozomen tells us,[7]

---

[1] The following examples of later oracles are not precisely synchronous. They illustrate the character of a long period, and the date at which we happen to hear of each has depended largely on accident.

[2] Damasc. ap. Phot. 348, φωνὴν λεπτοῦ συρίσματος. See also Paus. vii. 21.

[3] Procop. *Bell. Pers.* ii. 24. The practice of divining from sacrificial flame or smoke was of course an old one, though rarely connected with any regular seat of oracle. Cf. Herod. viii. 134. The πυρεῖον in the χωρίον Ἀδιαρβιγάνων which Chosroes consulted was a fire worshipped in itself, and sought for oracular purposes.

[4] Zosimus, *Ann.* i. 57.

[5] Macrob. *Sat.* i. 23. Fontenelle's criticism (*Histoire des Oracles*) on the answer given to Trajan is worth reading along with the passage of Macrobius as an example of Voltairian mockery, equally convincing and unjust. Cf. Amm. Marcell. xiv. 7 for a variety of this form of response.

[6] Amm. Marcell. xxix. 2, and xxxi. 1.

[7] Sozomen. vi. 35.

was enough to bring a man under the notice of the police. This theological rancour will the less surprise us, if we believe with some modern criticism that St. Paul himself, under the pseudonym of Simon Magus, had not escaped the charge, at the hands of a polemical Father, of causing the furniture of his house to move without contact, in obedience to his unholy will.[1]

Finally, to conclude this strange list with an example which may by many minds be considered as typical of the rest, it was in this age that, at the Nymphaeum at Apollonia in Epirus, an Ignis Fatuus[2] gave by its waving approach and recession the responses which a credulous people sought,—except that this Will-o'-the-Wisp, with unexpected diffidence, refused to answer questions which had to do with marriage or with death.

Further examples are not needed to prove what the express statement of Tertullian and others testifies,[3] that the world was still "crowded with oracles" in the first centuries of our era. We must now retrace our steps and inquire with what eyes the post-Socratic philosophers regarded a phenomenon so opposed to ordinary notions of enlightenment or progress.

Plato's theory of inspiration is too vast and far-reaching for discussion here. It must be enough to say that, although oracles seemed to him to constitute but a small part of the revelation offered by God to man, he yet maintained to the full their utility, and appeared to assume their truth. In his ideal polity the oracles of the Delphian god were to possess as high an authority, and to be as frequently consulted, as in conservative Lacedaemon, and the express decision of heaven was to be

---

[1] Pseudo-Clemens, *Homil.* ii. 32. 638, τὰ ἐν οἰκίᾳ σκεύη ὡς αὐτόματα φερό-μενα πρὸς ὑπηρεσίαν βλέπεσθαι ποιεῖ. Cf. Renan, *Les Apôtres*, p. 153, note, etc.

[2] There can, I think, be little doubt that such was the true character of the flame which Dio Cassius (xli. 45) describes : πρὸς δὲ τὰς ἐπιχύσεις τῶν ὄμβρων ἐπαύξει καὶ ἐς ὕψος ἐξαίρεται, etc. Maury's explanation (ii. 446) is slightly different. The fluctuations of the flame on Etna (Paus. iii. 23) were an instance of a common volcanic phenomenon.

[3] Tertullian, *de Anima*, 46 : Nam et oraculis hoc genus stipatus est orbis, etc. Cf. Plin. *Hist. Nat.* viii. 29 : Nec non et hodie multifariam ab oraculis medicina petitur. Pliny's oracular remedy for hydrophobia (viii. 42) is not now phar-macopœal.

invoked in matters of practical[1] as well as of ceremonial[2] import.

Aristotle, who possessed,—and no man had a better right to it,—a religion all his own, and to which he never converted anybody, delivered himself on the subject of oracular dreams with all his sagacious ambiguity. " It is neither easy," he said, " to despise such things, nor yet to believe them."[3]

The schools of philosophy which were dominant in Greece after the death of Aristotle occupied themselves only in a secondary way with the question of oracles. The Stoics and Academics were disposed to uphold their validity on conservative principles, utilising them as the most moral part of the old creed, the point from which its junction with philosophy was most easily made. Cicero's treatise on divination contains a summary of the conservative view, and it is to be remarked that Cratippus and other Peripatetics disavowed the grosser forms of divination, and believed only in dreams and in the utterances of inspired frenzy.[4]

Epicureans and Cynics, on the other hand, felt no such need of maintaining connection with the ancient orthodoxy, and allowed free play to their wit in dealing with the oracular tradition, or even considered it as a duty to disembarrass mankind of this among other superstitions. The sceptic Lucian is perhaps of too purely mocking a temper to allow us to ascribe to him much earnestness of purpose in the amusing burlesques[5] in which he depicts the difficulty which Apollo feels in composing his official hexameters, or his annoyance at being obliged to hurry to his post of inspiration whenever the priestess chooses "to chew the bay-leaf and drink of the sacred spring."[6]

---

[1] *Leges*, vi. 914.   [2] *Leges*, v. 428 ; *Epinomis*, 362.

[3] Ar. *Div. per Som.* i 1. He goes on to suggest that dreams, though not θεόπεμπτα, may be δαιμόνια.

[4] See Cic. *de Div.* i. 3.

[5] *Jupiter Tragoedus; Bis Accusatus*, etc. I need not remind the reader that such scoffing treatment of oracles does not now appear for the first time. The parodies in Aristophanes hit off the pompous oracular obscurity as happily as Lucian's. A recent German writer, on the other hand (Hoffmann, *Orakelwesen*), maintains, by precept and example, that no style can be more appropriate to serious topics.

[6] *Bis Accusatus*, 2. I may remark that although narcotics are often used to produce abnormal utterance (Lane's *Egyptians*, ii. 33 ; Maury, ii. 479),

The indignation of Oenomaus, a cynic of Hadrian's age, is of a more genuine character, and there is much sarcastic humour in his account of his own visit to the oracle of Apollo at Colophon; how the first response which he obtained might have been taken at random from a book of elegant extracts, and had also, to his great disgust, been delivered in the self-same words to a commercial traveller immediately before him; how, to his second question, "Who will teach me wisdom?" the god returned an answer of almost meaningless imbecility; and how, when he finally asked, "Where shall I go now?" the god told him, "to draw a long bow and knock over untold green-feeding ganders."[1] "And who in the world," exclaims the indignant philosopher, "will tell me what these untold ganders may mean?"

Anecdotes like this may seem to warn us that our subject is drawing to a close. And to students of these declining schools of Greek philosophy, it may well appear that the Greek spirit had burnt itself out; that all creeds and all speculations were being enfeebled into an eclecticism or a scepticism, both of them equally shallow and unreal. But this was not to be. It was destined that every seed which the great age of Greece had planted should germinate and grow; and a school was now to arise which should take hold, as it were, of the universe by a forgotten clew, and should give fuller meaning and wider acceptance to some of the most remarkable, though hitherto least noticed, utterances of earlier men. We must go back as far as Hesiod to understand the Neoplatonists.

For it is in Hesiod's celebrated story of the Ages of the World[2] that we find the first Greek conception, obscure though its details be,—of a hierarchy of spiritual beings who fill

---

this mastication of a laurel-leaf or bay-leaf cannot be considered as more than a symbolical survival of such a practice. The drinking of water (Iambl. *Myst. Aeg.* 72; Anacreon xiii.), or even of blood (Paus. ii. 24), would be equally in-operative for this purpose; and though Pliny says that the water in Apollo's cave at Colophon shortened the drinker's life (*Hist. Nat.* ii. 106), it is difficult to imagine what natural salt could produce hallucination.

[1] Eus. *Pr. Ev.* v. 23—

ἐκ τανυστρόφοιο λᾶας σφενδόνης ἱεὶς ἀνὴρ
χῆνας ἐναρίξειν βολαῖσιν, ἀσπέτους, ποιηβόρους.

[2] Hes. *Opp.* 109 *sqq.*

the unseen world, and can discern and influence our own. The souls of heroes, he says, become happy spirits who dwell aloof from our sorrow; the souls of men of the golden age become good and guardian spirits, who flit over the earth and watch the just and unjust deeds of men; and the souls of men of the silver age become an inferior class of spirits, themselves mortal, yet deserving honour from mankind.[1] The same strain of thought appears in Thales, who defines demons as spiritual existences, heroes, as the souls of men separated from the body.[2] Pythagoras held much the same view, and, as we shall see below, believed that in a certain sense these spirits were occasionally to be seen or felt.[3] Heraclitus held "that all things were full of souls and spirits,"[4] and Empedocles has described in lines of startling power[5] the wanderings through the universe of a lost and homeless soul. Lastly, Plato, in the *Epinomis*[6] brings these theories into direct connection with our subject by asserting that some of these spirits can read the minds of living men, and are still liable to be grieved by our wrong-doing,[7] while many of them appear to us in sleep by visions, and are made known by voices and oracles, in our health or sickness, and are about us at our dying hour. Some are even visible occasionally in waking reality, and then again disappear, and cause perplexity by their obscure self-manifestation.[8]

Opinions like these, existing in a corner of the vast

---

[1] It is uncertain where Hesiod places the abode of this class of spirits; the MSS. read ἐπιχθόνιοι, Gaisford (with Tzetzes) and Wolff, *de Daemonibus*, ὑποχθόνιοι.

[2] Athenag. *legat. pro Christo*, 21; cf. Plut. *de Plac. Phil.* i. 8.

[3] Porph. *vit. Pyth.* 384; reff. ap. Wolff. For obsession, see Pseudo-Zaleucus, ap. Stob. *Flor.* xliv. 20.

[4] Diog. Laert. ix. 6.   [5] Plut. *de Iside*, 26.

[6] I believe, with Grote, etc., that the *Epinomis* is Plato's; at any rate it was generally accepted as such in antiquity, which is enough for the present purpose.

[7] *Epinomis*, 361.   μετέχοντα δὲ φρονήσεως θαυμαστῆς, ἅτε γένους ὄντα εὐμαθοῦς τε καὶ μνήμονος, γιγνώσκειν μὲν ξύμπασαν τὴν ἡμετέραν αὐτὰ διάνοιαν λέγωμεν, καὶ τόν τε καλὸν ἡμῶν καὶ ἀγαθὸν ἅμα θαυμαστῶς ἀσπάζεσθαι καὶ τὸν σφόδρα κακὸν μισεῖν, ἅτε λύπης μετέχοντα ἤδη, κ.τ.λ.

[8] καὶ τοῦτ' εἶναι τότε μὲν ὁρώμενον ἄλλοτε δὲ ἀποκρυφθὲν ἄδηλον γιγνόμενον, θαῦμα κατ' ἀμυδρὰν ὄψιν παρεχόμενον.   The precise meaning of ἀμυδρὰ ὄψις is not clear without further knowledge of the phenomena which Plato had in his mind.   Comp. the ἀλαμπῆ καὶ ἀμυδρὰν ζωήν, ὥσπερ ἀναθυμίασιν, which is all that reincarnated demons can look for (Plut. *de Defect.* 10).

structure of Platonic thought, passed, as it seems, for centuries with little notice. Almost as unnoticed was the gradual development of the creed known as Orphic, which seems to have begun with making itself master of the ancient mysteries, and only slowly spread through the profane world its doctrine that this life is a purgation, that this body is a sepulchre,[1] and that the Divinity, who surrounds us like an ocean, is the hope and home of the soul. But a time came when, under the impulse of a great religious movement, these currents of belief, which had so long run underground, broke into sight again in an unlooked-for direction. These tenets, and many more, were dwelt upon and expanded with new conviction by that remarkable series of men who furnish to the history of Greek thought so singular a concluding chapter. And no part, perhaps, of the Neoplatonic system shows more clearly than their treatment of oracles how profound a change the Greek religion has undergone beneath all its apparent continuity. It so happens that the Neoplatonic philosopher who has written most on our present subject, was also a man whose spiritual history affords a striking, perhaps an unique, epitome of the several stages through which the faith of Greece had up to that time passed. A Syrian of noble descent,[2] powerful intelligence, and upright character, Porphyry brought to the study of the Greek religion little that was distinctively Semitic, unless we so term the ardour of his religious impulses, and his profound conviction that the one thing needful for man lay in the truest knowledge attainable as to his relation to the divine. Educated by Longinus, the last representative of expiring classicism, the Syrian youth absorbed all, and probably more than all, his master's faith. Homer became to him what the Bible was to Luther; and he spent some years in producing the most perfect edition of the *Iliad* and

---

[1] See, for instance, Plato, *Crat.* 264. δοκοῦσι μέντοι μοι μάλιστα θέσθαι οἱ ἀμφὶ Ὀρφέα τοῦτο τὸ ὄνομα (σῶμα *quasi* σῆμα) ὡς δίκην διδούσης τῆς ψυχῆς ὧν δὴ ἕνεκα δίδωσι, κ.τ.λ.

[2] G. Wolff, *Porph. de Phil.* etc., has collected a mass of authorities on Porphyry's life, and has ably discussed the sequence of his writings. But beyond this tract I have found hardly anything written on this part of my subject,—on which I have dwelt the more fully, inasmuch as it seems hitherto to have attracted so little attention from scholars.

Odyssey which had yet appeared, in order that no fragment of the inspired text might fail to render its full meaning. But, as it seems, in the performance of this task, his faith received the same shock which had been fatal to the early piety of Greece. The behaviour of the gods in Homer was too bad to be condoned. He discerned, what is probably the truth, that there must be some explanation of these enormities which is not visible on the surface, and that nothing short of some profound mistake could claim acceptance for such legends as those of Zeus and Kronos, of Kronos and Uranus, amid so much else that is majestic and pure.[1] Many philologists would answer now that the mistake, the disease of language, lay in the expression in terms of human appetite and passion of the impersonal sequences of the great phenomena of Nature; that the most monstrous tales of mythology mean nothing worse or more surprising than that day follows night, and night again succeeds to day. To Porphyry such explanations were of course impossible. In default of Sanskrit he betook himself to allegory. The truth which must be somewhere in Homer, but which plainly was not in the natural sense of the words, must therefore be discoverable in a non-natural sense. The cave of the nymphs, for instance, which Homer describes as in Ithaca, is not in Ithaca. Homer must, therefore, have meant by the cave something quite other than a cave; must have meant, in fact, to signify by its inside the temporary, by its outside the eternal world. But this stage in Porphyry's development was not of long duration. As his conscience had revolted from Homer taken literally, so his intelligence revolted from such a fashion of interpretation as this. But yet he was not prepared to abandon the Greek religion. That religion, he thought, must possess some authority, some sacred book, some standard of faith, capable of being brought into harmony with the philosophy which, equally with the religion itself, was the tradition and inheritance of the race. And such a rule of faith, if to be found anywhere, must be found in the direct communications of the gods to men. Scat-

---

[1] The impossibility of extracting a spiritual religion from Homer is characteristically expressed by Proclus (*ad. Tim.* 20), who calls Homer ἀπάθειάν τε νοερὰν καὶ ζωὴν φιλόσοφον οὐχ οἷός τε παραδοῦναι.

tered and fragmentary though these were, it must be possible
to extract from them a consistent system.[1] This is what he
endeavoured to do in his work, " On the Philosophy to be drawn
from Oracles," a book of which large fragments remain to us
imbedded in Eusebius's treatise " On the Preparation for the
Gospel."

Perhaps the best guarantee of the good faith in which
Porphyry undertook this task lies in the fact that he afterwards
recognised that he had been unsuccessful. He acknowledged,
in terms on which his antagonist Eusebius has gladly seized,
that the mystery as to the authors of the responses was too
profound, the responses themselves were too unsatisfactory, to
admit of the construction from them of a definite and lofty
faith. Yet there is one point on which, though his inferences
undergo much modification, his testimony remains practically
the same.[2] This testimony, based, as he implies and his
biographers assert, on personal experience,[3] is mainly concerned
with the phenomena of possession or inspiration by an unseen
power. These phenomena, so deeply involved in the conception
of oracles, and which we must now discuss, are familiar to the
ethnologist in almost every region of the globe. The savage,
readily investing any unusual or striking object in nature with
a spirit of its own, is likely to suppose further that a spirit's
temporary presence may be the cause of any unusual act or
condition of a human being. Even so slight an abnormality as
the act of sneezing has generally been held to indicate the
operation or the invasion of a god. And when we come to
graver departures from ordinary wellbeing—nightmare, con-
sumption, epilepsy, or madness—the notion that a disease-spirit
has entered the sufferer becomes more and more obvious.
Ravings which possess no applicability to surrounding facts
are naturally held to be the utterances of some remote intelli-

---

[1] ὡς ἂν ἐκ μόνου βεβαίου τὰς ἐλπίδας τοῦ σωθῆναι ἀρνόμενος (Eus. *Pr. Ev.* iv. 6)
is the strong expression which Porphyry gives to his sense of the importance of
this inquiry.

[2] There is one sentence in the epistle to Anebo which would suggest a contrary view, but the later *De Abstinentia*, etc., seem to me to justify the
statement in the text.

[3] See, for instance, Eus. *Pr. Ev.* iv. 6 : μάλιστα γὰρ φιλοσόφων οὗτος τῶν καθ'
ἡμᾶς δοκεῖ καὶ δαίμοσι καὶ οἷς φησι θεοῖς ὡμιληκέναι.

gence. Such ravings, when they have once become an object
of reverence, may be artificially reproduced by drugs or other
stimuli, and we may thus arrive at the belief in inspiration by
an easy road.[1]

There are traces in Greece of something of this reverence
for disease, but they are faint and few ; and the Greek ideal of
soundness in mind and body, the Greek reverence for beauty
and strength, seem to have characterised the race from a very
early period. It is possible indeed that the first tradition of

> " Blind Thamyris and blind Mæonides,
> And Teiresias and Phineus, prophets old,"

may have represented a primitive idea that the " celestial light
shone inward" when the orbs of vision were darkened. But the
legends which have reached us scarcely connect Homer's blindness with his song, and ascribe the three prophets' loss of sight to
their own vanity or imprudence. In nymph-possession, which,
in spite of Pausanias's statement, is perhaps an older phenomenon than Apolline possession, we find delirium honoured,
but it is a delirium proceeding rather from the inhalation of
noxious vapours than from actual disease.[2] And in the choice
of the Pythian priestess—while we find that care is taken that
no complication shall be introduced into the process of oracular
inquiry by her youth or good looks,[3]—there is little evidence
to show that any preference was given to epileptics.[4] Still less

---

[1] On this subject see *Prim. Cult.* chap. xiv. ; Lubbock, *Origin of Civilisation,* pp. 252-5, etc. The Homeric phrase στυγερὸς δέ οἱ ἔχραε δαίμων (*Od.* v.
396) seems to be the Greek expression which comes nearest to the doctrine of
disease-spirits.

[2] See Maury, ii. 475. Nymph-oracles were especially common in Boeotia,
where there were many caves and springs.—Paus. ix. 2, etc. The passage
from Hippocrates, *De Morbo Sacro,* cited by Maury, ii. 470, is interesting from
its precise parallelism with savage beliefs, but cannot be pressed as an authority for primitive tradition.

[3] Diod. Sic. xvi. 27.

[4] Maury (ii. 514) cites Plut. *de Defect. orac.* 46, and *Schol. Ar. Plut.* 39, in defence of the view that a hysterical subject was chosen as Pythia. But Plutarch
expressly says (*de Defect.* 50) that it was necessary that the Pythia should be
free from perturbation when called on to prophesy, and the Scholion on Aristophanes is equally indecent and unphysiological. Moreover, Plutarch speaks
of the custom of pouring cold water over the priestess in order to ascertain by
her healthy way of shuddering that she was sound in body and mind. This

can we trace any such reason of choice in other oracular sanctuaries. We find here, in fact, the same uncertainty which hangs over the principle of selection of the god's mouthpiece in other shahmanistic countries, where the medicine-man or angekok is sometimes described as haggard and nervous, sometimes as in no way distinguishable from his less gifted neighbours.

Nor, on the other hand, do we find in Greece much trace of that other kind of possession of which the Hebrew prophets are our great example, where a peculiar loftiness of mind and character seem to point the prophet out as a fitting exponent of the will of heaven, and a sudden impulse gives vent in words, almost unconscious, to thoughts which seem no less than divine. The majestic picture of Amphiaraus in the Seven against Thebes, the tragic personality of Cassandra in the Agamemnon, are the nearest parallels which Greece offers to an Elijah or a Jeremiah. These, however, are mythical characters; and so little was the gift of prophecy associated with moral greatness in later days, that while Plato attributes it to the action of the divinity, Aristotle feels at liberty to refer it to bile.[1]

It were much to be wished that some systematic discussion of the subject had reached us from classical times. But none seems to have been composed, at any rate none has come down to us, till Plutarch's inquiry as to the causes of the general cessation of oracles in his age.[2] Plutarch's temper is conservative and orthodox, but we find, nevertheless, that he has begun to doubt whether Apollo is in every case the inspiring spirit. On the contrary, he thinks that sometimes this is plainly not the case, as in one instance where the Pythia, forced to prophesy while under the possession of a dumb and evil spirit, went into convulsions and soon afterwards died.

---

same test was applied to goats, etc., when about to be sacrificed. There is no doubt evidence (cf. Maury, ii. 461) that the faculty of divination was supposed to be hereditary in certain families (perhaps even in certain localities, Herod. i. 78), but I cannot find that members of such families were sought for as priests in oracular seats.

[1] Plat. *Ion.* 5.—Ar. *Probl.* xxx.—I cannot dwell here on Plat. *Phaedr.* 153, and similar passages, which suggest a theory of inspiration which would carry us far beyond the present topic.

[2] Plut. *de Defect. orac.; de Pyth.; de EI apud Delphos.*

And he recurs to a doctrine, rendered orthodox, as we have already seen, by its appearance in Hesiod, but little dwelt on in classical times, a doctrine which peoples the invisible world with a hierarchy of spirits of differing character and power. These spirits, he believes, give oracles, whose character therefore varies with the character and condition of the inspiring spirit; and of this it is hard to judge except inferentially, since spirits are apt to assume the names of gods on whom they in some way depend, though they may by no means resemble them in character or power. Nay, spirits are not necessarily immortal, and the death of a resident spirit may have the effect of closing an oracular shrine. The death of Pan himself was announced by a flying voice to Thamus, a sailor, "about the isles Echinades;" he was told to tell it at Palodes, and when the ship reached Palodes there was a dead calm. He cried out that Pan was dead, and there was a wailing in all the air.[1]

In Plutarch, too, we perceive a growing disposition to dwell on a class of manifestations of which we have heard little since Homer's time,—evocations of the visible spirits of the dead.[2] Certain places, it seems, were consecrated by immemorial belief to this solemn ceremony. At Cumae,[3] at Phigalea,[4] at Heraclea,[5] on the river Acheron, by the lake Avernus,[6] men strove to recall for a moment the souls who had passed away, sometimes, as Periander sought Melissa,[7] in need of the accustomed wifely counsel; sometimes, as Pausanias sought Cleonice,[8] goaded by passionate remorse; or sometimes with no care to question, with no need to confess or to be forgiven, but as, in one form of the legend, Orpheus sought Eurydice,[9]

---

[1] This quasi-human character of Pan (Herod. ii. 146; Pind. *Fr.* 68; Hyg. *Fab.* 224), coupled with the indefinite majesty which his name suggested, seems to have been very impressive to the later Greeks. An oracle quoted by Porphyry (ap. Eus. *Pr. Ev.*) εὔχομαι βροτὸς γεγώς Πανὶ σύμφυτος θεῷ, κ.τ.λ., is curiously parallel to some Christian hymns in its triumphant sense of human kinship with the divinity.

[2] *Quaest. Rom.; de Defect. Orac.; de Ser. Num. Vind.*

[3] Diod. Sic. iv. 22; Ephor. ap. Strab. v. 244.   [4] Paus. iii. 17.

[5] Plut. *Cim.* 6.

[6] Liv. xxiv. 12, etc. The origin of this νεκυομαντεῖον was probably Greek. See reff. ap. Maury, ii. 467.

[7] Diod. iv. 22; Herod. v. 92 gives a rather different story.

[8] Plut. *Cim.* 6. Paus. iii. 17.   [9] Paus. ix. 30.

travelling to the Thesprotian Aornus, in the hope that her spirit would rise and look on him once again, and waiting for one who came not, and dying in a vain appeal.

But on such stories as these Plutarch will not dogmatically judge ; he remarks only, and the remark was more novel then than now, that we know as yet no limit to the communications of soul with soul.

This transitional position of Plutarch may prepare us for the still wider divergence from ancient orthodoxy which we find in Porphyry. Porphyry is indeed anxious to claim for oracular utterances as high an authority as possible ; and he continues to ascribe many of them to Apollo himself. But he no longer restricts the phenomena of possession and inspiration within the traditional limits as regards either their time, their place, or their author. He maintains that these phenomena may be reproduced according to certain rules at almost any place and time, and that the spirits who cause them are of very multifarious character. I shall give his view at some length, as it forms by far the most careful inquiry into the nature of Greek oracles which has come down to us from an age in which they existed still ; and it happens also that while the grace of Plutarch's style has made his essays on the same subject familiar to all, the post-classical date and style of Porphyry and Eusebius have prevented their more serious treatises from attracting much attention from English scholars.

According to Porphyry, then, the oracular or communicating demon or spirit,—we must adopt spirit as the word of wider meaning,—manifests himself in several ways. Sometimes he speaks through the mouth of the entranced "recipient," [1] sometimes he shows himself in an immaterial, or even in a material form, apparently according to his own rank in the

---

[1] δοχεύς, from δέχομαι, is the word generally used for the human intermediary between the god or spirit and the inquirers. See Lob. *Agl.* p. 108, on the corresponding word καταβολικός for the spirit who is thus received for a time into a human being's organism. Cf. also Firmicus Maternus *de errore prof. relig.* 13 : "Serapis vocatus et intra corpus hominis conlatus talia respondit ;" and the phrase ἐγκατοχήσας τῷ Σαράπιδι (*Inscr. Smyrn.* 3163, ap. Wolff, *de Nov.*)

invisible world.¹ The recipient falls into a state of trance, mixed sometimes with exhausting agitation or struggle,² as in the case of the Pythia. And the importance attached to a right choice of time and circumstances for the induction of this trance reminds us of Plutarch's story, already mentioned, of the death of a Pythian priestess compelled to prophesy when possessed by an evil spirit. Another inconvenience in choosing a wrong time seems to have been that false answers were then given by the spirit, who, however, would warn the auditors that he could not give information,³ or even that he would certainly tell falsehoods,⁴ on that particular occasion. Porphyry attributes this occasional falsity to some defect in the surrounding conditions,⁵ which confuses the spirit, and prevents him from speaking truly. For on descending into our atmosphere the spirits become subject to the laws and influences which rule mankind, and are not therefore entirely free agents.⁶ When a confusion of this kind occurs, the prudent inquirer should defer his researches,—a rule with which inexperienced investigators fail to comply.⁷

Let us suppose, however, that a favourable day has been secured, and also, not less important, a ⁸ "guileless inter-

---

¹ Porphyry calls these inferior spirits δαιμόνια ὑλικά, and Proclus (*ad Tim.* 142) defines the distinction thus : τῶν δαιμόνων οἱ μὲν ἐν τῇ συστάσει πλέον τὸ πύριον ἔχοντες ὁρατοὶ ὄντες οὐδὲν ἔχουσιν ἀντιτύπως, οἱ δὲ καὶ γῆς μετειληφότες ὑποπίπτουσι τῇ ἁφῇ. It is only the spirits who partake of earthly nature who are capable of being touched. These spirits may be of a rank inferior to mankind ; Proclus, *ad Tim.* 24, calls them ψυχὰς ἀποτύχουσας μὲν τοῦ ἀνθρωπικοῦ νοῦ, πρὸς δὲ τὰ ζῷα ἐχούσας διάθεσιν.

² οὐ φέρει με τοῦ δοχῆος ἡ τάλαινα καρδία (Procl. *in Rempublicam*, 380) is the exclamation of a spirit whose recipient can no longer sustain his presence.

³ Eus. *Pr. Ev.* vi. 5, σήμερον οὐκ ἐπέοικε λέγειν ἄστρων ὁδὸν ἱρήν.

⁴ *Ibid.* κλεῖε βίην κάρτος τε λόγων· ψευδήγορα λέξω : " Try no longer to enchain me with your words ; I shall tell you falsehoods."

⁵ ἡ καταστάσις τοῦ περιέχοντος. Eus. *Pr. Ev.* vi. 5, καὶ τὸ περιέχον ἀναγκάζον ψευδῆ γίνεσθαι τὰ μαντεῖα, οὐ τοὺς παρόντας ἑκόντας προστιθέναι τὸ ψεῦδος. . . . πέφηνεν ἄρα, adds Porphyry with satisfaction, πόθεν πολλάκις τὸ ψεῦδος συνίσταται.

⁶ Porph. ap. Philoponum, *de Mundi Creat.* iv. 20, with the comments of Philoponus, whose main objection to these theories lies in their interference with the freedom of the will.

⁷ *Pr. Ev.* vi. 5, οἱ δὲ μένουσι καὶ λέγειν ἀναγκάζουσι διὰ τὴν ἀμαθίαν.

⁸ *Ibid.* v. 8, κάππεσεν ἀμφὶ κάρηνον ἀμωμήτοιο δοχῆος.

mediary." Some confined space would then be selected for
the expected manifestations, "so that the influence should not
be too widely diffused."¹ This place seems sometimes to have
been made dark,—a circumstance which has not escaped the
satire of the Christian controversialist,² whose derision is still
further excited by the "barbarous yells and singing "³ with
which the unseen ⸴visitant was allured,—a characteristic, it
may be noticed in passing, of shahmanistic practices, where-
ever they have been found to prevail. During these proceedings the human agent appears to have fallen into an abnormal
slumber, which extinguished for the time his own identity,
and allowed the spirit to speak through his lips,—"to contrive
a voice for himself through a mortal instrument."⁴ In such
speeches, of which several are preserved to us, the informing
spirit alludes to the human being through whom he is speaking
in the third person, as "the mortal" or "the recipient;" of
himself he speaks in the first person, or occasionally in the
third person, as "the god" or "the king."⁵

The controlling spirits do not, however, always content
themselves with this vicarious utterance. They appear sometimes, as already indicated, in visible and tangible form. Of
this phase of the proceedings, however, Eusebius has preserved
to us but scanty notices. His mind is preoccupied with the
presumption and *bizarrerie* of the spirits, who sometimes
profess themselves to be (for instance) the sun and moon ;
sometimes insist on being called by barbarous names, and
talking a barbarous jargon.⁶ The precise nature of such
appearances had been, it seems, in dispute since the days of
Pythagoras, who conjectured that the apparition was an

---

¹ καὶ ἅμα ἀποστηρίζοντες αὐτὸ ἐνταῦθα ἔν τινι στερέῳ χωρίῳ ὥστε μὴ ἐπιπολὺ
διαχεῖσθαι, Iamb. *de Myst.* iii. 14. The maxims of Iamblichus in these
matters are in complete conformity with those of Porphyry.

² Eus. *Pr. Ev.* iv. 1, καὶ τὸ σκότος δὲ οὐ μικρὰ συνεργεῖν τῇ καθ᾽ ἑαυτοὺς
ὑποθέσει.

³ *Ibid.* v. 12, ἀσήμοις τε καὶ βαρβάροις ἤχοις τε καὶ φωναῖς κηλουμένοι.

⁴ *Ibid.* v. 8, αὐλοῦ δ᾽ ἐκ βροτέοιο φίλην ἐτεκνώσατο φωνήν.

⁵ φῶς, βροτός, δοχεύς. *Pr. Ev.* v. 9, λύετε λοιπὸν ἄνακτα, βροτὸς θεὸν οὐκέτι
χωρεῖ.

⁶ *Pr. Ev.* v. 10 (quoting Porph. *ad Aneb.*), τί δὲ καὶ τὰ ἄσημα βούλεται ὀνόματα
καὶ τῶν ἀσήμων τὰ βάρβαρα πρὸ τῶν ἑκάστῳ οἰκείων, etc.

emanation from the spirit, but not, strictly speaking, the spirit itself.[1]

In the Neoplatonic view, these spirits entered by a process of "introduction"[2] into a material body temporarily prepared for them; or sometimes it was said that "the pure flame was compressed into a sacred Form."[3] Those spirits who have already been accustomed to appear were best instructed as to how to appear again; but some of them were inclined to mischief, especially if the persons present showed a careless temper.[4]

After a time the spirit becomes anxious to depart; but is not always able to quit the intermediary as promptly as it desires. We possess several oracles uttered under these cir-

---

[1] Pythag. ap. Aen.; Gaz. ap. Theophr. p. 61, Boisson. πότερον θεοὶ ἢ δαίμονες ἢ τούτων ἀπόρροιαι, καὶ πότερον δαίμων εἷς ἄλλος εἶναι δοκῶν ἢ πολλοὶ καὶ σφῶν αὐτῶν διαφέροντες, οἱ μὲν ἥμεροι, οἱ δ᾽ ἄγριοι, καὶ οἱ μὲν ἐνίοτε τἀληθῆ λέγοντες οἱ δ᾽ ὅλως κίβδηλοι . . . . τέλος προΐεται δαίμονος ἀπόρροιαν εἶναι τὸ φάσμα.

[2] εἴσκρισις. See Lob. *Agl.* p. 730.

[3] *Pr. Ev.* v. 8:— ἱεροῖσι τύποις
συνθλιβομένου πυρὸς ἁγνοῦ.

I may just notice here the connection between this idea of the entrance of a spirit into a quasi-human form built up for the occasion, and that recrudescence of idol-worship which marks one phase of Neoplatonism. In an age when such primitive practices as "carrying the dried corpse of a parent round the fields that he might see the state of the crops" (Spencer's *Sociology*, § 154), were no longer possible, this new method of giving temporary materiality to disembodied intelligences suggested afresh that it might be practicable so to prepare an image as that a spirit would be content to live there permanently. An oracle in Pausanias (ix. 38) curiously illustrates this view of statues. The land of the Orchomenians was infested by a spirit which sat on a stone. The Pythia ordered them to make a brazen image of the spectre and fasten it with iron to the stone. The spirit would still be there, but he would now be permanently fixed down, and, being enclosed in a statue, he would no longer form an obnoxious spectacle.

[4] *Pr. Ev.* v. 8, ἔθος ποιησάμενοι τῆς ἑαυτῶν παρουσίας εὐμαθέστερον φοιτῶσαι καὶ μάλιστα ἐὰν καὶ φύσει ἀγαθοὶ τυγχάνωσιν, οἱ δὲ, κἂν ἔθος ἔχωσι τοῦ παραγίνεσθαι, βλάβην τινὰ προθυμοῦνται ποιεῖν, καὶ μάλιστα ἐὰν ἀμελέστερόν τις δοκῇ ἀναστρέφεσθαι ἐν τοῖς πράγμασι. This notion of a congruity between the inquirer and the responding spirit is curiously illustrated by a story of Caracalla (Dio Cass. lxxvii.), who ἐψυχαγώγησε μὲν ἄλλας τέ τινας καὶ τὴν τοῦ πατρὸς τοῦ τε Κομμόδου ψυχήν· εἶπε δ᾽ οὖν οὐδεὶς αὐτῷ οὐδὲν, πλὴν τοῦ Κομμόδου. Ἔφη γὰρ ταῦτα· βαῖνε δίκης ἆσσον, θεοὶ ἢν αἰτοῦσι Σεβήρῳ. No ghost would address Caracalla except the ghost of Commodus, who spoke to denounce to him his doom.

cumstances, and giving directions which we can but imperfectly understand. It appears that the recipient, for what reason we are left to conjecture, was in some way bound with withes and enveloped in fine linen, which had to be cut and unwrapped at the end of the ceremony.[1] The human agent had then to be set on his feet and taken from the corner where he had been outstretched, and a singular collaboration seems to have taken place, the spirit giving his orders to the bystanders by a voice issuing from the recipient's still senseless form.[2] At last the spirit departs, and the recipient is set free.

Eusebius, in a passage marked by strong common sense,[3] has pointed out some obvious objections to oracles obtained in this fashion. Some of these so-called "recipients," it appears, had been put to the torture and had made damaging confessions. Further penalties had induced them to explain how their fraud was carried out. The darkness and secrecy of the proceedings were in any case suspicious ; and the futility of the answers obtained, or their evident adaptation to the wishes of the inquirers, pointed too plainly to their human origin. The actual method of producing certain phenomena has exercised the ingenuity of other Fathers. Thus figures could be shown in a bowl of water by using a moveable bottom, or lights could be made to fly about in a dark room by releasing a vulture with flaming tow tied to its claws.[4]

But in spite of these contemptuous criticisms the Christian Fathers, as is well known, were disposed to believe in the genuineness of these communications, and showed much anxiety to induce the oracles, which often admitted the greatness and wisdom, to acknowledge also the divinity, of Christ.[5]

---

[1] *Pr. Ev.* v. 8 :—παύεο δὴ περίφρων ὀάρων, ἀνάπαυε δὲ φῶτα,
θάμνων ἐκλύων πολιὸν τύπον, ἠδ' ἀπὸ γυίων
Νειλαίην ὀθόνην χερσὶν στιβαρῶς ἀπάειρας.
And again, when the bystanders delay the release, the spirit exclaims—
σίνδονος ἀμπέτασον νεφέλην, λῦσόν τε δοχῆα.

[2] *Pr. Ev.* v. 8 :—ὑψίπρωρον αἶρε ταρσὸν, ἴσχε βάξιν ἐκ μυχῶν. And again,
ἄρατε φῶτα γαληθὲν ἀναστήσαντες ἑταῖροι, etc.

[3] *Pr. Ev.* iv. 2.

[4] Pseudo-Origen, *Philosophumena*, p. 73.

[5] *Pr. Ev.* iv. iii. 7. Aug. *de Civit. Dei*, xix. 23. Lact. *Instit.* iv. 13.

Eusebius himself, in another work,[1] adduces a letter of Constantine's describing an oracle said to have been uttered directly by Apollo "from a certain dark hole," in which the god asserted that he could no longer speak the truth on account of the number of saints who were now on the earth. But this has so little the air of an Apolline manifestation that it is suspected that a Christian man had crept into a cave and delivered this unauthorised response with a polemical object.[2]

Into so obscure, so undignified a region of mingled fraud and mystery does it seem that, by the admission of friends and foes alike, the oracles of Greece had by this time fallen. Compared with what had been stripped away, that which was left may seem to us like the narrow vault of the Delian sanctuary compared with the ruined glories of that temple-covered isle. There was not, indeed, in Porphyry's view anything inconsistent with the occasional presence and counsel of a lofty and a guardian spirit. There was nothing which need make him doubt that the Greeks had been led upwards through their long history by some providential power. Nay, he himself cites, as we shall see, recent oracles higher in tone than any which have preceded them. Yet as compared with the early ardour of that imaginative belief which peopled heaven with gods and earth with heroes, we feel that we are now sent back to "beggarly elements;" that the task of sifting truth from falsehood amid so much deception and incompetence on the part both of visible and invisible agencies,[3] of erecting a consistent creed on such mean and shifting foundations, might well rebut even the patient ardour of this most untiring of "seekers after God." And when we see him recognising all this with painful clearness, giving vent, in that letter to Anebo which is so striking an example of absolute candour in an unscrupulous and polemic

---

[1] *Vit. Const.* ii. 50 ; cf. Wolff, *de Noviss.* p. 4.

[2] The well-known story, Γρηγόριος τῷ Σατανᾷ Εἴσελθε—Greg. Nyss. 548 (and to be found in all lives of Gregory Thaumaturgus), illustrates this Christian rivalry with pagan oracles or apparitions.

[3] The disappointing falsity of the manifesting spirits who pretended to be the souls of departed friends, etc., is often alluded to ; *e.g.* in the *ad Anebonem :* οἱ δὲ εἶναι μὲν ἔξωθεν τίθενται τὸ ὑπήκοον γένος ἀπατηλῆς φύσεως, παντόμορφόν τε καὶ πολύτροπον, ὑποκρινόμενον καὶ θεοὺς καὶ δαίμονας καὶ ψυχὰς τεθνηκότων, etc.

age, to his despair at the obscurity which seems to deepen as he proceeds, we cannot but wonder that we do not see him turn to take refuge in the new religion with its offers of certainty and peace.

Why, we shall often ask, should men so much in earnest as the Neoplatonists have taken, with the gospel before them, the side they took ? Why should they have preferred to infuse another allegory into the old myths which had endured so much ? to force the Pythian Apollo, so simple-hearted through all his official ambiguity, to strain his hexameters into the ineffable yearnings of a theosophic age ? For we seem to see the issues so clearly! when we take up Augustine instead of Proclus we feel so instantly that we have changed to the winning side! But to Greek minds—and the glory of the Syrian Porphyry was that, of all barbarians, he became the most intensely Greek—the struggle presented itself in a very different fashion. They were fighting not for an effete mythology, but for the whole Past of Greece ; nay, as it seemed in a certain sense, for the civilisation of the world. The repulse of Xerxes had stirred in the Greeks the consciousness of their uniqueness as compared with the barbarism on every side. And now, when Hellenism was visibly dying away, there awoke in the remaining Greeks a still more momentous conception, the conception of the uniqueness and preciousness of Greek life not only in space but in duration, as compared not only with its barbarian compeers, but with the probable future of the world. It was no longer against the Great King, but against Time itself, that the unequal battle must be waged. And while Time's impersonal touch was slowly laid upon all the glory which had been, a more personal foe was seen advancing from the same East from whose onset Greece already had escaped, "but so as by fire." Christ, like Xerxes, came against the Greek spirit Συριήγενες ἅρμα διώκων, driving a Syrian car ; the tide of conquest was rolling back again, and the East was claiming an empire such as the West had never won.

We, indeed, knowing all the flower of European Christianity in Dante's age, all its ripening fruit in our own, may see that this time from the East light came ; we may trust and claim that we are living now among the scattered forerunners of such types of beauty and of goodness as Athens never knew. But if so much even of our own ideal is in the future still, how must it have been to those whose longest outlook could not overpass the dreary centuries of barbarism and decay ? So vast a spiritual revolution must needs bring to souls of differing temper very different fates. Happy were they who, like Augustine and Origen, could frankly desert the old things and rejoice that all things were become new. Happy too were those few saintly souls—an Antoninus or a Plotinus—whose lofty calm no spiritual revolution seemed able to reach or mar. But the pathetic destiny was that of men like Julian or Porphyry, men who were disqualified from leading the race onward into a noble future merely because they so well knew and loved an only less noble past.

And yet it is not for long that we can take Porphyry as an example of a man wandering in the twilight between "dying lights and dawning," between an outworn and an untried faith. The last chapter in the history of oracles is strangely connected with the last stage of the spiritual history of this upward-striving man.

For it was now that Porphyry was to encounter an influence, a doctrine, an aim, more enchanting than Homer's mythology, profounder than Apollo's oracles, more Christian, I had almost written, than Christianity itself. More Christian at least than such Christianity as had chiefly met Porphyry's eyes ; more Christian than the violence of bishops, the wrangles of heretics, the fanaticism of slaves, was that single-hearted and endless effort after the union of the soul with God which filled every moment of the life of Plotinus, and which gave to his living example a potency and a charm which his writings never can renew.[1] "Without father, without mother, without descent," a figure appearing solitary as Melchisedek on the scene of history, charged with a single blessing and lost in the unknown, we may yet see in this chief of mystics the heir of

---

[1] Eunapius (*vit. Porph.*) manages to touch the heart, in spite of his affectations, when he describes the friendship between Porphyry and Plotinus. Of Porphyry's first visit to Rome he says :—τὴν μεγίστην Ῥώμην ἰδεῖν ἐπιθυμήσας . . . ἐπειδὴ τάχιστα εἰς αὐτὴν ἀφίκετο καὶ τῷ μεγίστῳ Πλωτίνῳ συνῆλθεν εἰς ὁμιλίαν, πάντων ἐπελάθετο τῶν ἄλλων, κ.τ.λ.

Plato, and affirm that it is he who has completed the cycle of Greek civilisation by adding to that long gallery of types of artist and warrior, philosopher and poet, the stainless image of the saint.

It may be that the holiness which he aimed at is not for man. It may be that ecstasy comes best unsought, and that the still small voice is heard seldomer in the silence of the wilderness than through the thunder of human toil and amid human passion's fire.

But those were days of untried capacities, of unbounded hopes. In the Neoplatonist lecture-room, as at the Christian love-feast, it seemed that religion had no need to compromise, that all this complex human spirit could be absorbed and transfigured in one desire.

Counsels of perfection are the aliment of strenuous souls, and henceforth, in each successive book of Porphyry's, we see him rising higher, resting more confidently in those joys and aspirations which are the heritage of all high religions, and the substance of the communion of saints.

And gradually, as he dwells more habitually in the thought of the supreme and ineffable Deity, the idea of a visible or tangible communion with any Being less august becomes repugnant to his mind. For what purpose should he draw to him those unknown intelligences from the ocean of environing souls? "For on those things which he desires to know there is no prophet nor diviner who can declare to him the truth, but himself only, by communion with God, who is enshrined indeed in his heart."[1] "By a sacred silence we do Him honour, and by pure thoughts of what he is."[2] "Holding Him fast, and being made like unto Him, let us present ourselves, a holy sacrifice, for our offering unto God."[3]

And in his letter to the well-loved wife of his old age,—than which we find no higher expression of the true Platonic love (so often degraded and misnamed)—no nobler charge and

---

[1] *De Abstin.* ii. 54.

[2] *Ibid.* ii. 34, διὰ δὲ σιγῆς καθαρᾶς καὶ τῶν περὶ αὐτοῦ καθαρῶν ἐννοιῶν θρησκεύομεν αὐτῷ.

[3] *Ibid.* ii. 34, δεῖ ἄρα συναφθέντας καὶ ὁμοιωθέντας αὐτῷ τὴν αὐτῶν ἀναγωγὴν θυσίαν ἱερὰν προσαγαγεῖν τῷ θεῷ.

counsel of man to woman in all the stores which antiquity has bequeathed,—in this last utterance we find him risen above all doubt and controversy, and rapt in the contemplation of that Being whom "no prayers can move and no sacrifice honour, nor the abundance of offerings find favour in his sight ; only the inspired thought fixed firmly on Him has cognisance of God indeed."[1] It may seem that as we enter on this region we have left oracles behind. But it is not so. The two last oracles which I shall cite, and which are among the most remarkable of all, are closely connected with this last period of Porphyry's life. The first of them is found, by no chance we may be sure, on a leaf of the manuscript which contains his letter to Marcella. It is introduced to us by an unknown writer as "an oracle concerning the Eternal God."[2]

> O God ineffable, eternal Sire,
> Throned on the whirling spheres, the astral fire,
> Hid in whose heart thy whole creation lies,—
> The whole world's wonder mirrored in thine eyes,—
> List thou thy children's voice, who draw anear,
> Thou hast begotten us, thou too must hear !
> Each life thy life her Fount, her Ocean knows,
> Fed while it fosters, filling as it flows ;
> Wrapt in thy light the star-set cycles roll,
> And worlds within thee stir into a soul ;
> But stars and souls shall keep their watch and way,
> Nor change the going of thy lonely day.
>   Some sons of thine, our Father, King of kings,
> Rest in the sheen and shelter of thy wings,—
> Some to strange hearts the unspoken message bear,
> Sped on thy strength through the haunts and homes of air, —
> Some where thine honour dwelleth hope and wait,
> Sigh for thy courts and gather at thy gate ;
> These from afar to thee their praises bring,
> Of thee, albeit they have not seen thee, sing ;

---

[1] τὸ ἔνθεον φρόνημα καλῶς ἡδρασμένον συνάπτεται τῷ θεῷ.—See the *Ad Marcellam* passim.

[2] This oracle was very probably actually delivered in a shrine, as the utterances of this period were often tinged with Neoplatonism. I have followed Wolff's emendations, and must refer the reader to his *Porph. Fragm.* p. 144, and especially his *Addit. IV. de Daemonibus*, p. 225, in support of the substantial accuracy of my rendering. It is impossible to reproduce all the theology which this hymn contains ; I have tried to bring out the force of the most central and weighty expressions, such as ἀενάοις ὀχετοῖσι τιθηνῶν νοῦν ἀτάλαντον. The oracle will also be found in Steuchus, *de Perenni Philosophia*, iii. 14 ; Orelli, *Opusc. gr. vett. sentent.* i. 319 ; and Mai's edition of the *Ad Marcellam*.

> Of thee the Father wise, the Mother mild,
> Thee in all children the eternal Child,
> Thee the first Number and harmonious Whole,
> Form in all forms, and of all souls the Soul.

The second oracle above alluded to, the last which I shall quote, was given, as Porphyry tells us, at Delphi to his friend Amelius, who inquired, " Where was now Plotinus's soul ?"[1]

Whatever be the source of this poem, it stands out to us as one of the most earnest utterances of antiquity, though it has little of classical perfection of form. Nowhere, indeed, is the contest more apparent between the intensity of the emotions which are struggling for utterance and the narrow limits of human speech, which was composed to deal with the things that are known and visible, and not with those that are inconceivable and unseen.

Little, indeed, it is which the author of this oracle could express, less which the translator can render; but there is enough to show once more the potency of an elect soul, what a train of light she may leave behind her as she departs on her unknown way; when for those who have lived in her presence, but can scarcely mourn her translation, the rapture of love fades into the rapture of worship. Plotinus was " the eagle soaring above the tomb of Plato;" no wonder that the eyes which followed his flight must soon be blinded with the sun.

> Pure spirit—once a man—pure spirits now
> Greet thee rejoicing, and of these art thou ;
> Not vainly was thy whole soul alway bent
> With one same battle and one the same intent
> Through eddying cloud and earth's bewildering roar
> To win her bright way to that stainless shore.
> Ay, 'mid the salt spume of this troublous sea,
> This death in life, this sick perplexity,
> Oft on thy struggle through the obscure unrest
> A revelation opened from the Blest—

---

[1] Porph. *vit. Plot.* 22. It is seldom that the genuineness of an oracle can be established on grounds which would satisfy the critical historian. But this oracle has better external evidence than most others. Of Porphyry's own good faith there is no question, and though we know less of the character of his fellow-philosopher Amelius, it seems unlikely that he would have wished to deceive Porphyry on an occasion so solemn as the death of their beloved master, or even that he could have deceived him as to so considerable an undertaking as a journey to Delphi.

Showed close at hand the goal thy hope would win,
Heaven's kingdom round thee and thy God within.[1]
So sure a help the eternal Guardians gave,
From life's confusion so were strong to save,
Upheld thy wandering steps that sought the day
And set them stedfast on the heavenly way.
Nor quite even here on thy broad brows was shed
The sleep which shrouds the living, who are dead ;
Once by God's grace was from thine eyes unfurled
This veil that screens the immense and whirling world,
Once, while the spheres around thee in music ran,
Was very Beauty manifest to man ;—
Ah, once to have seen her, once to have known her there,
For speech too sweet, for earth too heavenly fair !
But now the tomb where long thy soul had lain
Bursts, and thy tabernacle is rent in twain ;
Now from about thee, in thy new home above,
Has perished all but life, and all but love,—
And on all lives and on all loves outpoured
Free grace and full, a spirit from the Lord,
High in that heaven whose windless vaults enfold
Just men made perfect, and an age all gold.
Thine own Pythagoras is with thee there,
And sacred Plato in that sacred air,
And whoso followed, and all high hearts that knew
In death's despite what deathless Love can do.
To God's right hand they have scaled the starry way—
Pure spirits these, thy spirit pure as they.
Ah, saint ! how many and many an anguish past,
To how fair haven art thou come at last !
On thy meek head what Powers their blessing pour,
Filled full with life, and rich for evermore !

This, so far as we know, was the last utterance of the
Pythian priestess. Once more, indeed, a century afterwards,
a voice was heard at Delphi. But that voice seems rather
to have been, in Plutarch's phrase, " a cry floating of itself over
solitary places," than the deliverance of any recognised priestess,
or from any abiding shrine. For no shrine was standing more.
The words which answered the Emperor Julian's search were
but the whisper of desolation, the last and loveliest expression
of a sanctity that had passed away. A strange coincidence !
that from that Delphian valley, whence, as the legend ran, had

---

[1] ἐφάνη γοῦν τῷ Πλωτίνῳ σκοπὸς ἐγγύθι ναίων· τέλος γὰρ αὐτῷ καὶ σκοπὸς
ἦν τὸ ἐνωθῆναι καὶ πελάσαι τῷ ἐπὶ πᾶσι θεῷ. Ἔτυχε δὲ τετράκις που, ὅτε συνήμην
αὐτῷ, τοῦ σκοποῦ τούτου ἐνεργείᾳ ἀρρήτῳ καὶ οὐ δυνάμει.—(Porph. vit. Plot.)

sounded the first of all hexameters,[1]—the call, as in the child-hood of the world, to "birds to bring their feathers and bees their wax" to build by Castaly the nest-like habitation of the young new-entering god,—from that same ruined place where "to earth had fallen the glorious dwelling," from the dry channel where "the water-springs that spake were quenched and dead,"—should issue in unknown fashion the last frag-ment of Greek poetry which has moved the hearts of men, the last Greek hexameters which retain the ancient cadence, the majestic, melancholy flow![2]

Stranger still, and of deeper meaning, is the fate which has ordained that Delphi, born with the birth of Greece, symbolis-ing in her teaching such light and truth as the ancient world might know, silenced once only in her long career, and silenced not by Christ, but by Antichrist, should have proclaimed in her last triumphant oracle the canonisation of the last of the Greeks, should have responded with her last sigh and echo to the appeal of the last of the Romans.

And here I shall leave the story of Greek oracles. It may be, indeed, that some strange and solitary divinities—the god Jaribolus at Palmyra,[3] the god Marnas at Gaza,[4] the god Besa at Abydos[5]—still uttered from time to time some perishing pro-phecy, some despairing protest against the new victorious faith. But that such oracles there still were is proved rather from Chris-tian legislation than from heathen records. On these laws I will not dwell, nor recount how far the Christian emperors fell from their divine ideal when they punished by pillage,[6] by torture,[7]

---

[1] ξυμφέρετε πτερά τ᾽ οἰωνοὶ κηρόν τε μέλιτται.—Plut. *de Pyth.* xvii.; and reff. ap. Hendess, *Orac. Graec.* p. 36.

[2] εἴπατε τῷ βασιλῆι, χαμαὶ πέσε δαίδαλος αὐλά·
οὐκέτι Φοῖβος ἔχει καλύβαν, οὐ μάντιδα δάφνην,
οὐ παγὰν λαλέουσαν· ἀπέσβετο καὶ λάλον ὕδωρ.
—Ge. Cedren. *Hist. Comp.* i. 304; and see Mr. Swinburne's poem, "The Last Oracle." The Pleistos is now called Xero-Potamo.

[3] *Inscr. Gr.* 4483 ap. Wolff, *de Noviss.* p. 27. There is, however, no proof of Jaribolian utterance later than A.D. 242.

[4] Marc. Diac. *vit. Porph. Episc.* ap. *Acta Sanctorum*, and Wolff, *de Noviss.* p. 26. Circ. A.D. 400.

[5] Amm. Marc. xix. 12 (A.D. 359).

[6] *Cod. Theod.* xvi. 10 (Theodosius I.)

[7] Amm. Marc. xxi. 12 (Constantius).

and by death[1] the poor unlearned " villagers," whose only crime
it was that they still found in the faith of their fathers the
substance of things hoped for, and an evidence of things not
seen. Such stains will mar the noblest revolutions, but must
not blind us to the fact that a spiritual revolution follows only
on a spiritual need. The end of the oracles was determined
not from without, but from within. They had passed through
all their stages. Fetishism, Shahmanism, Nature-worship,
Polytheism, even Monotheism and Mysticism, had found in
turn a home in their immemorial shrines. Their utterances
had reflected every method in which man has sought communion with the Unseen, from systematic experiment to
intuitive ecstasy. They had completed the cycle of their
scripture from its Theogony to its Apocalypse; it was time
that a stronger wave of revelation should roll over the world,
and that what was best and truest in the old religion should
be absorbed into and identified with the new.

And if there be some who feel that the youth, the *naïveté*,
the unquestioning conviction, must perish not from one religion
only, but from all; that the more truly we conceive of God, the
more unimaginable He becomes to us, and the more infinite, and
the more withdrawn; that we can no longer "commune with
Him from oak or rock as a young man communes with a
maid;"—to such men the story of the many pathways by
which mankind has striven to become cognisant of the Unseen may have an aspect of hope as well as of despondency.

For before we despair of a question as unanswerable we
must know that it has been rightly asked. And there are
problems which can become clearly defined to us only by the
aid of premature and imperfect solutions. There are many
things which we should never have known had not inquiring
men before us so often deemed vainly that they knew.

Suspense of judgment, indeed, in matters of such moment,
is so irksome an attitude of mind, that we need not wonder if

---

[1] *Cod. Justin.* ix. 18 (Constantius) ; *Theod. leg. Novell.* iii. (Theodosius II.).
These laws identify paganism as far as possible with magic, and, by a singular
inversion, Augustine quotes Virgil's authority (*Aen.* iv. 492) in defence of the
persecution of his own faith. See Maury, *Magie*, etc., p. 127. The last struggle
of expiring paganism was in defence of the oracular temple of Serapis at
Alexandria, A.D. 389.

confidence of view on the one side is met by a corresponding confidence on the other; if the trust felt by the mass of mankind in the adequacy of one or other of the answers to these problems which have been already obtained is rebutted by the decisive assertion that all these answers have been proved futile and that it is idle to look for more.

Yet such was not the temper of those among the Greeks who felt, as profoundly perhaps as we, the darkness and the mystery of human fates. To them it seemed no useless or unworthy thing to ponder on these chief concerns of man with that patient earnestness which has unlocked so many problems whose solution once seemed destined to be for ever unknown. " For thus will God," as Sophocles says in one of those passages (*Fr.* 707) whose high serenity seems to answer our perplexities as well as his own—

> " Thus then will God to wise men riddling show
> Such hidden lore as not the wise can know ;
> Fools in a moment deem his meaning plain,
> His lessons lightly learn, and learn in vain."

And even now, in the face of philosophies of materialism and of negation so far more powerful than any which Sophocles had to meet, there are yet some minds into which, after all, a doubt may steal,—whether we have indeed so fully explained away the beliefs of the world's past, whether we can indeed so assuredly define the beliefs of its future,—or whether it may not still befit us to track with fresh feet the ancient mazes, to renew the world-old desire, and to set no despairing limit to the knowledge or the hopes of man.

F. W. H. M.